BASIC PHOTOGRAPHIC MATERIALS AND PROCESSES

Basic Photographic Materials and Processes describes the three crucial stages of creating the perfect photograph—capture, processing and output—by providing a thorough technical investigation of modern, applied photographic technologies.

This new edition has been fully revised and updated to explore digital image capture, processing and output. It covers a wide range of topics including: the scientific principles of measuring and recording light, the inner workings of digital cameras, image processing concepts, color management and photographic output to screen and print media. With these topics come in-depth discussions of extending dynamic range, image histograms, camera characterization, display capabilities, printer and paper technologies. It also includes applied exercises that provide the reader with a deeper understanding of the material through hands-on experiments and demonstrations, connecting theoretical concepts to real-world use.

This comprehensive text provides photography students, educators and working professionals with the technical knowledge required to successfully create images and manage digital photographic assets. It is an essential resource for mastering the technical craft of photography.

Nanette L. Salvaggio is the Lecturer responsible for the Photographic Technologies class at the Rochester Institute of Technology. Her career in image quality, color science and the photography industry includes work with Eastman Kodak, Hughes Aircraft Corporation, TASC Inc. and Imagery Solutions, which she co-owned. She holds a Bachelor of Science degree in Imaging and Photographic Technology from the Rochester Institute of Technology.

Josh Shagam is a camera image quality engineer and photographer working in Silicon Valley. He previously worked on image quality for aerial imaging systems at Harris Corporation and before that taught photography at the Rochester Institute of Technology. He holds a Bachelor of Science degree in Biomedical Photographic Communications and a Master of Professional Studies degree from the School of Visual Arts.

BASIC PHOTOGRAPHIC MATERIALS AND PROCESSES

Fourth Edition

NANETTE L. SALVAGGIO
JOSH SHAGAM

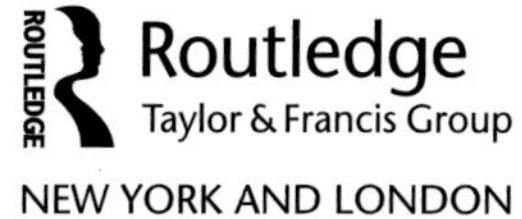

NEW YORK AND LONDON

Fourth edition published 2020
by Routledge
52 Vanderbilt Avenue, New York, NY 10017

and by Routledge
2 Park Square, Milton Park, Abingdon, Oxon, OX14 4RN

Routledge is an imprint of the Taylor & Francis Group, an informa business

First edition published by Focal Press 1990
Third edition published by Focal Press 2008

Library of Congress Cataloging-in-Publication Data
Names: Salvaggio, Nanette, author. | Shagam, Josh, author.
Title: Basic photographic materials and processes / Nanette L. Salvaggio and Josh Shagam.
Description: Fourth edition. | London ; New York : Routledge, 2020. | Rev. ed. of: Basic photographic materials and processes / Leslie Stroebel … [et al.]. c2000.
Identifiers: LCCN 2019017064| ISBN 9781138744363 (hbk : alk. paper) | ISBN 9781138744370 (pbk : alk. paper) | ISBN 9781315181097 (ebk : alk. paper)
Subjects: LCSH: Photography.
Classification: LCC TR145 .B25 2020 | DDC 576.8/8--dc23
LC record available at https://lccn.loc.gov/2019017064

ISBN: 978-1-138-74436-3 (hbk)
ISBN: 978-1-138-74437-0 (pbk)
ISBN: 978-1-315-18109-7 (ebk)

Typeset in Myriad Pro by Alex Lazarou

JOSH dedicates
this book to his wife of 3 years, Taylor.

NANETTE dedicates
this book to her husband of 33 years, Carl.

Thank you both for all of your patience and support during the time it took to write this book.

Contents

SECTION 3: OUTPUT

Abbreviations and Acronyms

AAC Advanced Audio Coding
ACE Adobe Color Engine
A/D Analog to Digital
AE Automatic Exposure
AEB Automatic Exposure Bracketing
AF Automatic Focus
AM Amplitude Modulation
ANSI American National Standards Institute
APS Active Pixel Sensor
AR Augmented Reality
ARTS Absorbed, Reflected, Transmitted, Scattered
AS-IPS Advanced Super In-Plane Switching
AV1 AOMedia Video 1
AVC Advanced Video Coding
AWB Automatic White Balance

B Byte
BD Blu-ray Disc
BID Binary Ink Developer
BMP Bitmap Image File
BRDF Bidirectional Reflectance Distribution Functions
BSI Backside Illuminated

CCD Charge-Coupled Device
CCFL Cold Cathode Fluorescent Lamp
CCM Color Correction Matrix
CCT Correlated Color Temperature
CD Compact Disc
CF Compact Flash
CFA Color Filter Array
CFL Compact Fluorescent Lamp
CIE Commission Internationale de l'Éclairage (International Commission on Illumination)
CMM Color Management Module or Color Matching Module
CMOS Complementary Metal Oxide Semiconductor
CMS Color Management System
CMYK Cyan, Magenta, Yellow, Key (Black)
CPU Central Processing Unit
CQS Color Quality Scale
CRI Color Rendering Index
CRT Cathode Ray Tube
CT Color Temperature

D50 CIE Standard Illuminant Daylight 5500K
D65 CIE Standard Illuminant Daylight 6500K
DAM Digital Asset Management
DCT Discrete Cosine Transform
DIB Device Independent Bitmap
DICOM Digital Imaging and Communications in Medicine
DLP Digital Light Processing
DNG Digital Negative
DOD Drop-on-Demand
DOF Depth of Field
DPI Dots Per Inch
DSLR Digital Single Lens Reflex
DSNU Dark Signal Non-Uniformity
DVD Digital Versatile Disc
DVI Digital Visual Interface
DWT Discrete Wavelet Transform

EIS Electronic Image Stabilization
eSATA External Serial Advanced Technology Attachment
ETTR Expose To The Right
EV Exposure Value
EVF Electronic Viewfinder
EXIF Exchangeable Image File Format

F2 CIE Standard Illuminant Fluorescent
FAT File Allocation Table
FLAC Free Lossless Audio Codec
FM Frequency Modulation
FPS Frames Per Second

GB Gigabyte
GeoTIFF Geostationary Earth Orbit Tagged Image File Format
GHz Gigahertz
GIF Graphics Interchange Format
GIS Geographic Information Systems
GOP Group of Pictures
GPS Global Positioning System
GPU Graphics Processing Unit
GRACoL General Requirements for Applications in Commercial Offset Lithography
GU Gloss Unit

HD High Definition
HDD Hard Disk Drive
HDMI High-Definition Multimedia Interface
HDR High Dynamic Range
HEIF High Efficiency Image File Format
HEVC High Efficiency Video Coding
HFR High Frame Rate
HMD Head Mounted Display
HTML Hypertext Markup Language
Hz Hertz

ICC International Color Consortium
IPS In-Plane Switching
IPTC International Press Telecommunications Council
IR Infrared
IS Image Stabilization
ISO International Standards Organization
ISOBMFF ISO Base Media File Format
ISP Image Signal Processor or Internet Service Provider
ITU International Telecommunication Union

JBOD Just a Bunch of Disks
JND Just Noticeable Difference
JPEG Joint Photographic Experts Group
JPEG-LS Joint Photographic Experts Group - Lossless Compression

K Kelvin
KB Kilobyte

LAN Local Area Network
LCD Liquid Crystal Display
LED Light-Emitting Diode
LPI Lines Per Inch
LUT Lookup Table
LZW Lempel–Ziv–Welch

MB Megabyte
MCS Material Connection Space
MJPEG Motion Joint Photographic Experts Group
MK Matte Black
MPEG Moving Picture Experts Group
MTF Modulation Transfer Function
mSATA Mini-Serial Advanced Technology Attachment

NAS Network-Attached Storage
ND Neutral Density
NIST National Institute of Standards and Technology
NTSC National Television Standards Committee

OBA Optical Brightener Agent
OIS Optical Image Stabilization
OLED Organic Light-Emitting Diode
OLPF Optical Low-Pass Filter
OS Operating System

PB Petabyte
PCIe Peripheral Component Interconnect Express
PCS Profile Connection Space
PIE Parametric Image Editing
PIP Photo Imaging Plate
PK Photo Black
PRNU Pixel Response Non-Uniformity
PNG Portable Network Graphics
POD Print On Demand
PPI Pixels Per Inch

PSB Photoshop Big
PSD Photoshop Document

QD Quantum Dot
QE Quantum Efficiency

RAID Redundant Array of Independent Disks
RAM Random Access Memory
RC Resin-Coated
RGB Red, Green, Blue
RGBAW Red, Green, Blue, Amber, White
RIP Raster Image Processor
RLE Run-Length Encoding
RPM Revolutions Per Minute
RW Rewritable

SaaS Software as a Service
SATA Serial Advanced Technology Attachment
SD Standard Definition or Secure Digital
SDHC Secure Digital High Capacity
SDUC Secure Digital Ultra Capacity
SDXC Secure Digital Extended Capacity
SDR Standard Dynamic Range
S-IPS Super In-Plane Switching
SLR Single Lens Reflex
SNR Signal to Noise Ratio
SoC System on a Chip
SPD Spectral Power Distribution or Silicon Photodiode
SSD Solid State Drive
SWOP Specifications for Web Offset Publications

TB Terabyte
TIFF Tagged Image File Format
TN Twisted Nematic
TRC Tone Response Curve
TTC Tone Transfer Compensation
TTL Through the Lens

UDMA Ultra Direct Memory Access
UHD Ultra High Definition
UHS Ultra High Speed
UI User Interface
USB Universal Serial Bus
UV Ultraviolet

VA Vertical Alignment
$V_M(\lambda)$ Photopic luminosity function of the human eye
VR Virtual Reality
VVC Versatile Video Coding

WCAG Web Content Accessibility Guidelines
WCG Wide Color Gamut
WORM Write-Once-Read-Many

XMP Extensible Metadata Platform

YC_bC_r Luminance, Chroma Blue, Chroma Red

Introduction

It's imperative that the modern image maker understands the workings of photography's latest tools and processes: this was our mindset when writing this textbook. This book is not a collection of step-by-step guides on photographic composition, studio lighting or editing in Adobe Photoshop. Instead, it's a deep dive into the medium's complex and interrelated workings. We've organized the information according to the basic pillars of a photographic workflow (capture, processing and output) but recognize that its content may not be read in a linear or single-sitting fashion (we'd be totally impressed if you did, though).

Furthermore, this book does not attempt to be a comprehensive or historical guide to all of photographic technology. It's instead a technical investigation of modern, applied photographic technology. We made the choice to write a forward-thinking resource not because we think "film is dead" (it's not!) but because many, many resources exist concerning analog processes and technologies, including previous editions of this book. While photographers of all types continue to explore film-based image-making, the reality is that wet process photography is more of a niche than a norm. Modern photographic technology inherited many core principles, terms and the insights made from hundreds of years of optical and material science. We are no longer in a transition from analog to digital and young photographers are exposed to film cameras and darkrooms only if they seek them out, not as ubiquitous cultural touchstones.

This new edition provides students studying photography for the first time or professionals working in this paradigm with the technical background required to create images and successfully manage digital photographic assets. This book covers a wide range of topics: the scientific principles of measuring and recording light, the inner workings of digital cameras, image processing concepts, color management and photographic output to both screen and print media. With these topics come in-depth discussions of extending dynamic range, image histograms, camera characterization, display capabilities, printer and paper technologies and more. We've also created sections at the end of select chapters called *Proof of Concept* that provide the reader with a deeper understanding of the material through hands-on experiments, exercises and demonstrations. These illustrative sections work to connect theoretical concepts to real-world use-cases.

It's our belief that a comprehensive book is needed to teach the science and technology that makes modern digital photography possible. This is not knowledge for its own sake—everything included on the following pages is connected to the applied practice of image-making. All of it is in the service of empowering your photographic vision and technical craft. Photography is a medium in constant flux with changes in aesthetics, technology and applications coming so frequently and fluidly that it is hard to pin down its epochs. In overhauling our first-year undergraduate course at Rochester Institute of Technology's School of Photographic Arts and Sciences, we learned a great deal about what newcomers must know to be proficient with the latest hardware and software tools. We hope that the content explored on the following pages proves insightful and empowering for your creative practice.

Section 1
CAPTURE

We begin our exploration of photographic processes and technologies with image capture. An image may start as a concept, a plan or idea; a photograph is truly born into existence at its moment of capture. There is no photographic capture without light, so we start this textbook section with photometry: the science of measuring light. Photometry establishes our definitions of visible light, light source technologies and the characteristics of light such as appearance and behavior.

Understanding light helps us to control and capture it. The chapters following photometry start with photographic optics and follow the path of light as it is transformed from photons to bits. We look at the designs and functions of lenses, perspective, distortions and approaches for evaluating image quality.

Forming an image on a plane is made permanent by recording it. We lay out the relevant digital camera technologies that detect, record and digitize light including camera apertures, focusing systems and sensors. A great camera can take a terrible photograph, so it's important to break down the mechanics of proper photographic exposure once we're familiar with the camera itself. The behaviors and interrelated effects of shutter speed, aperture and ISO are demystified in their own chapter.

Finally, we'd be remiss if we ignored motion video as a capture method. While not photography in the strictest sense, video comes with the territory due to the overlap of image-making and light-recording equipment.

There's a lot of ground to cover in this section as we take a comprehensive look at everything that goes into recording light to make photographs. Forge ahead to expand your knowledge of photographic technology and don't forget to take photographs as you go—test the concepts by experimenting and exploring with your eyes and your camera.

1 Light and Photometry

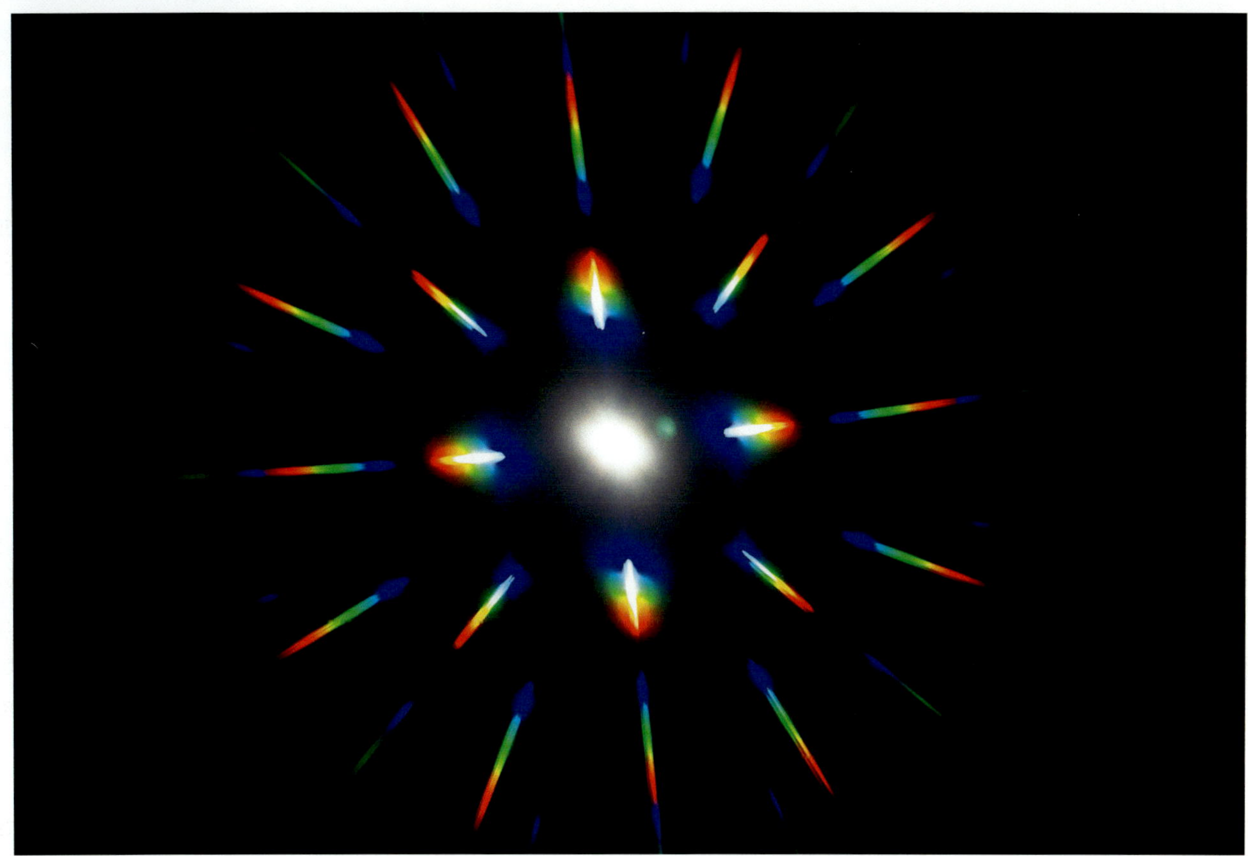

A smartphone camera LED flash viewed through a diffraction grating, an optical material that acts like a prism. The multicolored streaks radiating from the light source reveal its spectral energy components. Photograph by Rochester Institute of Technology photography student Hank Tilson

The potential for a photograph can begin as an idea in one's imagination or a confluence of circumstances and awareness, yet it is made real only when the materials and processes of photography are brought together to capture it. Light is the material that has defined photography since its invention; it is the basic ingredient for making photographs. For this reason, we start with photometry: the science of measuring and describing light. There's a lot of ground to cover: first we define light and its properties, then the many ways in which light is produced, described and measured. Finally, we highlight the light sources typically encountered by photographers. By chapter's end, you will know and understand light to confidently wield it for photographic ends.

The Nature of Light

Light is defined as the radiant energy that our visual system is sensitive to and depends upon for the sensation of vision. Light is fundamental to photography. The function of digital sensors and light-sensitive photographic materials is to capture light and record the patterns it creates. We use sunlight, lamps or electronic flash to produce light; exposure and color temperature meters to measure and characterize the light; and lenses, shutters, apertures and filters to control light falling on our light-sensitive recording medium. Our study of photography must start with understanding light.

Light is the subject of an enormous amount of experimentation and research spanning many centuries through to today. Isaac Newton was one of the first to make significant steps in understanding the nature of light. Newton performed a series of experiments in the seventeenth century and proposed that light is emitted from a source in straight lines as a stream of particles; this became known as the *corpuscular theory*.

Photographers know that light bends when it passes from one medium to another and that light passing through a very small aperture spreads out. These behaviors are not easily explained by the corpuscular theory. As a result, Christiaan Huygens proposed the *wave theory*, also in the seventeenth century, stating that light and similar forms of electromagnetic radiation are transmitted as a waveform in a medium. Thomas Young performed a number of experiments in the nineteenth century that supported Huygens' characterization. The wave theory satisfactorily explained many of the phenomena associated with light that the corpuscular theory did not, though it still did not explain all of them.

One of the notably unexplained effects is the behavior of *blackbody radiation*. Blackbody radiation is radiation produced by a body that absorbs all of the radiation that strikes it and emits radiation by incandescence (heat energy) depending on its temperature. In 1900, Max Planck hypothesized the *quantization of energy* to explain the behavior of blackbody radiation. This theory states that the only possible energies that can be possessed by a ray of light are integral multiples of a quantum of energy.

In 1905, Albert Einstein proposed a return to the corpuscular theory of light where light consists of *photons*, each photon containing a quantum of energy. These suggestions, along with others, developed into what is known today as *quantum theory* or *quantum electrodynamics*. Quantum theory combines aspects of the corpuscular and wave theories and satisfactorily explains all of the known behaviors of light. It states that light acts like both a wave and a particle: light exhibits a *wave-particle duality*. Unfortunately, this theory is difficult to conceptualize and can be rigorously explained only through sophisticated mathematics. As a result, the corpuscular and wave theories are still used where simple explanations of the behavior of light are required. Sometimes our observations of light behavior are best explained by its wave-like character. Other times, light behavior is better characterized by considering it as packets of energy.

Measuring Light Waves

Accepting that light moves as a wave function, the next step is determining the nature of the waves and the relationship of light to other forms of radiation. The light experienced with our visual system is a fractional part of a wide spectrum of radiant energy that exists in the universe, all of which can be thought of as traveling in waves. These forms of energy travel at the tremendous speed of approximately 186,000 miles ($3x10^8$ meters) per second. Radiant energy waves vibrate at right angles relative to their path of travel. The distance from the *crest* (the peak height) of one wave to the crest of the next is termed the *wavelength* represented by the Greek letter lambda (λ). Figure 1-1 illustrates this concept with a longitudinal cross section of a light wave; in reality, the wave vibrates in all possible right angles to the direction of travel. The number of waves passing a given point in 1 second is the *frequency* of vibration; the symbol f specifies this wave characteristic. The wavelength multiplied by the vibration frequency results in the speed or *velocity* (v) of the radiation. Thus, $v = \lambda \times f$.

Since the wavelength of radiant energy can be measured with far greater accuracy than the frequency, it is

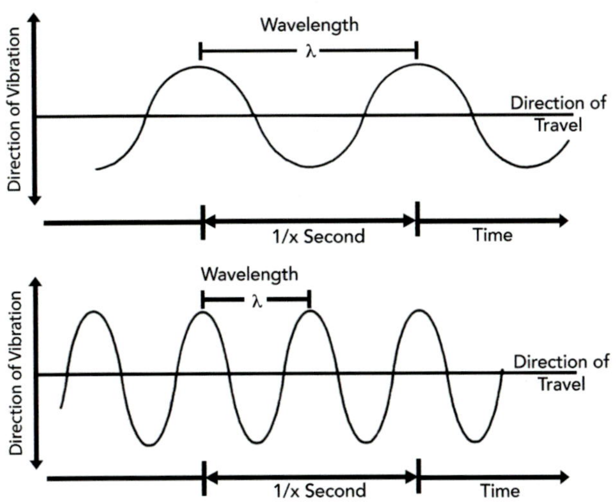

Figure 1-1 A simple form of a light wave illustrated in a longitudinal cross section. The second wave has a wavelength one-half that of the first and, therefore, a frequency twice as great.

Table 1-1 Units of length

Unit	Symbol	Length
Meter	m	1 m (38.6 in.)
Centimeter	cm	0.01 m (10^{-2} m)
Millimeter	mm	0.001 m (10^{-3} m)
Micrometer/Micron	μ (mu)	0.000001 m (10^{-6} m)
Nanometer	nm	0.000000001 m (10^{-9} m)
Angstrom	Å	0.0000000001 m (10^{-10} m)

common practice to specify a type of radiation by its wavelength. The unit of measure used for wavelength is the *nanometer* (nm) due to the extremely short wavelengths emitted by electromagnetic energy sources. A nanometer is equal to one-billionth of a meter. Table 1-1 summarizes units of length and their symbols to offer context for the scale of radiant energy wavelengths.

The Electromagnetic Spectrum

When the various forms of radiant energy are placed along a scale of wavelengths, the resulting continuum is called the *electromagnetic spectrum*. Although each form of radiant energy differs from its neighbors by an extremely small amount, it is useful to divide this spectrum into the generalized categories shown in Figure 1-2. All radiation is believed to be the result of electromagnetic oscillations. In the case of radio waves, the wavelengths are extremely long (on the order of 10^9 nm) and are the result of long electrical oscillations. Proof that such energy permeates our environment is easily demonstrated by turning on a radio. Radio waves are customarily characterized by their frequency, expressed in *cycles per second* or *Hertz* (Hz).

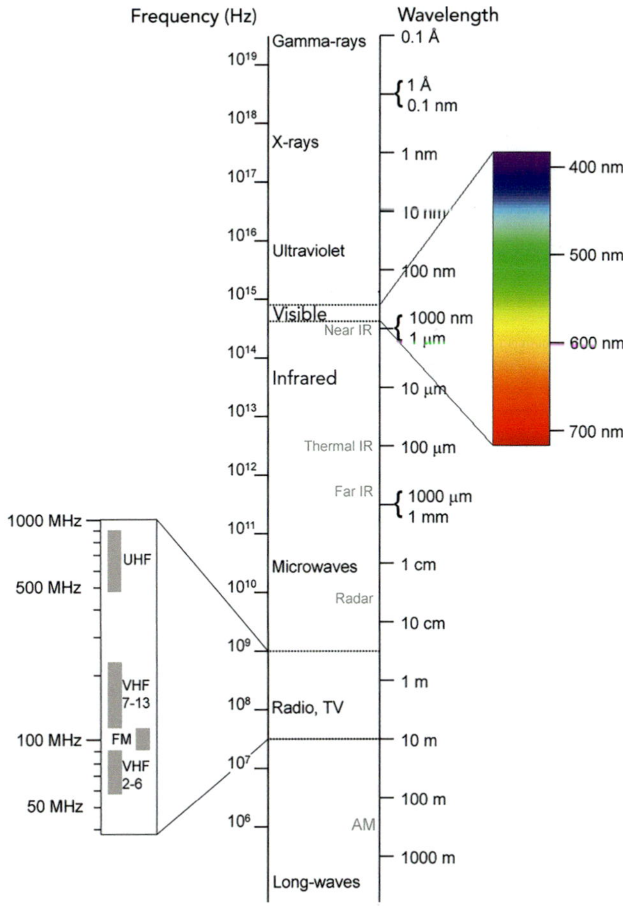

Figure 1-2 The electromagnetic spectrum.

The *infrared* region is the portion of the electromagnetic spectrum that we experience as heat. The origin of this type of radiant energy, which is shorter in wavelength than radio waves, is the excitation of electrons by thermal disturbance. When these electrons absorb energy from their surroundings, they are placed in an elevated state of activity. When they suddenly return to their normal state, they emit electromagnetic radiation. Experiments show that any object at a temperature greater than –459°F (–273°C) gives off infrared radiation. Thus, all the objects we come into contact with emit some infrared energy. In general, the hotter an object, the more total energy it produces and the shorter the peak wavelength.

If an object is heated to a high enough temperature, the wavelength of the energy emitted becomes short enough to stimulate the retina of the human eye and cause the sensation of vision. This region of the electromagnetic spectrum is labelled as *light* or *visible light*. Notice in Figure 1-2 that the visible region occupies a relatively narrow section of the spectrum between approximately 380 and 720 nm. Because the sensitivity of the human visual system is low at both extreme ends of this range, 400 and 700 nm are generally considered to be more realistic values.

Producing radiant energy shorter than 10 nm in wavelength requires that fast-moving electrons bombard an object. The sudden collision of these rapidly moving electrons striking the object produces extremely shortwave energy called *X-radiation*, or more commonly, *x-rays*. Still shorter wavelengths are produced if the electron bombardment intensifies, as occurs in a cyclotron (a type of particle accelerator used in nuclear medicine). In addition, when radioactive material decomposes, it emits energy shorter in wavelength than x-rays. In both cases, the energy is called *gamma rays*, which are 0.000001 nm (10^{-6} nm) in wavelength and shorter. Gamma rays are the most energetic, penetrating radiation known. Our Earth's atmosphere blocks a great deal of the gamma ray and x-ray radiation from space.

We begin to appreciate the usefulness of classifying the known forms of radiation using wave theory and the portion of the spectrum that we categorize as *light* in the context of human vision and photography.

The Visible Spectrum

Light energy is located near the middle of the electromagnetic spectrum called the *visible spectrum*. The boundaries of this region are solely dictated by the response characteristics of the human eye. In fact, the standard definition of the visible spectrum specifies that light is radiant energy experienced by a human observer as visual sensations via the retina. Simply put, light is the energy that permits us to see. By definition, all light is visible and for this reason the word *visible* is an unnecessary (and perhaps confusing) adjective in the common expression *visible light*. This definition also may be interpreted to mean that energy that is not visible cannot and should not be called light. It's also more accurate to talk about *ultraviolet radiation* (UV) and *infrared radiation* (IR), rather than ultraviolet light or infrared light. The popular use of such phrases as "blacklight" and "invisible light" to describe such radiation makes it impossible to determine what type of energy is emitted and should be avoided.

It helps to be familiar with how the human eye responds to light to better understand it. Figure 1-3 represents the *photopic luminosity function of the human eye*, $V_M(\lambda)$, as defined by the International Commission on Illumination (abbreviated as CIE from its French name, Commission Internationale de l'Éclairage). The plot illustrates the eye's sensitivity to different wavelengths of light. The data indicates that the sensitivity of the eye drops to near zero at 380 nm and at 720 nm. It also shows that the response of the eye is not uniform throughout the visible spectrum. Human vision is most sensitive to green light. If equal physical amounts of different colors of light are presented to an observer in turn, the green portion of the spectrum appears the brightest while the blue and red parts appear dim. This uneven response across the spectrum is key to working with light, color and digital image information as a whole; storage, transmission, compression and output of photographs are built on this foundational knowledge of our vision as we see in later chapters of this text.

Figure 1-3 plots the international *standard response function* for the measurement of light. This means that any light measurement device must possess a sensitivity

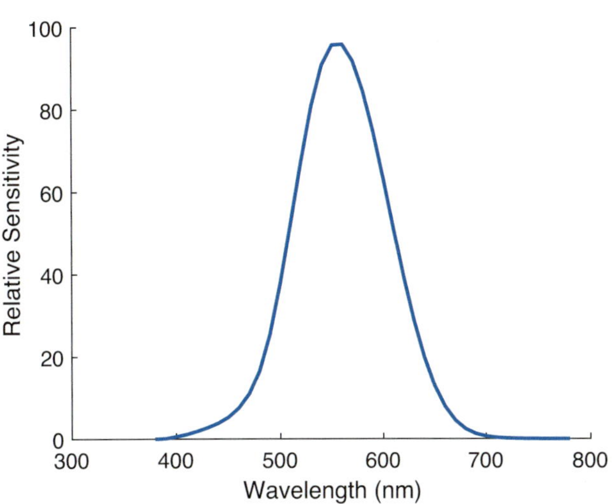

Figure 1-3 The photopic luminosity function or, more simply, the sensitivity curve of the human eye. The plot indicates the relative brightness of the energy at each wavelength.

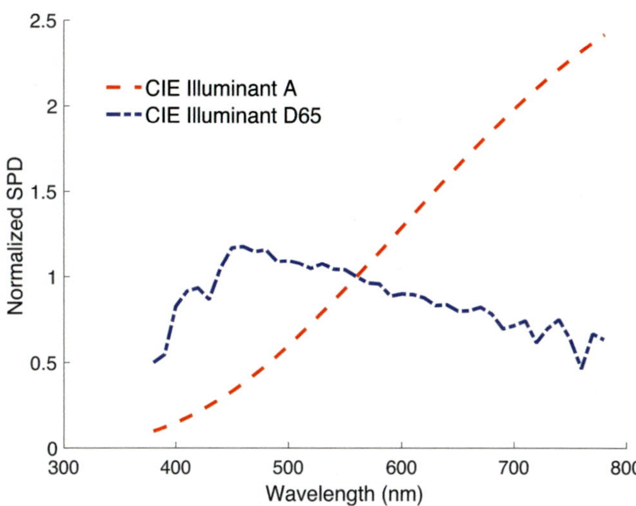

Figure 1-4 The spectral power distributions of a tungsten light source (CIE Illuminant A) and daylight at 6500K (CIE Illuminant D65).

function identical to it. Most photoelectric meters used in photography have response functions significantly different from the standard and are not properly called *light meters*, although the international standard curve can be approximated by using filters with some meters. Note that determining the proper f-number and shutter speed for a given photographic situation does not require a meter with this response function. It is more important for the meter to match the sensitivity of the image sensor or film emulsion used than that of the human eye.

When all of the wavelengths between approximately 400 and 700 nm are presented to the eye in nearly equal amounts, the light is perceived as white. There is no absolute standard for white light because the human visual system easily adapts to changing conditions in order to obtain the perception of a neutral "whiteness." For example, Figure 1-4 shows that the distribution of wavelengths of energy present in daylight are significantly different from those of tungsten light; however, both can be perceived as white due to physiological adaptation and the psychological phenomenon known as *color constancy*. Our eyes easily adapt to any reasonably uniform amounts of red, green and blue light in the prevailing illumination. Color constancy means that our eyes are not reliable for judging the color quality of the prevailing illumination for the purposes of color photography. To prove it to yourself, walk around with white notebook paper, moving from indoors to outdoors or between rooms with a variety of light sources. Your eyes and brain communicate that the paper is white in spite of the changes to the environment's dominant light source and the composition of the light energy reflected by it.

When a beam of white light passes through a glass prism as illustrated in Figure 1-5, the light is dispersed into its component colors (plus some energy we can't see on either end, ultraviolet and infrared). This separation of the colors occurs because wavelengths of light are bent by different amounts and is termed *dispersion*. Blue light, the shortest wavelength range in the visible spectrum, bends to a greater extent than the longer wavelength green and red light. The result is the rainbow of colors that spans deep violet to a deep red. Experiments indicate that human observers can distinguish nearly 100 different *spectral colors*. A spectral color is the result of a visual response to a single wavelength only. Such colors are the purest possible because they are unaffected by mixture with light of other wavelengths. It is also possible to specify a certain region or color of the spectrum by the bandwidth of the

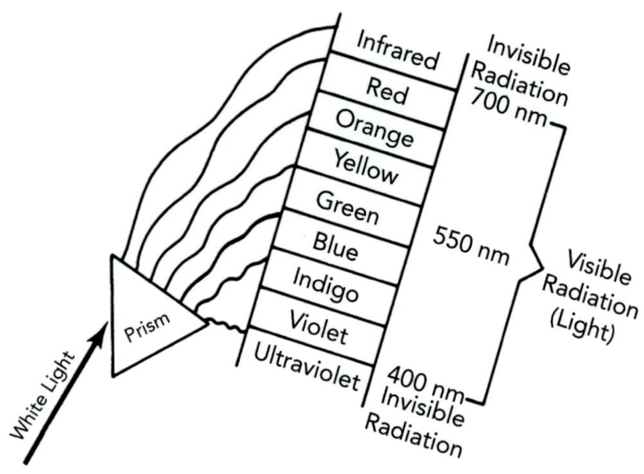

Figure 1-5 The dispersion of white light into the spectral colors.

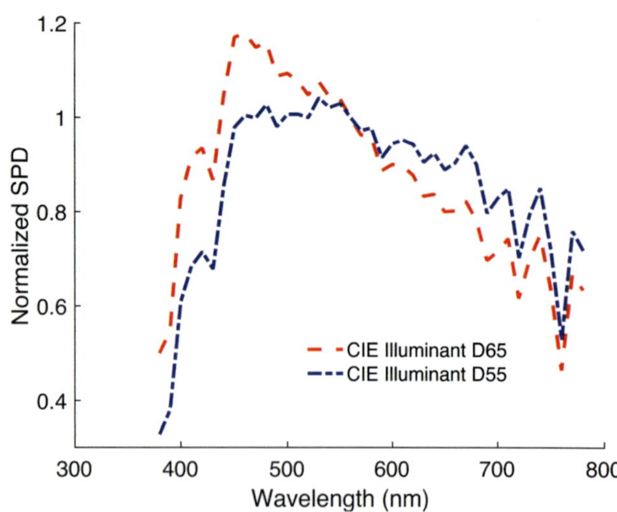

Figure 1-6 Spectral power distributions for D65 and D55 standard illuminants.

wavelengths. For example, the red portion of the spectrum is the region from 600 to 700 nm. It's estimated that we can see approximately 10 million colors when combining wavelengths of energy. However, the visible spectrum is often arbitrarily divided into the seven colors labeled in Figure 1-5: red, orange, yellow, green, blue, indigo and violet (ROY G BIV is commonly taught in grammar school). Our description of the visible spectrum is further simplified in the photography world into just three regions: red, green and blue.

Spectral Power Distributions

The ability to separate white light into its individual wavelengths via dispersion means that we can measure a light source by wavelength using a *spectroradiometer*. The resulting measurements, plotted as a function of energy at each wavelength, comprise a *spectral power distribution* (SPD). The amount of energy emitted across wavelength bands is plotted on an SPD plot to accurately describe a light source's energy emission. Figure 1-4 shows the SPD for two example tungsten and daylight sources. Notice that the tungsten line is smooth and continuous (without any breaks or gaps). As a result, tungsten sources are called *continuous sources* and their SPDs simulate that of a blackbody radiator.

Planck's equation is used to determine the SPD of a blackbody radiator at any temperature (see Equation 1.1). All of the terms in this equation are constant except for wavelength.

$$M = \frac{2hc^2}{\lambda^5(e^{hc/\lambda kT} - 1)} \qquad \text{(Eq. 1.1)}$$

where
h is Planck's constant of 6.6262 x 10^{-34} J-s
c is the speed of light with a value of 2.9979 x 10^8 m/s
λ is the wavelength of energy in meters
k is Boltzmann's constant of 1.3807 x 10^{-23} J/K, and
T is the absolute temperature of the light source in degrees Kelvin.

Standard illuminants are established models referenced for artificial light sources to describe their spectral power distribution relative to sunlight, our primary natural light source. An *illuminant* is another way to refer to a light source. The standard illuminant called *D65* defines the SPD for noon daylight in the shade. *D55* is another standard illuminant which defines noon daylight; we break down the difference between daylight and sunlight later in this chapter. Figure 1-6 shows these standard illuminants on a combined SPD plot.

Solid-Object Sources and the Heat-Light Relationship

Light is a form of energy that can only be produced from some other form of energy. The simplest and perhaps most common method is from heat energy, a process called *incandescence*. Whether the source is the filament in a tungsten bulb, a candle flame, or anything heated until it glows, incandescence is always associated with heat. The amount and color of light produced by an incandescent source is directly related to its temperature. Consider, for example, an iron poker with one end placed in a fire. Holding the opposite end feels cold, but as it is left in the fire its temperature rises and it begins to feel warm. By increasing the temperature of the poker, we become aware of a change in its radiating properties through our sense of touch even as it looks the same. Soon the poker becomes too hot to touch and we sense its radiation as heat from a short distance. As the temperature rises even higher, the poker reaches its point of incandescence and begins to emit a deep red glow. If the poker is allowed to get hotter still, the light grows brighter and becomes more yellowish. At extremely high temperatures, the end of the poker looks white and ultimately blue while becoming brighter still. This example illustrates that a solid object heated to its point of incandescence and higher produces light that varies in color as a function of its temperature. We use the absolute or Kelvin scale when describing the temperature of such sources because all objects emit some infrared energy at temperatures above absolute zero.

The best solid-object radiator is a *blackbody* as it absorbs all of the energy that strikes it. All light sources are radiators, though some are more efficient than others. Since a perfectly black object would absorb and emit energy but not reflect it when heated, it is the most efficient source. A blackbody source is achieved in practice by the design shown in Figure 1-7 consisting of an enclosure surrounded by a boiling material. Since the interior surface of the object is darkened and concave, any entering light is absorbed (immediately or after one or more reflections). Consequently, the hole appears perfectly black. As the walls are heated, they emit radiant energy in all directions. The energy that escapes through the hole is blackbody radiation. When such an experiment is performed and the blackbody is heated to a variety of temperatures, the spectral power distribution changes.

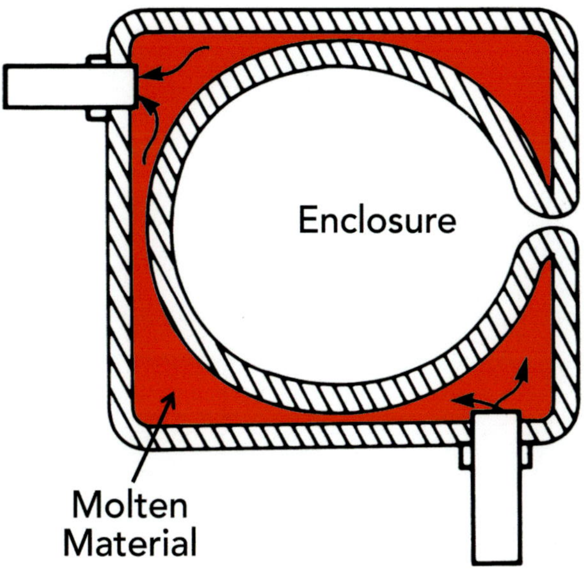

Figure 1-7 Cross section of a simple blackbody radiator consisting of an enclosure surrounded by boiling or molten material.

Vapor Sources and the Effect of Electrical Discharge

A fundamentally different method for producing light involves passing an electrical current through gases. Sources that employ this method are called *discharge* or *vapor lamps* and generally consist of a glass tube containing an inert gas with an electrode at each end. An electrical current is passed through the gas to produce light and ultraviolet energy. This energy may be used directly or to excite phosphors coated on the inside of the glass tube, as in a fluorescent lamp.

The basic process involved in the production of light is the same for all vapor lamps. Light emission from the vapor is caused by the transition of electrons from one energy state to another. When the electrical current is applied to the lamp, a free electron leaves one of the electrodes at high speed and collides with one of the valence electrons of the vapor atom. The electron from the vapor atom is

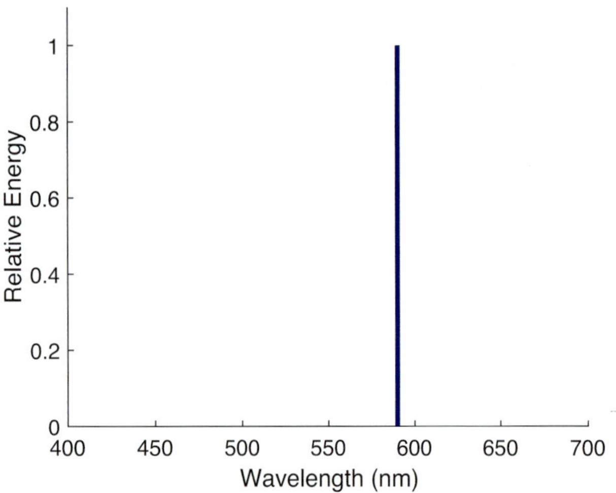

Figure 1-8 Spectral power distribution of a low-pressure sodium-vapor source. This source appears yellow.

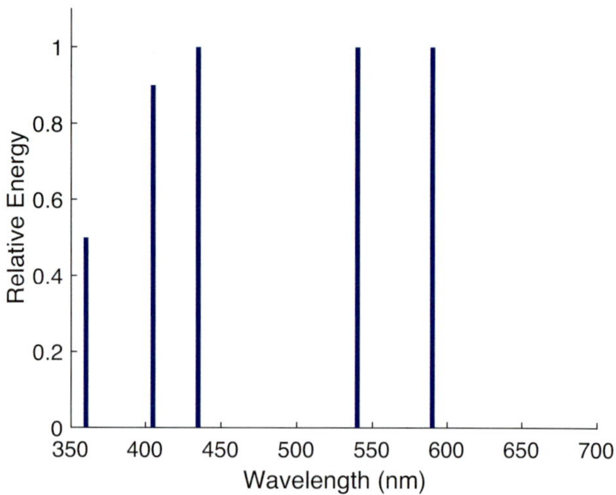

Figure 1-9 Spectral power distribution of a low-pressure mercury-vapor source. This source appears violet.

bumped from its normal energy level to a higher one and exists for a short time in an excited state. After the collision, the free electron is deflected and moves in a new direction at a reduced speed. However, it excites several more electrons before it completes its path through the lamp. The excited electron eventually drops back to its former energy level and emits some electromagnetic radiation in the process.

Each type of vapor atom, when excited, gives off energy at wavelengths determined by its structure. Some gases emit radiation only at a few wavelengths while others emit energy at many different wavelengths. These sources are said to show a *discontinuous spectrum* represented by a line on a spectral-energy plot. For example, the spectrum of sodium vapor shows a bright yellow line near 600 nm, as shown in Figure 1-8, while mercury vapor produces energy at many different wavelengths, both in the ultraviolet region and in the visible region, shown in Figure 1-9. The spectral characteristics of the emitted light are primarily dictated by the vapor in the tube.

The pressure under which the vapor is dispersed in the tube has a significant effect on the amount of energy emitted. Vapor lamps are categorized as *low pressure* or *high pressure*; low pressure indicates some small fraction of atmospheric pressure while high pressure describes sources working above atmospheric pressure. High-pressure sodium-vapor lamps are traditionally used for illuminating streets and parking lots at night. Low-pressure mercury-vapor sources are used in greenhouses as plant lights because the ultraviolet energy they emit is beneficial to plant growth.

Perhaps the most common vapor sources in daily life are *fluorescent lamps*. These are typically low-pressure mercury-vapor tubes with phosphors coated on the inside of the glass envelope (another name for the bulb enclosure). When bombarded by the large amount of ultraviolet radiation emitted by the mercury vapor, these phosphors begin to glow and give off visible energy at all wavelengths in the visible spectrum. Thus, the light emitted by a fluorescent lamp is the result of both the discontinuous energy emitted by the vapor and the continuous energy emitted by the fluorescing phosphors.

There are many classes of phosphors that can be used for this purpose. Each phosphor emits its own color of light. Figure 1-10 illustrates the spectral-energy distribution for a typical cool white fluorescent lamp. The light that corresponds to the discontinuous line spectrum produced by the mercury vapor may not be apparent to a human observer because of color constancy, described in Chapter 13.

Fluorescent lamps excite gas molecules within the tube with electrons to produce energy of discrete wavelengths, largely in the blue and ultraviolet regions (primarily dependent on the gas elements in the tube). Some of this

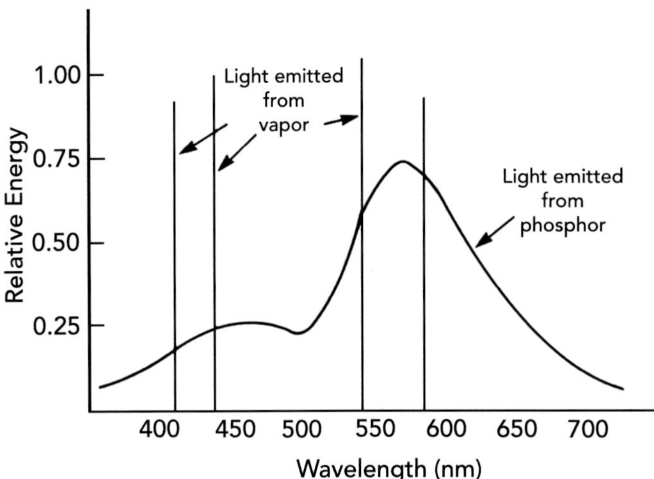

Figure 1-10 Spectral power distribution of a cool white fluorescent lamp.

energy is absorbed by phosphors coated on the inside of the tube and is converted to longer-wavelength, visible radiation. The color of the fluorescent emission is highly dependent on the phosphor material and the activators incorporated in it.

Luminescence, Fluorescence and Phosphorescence

Luminescence is the emission of light from a substance by means other than incandescence. Luminescence is a form of *cold body radiation* as it usually occurs at low temperatures. It is generally caused by the emission of photons from atoms excited by energy of relatively short wavelengths. As the electrons return to a lower energy level, energy of longer wavelengths is released. The rate at which this occurs can be affected by the presence of an activator made up of ionized atoms that trap and release electrons slowly for recombination. The exciting energy is usually in the ultraviolet region but can be caused by energy in the visible and infrared regions as well. There are many forms of luminescence.

Chemiluminescence is the result of a chemical reaction. A common example of chemiluminescence is found in forensics laboratories that use luminol, a chemical solution that indicates the presence of blood on a material or surface. The blood glows when it comes in contact with the iron in luminol. When chemiluminescence happens in a living organism, it is called *bioluminescence*. Bioluminescence is the result of biochemical reactions and is seen in fireflies and dinoflagellates (a type of plankton).

Triboluminescence occurs when rubbing breaks the asymmetrical bonds in a crystal, crushing or breaking the material. Examples include grinding sugar with a mortar and pestle or the sparks seen when biting into a Wint-O-Green Life Savers Mint in a dark room. Solid substances that luminesce are called phosphors.

Photoluminescence includes *fluorescence* and *phosphorescence* and is caused by a chemical compound absorbing photons, which elevates it to a higher energy state. Here the light photons are given off until the compound returns to its original energy state. The length of time this takes is typically around 10 nanoseconds.

Fluorescence is an emission of electromagnetic radiation in the visible region that occurs during the time of excitation. Thus, phosphors that are irradiated with ultraviolet energy fluoresce. The fluorescence emission ceases quickly when the excitation is removed: somewhere between 10^{-8} and 10^{-1} seconds depending on the activator. Fluorescence imaging is a key tool for imaging microscopic structures and biological processes.

Phosphorescence is similar to fluorescence but with a slower rate of decay. An example of phosphorescence can be found in glow-in-the-dark children's toys. Phosphorescence emission occurs after the excitation stops and lasts anywhere from 10^{-8} seconds to several hours. Its duration is largely dependent on temperature.

Some dyes fluoresce, including fluorescein, eosin, rhodamine and a collection of materials used as optical brighteners in materials like paper and fabric. Many modern photographic and digital printing papers are treated with brighteners to give them cleaner and more brilliant white appearances. This is a distinguishing characteristic when comparing modern prints to those made 40 or 50 years ago that did not use fluorescing agents. Fluorescence and phosphorescent dyes are also used in *organic light-emitting diode* (OLED) technologies that are becoming commonplace as display and lighting solutions.

Methods of Measuring Light

Candles were the standard light source when the field of photometry was established in the early 1900s. Consequently, many of the definitions and units of light measurement were based on the candle. It wasn't until 1940 that the international standard unit for light measurement became defined based on the light emitted by 1 square centimeter of a blackbody radiator heated to the temperature of solidification of platinum. This unit is called the *candela* and it's more exact and reproducible than relying on candles.

Starting with a clearly defined light source is important but we also need to know exactly how to measure that light source. Do we take a single measurement directly next to the source? Should we take multiple measurements all around a room lit by that source? What is the end goal for taking this measurement? Let's review the options.

Intensity

Intensity (also called *luminous intensity*) is a measure of the rate at which the source emits light in a given or single direction. Initially, the intensity of a source could be determined by comparison to the old standard candle, with the result expressed as *candlepower*. A 50-candlepower source emits light equivalent to amount of light from 50 standard candles. The modern equivalent is the *candela*. One candela is one-sixtieth the light from 1 square centimeter blackbody heated to the freezing temperature of platinum. Admittedly more of a mouthful, but decidedly more precise.

Tungsten lamps and fluorescent tubes always vary in their intensity with direction and therefore no single measurement of intensity can completely describe them. Perhaps the easiest way to understand the concept of intensity is to think of a ball-shaped lawn sprinkler with many holes through which the water sprays. Measuring the intensity of a light source is similar to measuring the rate at which water is sprayed through one of the sprinkler holes in a specific direction. Such information is of limited value since it does not describe the variation in intensities around the ball nor the total amount of water being emitted by the sprinkler.

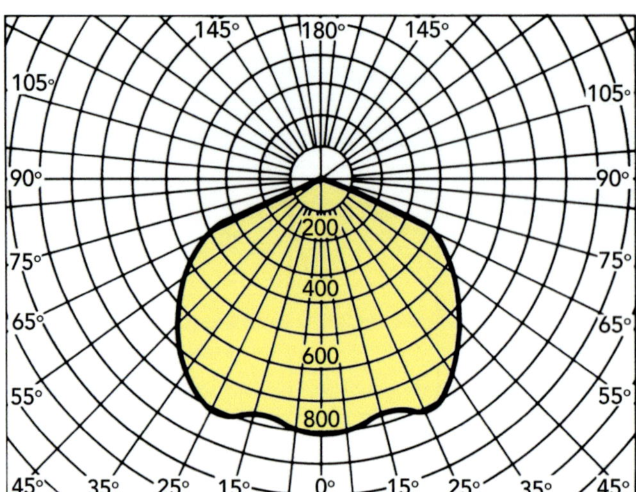

Figure 1-11 Polar coordinate plot of intensities for a lamp-reflector combination in candelas.

Since the intensity of a light source changes with direction, it helps to know the distribution of intensities. This information is often provided by the lamp manufacturer in the form of a two-dimensional graph based on polar coordinates, an example of which is shown in Figure 1-11. Intensity is plotted against the angle using a special graph called a polar-coordinate plot. The zero angle is head-on with the lamp, with the intensity in this direction known as the *beam intensity*. A lamp's intensity at any desired angle is derived from this plot.

The lamp-reflector combination illustrated in Figure 1-11 indicates that the beam intensity is approximately 800 candelas. This intensity is nearly uniform within 25° on either side of the beam position, indicating that this lamp-reflector combination provides nearly uniform illumination over a 50° angle of projection. At 65° off the beam position, the intensity drops to nearly 400 candelas. The same lamp equipped with a more narrowly curved reflector produces a distribution of intensities much narrower than what is shown in Figure 1-11. Understanding the distribution of intensity is particularly helpful when using artificial light sources in photography because it may mean the difference between spotlighting a subject's face in a portrait and lighting an entire set with an even glow.

There are three ways in which the intensity of a light source can be reported as a single value illustrated in Figure 1-12. In the simplest case, the intensity is

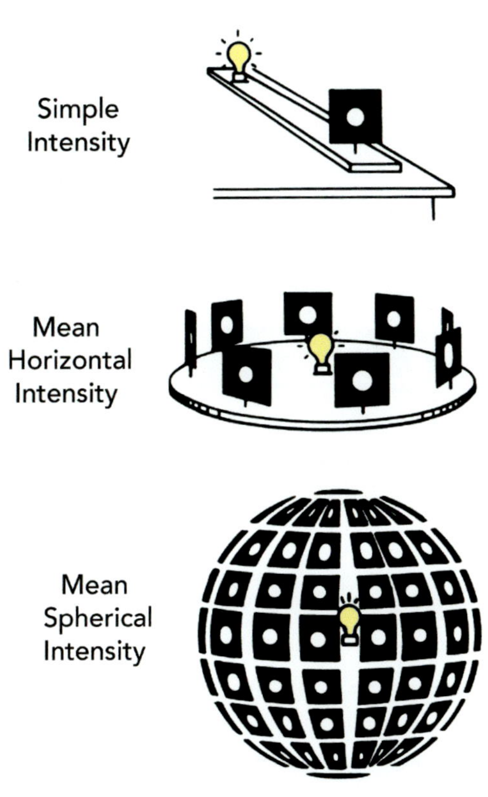

Figure 1-12 Three ways to measure light source intensity.

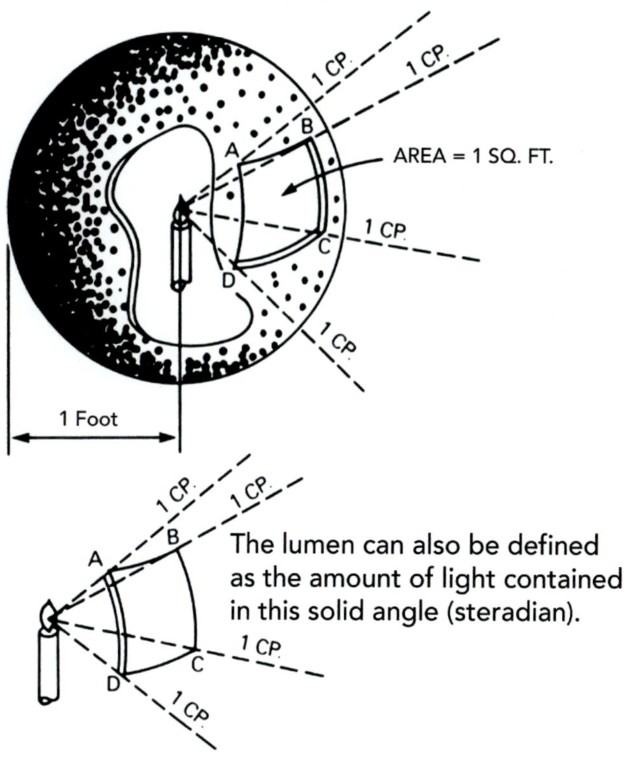

Figure 1-13 The relationship between candlepower or candelas and lumens.

measured in a single direction and reported as a single candela value. When a number of readings are taken at uniform intervals on a horizontal plane around the source and then averaged, the result is the *mean horizontal intensity* (candlepower) of the light source. Instead of taking a large number of individual readings, this result is obtained by rotating the source rapidly upon its vertical axis while repeated readings are taken. The intensity of light in all directions is determined by measuring intensities at uniform intervals around the light source. An average of these readings gives the *mean spherical intensity* (candlepower) of the illuminant. Note that this value is related to the total light output of the lamp. In each of these cases, the intensity is determined through comparison to a standard lamp at a variety of distances.

Flux

Another method of measuring light uses *flux* (sometimes called *luminous flux*), the rate at which a source emits light in all directions. The flux of a light source is calculated from intensity measurements and is closely related to the measurement of mean spherical intensity. The unit of measurement for flux is the *lumen*. The lumen is defined as the amount of light falling on a surface 1 square foot in area, every point of which is 1 foot from a uniform source of 1 candela. It is a three-dimensional concept as it concerns the light output in all possible directions in space. The relationship between the candela and the lumen is illustrated in Figure 1-13.

If the opening indicated by A, B, C, D in Figure 1-13 is 1 square foot of the surface area of a sphere with a 1-foot radius, the light escaping is 1 lumen. The light escaping becomes 2 lumens if the area of the opening is doubled.

The total surface area of a sphere with a 1-foot radius is 12.57 square feet (that is, $4\pi r$ where the radius is 1 foot). It follows that a uniform 1-candela source of light emits a total of 12.57 lumens. An area of 1 square foot on the surface of a sphere with a 1-foot radius subtends a unit solid angle (1 *steradian*) at the center of that sphere. The lumen is also defined as the amount of light emitted in a unit solid angle by a source with an average intensity of 1 candela throughout the solid angle. All of this is to say that, when considering a point source that emits light equally in all directions, there are 12.57 (4π) lumens of flux for every candela of intensity.

Illuminance

Candelas and lumens are both measurements of the light source but neither one considers the effect of the light on a surface or environment, only the source of it. For this, we turn to *illuminance*, the light incident upon a surface. Illuminance is measured in *footcandles*. A footcandle is the illumination at a point on a surface that is 1 foot from, and perpendicular to, the light rays from a 1-candela source. For example, if the light source in Figure 1-14 has an intensity of 1 candela, the illuminance at point A (1 foot distant from the source) is equal to 1 footcandle. The illuminance at points B and C is less because they are at distances greater than 1 foot. Therefore, an illuminance reading applies only to the particular point where the measurement is made. We determine the average illumination by averaging the footcandle measurements at a number of locations at our surface.

The footcandle is the unit of measure most closely associated with the everyday use of light. To get an idea of how much light 1 footcandle is, hold a lit candle 1 foot from a print in a dark room. The result is approximately 1 footcandle of illumination. A full moon on a clear night emits approximately 0.02 footcandles; a well-lit street at night gives approximately 5 footcandles; a well-lit classroom has nearly 50 footcandles of illumination. Direct sunlight is approximately 12,000 footcandles.

Referring again to Figure 1-13, the surface A, B, C, D fulfills the conditions for a surface illuminated to a level of 1 footcandle. Every point on this square foot of surface

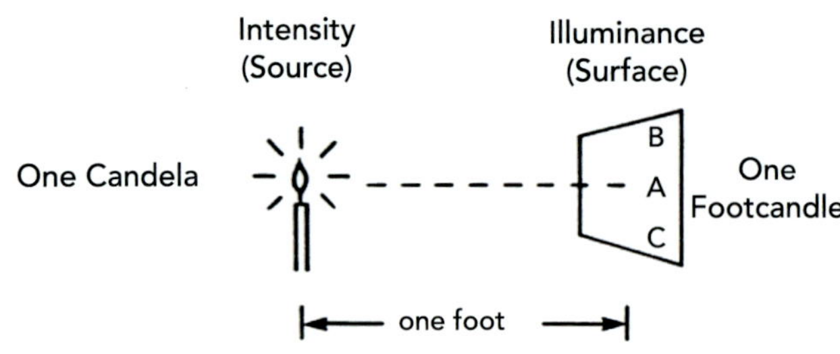

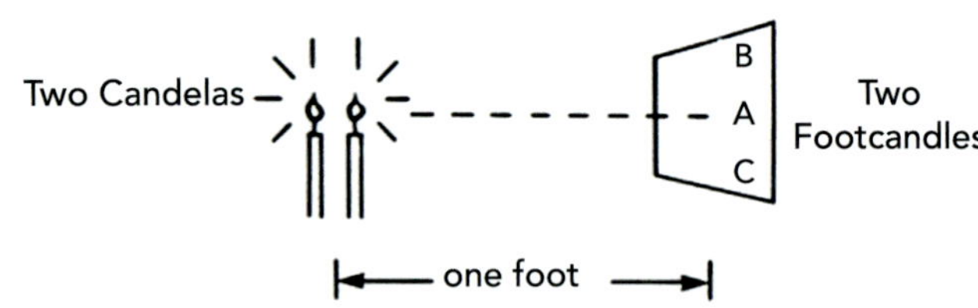

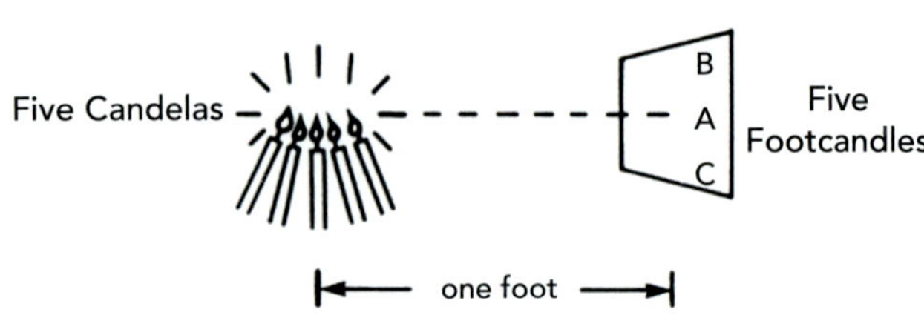

Figure 1-14 The relationship between intensity and illuminance at a constant distance of 1 foot.

is perpendicular to the rays of a 1-candela source placed 1 foot away. This illustrates an important relationship between lumens and footcandles. A lumen is the light flux spread over 1 square foot of area that illuminates that area to a level of 1 footcandle. Therefore, 1 footcandle is equal to 1 lumen per square foot. This forms the basis of a simplified approach to lighting design known as the *lumen method*. When the square footage of an environment is known and the desired level of illumination determined, it is simple to determine the number of lumens required.

With a 1-candela source, as shown in Figure 1-15, the level of illumination on point A 1 foot away is 1 footcandle. If plane A is removed and the same beam of light passes on to plane B, which is 2 feet away, this same beam of light now covers an area four times that of plane A. The average illumination on plane B is one-quarter as great as that on plane A, which is equal to one-quarter of a footcandle. If the beam of light is allowed to fall upon plane C, 3 feet

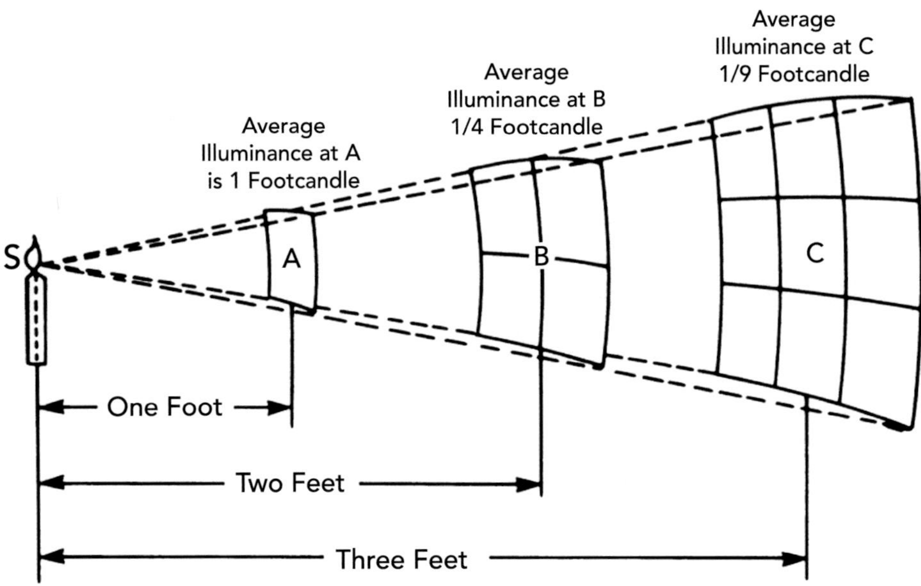

Figure 1-15 The relationship between intensity and illuminance for a constant intensity and varying source-to-surface distances, illustrating the inverse square law.

away from the source, it's spread over an area nine times as great as plane A, and so on.

From this we conclude that illumination falls off (or decreases) not in proportion to the distance but in proportion to the square of the distance. This relationship is known as the *inverse square law*. Put another way, this law shows us that doubling the distance of a light source from our subject results in one-quarter of the light. We instinctively know that moving a light farther away decreases the light available to make an exposure, though we might not intuitively grasp just how dramatic and rapid that decrease is as the distance grows. The light travels farther and also wider in its scope (i.e. the area illuminated increases with distance). The inverse square law is based on a *point source* of light from which the light rays diverge. In practice, it applies with close approximation when the diameter of the light source is no greater than approximately one-tenth the distance to the illuminated surface. In other words, a light behaves according to the inverse square law assuming it approximates a point source: the illumination must derive from a very small point (a tungsten bulb is one example). If a light source appears to emit light from a broad area, such as a softbox in the studio, it does not behave according to this law. Equation 1.2 defines the formula for the inverse square law:

$$F = \frac{I}{d^2} \qquad \text{(Eq. 1.2)}$$

Where *E* is the illuminance in footcandles, *I* is the intensity of the source in candelas and *d* is the distance of the surface from the source in feet. Illuminance measurements can be used to determine the intensity (expressed as candelas) of a source by solving the above equation for *I* as shown in Equation 1.3:

$$I = E \times d^2 \qquad \text{(Eq. 1.3)}$$

An alternative unit for measuring illuminance in photography is the *metercandle*. The definition of a metercandle is similar to that of a footcandle except the distance from the source; S to point A in Figure 1-14 is 1 meter. One metercandle is the amount of light falling on a surface at a point 1 meter from a 1-candela source. There are approximately 3.28 feet in 1 meter, making 1 metercandle equal to 0.0929 footcandles. Or, 1 footcandle is equal to 10.76 metercandles. The term metercandle is not used with great

Table 1-2 Standard illuminance levels for viewing reflection prints and luminance levels for viewing transparencies.

ANSI PH2.30-1989	
Comparison viewing/critical appraisal	2,200 ± 470 lux
Display, judging and routine inspection	800 ± 200 lux
Transparency viewing	1,400 ± 300 cd/m^2
ISO 3664:2009	
Prints and Proofs	2,000 ± 250 lux (preferred) 2,000 ± 500 lux (required)
Transparencies	1,270 ± 160 cd/m^2(preferred) 1,270 ± 320 cd/m^2 (required)

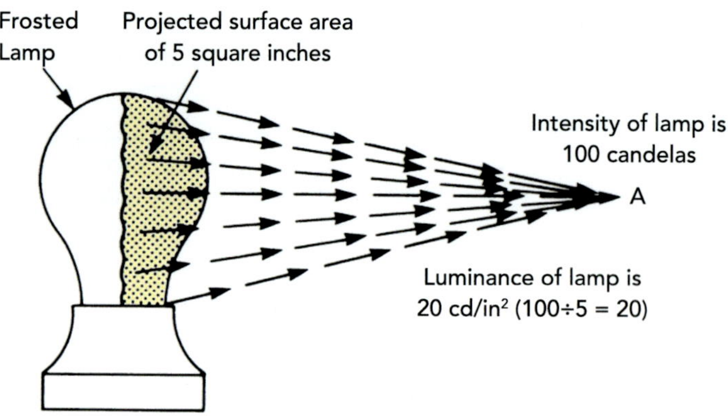

Figure 1-16 Measuring luminance as a function of intensity and surface area.

frequency today; the preferred term is *lux*. One lux is equal to 1 metercandle—an easy conversion to remember.

When exhibiting photographic prints, the level of illumination in the environment can have a significant impact on their appearance. Consequently, a number of standard conditions are specified for viewing purposes and are summarized in Table 1-2. The variety of levels suggested is due in part to the differing visual tasks being performed. For example, the viewing of prints for comparison purposes requires a higher level of discrimination and, therefore, a higher illuminance level than does the viewing of a pictorial display. Further, since print judging and display involve subjective opinions, it should not be surprising that a variety of standards exist.

Luminance

The rate at which the unit area of a source emits light in a specific direction is called *luminance*. If a source is not a point source but has an appreciable size (as all real sources do), it is less useful to describe the intensity of such a source than to specify its luminance. Luminance is derived from intensity measurements, which are then related to the projected surface of the source.

Luminance is expressed in *candelas per unit area* (candelas per square foot, candelas per square inch or candelas per square centimeter depending upon the size of the surface area considered). For example, Figure 1-16 shows a frosted tungsten lamp with an intensity of 100 candelas in the direction of point A. This lamp's projected area is 5 square inches. The luminance is equal to 100 candelas divided by 5 square inches, or 20 candelas per square inch.

Luminance is the photometric quantity that relates closely to the perceptual concept of *brightness*. Brightness is used exclusively to describe the perceived appearance of a source to the human eye and cannot be directly measured.

Generally, as the luminance of a source increases, so does the brightness of that source. If two 60-watt tungsten lamps are placed side by side—one lamp is frosted while the other is clear—the clear lamp looks much brighter. Both bulbs use the same amount of electrical energy and they both use a tungsten filament, so the intensities of the two lamps should be the same. However, the luminance of the clear bulb is greater because the projected area of the filament is smaller than the projected area of the glass envelope on the frosted lamp. We conclude from this observation that knowing a light source's intensity is less valuable than knowing its luminance. Consequently, luminance data for real sources is always preferred over intensity data when we want to better understand their visual appearance.

Measuring luminance applies to reflecting and transmitting surfaces as well, since it makes no difference whether the surface being considered is emitting the light or merely reflecting or transmitting it. In this respect, if all of the light falling on a perfectly diffusing surface were re-radiated by the surface, the luminance would be numerically equal to the illuminance. This does not happen in practice because real surfaces never reflect 100% of the light that strikes them. For this reason, it is necessary to determine the *reflection factor* of the surface, the ratio of reflected light to incident light. The following formula is used:

$$\text{Reflective Factor } (K) = \frac{\text{Reflected Light}}{\text{Incident Light}} \quad \text{(Eq. 1.4)}$$

Applying this formula to a perfectly diffusing surface, luminance equals illuminance multiplied by the reflection factor. The most commonly used unit of luminance when considering reflecting surfaces is *candelas per square foot* and the formula is:

$$L = \frac{K \times E}{\pi} \quad \text{(Eq. 1.5)}$$

where L is the surface luminance in candelas per square foot, E is footcandles incident on the surface and K is the reflection factor of the surface.

As illustrated in Figure 1-17, the product of the reflectance and the illuminance must be divided by π (3.14) since the light is emitted into a hemisphere of unit (1-foot) radius and IT is the ratio of the radius to the surface area of the hemisphere ($IT = A/(2r)^2$). For example, if a perfectly diffusing surface with 18% reflectance is illuminated with 100 footcandles of light, we calculate the luminance of that surface by multiplying 0.18 by 100 divided by 3.14, which equals 5.73 candelas per square foot.

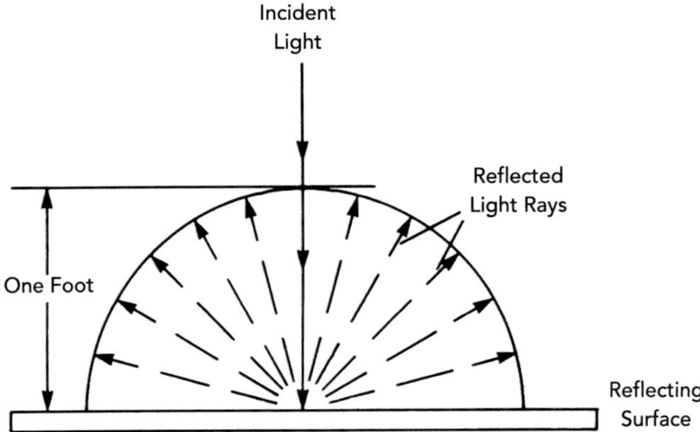

Figure 1-17 A perfectly diffusing surface; sometimes referred to as a Lambertian surface.

The *footlambert* was invented to avoid the need to divide by π all of the time. The footlambert is defined as one divided by π candelas per square foot. Thus, the previous relationship reduces to:

$$L = K \times E \quad \text{(Eq. 1.6)}$$

where L is now expressed in footlamberts.

The footlambert is actually defined as the luminance of a 100% reflecting surface illuminated by 1 footcandle of light. Therefore, the luminance of the previously described surface is calculated by multiplying 0.18 by 100 footcandles, which equals 18 footlamberts. Although the calculations are simpler for footlamberts, modern light meters read luminance directly in candelas per square foot. Candelas per square foot is the more commonly used unit of light measurement in photography.

Note that these examples assume that the illuminated surfaces are perfectly diffusing or reflecting equally in all directions. This is approximately true for matte surfaces. However, shiny surfaces give highly directional reflections and do not follow these formulas.

Luminance is particularly useful in photography since it provides a way of describing the light reflected from the surfaces of the subject being photographed. Whenever a reflected light meter reading is made, we're measuring luminance. Luminance measurements have the unique characteristic of being independent of the distance over which the measurement is made. For an example, if we use a handheld meter with a 50° angle of view to measure the reflected light from a surface, the luminance value obtained is identical to one taken with a spot meter from the camera location (light meters are discussed further in Chapter 4). The amount of light measured from the original area decreases with increasing distance and the projected surface area included in the angle of view increases in direct proportion. Thus, the number of candelas per square foot remains the same. This assumes a clear atmosphere exists between the meter and the surface area being measured, which is usually the case. The various conversions of illuminance data to luminance data are summarized in Table 1-3.

Table 1-3 Illuminance–luminance conversions based on an 18% reflectance neutral test card.

Illuminance to Luminance
Luminance = illuminance × reflectance
1. Footlambert = footcandle × reflectance Luminance = 1.0 footcandle × 0.18 = 0.18 footlambert
2. Candela per square foot = footcandle × reflectance/π Luminance = 1.0 footcandle × 0.18 = 0.18 / 3.1416 = 0.057 Cd/ft^2
3. Candela per square meter = metercandle × reflectance/π Luminance = 1.0 metercandle × 0.18 = 0.18 / 3.1416 = 0.057 Cd/m^2
Luminance to Illuminance
Illuminance = luminance / reflectance
1. Footcandle = footlambert / reflectance Illuminance = 1.0 footlambert / 0.18 = 5.56 footcandles
2. Metercandle = apostilb / reflectance Illuminance = 1.0 apostilb / 0.18 = 5.56 metercandles
3. Footcandle = candela per square foot × π/reflectance Illuminance = 1.0 candela/ft.^{2} × 3.1416 / 0.18 = 17.45 footcandles
4. Metercandle = candela per square meter × π/reflectance Illuminance = 1.0 candela/m^2 × 3.1416 / 0.18 = 17.45 metercandles

Notes:
1. A perfectly diffusely reflecting surface (100%) illuminated by 1 footcandle (1 lumen per square foot) reflects 1 footlambert (1 lumen per square foot or 1/π candela per square foot).
2. Metric: A perfectly diffusely reflecting surface (100%) illuminated by 1 metercandle (1 lumen per square meter or 1 lux) reflects 1 apostilb (1 lumen per square meter or 1/π candela per square meter).

Candle 1850K
Tungsten 2400K
Warm Fluorescent 3000K
Studio Lamp 3200K
Horizon Daylight 5000K
Xenon Lamp 6200K
Overcast Day 7000K
Hazy Sky 8000K
Clear Sky 10,000K

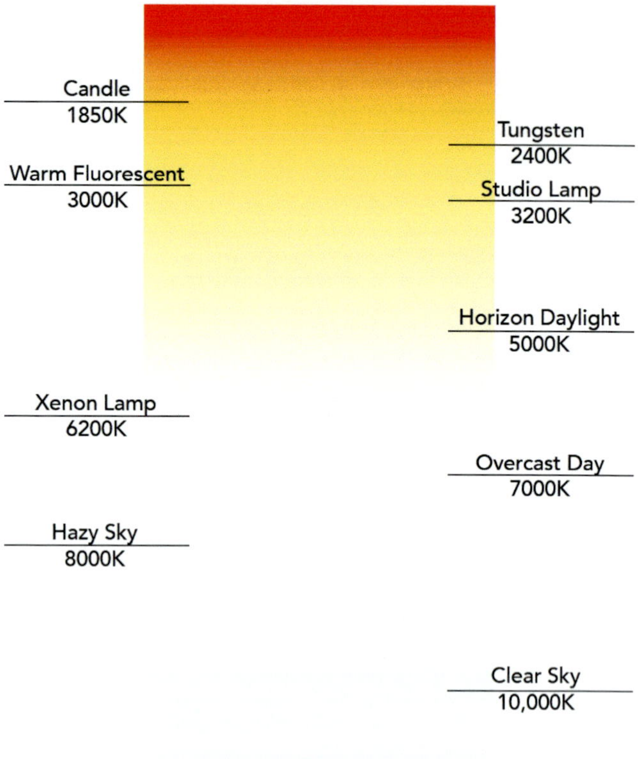

Figure 1-18 The range of color temperatures from warm to cool appearances.

Color Temperature

Since the amount and color of radiation emitted by a solid-object source is temperature-dependent, the color of light emitted from such a source can be completely specified by the Kelvin temperature (K) at which it is operating. Such a rating is referred to as the *color temperature* of the source. A color temperature is assigned to a light source by visually matching it to a blackbody radiator. The temperature of the blackbody radiator is raised until the color of its light visually matches that from the light source. The Kelvin temperature of the blackbody is then assigned as the color temperature of the light. The use of color temperature in photography presumes that the light source adheres to the same heat-to-light relationship as the blackbody radiator, meaning the plot of their spectral power distributions are continuous (see Figure 1-4). This presumption is correct for incandescent illuminants. However, the color of light emitted by some sources, such as fluorescent lamps, has no relationship to the operating temperature (see Figures 1-8, 1-9 and 1-10). In these cases, the measurement *correlated color temperature* (CCT) is required to indicate that the color of light emitted by a blackbody radiator of that temperature produces the closest visual match that can be made with the source in question.

The color temperatures of common light sources are shown in Figure 1-18. Counterintuitively, the color of a light becomes cooler or colder (read: more blue, less yellow) as

Table 1-4 Color temperatures of common light sources.

Light Source	Temperature (K)	Mired Value
Candle	1800–1900	555–526
Continuous LED studio lights	2700–6500 (variable)	370–153
Tungsten lamp	2800	357
CIE Tungsten illuminant or Illuminant A	2856	350
CIE Cool White Fluorescent	4100	244
Direct sunlight	4500	222
CIE D50 or horizon light	5000	200
Electronic flash	5500–6000	182–166
CIE D65 or noon daylight	6500	154
Sky light (overcast sky)	8000	125
North sky light	~15,000	67

the color temperature increases. This flies in the face of our everyday experiences with temperature—usually hotter things look more yellow or orange than blue. It is consistent, though, with the property of light that tells us shorter wavelength radiation has more energy.

Four CIE Standard Illuminants are listed in Table 1-4. Standard illuminants are theoretical light sources and do not represent specific consumer products. *Illuminant A*, introduced in 1931, represents a typical tungsten-filament light with a color temperature of 2856K. CIE *Cool White Fluorescent* or *F2* is one of 12 defined fluorescent standards. D50 and D65 represent daylight at 5000K and 6500K respectively. D50 is used in the printing industry while D65 is more often used in photography as it is a practical stand-in for average midday light.

Photographers are faced with a tremendous range of color temperatures, from the yellowish color of a candle at about 1800K to the bluish appearance of north skylight, rated at 15,000K. Though Figure 1-18 shows an approximate color temperature for a tungsten source, the actual color temperature encountered can vary significantly as a result of reflector and diffuser characteristics, changes in the power supply and the age of the bulb. Consequently, it is more accurate to measure a light source directly with a color temperature meter or to photograph a neutral-tone reference image (an 18% gray card works well) from which to calibrate a photograph's accurate color reproduction.

Light-emitting diode (LED) panels and bulbs are increasingly popular for photographic use for a variety of functional and practical reasons (weight, cost, minimal heat output). LED sources are particularly interesting in this context because, unlike tungsten sources, varying the voltage applied (i.e. using a dimmer control) does not change their color temperature. LED panels offer variable color temperature capabilities by using red, green and blue LEDs to make white light. Varying the brightness of each RGB cluster produces white light with a cooler or warmer color cast. This is a handy feature when looking to match a light's color temperature to an environment's existing light. Some panels feature amber and white LEDs in addition to red, green and blue (referred to as RGBAW) to ensure a pure, neutral white and warmer color temperature output options.

Color temperature meters employ three silicon photodiodes filtered for red, green and blue that approximate the sensitivity of image sensors. These meters measure the amount of energy present in each of the three regions of visible light and determine the color temperature by finding the closest match to a blackbody curve. They work best with continuous-spectrum light sources. If a color temperature meter is used to measure a vapor source that produces a discontinuous spectral power distribution, the results can be misleading and inaccurate due to significant differences in the measured response compared to the blackbody curves.

All color photographs have some notion of a neutral reference point in order to faithfully render the colors of a scene. In order to do this, cameras estimate or assume the color temperature of the primary light in the scene. Sometimes this works automatically without issue, but not always. Photographers have several options when the color temperature of the light does not match the response of the camera's sensor or if the software interpretation gets it wrong. Note that while the term color temperature is descriptive of the light source's appearance relative to a blackbody radiator, *color balance* is used to describe the color appearance of light rendered in a photograph. The term is often used interchangeably within the context of making images because we rarely care about a light source's characteristics for their own sake, we're interested in how it impacts any resulting photographs. Since a balance of color necessitates a definition of a neutral tone, like white, it's also called *white balance*. All three terms are reasonably used when describing a photograph, though color balance and white balance are not used to describe a light's character.

Cameras have several built-in white balance settings that correspond to commonly encountered color temperatures such as sunny daylight, cloudy daylight, indoor incandescent or indoor fluorescent. We can choose the white balance setting that appropriately corresponds to the scene. This may or may not give satisfactory results, especially knowing that there is considerable variability in the color of outdoor sunlight or indoor light bulbs. Take the example of an indoor incandescent light: the published color temperature for a light bulb in a living room is 2850K and the incandescent setting on our camera is calibrated to 3000K (an averaged value). This discrepancy may cause a color cast in the image. The second option available is establishing a custom white balance setting. It requires an extra step, but the results are much more likely to accurately render a scene's color. Setting a custom white balance involves taking a photograph of a neutral-toned object (white or gray works best) in the scene and selecting this image in the camera's menu as a reference photograph. An 18% gray card or neutral patch on a ColorChecker are ideal subjects because they are specifically created for colorimetric accuracy. The camera uses this reference image to understand the color temperature of the scene and assigns a custom value for use on all subsequent photographs. In effect, we help to calibrate the camera's understanding of the color quality of our scene. A third option is to disregard the issue altogether and wait until post-processing—not the most efficient workflow but one that does not negatively impact color reproduction or image quality in any way.

The Mired Scale

Although color temperature provides a useful scale for classifying the light from continuous-spectrum sources, it has limitations. A 500K change at the 3000K level, for example, does not produce the same visual or photographic effect as a 500K change at the 7000K level. This is because of the nonlinear relationship between changes in a source's color temperature and the changes in the color of light it produces, which is illustrated in Figure 1-19.

This awkwardness is eliminated using the *mired value*. The mired value is the reciprocal of the color temperature and exhibits a nearly linear relationship between the numeric value and the visual change. Mired is an acronym for the

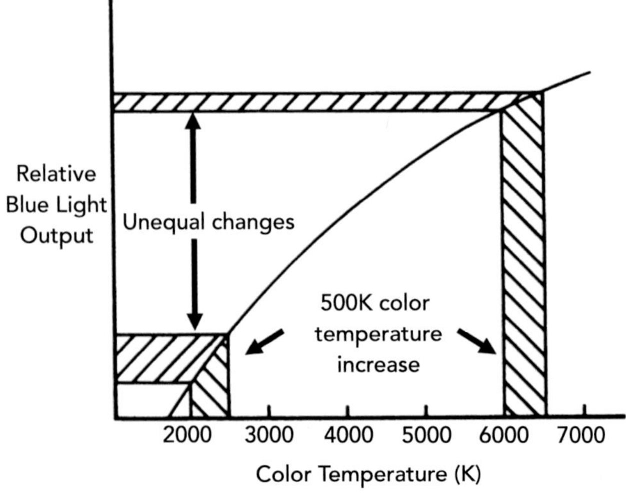

Figure 1-19 The relationship between color temperature and the relative amount of blue light emitted by a solid-object source.

term *micro-reciprocal degrees*. The reciprocal of color temperature value is quite small, so multiplying it by one million gets us a number that's easier to intuit. Convert color temperatures to the mired scale using the following formula:

$$mired = \frac{1{,}000{,}000}{color\ temperature} \quad \text{(Eq. 1.7)}$$

Color temperature meters can read out directly to mired values. *Decamired* is sometimes used for convenience; each decamired containing 10 mireds. For example, a mired value for a color temperature of 125,000K is 80, or 8 decamireds.

Figure 1-20 illustrates the relationship between changes on the mired scale and changes in the resulting effect. It shows that equal changes in the mired scale produce equal changes in the effect. The relationship between color temperature and mireds is illustrated in Figure 1-21, which indicates that the higher the color temperature, the lower the mired value. Bluish sources with very high color

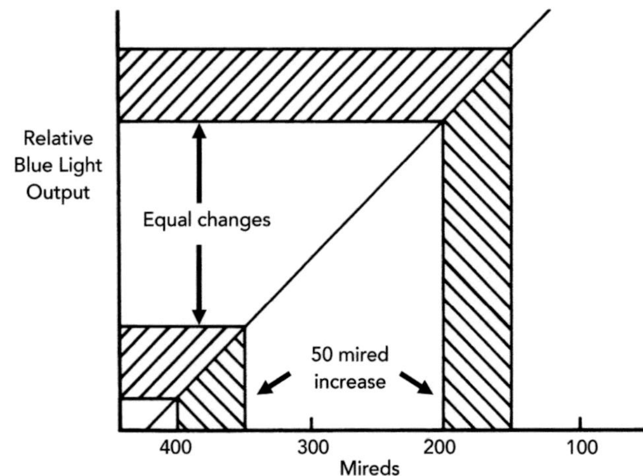

Figure 1-20 The relationship between mireds and the relative amount of blue light emitted by a solid-object source.

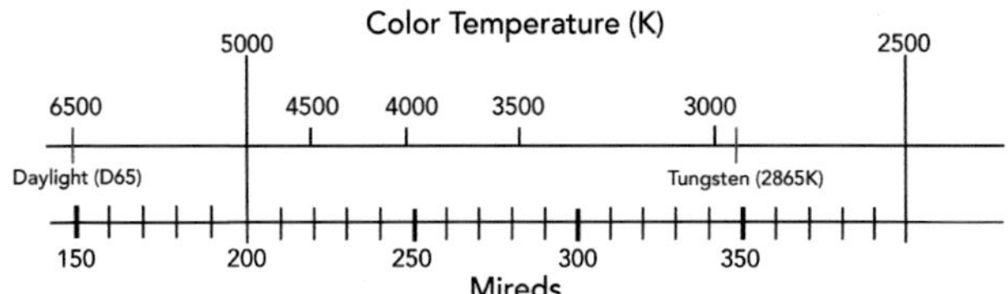

Figure 1-21 A comparison of color temperature and mired scale.

Table 1-5 Light measurement terms with typical examples of each. Note: Concepts 1–8 apply to light sources. Concept 8, Luminance, also applies to reflected and transmitted light. Concepts 9–10 apply to light falling on a surface.

Popular Concept	Technical Term	Symbol	Unit	Abbreviation	Measurement (Practical)
1. Strength	Luminous intensity	I	Candela	c	Compute from illuminance and distribution
2. Strength	Luminous flux	F	Lumen	lm	(Manufacturer data) or estimate watt × luminous efficiency
3. Strength/watt	Luminous efficiency	μ	Lumens/watt	lm/W	(Manufacturer data)
4. Total light	Luminous energy	Q	Lumen-second	lm-sec	(Manufacturer data) or integrate area under curve
5. Color	Wavelength	λ	Nanometer	nm	Spectrometer (electronic) Spectroscope (visual) Spectrograph(photographic)
6. Color Balance	Color Temperature	CT	Degree Kelvin	K	(Manufacturer data) or color-temperature meter
7. Source conversion	Mired shift	(N/A)	Mired	MSV	(Manufacturer data) or compute
8. Brightness	Luminance	L	Candela/sq. foot	c/ft.^{2}	Reflected-light meter
9. Illumination	Illuminance	E	Footcandle Metercandle Lux	ftc (fc) mc	Incident-light meter with flat surface
10. Exposure	Photographic exposure	H	Footcandle-second Metercandle-second	ftc-sec mc-sec	Compute H = illuminance × time

temperatures have very low mired values, while reddish-appearing sources with low color temperatures have high mired values.

In the past, photographers used the mired scale to determine which correction filters to place over the lens when the color balance of a light and the film were mismatched. In the digital realm, we use the mired scale to make corrections to the in-camera white balance. Since we discussed how color temperature values are not linear to the appearance of color changes, the mired scale is the logical and intuitive choice for user-controlled tweaks to color balance. We've encountered cameras with color balance menus allowing for a manual shift in color balance with mireds as the unit of change (i.e. +5 Green, −10 Magenta).

Table 1-5 summarizes many of the light measurement terms and presents typical values for comparison purposes. It is obvious from this table that light sources can be described in a wide variety of ways. It is important to understand the differences in order to obtain appropriate information.

Cool White
Relative Output (%)
100
50
0
400
500
600
700
Wavelength (nm)
Less red energy produced by this source.

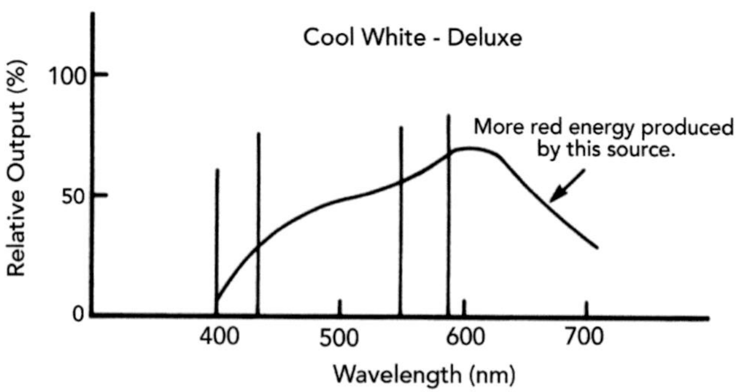

Figure 1-22 Spectral power distributions for two fluorescent lamps with the same correlated color temperature (4200K). Their CCT values can be the same despite the differing appearance of objects lit by them.

Color Rendering Index

Color temperature is a great way to quantify the visual appearance of a light source. It does not tell us anything about an object's color appearance under that same source. Since an object's color is a function of the light it reflects, it stands that its color appearance can change based on the light source's spectral emission. The following example illustrates why this matters.

The spectral-energy distributions for two fluorescent lamps of equal correlated color temperature are shown in Figure 1-22. The Cool White Deluxe lamp produces more red light than the Cool White lamp, resulting in widely different color rendering for some objects. If a person's face is illuminated by these sources, the Cool White Deluxe lamp casts more red light, some of which reflects back to the camera. This results in a healthier, more natural skin complexion appearance than that given by the Cool White lamp.

The CIE developed the *color rendering index* (CRI) in 1965 to quantify a light source's ability to accurately reproduce the perceived color of an object when compared to an ideal, standard light source. For light sources with a color temperature between 2000K and 5000K, the standard is the blackbody radiator. For sources above 5000K, the standard is D65. Two evaluated sources can only be compared to each other if their reference sources are similar (within approximately 200K). Spectral power distribution is the key characteristic dictating a light's CRI: the more a light source differs from the spectral power distribution of natural daylight, the lower its CRI is likely to be. Color rendering index and color temperature are independent characteristics.

The color rendering index was designed to evaluate continuous-spectrum tungsten or incandescent light sources. The reference source always has a CRI of 100. The higher the CRI for a given source, the more closely object colors appear to their counterparts under the reference source and the better the color rendition. A CRI value of 100 indicates that there is no color difference between the standard and the evaluated light source, offering perfect

Table 1-6 Color temperatures and color rendering indexes for a variety of light sources. There are often premium models alongside standard versions offering higher CRIs.

Bulb Type	Color Temperature	Color Rendering Index
Tungsten: Warm White	3000K	53
Tungsten: Warm White Deluxe	2900K	75
Tungsten: White	3500K	60
Tungsten: Cool White	4200K	66
Tungsten: Cool White Deluxe	4200K	90
LED: Daylight	5000K	85
LED: Soft White	2700K	80
Tungsten Halogen	2850K	100
Compact Fluorescent	2700K–6500K	80
Mercury Vapor	4200K	20

color rendering. A score of 80–90 is very good; anything over 90 is an excellent color rendering light source. A negative CRI value can exist, though this should not be surprising to anyone that's stood out in a parking lot at night: sodium vapor lights are one example.[1] These illuminants are particularly poor in producing accurate color appearances. Photographing under high CRI-scored light sources is not required for color photography in general, but it is desirable when color accuracy counts. Table 1-6 lists common light sources, their color temperatures and their color rendering index values.

Determining the color rendering index for a light source requires knowing the spectral power distribution and the color temperature (or CCT in the case of non-continuous spectrum sources) so that an appropriate reference source can be selected. First, we measure the CIE chromaticities of eight Munsell color samples with low to medium chromatic saturation under the evaluated source (more on what this measurement means in Chapter 14). Next, we do the same under the reference source. The differences between the two sets of data indicate the color shift; the eight differences are averaged to arrive at the color rendering index. This method can be misleading because poor scores on a few of the samples can still yield a desirable CRI. The calculation also uses a color space considered obsolete by color science experts today and the eight color samples have proven to work poorly under modern light sources like LEDs. The color rendering index calculation was last revised in 1995. The CIE recently called for an additional revision, but one has not yet been established.[2,3] The Illuminating Engineering Society published a promising metric in 2015 aimed at replacing CRI called *TM-30*; it is not officially endorsed by CIE.[4,5]

The Color Quality Scale

The National Institute of Standards and Technology (NIST) recently developed a new method for evaluating a light source's color rendering ability that addresses the shortcomings of CRI called the *Color Quality Scale* (CQS).[6] CQS and CRI are similar in that they use averages of color differences. They differ in that the CQS uses 15 color samples to the CRI's eight.

NIST selected the 15 samples from the Munsell Book of Color. All of them have the highest chroma available for their hues (remember, CRI uses low and medium chroma) and sample the Munsell hue circle with approximately even spacing. They selected these samples to more accurately span the color of normal objects and to include saturated colors that include the peak wavelengths of modern light sources. These samples are also commercially available from X-Rite Incorporated, the owner of Munsell. The CQS uses the 1976 L*a*b* (CIELAB) color space for its calculations because it is the CIE-recommended color space and is considered visually uniform. The Munsell System and CIELAB systems are also discussed in Chapter 13.

At the time of publication, the CIE recognizes the flaws with CRI and is investigating an update to the CRI metric. They do not yet endorse the CQS but published the following statement on revisions or new approaches to color rendering metrics: "The CIE . . . recommends that important lighting metrics such as the Colour Rendering Index require formal international agreement. New metrics introduced at the regional level could cause confusion in the global lighting market."[7]

Describing the Appearance of Light

We describe the appearance of light as being either *specular* or *diffuse*. Point sources (bare light bulbs, bright sun on a clear day) produce specular, directional light. This type of light is characterized by having hard-edged, well-defined shadows, bright highlights and specular highlights in reflective areas or surfaces. Reflective surfaces reflect a large percentage of the incident light rays in an orderly fashion which leads to such bright highlights. *Broad sources* (studio softboxes, overhead office lighting) produce diffuse, non-directional light. This type of light is characterized as having soft, ill-defined shadows (if it produces any at all) and low contrast between highlights and shadows.[8] Rough, uneven or textured surfaces act to further scatter incident light and lead to diffuse reflections even if that light is specular.

Figure 1-23 shows a pair of tomatoes photographed with a point light source and with a diffuse light source in a studio. In addition to identifying that the primary light source is specular, we also identify:

1. Highlights: the bright, directly illuminated portion of the subject.
2. Specular highlights: the brightest and most reflective parts of the subject, often rendered as pure white.
3. Shadows: the darker areas blocked from direct light by the subject. Note how this area is not devoid of light entirely but instead illuminated by indirect light bouncing off of the environment.

Identifying light in an environment or crafted studio setup is important for two reasons. First, it helps avoid making poor metering decisions. Making light measurements from a specular light source can be misleading due to its high contrast between bright and dark areas. Second, the appearance of light and its characteristics relative to the illuminated subject influences our perception of that subject. Since specular highlights are a consequence of reflectivity, we're highly attuned to seeing them when a surface has a glossy or shiny texture. This could be due to the material (metal, mirrors) or the subject's condition

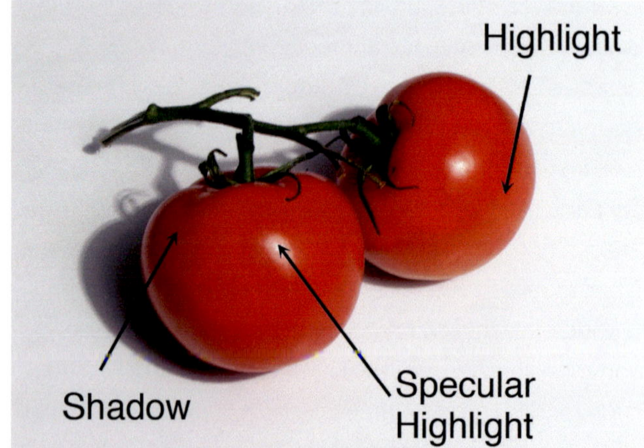

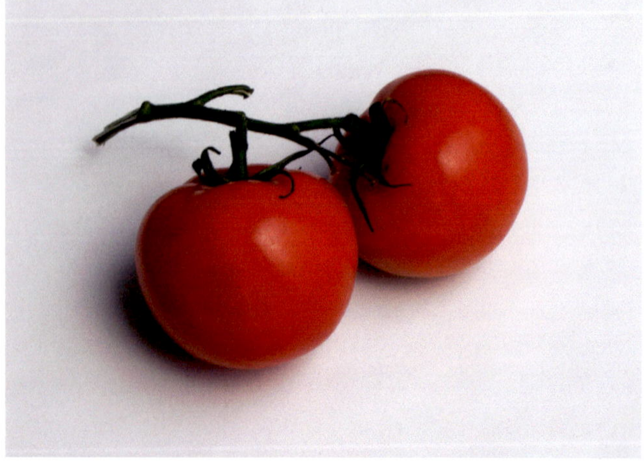

Figure 1-23 The same subject can look different when lit primarily by a point light source (top) or diffuse light source (bottom).

(freshly polished, wet). We subconsciously infer a subject's texture or material composition by the presence or absence of these specular highlights.

Earlier, we defined skylight as the light scattered by molecules in the Earth's atmosphere. This indirect light is important because it adds a diffuse quality to sunlight. Direct sunlight acts as a point source because it is one small spot in the sky. When some of that light bounces around in our atmosphere, especially on an overcast day where it scatters through thick clouds, sunlight takes on a completely different appearance. Instead of a single, intensely bright source, the sun effectively becomes a dimmer, spread out one. You can block the sun from your eyes by putting a hand up in front of your face, but consider the scale of the light source when it's spread across the entire visible sky on a cloudy day. Think of this the next time you're looking to do an outdoor portrait shoot—an overcast day might be more desirable than one with clear skies.

The sun also illustrates that a light source's *effective size* is a defining characteristic of light quality. There is no light source in our solar system physically larger than the sun (a star with a diameter more than 100 times that of Earth). Yet it's distance from us is so great that it's effective size in the sky is actually quite small. The quality of light provided by the sun on a clear day (acting as a point source) falling on a building is comparable to a lamp illuminating a pair of playing dice on a desk. The effective size of a light source considers the size and position of the light relative to the subject. Bringing the lamp close to the dice dramatically changes the light quality and renders them just as it would if the Earth were moved much closer to the sun. Both subjects get considerably warmer, too.

The Polarization of Light

As discussed at the start of this chapter, light appears to travel in a wave-like motion. The vibrations of these light waves occur in all directions at right angles to the path of travel, as illustrated by the light beam to the left of the filter in Figure 1-24. This is an *unpolarized light beam*. When light waves vibrate exclusively in one direction it is *polarized*. The light beam on the right of the filter illustrates this condition.

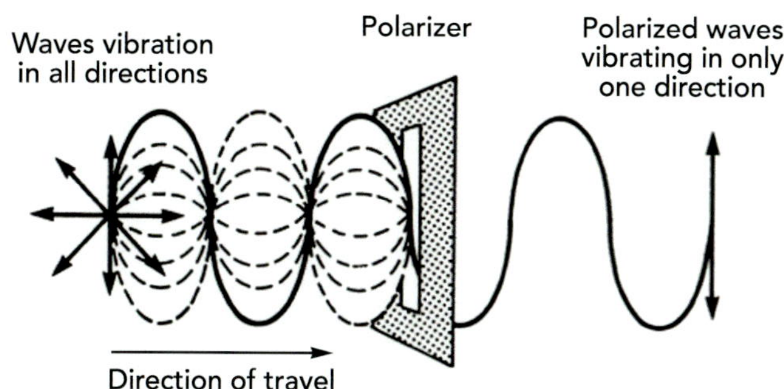

Figure 1-24 The polarization of light.

The polarization of light occurs naturally in a number of ways:

1. Light emitted from a portion of clear blue sky, at right angles to a line connecting the viewer (or camera) and the sun, is highly polarized. The scattering of the light rays is caused by very small particles in the atmosphere such as dust, molecules of water vapor and other gases. As the angle decreases, the effect also decreases, illustrated in Figure 1-25. A portion of the light blue sky encountered in typical outdoor scenes is polarized.
2. Light becomes polarized when it is reflected from a flat, glossy, non-metallic surface like glass, water and shiny plastics. This effect is maximized at an angle whose tangent is equal to the refractive index of the reflecting material; this is known as the *Brewster angle*. For surfaces

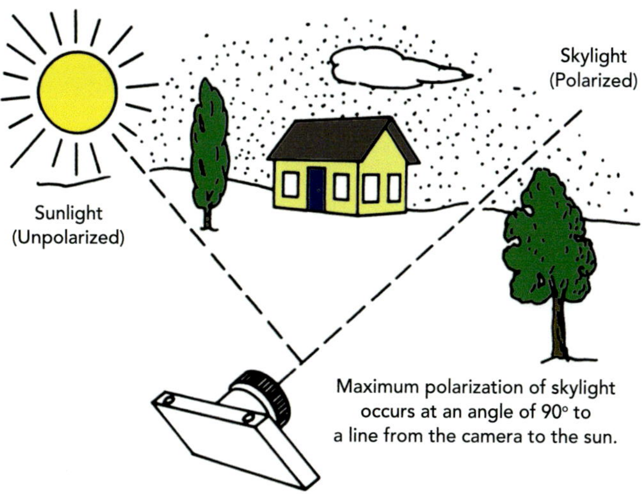

Figure 1-25 The polarization of skylight.

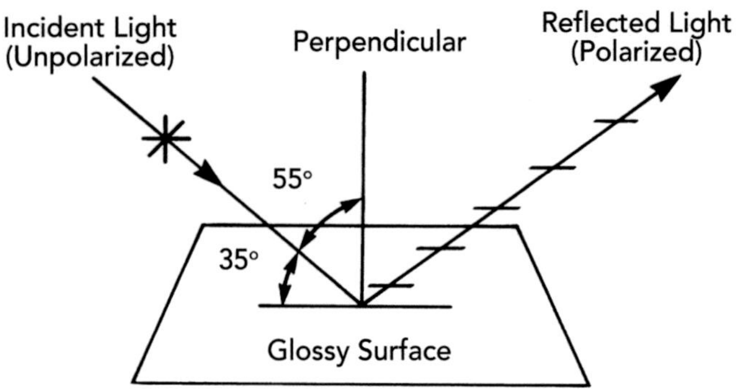

Figure 1-26 The polarization of light reflected from a glossy surface.

like glass and water, this angle is approximately 55° from the perpendicular (35° from the surface) and is illustrated in Figure 1-26.

3. Light becomes polarized when it is transmitted through certain natural crystals or commercially manufactured polarizing filters. Tourmaline is an example of a dichroic mineral that polarizes the light it transmits. *Dichroic* means that the material exhibits multiple refractive indices, causing light to move through it differently than standard materials. When a beam of unpolarized light passes through a thin slab of tourmaline, the only light transmitted is oriented along a single plane. This property is demonstrated by rotating a second slab of tourmaline across the direction of polarization as illustrated in Figure 1-27. When the second slab is rotated to a position of 90° from that of the first, no light is transmitted through the second filter. Commercially available polarizing filters are made from materials whose chemical composition calls for the grouping of parallel molecular chains within the filter. This is the nature of the filters illustrated in Figures 1-24 and 1-27.

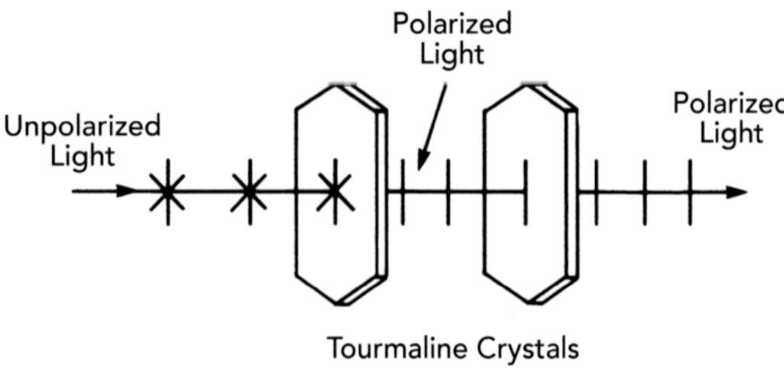

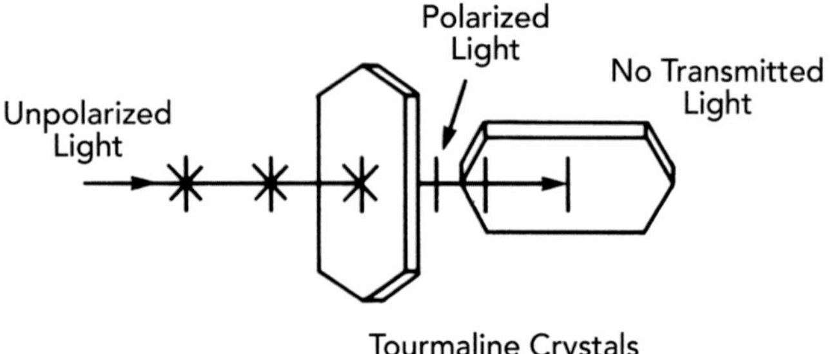

Figure 1-27 The polarizing effect of a tourmaline crystal.

Polarized light becomes depolarized when it strikes a scattering medium. This most frequently occurs when the light reflects off of a matte surface, such as a sheet of white photo paper. It can also become depolarized upon transmission through a translucent material like a sheet of acetate.

Commonly Encountered Light Sources

So far, our discussion of light has centered on methods of production, its properties and measurement. Presumably, you'd like to take a photograph at some point! Let's review the light sources most often encountered by photographers. Broadly speaking, light sources come in two varieties: artificial or natural. The primary natural light source is, of course, the sun. Artificial sources can be subcategorized as *continuous* or *discontinuous* in duration (try not to mix this up with their spectral emission continuity—here we're describing emission as a function of time). Sunlight, tungsten bulbs and LEDs are all continuous as they provide illumination for as long as we may wish to take a photograph, even if that's a duration spanning many minutes. Studio strobes or handheld flash units, on the other hand, are generally considered to be discontinuous because they illuminate for brief fractions of a second. Let's dive into our light sources in greater detail.

Sunlight

The sun produces enormous amounts of radiation in all directions through space. The radiation that we see travels through the vacuum of space, through our planet's atmosphere, onto the surfaces of everything around us. Luckily, that atmosphere mostly protects us from the forms of radiation our bodies find harmful while allowing quite a lot of visible light radiation through. We often consider the sun as a fairly simple light source: it's always the same size in the sky, we learn from an early age to draw it as a yellow circle and we have interactions with it many hours a day (unless you retreat to a dark room with shut curtains in the hopes of completing a textbook). However, its qualities vary with a complex combination of variables. The time of year, your elevation relative to sea level, air quality, weather conditions and time of day all change the appearance of sunlight.

Daylight is composed of at least two different sources of light: direct sunlight, which travels directly through Earth's atmosphere; and *skylight*, the light scattered and reflected within the atmosphere. Skylight is blue because the small particles in the atmosphere selectively scatter light—especially the short wavelengths—away from the direction of travel of the sunlight. This effect is known as *Rayleigh scattering* and it varies inversely with the fourth power of the wavelength. In other words, the scattering at 400 nm is 9.4 times greater than at 700 nm. The color temperature of blue skylight ranges between 10,000 and 20,000K. Additional light may also reach the subject by reflecting off of objects. *Mie scattering* is an effect caused by water droplets suspended in clouds that are similarly sized to light wavelengths (indiscriminately across the visible light wavelength range) and explains why clouds are white.

The amount of direct sunlight is at a maximum when the sky is clear. This results in 88% of the total light on the ground, producing a lighting ratio of approximately 8:1. The ratio decreases as the amount of overcast increases. Skylight supplies significant "fill" in the sense that shadowed areas not receiving direct sunlight are still very well illuminated. We can appreciate the contribution of skylight in illuminating our world by observing its absence: the moon has no atmosphere and thus no skylight, only direct sunlight illumination. Photographs taken on the moon show a world with harsh, contrasty light and deep, impenetrable shadows. Even if it had air to breathe, photographers would have a considerable challenge making flattering glamour portraits on the moon.

While you're thinking about the moon, consider that it's got the same spectral power distribution as daylight—it's a D65 illuminant—albeit at a fraction of the intensity, since moonlight is simply sunlight reflecting off of the moon's surface.[9] It's a moot point for our vision since we don't perceive color at extremely low light levels, but it may come in handy when shooting a nighttime exposure lit exclusively by the moon.

Back to the sun: its energy distribution outside of Earth's atmosphere closely approximates that of a blackbody source at 6500K. A considerable amount of this light is lost as it travels through the atmosphere, particularly in the blue region of the spectrum. The color temperature of sunlight combined with the scattered skylight varies between 5000K and 6000K measured from the ground at midday (noon). Daylight white balance presets on cameras are typically tuned to a color temperature of 5500K. Variations in color temperature with the time of day are illustrated in Figure 1-28, illustrating how a one-size-fits-all setting for daylight is not ideal. This is especially true when taking photographs at sunrise or sunset because the sun's oblique angle relative to the viewer causes light to travel through more of the Earth's atmosphere, illustrated in Figure 1-29 (overleaf). During these brief but beautiful times of the day, that additional atmosphere in the light's path scatters much of the blue and green bands, rendering warm red and orange hues. Photographers refer to this as the *golden hour*, though its true duration and probability of occurring is largely dependent on

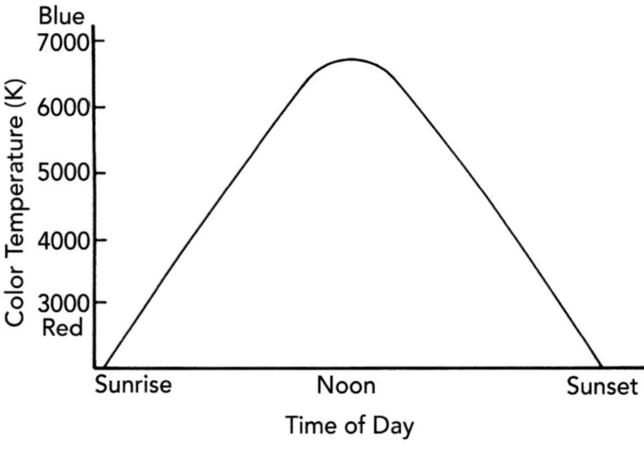

Figure 1-28 The variation in light color temperature with time of day at the surface of the Earth (no cloud cover).

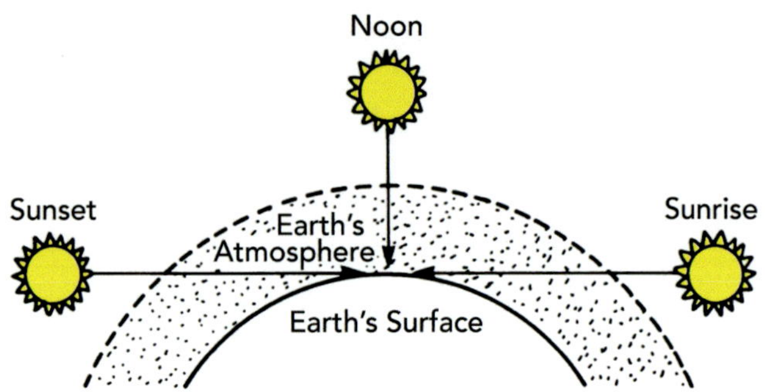

Figure 1-29 The relationship between position of the sun and the length of the sunlight's path of travel through Earth's atmosphere.

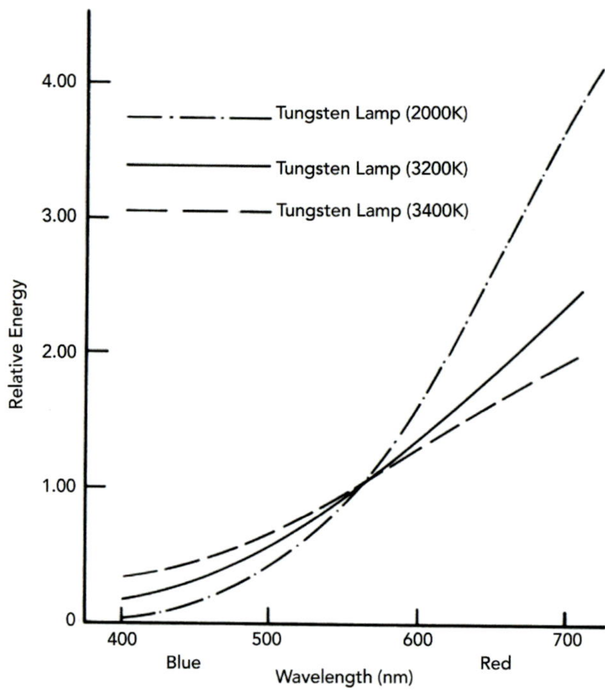

Figure 1-30 Relative spectral power distributions for three incandescent sources.

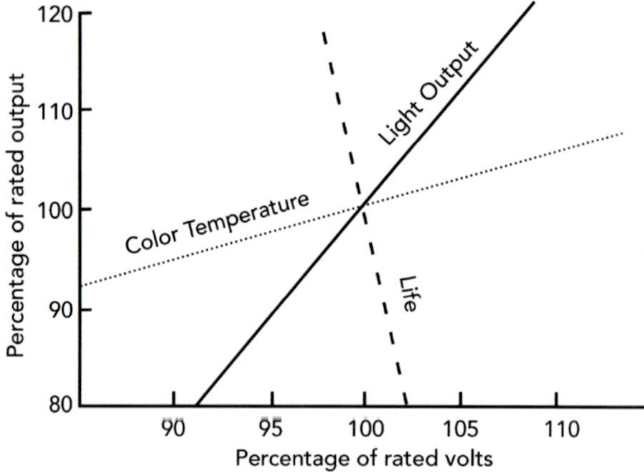

Figure 1-31 The variation in light output, color temperature and life of a tungsten lamp at different voltages.

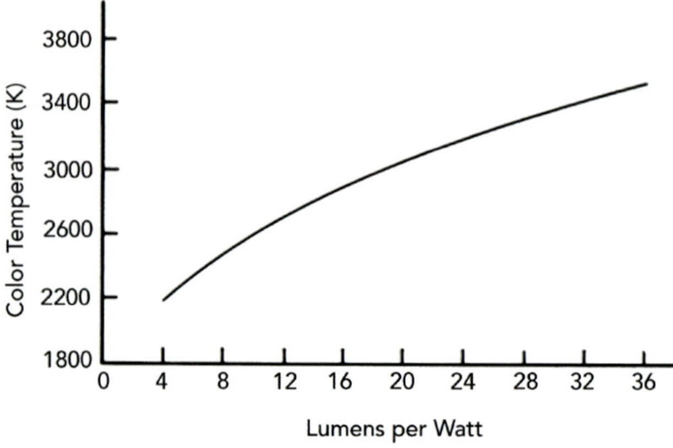

Figure 1-32 The average relationship between luminous efficiency and color temperature of tungsten-filament lamps.

weather and geographic location. Morning light tends to be less intense and often cooler in color temperature compared to sunsets due to the air's humidity in transitioning from cooler nighttime temperatures.

Tungsten-Filament Lamps

Incandescent lamps emit light when the tungsten-filament wire reaches a high temperature as the result of its resistance to the passage of electricity. Electricity is converted to heat which is then converted to light. The filament is housed in a glass envelope (the bulb) containing an inert gas such as nitrogen or argon and it evaporates as it heats up, ultimately settling on the inside surface of the envelope—this is why a dead tungsten bulb appears blackened or opaque. The upper temperature limit for this type of source is 3650K: the melting temperature of tungsten. The color temperature of light emitted by tungsten-filament lamps ranges from 2700K for a 15-watt household light bulb to 3200K for photographic studio lamp. Figures 1-30, 1-31 and 1-32 highlight the relationships of spectral-energy distribution, voltage, color temperature and energy efficiency.

Tungsten bulbs are waning in popularity due to their low energy efficiency relative to alternatives like LED bulbs; they can waste up to 90% of the input energy through heat emission rather than light emission. Many countries have already started the phase out of these bulbs in favor of more efficient modern bulbs for basic infrastructure projects like street lamps.

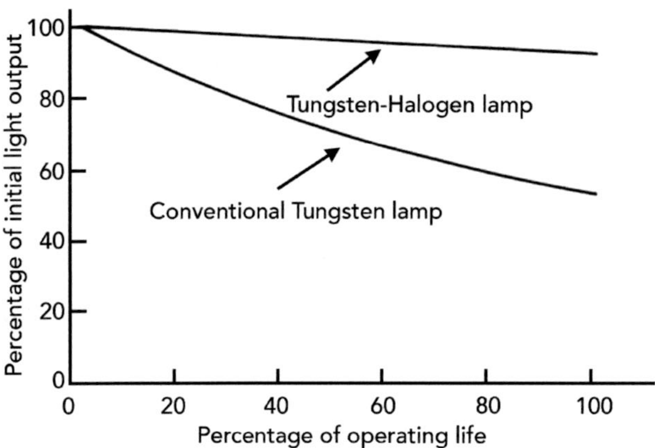

Figure 1-33 Typical lamp depreciation for a conventional tungsten lamp and a tungsten-halogen lamp.

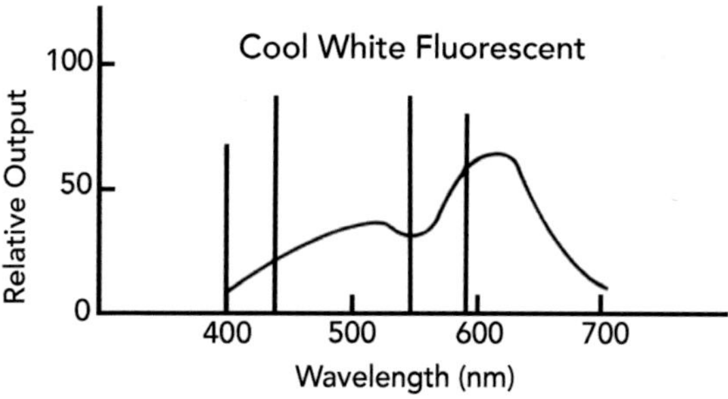

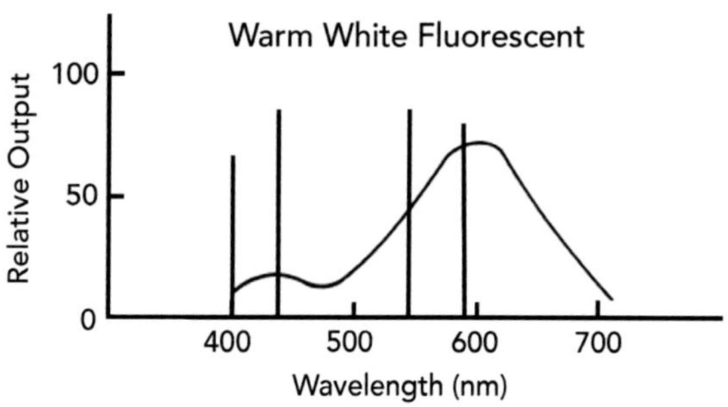

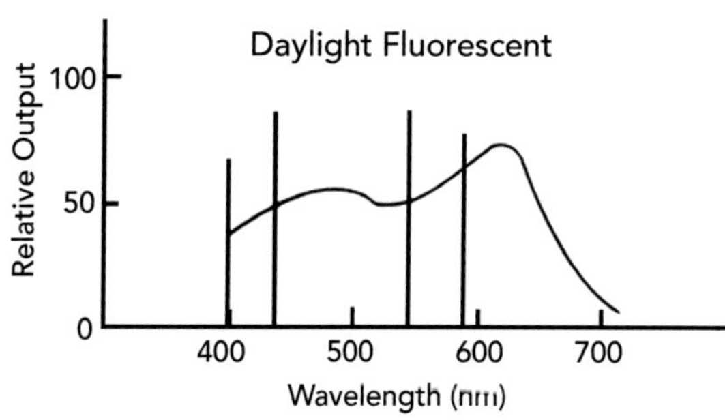

Figure 1-34 Spectral power distributions of three different fluorescent lamps.

Tungsten-Halogen Lamps

Tungsten-halogen lamps are sometimes called quartz-iodine or simply halogen lamps and emit light through incandescence. They differ from conventional tungsten lamps in that iodine or bromine gas is added and the bulb is made from quartz or a similar high-temperature glass. The iodine combines with the tungsten evaporating from the filament which, combined with the high temperature of the filament, produces a decomposition that redeposits tungsten on the filament. This chemical reaction increases the life of the filament and prevents the deposit of tungsten on the bulb enclosure.

The tungsten-halogen design offers high luminance output consistently over a lifespan that exceeds that of a traditional tungsten lamp. The filament also burns hotter, meaning that its color temperature more closely approaches daylight. Figure 1-33 plots the loss in total light output for conventional tungsten lamps and tungsten-halogen lamps over time.

Fluorescent Lamps

Fluorescent lamps produce light by establishing an arc between two electrodes in an atmosphere of very low-pressure mercury vapor contained in a glass tube. This low-pressure discharge produces ultraviolet radiation at specific wavelengths that excite crystals of phosphors lining the wall of the tube. Phosphors such as calcium tungstate have the ability to absorb ultraviolet energy and to re-emit it as light. The color of light emitted by a fluorescent tube depends largely on the mixture of fluorescent materials used in the phosphor coating.

The light that reaches the eye or camera from such a lamp, therefore, consists of the light given off by these fluorescent compounds plus part of the light from the mercury vapor that gets through them without being absorbed. The result is a continuous spectrum produced by the fluorescent material superimposed upon the line spectrum of energy produced through the electrical discharge of the mercury vapor. The spectral-energy distributions for three commonly encountered fluorescent lamps are shown in Figure 1-34.

Fluorescent lamps with a correlated color temperature of 5000K (such as the General Electric Chroma 50®) are believed to give a better match to daylight and are now specified in American National Standards Institute (ANSI) standards for transparency illuminators and viewers. Fluorescent lamps find widespread use because they generate minimal heat and are less expensive to operate (that is, they have higher luminous efficiency) than tungsten lamps. Additionally, they are low luminance sources due to their larger surface areas relative to tungsten lamps. The result is that these lamps have less glare and produce more diffuse illumination. Fluorescent lamps are nearly always used for commercial lighting and, consequently, photographers working under such light conditions should be familiar with their characteristics.

The luminous efficiency of fluorescent lamps is generally higher than that of tungsten sources, ranging between 40 and 60 lumens/W. Additionally, the average life of a fluorescent lamp is approximately 5,000 hours, which is nearly five times as long as that of a conventional tungsten lamp.

Compact Fluorescent Lamps

Compact fluorescent lamps (CFLs) operate similarly to a traditional fluorescent lamp but are designed in form factors that allow it to take the place of tungsten light bulbs. CFL bulbs take on a variety of shapes, always consisting of a tube containing argon and mercury vapor. They have built-in ballasts that produce the necessary electrical current to excite the gas molecules, the result of which is the emission of ultraviolet radiation. The ultraviolet radiation stimulates the fluorescent material coated on the inside of the tube, which absorbs and re-emits the energy as visible light. CFL bulbs are more energy efficient than tungsten-filament bulbs, produce less heat as a by-product and have longer lifespans. Some CFL bulbs, particularly older ones, take several minutes to achieve full brightness when switched on. This trait is worsened when operating in colder temperatures. Once looked at as a potential successor to traditional tungsten, CFLs are taking the backseat to LED as the desired light source of the future. Figure 1-35 is a sample spectrum for a CFL bulb.

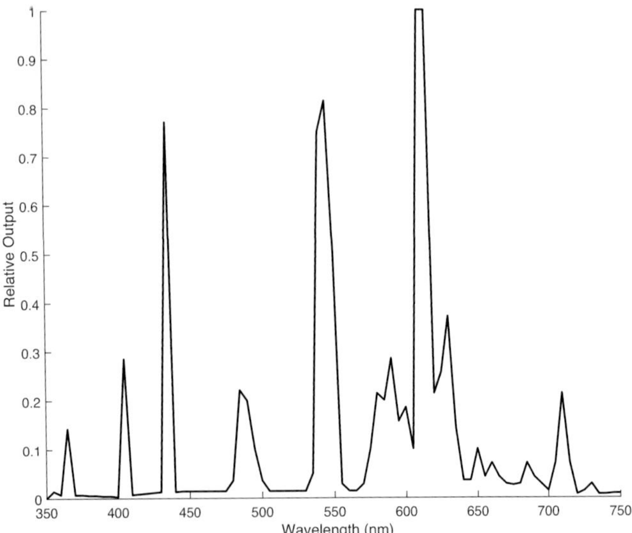

Figure 1-35 A sample compact fluorescent lamp bulb spectrum.

High-Intensity Discharge Lamps

Similar in operation to fluorescent lamps, *high-intensity discharge lamps* produce light by passing an arc between two electrodes that are only a few inches apart. The electrodes are located in opposite ends of a small sealed transparent or translucent tube. Also contained within the tube is a chemical atmosphere of sodium and/or mercury. The arc of electricity spanning the gap between the electrodes generates heat and pressure much greater than in fluorescent lamps and for this reason these lamps are also referred to as *high-pressure discharge sources*. The heat and pressure generated are great enough to vaporize the atoms of the various metallic elements contained in the tube. This vaporization causes the atoms to emit electromagnetic energy in the visible region. Since the physical size of the tube is small, it allows for the construction of optical sources that have excellent beam control. Such sources are frequently employed for nighttime illumination of sports stadiums, highways, exteriors of buildings and the interiors of large industrial facilities.

As in the operation of low-pressure discharge sources, high-intensity discharge lamps produce spikes of energy at specific wavelengths. These peaks are the result of specific jumps of the electrons within the atomic structure of the metallic elements. Energy is emitted in peaks located in different positions of the visible spectrum for each element.

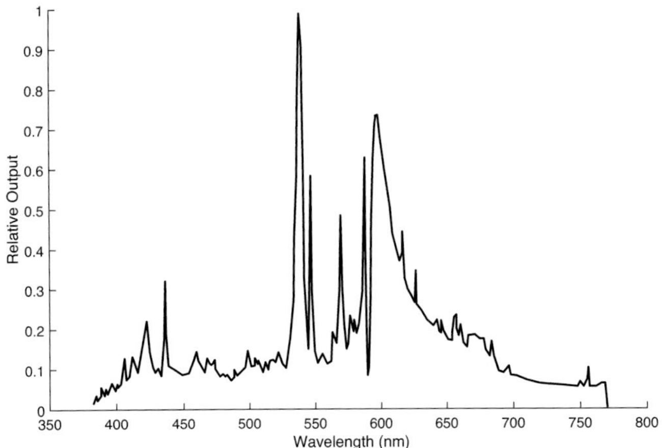

Figure 1-36 Spectral power distribution of a high-pressure metal halide lamp, ConstantColor™ CMH by General Electric. It is a modern, energy efficient replacement for high-pressure sodium bulbs.

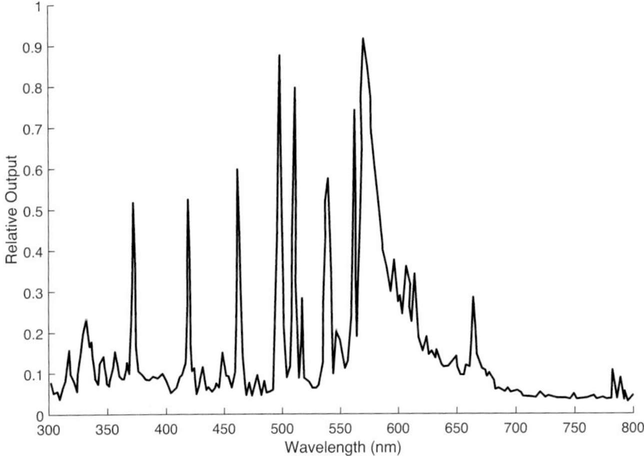

Figure 1-37 Spectral power distribution of a high-intensity metal halide discharge source, the General Electric Multi-Vapor™ lamp.

Thus, these lamps do not have a true color temperature, since they are not temperature dependent for the color of light emitted. The SPDs of two commercially available, high-intensity discharge sources are shown in Figures 1-36 and 1-37.

Electronic Flash

An *electronic flash lamp* consists of a glass or quartz tube filled with an inert gas such as xenon with electrodes placed at either end. When a high-voltage current from the discharge of a capacitor passes between the electrodes, the gases glow, producing a brilliant flash of light. The total

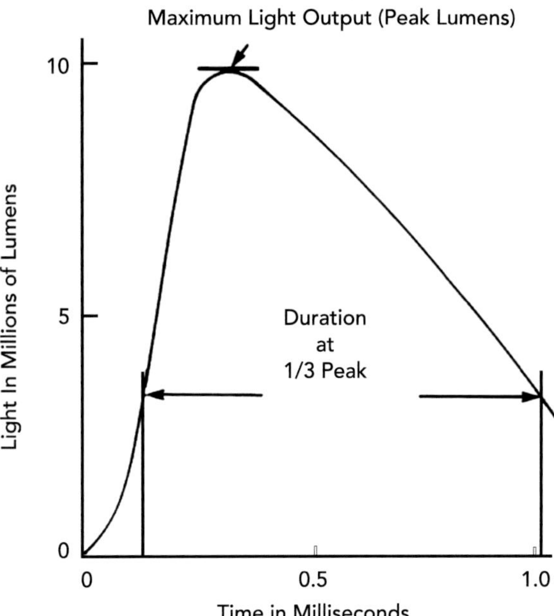

Figure 1-38 Light output curve of an electronic flash unit.

time of operation is exceedingly short, with the longest times being on the order of 1/500 second and the shortest times approaching 1/100,000 second. The time-light curve for a typical electronic flash unit is plotted in Figure 1-38. The effective flash duration is typically measured between one-third peak power points and the area contained under the curve between these limits represents nearly 90% of the total light produced.

The spectral power distribution of these sources shows a line spectrum, the exact nature of which is determined by the type of gas dispersed in the tube. Although the gas gives a line spectrum, there are so many lines and they are so well distributed throughout the visible spectrum that no serious error is involved in considering the spectrum to be continuous, as shown in Figure 1-39 (overleaf). The spectrum from the gas in these tubes approaches incandescence due to the high-current density at the time of discharge. The resulting light has a correlated color temperature of approximately 6000K, which is conveniently close to the 5500K used as the typical daylight white balance setting on a camera. A color-correction coating or filter is built-in to the flash unit to ensure an output of 5500K.

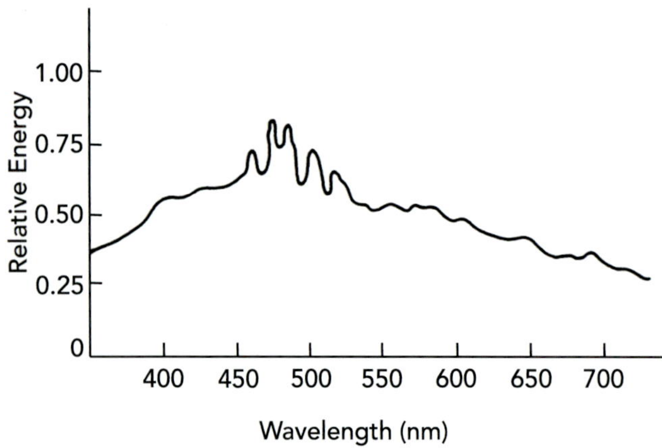

Figure 1-39 Relative spectral power distribution of a typical xenon-filled electronic flash unit.

The total light output for an electronic flash unit depends upon the design of the flash lamp and reflector, the voltage, and the capacity of the capacitor. In the early days of electronic flash photography, exposure was controlled by setting the f-number as the number obtained by dividing a guide number by the flash-to-subject distance. Portable electronic flash units today have built-in sensors that monitor the light reflected from the subject. Alternatively, they may measure the light falling on the imaging sensor and quench the flash when sufficient light produces the desired exposure.

Electronic flash units have proven to be an incredibly useful source of light for photographers. Their consistency in color output, quantity of light output and their extremely short duration are all reasons for their widespread use.

Light-Emitting Diodes

Relatively new to the light source scene is the light-emitting diode or LED. An LED is unique in that it does not use phosphors, gases or filament to create light. Instead, it produces light through electroluminescence when an electrical current is passed through semiconductor materials. This process also produces heat as a by-product, though much less so than tungsten sources. A heatsink plate is incorporated into the design of an LED to move heat away from the diode and prevent damage.

The electroluminescence created by an LED happens when electrons move within the semiconductor, introduced from an input voltage through a *p-n junction*. One semiconductor material called the *p-type* is the positive carrier and another semiconductor material, the *n-type*, is the negative carrier. Energy flows in one direction from the n-type to the p-type. The junction that forms between them allows electrons to change state, giving off energy in the form of photons. The color of an LED is determined by the semiconductor materials and the amount of energy flowing through them. The resulting electroluminescent light produces enough heat to necessitate a heatsink but not so much that it can be felt by us except in extremely close proximity—perfect for when a situation calls for lighting with heat-sensitive subjects like a portrait or an ice cream still life.

A single LED can be very bright, though it is more common today to see groups or arrays of LEDs to produce brighter and larger light sources. LEDs may be two-dimensional panels or more unique in shape to create a form factor that mimics that of a tungsten-filament bulb (allowing for compatibility with existing light fixtures). LED panels arrange dozens or even hundreds of diodes in a circular or rectangular shape to create a broad source.

Since the wavelength emission of LEDs is partially dictated by the amount of energy set through the p-n junctions, some light sources offer variable color temperature capabilities. Some sources are comprised of red, green and blue LEDs that visually combine to create white light, allowing for tunability to different colors when desired. Others encase the diode in a material that filters the light emission to the desired wavelength. Specialized LED sources exist that emit in the UV and IR portions of the spectrum for scientific applications.

Most LED-based studio lighting is designed for recording video, as studio strobe lighting does not produce continuous duration light and tungsten lights tend to be hot and physically large. See Figure 1-40 for one example of a studio light using an LED array. These lighting solutions have the additional benefit of being portable and power efficient. Primary characteristics to consider for these solutions are maximum light output, degree of control over color and brightness and form factor or shape.

A form of LED technology is used to backlight television, computer monitor and smartphone screens. While this incarnation of LEDs is not frequently used as a

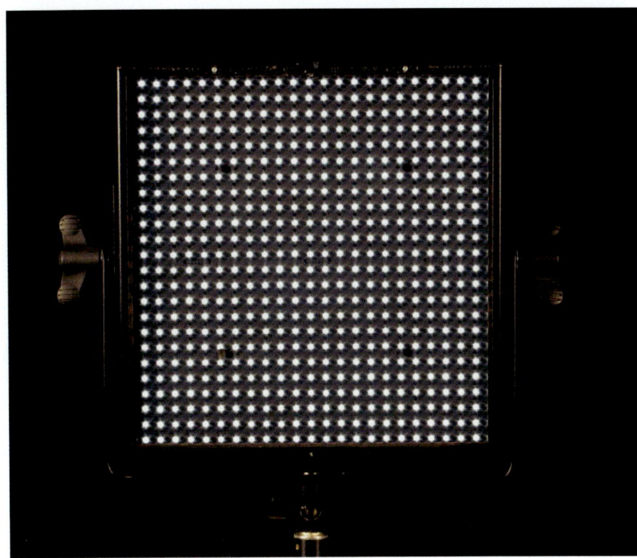

Figure 1-40 An LED panel for photography and videography.

photographic light source, we do live in a world illuminated by screens. Chapter 15 details more on LEDs and display technologies.

LED lights have a very long life of up to 50,000 hours (compared to between 1,000 to 2,000 for a tungsten bulb) and do not burn out in the same way that tungsten-filament does, though they do get dimmer over their lifetime. Products on the market claim CRI values around 80 and 90; this is one characteristic that is hard to match with tungsten's typical CRI of 100. LEDs have been in use for about 50 years but saw rapid adoption as a primary light source technology in homes and in photo and video production in the last decade as costs have fallen. Given the efficiency, considerable lifespan and degree of control offered by LED bulbs, the future is destined to be lit by LEDs in their many form factors.

Proof of Concept: Visualizing the Spectral Output of Light Sources

We've explored the numerous ways of characterizing light in this chapter. The following demonstration showcases a unique way in which we observe the spectral emissions of common artificial light sources. The spectral emission of a light source tells us about the composition of the visible light radiation produced and comparing multiple sources reveals that seemingly similar bulbs can make highly varied light.

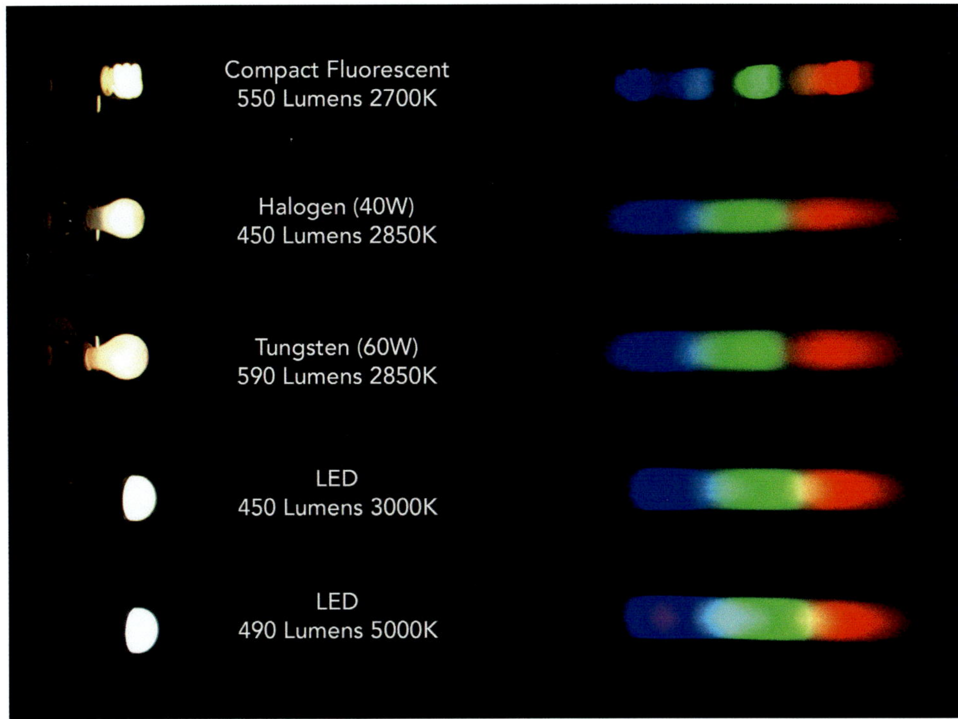

Figure 1-41 Five light bulbs photographed through a diffraction grating to reveal their spectral output.

We gathered a set of light bulbs: traditional tungsten, halogen, compact fluorescent and two LED designs. The specifications listed in Figure 1-41 come from the bulbs' advertised intensity and color temperature. If you walk past the displays in the light bulb aisle of a home improvement store, you can quickly spot differences in color. This is harder to do when viewing a single light source illuminating an environment and the variety of bulb technologies makes it less obvious why it appears the way it does. If we can see the light energy emitted by each bulb in relation to the complete visible spectrum, it's easier to understand why some sources appear "warm" and others "cool," i.e. why they vary in their color temperatures.

To make the photograph shown in Figure 1-41, we lined the bulbs up on a table and photographed them in a dark room. A special optical material called a *diffraction grating* was positioned in front of the camera lens. This material splits white light into its components similar to a prism. The result is the visual equivalent of what is shown in a spectral power distribution plot—varying energy emission across the visible spectrum.

Consider the following questions and see if you can answer them based on the image:

1. One of the five lights does not produce a continuous spectrum of white light. Which bulb is it?
2. What visual evidence supports the provided information that one LED bulb is 5000K and another is 3000K?
3. Which light source exhibits the least red energy emission? Does this result in a warm or cool color temperature appearance?

Notes

1 Whelan, M., and R. DeLair. *History and Types of Speakers*, 2013, www.edisontechcenter.org/SodiumLamps.html.

2 Whitehead, Lorne. "Prof. Lorne Whitehead: 'Improving the CIE Color Rendering Index – How This Can Be Done and Why It Matters.'" *SCIEN Blog Posts RSS*, Stanford University, Feb. 21, 2012, scien.stanford.edu/index.php/lorne-whitehead/.

3 "Position Statement on CRI and Colour Quality Metrics." *Position Statement on CRI and Colour Quality Metrics (October 15, 2015) | CIE*, International Commission on Illumination, Oct. 15, 2015, cie.co.at/publications/position-statement-cri-and-colour-quality-metrics-october-15-2015.

4 Wright, Maury. "IES Publishes TM-30 Defining New Color Metrics for Characterizing Lighting." *LEDs*, Aug. 19, 2015, www.ledsmagazine.com/articles/2015/08/ies-publishes-tm-30-defining-new-color-metrics-for-characterizing-lighting.html.

5 Royer, Michael, and Kevin Houser. "WEBINAR: UNDERSTANDING AND APPLYING TM-30-15." *Department of Energy*, Sept. 15, 2015. www.energy.gov/eere/ssl/webinar-understanding-and-applying-tm-30-15.

6 Davis, Wendy L., and Yoshihiro Ohno. "Development of a Color Quality Scale." *NIST*, Feb. 6, 2006, www.nist.gov/publications/development-color-quality-scale-0.

7 "Position Statement on CRI and Colour Quality Metrics." *Position Statement on CRI and Colour Quality Metrics (October 15, 2015) | CIE*, International Commission on Illumination, Oct. 15, 2015, cie.co.at/publications/position-statement-cri-and-colour-quality-metrics-october-15-2015.

8 Hunter, Fil, et al. *Light – Science & Magic: An Introduction to Photographic Lighting*. Focal Press, 2015.

9 MacEvoy, Bruce. "Light and the Eye." *Handprint : Modern Color Theory (Concepts)*, Aug. 1, 2015, handprint.com/HP/WCL/color1.html.

2 Photographic Optics

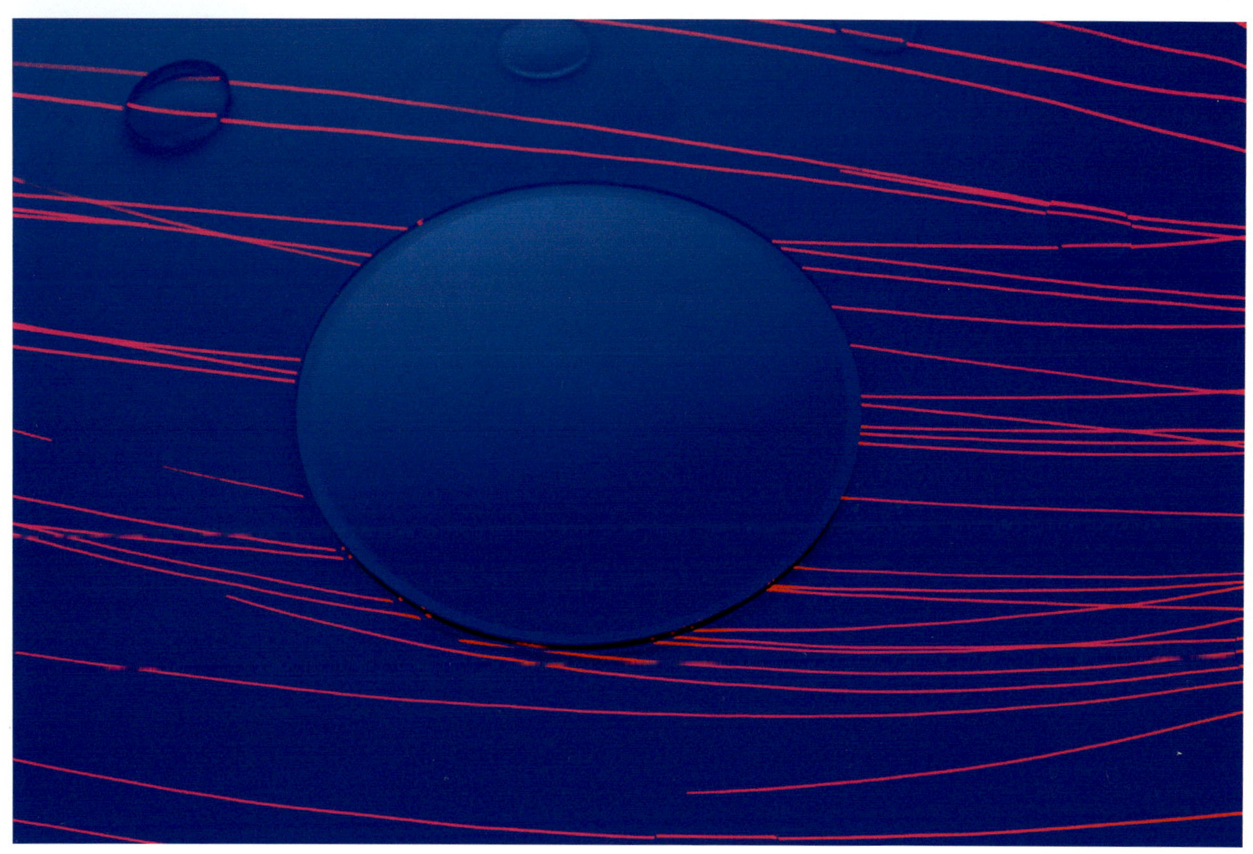

Photograph by Rochester Institute of Technology photography student Erin Percy

If understanding light is the first step toward the photographic image, step two is controlling light to form bright, well-resolved recordings of the world. Controlling light is best accomplished by directing its path and its behavior as it travels through the camera. The simplest way to start controlling light is with a small opening—a pinhole—but that's just the starting point. Photographic optics provide the technical means to make sharp, detailed images of our world from many distances, environments, speeds, magnifications and lighting conditions. This chapter covers the principles of image formation, camera lenses, depth of field and considerations for evaluating image quality from an optical imaging system. The last section brings many of the chapter's concepts together in an applied shooting exercise to better appreciate the relationships between lens choice and camera position.

Image Formation with a Pinhole

The pinhole as an image-forming mechanism played an important role in the evolution of the modern camera. The observation of images formed by a small opening in an otherwise darkened room goes back at least to Aristotle's time, about 350 B.C.—and the pinhole camera still fascinates photography students because of the simplicity with which it forms images. The *camera obscura*, Latin for "darkened room," evolved into a portable room or tent large enough to accommodate a person. In fact, any space can be turned into a camera obscura by restricting light exclusively to a small opening in a given space, though the image that results can be quite dim depending on the scene outside. The light that travels through the small opening projects onto an image plane: the location at which an image is formed. The portable room concept shrank to a portable box with a small pinhole opening and tracing paper, used as a drawing aid. By 1570, the pinhole was replaced by a simple glass lens to produce a brighter, easier to trace image.

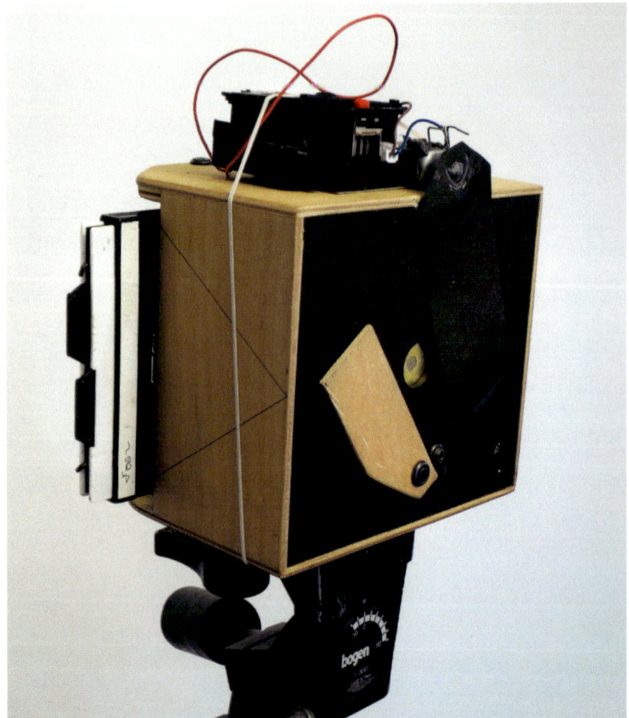

Figure 2-1 This homemade pinhole camera uses sheet film and electronic components to control when and for how long the pinhole lets light through. Photograph by Joe Ziolkowski

A handheld, light-tight box with a tiny opening at its front creates a *pinhole camera* when a light sensitive medium is placed opposite the opening. Figure 2-1 is an example of a homemade pinhole camera. We typically think of pinhole cameras using film or photographic paper and darkroom chemistry. These materials were cheap and accessible for many decades. It is increasingly difficult today to find a darkroom within which we can easily load and process the photographs from these simple cameras. Pinhole photography lives on in the digital realm with the same mechanical and optical principles applied. Swapping the light-sensitive film or paper with a digital sensor replaces the need for chemistry and safe lights while retaining the simplicity and craft that pinhole imaging allows. We recommend browsing pinhole.org, a community of active photographers and the creators of an annual Worldwide Pinhole Photography Day.

We described the behavior of light in terms of the corpuscular theory in Chapter 1. Pinholes form images because the corpuscular theory tells us that light travels in a straight line and for each point on an object, a reflected ray of light passing through a pinhole falls on exactly one spot on the image plane. Because light rays from the top and bottom of the scene and from the two sides cross at the pinhole, the image is reversed vertically and horizontally so that objects in a scene appear upside-down and backward at the location of the sensor as illustrated in Figure 2-2. Thankfully, our camera viewfinders flip the

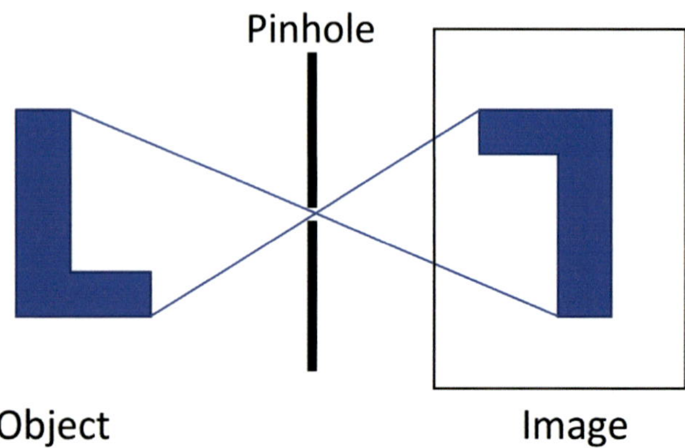

Figure 2-2 Reversal of the image vertically and horizontally by the crossing of the light rays at the pinhole produces an image of the letter L that is upside-down and backwards.

image of our scene to appear as we perceive it—right-side-up and forward. Optical viewfinders accomplish this with mirrors; electronic viewfinders use software to make the correction.

A pinhole camera offers two adjustable parameters for dictating the character of its image: the pinhole-to-image-plane distance and the diameter of the pinhole opening. Image size increases in direct proportion to the pinhole-to-image-plane distance, meaning that using a pinhole with a large format view camera (which uses bellows to extend the image distance) results in a telephoto effect. The angle of view, on the other hand, decreases as the image distance increases (see Figure 2-3). A pinhole controls the amount of light but it does not focus it, so changing the image distance has little impact on the apparent sharpness of the image. That said, critical examination of the image reveals an optimal pinhole-to-image-plane distance for a pinhole of a given diameter.

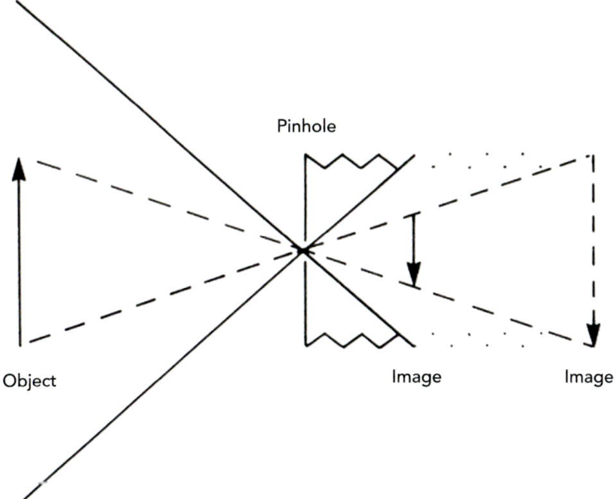

Figure 2-3 As the pinhole-to-sensor distance increases, the image size increases and the angle of view decreases.

Increasing the size of a pinhole beyond the optimal size allows more light to pass, increasing illuminance at the image plane and reducing the exposure time required. It also reduces image sharpness. When the pinhole size is decreased below the optimal size for the specified pinhole-to-image plane distance, *diffraction* causes a decrease in sharpness (see Figure 2-4).

Diffraction is the behavior of waves disrupted by an object or opening; it causes light waves to bend and spread out. Too little diffraction (like not using a pinhole at all) and an image fails to resolve at all. Too much diffraction introduced into an imaging system leads to destructive interference of the bent light waves in a way that degrades resolved detail. Thus, a Goldilocks set of pinhole size and image distance parameters helps produce the best

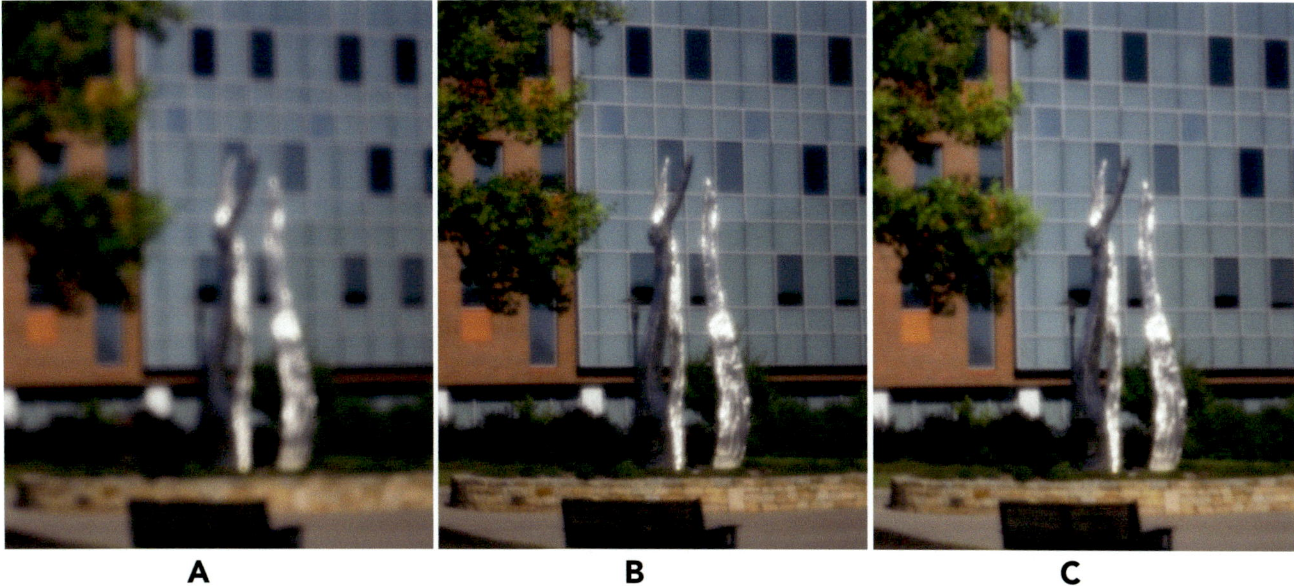

Figure 2-4 Three photographs made with pinholes of different sizes: (A) one-half the optimal size, (B) the optimal size and (C) twice the optimal size. These represent small sections cropped from the full-sized photographs.

possible image. The optimal pinhole size is calculated with the formula:

$$D = \frac{\sqrt{f}}{141} \quad \text{(Eq. 2.1)}$$

where D is the diameter of the pinhole in inches and f is the pinhole-to-image plane distance in inches (see Table 2-1). When photographing relatively close subjects, the value of f is found by substituting the object distance (u) and the image distance (v) in the formula $1/f= 1/u+ 1/v$. Note that the formula changes when measuring pinhole diameter, D, in millimeters:

$$D = \frac{\sqrt{f}}{28} \quad \text{(Eq. 2.2)}$$

To take one example, using an image distance of 8 inches dictates that the optimal pinhole diameter is about 1/50 inch. A No.10 sewing needle produces a pinhole of approximately this size, a helpful fact for photographers looking to make use of their sewing kits.

Table 2-1 Optimal pinhole diameters for different pinhole-to-image plane distances.

f (Distance)	D (Diameter)	F-number
1 in.	1/140 in.	f/140
2 in.	1/100 in.	f/200
4 in.	1/70 in.	f/280
8 in.	1/50 in.	f/400
16 in.	1/35 in.	f/560

Image Formation with a Lens

Making images with pinholes is a great way to observe the principles of image formation and the parameters that control its behavior. Pinholes are limiting, however, because they do not efficiently collect and focus light to the degree that we have come to expect from our image-making tools. The rest of this chapter focuses on lenses as a consequence of this limitation.

The speed of light travelling in a vacuum is 186,000 miles per second. Other than photographing stars from a space telescope, we're concerned with light as it travels through air and other materials. When it does, its speed decreases. All photographic lenses rely on a material's ability to bend light rays as they travel from subject to sensor. *Refraction* is the behavior of light rays changing direction, or bending, due to a speed change as they move through from one medium to another. *Snell's Law of Refraction* is used to calculate how much a medium changes the direction of light rays depending on their angle of incidence. Any material that transmits some amount of light—glass, plastic, water—has an *index of refraction* that indicates how quickly light travels relative to its behavior in air. It's this change from one medium to another, say from air to glass and back to air again, that introduces the path changes of light rays.

$$\text{Refractive index } (n) = \frac{\text{Speed of light in a vacuum}}{\text{Speed of light in a medium}} = \frac{c}{v} \quad \text{(Eq. 2.3)}$$

We approximate air's refractive index as 1.0, not far off from that of a vacuum where light does not bend or slow at all. Any material that refracts light more than air has a refractive index greater than 1. Index of refraction is unitless because it's a ratio of the speed of light in a vacuum relative to its speed in a medium. Wavelength-independent refraction is called *dispersion*, mentioned in Chapter 1 to explain why a glass prism creates a rainbow of colors out of white incident light.

Optical materials like glass and plastic have refractive indices higher than air. Light traveling through them bends toward the perpendicular or *normal* as illustrated in Figure 2-5. We've all seen an example of refraction when looking at a straw in a glass of water: it appears broken or in two places at the same time, as part of the straw is submerged in the liquid while the rest is surrounded by air. This is the same phenomenon that makes it challenging to spear a fish in a stream (a traditional rite of passage for all photographers). Our eyes perceive the bent light rays and incorrectly estimate the actual position of the fish where it exists below the water's surface.

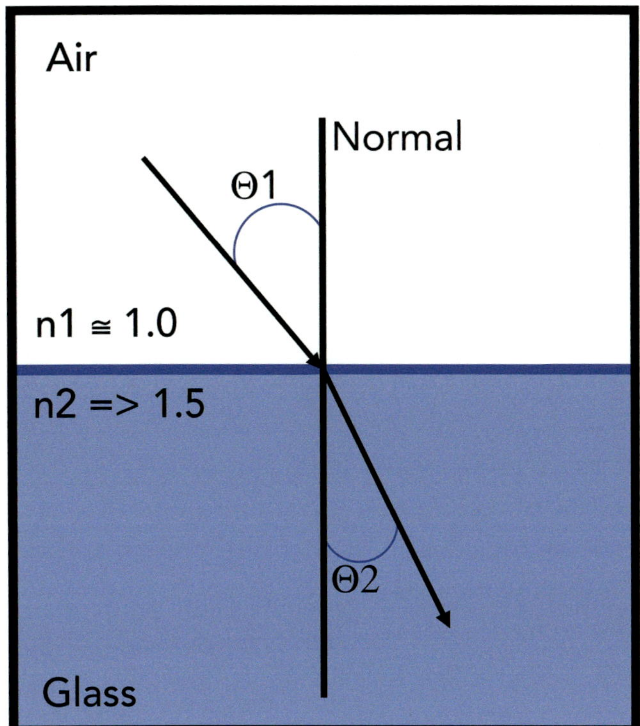

Figure 2-5 Light travelling through a medium at an angle with a refractive index greater than 1.0 bends toward the perpendicular.

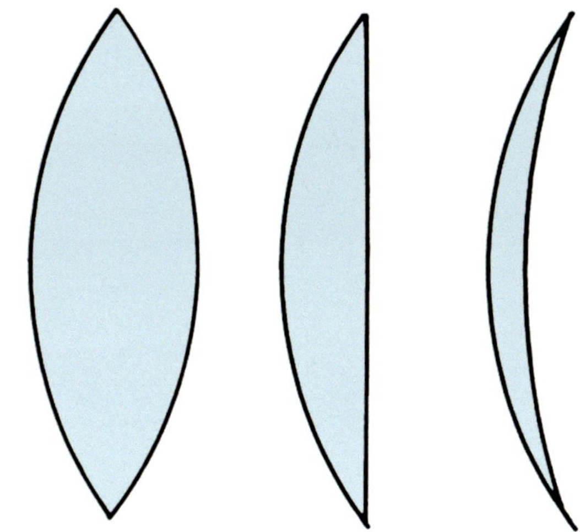

Figure 2-6 Three types of positive lenses: double convex (left), plano-convex (center) and positive meniscus (right).

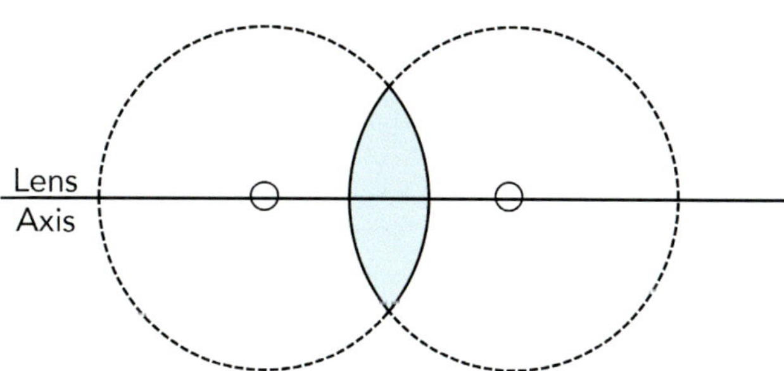

Figure 2-7 The lens axis is a straight line through the centers of curvature of the lens surfaces.

The refractive index of glass is 1.5, sometimes higher for particular types of glass. This makes it a great candidate for bending light to form images, which is exactly why we use glass for photographic lenses. Certain plastics are also used in smartphone camera system optics in the interest of size, cost and weight. Water's refractive index is 1.333, making it a viable but less effective candidate for image formation.

The shape of a lens controls how it bends light to form an image. A *positive lens* is easily recognized as thicker at the center than the edges. It must have one convex surface. The other surface can be convex (*double convex*), flat (*plano-convex*) or concave (*positive meniscus*) as illustrated in Figure 2-6. The curved surfaces of positive lenses are typically spherical like the outside (convex) or inside (concave) surface of a hollow ball. If the curvature of a spherical lens surface is extended to produce a complete sphere, the center of that sphere is identified as the *center of curvature* of the lens surface. A straight line drawn through the two centers of curvature of the two lens surfaces is defined as the *lens axis* or *optical axis* (see Figure 2-7). If one of the surfaces is flat, the lens axis is a straight line through the one center of curvature and perpendicular to the flat surface.

A positive lens produces an image by refracting or bending light such that all of the light rays from an object point falling on its front surface converge to a point behind the lens (see Figure 2-8, overleaf). If the object point is at infinity or a large distance, the light rays enter the lens traveling parallel to each other. The location where they come into focus is the *principal focal point*. We determine the focal length of the lens by measuring the distance from the principal focal point to the *back nodal point*—roughly the middle of a single-element lens (see Figure 2-9, overleaf). Reversing the direction of light through the lens with a distant object on the right produces a second principal focal point and a second focal length to the left of the lens, as

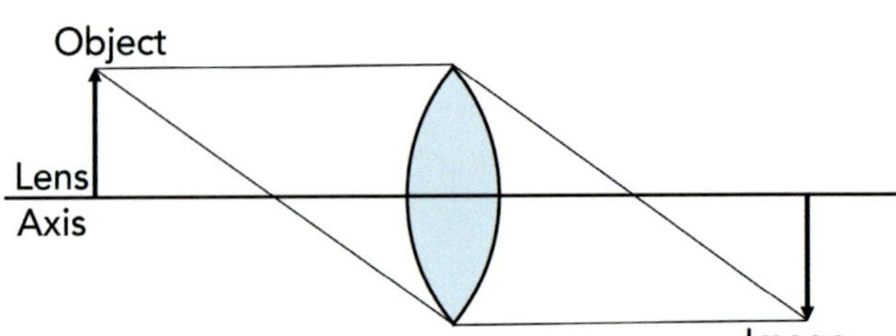

Figure 2-8 Image formation with a positive lens.

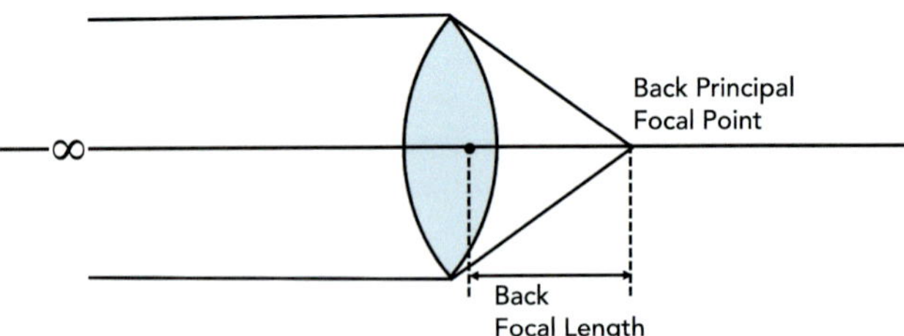

Figure 2-9 The back focal length is the distance between the back nodal point and the image of an infinitely distant object.

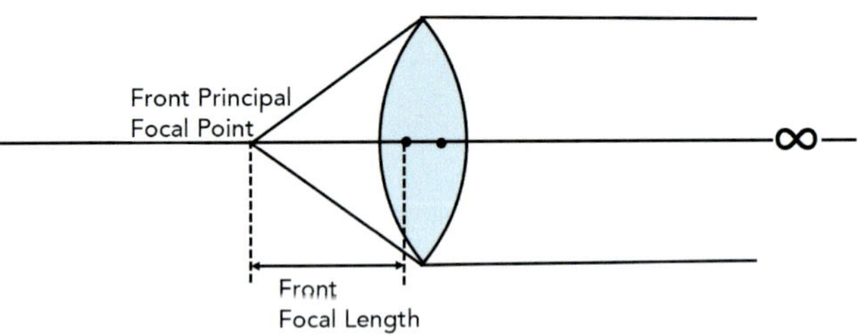

Figure 2-10 The front focal length is found by reversing the direction of light through the lens.

well as a second nodal point (see Figure 2-10). The two sets of terms are distinguished using the designations of *object* (or front) and *image* (or back). For example: *front principal focal point* and *back principal focal point.*

A *negative lens* cannot form an image alone and is easily identified as thinner in the center than at its edges. Light rays entering a negative lens travelling parallel to each other diverge and never form an image. Its focal length is determined by extending the diverging rays back toward the light source where it forms a *virtual image* (see Figure 2-11). Note that light rays traveling through the center of a lens (negative or positive) are *undeviated* and continue behind the lens the same as they entered it.

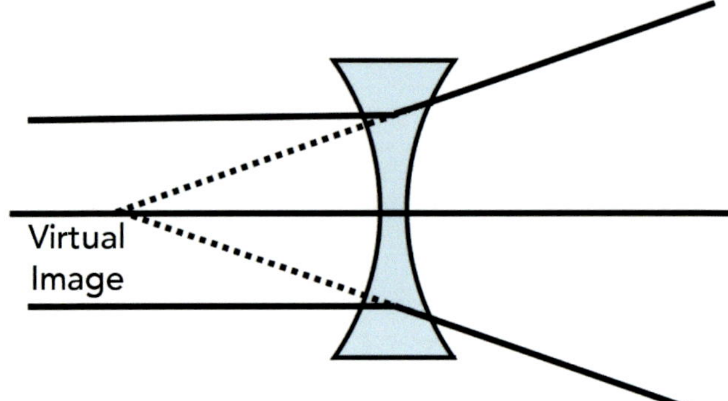

Figure 2-11 Image formation with a negative lens.

Let's pause here because most of us grow up thinking that images, by definition, are the things we see with our own eyes. Though accurate, this is an incomplete understanding of image formation and optics. When we talk about a positive lens forming a *real image*, it's an image that can be captured by a sensor or projected onto a surface where we can see it for ourselves. Positive lenses are *converging lenses* because they bring light rays together to form the real image we see. Their counterpart, negative lenses, are *diverging lenses* because they never allow light rays to focus at a point in front of them. Instead, a negative lens forms an image behind itself—we call this a virtual image because it cannot be captured or projected.

The *optical center* of a lens is a point on the lens axis where an off-axis, undeviated ray of light crosses the lens

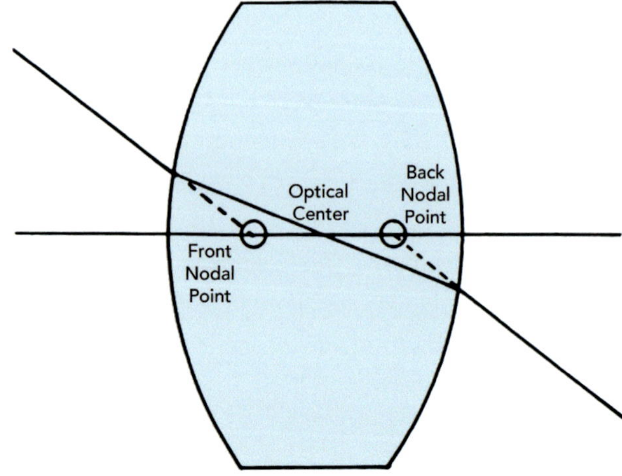

Figure 2-12 All light rays passing through the optical center leave the lens traveling parallel to the direction of entry. Nodal points are identified by extending the entering and departing portions of an undeviated ray of light in straight lines until they intersect the lens axis.

axis. All rays of light that pass through the optical center are undeviated—that is, they leave the lens traveling parallel to the direction of entry (see Figure 2-12). Object distance and image distance are measured to the optical center when great precision is not needed. When precision is required, the object distance is measured from the object to the front (or object) nodal point and the image distance is measured to the back (or image) nodal point.

We locate the front nodal point on a lens diagram by extending an entering, undeviated ray of light in a straight line until it intersects the lens axis. We locate the back nodal point by extending the departing ray of light backward in a straight line until it intersects the lens axis.

Manufacturers do not mark nodal points on lenses, however, we can find their locations with a simple experiment. We first place the lens in a *nodal slide*, a device that allows for pivoting the lens at various positions along its axis. A simple trough with a pivot on the bottom like the one in Figure 2-13 works for crude measurements. Professional optical benches like the one shown in Figure 2-14 are used when greater precision is required. We focus the lens on a distant light source with the front of the lens facing the light. Then we pivot the lens slightly from side to side while observing the image it forms on a flat plane (a board or piece of paper works well). If the image does not move as the lens pivots, this pivot point is the back (image) nodal point. If the image does move, however, we have to move the lens toward or away from the light source on the nodal slide, focus the image on the paper by moving the whole nodal slide and try pivoting it again. We repeat this process until the image remains stationary when the lens is pivoted. The front (object) nodal point is determined the same way with the lens is reversed so that the back of the lens is facing the light source. Knowing the nodal point locations on lenses is particularly helpful with certain applications requiring optical precision. If it were up to us, lenses would be labeled with this information directly from the manufacturer.

Here are three practical applications of knowing the nodal point locations:

1. When accuracy is required, such as during lens design, the object distance is measured from the object to the front nodal point and the image distance from the image to the back nodal point. Accurate determination of the focal length requires measuring the distance from the sharp image of a distant object to the back nodal point. Measurements to the nodal points are also made when using lens formulas to determine image size and *scale of reproduction* (see Figure 2-15, overleaf). With conventional lenses that are relatively thin, little error is introduced by measuring to the physical center of the lens rather than to the appropriate nodal point. With thick lenses and some lenses of special design—such as telephoto, reversed telephoto and variable focal length lenses—considerable error is introduced by measuring to the center of the lens. Here, the nodal points can be some distance from the physical center of the lens

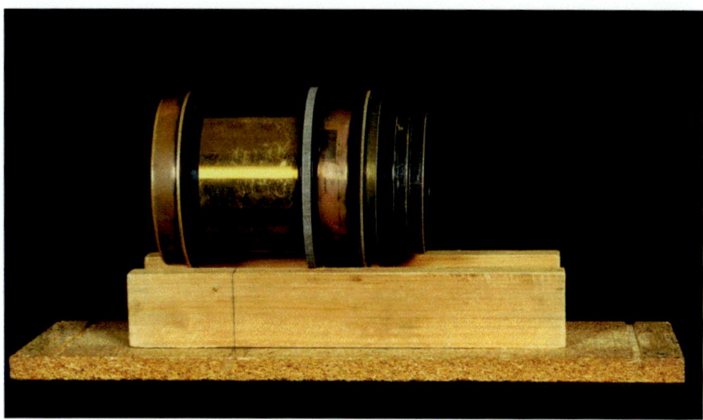

Figure 2-13 A simple nodal slide. The line on the side identifies the location of the pivot point.

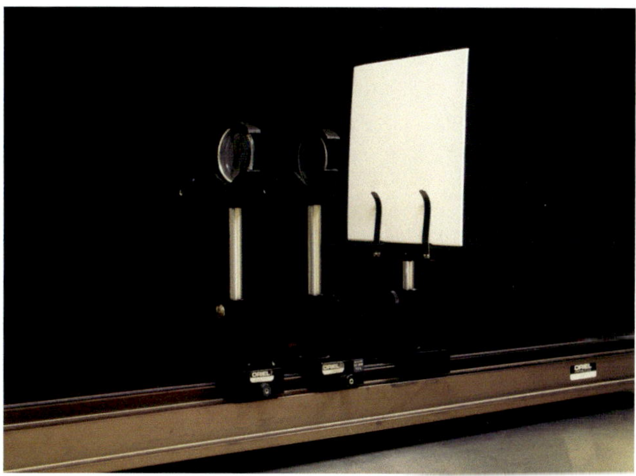

Figure 2-14 A professional optical bench permits microscopic examination of the aerial image formed by a lens.

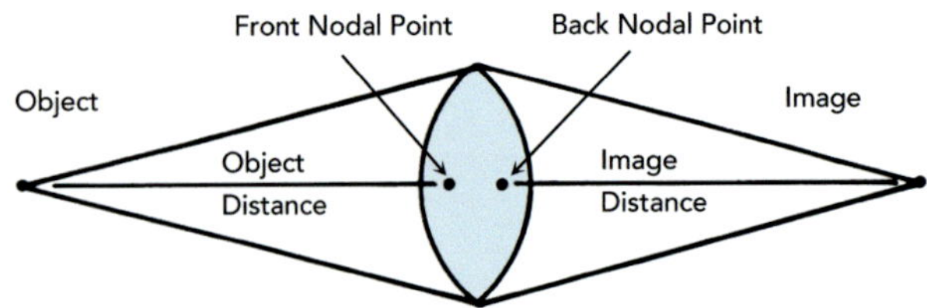

Figure 2-15 For an object point on the lens axis, object distance is measured to the front nodal point and image distance is measured from the image to the back nodal point.

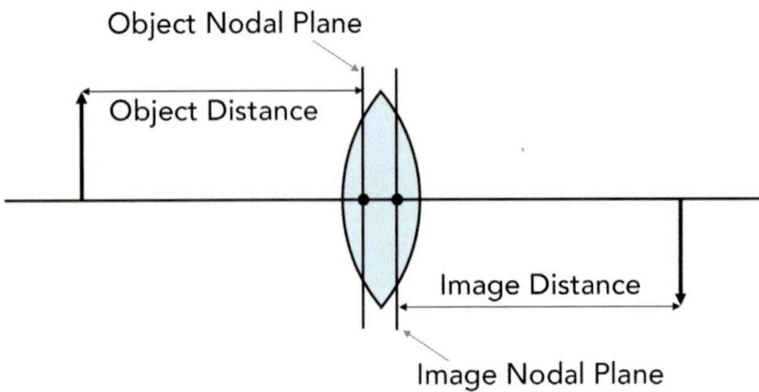

Figure 2-16 For an object point off the lens axis, object and image distances are measured in a direction that is parallel to the lens axis, to the corresponding nodal planes.

and may even be in front of or behind the lens. When distances are measured for objects or images that are not on the lens axis, the correct procedure is to measure the distance parallel to the lens axis to the appropriate nodal plane rather than to the nodal point. The nodal plane is a plane that is perpendicular to the lens axis and that includes the nodal point (see Figure 2-16).

2. Panoramic photography is easier with more seamless and easily stitched results if the camera is rotated on the back nodal point. Special tripod mounts like the one shown in Figure 2-17 make this a practical and straightforward technique. The setup allows for taking multiple frames as the camera is rotated that are later blended and stitched together.
3. Making lens diagrams to illustrate image formation is greatly simplified using nodal points and planes rather than lens elements. Whereas lens designers must consider the effect that each surface of each element in a lens has on a large number of light rays, many problems involving image and object sizes and distances are illustrated and solved using the nodal planes to represent the lens in the drawing, regardless of the number of lens elements. We adhere to this procedure in the following section.

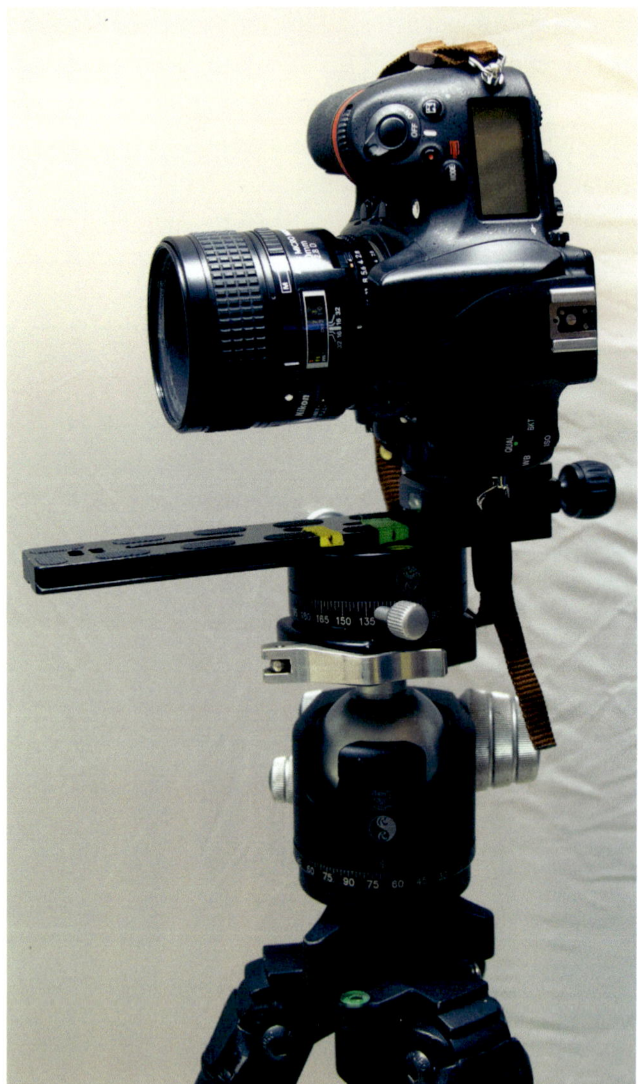

Figure 2-17 A tripod mount designed to place the point of rotation at the back nodal point of the lens. The nodal points of the photographer's favorite lenses are marked with tape.

Lens Focal Length

Let's step back and speak practically about photographic optics. We believe it's important to know how an image is formed and why, but a photographer just starting out is not going to wrestle with the details—rather, you're going to pick up a camera with a lens attached and start shooting.

The key concept to understand from the moment you put the camera's viewfinder up to your eye is lens focal length. We've defined *focal length* as the distance from the principal focal point to the back nodal point of the lens. It's a measure of the distance it takes the optics to bend light to a point of focus at the image plane. The problem with this definition is that you won't find *principle focal point* or *back nodal point* labeled on the lens barrel. Instead, photographer's associate lens focal lengths with their resulting *field of view*, the amount of a scene that is projected to fit onto the image sensor. Focal length also dictates *subject magnification* as it appears on the sensor and *perspective* (the relative sizes of objects in a scene). In other words, pick a lens based on how much of the scene you wish to capture, the distance from which you can capture it, how subjects at different distances appear relative to each other, or some combination of the three. The right lens choice won't leave you surprised or frustrated when putting an eye up to the viewfinder.

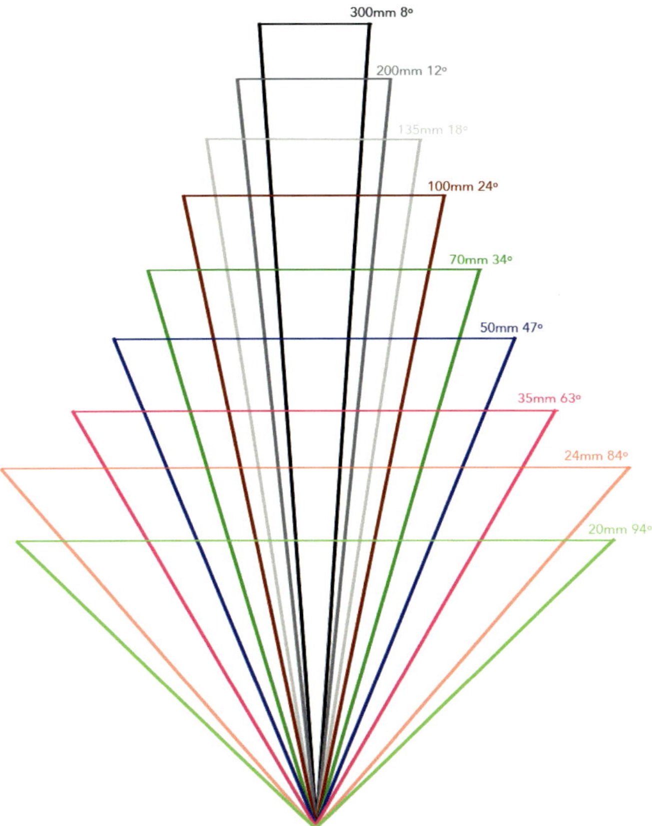

Figure 2-18 A range of focal lengths and the fields of view that result when using a full frame sensor. Field of view decreases as focal length increases.

Lens focal length is commonly described in millimeters. Figure 2-18 illustrates a range of focal length lenses for a full frame camera and the corresponding field of view of each. Note that all of these are actually *compound lenses* in that they consist of many separate lens elements manufactured and arranged to achieve the desired focal lengths with high image quality. Focal length and field of view have an inversely proportional relationship: the longer the focal length, the smaller the field of view.

It's tempting to take a mental shortcut and memorize a given focal length in millimeters with a corresponding field of view. However, there is no single measurement for each category of lens: the focal length that achieves a desired field of view is different depending on the sensor size. Lenses of different focal lengths are required to achieve equivalent fields of view between smartphone camera sensors, crop sensors, full frame sensors and medium format sensors.

Focal length varies based on the degree or amount that the lens bends light, a function of light refraction. Short focal length lenses bend light very sharply, bringing light to a point of focus just a short distance away from the back of the lens. Long focal length lenses, in contrast, bend the light much less and over a longer distance, bringing light to a point of focus farther from the back of the lens. Longer focal length lenses always necessitate additional physical distances between the front lens elements and the sensor, which is part of the reason that portable camera options shy away from long focal lengths.

Professional photographers gravitate toward camera equipment featuring the ability to change lenses, commonly known as *interchangeable lens* camera systems. Swapping out the optics provides creative and functional flexibility with regard to image formation and is much cheaper than buying a set of cameras with unique focal length lenses on each one. That said, we doubt you'll fail to capture a fleeting, special moment simply because you had an 80mm lens instead of an 85mm. In this way, small value differences in focal lengths are not nearly as important as their general type: photographers work with *normal*, *wide-angle*, *telephoto* and *variable focal length* (*zoom*) lenses and tend to group them as such. We'll step through each category and identify their particular qualities. The numbers we use apply to full frame cameras, so a wide-angle lens described later does not function as such on a medium format sensor.

Normal Focal Length

The go-to standard focal length on any camera system is one that achieves an *angle of coverage*, or field of view, approximating 55°. Where did we come up with this number? Studies show that the functional field of view of the human eye is 55°. We use the designation of *normal* because photographs taken with this field of view appear natural and in-line with our perceptual experience of the world. That doesn't necessarily make it the best or most effective focal length for a given photograph, it's simply helpful to establish as a baseline from which to compare. Anything wider than normal renders a scene with a greater field of view than we experience ourselves while anything narrower than normal renders a scene with a lesser field of view.

If 55° doesn't seem like very much for our vision, keep in mind that our eyes are different from a camera capture in one important dimension: time. Our eyes can change shape, iris dilation and position many times in just fractions of seconds, with the perceived visual data being continually processed by the brain. A still image is locked into one combination of lens focal length, exposure time, aperture setting and focus distance. Additionally, the camera contains only a single sensor whereas we have two eyes and two light-sensing retinas. We do perceive the world beyond the 55° field of view range, just not with the same level of visual acuity or attention and not all in one singular instance in time. Field of view can be measured horizontally, vertically or diagonally—having a single value instead of three makes our lives easier. In light of all of this, we specify that 55° is equivalent to the eye's *visual cone of attention.*[1] You can sense someone approaching out of the "corner of your eye" (an expression, obviously, as our spherical eyeballs don't have corners), though it's more of a light-difference sensation than full visual acuity. More on human vision and its role in photography in Chapter 13.

Determining what focal length provides a field of view equivalent to 55° on a given sensor requires some measurements and calculation. First, we determine the diagonal dimension of the rectangular sensor. A standard, full frame sensor measures 24mm by 36mm and the Pythagorean theorem tells us:

$$a^2 + b^2 = c^2 \qquad \text{(Eq. 2.4)}$$

or

$$c = \sqrt{a^2 + b^2}$$

$$c = \sqrt{24mm^2 + 36mm^2}$$

$$\sqrt{1{,}872} = 43.3mm$$

The full frame sensor diagonal dimension is 43.3mm. With this number in-hand, we calculate a normal focal length providing a desired field of view of 55°:

$$Focal\ length = \frac{sensor\ diagonal}{2\tan\left(\frac{field\ of\ view}{2}\right)} \qquad \text{(Eq. 2.5)}$$

$$Focal\ length = \frac{43.3}{2\tan\left(\frac{55}{2}\right)}$$

$$Focal\ length = 41.6mm$$

Our target focal length is 41.6mm to achieve the standard 55° field of view. With some rounding out of convenience, 50mm or 55mm are traditional normal focal lengths, though the range from 35mm to 85mm is broadly considered to qualify as well.

Alternatively, algebraically rearranging the previous equation allows us to calculate the field of view if sensor size and lens focal length are known:

$$Field\ of\ View = 2\tan^{-1}\left(\frac{sensor\ diagonal}{2 \times focal\ length}\right) \qquad \text{(Eq. 2.6)}$$

Normal focal length lenses are invaluable and often inexpensive compared to other lens types that require more complex optical engineering or more material. Figure 2-19 shows a photograph taken with a normal focal length lens considered against the same subject photographed using telephoto and wide-angle lenses.

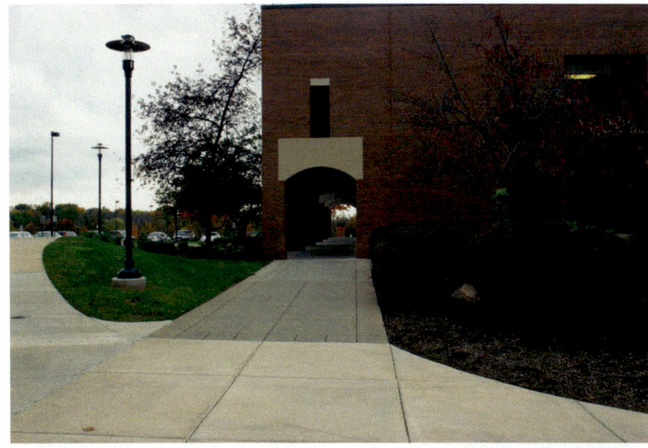

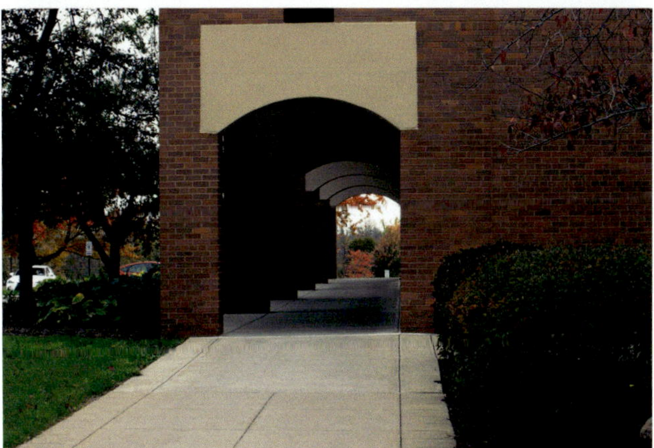

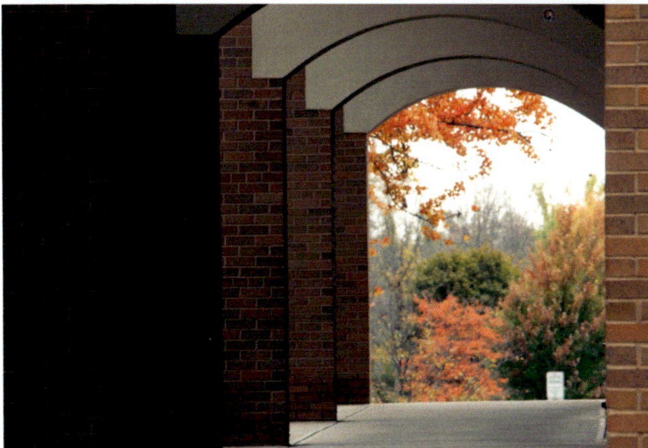

Figure 2-19 A scene photographed with a full frame SLR using 20mm, 50mm and 200mm focal length lenses, respectively. The photographer stayed in the same location for all three. Photographs by Rochester Institute of Technology photography student Serena Nappa

In the past, it was safe to assume that a typical consumer camera with a non-interchangeable lens used a focal length of approximately 35mm, producing a slightly wide field of view, or a zoom lens that included this focal length in its zoom range. However, phone cameras in particular ushered in an era of wider focal length lenses based on how the average user photographed: with a particular interest in capturing a wide field of view. We continue to define a normal focal length as equivalent to 50mm on a full frame system because it offers minimal distortion, represents our first person visual experience closely and serves as a convenient reference point for all focal lengths wider or longer. Having said that, it may very well be true that the majority of cameras out in the world shoot with wide-angle lenses.

This is a good time to point out a common oversimplification regarding focal length. Stand in one place, take a photograph with a 50mm lens, swap it for a 25mm lens and take another photograph. You might conclude that the lenses always change subject magnification. By only changing focal length, you've made two photographs of a subject rendered at different sizes on the sensor. Repeat this experiment while adding a second variable: distance. By moving closer to the subject and taking that second photograph at 25mm, you achieve the same subject magnification as the 50mm at the original distance. This shows us that focal length dictates *working distance*, the distance between the front of the lens and the subject photographed. Both 50mm and 25mm lenses can achieve the same subject magnification; they differ in the working distance required to achieve it. Longer focal length lenses mean photographers can be a considerable distance from the subject (a critical detail for venomous spider photographers). Shorter focal length lenses mean photographers can get right in the middle of the action (a boon for puppy photographers). Sometimes you'll choose focal length not because of its field of view but rather for its ability to solve a problem in working distance, either when you can't get closer or when you specifically can't get away. The secondary effect of changing working distance is changes in perspective, which we'll talk about a little later in this chapter.

Telephoto Focal Lengths

Telephoto lenses offer increased subject magnification and decreased field of view when object distance is held constant. They also tend to compress perspective. Telephoto focal lengths are anything above the normal 50mm on a full frame sensor. There's overlap in each of these categories, though, so most photographers don't consider a lens to be a telephoto until it's 85mm or greater. The overlap is also due to the fact that true telephoto lens designs have unique lens element arrangements. Photographers are not usually concerned with the actual design and instead simplify telephoto as a function of focal length. Generally speaking, 80mm to 300mm is described as telephoto and anything greater is a *super telephoto* focal length.

The basic design for a telephoto lens consists of a positive element in front of (but separate from) a negative element as illustrated in Figure 2-20. When a telephoto lens and a normal-type lens of the same focal length are focused on a distant object point, both images come to a focus one focal length behind the respective back (image) nodal planes. However, the lens-to-image distance is smaller with the telephoto lens. This reduced lens-to-image distance is due to the fact that the back nodal plane is located in front of the lens with telephoto lenses rather than near the center, as with normal lenses. It is easy to locate the position of the back nodal plane in a ray tracing of a telephoto lens focused on a distant object point, as in Figure 2-20 (top), by reversing the converging rays of light in straight lines back through the lens until they meet the entering parallel rays of light. To determine the position of the back nodal point with a telephoto lens, we pivot the lens in various positions along the lens axis on a nodal slide until the image of a distant object remains stationary. Alternatively, the lens and camera can be focused on infinity, whereby the back nodal point is located exactly one focal length in front of the image plane. The position of the back nodal plane is noted in relation to the front edge of the lens barrel, since this relationship remains constant.

Wide-Angle Focal Lengths

Wide-angle lenses are broadly defined as any focal length below than the normal focal length. Again, though, there's wiggle room in these categories and photographers typically consider lenses wider than 35mm to be truly wide-angle. These focal lengths offer decreased magnification and increased field of view at a constant working distance relative to a normal lens. They can exhibit exaggerated perspective, sometimes to the point of distortion. *Ultra wide-angle* lenses like 8mm or 12mm on a full frame

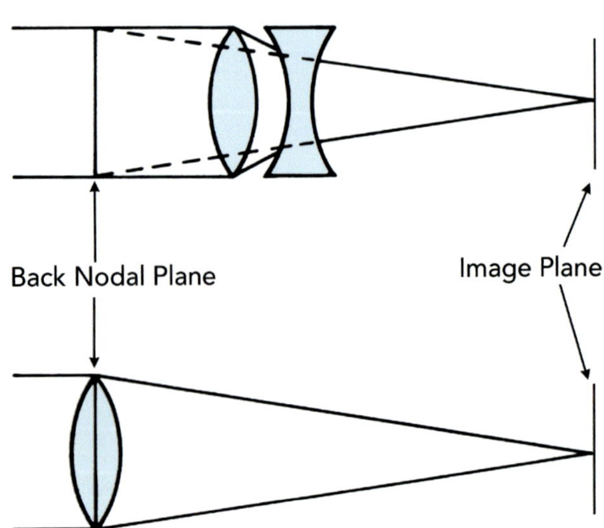

Figure 2-20 The lens-to-sensor distance is shorter for a telephoto lens (top) than for a normal-type lens (bottom) of the same focal length.

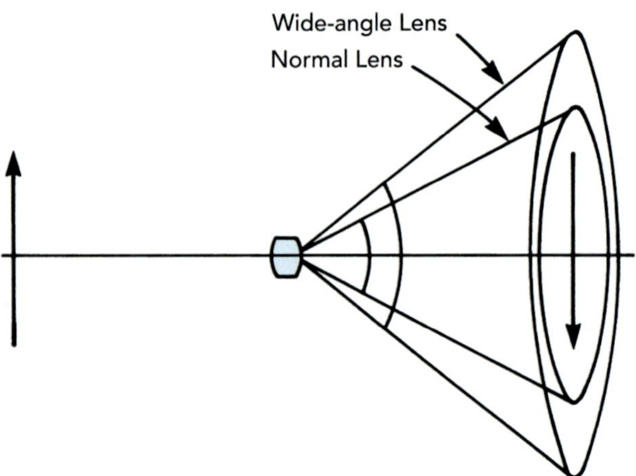

Figure 2-21 The covering power of a wide-angle lens compared to that of a normal-type lens of the same focal length. The images formed by the two lenses are the same size.

sensor are called *fisheye* because of their characteristic bulging, circular image distortion. Fisheye lenses can achieve a field of view approaching 180° by foregoing the formation of a rectilinear image and instead rendering straight lines as curved, particularly near the image frame edges.

A wide-angle lens is optically defined as a lens having an angular covering power significantly larger than the 55° angle of coverage provided by a normal-type lens, or as having a circle of good definition with a diameter considerably larger than the focal length when focused on infinity (see Figure 2-21). Most modern wide-angle lenses have a considerable number of elements and they generally produce good definition even at the maximum aperture, with much less fall-off of illumination toward the corners than the earlier lenses.

Variable Focal Length

Having the right lens at the right moment is both logistically challenging and potentially expensive (there are a lot of lenses to own and then you have to carry them all). An ideal solution is to have a single, versatile lens that adjusts to multiple focal lengths. Variable focal length lenses offer us this functionality, though not without some compromise. Their designs allow the photographer to change the distances between lens elements inside the lens barrel to achieve different focal lengths. Focal length is altered continuously while the image remains in focus. The relationship is illustrated with a simple telephoto lens where the distance between the positive and negative elements is varied, as illustrated in Figure 2-22. This change in position of the negative element changes the focal length (as well as image size and angle of view), but the image does not remain in focus. Other problems include aberration correction and keeping the relative aperture constant at all focal length settings.

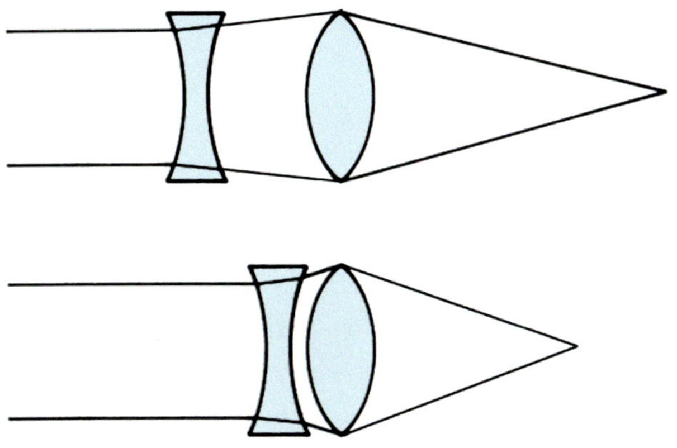

Figure 2-22 Changing the distance between the positive and negative elements of a telephoto lens changes the focal length.

Two methods are used for the movement of elements in zoom lenses. One method is to link the moveable lens elements so that they move the same distance. This is called *optical compensation*. The mechanical movement is simple; the optical design is complex and requires more elements. The other method is *mechanical compensation* and involves moving multiple elements by different amounts and requires a complex mechanical design. For the problem of maintaining a constant f-number as the focal length is changed, an optical solution is incorporating an afocal attachment at or near the front of the lens so that the aperture diameter and the distance between the diaphragm and the sensor remains fixed. An alternative mechanical solution adjusts the size of the diaphragm opening as the focal length is changed.

There are also mechanical and optical methods for keeping the image in focus. The mechanical method consists of changing the lens-to-sensor distance, as with conventional lenses. The optical method involves using a positive element in front of the afocal component that is used to keep the relative aperture constant.

The primary disadvantage of variable focal length lenses concerns their ability to resolve sharp images. Compared to fixed focal length lenses (also called *prime lenses*), variable focal length lenses are less optimized for sharpness at any one setting. If you find that you frequently photograph at 85mm, invest in an 85mm prime lens; an 85mm prime produces a sharper photograph than a variable 35–135mm zoom lens set to 85mm. Additionally, zoom lenses have smaller maximum apertures (the impact of which is described later on in this chapter).

The Relationship Between Focal Length and Perspective

Understanding how to control perspective in photography is essential yet often misunderstood. *Perspective* is the perception of space and the relationships of objects in that space, including scale, distance and size. We've used the term in this chapter thus far to categorize lens focal lengths. Perspective is also influenced by depth of field, lighting, subject overlap, color and aerial haze. Our brain uses details like shadows and color saturation to get a sense of objects in three-dimensional space that photographers can exploit to further their visual goals. Stereoscopic vision, thanks to our pair of eyes, gives us additional information about depth and distance; traditional, single-lens camera systems do not have stereoscopic information.

Linear perspective in an image only changes when the camera location changes relative to your subject. Consider the example of taking two photographs, framing the subject similarly, first with a telephoto and second with a wide-angle lens. The perspective in the resulting two photographs is different. Many people assume that the perspective change is due to the lens focal length change because it is the obvious variable in the scenario. However, the change in perspective is actually due to the difference in distance between the camera and subject. To achieve similar framing, the two focal length lenses require the photographer to move closer or farther away to achieve similar framing. While the lens change is an important part of the story, the true source of the perspective change is the distance from the photographer to the subject.

Changes in linear perspective happen when there are changes in camera position and the focal length of camera lenses. If the definition of linear perspective were limited to the relative image size of objects at different distances (or the angle of convergence of parallel subject lines), the photographer's control would be limited to the choice of camera position (object distance). If changes in the appearance of linear perspective were included even when there is no change in the relative image sizes of objects at different distances, then lens focal length would have to be included as a control. Two basic concepts important to an understanding of the control of linear perspective are:

1. Image size is directly proportional to focal length.
2. Image size is inversely proportional to object distance.

Focal Length and Image Size

Photographers like to have more than one focal length lens available to control image size and the corresponding angle of view. Let's examine our first concept, image size is directly proportional to focal length, using the following example. We photograph a building that reproduces ¼ inch high on our sensor when using a 50mm focal length lens on a full frame camera. Now we switch to a 100mm focal length lens while keeping the camera in the same position. The building is now ½ inch high on the sensor. The relationship between image size and focal length is a direct one: doubling the focal length doubles the image size. It also doubles everything else in the scene, though it does not change the ratio of image sizes for objects at different distances (see Figure 2-23).

This relationship holds true with the image distance approximately equal to the focal length of the lens, which is the case when photographing objects that are at a moderate to large distance from the camera. Photographing objects that are close to the camera causes the image distance to be larger than the focal length, causing this relationship to fail.

Object Distance and Image Size

Consider an example of placing two objects of equal size at distances of 1 foot and 2 feet from a camera lens. This produces images that vary in size in a 2:1 ratio with the object at 1 foot appearing twice as large as the object at 2 feet. Actual image sizes can be determined given the object size, focal length and object distances with either graphical drawings or lens formulas. For now, we are only concerned with relative image sizes.

Linear perspective is based on the ratio of image sizes for objects at different distances. Figure 2-24 shows two objects of equal size at distance ratios of 1:2, 1:3 and 1:4.

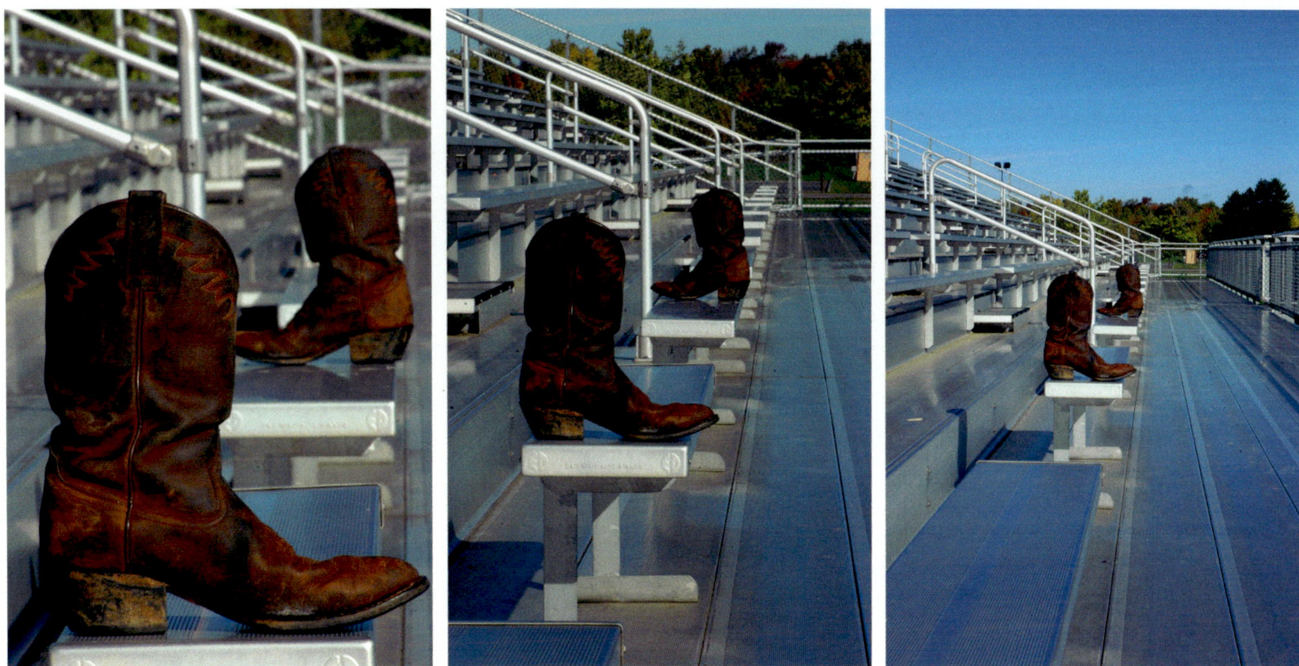

Figure 2-23 Photographs made from the same position with 135mm (left), 55mm (middle) and 28mm (right) focal length lenses. Image size changes in proportion to focal length. Relative sizes for objects at different distances remain constant.

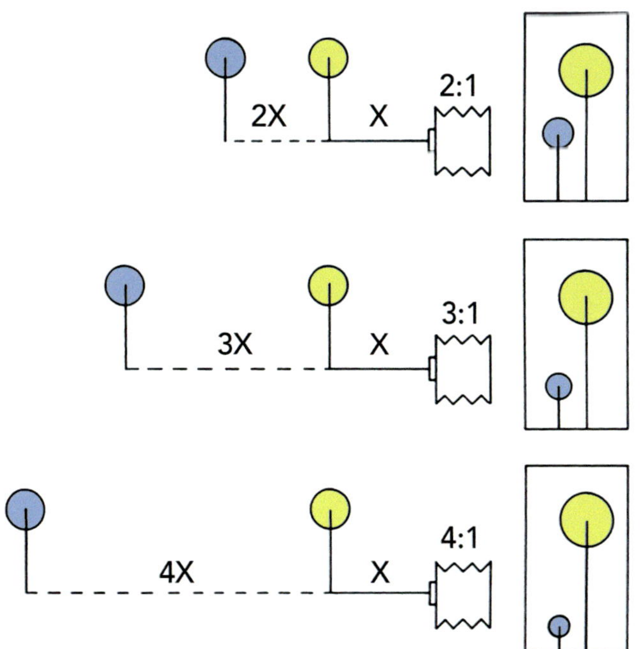

Figure 2-24 Image size is inversely proportional to object distance. The ratios of the object distances from top to bottom are 2:1, 3:1 and 4:1.

The sizes of the resulting images are in ratios of 2:1, 3:1 and 4:1. If we have movable objects, the relative image sizes and linear perspective are easily modified by changing the object positions within the scene. Many times, however, we photograph objects that cannot be moved and therefore the options available to control perspective or alter image size are either moving the camera or changing the lens focal length.

Consider two objects at a distance ratio of 1:2 from the camera (see Figure 2-25, overleaf). The ratio of the image sizes is 1:2. Next, we move the camera away to double the distance from the closer object. This does not double the distance to the farther object. Therefore, the ratio of the image sizes does not remain the same. The ratio of object distances changes from 1:2 to 2:3 by moving the camera; the ratio of image sizes changes from 2:1 to 3:2 (or 1.5:1). Moving the camera farther away from the subjects reduces the size of both objects in the image and also makes them appear nearly equal in size. The two images will never be equal in size no matter how far away we move the camera. However, with very large object distances, the differences in size becomes insignificant.

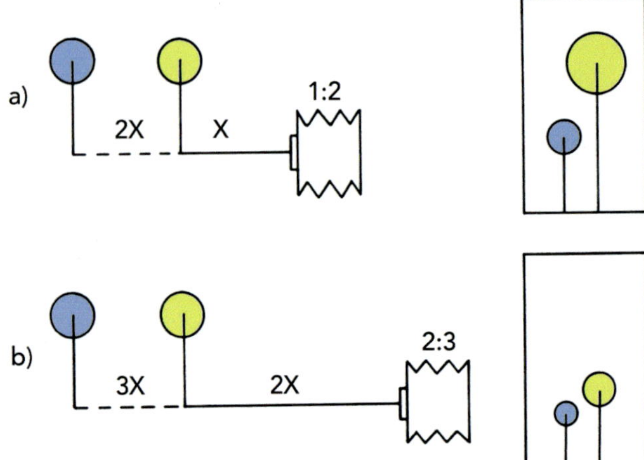

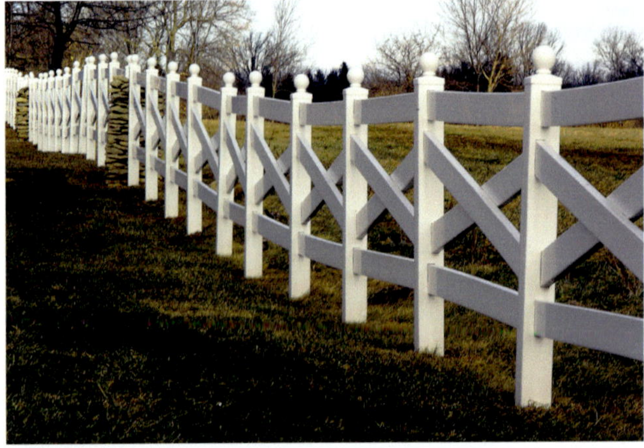

Figure 2-25 Doubling the distance from the camera to the near object changes the ratio of distances to the two objects from 1:2 to 2:3.

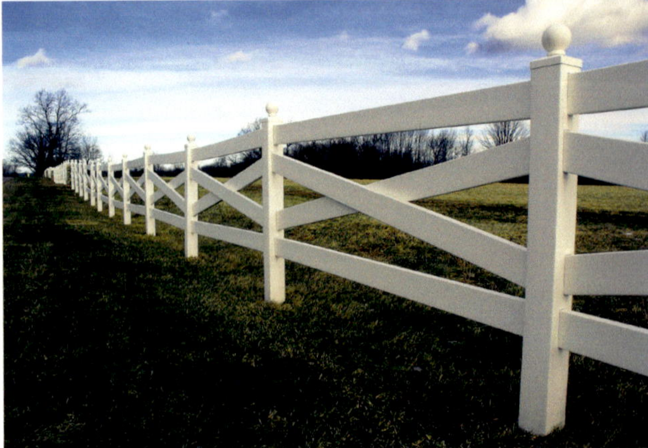

Figure 2-26 Space appears compressed in the top photograph, made with a 150mm lens, compared to the bottom photograph made with a 50mm lens from a closer position.

The linear perspective produced by moving the camera farther from the objects is referred to as a *weaker perspective* than that produced with the camera in the original position. Thus, weak perspective is an attribute in a picture in which image size decreases more slowly with increasing object distance. With weak perspective, space appears compressed as though there were less distance between nearer and farther objects than actually exists (see Figure 2-26).

Conversely, moving a camera closer to the two objects increases the image size of the nearer object more rapidly than that of the farther object, producing a *stronger perspective*. Strong perspective is especially flattering to architectural photographs of small rooms because it makes the rooms appear more spacious. All of these examples teach us that linear perspective is dictated by the camera-to-subject distance, not focal length of the lens.

Focal Length and Object Distance

Photographers commonly change focal length and object distance simultaneously to control linear perspective and overall image size. If the perspective appears too strong and unflattering in a portrait shoot when taken with a normal focal length lens, the photographer can substitute a longer focal length lens and move the camera farther from the subject to obtain about the same size image but with a weaker and more flattering perspective. Because short focal length, wide-angle lenses tend to be used with the camera close to the subject and telephoto lenses are often used with the camera at relatively far distances, strong perspective is associated with wide-angle lenses and weak perspective is conversely associated with telephoto lenses. However, it is the camera position and not the focal length or type of lens that produces the abnormal linear perspective.

The change in linear perspective with a change in object distance is seen most vividly when a corresponding change is made in the focal length to keep an important part of the scene the same size. In Figure 2-27, the focal length of the lenses and the camera positions were adjusted to keep the images of the nearer object the same size. The difference in

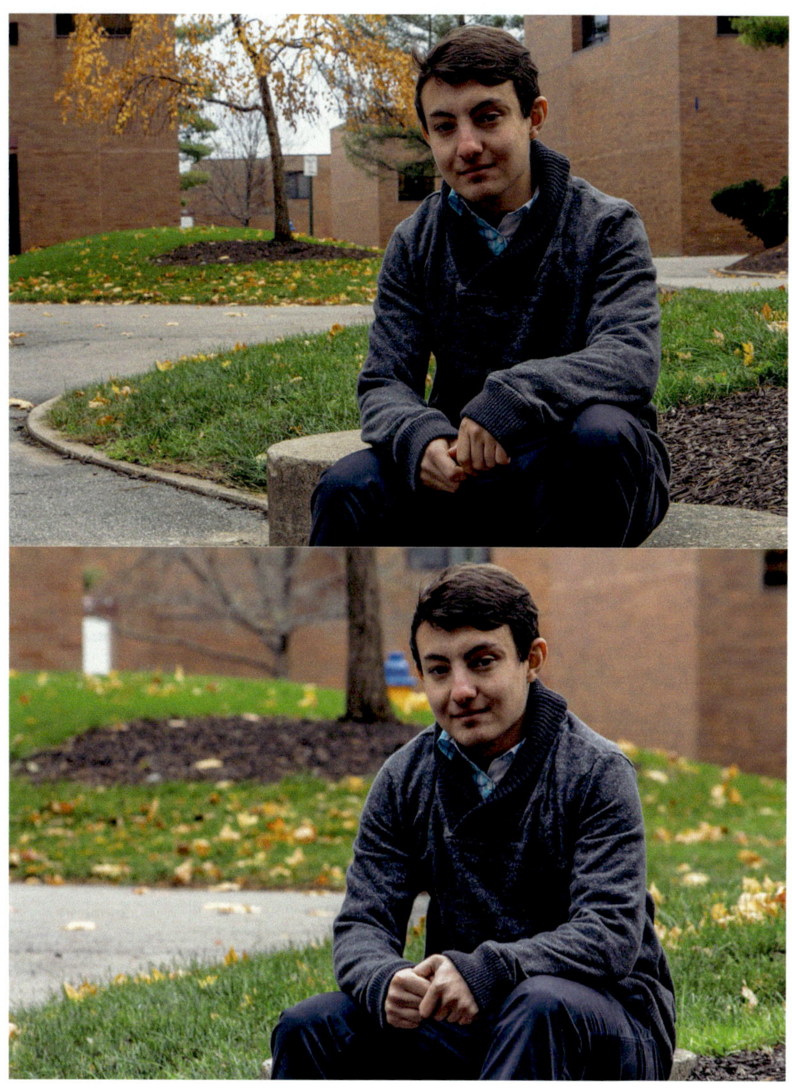

Figure 2-27 Photographs made with a 50mm focal length lens (top) and 135mm focal length lens (bottom) with the camera moved closer to match the image size. The change in the relative sizes between the subject and background elements is due to the camera position change. Photographs by Rochester Institute of Technology photography students Daniel Bacon and Jesse Wolfe

linear perspective is revealed by the difference in size of the images of the farther object.

In situations where a certain linear perspective contributes significantly to the photograph's effectiveness, the correct procedure is to first select the camera position that produces the desired perspective and then select the focal length lens that produces the desired image size. A zoom lens offers the advantage of providing a range of focal lengths. With fixed focal length lenses, if the desired focal length is not available and changing the camera position reduced the effectiveness because of the change in perspective, an alternative is to use the next shorter focal length lens available and enlarge and crop the resulting photograph.

Drawing Lens Diagrams

Lens diagrams of complex lens systems become quite cluttered and difficult to follow. Luckily, they can be simplified and serve as a helpful alternative to mathematical formulas. In an effort to simplify the drawings, we employ the *thin lens* treatment: the two nodal planes of a lens element are considered close enough to each other that they can be combined into a single plane without significant loss of accuracy. The two drawings in Figure 2-28 (overleaf) show a comparison between using lens elements and using nodal planes. Provided here are the instructions for creating a scaled-down lens diagram using a single nodal plane like the one in Figure 2-29 (overleaf).

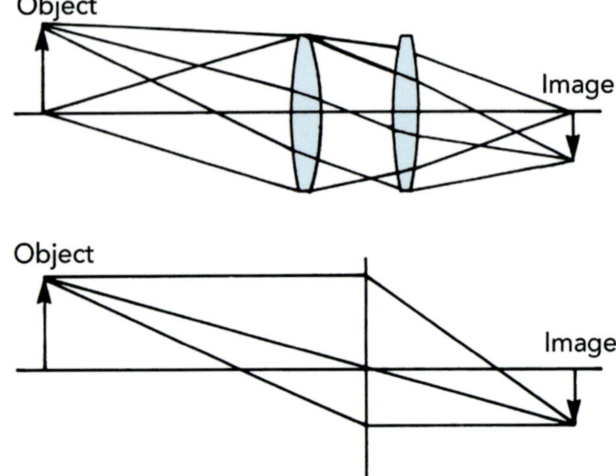

Figure 2-28 Lens diagrams showing image formation using the lens elements (top) and the simpler thin-lens procedure (bottom).

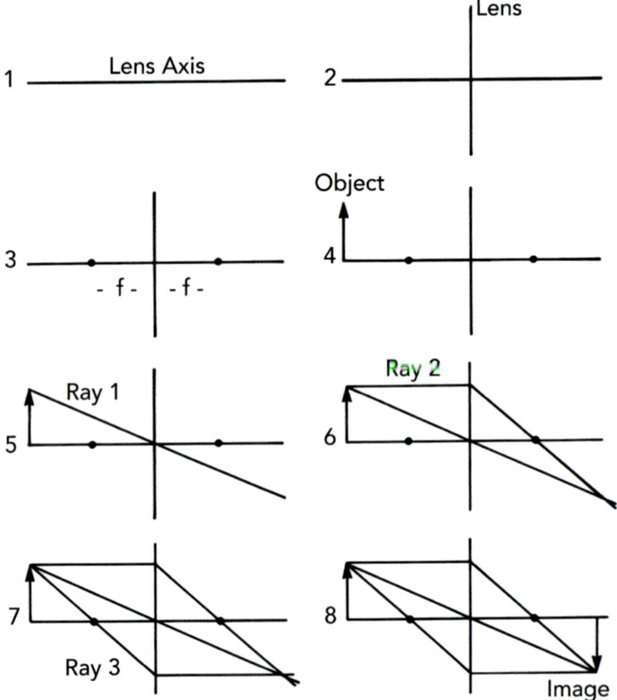

Figure 2-29 Making an actual-size or scale lens diagram in eight steps.

1. Draw a straight, horizontal line to represent the lens axis.
2. Draw a line perpendicular to lens axis to represent the nodal plane of the lens.
3. Place marks on the lens axis one focal length in front and behind the lens. In this example, the focal length is 1 inch. These two marks represent the front and back principal focal points.
4. Draw the object at the correct distance from the lens. In this example, the object is 1 inch tall and located 2 inches from the lens.
5. Draw the first ray of light from the top of the object straight through the optical center of the lens (that is, the intersection of the lens axis and the nodal plane).
6. Draw the second ray parallel to the lens axis, to the nodal plane, then through the back principal focal point.
7. Draw the third ray through the front principal focal point to the nodal plane, then parallel to the lens axis.
8. The intersection of the three rays represents the image of the top of the object. Draw a vertical line from that intersection to the lens axis to represent the entire (inverted) image of the object.

We determine the correct size and position of the image from the original drawing using a ruler. The image size is 1 inch and the image distance is 2 inches. From this we can generalize that placing an object two focal lengths in front of any lens produces a same-sized image two focal lengths behind the lens.

Changing the distance between the object and the lens produces a change in the image formation location. The

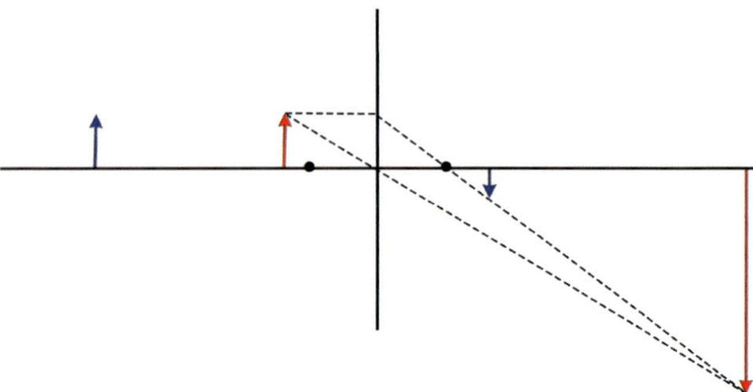

Figure 2-30 Moving an object closer to the lens results in an increase in both image distance and image size.

relationship is an inverse one, so as the object distance decreases, the image distance increases. Since the two distances are interdependent and interchangeable, they are called *conjugate distances*. Image size also changes as the object and image distances change. Moving an object closer to the lens results in an increase in both the image distance and the image size. These relationships are illustrated in Figure 2-30.

The closest distance that an object can be placed in front of a lens that yields a real image is, theoretically, slightly more than one focal length. Placing an object at exactly one focal length from the lens causes the light rays from an object point to leave the lens traveling parallel to each other. As a result, we think of an image only as forming at infinity. In practice, the closest an object can be placed in front of a lens while still obtaining a sharp image is determined by the maximum distance that the sensor can be placed from the lens. Problems like these are solved with lens diagrams. If the maximum image distance is 3 inches for a camera equipped with a 2 inch focal length lens, an actual-size or scale drawing is made starting with the image located 3 inches to the right of the lens. Three rays of light are then drawn back through the lens, using the same rules as before, to determine the location of the object.

If we work with lenses too thick to generalize as thin lenses, or where greater accuracy is required, only small modifications must be made to the thin-lens treatment. If we know that the front and back nodal planes are separated by a distance of 1 inch in a certain lens, two vertical lines are drawn on the lens axis to represent the two nodal planes, separated by the appropriate actual or scale distance. The three rays of light are drawn from an object point to the front nodal plane, as before, but they are drawn parallel to the lens axis between the two nodal planes before they converge to form the image (see Figure 2-31).

It's not just image and object distances that we derived from lens diagrams. *Angle of view*, a measure of how much of the scene is recorded on the sensor, is also determined through these drawings. Angle of view is typically measured for the diagonal dimension of the sensor, although two angles of view are sometimes specified: one for the sensor's vertical dimension and one for the horizontal. Angle of view is determined with the sensor placed one focal length behind the lens which corresponds to focusing on infinity. We first draw a horizontal line for the lens axis and a vertical line to represent the nodal planes, just as we did with the thin-lens treatment. Next, we draw a second vertical line one focal length (actual or scale distance) to the right of the nodal planes. The second vertical line represents the sensor diagonal, so it must be the correct (actual or scale) length.

The drawing in Figure 2-32 represents a 50mm lens on a camera whose sensor diagonal is approximately 43mm. Lines drawn from the rear nodal point (that is, the intersection of the nodal planes and the lens axis) to opposite corners of the sensor form an angle that can be measured with a protractor. No compensation is necessary for the drawing's scale since there are 360° in a circle no matter how large the circle is drawn. The angle of view in this example is approximately 47°.

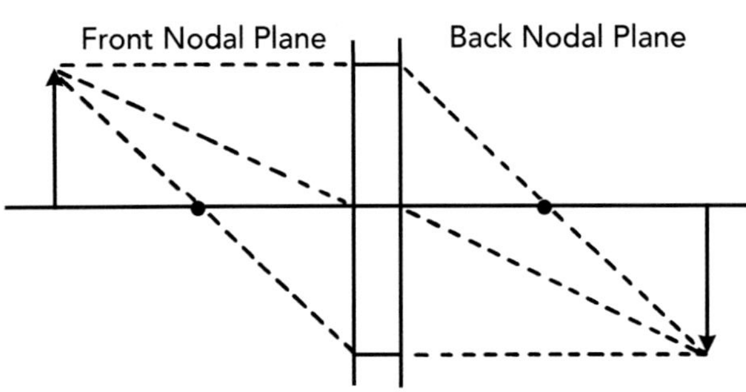

Figure 2-31 The nodal planes are separated by an appropriate distance for thick-lens diagrams.

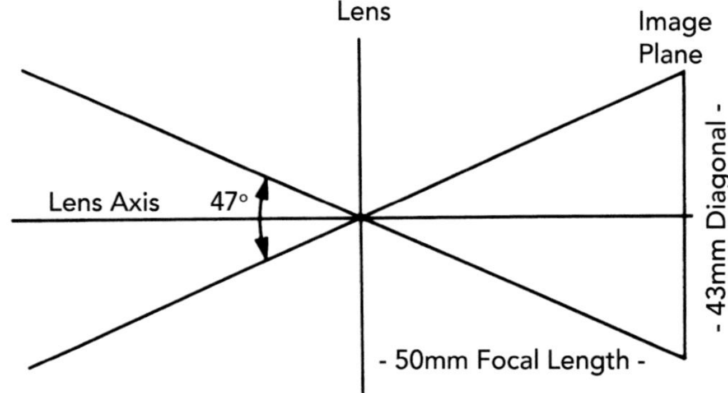

Figure 2-32 The angle of view of a lens-sensor combination is determined by drawing a line with the length equal to the sensor diagonal at a distance of one focal length from the lens. The angle formed by the extreme rays of light is measured with a protractor.

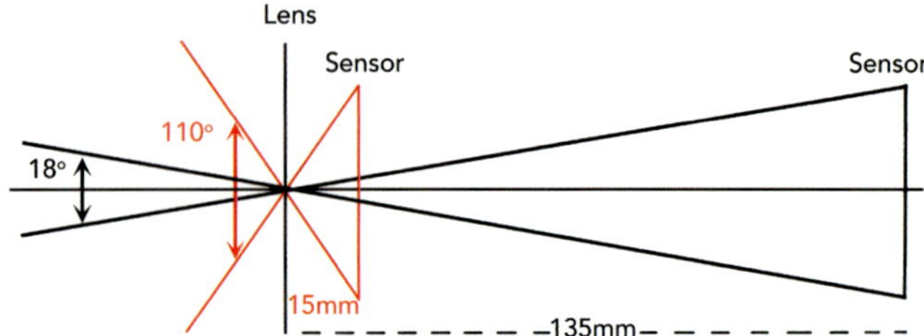

Figure 2-33 Angles of view for 15mm and 135mm focal length lenses on a full frame camera.

Two other focal length lenses, 15mm and 135mm, are represented in the drawing in Figure 2-33. The measured angles of view are approximately 110° and 18°. It's apparent from these drawings that using a shorter focal length lens on a camera increases the angle of view, whereas using a smaller sensor decreases the angle of view. When a camera is focused on nearer objects, the lens-to-sensor distance increases and the effective angle of view decreases.

Lens diagrams are especially helpful for new photographers because they make it easy to visualize the relationships involved in image formation. With experience, it's more efficient to solve problems relating to distances and sizes using mathematical formulas. Most problems of this nature encountered by practicing photographers can be solved by using these five simple formulas:

$$\frac{1}{f} = \frac{1}{u} + \frac{1}{v} \quad \text{(Eq. 2.7)}$$

$$R = \frac{v}{u} \quad \text{(Eq. 2.8)}$$

$$R = \frac{(v - f)}{f} \quad \text{(Eq. 2.9)}$$

$$R = \frac{f}{(u - f)} \quad \text{(Eq. 2.10)}$$

$$R = f(R + 1) \quad \text{(Eq. 2.11)}$$

Where
f = focal length
u = object distance
v = image distance
R = scale of reproduction, which is image size/object size, or I/O.

What happens if we don't know the focal length of a lens? No problem! Set the lens to form a sharp image of an object on an optical bench (or equivalent low-tech solution), measure object and image distances and use Equation 2.7 to solve for *f*. For example, if the object and image distances are both 8 inches, the focal length is 4 inches (or 101.6mm). This formula demonstrates the inverse relationship between the conjugate distances *u* and *v*, whereby moving a camera closer to an object requires increasing the lens-to-sensor distance to keep the image in sharp focus.

It also illustrates that *u* and *v* are interchangeable, meaning that sharp images can be formed with a lens in two different positions between an object and the sensor. For example, if a sharp image is formed when a lens is 8 inches from the object and 4 inches from the sensor, another (and larger) sharp image forms when the lens is placed 4 inches from the object and 8 inches from the sensor (see Figure 2-34). Exceptions to this rule: 1) when the object and image distances are the same, which produces an image that is the same size as the object; 2) when an image distance is larger than a camera body can realistically achieve between

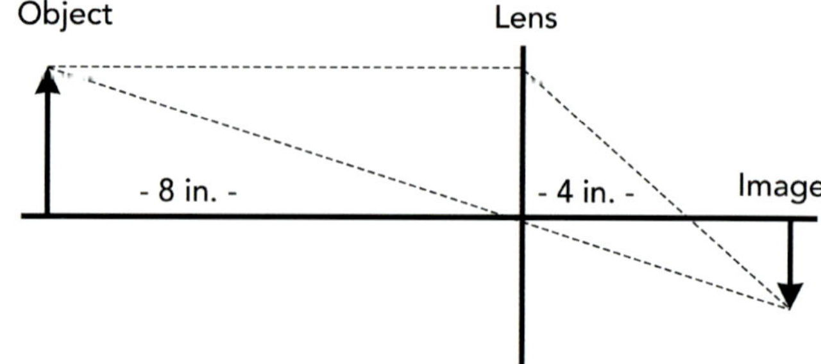

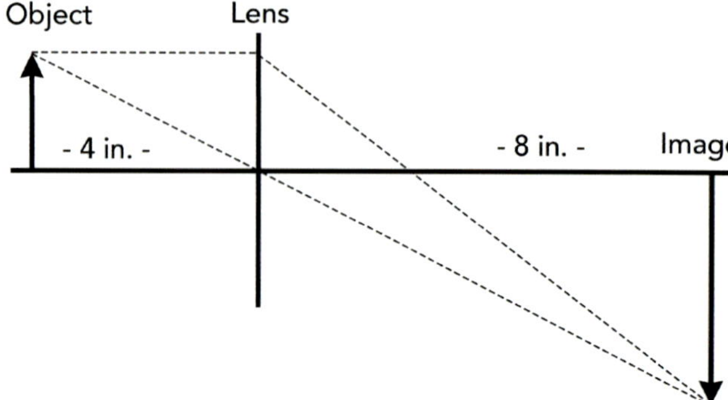

Figure 2-34 Since the object and image distances are interchangeable, sharp images can be made with a lens in two different positions between object and sensor.

the lens and the image plane to form the second sharp image.

Photographers may encounter the problem of determining how large a scale of reproduction (R) is obtainable with a certain camera-lens combination. If a view camera's maximum bellows extension (v) is 16 inches and is equipped with an 8 inch focal length (f) lens, we use the formula $R = (v - f)/f = (16 - 8)/8 = 1$, where the image is the same size as the object. A longer focal length lens can be used to obtain a larger image when the camera cannot be moved closer (see Equation 2.4). However, a shorter focal length lens is preferred in close-up work because the maximum bellows extension is the limiting factor. Replacing the 8 inch lens with a 2 inch lens increases the scale of reproduction from R = 1 to R = 7.

Calculating focal length when an imaging system employs a combination of lenses requires the following formula:

$$\frac{1}{f_c} = \frac{1}{f_1} + \frac{1}{f_2} \qquad \text{(Eq. 2.12)}$$

Where
f_c = the combined focal length
f_1 = the focal length of the first lens
f_2 = the focal length of the second lens

If the lenses are separated by a physical space or distance (d) from the current lens, we use the following formula:

$$\frac{1}{f_c} = \frac{1}{f} + \frac{1}{f_s} - \frac{d}{(f x f_s)} \qquad \text{(Eq. 2.13)}$$

Where
f_c = the combined focal length
f = the focal length of the current lens
f_s = the focal length of the supplementary lens
d = distance between f and f_s

Depth of Field

Camera lenses focus on one object distance at a time. In theory, objects in front of and behind the object distance focused on are not imaged sharply on the sensor. In practice, acceptably sharp focus is seldom limited to a single plane. Instead, objects somewhat closer and farther away appear sharp. This is referred to as *depth of field* (DOF). Depth of field is the range of object distances within which objects are imaged with acceptable sharpness. It is not limited to the plane focused on because the human eye's resolving power is finite; a circle up to a certain size appears as a point to our visual system (see Figure 2-35). The largest circle that appears as a point is referred to as the *permissible circle of confusion.*

The size of the largest circle that appears as a point depends on viewing distance. For this reason, permissible circles of confusion are generally specified for a viewing distance of 10 inches and 1/100 inch is commonly cited as an appropriate value for the circle diameter. Even at a fixed distance, the size of the permissible circle of confusion varies with factors including differences in individual eyesight, the tonal contrast between the circle and the background, the level of illumination and the viewer's criteria for sharpness.

Although many photography books that include the subject of depth of field accept 1/100 inch as appropriate,

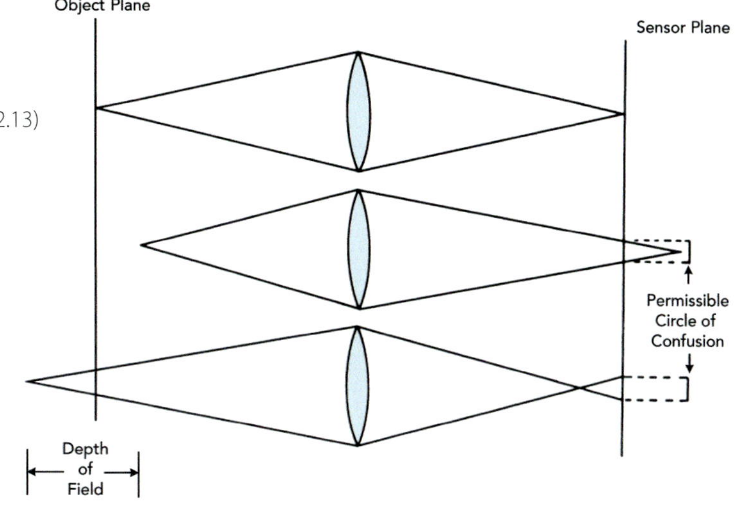

Figure 2-35 Depth of field is the range of distances within which objects are imaged with acceptable sharpness. At the limits, object points are imaged as permissible circles of confusion.

there is less agreement among lens manufacturers. A study involving a small sample of cameras designed for advanced amateurs and professional photographers revealed that values ranging from 1/70 to 1/200 inch were used—approximately a 3:1 ratio. We consider two different methods for evaluating depth of field scales and tables for specific lenses.

One method is photographing a flat surface with fine texture or detail at an angle of approximately 45°, placing markers at the point focused on and at the near and far limits of the depth of field as indicated by the depth of field scale or table, as shown in Figure 2-36. The first photograph should be made at an intermediate f-number with additional exposures bracketing the f-number one and two stops on both sides, with appropriate adjustments in exposure time. A variation of this method is using three movable objects, focusing on one and placing the other two at the near and far limits of the depth of field as indicated by the scale or table.

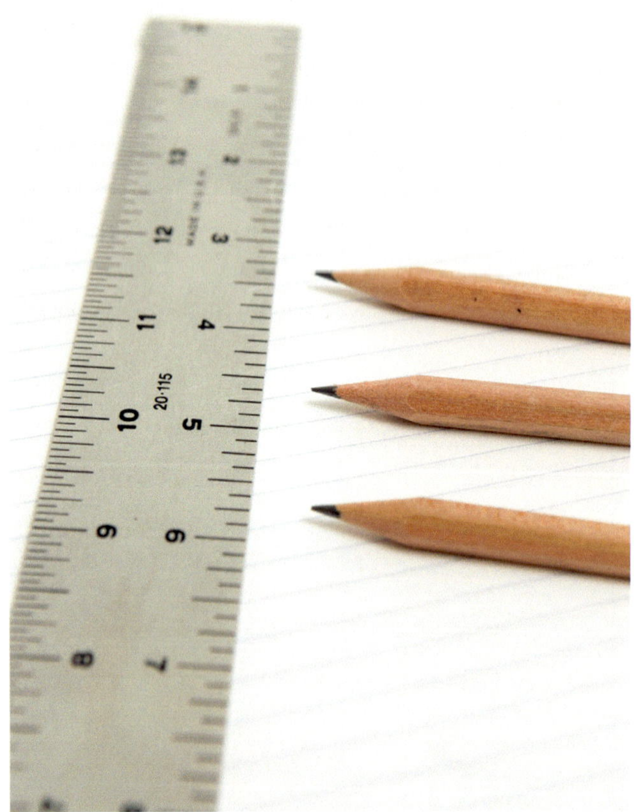

Figure 2-36 Validating depth of field scales and tables by photographing an object at an angle with markers at the focus location and the indicated near and far limits. Photograph by Rochester Institute of Technology photography alumnus Oscar Durand

To judge the results, output 6x8 inch or larger prints to view from a distance equal to the diagonal of the prints. The diagonal of a 6x8 inch print is 10 inches, which is considered to be the closest distance at which most people can comfortably view photographs or read. If the photograph made at the f-number specified by the depth of field scale has either too little or too much depth of field when viewed at the correct distance, the photograph that best meets the viewer's expectation should be identified from the bracketing series. A corresponding adjustment can be made when using the depth of field scale or table in the future.

The second method involves determining the diameter of the permissible circle of confusion used by the lens manufacturer in calculating the depth of field scale or table. No photographs are needed for this approach. Instead, substitute values for the terms on the right side of the formula:

$$C = \frac{f^2}{(f\text{-}number \times H)} \qquad \text{(Eq. 2.14)}$$

Where *C* is the diameter of the permissible circle of confusion on the sensor, *f* is the focal length of the lens, *f-number* used and *H* is the hyperfocal distance at the indicated f-number.

The *hyperfocal distance* is defined as: a) the closest distance that appears sharp when a lens is focused on infinity; or b) the closest focus distance that renders an object at infinity to appear sharp. When a lens is focused on the hyperfocal distance, the depth of field extends from infinity to one-half the hyperfocal distance (see Figure 2-37). If f/16 is selected as the f-number with a 2 inch (50mm) focal length lens, the hyperfocal distance can be determined from a depth of field table, a depth of field scale on the lens or by noting the near distance sharp at f/16 when the lens is focused on infinity. If the near-limit marker on a DOF scale falls between two widely separated numbers, making accurate estimation difficult, set infinity opposite the far-limit marker as shown in Figure 2-38 and multiply the distance opposite the near-limit marker by two.

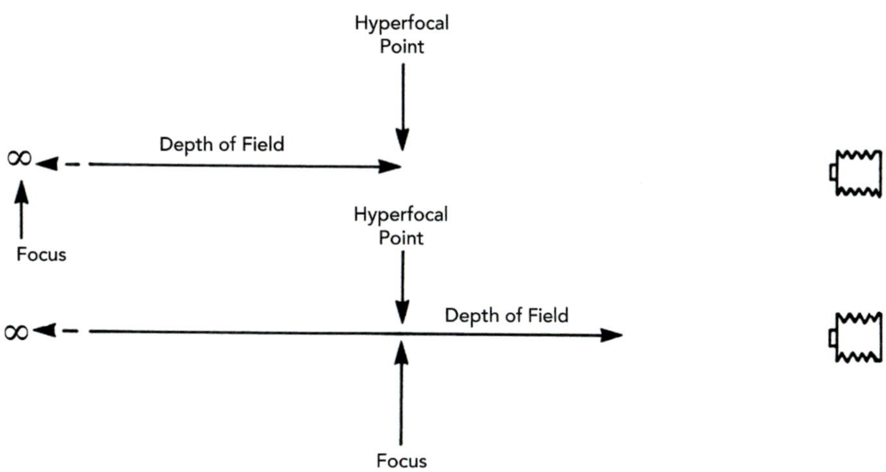

Figure 2-37 The hyperfocal distance is the closest distance that appears sharp when a lens is focused on infinity (top), or the closest distance that can be focused on and have an object at infinity appear sharp (bottom).

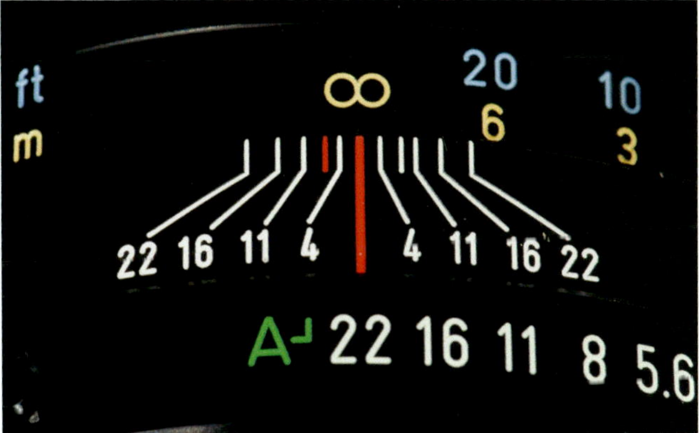

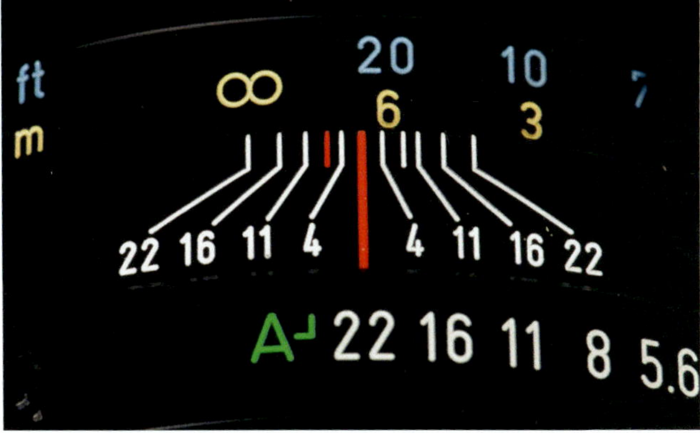

Figure 2-38 The hyperfocal distance can be determined from a depth of field scale by focusing on infinity and noting the near-distance sharp at the specified f-number (top) or by setting infinity opposite the far-distance sharp marker and multiplying the near distance sharp by two (bottom). Photograph by Rochester Institute of Technology photography alumnus James Craven

Since the circle of confusion is commonly expressed as a fraction of an inch, the hyperfocal distance and the focal length must be in inches. The hyperfocal distance at f/16 for the lens illustrated is 24 feet (288 inches). Substituting these values in the formula from Equation 2.14 equates to 22/(16 x 288) or 1/1,152 inch. This is the size of the permissible circle of confusion on a full frame sensor, but this image must then be magnified six times to make a 6x8 inch print to be viewed at 10 inches. Thus, 6 x 1/1,152 = 1/192 inch, or approximately half as large a permissible circle of confusion as the 1/100 inch value commonly used.

Note that the size of the permissible circle of confusion used by a lens manufacturer in computing a depth of field table or scale tells us nothing about the quality of the lens itself. The manufacturer can arbitrarily select any value and in practice a size is selected that is deemed appropriate for the typical user. If a second depth of field scale is made for the lens in the preceding example based on a circle with a diameter of 1/100 inch rather than approximately 1/200 inch, the new scale indicates that it is necessary to stop down only to f/8 in a situation where the original scale specified f/16. Lens definition, however, is determined by the quality of the image for the object focused on and not the near and far limits of the indicated depth of field.

Depth of Field Controls

Photographers have three controls over depth of field: f-number, object distance and focal length. Since viewing distance also affects the apparent sharpness of objects in front of and behind the object focused on, it is generally assumed that photographs are viewed at a distance approximately equal to the diagonal of the picture. At this distance, depth of field is not affected by making differently sized prints from the same file. For example, the circles of confusion at the near and far limits of the depth of field are twice as large on a 16x20 inch print as on an 8x10 inch print from the same image file. However, the larger print would be viewed from double the distance, making the two prints appear to have the same depth of field. If the larger print is viewed from the same distance as the smaller print, it appears to have less depth of field. Cropping when enlarging decreases the depth of field because the print size and viewing distance do not increase in proportion to the magnification.

Depth of Field and F-Number

The relationship between f-number and depth of field is a simple one: depth of field is directly proportional to the f-number, or $D1/D2 = f\text{-}number_1/f\text{-}number_2$. If a lens' available f-numbers range is from f/2 to f/22, the ratio of the depth of field at these settings is $D1/D2$ = (f/22)/(f/2) = 11/1. Changing the f-number is generally the most convenient method of controlling depth of field, but occasionally insufficient depth of field is obtained with a lens stopped down to the smallest diaphragm opening or too much depth of field is obtained with a lens wide open. Other controls must be considered in such circumstances.

Depth of Field and Object Distance

Depth of field increases rapidly as the distance between the camera and the subject increases. For example, doubling the object distance makes the depth of field four times as large. The differences in depth of field with very small and very large object distances are dramatic. In photomacrography, where the camera is at a distance of two focal lengths or less from the subject, the depth of field at a large aperture sometimes appears to be confined to a single plane (see Figure 2-39).

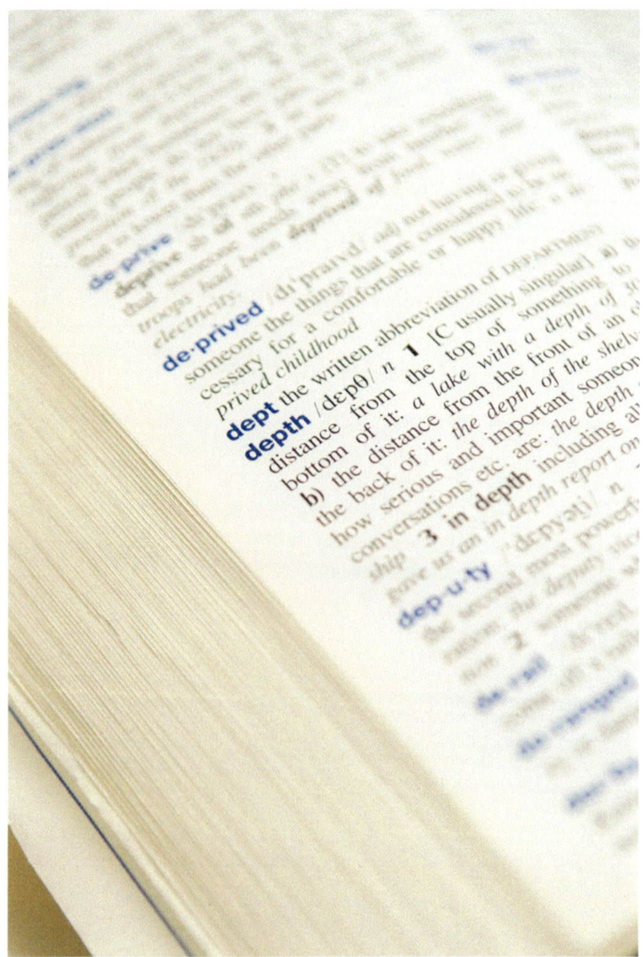

Figure 2-39 Depth of field varies in proportion to the object distance squared. Photographs made at a scale of reproduction of 1:1 and larger tend to have a shallow depth of field. Photograph by Rochester Institute of Technology photography alumnus Oscar Durand

At the other extreme, by focusing on the hyperfocal distance, depth of field extends from infinity to within a few feet of the camera with some lenses (see Figure 2-40). The mathematical relationship between depth of field and object distance (provided the object distance does not exceed the hyperfocal distance) is represented by the formula $D_1/D_2 = u_1^2/u_2^2$ where u is the object distance. For example, if two photographs are made with the camera 5 feet and 20 feet from the subject, the ratio of the depths of field is as follows:

$$\frac{D_1}{D_2} = \frac{20^2}{5^2} = 16$$

If the object distance is increased to achieve a larger depth of field when the camera lens cannot be stopped down far enough, it is necessary to take into account the enlarging and cropping required to obtain the same image size as with the camera in the original position. There is still a net gain in depth of field in moving the camera farther from the subject, even though some of the increase is lost when the image is cropped in printing. The net gain is represented by the formula $D_1/D_2 = u_1/u_2$, which is the same as the preceding formula with the square sign removed.

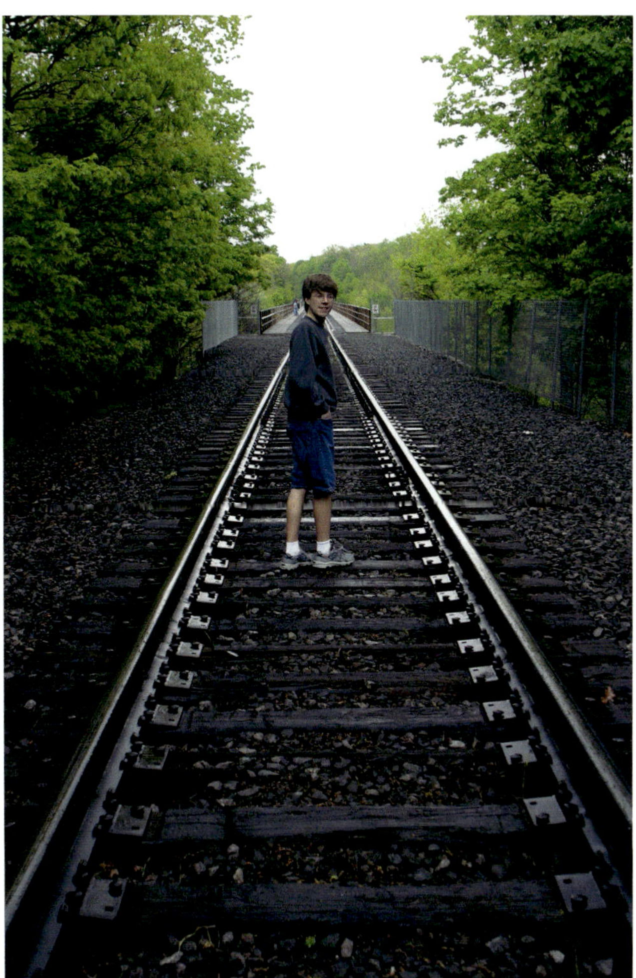

Figure 2-40 Focusing on the hyperfocal distance produces a depth of field that extends from infinity to one-half the hyperfocal distance.

Depth of Field and Focal Length

There is an inverse relationship between focal length and depth of field: as focal length increases, depth of field decreases. Using a 50mm focal length lens and a 300mm focal length lens on the same camera produces a dramatic difference in depth of field. The mathematical relationship is $D_1/D_2 = (focal\ length_2)^2/(focal\ length_1)^2$. This relationship holds true only if the camera remains in the same place relative to the subject.

Depth of Focus

Depth of focus is the focusing latitude present when photographing a two-dimensional subject. It is the distance the sensor plane can be moved in both directions from optimum focus before the circles of confusion for the image of an object point match the permissible circle of confusion used to calculate depth of field. Note that depth of field calculations assume the image plane occupies a single flat plane while depth of focus calculations assume the subject occupies a single flat plane (see Figure 2-41). If a three-dimensional object completely fills the depth of field space, there is only one position for the sensor, there is in effect no depth of focus and no tolerance for focusing errors.

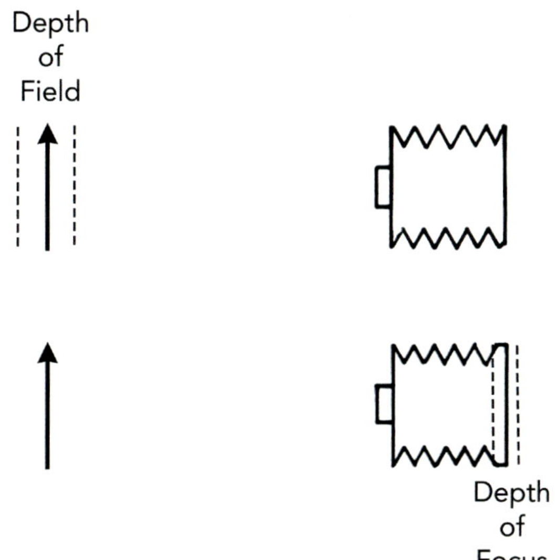

Figure 2-41 Depth of field calculations are based on the assumption that the two-dimensional image plane is in the position of optimum focus (top). Depth of focus calculations are based on the assumption that the subject is limited to a two-dimensional plane (bottom).

Depth of focus for a two-dimensional subject is calculated by multiplying the permissible circle of confusion by the f-number by 2. Using 1/200 inch for the permissible circle of confusion on a 6x8 inch print or 1/1200 inch on a full frame sensor, the depth of focus is *C* x *f-number* x *2* = *1/1200* x *f/2* x *2* = *1/300 inch*. From this formula we can also see that depth of focus varies in direct proportion to the f-number, as does depth of field.

Depth of field decreases when the camera is moved closer to the subject, however at the same time the depth of focus increases. As the object distance decreases, the lens-to-sensor distance must be increased to maintain sharp focus of the image. This increases the effective f-number. It is the effective f-number, not the marked f-number, that is used in the formula above.

Although increasing focal length decreases depth of field, it does not affect depth of focus. At the same f-number, both the diameter of the effective aperture and the lens-to-sensor distance change in proportion to changes in focal length. Consequently, the shape of the cone of light falling on the sensor remains unchanged. It follows that as focal length does not appear in the formula *C* x *f-number* x *2*, it has no effect on depth of focus.

Although changing sensor size does not seem to affect depth of focus, using a smaller sensor reduces the correct viewing distance and, therefore, the permissible circle of confusion. Substituting a smaller value for C in the formula C x f-number x 2 reduces the depth of focus.

Specialty Lenses

So far we've covered normal, telephoto and wide-angle lenses. That trio works as an excellent set for photographers that shoot a variety of subjects and scenes, allowing us to shoot across a range of distances and fields of view. Normal, telephoto and wide-angle focal length lenses are a versatile combination in any camera bag. We turn to specialty lenses for specific applications, effects or image-making requirements.

Macro Lenses

Lenses producing excellent quality images with objects at moderate to large distances may not perform well when used at small object distances. *Macro lenses* are designed specifically for photographing at small object distances while rendering the subject at or greater than life size on the sensor. They are designed with additional aberration corrections that are otherwise apparent at such magnifications such as focus fall off along image edges (shown in Figure 2-42).

It's common to see lenses boasting macro capabilities despite not being able to render the subject greater than life size. Here the use of the term is misleading, replacing its technical definition with one broadly describing an ability to focus at close distances (which we would

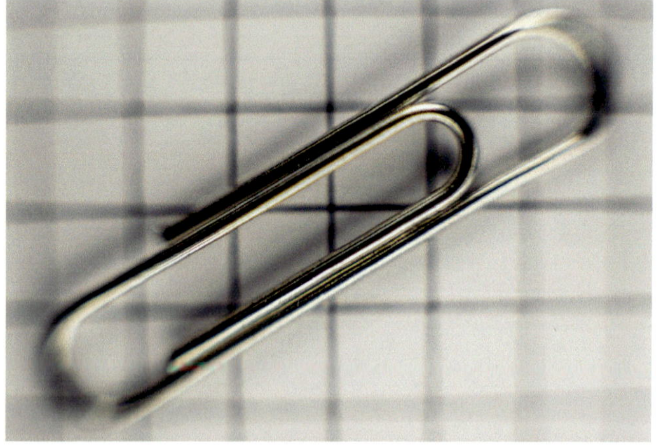

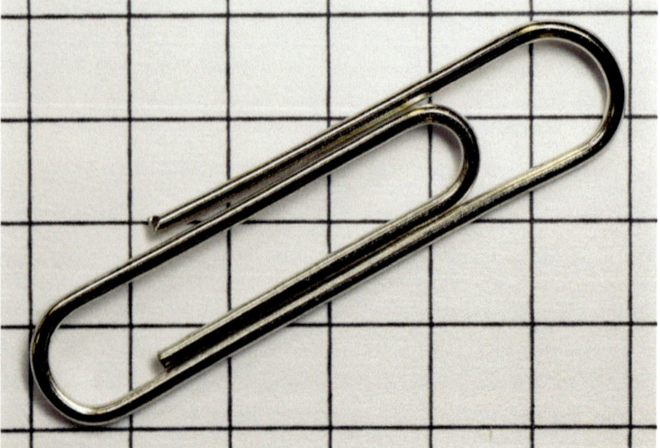

Figure 2-42 Photographs of a small object made with a standard camera lens (top) and a macro lens (bottom), both at their maximum aperture. Photograph by Rochester Institute of Technology photography student Kristina Kaszei

presumably do with small subjects). These lenses tend to produce a maximum scale of reproduction no larger than 1:2. If you need to occasionally photograph larger subjects at very close distances, such a "macro" lens is perfectly adequate—but you'll need a true macro lens to photograph particularly tiny subjects like insect eyes or pollen grains on a flower.

Perspective Control Lenses

Also known as *tilt-shift, perspective control* lenses introduce perspective or distortion controls on SLRs that have historically only been available with view cameras. The lens housing of a tilt-shift lens introduces a variable positioning of the optics relative to the sensor plane, whereas a traditional lens uses optics in a fixed position and distance. As a consequence, perspective control lenses can be a range of focal lengths and behave exactly like their non-tilt-shift counterparts when set in a neutral position. Adjusting the lens housing positioning knobs shifts the optics up, down, left or right and can also tilt up or down (hence the nickname).

There are two outcomes when employing a perspective control lens. The first is counteracting the natural perspective convergence of rectilinear lines like the ones seen in Figure 2-43. Left uncorrected, the vertical building elements appear to lean. Architectural photography is a smart fit for perspective control lenses as shifting helps render subjects as they are without distortion.

A normal lens allows us to focus in one plane perpendicular to the optical axis of the lens; the tilt function allows for manipulation of the plane of focus from the perpendicular. Carefully considered tilt-shift movements help to extend the plane of focus to minimize focus fall-off.

Figure 2-44 (overleaf) highlights the other outcome whereby intentionally introducing extra distortion or unusual focus fall-off. Interestingly, a unique side effect of this imaging method is the illusion of miniaturization. We're used to seeing tiny things up close with limited depth as our eyes adjust to the close focusing distance and small scale. When we see extremely shallow depth of field on scene—especially at elevated vantage points—more commonly photographed with everything in focus, we start to perceive them as miniaturized. Unusual placement of the in-focus sweet spot can be used for other compositional effects, though this is also possible by holding any normal lens in front of the camera body without mounting it.

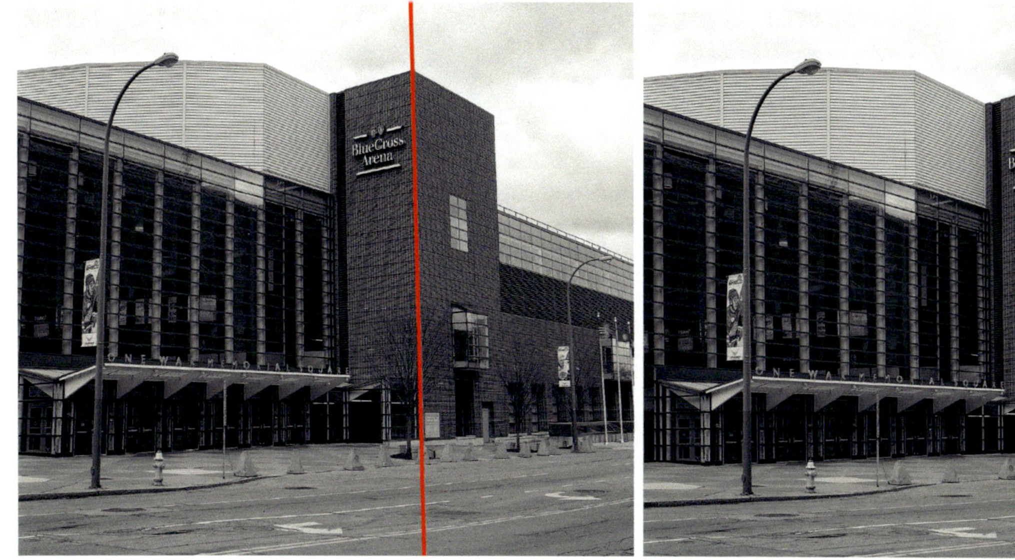

Figure 2-43 Before (left) and after (right) perspective correction using a tilt-shift lens. Photograph by Rochester Institute of Technology student Adam Montoya

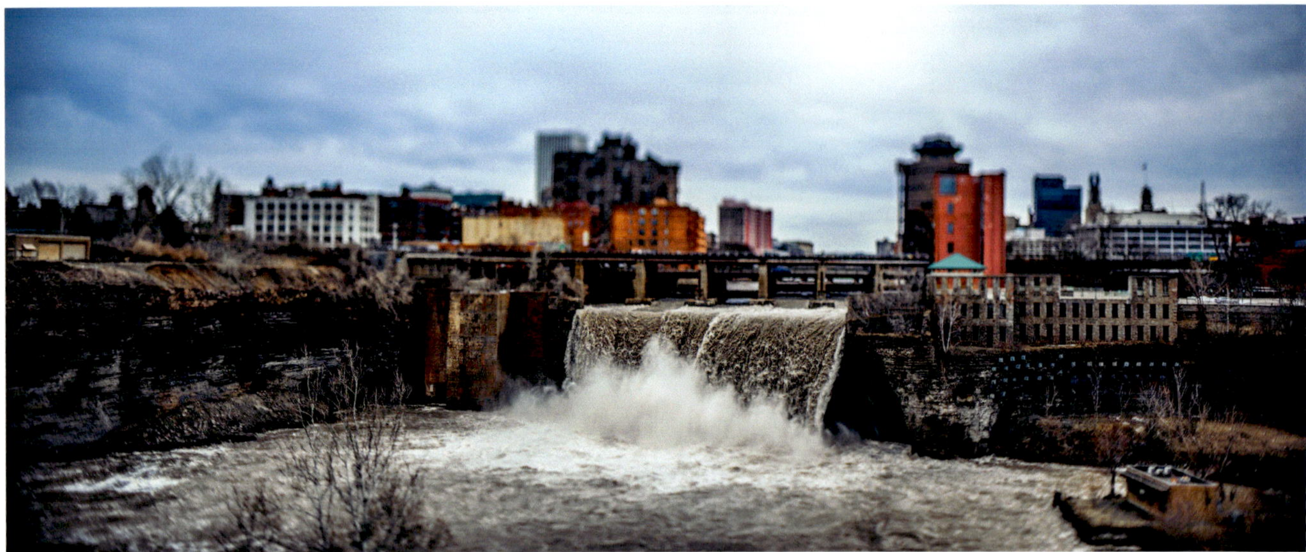

Figure 2-44 A miniaturization effect is introduced with a tilt-shift lens by manipulating the focus plane to drastically decrease depth of field and focus fall-off. Photograph by Rochester Institute of Technology photography student Joel Beckwith

Catadioptric Lenses

Notwithstanding the shorter lens-to-sensor distance obtained with telephoto lenses compared to normal lenses of the same focal length, the distance becomes inconveniently large with long focal length lenses. *Catadioptric lenses* achieve a dramatic improvement in compactness through the use of folded optics, combining glass elements and mirrors. The name catadioptric is derived from dioptrics (the optics of refracting elements) and catoptrics (the optics of reflecting surfaces). Similar designs are employed for telescopes.

Figure 2-45 illustrates the principle of image formation with a catadioptric lens. A beam of light from a distant point passes through the glass element, except for the opaque circle in the center; it is reflected by the concave mirror and again by the smaller mirror on the back of the glass element and it passes through the opening in the concave mirror to form the image at the sensor plane. The glass element and the opaque stop reduce aberrations inherent to the mirror system.

Catadioptric lenses are capable of producing images with excellent image quality with some drawbacks. Their design makes it impractical to contain a variable-diameter aperture, so exposure must be regulated by other means and depth of field control is nonexistent. It also requires very large lens diameters to achieve long focal lengths. Finally, these lenses have a signature (and not necessarily desirable) image artifact in out-of-focus areas that look like rings or donuts.

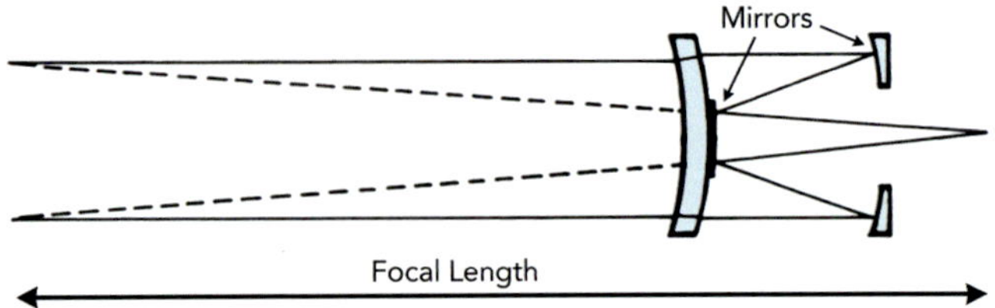

Figure 2-45 Catadioptric lenses make use of folded optics to obtain long focal lengths in relatively short lens barrels.

Reversed Telephoto Wide-Angle Lenses

Reversed telephoto wide-angle lens designs are used to avoid interference between the lens and the mirror. Problems may be encountered when using conventional design, short focal length wide-angle lenses because of the resulting short lens-to-sensor distances. The lens designer's solution is to reverse the arrangement of the elements in a telephoto lens, placing a negative element or group of

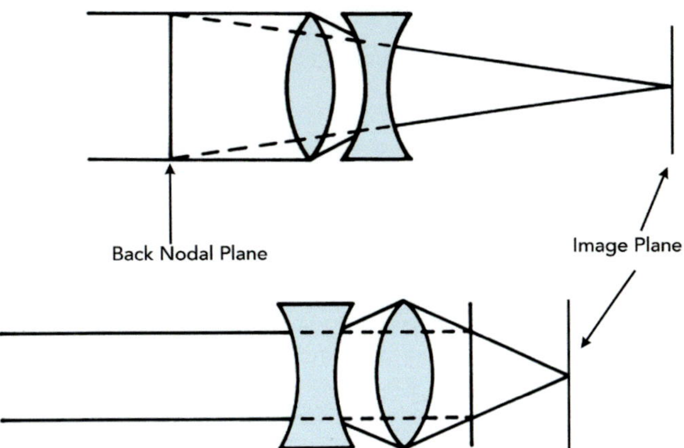

Figure 2-46 The back nodal plane is behind the lens with reversed telephoto wide-angle lenses, providing a larger lens-to-sensor distance than for a normal-type lens of the same focal length.

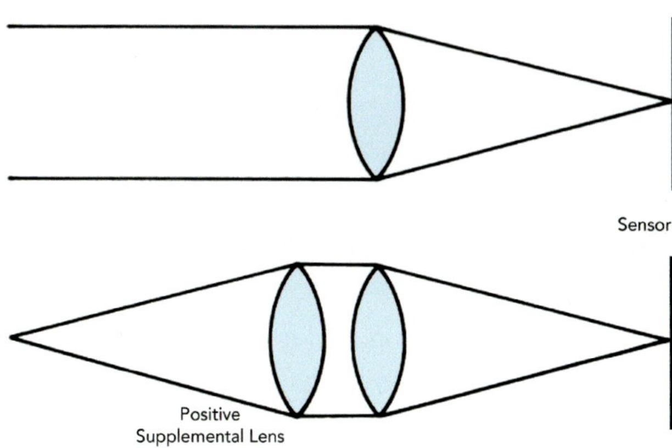

Figure 2-47 Positive supplemental lenses enable the camera to focus on near object without increasing the lens-to-sensor distance.

elements in front of and separated from a positive element or group of elements. This design places the image nodal plane behind the lens (or near the back surface), which effectively moves the lens farther away from the sensor (see Figure 2-46). Lenses of this type are called reversed telephoto, inverted telephoto and retrofocus wide-angle lenses.

Supplemental Lenses

Photographers can use a lower-cost, single element *supplemental lens* to give their general-purpose lens more functionality. A supplemental lens alters focal length when attached to a lens. Adding a positive supplemental lens produces the equivalent of a shorter focal length. These supplemental lenses are attached close to the front surface of the camera lens, making it possible to calculate the focal length of the lens combination with reasonable accuracy using the formula $1/f_c = 1/f + 1/f_s$, where f_c is the combined focal length, f is the focal length of the camera lens and f_s is the focal length of the supplemental lens.

Supplemental lenses are commonly calibrated in *diopters*. Diopter power equals the reciprocal of the focal length in meters of $D = 1/f$. To convert the diopter value to a focal length the previous equation becomes $f = 1/D$. Diopters are the measure of lens power used for corrective eyeglasses and contacts, which may make it easier to remember how supplemental lenses behave. Adding a positive supplemental lens lowers the focal length; it cannot convert a normal lens into a wide-angle one. Therefore, using a supplemental lens when photographing objects at far distances may not provide the desired covering power. However, using a positive supplemental lens allows you to focus on new objects without increasing the lens-to-sensor distance (see Figure 2-47).

Extension Tubes and Teleconverters

Supplemental lenses are not the only way to modify the image produced by a camera lens. *Extension tubes* increase the image distance between the lens elements and the sensor. They do not contain any additional optics and instead act as a physical separator to position the back of the camera lens farther from the camera body mount. They increase magnification and allow for closer focusing distances. The downside to using extension tubes is light loss. With additional distance to travel, the additional light fall-off raises the effective f-number of the attached lens. Adding optical elements to further increase image magnification results in a *teleconverter*. These have the same drawbacks as extension tubes when it comes to reducing the amount of light reaching the sensor. Teleconverters are often categorized by the amount of magnification they introduce, i.e. 1.4x or 1.5x. It's possible to chain together a long focal length lens and multiple teleconverters to achieve very long effective focal lengths, though the weight and physical length introduced by this assembly is unwieldy for handheld or portable use.

Lens Shortcomings and Aberrations

It's difficult to make a single, perfect lens for making photographs. Earlier in this chapter we defined concepts of photographic optics using simple lenses due to their straightforward design. However, nearly every lens used for making pictures is actually a *compound lens* consisting of groups or sets of different optical components in series. Compound lens systems are necessary for minimizing the optical imperfections of any one lens. Photographic optics have shortcomings that, unmitigated, result in *aberrations* or departures from the ideal image that appear as unwanted image artifacts or imperfections. Lens shortcomings can be grouped into four categories relating to image definition, image shape, image illuminance and image color.

Here we describe the aberrations most commonly encountered by photographers. It is not a comprehensive list; some optical shortcomings are only problematic in specific use-cases like microscopy or telescopes, so we've put those to the side. Distortions, color fringing and focus aberrations tend to be more extreme and noticeable along frame edges.

Chromatic Aberration

We understand now that positive lenses work by bringing light rays to a single point of focus at the location of our camera's sensor. Lenses accomplish this by the principle of refraction whereby light changes direction when it travels through the lens material. The catch is that light changes direction or bends to varying degrees based on its wavelength (dispersion). Blue light rays do not come into focus at the same position as red light rays—a problem when visible light consists of a whole variety of wavelengths. Unless actively corrected, shorter wavelengths (blues) bend more and come into focus in front of the image plane while longer wavelengths (red) bend the least and come into focus behind the image plane (see Figure 2-48). This is called *chromatic aberration*. We're simplifying these groupings, but the bottom line is that our full color image is at risk of forming across multiple planes when our sensor can only capture one.

Chromatic aberration appears as *color fringing* along subject edges in a photograph and it is especially noticeable along edges with considerable contrast, such as an object's silhouette against a bright sky. They are not necessarily red, green or blue. In fact, chromatic aberration in modern lenses is often yellow and/or magenta (see Figure 2-49). Wide-angle lenses are particularly susceptible to color fringing due to the extreme angles that light enters and bends through them. Generally speaking, chromatic aberration appears most prominently near the corners of a photograph where the optics are the least corrected.

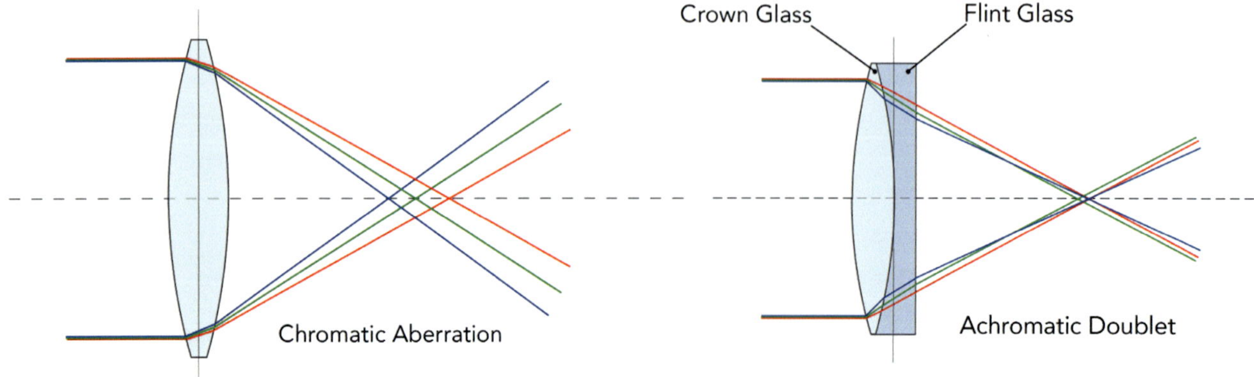

Figure 2-48 Chromatic aberration as light travels through a positive lens. It is commonly corrected using an achromatic doublet lens. Adapted from images by Andreas 06 and DrBob, released into the Public Domain under a Creative Commons license

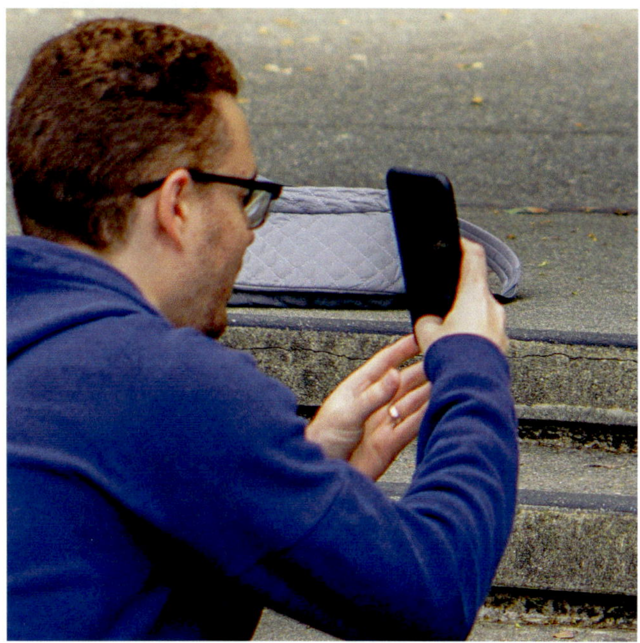

Figure 2-49 Chromatic aberration visible along contrasty edges. Photograph by Ruben Vargas

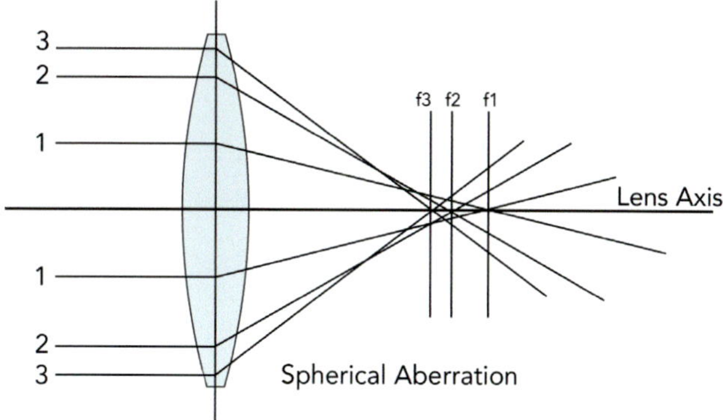

Figure 2-50 Spherical aberration as light travels through a positive lens.

A common optical solution to counteract this aberration is *achromatic doublet* lens elements. This two-lens system pairs a positive, low index of refraction *crown* glass with a negative, high index of refraction *flint* glass. The differing indices of refraction effectively correct the shortcomings of the system and reduce chromatic aberration in the final image.

Interestingly, our eyes also suffer from chromatic aberration. There are a few things that help minimize its appearance. There are no blue-sensitive light detectors or S cones at our centralmost vision (the fovea), only red (L cones) and green (M cones) sensitive ones. Additionally, the brain mitigates the perception of chromatic aberration when it processes the signals from our eyes. It's believed that the chromatic aberration inherent to human vision is interpreted to better understand depth and drive accommodation, though we are not consciously aware of it.[2]

Spherical Aberration

Some light rays travel through the center of a lens while others travel through its periphery. This can mean that the light rays travel through different amounts of the lens medium; remember, positive lenses form images by bending light to bring an image into focus. Light passing through the edges of the lens bend more than the light traveling through the center as illustrated in Figure 2-50. This results in an unsharp image and is called *spherical aberration*. As with chromatic aberration, combinations of additional lens elements in the optical system are introduced to mitigate this image quality degradation. Aperture size can also reduce spherical aberration by blocking the light from the outside edges of the lens. Spherical aberration is reduced as the lens aperture is stopped down, giving the photographer some control over the degree of unsharpness.

We often get caught up in chasing perfectly sharp, well-defined photographs. Sometimes artistic intent dictates something decidedly less accurate or optically precise. Soft-focus specialty lenses under-correct for spherical aberration, leaving us with a unique effect sometimes used in portrait photography or pictorialist-style aesthetics.

Diffraction

Diffraction is the only lens aberration that affects the definition of images formed with a pinhole. The principles of geometrical optics tell us that image definition increases indefinitely as a pinhole is made smaller. In practice, there is an optimal pinhole size and image definition decreases due to diffraction as the pinhole is made smaller. The narrow beam of light passing through the pinhole from an object point spreads out not unlike water coming out of a hose nozzle. The smaller the pinhole, the more apparent the effect.

Diffraction happens when light bends around the edge of an object which, in our case, is an aperture. The amount of bending depends on the wavelength of the light and the size of the opening. When the aperture is much larger than the wavelength, the diffraction is barely noticeable. When the wavelength of the light and the size of the aperture are nearly the same, diffraction is noticeable to the eye and renders the image soft.

In practice, the definition of an image formed by an otherwise perfect lens is limited by diffraction. Some lenses are *diffraction-limited* because under the specified conditions they approach optical perfection. Using resolution as a measure of image definition, the diffraction-limited resolving power is approximated with the formula:

$$R = \frac{1{,}800}{f\text{-}number} \qquad \text{(Eq. 2.15)}$$

where:
R = the resolving power in lines per millimeter
1,800 = constant for an average wavelength of light of 550 nm

Applying this to a hypothetically perfect lens with minimum and maximum f-numbers of f/2 and f/22, this equation tells us that its diffraction-limited resolving power is 900 and 82 lines/mm, respectively.

Vignetting

Vignetting or *light fall-off* is the reduction in brightness from the center to the outer edges of an image. There are several causes and therefore categories of vignetting: natural, optical, mechanical and artificial. Every lens exhibits some optical and natural vignetting as a reality of lens design.

Optical vignetting appears as a gradual darkening from the center to the edge of the image and can be seen in Figure 2-51. It's caused by the lens barrel that houses the optical and mechanical elements of a complete lens system. We can't remove the barrel, so we can't entirely eliminate this type of vignetting. Optical vignetting becomes more apparent as the aperture is adjusted to larger, more open settings. Some of the light rays entering the lens from the edges of the scene are blocked by the lens barrel and are rendered with less exposure or no exposure at all, causing the vignette. The effect is minimized by stopping down the lens. This particular issue can rear its ugly head with cheaper lenses that can suffer from noticeable vignetting at wider apertures, leaving you with the choice between minimizing vignetting and using a desired, stopped-down aperture setting. Holga film cameras are known for—and sought out specifically because of—their cheap design that frequently exhibits strong vignetting.

Natural vignetting also appears as a gradual darkening or reduction in brightness from the center of the image to the edges. Its root cause is different from optical vignetting, however. Light rays entering the lens at its center travel in a straight line and have a shorter distance to travel to the sensor compared to rays that enter at an angle. The center of a sensor or film plane receives more light and therefore more exposure than at its periphery. The *cosine fourth law* quantifies this type of vignetting.

Pixel vignetting appears the same as natural vignetting. It's caused by the physical photosite that receives the light rays collected by the lens optics. The effect of the cosine fourth law is at play here because a photosite is not a flat, two-dimensional light detector. Instead they can be thought of like trenches or wells; as light rays travel toward the photosites, those that are headed straight into the opening make it with greater success than ones traveling off-axis.

Imagine the classic carnival game of ping pong toss. The player throws balls into a tightly arranged array of fish bowls and observes that many shots bounce off the bowl edges instead of landing inside them. The game would be much easier if the player is positioned directly above the table of fish bowls, dropping ping pong balls straight down. The odds of winning increase when there's minimal reliance on perfectly thrown, carefully calculated parabolic arcs made from an oblique angle. The carnival game gets harder when the player's distance from the bowls is greater and the ping pong balls' angle of travel is less direct. Similarly, light rays headed toward photosites have a lesser probability of making it into the well if they approach at an angle. Blocked light rays become a form of light vignetting. It's an unavoidable reality of image formation and our best strategy is mitigation. Microlenses are installed atop photosite wells to better collect or catch incoming light. If carnival game analogies aren't helping to visualize the problem, jump to Chapter 3 for digital sensor illustrations.

Mechanical vignetting is a very abrupt artifact caused by a physical obstruction in the light path. A long lens hood or a filter holder attached to the front of the lens barrel are likely culprits, especially if they are designed for focal length lenses different from the ones used. Mechanical vignetting is eliminated by removing the obstruction.

The last type is *artificial* or *post-processing vignetting*. Photo editing software offers tools that allow us to add a darkening effect that emulates natural or optical vignetting for aesthetic effect (see Figure 2-51). It's useful for drawing the eye toward the center or toward a brighter, highlight area of the composition. On the right image and with a delicate hand, the tool is a valuable one. However, it is easy to overdo and risks becoming a cheap shortcut to better composition and refined tone adjustments.

Optical vignetting correction is offered in professional image editing software. The software can leverage image file metadata containing the lens focal length and model against a lens characteristic database created by software developers. These developers quantify the vignetting behavior of most major lens manufacturer offerings by conducting controlled lab shoots. From this information a counter-vignette is applied to the image, lightening edge pixels that are known to be darker than their center counterparts. This same strategy is used by camera manufacturers, though the process happens in-camera when saving to JPEG; often the proprietary lens characterization information is readable only by their respective software for raw captures. Third party image editing tools have to create the information on their own and do not necessarily have prepared vignette correction for obscure or rare camera lenses.

Bokeh

The blurry, out-of-focus areas that result from points of light not at the plane of focus are called *bokeh*. This term is colloquially derived from *boke*, Japanese for "blur" or "haze" in the context of photography. While not an aberration per se, bokeh is a characteristic inherent to a camera lens that some photographers pay particular attention to.

The shape of out-of-focus areas, especially bright points of light, is a direct consequence of the aperture opening shape. The aperture opening is created by a set of

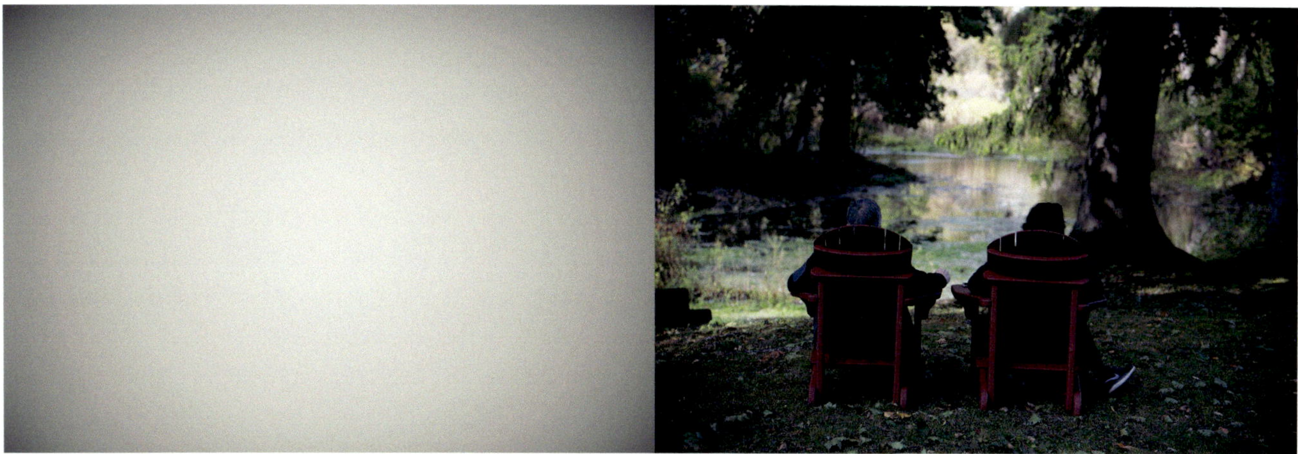

Figure 2-51 Photographing a flat, uniformly lit surface is a quick way to spot vignetting (left). Darkened edges, either optical or artificial (post-processing) means, can be an attribute to the final image's appearance and visual focal point (right).

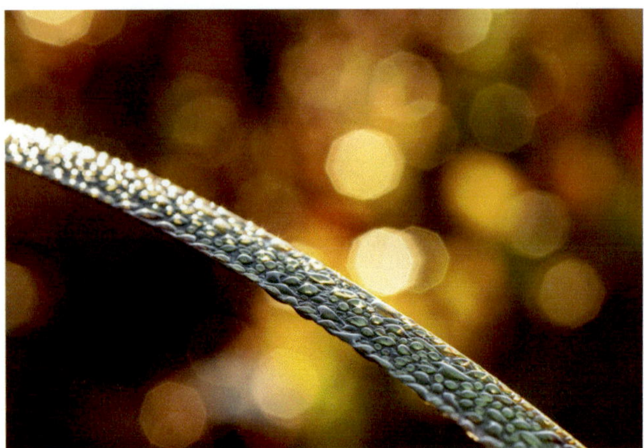

Figure 2-52 The aperture opening shape is seen in out-of-focus specular highlights. This photograph shows the bokeh quality for a 100mm macro lens set to f/8 with considerable distance between the subject and background elements.

overlapping metal petals or blades attached to a mechanism that can dilate or constrict its diameter. The petals themselves have straight edges and therefore create small angles at the points of overlap. The opening that results is similar to drawing a perfect circle using a ruler instead of a compass: you have to draw a group of straight lines at consistent angles to close the circle. Lens apertures are designed using anywhere from 5 to 20 individual blade segments. The more segments, the closer the opening shape resembles a true circle. The closer the opening is to a circle, the more circular the bokeh appears.

Lens bokeh is most apparent when shooting at wider apertures or when focused at close distances with a distant background as evident in Figure 2-52. While the shape of the blurred points of light is closely related to the aperture shape, it is not the only influencing factor. The optical design of the lens also dictates the way in which out-of-focus points are blurred. Some lenses have better correction at their center than at their edges, meaning that bokeh near the frame corners can be further distorted or blurred.

Barrel and Pincushion Distortion

Barrel and *pincushion* distortion are common image-formation pitfalls. Barrel distortion is when straight lines bend outward, similar to how a wooden barrel bulges out at the sides. The image distortion is greatest at the edges of the frame and the least at its center. Super wide-angle lenses exhibit barrel distortion, as it's an inherent consequence of refracting extremely oblique angles of light onto the camera sensor (see Figure 2-53). Pincushion distortion is the opposite effect where straight vertical lines bend inward toward the center of the frame. Here, too, the distortion is at its most extreme near the image frame edges. Either type renders shapes differently from how they appear in the world. Telephoto lenses can suffer from pincushion distortion though not to the obvious degree that a fisheye lens suffers from barrel distortion (see Figure 2-54). Both can be largely corrected in post-processing, particularly if reference data exists that document the exact degree of distortion introduced by a lens—called *lens profiles*. Lens profiles are created by photographing reference targets and mathematically determining the distortion introduced by a lens. They offer a type of engineering instructions to undistort image content when applied by post-processing software. The only downside to using lens profiles to correct for significant distortion is that cropping may be required to retain a rectilinear image frame.

Flare

Flare is non-image forming light in our imaging system that degrades image quality at capture. With all photographic optics, our goal is to control and direct light to form an image of a scene to be recorded by the light-sensitive medium. For the most part, our lenses do this well, especially because lens manufacturing includes steps to coat lens elements with a number of special optical materials to minimize internal reflections. However, there is inevitably some light that scatters or otherwise bends at angles that results in a washed out, low contrast image. The cinematic flare bursts that appear near the sun in scenic landscapes have aesthetic appeal, but that's the crowd-pleasing side of flare. The not-so-desirable flare is the kind that brings a general haziness to photographs and is often tough to spot in the moment. This flare happens when a bright light source is either directly within the lens' line-of-sight or when one is at an extreme, oblique angle relative to the lens' front element. In both cases, light enters the lens and

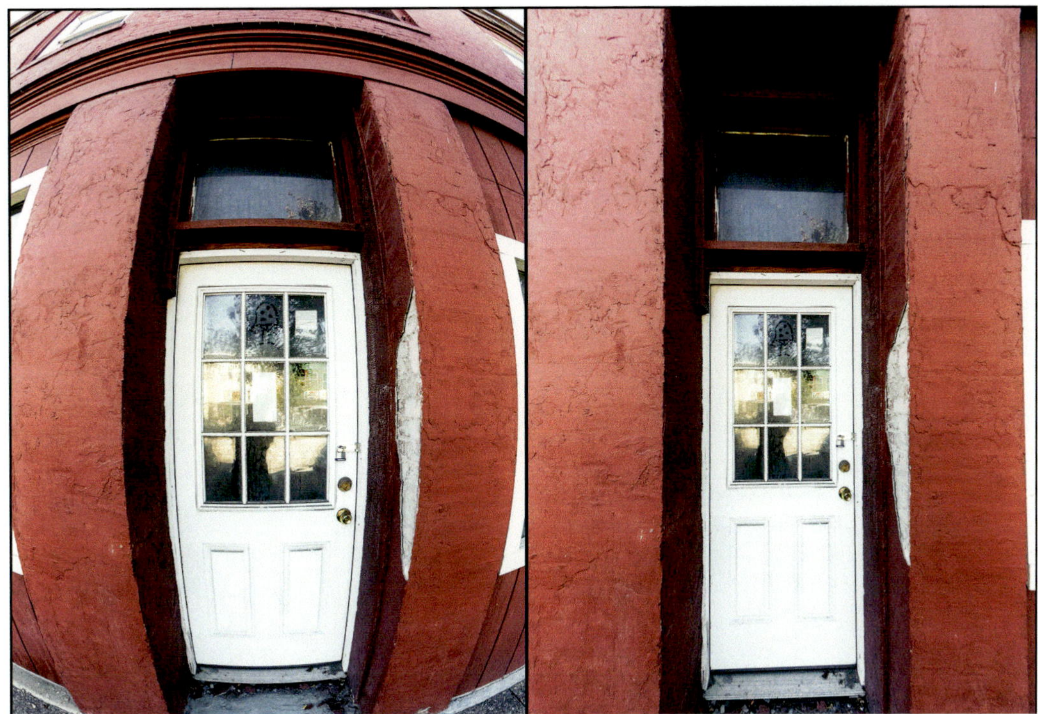

Figure 2-53 Barrel distortion using a fisheye lens at 15mm (left). Even this extreme distortion can be counteracted with distortion correction controls in post-processing software, though cropping from the original framing is necessary (right).

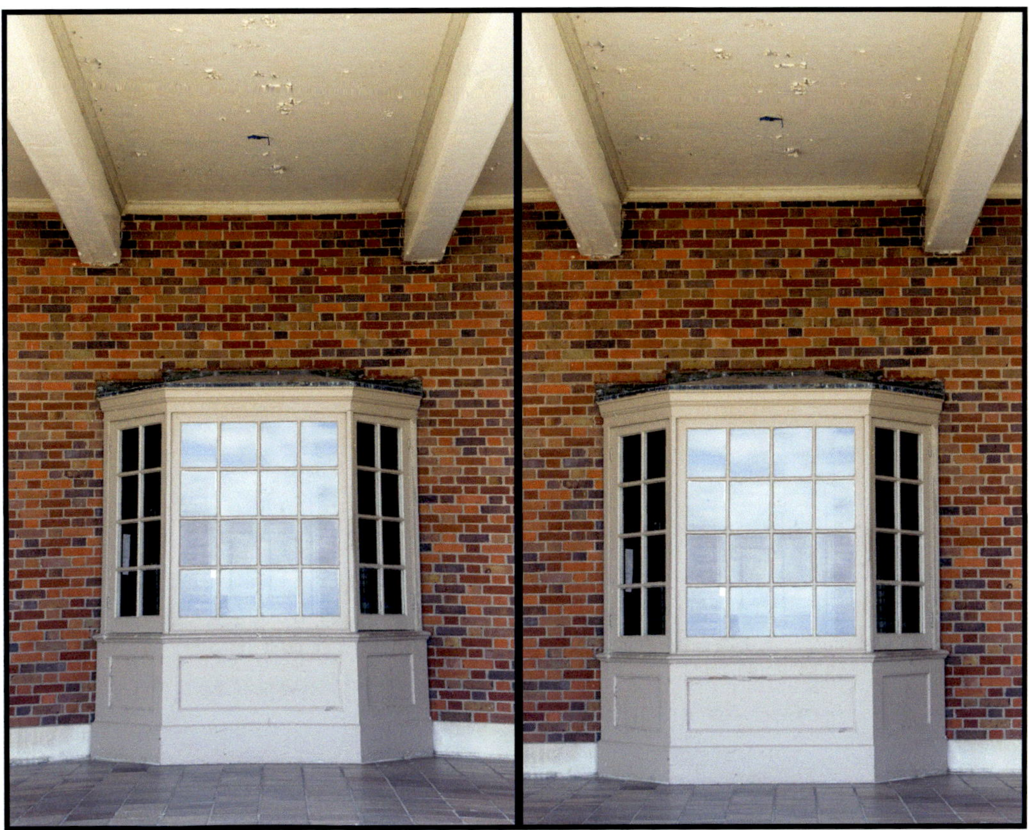

Figure 2-54 Pincushion distortion using a telephoto lens at 70mm (left). Distortion correction helps to keep the rectilinear architecture lines straight (right).

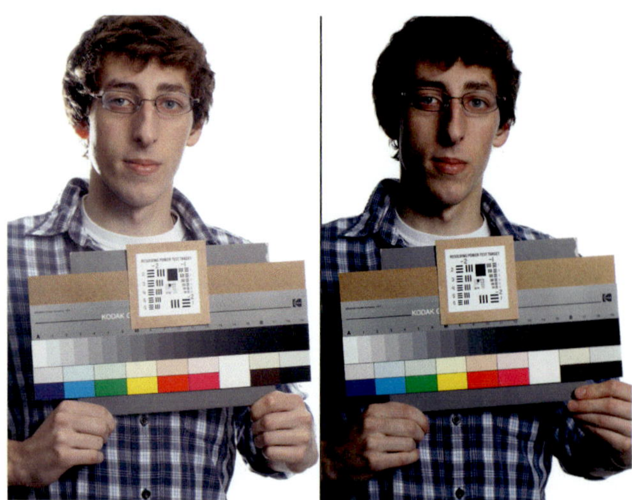

Figure 2-55 A studio lighting setup with (left) and without (right) a light aimed at the camera lens within its field of view. The light introduces significant flare that reduces image contrast.

bounces around in a random way, eventually reaching the sensor and adding exposure to areas that shouldn't receive it. This reduces contrast because dark areas become lighter, as can be seen in the grayscale patches on the target in Figure 2-55. In a way, flare is like a kind of noise or static in the form of light hitting our sensor that isn't contributing to forming an accurate image of our scene.

Flare can also be introduced or exacerbated by the camera design. Light travels through the lens, out through the rear lens element, through air (a small distance within the camera body) and finally reaches the sensor. Reflective materials in the camera body or a poorly light-sealed connection between the lens and camera can introduce flare. This is why you won't see cameras designed with anything other than black on the inside. Nor do you want a camera body made out of transparent plastic. Apple learned this the hard way when designing the iPhone 4 in black and white models: it's speculated that they delayed the white model for months once they discovered that its camera suffered from excessive flare due to some of the materials used.[3]

A multi-pronged strategy is the way to go when avoiding flare:

1. Treat the lens elements with special coatings that limit unpredictable light spreading and internal reflections. Unless you're reading this from a cubicle at an optical engineering lab, we assume this part is taken care of by the time you buy a lens. You may be familiar with such coatings if you wear eyeglasses since the same problem exists there. These coatings help but they can never entirely eliminate flare.
2. Use a *lens hood* attached to the front of the lens barrel. These tube-like or petal-like attachments block extraneous and oblique angle light from entering the lens. Lens hoods can be low-tech or makeshift. As long as they don't creep into the field of view, anything that works to minimize flare is worthwhile. Well-designed lens hoods are coated on their inside surface with flocking material (think black velvet or felt) that absorbs light rays before they have a chance to enter the lens at flare-inducing angles. This same material is used inside the lens barrel for the same functional purpose. Lens hoods exist for most focal lengths.
3. Avoid pointing the camera right at a light source. It's often unavoidable to have the sun in a landscape scene but we're not suggesting that you photograph only in the shadows and scorn the daylight. It's a matter of awareness: in the studio, it's easy to unwittingly position a light source seemingly off-camera that introduces contrast-deteriorating effects as demonstrated in Figure 2-55.
4. Keep everything clean. Fingerprints, smudges, dirt or any other debris that deposits on an exposed lens surface act as a light scattering medium. We've all seen terrible smartphone images due to a smudged, fingerprint-oil covered lens. Keep a microfiber lens cleaning cloth handy and stay vigilant: when bright spots or light sources in a scene start showing up in photographs as smeary streaks, it's a strong indication that your optics hygiene needs work.

Proof of Concept: Focal Length, Subject Distance and Portraits

The principles of perspective in photography are observable by taking a sequence of portrait images using varied focal length lenses and subject distances. Portraits are particularly important because we're highly attuned to human faces and how ourselves and others appear in images. Let's look at the effect of altering both lens focal length and subject distance simultaneously by taking a sequence of photographs with the following steps:

1. Obtain three focal length lenses: a lens in the range of 18 to 24mm, a 50mm lens and a lens in the range of 150 to 200mm.
2. Find a location where your model can sit or stand in place.
3. Start with the shortest focal length lens on the camera and fill the frame with your subject. We suggest a tight crop on the subject's head and shoulders to maximize the effect. Capture an image.
4. Switch to the 50mm lens. Work to maintain a similar framing as the previous image by moving farther away. The larger focal length lens means that a farther distance is needed to maintain an equivalent field of view. Keep f-number the same and capture a second image.
5. Switch to the long focal length lens and reposition yourself relative to your subject to again maintain an equivalent framing as the previous exposures. Keep f-number the same and capture a third image.

Questions to consider when reviewing the resulting photographs:

- How does the relative distance between the subject and the background appear to change when shooting between the shortest to longest focal length lenses?
- How do the subject's features appear to change between the shortest and longest focal lengths? Which version is the most flattering or most representative of how you view this person in face-to-face interactions? Can you imagine scenarios where you would pick the focal length for its unique traits?
- Which lens emphasizes the background? Which lens minimizes the background?

Figure 2-56 shows one set of results from this exercise. Focal length and camera position change in each image such that our subject, the young man, stays relatively the same. Notice how the background appearance changes

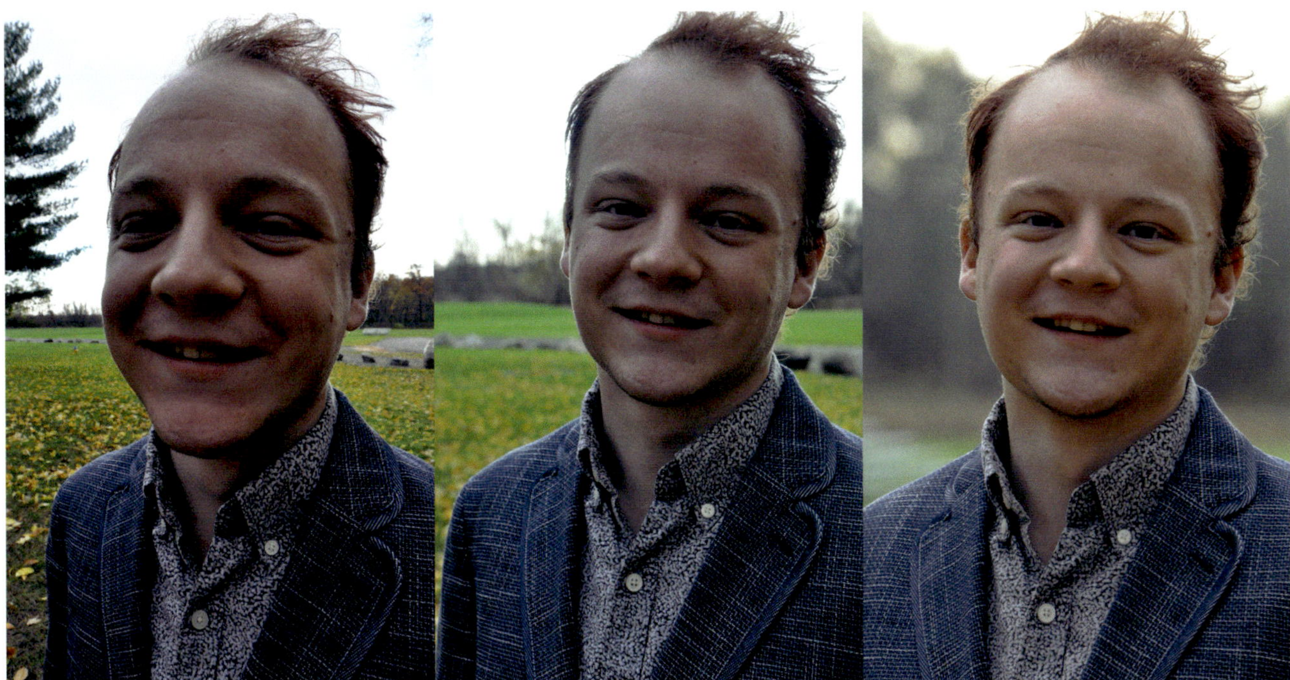

Figure 2-56 A sequence of portraits made by changing lens focal length and subject distance. Photographs by Rochester Institute of Technology photography students Dorothy Marquet and Ben Morrow

dramatically from image to image. Though the frame is dominated by the subject, his apparent relationship to the background and environment is altered. Altering the camera location and the focal length used allows us to either emphasize or diminish the background in the scene. This applies our understanding of photographic perspective to intentionally create a desired visual effect. Don't blame your environment for poor photographs when you can solve it with smartly chosen photographic optics and positioning. Also consider the impact to facial features: longer focal lengths are generally more flattering! The added subject distance required at longer focal lengths can make your subject more comfortable and at ease, while short focal lengths require you to move into someone's personal space.

Notes

1 Goolkasian, Paula. "Size scaling and spatial factors in visual attention." *American Journal of Psychology*, vol. 110, 1997, p. 397.

2 Cholewiak, S.S., G.D., Love, P.P. Srinivasan, R. Ng, and M.S. Banks. "ChromaBlur: Rendering chromatic eye aberration improves accommodation and realism." *ACM Transactions on Graphics*, vol. 36, no. 6, 2017, Article 210.

3 Camm-Jones, Ben. "Apple explains white IPhone 4 delay." *PCWorld*, PCWorld, Apr. 28, 2011, www.pcworld.com/article/226520/Apple_Explains_White_iPhone_4_Delay.html.

3 Digital Camera Technology

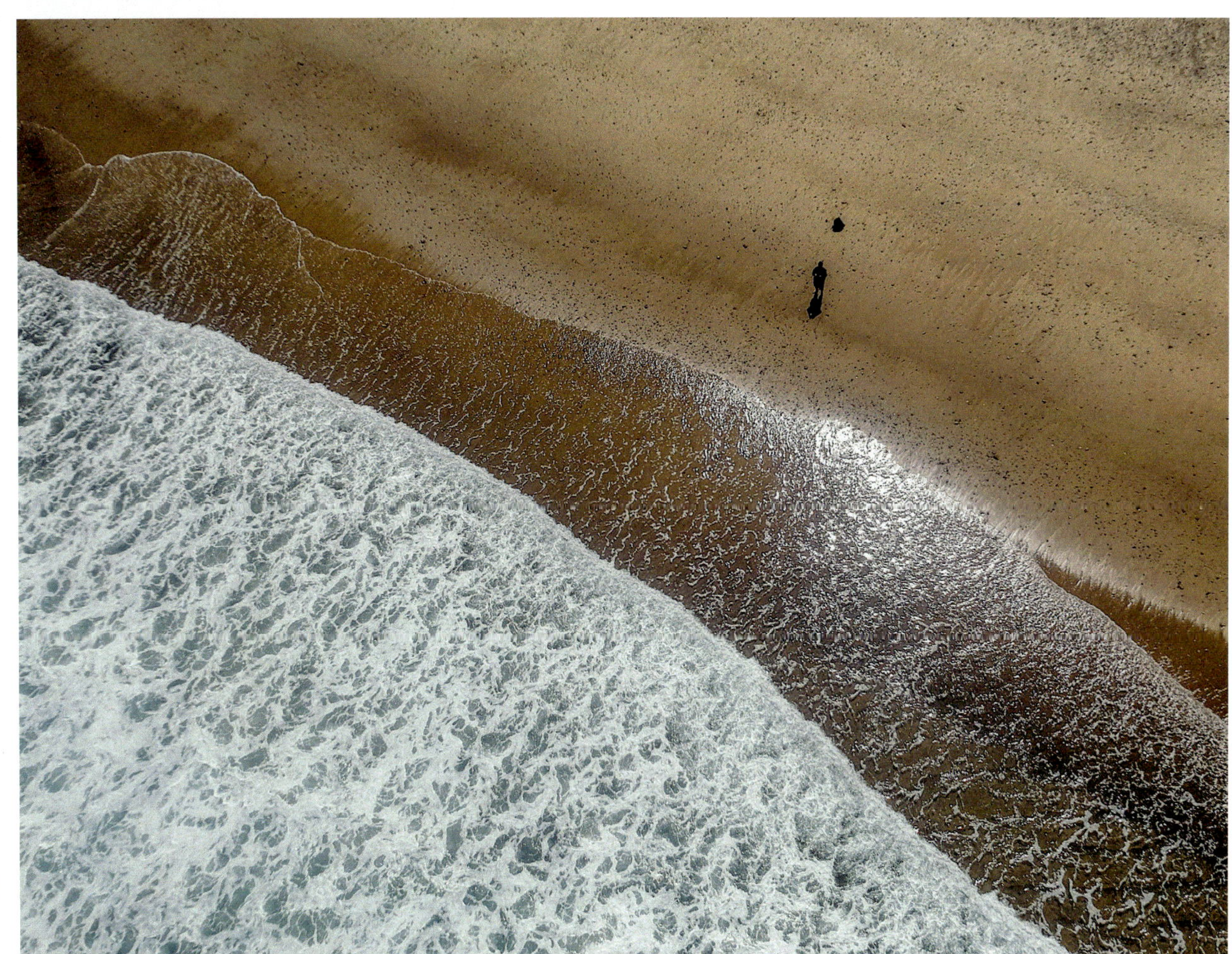

Photograph by Rochester Institute of Technology photography alumnus Dan Wang

The previous chapter concentrated on optics forming an image on the image plane, the location at which a light-sensitive material is placed. The image-recording technology of choice for more than 150 years was film: an analog and chemistry-dependent medium. Today, the dominant light-sensitive material in cameras is the *image sensor*, a digital and electronics-dependent medium. The goal is the same today as it was 150 years ago: to record light information in a permanent way. If we consider the sensor as the heart of the camera, we have to support and understand the additional anatomy that gives life to digital photographs. This chapter dives into that anatomy: the sensors, apertures, shutters and other advanced hardware and software mechanisms that work in harmony to control and record light as electronic information. Camera technology is always evolving to meet new demands and expand image-making capabilities, yet the primary components remain the same.

The Single Lens Reflex Camera Design

Studying the *single lens reflex* (SLR) camera design is a great way to understand the components and functionality of a digital camera. Keep in mind that the fundamental design is adapted from its film predecessors, with the image plane swapping analog for digital. Solely going off of appearance, it's difficult to appreciate how differently SLRs operate from point-and-shoots or other camera designs. The primary difference at a glance is the large lens attached to the camera body. One of the key aspects of the SLR design is its *interchangeable lens* system. A mount on the body allows for the entire set of optical components to be changed out with different lenses. Professional photographers find unmatched utility in being able to swap lens focal lengths at a moment's notice. There's much more going on inside, though, that makes the SLR distinct from a smartphone with clip-on lens attachment.

Figure 3-1 is a cutaway illustration of a single lens reflex camera's internal components. Light reflected from an object in front of the camera enters the lens (1) and is focused on the main *reflex mirror* (2). Here the light takes two possible paths. Most of the light is directed through the *focusing screen* (7) and *condenser lens* (8) up to the *pentaprism* (9) which is located just in front of the *viewfinder* (10). Chapter 2 explained that the image formed by a lens is inverted and reversed (or upside-down and backwards). The pentaprism is an arrangement of five mirrors that flip the object image back to normal so we see it in the viewfinder as it appears in front of us. The image in the viewfinder is the same as the one seen by the sensor, offering up a synchronized experience between framing the shot and the resulting capture. The reflex mirror also allows some of the light to pass through to a *secondary mirror* (4) which

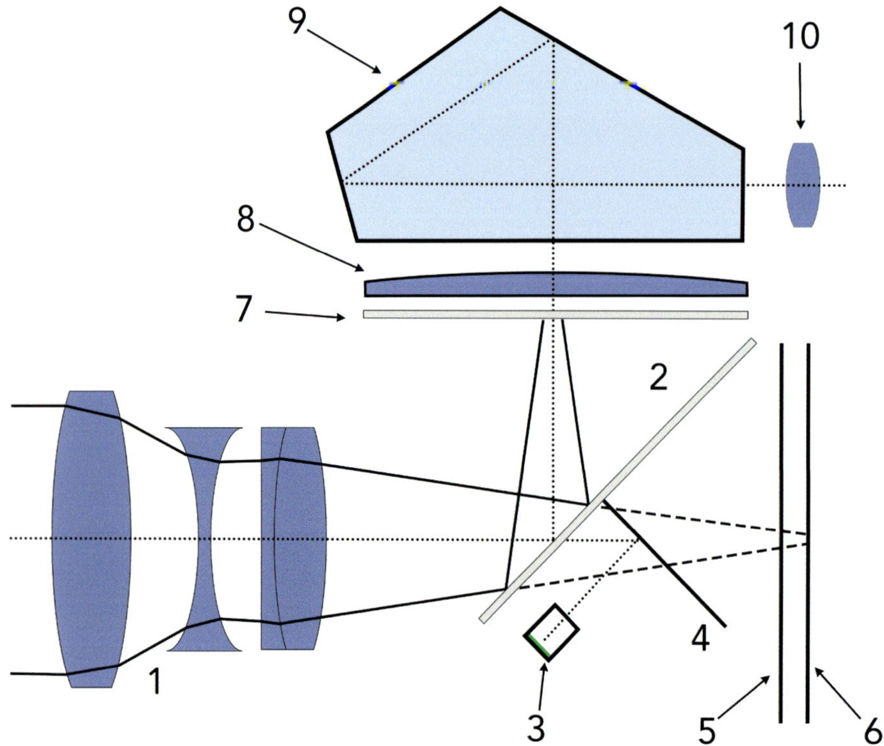

Figure 3-1 A cross section view of a single lens reflex camera reveals the multiple paths traveled by the image before, during and after capture.

directs the image to a light sensor that determines exposure, a phase detection autofocus sensor, or both (3). When the shutter button is pressed, the main reflex and secondary mirrors flip up out of the light path, allowing the image formed by the lens to reach the image sensor (6). The sensor detects and records the light. Once the *shutter curtains* (5) complete their opening and closing event, the mirrors flip back down to their original positions. During exposure, light is blocked from traveling to the viewfinder and the light and/or focus sensors as it is all redirected to the image sensor.

Recording Light with Digital Image Sensors

Our image sensors record light using a two-dimensional array or grid of light detectors called *photodiodes*, *photosites* or *silicon photodiodes* (SPDs). Photosites is preferred for brevity's sake and we use it throughout this text, though the other terms are accurate alternatives. Photosites are simple in that they detect light that varies from very dark to very bright. They do not inherently understand or record anything about the color of a scene, only the range of tones in it. These light detectors are placed close together yet there is always some miniscule space between them. Additionally, they need to pass along the amount of light they detect to digital circuitry, which has to be close by if the data is going to stay true and accurate. So where does this circuitry go? What happens to light that lands in between the photosites? Where does color come into play? How do light photons become digital values? It's easy to say that the sensor records the scene focused by a lens but there are many details that make such a feat possible.

An image sensor translates an optical image, comprised of many millions of photons, into an electrical signal that is stored and interpreted by a computer. The sensor's photosites contain a material (often silicon) that produces electric charges when struck by these photons, a behavior called the *photoelectric effect*. The more photons that reach a photosite, the more charge is generated. The greater the charge, the brighter the resulting pixel value. This charge is recorded as voltage: an analog phenomenon. In a perfect world, every photon of light is faithfully detected and recorded as a voltage by the sensor. The reality, however, is that some of those photons are left unrecorded. The ratio of incoming photons to electric charges collected describes the *quantum efficiency* (QE) of the sensor. The higher the quantum efficiency, the less light is wasted in the process. QE is wavelength-dependent, meaning that a sensor's efficiency is different if it's recording mostly blue light compared to red (just as one example). If you see a single value describing QE of a sensor, it's likely an average performance across its sensitivity spectrum. Alternatively, a photosite may receive zero photons if no light is present. Photosites with no photoelectric activity during exposure end up as black pixels in the image file.

Two things have to happen next: first, the voltage is amplified to a usable level (the initial voltage is too small to create a viable photograph). The voltage amplification has shortcomings, as we'll see when we take a deeper look at photographic noise. Second, our analog input signal must be converted to digital information—zeroes and ones, the language that computers speak—this is called the *analog to digital conversion*. Each photosite's electrical voltage becomes a digital value or *digital count*, one of a defined set of values that represents a brightness. Furthermore, these digital values must be discrete, whole numbers, whereas analog light signals in nature can be a continuous spectrum of values (see Figure 3-2).

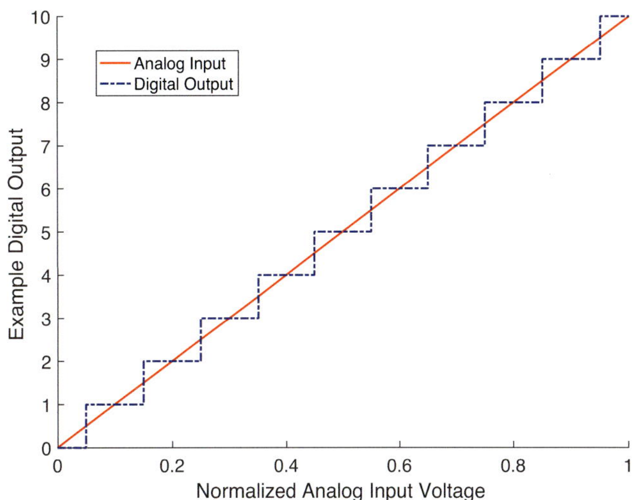

Figure 3-2 Converting analog light information into digital counts requires quantizing, making an infinite amount of variability into a discrete and finite set of numeric values.

Pixel defects are another unavoidable artifact in recording digital images. Making a sensor that is totally free of defects is nearly impossible because of the large number of pixels and the complex manufacturing processes involved in making sensors. There are *hot pixel defects*, in which the pixel has a high dark-current noise, and there are *dark pixel defects*, in which the pixel has a lower response than surrounding pixels. Other than scrapping the sensor and manufacturing a new one, there's no easy fix for these defects. Instead, cameras may incorporate a form of masking whereby the internal software evaluates its sensor for defects, notes their locations and borrows from neighboring photosites to fill in the defective spots. This may be bypassed when shooting raw files but is often an automatic process in JPEG capture.

Photosites are covered with color filters to record color information from a scene. When a blue filter is placed over a single photosite, for example, the only light energy that travels to the light-sensitive material and recorded as a charge is the blue light present. If there is no blue light, the photosite doesn't record much of anything. Since every color can be made through a combination of red, green and blue (see Chapter 13), it follows that filtering an image sensor with a combination of red, green and blue filters gets us closer to a full color recording. Introducing any color filters means a little less light sensitivity, as we're preventing some of the incident light from traveling to the photosite. In this way, a monochrome sensor needs less light to generate an exposure equivalent to one made with a color-filtered sensor. Today, photographers have the option of buying cameras with monochrome sensors, sans color filtering. These are niche products, though, and often come with higher price tags in exchange for specialized functionality.

Now's a good time to point out that you often hear photographers call the photosites *pixels* since we ultimately get a photographic image file from a sensor's capture comprised of pixels (the fundamental building block of a digital image). However, it's best to use *photosites* when discussing the sensor, as there is not always one-to-one relationship between the number of photosites and the number of pixels. We'll look at this challenge of color filtering the photosites and translation to color pixels a little later.

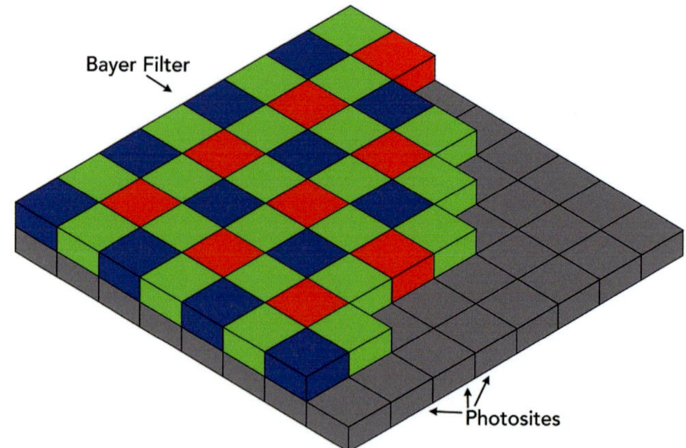

Figure 3-3 The Bayer color filter pattern sits above the light-sensitive photosites.

Bayer Pattern Color Filter Array

The *color filter array* (or CFA) most commonly found on camera sensors is the *Bayer Pattern filter*, invented in 1976 by Bryce Bayer at Kodak. This pattern alternates the filter colors between red, green and blue. Rather than having an even distribution of each, this pattern uses twice as many green filters as it does red and blue: the ratio of a Bayer pattern CFA is 50% green, 25% red and 25% blue (illustrated in Figure 3-3). This results in photosite data for only one-third of the color information needed to render a full color photograph. The other two-thirds are algorithmically derived through the process of *demosaicing*. Many demosaicing algorithms exist. The simplest method averages the surrounding pixels to interpolate the missing data. This method is applied to every pixel location, though rarely is such a simple approach used today. Most demosaicing algorithms include additional strategies for identifying and preserving edges, weighting local brightness trends and pixel groupings. In addition to the CFA, an infrared blocking filter is fitted in front of the sensor due to the natural sensitivity of silicon to infrared radiation.

X-Trans Color Filter Array

Fujifilm developed an alternative approach that forgoes the Bayer filter array for one of its own devising. First appearing in Fujifilm cameras in 2012, the *X-Trans color filter array* uses a larger 6x6 pattern of red, green and blue photosite filters.

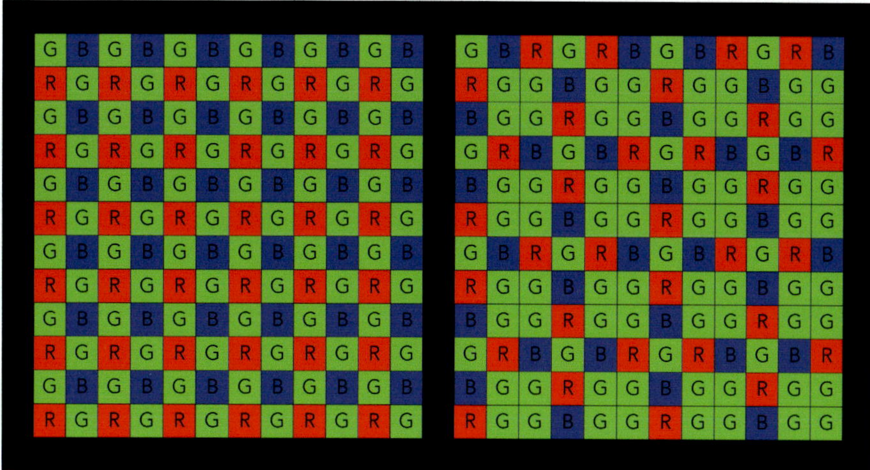

Figure 3-4 The traditional Bayer CFA pattern compared to the X-Trans™ CFA developed by FUJIFILM. Illustration courtesy of Jonathan Liles

Figure 3-4 shows that, unlike the Bayer pattern, there are adjacent green photosites. This arrangement promises to minimize moiré patterns (discussed later in this chapter) and other artifacts inherent to color filtering photosites coupled with demosaicing algorithms. Real-world testing shows the X-Trans CFA to be extremely capable but not necessarily superior to the Bayer CFA.[1] The raw mosaicked image file captured by an X-Trans CFA requires its own special algorithm for demosaicing.

Camera Sensor Technologies

Imaging sensors are made of silicon and are semiconductor devices. Sensors convert photons of light that strike them into an electrical current. In this process, free electrons are released from the material, which in turn produce the electrical charge recorded and converted to a digital signal. There are several different sensor types that exploit this behavior to record digital photographs.

Charge-Coupled Device Sensor

One of the earliest image sensor technologies is the *charge-coupled device*, or CCD, invented in 1969 by Willard Boyle and George Smith at AT&T Bell Labs. Boyle and Smith received the 2009 Nobel Prize in Physics for the invention of the CCD as it profoundly transformed consumer electronics and photography. In the early days of digital cameras, CCD sensors could be found in all types of form factors ranging from point-and-shoot to SLRs and medium format backs. You might find CCD sensors in some low-end point-and-shoot models today but their popularity is waning in consumer camera hardware.

The CCD builds up a charge within each photosite that is proportional to the amount of light that strikes it. The CCD uses *shift register electronics* to move the charges from their respective locations on the sensor array to circuitry along the edge of the chip. The electrical charges are fed, pixel by pixel, row by row, to the *analog to digital* (A/D) *converter* as illustrated in Figure 3-5 (overleaf). When the first line is completed, all the lines shift down and the process starts again. This method is efficient in that it only requires a single A/D converter through which all signals are processed. On the other hand, the serial, pixel-by-pixel readout takes time and leads to an unavoidable delay between a photographic exposure taken, readout and saved and when a new exposure can be made.

Astronomers were among the early adopters of CCD technology. CCD technologies have a quantum efficiency of ~90%, meaning that they convert 90% of the light that strikes them into pixel values.[2] CCD photosites are particularly sensitive to ultraviolet and infrared radiation, which happens to be the makeup of many celestial objects'

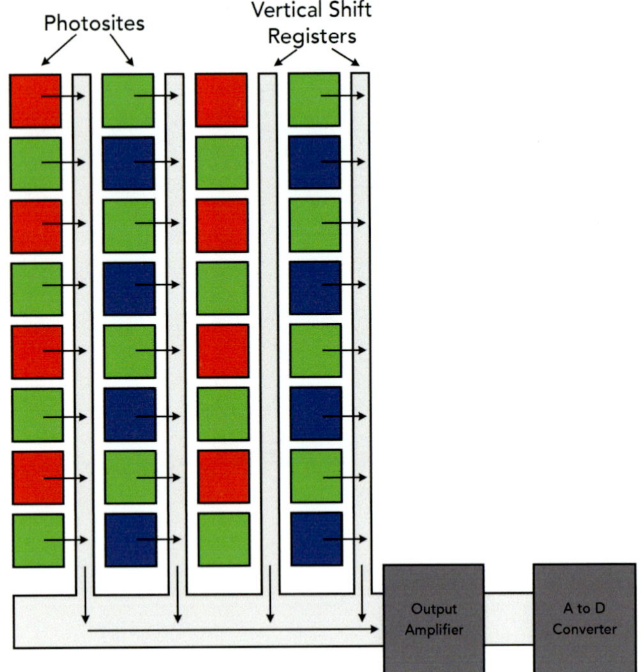

Figure 3-5 A simplified illustration of a CCD sensor readout.

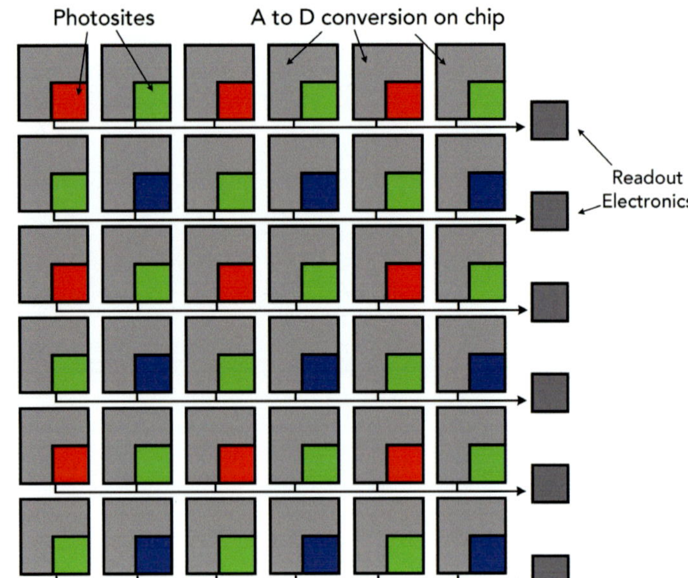

Figure 3-6 A simplified illustration of CMOS sensor readout. Analog to digital conversion happens at each photosite and that signal is sent to readout electronics on the chip.

emitted radiation. CCDs produce low amounts of noise, especially when kept at cold operating temperatures using special cooling devices.[3] Lastly, CCDs have a linear response to light which makes them excellent measurement devices.

Sparse Color Filter Array Sensor

Kodak developed a special color filter array for CCDs called *TrueSense*. Also known as a *sparse color filter array*, the design differs from the traditional Bayer pattern in that it includes "white" photosites alongside the red, green and blue ones. These *panchromatic* photosites do not use a color filter and instead collect all of the available light to record brightness. Removing the color filter allows 66% more light to reach to the photosite. By including these color-indifferent collectors, the sensor is able to make use of increased luminance data for improved image quality and light sensitivity. This technology is now owned by ON Semiconductor.[4]

Complementary Metal Oxide Semiconductor Sensor

The *complementary metal oxide semiconductor* (CMOS) sensor came along after the CCD and, early in its existence, exhibited worse image quality performance. The photosites on a CMOS sensor are called *active pixel sensors* (APS) and consist of the photodetector, an amplifier and integrated circuitry. This is a key distinction from CCD technology: CMOS photosites independently convert their detected voltages into digital signals and can be read out individually, all at once, instead of row by row as illustrated in Figure 3-6. This allows for more complex behaviors like triggering specific rows or groups of pixels to expose for durations different than that of the other photosites in the array. Sometimes the CMOS sensor as a piece of electronics is confusingly described as an APS-type sensor, when the sensing is actually being done by many millions of photosites.

Since a CMOS sensor's photosites use additional circuitry, gaps or trenches exist between the light-sensitive areas. It's also necessary to use barriers to separate each

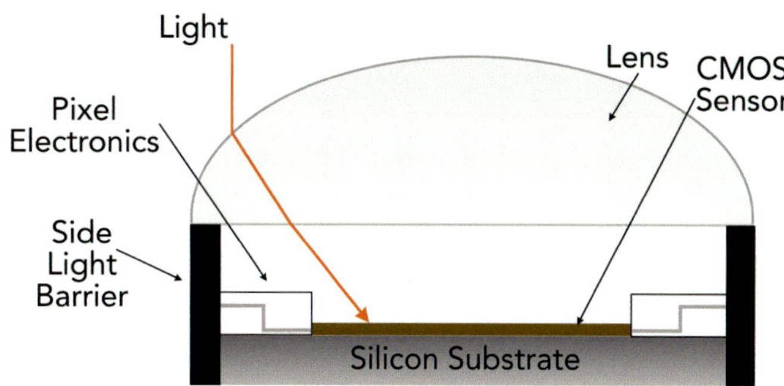

Figure 3-7 A cut-away view of a CMOS photosite with a microlens.

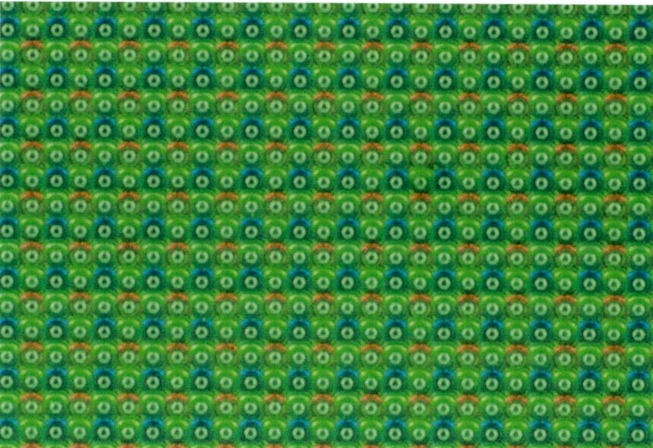

Figure 3-8 A photograph of a CMOS sensor taken under a microscope. The bright rings are reflections of the light source on the curved surfaces of the photosite microlenses.

photosite to minimize *crosstalk* where photons land in one well but get recorded by a neighboring one (see Figure 3-7). A notable amount of light is lost if the sensor design doesn't account for these trenches. Consider collecting photons like collecting raindrops with buckets. Arranging the buckets along the ground as close together as possible helps collect the rain falling in your yard, yet there's some space between the buckets that fails to catch a percentage of the rainfall. One solution is to introduce large funnels atop the buckets to redirect the maximum amount of raindrops to their collection vessels. Similarly, CMOS sensors employ *microlenses* to help gather light energy that otherwise strikes light-insensitive edges of the photosite architecture. Each photosite has its own microlens directly above it as shown in Figure 3-8. These lenses increase sensor efficiency as they help capture a higher percentage of the photons reaching the sensor plane. CMOS sensors have a quantum efficiency of approximately 50%.

The architecture of a CMOS sensor helps it to maximize light collection but its overall quantum efficiency is an average across wavelengths and doesn't consider the role of the incident light's wavelength. Figure 3-9 plots the spectral sensitivity of unfiltered CMOS photosites across the visible spectrum. Notice that there is relatively low sensitivity around 400 nm (the blue region). On the other end, there is an increasing sensitivity beyond 750 nm, heading into the infrared region of the spectrum. From this we understand that photosites record a weaker signal from blue light than from green or red; image processing has to accommodate by boosting the blue-filtered photosites' signal. It also explains why CMOS sensors are designed with infrared-blocking filters in addition to the microlenses on their surface. If left unfiltered, a great deal of IR radiation travels to the photosites and records signal. The optical filter prevents this energy from making it that far via interference.

One potential pitfall with smartphone cameras and similarly small form factors in regard to this IR-cut filter is the possibility for *color shading*, an image quality artifact. Color

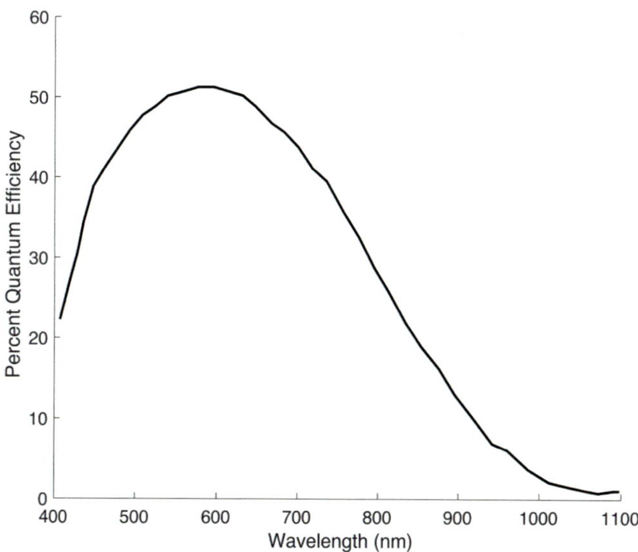

Figure 3-9 The spectral sensitivity of an unfiltered CMOS photosite.[6]

shading happens when IR light traveling at oblique angles (due to the short image distances rendered by wide-angle lenses in compact spaces) manages to transmit through the filter. Compact camera systems employ a combination of IR filtering material and glass absorption filters; the efforts of the two in combination ensures minimal IR transmittance. Without this hybrid approach, these cameras can suffer from color non-uniformity between the center and edges of their images.[5]

CCD was a superior technology choice in the early years of consumer digital photography for price, low light sensitivity and overall image quality. However, advances in CMOS designs, manufacturing and their ubiquity in so many consumer devices flipped that relationship. It continues to be expensive and difficult to produce very large CMOS chips. Still, the majority of imaging devices used by photographers today use CMOS sensor designs.

Backside Illumination Detectors

As discussed, CMOS sensors have circuitry at every photosite in order to independently read detected voltages. The drawback of this arrangement is that the circuitry occupies a certain surface area, lessening the area available for light-sensing. Microlenses above each photosite help gather the light toward the light-sensitive well of the photodiode. We gain additional light-sensitivity and efficiency by moving the electronics underneath the well. This is the premise behind *backside illuminated* (BSI) detectors, a type of CMOS technology that is particularly prevalent in smartphone cameras. BSI sensors detect more light reaching them compared to conventional CMOS photosite construction.

Foveon Sensor

Sigma has its own approach to recording color on a CMOS image sensor called *Foveon* currently found in their mirrorless cameras. The Foveon sensor uses three layers of photosites, one stacked on top of the other. Light of varying wavelengths travels different depths such that the top layer records blue, the middle layer records green and the bottom, red. Incoming light travels through silicon, a material whose properties dictate that light is absorbed differently depending on its wavelength, making this approach possible. Foveon technology is described as a "direct imaging" sensor since it does not rely on interpolation. However, the latest incarnation, the X3 Quattro, isn't quite this simple. It uses a higher density of photosites at its blue layer (four times as many as the other two layers), meaning that additional image processing considers four photosite data points for every two red and green at a given location. Why does blue light get special treatment when we often hear about green being the favored part of the visible spectrum? Our recording material is less sensitive to blue wavelengths and thus needs help in recording enough data to match what gets recorded at other wavelengths. Sigma's solution samples four times as many blue photosites, kind of like giving the scrawny one of your three kids extra glasses of milk. The Foveon-type sensor offers advantages in color reproduction and sharpness, though it's not a clear-cut race with other options; its exclusivity to Sigma cameras means that it simply isn't as common to come across in the photography world.

Image Sensor Sizes

The size of the sensor is often dictated by the camera's form factor and its size. Using a larger sensor requires more physical space in the camera's body to house it and to support the necessary optics for forming an image large enough. Smaller sensors are easier to fit into compact camera bodies but lack some of the image quality benefits of larger ones. Consider again the analogy of collecting raindrops in your yard. Arranging buckets over a small area of the yard is effective, yet arranging them over a larger area offers the greatest collection potential.

When it comes to defining image sensor sizes offered by camera manufacturers, think of it like choosing the size of popcorn at the movie theater (small, medium, large and bucket). Perhaps the four options started out as standard and uniform sizes across the industry. As time went on, each movie theater decided to use their own unique bag sizes, making the size categories imprecise and context-specific. A small popcorn at one location could be the size of a medium at another. In the sensor world you can still get the equivalent of a bucket of popcorn but there are more sizes to choose from and most of us rarely need or take advantage of it—a larger image sensor is not a necessity in many imaging applications.

Common throughout the sensor size categories is the moniker *APS*. This term originally started with a camera system developed by Kodak and released in 1996 (one of the authors worked on the team that developed the color balance algorithm for this system). APS stood for *Advanced Photo System* to describe the film format used. The film included a magnetic strip along its edge that recorded information about each exposure as a form of capture metadata. That information, such as shutter speed, aperture, time of the exposure and print aspect ratio, was used at the time of printing to improve quality. Kodak marketed it under the brand name *Advantix* while Konica, Agfa and Fujifilm marketed it under different names. This was a major step forward in imaging technology. The APS acronym has since morphed into use to designate an active pixel sensor, describing the modern silicon photosites that comprise the sensor's light detectors.

Full frame sensors are the dominant choice of professional photographers as they offer exceptional image quality and a traditional form factor. The designation comes from a legacy film standard: 24x36mm, the dimensions of a 35mm film frame. This size also produces a 3:2 width to height ratio. Though common today, the early years of digital photography saw much smaller sensors due to the cost and complexity of manufacturing sensors of this size. Most SLR-style cameras house full frame sensors with lenses to match.

Any larger than full frame and we enter *medium format sensor* territory. This, too, follows in the footsteps of film photography standards. Medium format cameras are a larger form factor themselves, primarily in service of housing such a massive light-recording material. Medium format film comes in a variety of sizes but is commonly more square in aspect ratio; image sensors in this category follow suit. Medium format sensors offer some of the highest megapixel resolutions available. Film photography also has a category of large format sizes but we don't see many digital equivalents due to the cost and manufacturing challenges.

Sensors smaller than full frame yet designed for SLR bodies and lenses are called *crop sensors* because they crop the image formed by the lens if all things are kept the same. Crop sensors vary in their dimensions as manufacturers adopted their own standards, though they all use the shorthand of *APS-C* to indicate this size category. You may see a sensor described by the *crop factor* (example: 1.5x) which describes the multiplier necessary to calculate the effective focal length resulting from its use with a lens designed for full frame sensors. Crop factor is simple enough to calculate:

$$\textit{Crop Factor} = \frac{\textit{Diagonal of full frame}}{\textit{Diagonal of smaller sensor}} \quad \text{(Eq. 3.1)}$$

Going smaller still, the *Four-Thirds* or *4/3 sensor* was developed by Eastman Kodak and Olympus for a generation of smaller, mirrorless cameras with new lens designs to match. These tend to be about 30–40% smaller in area than full frame sensors. There are also many sizes smaller than 4/3 used in modern cameras, particularly those found in phones, tablets and laptops. As Figure 3-10 shows, these sizes are quite small—some fractions of an inch in height and width.

Sensor size naming conventions are decidedly confusing. There's 4/3, 2/3, 1/3 and 1", APS-C, APS-H and the list goes on. So where do these come from? It turns out that these are left over from 1950s television standards. The sizes are not defined by the TV diagonal as some assume; they refer to the diameter of the glass envelope of the TV tube. The usable area of the imaging plane was approximately two-thirds of the tube.

As we moved from film to small digital sensors, experienced photographers quickly noticed that looking through

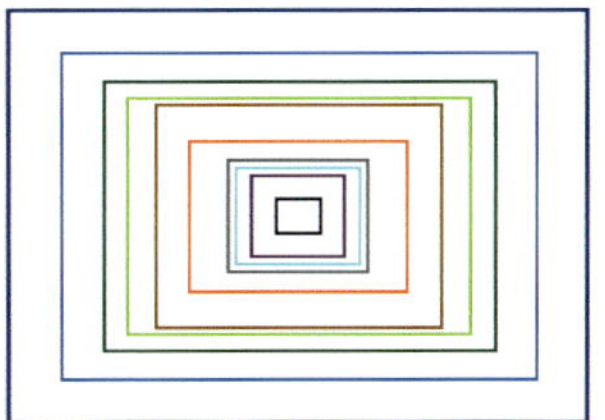

Full Frame 36x24mm
APS-H (Canon) 28.7x19mm
APS-C (Nikon DX) 23.6x15.7mm
APS-C (Canon) 22.2x14.8mm
Foveon 20.7x13.8mm
Four Thirds System 17.3x13mm
1" (Sony,Nikon) 13.2x8.8mm
2/3 (Fujifilm) 8.6x6.6mm
1/1.7" 2.6x5.7mm
1/2.5" 5.76x4.29mm

Figure 3-10 A sampling of common image sensor sizes stacked against one another.

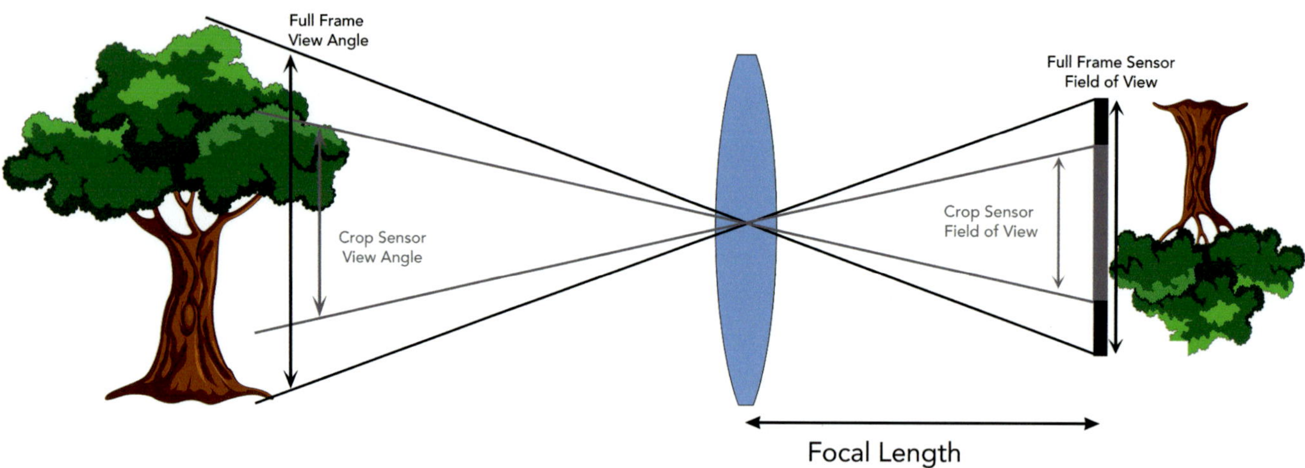

Figure 3-11 The effective field of view is lessened when using a crop sensor relative to a full frame sensor. Here, the full frame system images the tree in its entirety while the crop sensor system's view is limited to a portion of it.

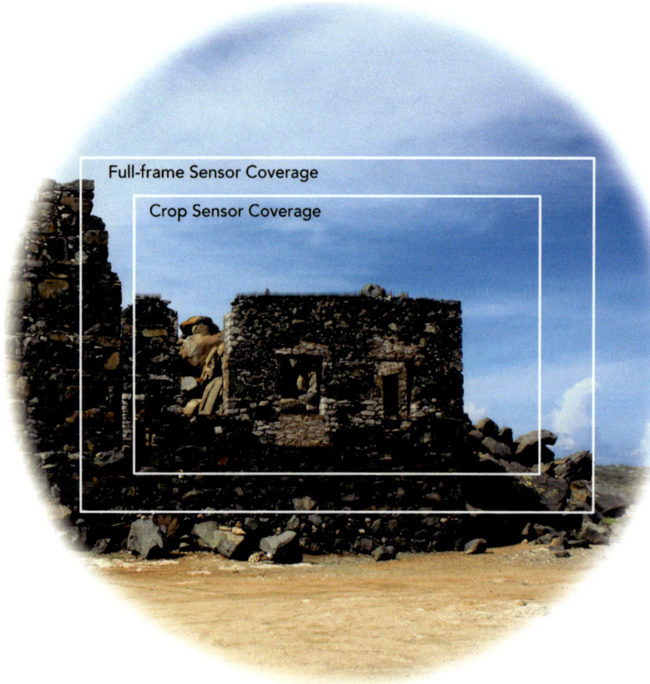

Figure 3-12 A lens projects a circular image at the imaging plane. A sensor is sized and positioned such that it records image content from edge to edge; a crop sensor positioned similarly to a full frame sensor records a lesser field of view.

a full frame DSLR with a 50mm lens compared to a 50mm lens on a crop sensor, the field of view looked different (see Figure 3-11). The "normal" field of view expected with a 50mm lens appeared narrower. A lens produces a circular image and yet a sensor is square or rectangular (see Figure 3-12). A full frame sensor captures a larger field of view (the image area) relative to a smaller crop sensor at the same location. The crop factor provides the effective focal length of the lens. For example, a 50mm lens used on a camera with a 1.6x crop factor has an effective focal length of 80mm.

Sensors also differ in their *aspect ratio*, the rectilinear shapes made by varying width and height independently. The traditional aspect ratio of still photography is 1:5:1 which is the same aspect ratio of full frame sensors and 35mm film before them. Medium format sensors are typically 1:33:1, more square than rectangular.

Finally, sensors are no longer constrained to a flat plane: *curved sensors* where the edges curve outward toward the lens are a forthcoming technology.[7] This design tweak means that light travels an equal distance from the lens to both the center and the corners of the light-sensitive array. From an image quality standpoint, this lessens light fall-off and sharpness fall-off at the edges of the frame without the need for expensive and complex optical corrections in lenses.[8,9] Curving the sensor plane simplifies the optical components. It may even offer additional light sensitivity.[10] Since new lenses have to be designed specifically for this type of sensor, you won't be upgrading your SLR to a model with a curved sensor to use with an older set of lenses. On the other hand, it can make fixed focal length cameras embedded in a variety of electronics cheaper and lighter. Unlike the short-lived trend of curved televisions, the added dimensionality of a curved sensor offers measurable quality improvements and not just a novelty shape.

Camera Sensor Resolution

Image sensor dimensions vary depending on the application or camera type but it's not the only aspect that characterizes a photograph. *Spatial resolution* describes the number of picture elements (pixels, in this case) that comprise a photographic image. The more photosites on a sensor, the greater the image resolution recorded. Just like the convenience of describing a plank of wood by its dimensions (i.e. "2x4"), describing the spatial resolution of a sensor is accomplished by counting the number of photosites in the horizontal and vertical dimensions (i.e. 5,632 x 3,750). These numbers don't roll off the tongue or offer easy commitment to memory. Instead, multiplying the horizontal dimensions by the vertical gives us the total number of pixels (21,120,000, for example) which we then shorten to an easy-to-remember value like 21.1. This value describes the *megapixels* or the number of millions of pixels.

Pixel Pitch

Spatial resolution tells us the number of detectors but doesn't specify that number in the context of a physical area. If an airline announces that its popular flight routes have an additional 50 available seats yet they continue to use the same aircraft, you'd suspect that they lessened the legroom to cram in additional rows. A bigger number doesn't guarantee a better, or even equivalent, experience. The same logic applies to sensor resolution: the amount detectors matters but it should always be considered against the physical dimensions of the array.

The larger the photosites, the more light-gathering ability. A 50 megapixel full frame sensor produces an image file with the same number of pixels as a 50 megapixel compact camera sensor but these two are not completely equivalent. Fitting 50 million photosites onto a compact camera sensor means designing similarly tiny photosites. Thus, the light-gathering ability and consequently the image quality performance of the two sensors is unlikely to be equal. We describe the size of photosites as *pixel pitch* and measure their dimensions in microns. A sensor with a smaller pixel pitch uses smaller photosites which in turn records lesser amounts of light at each location. Less light equals less signal relative to noise, ultimately resulting in lesser image quality, particularly in low light situations. Smartphone camera sensors have pixel pitches of approximately 1–2 microns whereas full frame SLR sensors have pixel pitches in the 5–8 micron range. The difference in light-capturing potential between the two is like the odds of you successfully hitting a ping pong ball with a ping pong paddle versus a tennis racket. More surface area means more opportunities for successful contact between ping pong ball and racket in the same way that it means more opportunities for photons of light to strike the photosite well.

Image Bit Depth

Pixels in an image have numeric values. The range of these values is dictated by *bit depth.* Since all digital data is built by *bits*, binary values of either 0 or 1, a greater number of bits means a greater number of possible combinations available to describe a pixel's value. Bit depth defines the range of potential values that a pixel describes sort of like knowing that a gallon jug of milk contains some amount of milk anywhere between zero and one gallon. A gallon jug of milk doesn't necessarily have to hold a gallon, it dictates the range of milk it could hold. A sensor's bit depth tells us how many bits are available to describe any given pixel in an image at the time of capture.

What amount of bit depth is needed or desired when making photographs? The leftmost version of the photograph in Figure 3-13 (overleaf) shows a *bitonal* image, that is, an image constructed from only two possible tones: black or white. This is a black and white photograph in

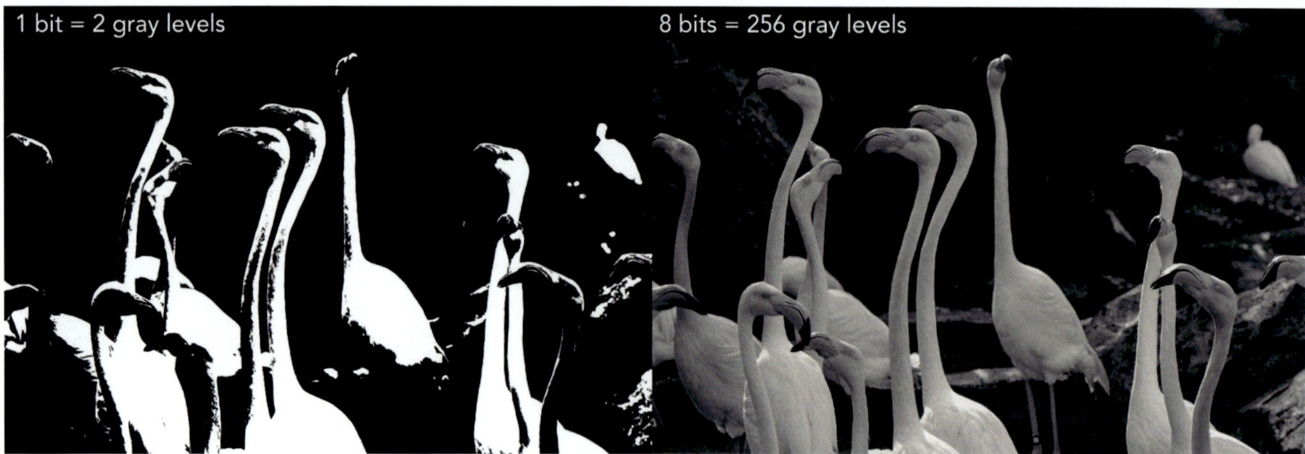

Figure 3-13 A 1-bit version of a scene (left) and an 8-bit version (right) that has up to 256 shades of gray to represent the scene.

the most literal sense. A 1-bit representation of tone is good enough for text and simple graphics and not nearly enough for a true-to-life photograph. The rightmost version of the photograph in Figure 3-13 uses 8-bits, or 256 gray levels, to more closely represent continuous tone as we see it with our eyes.

The more possibilities for how bright or dark a pixel can be, the more exact our recording becomes and the more gradual and natural the transitions between brightnesses appear. The bit depth of an image describes the amount of tones (gray levels) represented as shown in Figure 3-14.

This only describes a photographic image in shades of gray. Where does the color come into play? A color image is actually three sets of pixel data: one for red, one for green and one for blue. These sets are called *channels*, and color photographs always have three. In order to have 256 possible brightness values—the standard bit depth established for grayscale images—for each color channel, the total amount of bits (8-bits x 3 channels) is 24. Combinations of values in each of the three color channels yields a wide range of observable colors: 16.7 million, in fact. This number is calculated by raising 2 to the 24 power (2^{24}).

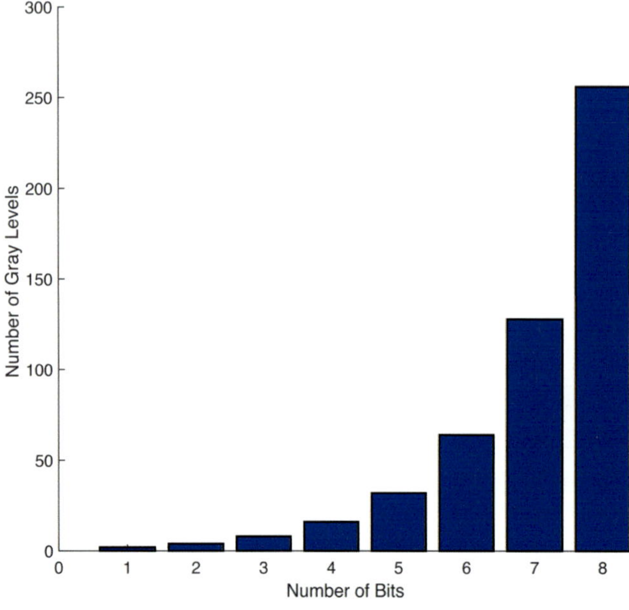

Figure 3-14 Gray levels in an image per number of bits.

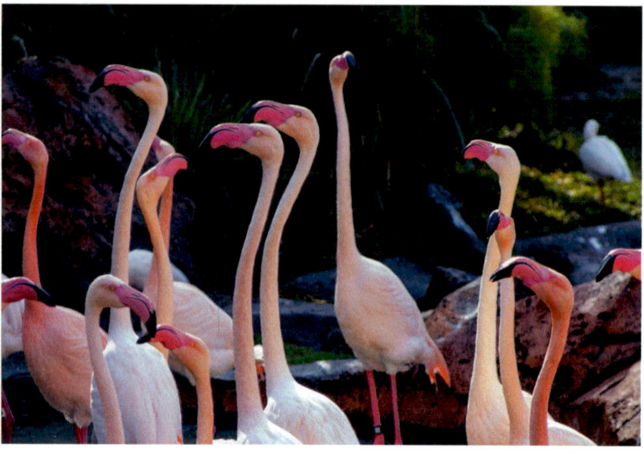

Figure 3-15 A full color photograph made from 8-bits of data in each of the three color channels, or 24-bits in total.

Figure 3-15 uses 8-bits per color channel, or 24-bits in total, to create a full color photograph.

Confusingly, a full color image file is often referred to as 8-bit even though we understand that, taken literally, this makes a pretty ugly looking photograph. The confusion is abated by specifying if that number describes *bits per channel* (which it does) or *bits per pixel* (which it does not). The images seen regularly on websites have bit depths of 8 bits per channel. Importantly, photographers have the option of shooting and editing images in formats that support up to 16-bits per channel. Recent video formats and playback support mean that traditional, 8-bit video will soon be supplanted by 10-bit encoded video to extend the dynamic range of video content.

Research shows that 5-bits per color is typically enough information to represent continuous tone and natural color gradations in both display and print output. It is also unlikely that the average viewer on a given display detects a difference between, say, a 7-bit image and an 8-bit one. This will change as displays evolve in their capabilities; for now we understand that 8-bits is the appropriate volume of bit depth for most applications of sharing and viewing images.

In the context of the camera sensor, the *capture bit depth* is an inherent and static characteristic. It describes the total range of values that can be detected and recorded when photons strike the silicon material and produce an electric signal. Many sensors record in 10- or 14-bits. The bottleneck isn't the photosites, it's the analog to digital converter. A cheaper A/D might limit the nuance of brightnesses translated to digital signals even if the photosites capture a larger range of voltages. This information is stored in a raw file format that's adjustable later down the line when processing and exporting photographs on the computer; not all file formats support a bit depth as great as that captured by the camera. Higher bit depth information must be downsampled, often with minimal visual degradation, to exist in these other formats. Chapter 8 offers more on image file formats.

Aliasing and Moiré Patterns

Earlier, we showed that the image sensor is covered with color filters and an IR-blocking filter. It's also common to have an *optical low-pass* or *anti-aliasing filter* in the imaging system. This filter introduces a slight blurring to the image. This may make you shout "why on Earth?" since it seems to undermine all the hard work our optical components do to resolve a sharp image. We run into some trouble when details in a scene are so small and fine that they hit the resolving power limit of our optics. This is exacerbated by the demosaicing algorithms that struggle to accurately interpolate detail edges and patterns. In essence, the subject detail exceeds the detail our camera system records. The visual artifact that results in this circumstance is called *moiré* and looks like wavy-lined patterns not actually present in the scene (see Figure 3-16). *Aliasing* is similar in

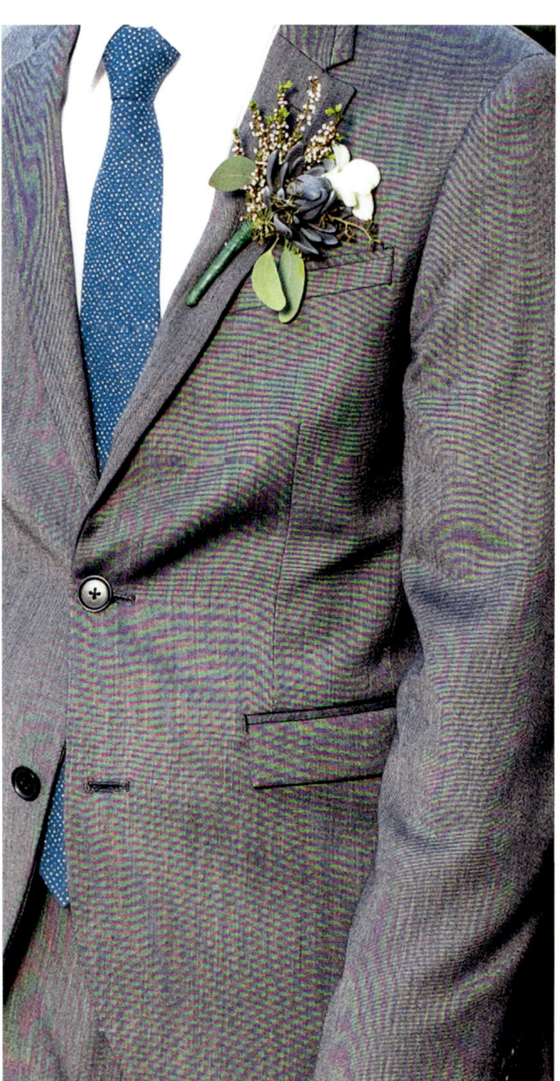

Figure 3-16 Moiré pattern artifacts captured by a camera lacking a low-pass filter. The fine detail of the suit fabric is not faithfully reproduced after capture and demosaicing. Photograph by Hieu Pham

that it renders straight, continuous lines as stair-stepped and jagged due to a lack of resolved detail. These artifacts are unavoidable if left alone but are negated if the image is slightly blurred right before it reaches the photosites. That's the job of the optical low pass filter: a slight bit of blurring is the tradeoff to avoid unnatural and distracting artifacts.

Low-pass filters were typically installed on every consumer digital camera on the market. Today, photographers have the option of buying cameras with sensors that specifically omit the low-pass filter. At the risk of recording moiré patterns, this translates to sharper images right out of the gate. The Achilles heel of such cameras is clothing and fabrics. These subjects often feature fine details, textures and patterns that threaten to introduce significant moiré artifacts. The primary way to minimize the artifacts, assuming they're noticed during a shoot, is to change the subject distance from the camera. Otherwise, it's difficult to mitigate the artifact without significant, manual retouching.

As sensor designs continue to push more photosites into small areas, we approach the *Nyquist frequency*. The *sampling Nyquist theorem* states that the minimum rate for sampling a signal without introducing errors is twice the highest frequency present. With light and images, this frequency is related to object size. Small objects and fine details in an image are considered *high frequency content* or signal. The *imaging sample rate* or pixel size, then, must be half the size of the smallest object or detail recorded to avoid visible artifacts. Moiré and aliasing artifacts are often a direct result of having undersampled the scene.

Apertures

The *aperture* is the opening at the center of a lens through which light passes. The concept of an aperture is fundamental to the conception of the camera. The camera obscura, the precursor to photography, is effectively an aperture opening allowing light into a dark room. The larger the opening in a lens, the more light passes through to the light-sensitive recording medium. A smaller opening means less light but potentially greater resolved detail and in-focus scene content.

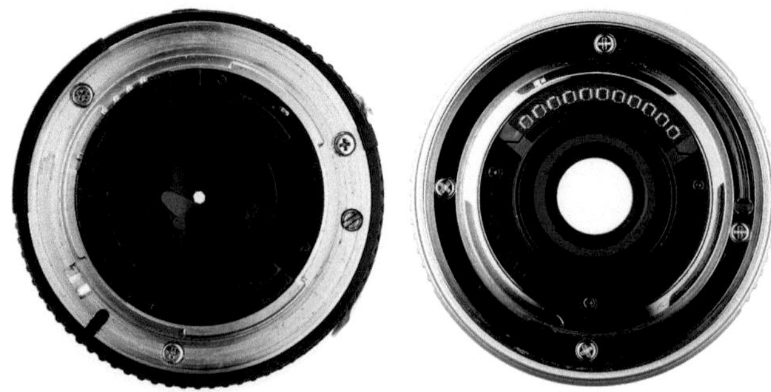

Figure 3-17 Aperture shapes can vary with lens design. The left lens is stopped down to a high f-number with the aperture blades forming a heptagonal opening. The right lens is set to a low f-number with an opening approximating a circle.

Setting the aperture means changing the size of the opening. The mechanism that accomplishes this is the *aperture diaphragm*, a set of overlapping blades or petals that form a circular opening at their center pictured in Figure 3-17. The range of diameters of an adjustable aperture diaphragm is lens-dependent and has implications for how that lens may be used (see Chapter 4). Traditional camera apertures approximate a circular opening. They may also appear as hexagonal or octagonal with flat-edged sides. The discrete positions of the aperture's overlapping blades are called *f-stops*.

The aperture shape dictates the shape of a point of light formed on the image plane; the closer this shape is to a circle, the closer small resolved points of the image are rendered as circular points. This is not the only way to form an image but it's the most common and visually pleasing approach. Creative visual effects are possible using a uniquely shaped aperture opening. This shape could be a star, an amorphous blob or any other geometric, two-dimensional form. All form a usable photographic image, yet their differences become apparent in out-of-focus areas, particularly specular highlights, that take on the appearance of the aperture shape.

The aperture diaphragm mechanism quickly adjusts the size of the opening with automatic, electronic programming. A key behavior of electronically controlled apertures is that they often stay at their maximum opening until the shutter button is pressed. In the milliseconds that follow, the camera electronics tell the aperture diaphragm to move into the predetermined position—say, f/8.0, as dictated by the user manually or from automatic exposure calculations. The shutter opens immediately following this change to create an exposure. This is notable because it means that what the photographer sees in the moments before pressing the shutter button will likely be different from the recorded image.

SLR cameras typically have a *depth of field preview* button that, when held, temporarily changes the aperture diaphragm to the position used during an exposure. This darkens the observable image through the viewfinder or the electronic live preview since it's stopping down the aperture from its maximum opening. The main benefit, as the name implies, is in previewing the depth of field of the about-to-be-captured exposure. A fully manual lens or an analog camera inherent provides this behavior since the user directly adjusts the aperture setting when composing.

Smaller cameras including smartphones use fixed apertures. These are typically large openings like f/1.4 or f/2.8 to keep exposure times short and to maximize light detection on their relatively small sensors. A few recent smartphones introduced variable apertures that adjust based on light level; these mechanical components are challenging to build in small form factors.

Lenses designed for motion video or cinema cameras use a unique aperture design called *transmission stops* or *t-stops*. These are precisely calculated to control light transmission in video exposure and allow for continuous adjustment from the widest to the narrowest aperture opening. This is notably different from a traditional still camera whose f-stops are discrete and abrupt steps in aperture blade position. The t-stop design is critical for motion video work in creating smooth, gradual changes to the aperture setting during recording.

Shutters

All photographs require that the image sensor receives exposure for a short period of time. Back in the earliest days of photography, this was achieved in the simplest of ways: a photographer removed a lens cap from the lens, counted out the exposure time and then placed the cap back over the lens. Cheap and easy but not at all consistent. Those early cameras used film that was relatively insensitive to light and therefore a photograph's exposure was measured as a function of minutes. Today we use exposure times on the scale of fractions of seconds. Even the quickest-draw lens capper can't nail a 1/8000th exposure time. Instead, our cameras house *shutters* that control when and for how long light reaches the image sensor. These shutters operate mechanically, electronically or a combination of the two for a duration called the *shutter speed*. The physical button on the camera body that signals a shutter action is the *shutter button* or *shutter release*, though other triggering options include sound, timers or even face detection via software algorithms (only capturing when the subject smiles, for example). The physical shutter button is most commonly designed with two stages of travel, meaning that it can be pressed down halfway to indicate a forthcoming exposure trigger or to lock a focus position or light meter reading. Pressing it down completely initiates the shutter action to capture an image.

Leaf Shutters

A *leaf shutter* is a set of overlapping metal blades (also called leaves), much like the lens aperture. The difference is that the leaf shutter blades close down completely; aperture blades always allow for a small opening at their center. When triggered, a leaf shutter opens and dilates from its center, exposing the image plane to light as it eventually expands beyond the sensor area. Figure 3-18 (overleaf) shows a sequence of leaf shutter positions from closed to completely open. After the length of time set by the photographer for shutter speed, the blades close until the image plane is once again blocked from all light.

The primary advantage of a leaf shutter is in its ability to expose the entire sensor at once: if a short-duration flash is used, say, in a studio setting, we know that the whole frame receives that flash as part of the exposure. Put another way, leaf shutters are *flash-synchronous* at any speed. This is put to great use when mixing flash and ambient light for on-location shooting. It's easier to work out functional exposure times that get the best of both artificial

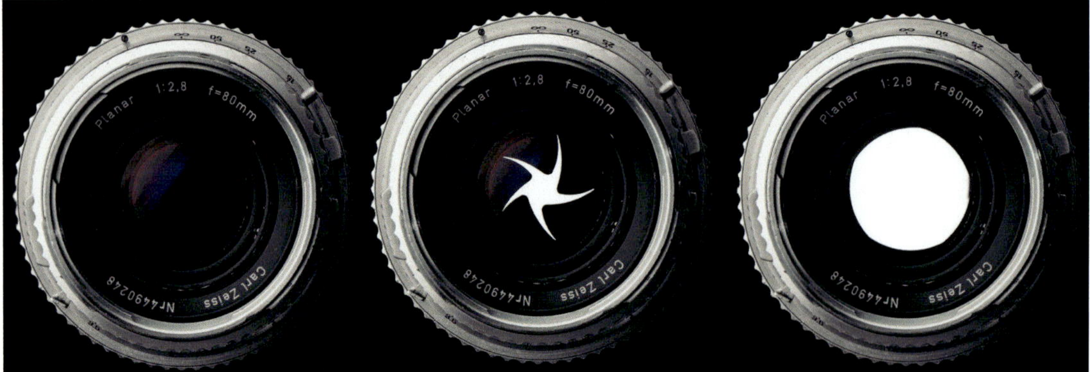

Figure 3-18 A leaf shutter in stages of opening as seen in a medium format lens. Photographs by Rochester Institute of Technology photography alumnus Dan Wang

and natural lighting, especially under bright sunlight. Shutter speed is measured as the duration of time that the leaf shutter remains completely open.

Leaf shutters are not common in consumer cameras and are typically only found in professional medium and large format cameras. There are exceptions to everything, of course, and a few select mirrorless cameras feature such shutter designs. One notable shortcoming of the leaf shutter design is the speed ceiling: they cannot achieve the fast shutter speeds that other methods offer. Another shortcoming is cost. Leaf shutters must be placed in the lens, rather than the camera body, meaning that each lens is more complex and expensive to make and you pay for it each time you buy a lens rather than once as part of the camera body cost.

Focal Plane Shutters

A *focal plane shutter* is a set of curtains that travel in tandem forming a slit opening in front of the image sensor, usually from top to bottom. As one curtain moves downward, the second curtain waits some fraction of a second before following, leaving a small, horizontal opening through which light reaches the focal plane. The curtains then move upwards to reset their position, this time without leaving a gap between them. The amount of time set for the shutter speed determines how much time the sensor is exposed to light before that second curtain blocks it again. Longer shutter speeds have a long enough delay of the second curtain that both remain out of the way for a time, leaving the entire sensor exposed.

The downside to using a moving slit to expose the sensor reveals itself when using an electronic flash. Its duration is many times shorter than that of the shutter curtains and a poorly synchronized exposure could see the flash exposing only a small slit of the sensor while the rest receives only ambient light. This creates *partial frames* as shown in Figure 3-19. Cameras tend to include an automatic shutter speed adjustment when they're attached to electronic flash sources to avoid this problem and to give the photographer one less thing to have to remember.

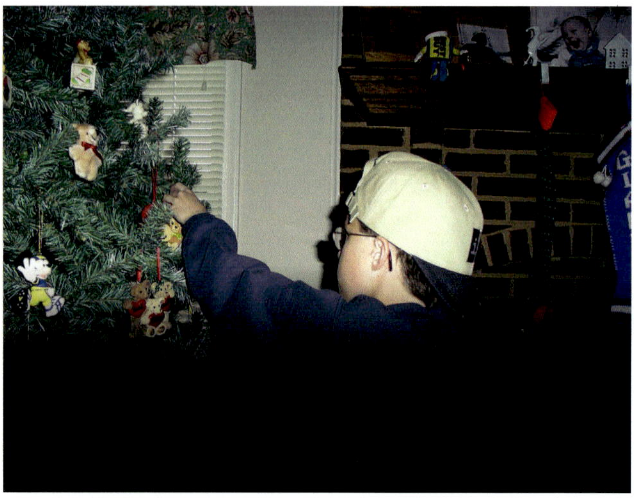

Figure 3-19 A partial frame due to an improper focal plane shutter speed used with electronic flash.

Electronic Shutters

So far we've described physical camera components that block light from reaching the sensor save for a brief instant when they move out of the way. This is the only way to control exposure time in analog systems because film reacts to light the moment the two are introduced to one another. A digital image sensor isn't so reactionary. It only pays attention to light when it's switched on and recording photons. If we leave it switched off, it pays no mind to any incident light. It follows, then, that flipping the electronic switch on and off for a short time has a similar effect as a physical, light-blocking shutter would.

CCDs aren't a great candidate for the *electronic shutter* approach as they can't turn on and off as rapidly as typical photographic exposures require. CMOS, on the other hand, can be turned on, record light and then turned off in extremely short durations. Since CMOS photosites are self-contained units with their own circuitry, we can go one step further and command specific photosites or rows of photosites at will. Thus, a simulation of a focal plane shutter is created by triggering the topmost line of sensor photosites to record, then the next line, the next, and so on, turning each trailing line off in sequence. If we're really feeling crazy, some sensors and accompanying programming allow for multiple exposures to be recorded at effectively the same time: every even photosite turns on for one duration and every odd photosite exposes for a different duration, for example. Handling these disparate exposures becomes a challenge for processing yet it offers a unique opportunity in simultaneous capture that is not available with analog methods.

The common electronic shutter method used by CMOS sensors is called a *rolling shutter* which records and reads out exposure line by line rather than with the entire sensor area all at once. Each row receives the same amount of exposure; the row exposures are offset in time. Reading each line in sequence allows the sensor and accompanying electronics to process the huge amount of light data recorded in video capture and avoids the need for a physical shutter in the small form factor. This can be a problem when filming fast-moving subjects. The subject may be at one location when the top lines of the sensor are recorded and at a very different location by the time the bottom lines are recorded. The *rolling shutter artifact* that results is described as jelly-like: solid objects like buildings or cars appear to warp, undulate or skew. Figure 3-20 shows one such example of an aerial imaging system that was moving quickly as the sensor exposed the scene using a rolling shutter. The larger the sensor (in terms of number of photosites and number of rows), the longer it takes to read out exposure from top to bottom. Higher-end cameras used for video recording in particular use CMOS with *global shutters*. Global shutters capture all sensor rows at the same time. As mobile processors become more powerful, we expect to see global shutter methods incorporated into smaller and cheaper camera systems.

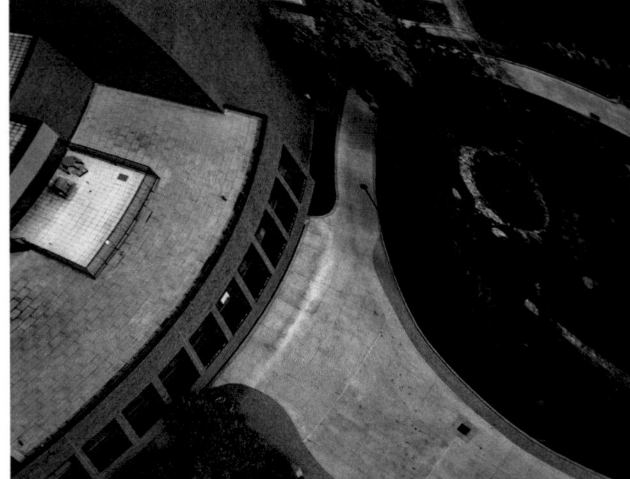

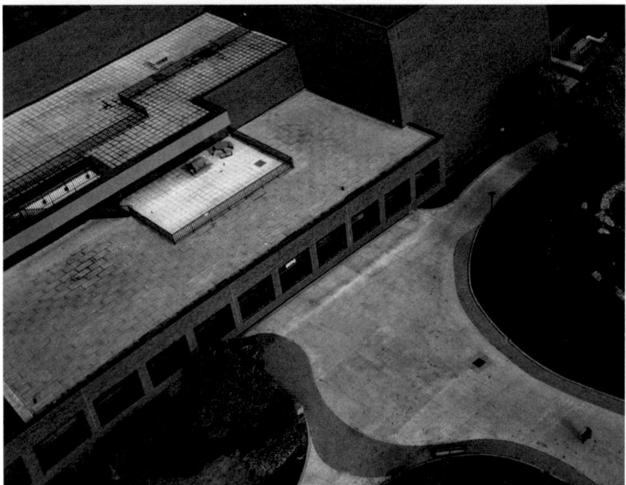

Figure 3-20 The visual artifact resulting from a rolling shutter with fast camera movement (top) and an undistorted view of the same scene (bottom).

Electronic first curtain shutter is a technique that uses both mechanical and electronic behaviors. An exposure begins when each successive line of the CMOS sensor is switched on to detect photons and a mechanical curtain moves to cover up the sensor to end exposure. This allows for faster exposure times using a partially electronic shutter, reducing in-camera vibration and shutter noise.

Automatic Exposure and Metering

Cameras determine the amount of light required for photographic exposure in one of two ways. They evaluate the light hitting the sensor (by opening the shutter), effectively taking photographs that aren't permanently saved. This means using the imaging sensor as a light sensor: they're one in the same. The downside to this method is that the camera must take initial guesses as to a correct exposure. If it's way off, it must continue to guess and check until it zeroes in on the amount of available light.

The second approach involves a dedicated light sensor inside the camera body. This is called *through the lens* (TTL) metering as it measures light coming into the camera to determine exposure (refer back to Figure 3-1). A basic TTL meter offers three modes: matrix, spot and center-weighted. In more advanced cameras, the TTL meter can be tied to the autofocus mode. The two behaviors work hand in hand to create the proper exposure for the area of interest in a composed scene. TTL metering takes into account stray light entering the lens, the angle of view and close-up exposure corrections that handheld meters cannot. On the other hand, it's only capable of reflective light readings by virtue of its location in the camera and position relative to the subject. This fact can be limiting with very bright or dark subjects. Through the lens metering is discussed further in Chapter 4.

Automatic Focus

Manual focus is nearly always an option on professional cameras and many prefer to trust their hand-eye coordination to adjust the lens moments before capture. We view the scene through the viewfinder while rotating a ring on the lens barrel, trusting our eye to set the camera focus to the sharpest position for the scene. There is no question, though, that *automatic focus* is convenient and relied upon by many to get photographs in sharp focus. The basic functionality behind automatic focus is described in the following paragraphs. Note that today's camera systems increasingly layer strategies with additional algorithms to infer subject priority or anticipated motion. Face detection, for example, identifies likely human faces in the frame and ensures that the face is in focus above all other subjects.

There are two components required for a system offering automatic focusing. The first is mechanical, as the internal lens elements must be electronically controllable to adjust focus. The second is either a combination of hardware and software or exclusively software that determines how the lens must be adjusted to achieve optimal focus. For traditional, interchangeable lens systems, mechanical focusing is accomplished with small motor drives in the lens housing. There's no room for gear-driven motors in smaller camera form factors. Instead, these cameras use *voice coil motors* that rapidly move tiny lens elements using electromagnets and applied voltage. The physical movement of lens elements and the whirr of the motors introduces both speed and noise considerations when evaluating lenses for a photoshoot. Video recording specifically demands quiet motor drive systems if the audio recording equipment is anywhere near the lens; sports photography demands the quickest possible adjustments to achieve focus with fast-moving subjects. All camera systems with autofocus capabilities use the strategies of phase detection, contrast detection or a combination therein.

Phase Detection Autofocus

Phase detection autofocus takes a beam of light entering the system and splits it into two beams. Each of these new beam strikes one of two adjacent photosites. The signals detected on these photosites are compared. If they are the same, they are *in phase* and the image reaching the sensor is in focus. If they are not the same, or *out of phase*, the camera focus point is adjusted and the process is repeated until the correct focus point is located. This phase detection information is used to calculate subject distance and is fast at getting the camera system focused. The out-of-phase detection information is explicit in indicating front- or back-focusing, further speeding up the process of finding correct focus.

Phase detection often occurs on a separate sensor within the camera. For every focus point in the viewfinder (often indicated by overlayed dots or boxes), there are two dedicated photosites that perform phase detection focusing. Manufacturers sometimes advertise the focus point patterns of these detectors as a means of indicating effectiveness. Phase detection can also occur on the main sensor by splitting designated "focusing pixels" in two using microscopic masks over photosites. This system allows phase detection focusing to be used when the camera is in "live view" as well as when composing through the viewfinder. This approach is increasingly common on small camera form factors including smartphones because it adds minimal complexity to their design. However, the signal must be clean enough to make accurate measurements and camera systems may struggle to leverage phase detection autofocus in low light conditions.

Contrast Detection Autofocus

Contrast detection autofocus is used most commonly in compact cameras, mirrorless cameras and when shooting in live view modes on SLRs. The image sensor itself is employed to detect contrast and determine optimal focus rather than having a separate, dedicated sensor in the camera body. A major upside to this approach is that the full resolution image sensor is leveraged to look at any and all areas of the frame, if desired, to find sharp focus. Phase detection sensors are typically lower resolution and only look for focus points in specific, patterned areas. Using contrast detection autofocus means having thousands of spatially sampled points when phase detection might have dozens.

Contrast detection evaluates the contrast of the initial image using image processing algorithms. The highest contrast is achieved when the image is in focus. The lens moves back and forth while evaluating contrast and settles in at the highest contrast. This strategy is slower than phase detection and does not provide decisive guidance to the lens focusing motors to know which direction to move. This may lead to *focus seeking* where the system adjusts focus distance all the way in one direction before doubling back and trying in the other direction before settling. Focus seeking can easily lead to missed shots, particularly with fast motion events, as it may take entire seconds before getting the scene in focus. Contrast detection autofocus is well-suited for studio still life shooting as it's unlikely to encounter constantly changing focus needs. It may also be the only option in low light conditions where a phase detection system's signal is too noisy to rely on. Some hybrid systems exist that use the best of both strategies: phase detection quickly hones in on an approximate focus distance, then contrast detection fine-tunes the exact setting.

Active Autofocus

Phase and contrast detection methods work by measuring the light coming into the system, functioning as passive detectors of image focus. Another approach is to actively emit a signal, either infrared or ultrasonic, that reflects off of the scene and back to onboard sensors to measure subject distance. The camera measures the time it takes for the signal to return, calculates it against the speed of the signal and drives the autofocus mechanisms to focus the lens at the sensed subject distance. This is called *active autofocus.*

Active autofocus sensors can work in complete darkness but are more effective at close ranges as the emitted signal takes longer to return and is more likely to scatter with farther subject distances. They can also fail if the subject absorbs the emitted energy rather than bouncing it back. Additionally, infrared active sensors can also be confused by other heat energy sources in a scene.

Autofocus Points

Similar to auto exposure techniques, cameras can use either a single autofocus point or multiple points to average or calculate a best-guess estimate for focus distance. Autofocus points light up in the traditional SLR's viewfinder

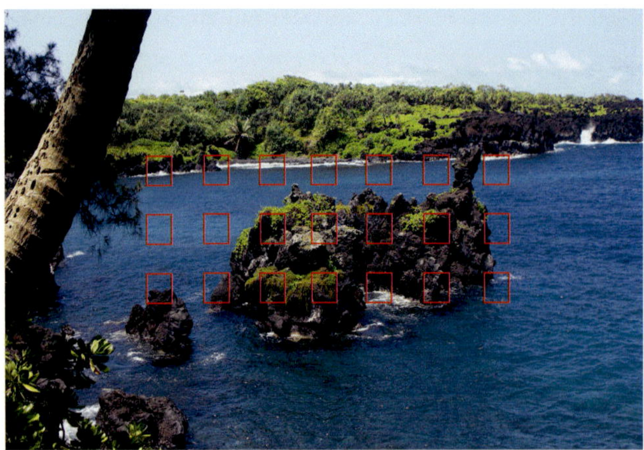

Figure 3-21 An illustration of the autofocus point overlay seen through an SLR viewfinder.

when the shutter button is pressed halfway (see Figure 3-21). Depending on the manufacturer and model, these points may appear in different patterns or shapes and light up to indicate subject detection. They also appear as a graphic overlay on the preview screen when using live view. SLR models featuring touchscreens allow the photographer to tap a location in the image frame to direct autofocus. This is particularly helpful when there are objects at multiple distances from the camera.

Detecting movement and focus in different zones of the image frame allows for subject motion prediction. For example, if the system detects a subject at the left edge of the frame moving toward the right, it may opt to lock focus for this area rather than at the frame center, which might otherwise put the focus farther back. Using autofocus with moving objects takes practice to achieve good results for every exposure.

Finally, focus behavior is further specified by setting the camera to either *single servo focus* or *continuous servo*. In the former, the lens focus distance locks when the shutter is pressed halfway. The camera assumes that subject position remains static until the shutter is fully pressed and a capture is recorded. In the latter behavior, pressing the shutter button halfway down causes the autofocus mechanisms to constantly evaluate and adjust focus position. This active, responsive behavior is excellent for catching proper focus with quick-moving subjects but it requires a constant power draw to run the lens motors. Experienced photographers enjoy the level of control afforded by toggling between different focusing behaviors depending on the shooting context; entry-level cameras may bury their selection in menus while higher-end cameras include dedicated hardware buttons or switches.

Image Stabilization

Image stabilization (IS) counteracts camera shake that otherwise leads to blurry images. Excessive camera shake means that the image is rapidly changing and moving around. Sometimes the shake comes from the photographer while other times it's introduced by the environment or shooting platform. Fast shutter speeds are somewhat immune to this movement because they expose for such a relatively brief moment of time, successfully freezing a sharp image at capture. It becomes harder to keep the camera steady as focal length increases due to its weight and its field of view; the longer the lens, the more susceptible your images are to camera shake. There is also a direct relationship between the amount of camera shake relative to the amount of caffeine consumed by the photographer. A low-tech image stabilization technique involves controlled breathing, keeping the camera close to your body and keeping shutter speeds as fast as possible. This is a functional approach until light levels or other exposure considerations paint you in a problem-solving corner: sometimes there's simply not enough light to get a good exposure at a fast shutter speed. This is where we look to other solutions for image stabilization.

Lens-Based Optical Image Stabilization

Optical image stabilization (OIS) allows for slower shutter speeds while still getting sharp images. In lens-based OIS, a single floating lens element is positioned within the compound lens. This lens shifts to compensate for the camera (and therefore image) movement. It makes sure that the projected image is stable by the time it reaches the sensor. Disregarding the technical merits of the analogy, lens-based stabilization is like really good suspension in a car where your sharp image is the comfy passenger on the bumpy road of camera shake. The downside is that the approach requires additional components built into the lens, making it an expensive proposition with a camera system that encourages swapping lenses. Each lens must bring its own OIS solution to the table. There's a price premium for lenses with built-in OIS relative to ones without it.

Camera-Based Image Stabilization

If we want to pay for a stabilization technology once when buying the camera instead of every time we buy a new lens, *camera-based image stabilization* is the answer. Here, the sensor moves to compensate for shaky camera movement instead of a lens in front of it. This way, even with an interchangeable lens system, every setup used can take advantage of the image stabilization. The degree of correction or movement compensation may be less than that which is achieved with a lens-based solution, however.

Both lens- and camera-based image stabilization strategies can be damaging to the equipment if left on when shooting with a tripod. The system may attempt to correct for movement when there is none and puts wear on the moving components. It may also lead to more camera shake, ironically, as it introduces vibrations and image movement artificially as it struggles to operate. Both forms of image stabilization are also power-hungry and drain batteries faster than non-image-stabilized setups, and so they should be toggled on only when needed.

Aside from photographer-induced shakiness, a small amount of vibration is introduced by the mirror-flipping mechanisms in SLR cameras. It may not feel like much but at longer focal lengths and at close working distances, the vibration can very quickly reduce image sharpness. *Mirror-lock up* is an option typically found in camera firmware that lessens the effect of mirror vibration during exposure. In this mode, one press of the shutter flips the reflex mirror into position for capture and the sensor curtains remain closed. Pressing the shutter again opens the curtains for the determined shutter speed duration, followed by the mirror flipping back to their default position. In between, there is no image redirected to the pentaprism or viewfinder. This means you're temporarily unable to see what you're photographing with the benefit being that you've eliminated some of the physical components moving around immediately preceding exposure. Electronic first curtain shutter, mentioned earlier, is another available setting for minimizing vibration.

Electronic Image Stabilization

Lastly, software processing can offer *electronic image stabilization* (EIS). While it cannot rely on physical hardware to counteract or minimize physical camera movement, it works with the captured pixels to reduce blur. Still photographs benefit from merging or fusing multiple, rapid captures to achieve sharpness. Recording video at higher resolutions than the final intended capture, a technique called *overscan*, is valuable for realigning consecutive frames to correct for temporal camera shake. Advanced video editing software can additionally offer frame warping to minimize distortion or framing changes despite camera movement. Electronic image stabilization is ultimately limited by the quality of its input. The best strategy is to eliminate the effects of camera shake as early in the image-making pipeline as possible for best results.

Camera Viewfinders

Composition is a key skill for photographers. While cropping at the post-processing stage is an option, we rely on getting most of the way to a perfect shot using a viewfinder. Holding the camera out at arm's length and shooting wherever we happen to be looking is simply too dependent on sheer luck; instead we prefer to see as the camera sees and commit to a capture when everything aligns. The viewfinder is critical for framing, timing, focus, exposure determination—pretty much everything that the photographer needs to see and know. There are several methods of providing such feedback in camera design, either optically or electronically.

Optical Viewfinders

The SLR camera's design uses an *optical viewfinder* where we place our eye to see the image as rendered through the camera optics. The image seen is right-side up in orientation (recall from Chapter 2 that a lens forms an image that is upside-down and backwards). The SLR camera's reflex mirror sits at a 45° angle and directs the light coming through the lens to a ground glass above it. The image is formed on this ground glass, passes to the pentaprism which re-inverts the image via mirror reflections. The optical viewfinder goes dark and the photographer's view is momentarily obstructed during exposure as the light is redirected to the sensor.

A notable limitation of SLR optical viewfinders is their reliance on available light. A dark scene viewed through the viewfinder is at least as dark, likely darker, than how it appears to the eye. Light loss through the optics and any attached lens filters results in a dim preview. This is further exacerbated by the aperture setting. A stopped down aperture significantly cuts down the available light for real-time viewing even if the eventual exposure uses a long shutter speed or high ISO to compensate. The solution that camera manufacturers settled on involves leaving the aperture wide open until the milliseconds before the shutter opens for exposure. We must explicitly command the camera to adjust the aperture to the desired diameter when composing through the viewfinder. This is typically accomplished with a depth of field preview button. Otherwise, the viewfinder preview does not accurately reflect the depth of field that results in the final capture.

An honorable mention here is *waist-level viewfinders*, most commonly encountered on analog medium format cameras. Forgoing the pentaprism (and therefore yielding a backwards image), this unique viewing mechanic projects the lens image onto a ground glass along the top facet of the camera. Holding the camera at waist height allows the photographer to look down at the ground glass, sometimes shrouded in a foldable, pop-up hood, to focus and compose.

Another optical approach is found on rangefinder-type cameras. A rangefinder uses two lenses that place the two images into a single eyepiece using prisms. When the camera lens is in focus, the two images are in alignment and the distance or range to the object is determined. Once known, the range is used to set the focusing mechanism on the camera. In later rangefinder designs, these optical mechanisms became internalized in the camera design for easier focusing.

Electronic Viewfinders

Electronic viewfinders (EVFs) take a live feed from the sensor and transmit it to a miniature screen in the camera body, viewable only when the user puts an eye up to the opening. This is not necessarily a strict, unedited video feed, as the image can undergo additional processing in real time to boost brightness, introduce software filter effects or otherwise overlay relevant metadata. Early implementations were low resolution, laggy and not particularly good replacements for optical viewfinders. This is changing quickly as microdisplay technologies evolve with higher pixel densities and faster refresh rates. EVFs are advantageous in bright light, outdoor conditions because the space formed between the eye and the display blocks extraneous light. They also work to keep form factors small, eliminating the need for mirrors and alternate light paths in the camera body. The downside comes in the form of power consumption: using the viewfinder means powering that small display and running the sensor continuously. Where optical viewfinders are effectively passive and require no battery power to help you compose, EVFs need a steady flow of power from the battery pack.

Alternatively, the live view continuous video feed from the sensor can be piped to a relatively large screen on the back of the camera. SLR cameras offer this functionality in addition to their optical viewfinder. Compact point and shoot digital cameras exclusively rely on this approach. Using live view on an SLR necessitates locking the reflex mirror in its upright position to direct all incoming light directly to the image sensor. This behavior eliminates some camera shake and shutter noise when it's time to take the still photo capture. However, it also means bypassing the autofocus and light meter sensors. The camera instead relies on signal detected at the image sensor and a layer of image processing algorithms to evaluate focus and exposure (using techniques like contrast-based autofocus and edge detection).

Electronic Flash

Sometimes sunlight isn't available or enough for making photographs. At the same time, artificial lights indoors, such as lamps and ceiling fixtures, are not necessarily bright enough for the camera sensor and lens combination. *Electronic flash* offers bright illumination with extremely short durations as described in Chapter 1. Flash is typically triggered by the camera shutter press and lasts just long enough for photographic exposure, appearing only briefly to our eyes. We mentioned flash synchronization earlier in this chapter with regard to shutter types; using electronic flash limits the available shutter speeds with focal plane shutters found on SLRs. You may even notice that, when flash units are connected to your camera, the camera programming automatically adjusts shutter speed (often defaulting to 1/125th second).

Many SLR cameras include a built-in or pop-up flash unit or the ability to add an on-camera flash unit via *hot shoe* connection. There are drawbacks to these smaller light sources despite their convenience. The first issue with built-in flash in particular is the small size. Recall from light's inverse square law that light falls off with the distance squared. The effectiveness of the built-in flash drops off sharply as the distance to the subject increases and since it's always going to be at the location of the camera, its illumination ability is not effective when the subject is more than a few feet away. This can be countered by higher illumination output but a brighter flash requires a larger energy storage capacity. On-camera flash employs small capacitors in the camera fueled by the camera's battery, limiting voltage and number of discharges. We trade flash output capacity and size for convenience.

Another challenge with on-camera flash is *red eye* in portrait photos (see Figure 3-22). Why does this happen? It's common to use flash in low light situations where our pupils naturally dilate for scotopic vision (more on this in Chapter 13). On-camera flash is very close to the optical axis of the lens and sensor. When the flash fires, light bounces off the fundus at the back of the eye and reflects back to the lens. The red color comes from the choroid layer of the eye which provides the blood supply to the retina. Since your subject's pupils are likely to be dilated in a low light environment, the reflection is large and noticeable. The only way to completely avoid red eye in portraits is to use off-axis flash. Some camera's offer red-eye reduction modes that introduce a lower-intensity *pre-flash* before the full flash output and camera capture. This first burst of light causes your subject's pupils to constrict prior to taking the photograph. The smaller pupil size minimizes the appearance of the red reflection off of the fundus. It does not entirely eliminate red eye.

Using a dedicated flash unit mounted to the camera offers many more creative options for light direction and quality. Aiming the flash head allows for bouncing the light off of the ceiling or wall to reduce harsh shadows.

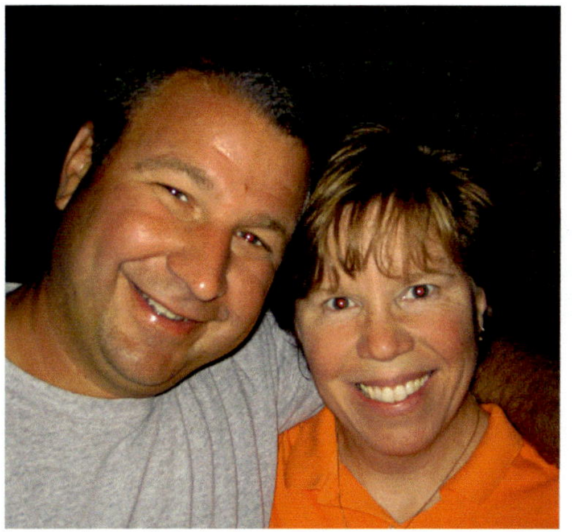

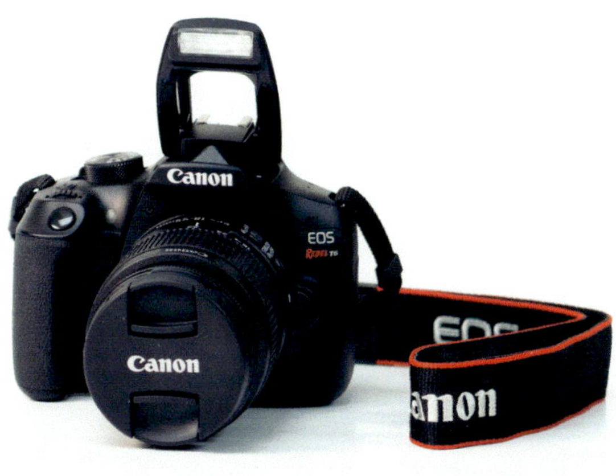

Figure 3-22 An on-camera flash often causes red eye. Photograph by Rochester Institute of Technology photography student Genae Shields

Placing a diffuser on the flash unit provides soft, diffuse illumination.

Off-camera flash units range in size, portability and light output. A *sync cable* is the cheapest method of synchronizing the shutter and flash discharge, though some camera models require additional peripherals to support these cables. Off-camera flash equipment can also be triggered via radio frequency communication or optical sensors. *Studio strobes* are large electronic flash units that either use built-in power packs or require tethering to large capacitors and controllers. Studio strobes typically include a combination of bulbs to provide the extremely bright, instantaneous flash as well as continuous tungsten illumination for previewing light quality and generally lighting the scene between exposures.

We defer to the lighting experts when it comes to modifying and controlling electronic flash with lighting accessories; for more on the topic look to *Light Science and Magic: An Introduction to Photographic Lighting* by Hunter, Biver and Fuqua published in 2015 by Focal Press.

Camera Form Factors and Characteristics

Camera form factors are many and their features varied. Few of us are shooting with equipment identical to that used in the early decades of photography's birth yet they all share the principles of recording light. The single lens reflex camera was a staple of the field-shooting professional photographer for many decades. Medium format was the studio photographer's go-to. SLR and medium format camera types are used by professionals today but there exists considerably more variety in form factor, sensor design, viewfinder style and price points that open up availability to prosumers (semi-professional/consumer/hobbyist types) and beyond. These cameras offer a host of buttons, dials, displays and touchscreen interfaces for control and review of camera captures.

Above most other features discussed in this chapter, the primary delineation of camera form factors comes down to those with interchangeable lens capabilities and those without (sometimes called *dedicated lens* cameras).[11] Cameras of many shapes and sizes theoretically offer the ability to swap lenses, though the designs of some, like smartphones, are self-contained. Any change to focal length must be accomplished by adding supplemental optics in front of the existing ones.

Single Lens Reflex Cameras

Mentioned many times already in this chapter, the classic SLR form factor features an interchangeable lens mount, mirror system to support an optical viewfinder and a 35mm film equivalent (24x36mm) sensor size. Crop sensor variants eschew the more expensive full frame sensor for smaller sensor sizes that sit at the same focal plane in the camera body. The mirror system allows for additional components like light and focus sensors. The SLR form factor was a staple of analog photography, so it was the obvious choice for early, professional digital cameras. Replacing the film plane with a digital image sensor was the first step, then came replacing mechanical light sensors, lens controls and other components with ones that all feed to an onboard computer for automatic control and processing. The *digital SLR* (or DSLR) is most common today, though for our purposes we use the terms SLR and DSLR interchangeably in this text.

The ergonomics of the SLR and its rectangular sensor require rotating the entire camera to change framing orientations between portrait and landscape compositions. Portrait photographers may opt for an additional body attachment that adds shutter buttons and other controls in more comfortable locations when holding the camera sideways is a frequent requirement. SLR models designed for a variety of applications beyond studio photography include hot shoe mounts atop the pentaprism for connecting portable flash units. Additional features can include Global Positioning System (GPS) modules, motion and orientation sensors, wireless transceivers and articulating displays.

Medium Format Cameras

When 35mm film wasn't large enough for commercial applications and reproduction, photographers turned to *medium format cameras* with film sizes like 6x4.5cm (also known colloquially as "645"), 6x6cm and 6x7cm. Note that some of these aspect ratios adhere to a more square relationship between frame height and width compared to 35mm film. Analog medium format cameras featured hot-swappable film backs for alternating between film types and quick reloading. Borrowing a trick from interchangeable lens mounts, these designs allow for removing the back portion of the camera that houses a roll of film like a cartridge. Analog medium format cameras also feature reflex mirrors but forgo the pentaprism viewfinder for *ground glass* to focus and compose.

Digital medium format cameras do not necessarily offer sensors equal in physical size to their film counterparts (it is perpetually expensive to make such large sensors), nor do they adhere to the square or square-ish aspect ratios. They do use sensors larger than 35mm; in comparison to a full frame 24x36mm sensor, a medium format camera may house one as large as 40x53mm. Larger sensors can translate to higher pixel counts without compromising light sensitivity or dynamic range. Medium format cameras offer some of the highest megapixel counts available. In addition to fully digital models, medium format shooting is possible by means of *digital backs* that attach to traditional film bodies using the unique, detachable camera back mount.

This form factor is decidedly heavier, not as well-suited for field shooting and instead sees its primary application in photography studios where super high-resolution images are needed for retouching, compositing and general commercial use. Their high price points make them available primarily to working professionals that need the high-end performance and are not as commonly seen in the hands of prosumers or hobbyist photographers.

Rangefinders

Rangefinders are handheld, field shooting cameras that use a double-lens system. The optical viewfinder is independent from the optics used to record an image on the film or image sensor. Since the two components are a few inches apart in the camera body, it results in a slight mismatch between what the photographer frames up in the viewfinder and the recorded image. This also means that rangefinders are not a good choice when telephoto focal lengths are required, as the viewfinder field of view is static. Wide focal lengths fare much better. This form factor forgoes any mirror system, allowing the camera body and lens-to-sensor distance to be slimmer than that of an SLR.

Rangefinders get their name from their unique focusing mechanic: to accurately focus at different distances, the viewfinder uses a split-image view. A centered subset of the frame shows two split reflections of the scene that align perfectly when optimal focus is set. When it's out of focus, this subset area shows two misaligned or mismatched images. The viewfinder is positioned such that the photographer keeps one eye on the scene, unobstructed by the camera, while the other sees through the camera. This provides additional context and situational awareness.

Rangefinders are not common in the digital realm—the main true-to-form models are made by Leica Camera AG—though their split-image focusing mechanic exists as a digital emulation in electronic viewfinder interfaces.

View Cameras

View cameras are the largest of the traditional camera formats with design roots reaching back to the earliest cameras. Also known as *large format* and *technical cameras*, they house the largest image plane and therefore accommodate large sheets or plates of photographic material (typically film). View cameras consist of two components called *standards*: one houses the lens assembly (including a leaf shutter) and the other the ground glass which functions as a viewfinder and the location at which film is loaded at the time of capture. The image projected onto the ground glass is upside-down and backwards, helping you to appreciate the thankless work done by the pentaprism in our SLRs. Large format cameras are simple in that the area between the optics and the image plane is devoid of mechanical components, mirrors or additional optics. The *bellows* are accordion-like folded black material that serve to adjust the image distance; they make the black box longer or shorter to adjust focus and magnification.

Portable variants are called *field cameras* featuring foldable designs for easier transportation; studio versions are called *monorail* or *studio* view cameras. Standard film sizes are 4x5 inches and 8x10 inches. Changing from portrait to landscape orientation is simply a matter of rotating the back standard's film holder.

Mirrorless Cameras

Mirrorless cameras offer many of the features of SLRs including full frame sensors but are able to fit it all in smaller form factor bodies. By removing the need for the mirror reflex system and optical viewfinder, the camera housing is much more compact with a shorter distance needed between the back of the lens and the sensor plane.

Mirrorless cameras grew in popularity in the mid-2010s, spearheaded by Sony and Fujifilm. Canon and Nikon, the industry leaders in SLRs, continued to iterate on their full frame models. It is only recently as of this writing that the two companies have brought professional mirrorless, SLR-replacement models to market.[12] Taking advantage of the smaller body sizes, these newer models have their own lens systems that are also more compact and lightweight. Nearly all mirrorless cameras have optional lens adaptors available that bring compatibility for SLR lenses.

The principle of mirrorless camera form factors is building a camera's internals and technological capabilities from the ground up with the latest imaging capabilities. In many ways, the DSLR is an analog film camera design with its internals converted for a digital sensor. The evolution was logical and functional. Mirrorless designs promise an exciting future for camera form factors as they build around digital-exclusive functionality. The balance they strike between small hardware with minimal moving parts and high-quality sensors makes them an excellent choice for aerial imaging with remotely piloted drone platforms (unmanned aerial vehicles).

Compact Cameras

Compact or *small format cameras* are a category that started with Kodak in the late 1880s when the only previously available option was large format. In the nearly 150 years since, the compact camera has seen evolutions in materials, image quality and transitioned from analog to digital imaging technologies. Even in the earliest days, the allure of the compact camera was the simple controls and consumer convenience. This idea spawned ideas like the one-time-use, disposable plastic camera that consumers used to expose a roll of film, mail or drop off at a camera store, and received a set of prints. These disposable cameras used fixed aperture, shutter speeds and focus distances. They are alternatively named *point-and-shoot cameras* as a result of their ease of use and are almost always dedicated lens (non-interchangeable) form factors. Unconventional compact cameras include instant-film types like the Polaroid and Fujifilm Instax that continue in popularity due to their uniquely analog output.

Digital compact cameras came about in the early 2000s with affordable pricing and put the power back in the user's hands to manage, edit and print their image files. Focal lengths tend to be normal (around 50mm full frame equivalent) or zoom/telephoto. They also feature built-in flashes that are notorious for causing red eye in portraits. They sometimes employ physical shutters though the available shutter speeds are lesser in range than what an SLR can achieve. Compact cameras stick with fixed apertures for the sake of mechanical convenience and because the average user takes similar-style images in bright light while expecting everything to be in focus.

The compact camera category is shrinking due to mobile device cameras. Offering the same convenience and user-friendliness, they've eclipsed the need for separate, single-function hardware for casual photography. Some limited compact camera models exist that target prosumers looking for raw capabilities and a degree of advanced controls, featuring nearly pocketable designs and the latest sensor technologies.

Mobile Phone Cameras

It's impossible to understate the sea change in democratized image-making brought about by cellphones in the last decade. The early 2000s saw the earliest integrations of camera systems into cellphones as full color screens and data networks became available. The birth of smartphones in the middle of that decade then brought high-resolution screens, touch interfaces, mobile operating systems, capable processors and internet connections to devices whose previous, primary function was voice calling. The embedded camera offerings matured quickly after that. Today, camera systems are a staple hardware feature on every consumer smartphone and eschew traditional image processing workflows for mobile apps and instant upload to social media platforms.

The ubiquitous form factor of smartphones is that of a thin metal and glass slab with a few physical buttons on either side. This is radically different from any traditional camera design and presents serious challenges to designing an imaging system within it. Phone cameras are afforded extremely small footprints for compound lenses and image distances to the sensor. They feature very small sensor sizes, fixed apertures, electronic shutters and fixed focal lengths. The sensors can rival professional SLR megapixel counts but do so with smaller pixel pitches and therefore greatly diminished low light performance. LED flash units are often positioned near the primary imaging lens which often leads to red eye in portraits. Optical image stabilization is available on some; others opt for electronic image stabilization to minimize the impact of handshake (which is ever-present given the ergonomics). Phase detection and contrast detection may be used for autofocus. Since smartphones have computing demands beyond running the camera, processors and therefore image processing capabilities of phone cameras are very capable. Fortunately so, as some image quality shortcomings from these tiny imaging systems can be mitigated with image processing corrections.

Smartphones are permanent mobile computing fixtures in our modern lives. It's likely that the imaging capabilities of our devices will continue to grow in quality, complexity and features. Developing trends in this form factor include multi-camera arrangements (adding supplemental focal lengths, depth detection or otherwise specialized modules), miniaturized variable apertures and more. Truly, exciting developments in the mobile camera space are pushing the medium forward as *computational photography* leverages software to create previously unimaginable image assets with mobile hardware. It remains to be seen how imaging systems may be integrated into wearable computing like watches and smart glasses.

Action Cameras

A niche but notable category, *action cameras* are a class of ultraportable all-in-one imaging systems designed primarily for video capture with fixed focal lengths and remote tethering. These cameras feature a similar class of sensors used in smartphones and often use super wide-angle lenses or multiple sensor and lens combinations to extend the field of view to 180° or 360°. Action cameras come with a slew of waterproofing, stabilizing and mounting accessories in order to get cameras into places they were previously unable to access. While they are largely advertised for high-definition video recording, still photos (sometimes offering raw capture) can be of high enough resolution for professional output and reproduction. Action cameras are frequently mounted or built into drones and other remotely operated motion platforms.

We've listed the common form factor categories, a selection of which are shown in Figure 3-23 (overleaf). It's growing increasingly difficult to sort cameras into these discrete categories, however. For example, the Fujifilm GFX 50R houses a medium-format-sized sensor, uses a mirrorless imaging pathway and uses a compact body design reminiscent of a rangefinder.[13] Some camera manufacturers are leveraging the familiarity of smartphone interfaces and software, running mobile operating systems directly on dedicated camera hardware. The industry continues to evolve with a combination of technological advances and user preferences. Camera form factors are increasingly bolstered and reliant upon complex software with important integrations to our networks, remote workstations, cloud storage and social web platforms.

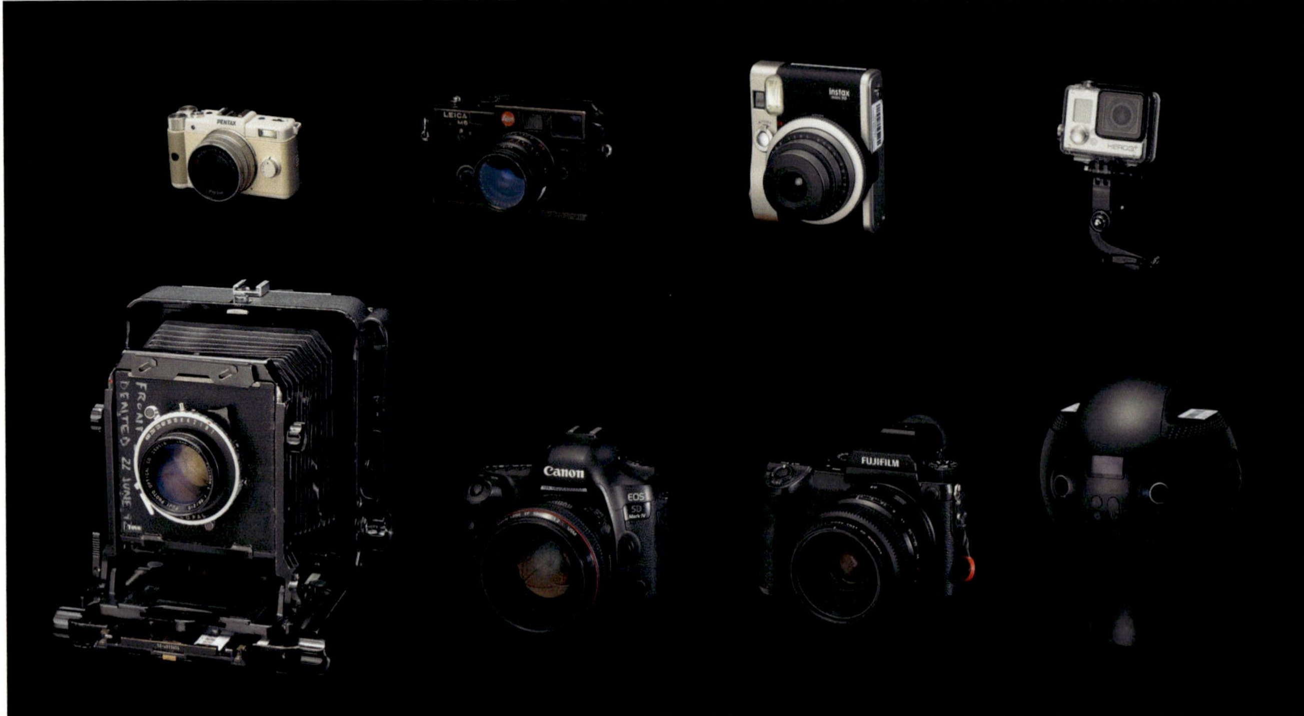

Figure 3-23 Camera technology comes in many shapes and sizes. Pictured along the top row from left to right: a compact camera with interchangeable lens capability, a rangefinder, an instant film camera and an action camera. Pictured along the bottom row is a 4x5 view camera, a full frame DSLR, a full frame medium format camera and a 360° stereoscopic camera. Photographs by Rochester Institute of Technology alumnus and Lecturer Dan Hughes

Camera Storage Media

Removable, solid state *flash memory* is the go-to in-camera capture storage solution. Every exposure must be stored, at least temporarily, into local memory before it is transferred to other storage media. Flash memory is ideal because it offers small form factors, quickly reads and writes digital information, has no moving parts and can be swapped out as needed. This is particularly welcome if you are old enough to recall the awkward growing phases of digital cameras that used floppy disks or compact discs as image file storage solutions built into the camera body. Some cameras today offer built-in flash memory storage for emergency use, though the capacities are rarely enough to get by for long without an additional memory card. A well-prepared photographer keeps a set of cards on-hand when shooting, protected from dust and debris in plastic cases or card wallets.

The two common camera storage flash memory formats are *CompactFlash* (CF) and *Secure Digital* (SD). Many proprietary, manufacturer-specific memory card formats have come and gone while SD and CF have withstood waves of technology evolutions and ever-increasing storage needs. Though market competition has whittled the options down to these two contenders, there's no shortage of variants, tiers and new generations of each. We recommend checking online for the latest numbers and product developments, buying the best you can afford for the work you'll be shooting in the near-term. It's a dizzying blend of spec bumps and marketing speak. A bit of research before purchasing ensures an educated purchase.

CompactFlash was developed by SanDisk in the mid-1990s along with the establishment of the CompactFlash Association. Versions of CF cards offering increasing read/write speeds add nomenclature like *Ultra* and *Extreme* to the product names. CF slots exist on a number of camera models available today and capacities top out around 512GB. Their read/write speeds are marketed in terms of an *Ultra Direct Memory Access* or UDMA rating; the higher the UDMA, the faster the card. The highest UDMA available is 7.[14] The XQD format, also created by SanDisk, was proposed in 2011 as a faster, non-backwards-compatible successor to CF with a smaller form factor.[15] Its use is supported in some Sony and Nikon camera systems.

Secure Digital cards are smaller than CompactFlash but offer similar storage sizes, read/write speeds and ubiquity in camera system support. The SD format was developed in the late 1990s by the SD Association, an organization formed by SanDisk, Toshiba and Panasonic.[16] The SD memory card format expanded over the years to include variations like SD High Capacity (SDHC), SD Extended Capacity (SDXC) and most recently, SD Ultra Capacity (SDUC). The largest capacity of an SDXC card is 2TB and SDUC expands that up to 128TB.[17] Iterative versions of SD cards offer faster read/write speeds for large raw files, increased rapid-capture frames per second and video recording. SD cards are also marketed with *Ultra High Speed* (UHS) ratings and classes that indicate minimum and maximum read/write speeds.[18] They use a video class ("V" class) label on cards specifically designed for handling high-resolution video recording. If you work with large raw files or rely on continuous shooting for fast-action events, research the latest versions of memory cards that are compatible with your camera as the advertised speeds may not be achievable with older camera models. The *microSD* card is an even smaller variant used for expandable storage for electronics like action cameras. The microSD form factor comes in the same flavors as its larger, standard SD form factor sibling.

Some professional cameras include multiple memory card slots, either of matching design (dual SD, for example) or mixing different card types (SD and CF). Camera firmware offers different configurations of the memory slots to further expand the total number of captures or to have one function as a mirrored backup of the other.

Reading and writing activity on a removable memory card is commonly indicated with an LED on the camera body. Never take a card out of the camera when it is actively reading or recording an image as it can corrupt the data or otherwise interrupt its processing. As mentioned earlier, any memory cards that reside outside of the camera should be stored in cases or sleeves to protect the metal contacts. Haphazardly handling the cards or throwing them in your lint-filled pocket alongside car keys is an excellent way to render the card unusable by your camera and card reader.

Writing camera captures to a memory card is short-term solution and truly the only convenient one when shooting in the field. Transferring them to desktop storage is accomplished using an external memory card reader or by connecting the camera to a computer via USB cable. Higher-end cameras offer ethernet connections to tether directly to a computer or network storage solution (ideal for studio shooting or a fully equipped field production) and offer the fastest transfer speeds. Cameras across all categories are increasingly including WiFi or Bluetooth connectivity to support file transfers to phones, tablets or laptops. These functions eliminate the steps of plugging a cable from the camera to a computer, or removing the memory card and inserting it into a wired card reader. However, your particular use-case should consider the data transfer rates of each to best serve your workflow: don't get caught waiting for huge raw files to download one at a time over a slow WiFi network, for example. We review storage options in Chapter 8.

Notes

1 Liles, Jonathan Moore. "X-Trans vs Bayer sensors: Fantastic claims and how to test them." *PetaPixel*, Mar. 3, 2017, petapixel.com/2017/03/03/x-trans-vs-bayer-sensors-fantastic-claims-test/.

2 Spring, Kenneth R., and Michael W. Davidson. "Concepts in digital imaging technology quantum efficiency." *Hamamatsu Learning Center: Avalanche Photodiodes*, hamamatsu.magnet.fsu.edu/articles/quantumefficiency.html.

3 "What is a CCD?" *What is a CCD? Charge Coupled Device*, Special Instruments Inc., www.specinst.com/What_Is_A_CCD.html.

4 "ON Semiconductor to acquire Truesense Imaging, Inc." *LM317T: 3-Terminal 1.5 A Positive Adjustable Voltage Regulator*, Apr. 2, 2014, www.onsemi.com/PowerSolutions/newsItem.do?article=3076.

5 "More information about color shading." DXO Labs, 2003, web.archive.org/web/20180503071520/https://www.dxo.com/us/more-information-about-color-shading.

6 DeVriere, Frederic. "Quantum efficiency advances sensors for night vision." *Photonics Media*, Photonics.com, Jan. 10, 2014, www.photonics.com/Articles/Quantum_Efficiency_Advances_Sensors_for_Night/a51008#Comments.

7 Sanyal, Rishi. "UPDATED: Sony's curved sensors may allow for simpler lenses and better images." *DPReview*, DPReview, July 7, 2014, www.dpreview.com/articles/6229436014/sony-s-curved-sensors-may-allow-for-simpler-lenses-and-better-images.

8 Courtland, Rachel. "Sony creates curved CMOS sensors that mimic the eye." *IEEE Spectrum: Technology, Engineering, and Science News*, IEEE Spectrum, June 12, 2014, spectrum.ieee.org/tech-talk/semiconductors/devices/sony-creates-curved-cmos-sensors-that-mimic-the-eye.

9 Guenter, Brian, et al. "Highly curved image sensors: A practical approach for improved optical performance." *Optics Express*, vol. 25, no. 12, 2017, p. 13010., doi:10.1364/oe.25.013010.

10 Reshidko, Dmitry and José Sasian. "Current trends in miniature camera lens technology." *SPIE Newsroom*, 2016, doi:10.1117/2.1201602.006327.

11 Modrak, Rebekah and Bill Anthes. *Reframing Photography: Theory and Practice*. Routledge, 2011, p. 64.

12 "Nikon introduces the new Nikon Z mount system, and releases two full-frame mirrorless cameras: The Nikon Z 7 and Nikon Z 6." *Nikonusa.com*, Aug. 23, 2018, www.nikonusa.com/en/about-nikon/press-room/press-release/jktu9ets/Nikon-Introduces-the-New-Nikon-Z-Mount-System%2C-and-Releases-Two-Full-Frame-Mirrorless-Cameras%3A-the-Nikon-Z-7-and-Nikon-Z-6-.html.

13 "FUJIFILM GFX 50R." *Fujifilm Value from Innovation*, www.fujifilm.com/products/digital_cameras/gfx/fujifilm_gfx_50r/.

14 "SanDisk CompactFlash read/write speeds and UDMA information." *SanDisk*, Aug. 21, 2014, kb.sandisk.com/app/answers/detail/a_id/31/~/sandisk-compactflash-read%2Fwrite-speeds-and-udma-informatio.

15 "The CompactFlash Association announces the recently adopted XQDTM specification as a new memory card format." *Compact Flash Association*, Dec. 7, 2011, www.compactflash.org/assets/docs/cfapress/xqd_111207.pdf.

16 "SD Association celebrates 10 years of innovation at CES 2010." *Hughsnews.ca*, Jan. 5, 2010, www.hughsnews.ca/sd-association-celebrates-10-years-00970.

17 Gaz, Bryan. "SD express SDUC memory cards will give you 985MB/s transfer speeds and 128TB of storage." *DPReview*, DPReview, June 29, 2018, www.dpreview.com/news/7847794311/sd-express-sduc-memory-cards-association.

18 "Difference between speed class, UHS speed class, speed ratings (performance) and video speed class for SD/SDHC/SDXC cards." *SanDisk*, Apr. 11, 2017, kb.sandisk.com/app/answers/detail/a_id/1996/~/difference-between-speed-class%2C-uhs-speed-class%2C-speed-ratings-%28performance%29.

4 Photographic Exposure

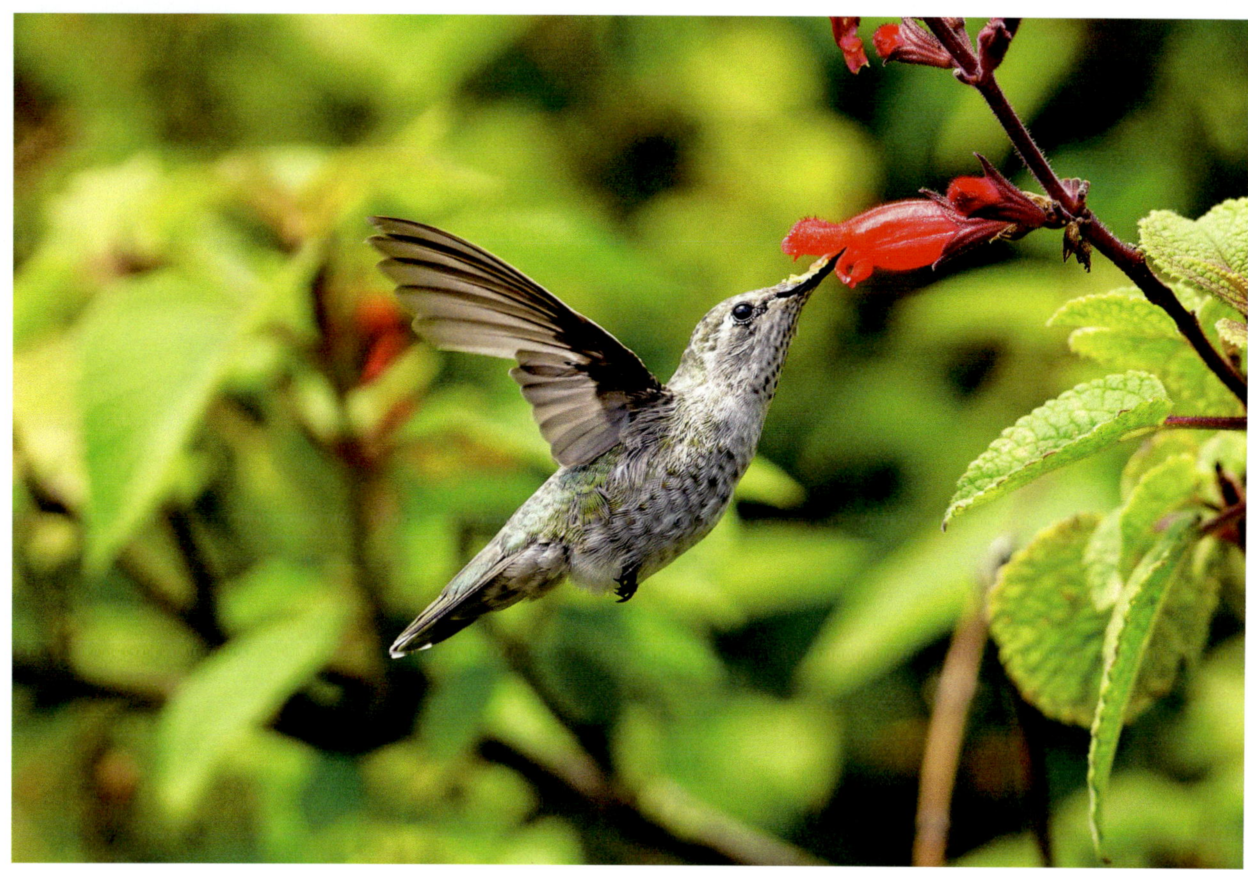
Photograph by Ruben Vargas

Photographers with a clear understanding of light, optics and camera components are primed to fully explore and master photographic exposure. We spend a considerable amount of time with cameras in hand chasing good light in the field and in the studio. We must be equally good at recording it as we are at finding it. This chapter fully explores what photographic exposure entails. This includes how exposure is calculated and how to work with the camera controls of shutter speed, aperture and ISO. It also requires a complete understanding of scene dynamic range, image histograms and light metering methods. It is both a technical topic and a constant creative puzzle that photographers are challenged to solve with every captured frame. The last section of this chapter offers a shooting exercise to test your understanding of exposure variables, metering and image quality tradeoffs by shooting bracketed exposures of a challenging nighttime scene.

Exposure Determination

First and foremost: exposure is not an acceptable form of payment from a potential client! More seriously, exposure is a combination of:

- *Light intensity* from the scene
- *Light volume* permitted through the lens aperture opening
- *Light duration* on the sensor dictated by the shutter opening
- The *sensitivity of light recording* via the sensor itself

A studio environment allows for complete control of a scene's light intensity while natural or uncontrolled environments leave the other three variables available for dictating a photographic exposure.

We've seen numerous attempts to draw diagrams explaining photographic exposure (search for "exposure triangle" online) that are more confusing than useful. So, we're keeping it simple. The amount of light, the time it's allowed to hit the sensor and the electronic configuration of that sensor must be assigned in harmony with one another based on light measured from the scene to achieve a proper exposure. Each of these variables presents its own trade space (in other words, pro's and con's) to weigh based on circumstance, aesthetics and sometimes simple personal preference.

There are two types of exposures to review. The first is *photographic exposure* (H) defined as the quantity of light per unit area reaching the sensor and is calculated by multiplying the *illuminance* (E) and the *exposure time* (t). Photographic exposure is expressed as $H = E \times t$. The second type is *camera exposure*, referring to the combination of shutter speed, f-number and ISO speed used to properly expose an image.

Photographers are primarily concerned with achieving the proper camera exposure (avoiding an overly dark or bright image). Proper camera exposure makes the most of the camera sensor's capabilities and renders the scene with visually pleasing tonality. We explore all of the components needed to achieve an optimal exposure over the next several sections.

Determining the correct exposure is done through light metering. The goal of metering light is to determine the average scene brightness to then determine the correct camera exposure. This is the basis of spot metering and is the basic camera metering approach. However, complex metering systems and software algorithms mean that there are many different ways to reach an opinion on optimal exposure. No matter the method of determination, proper exposure is just a planning step—configuring the camera and executing is what gets us recorded photographs.

Before going further, let's define the universal photographic exposure descriptor: the *stop*. A stop is one full step change in exposure. A one stop change equates to a halving or doubling of light relative to the original conditions. Stops are used to indicate changes in aperture, shutter speed, ISO and even flash output. The contributing factors might be a mix of any of those exposure parameters as long as the result is a full doubling or halving of light in the captured image. Camera exposure indicators in viewfinders typically show a scale or bracket with a pointer or needle. The center of this scale indicates the optimal photographic exposure as determined by the internal light meter. Any time that the pointer moves to the left or right of this center point is an indication that the exposure resulting from your current settings will yield an underexposed or overexposed frame, respectively. This scale is often marked with reference points to indicate whole stop increments of underexposure and overexposure.

Dictating Exposure Time with Shutter Speed

Shutter speed is a measure of the *exposure time* or the amount of time that light is collected by the sensor. DSLRs offer shutter speeds in increments as small as ⅓ stop and with ranges spanning from as quick as 1/8000th second to 30 seconds. Figure 4-1 lists the common whole stop shutter speeds, though many cameras allow for incrementing exposure in half, third and quarter stops between these settings. Exposure times longer than 30 seconds rely on the *bulb mode* where the photographer actively opens and closes the shutter and uses a handheld timer. Don't get too hung up on the term as it's a remnant of analog camera designs where the shutter was triggered by a shutter release cable. Early cables used a rubber bulb that used air pressure to physically depress the shutter button. The term persists even though the mechanics of initiating exposures longer than 30 seconds are different today.

Shutter speed selection dramatically impacts the final image if there are moving objects in the scene or when there is camera motion. Let's use a merry-go-round as an example. To get a picture of a child on the ride, we select a short shutter speed to stop the motion and have a sharp image of the entire merry-go-round and the child. To instead highlight the motion of the merry-go-round, we select a much slower shutter speed to introduce motion blur.

A second consideration when selecting shutter speed is equipment: are you hand holding the shot or is the camera mounted to a tripod? Additionally, what lens are you using? Hand holding a camera at too slow of a shutter speed often introduces blur in the image, as it is difficult to remain perfectly still during exposure. Here we turn to the *hand-held shutter speed rule of thumb*. It states that the minimum shutter speed to avoid camera shake and blur is found with the equation: *minimum handheld shutter speed* = 1/(*effective lens focal length*). We specify effective focal length as the lens focal length may need to consider a crop sensor's crop factor. As an example, this rule dictates that the minimum shutter speed for shooting handheld with a 500mm lens on a full frame camera is 1/500th of a second. Notice the inverse relationship between shutter speed and focal length. The minimal acceptable shutter speed increases as focal length increases. Using a crop sensor requires changing the equation to: *minimum handheld shutter speed* = 1/(*focal length* x *crop factor*). This rule of thumb helps to estimate the slowest shutter speed to safely use without risking handshake or blur. That said, lenses with built-in optical image stabilization help to lower the minimum handheld shutter speed. Refer back to the Image Stabilization section in Chapter 3 for more on this topic.

	ISO	f-number	Shutter Speed
More Exposure	102,400	1.4	1
↑	51200	2	1/2
	25600	2.8	1/4
	12800	4	1/8
	6400	5.6	1/15
	3200	8	1/60
	1600	11	1/125
	800	16	1/500
	400	22	1/1000
	200	32	1/2000
↓	100	45	1/4000
Less Exposure	50	64	1/8000

Figure 4-1 A reference scale of whole stop ISO, aperture and shutter speeds. Note that the three columns are not directly tied to one another.

A section on shutter speed would not be complete without providing a list of common whole stop increments of shutter speed: 1/1000s, 1/500s, 1/250s, 1/125s, 1/60s, 1/30s, 1/15s, 1/8s, 1/4s, 1/2s, 1s. Since one full stop change halves or doubles the exposure, additional shutter speeds in either direction are easily determined. Figure 4-2 shows a spinning black and white disc photographed with a sequence of shutter speeds, going from

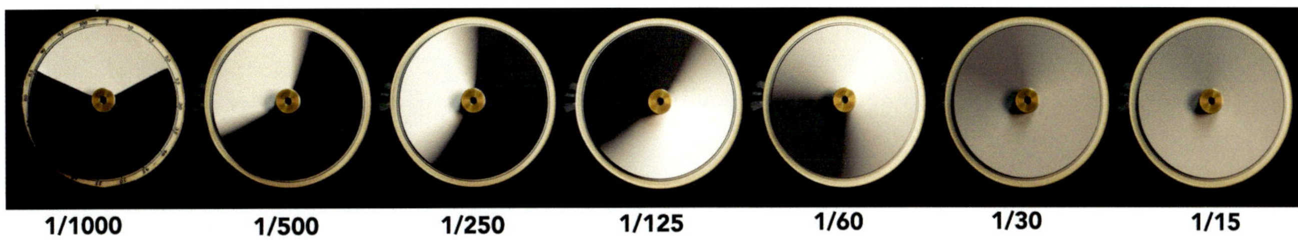

Figure 4-2 A spinning black and white disc photographed with decreasing shutter speeds.

fast to slow, as other exposure parameters are adjusted to compensate for the change in brightness. The portions of black to white are accurately depicted at 1/1000th of a second, as the short shutter speed captures the disc in motion.

Not all cameras have physical shutters. The exposure behavior whereby the sensor detects and records a light signal is described as the *integration time*. The photosites are controlled electronically to "turn on" and "turn off" such that they record incoming light exclusively during the time in between. Integration time is a function of time lapsed and can adhere to the same traditional set of speeds like 1/30s, 1/60s and so on. We can say that a smartphone camera exposure uses an integration time of 1/30s to accurately describe capture behavior of the shutterless system. This integration exposure process happens in rapid succession, over and over again when watching the live video preview in our camera app.

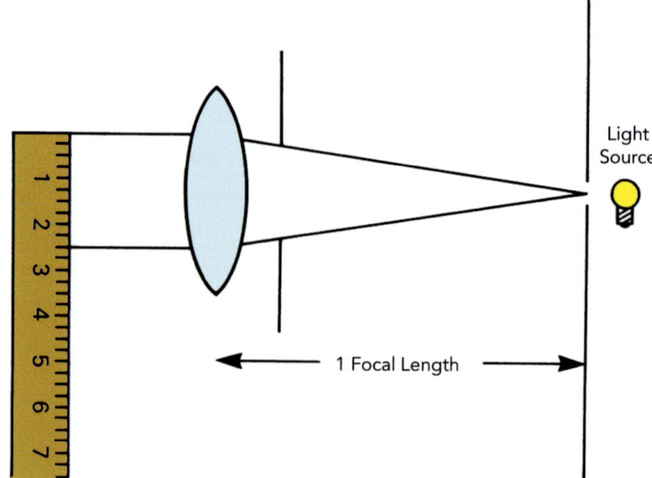

Figure 4-3 Determine the effective aperture by placing a point source of light one focal length behind the lens and measure the diameter of the beam of light that emerges from the front of the lens.

Dictating the Amount of Light with F-Number

Shutter speeds are easy to keep track of because they are described as a function of time. When setting the shutter speed to 2 seconds and then again to 1/30th second, you have a general, intuitive sense for how this change translates to a mechanical action. Aperture is not as intuitive but using the standard unit of exposure measurement, the stop, you can quickly become fluent in anticipating its influence on exposure.

Relative aperture or *aperture* are alternative names for *f-number*. The value of the relative aperture or f-number depends upon two things: the focal length of the lens and the *effective aperture*. The effective aperture is defined as the diameter of the entering beam of light that just fills the opening in the diaphragm of a camera lens or other optical system. The diameter of the opening in the diaphragm is known as the aperture. When the diaphragm is located in front of a lens, the effective aperture is found by measuring the diaphragm directly. Rarely is the diaphragm located in front of a photographic lens, so it's necessary to take into account how the light rays may change direction between the time they enter the lens and when they pass through the diaphragm opening.

F-numbers are calculated by dividing the lens focal length (f) by the effective aperture (D), or *f-number = f/D*. The effective aperture is rarely the same size as the aperture (the physical opening in the diaphragm); the diameter of the entering beam of light that just fills the diaphragm opening must be measured. One method to determine this diameter is to place a point source of light one focal length behind the lens so the diaphragm opening restricts the beam of light emerging from the front of the lens. This beam is the same size as an entering beam that just fills the diaphragm opening (see Figure 4-3). The diameter of a beam of light is measurable with a ruler in front of the lens.

This would be a quick calculation if all lenses featured fixed apertures. Instead, most lenses have a range of apertures to pick from when selecting photographic exposure. It's useful to know the series of f-numbers that represent whole stops changes: f/0.7, 1.0, 1.4, 2.0, 2.8, 4, 5.6, 8, 11, 16, 22, 32, 45, 64. The f-number series is extended in either direction by understanding that the factor for adjacent numbers is the square root of 2, or approximately 1.4. Also note that alternate f-numbers vary by a factor of 2, with a small adjustment between 5.6 and 11, and between 22 and 45, to compensate for the cumulative effect of fractional units.

Each time that the diaphragm is stopped down one stop (i.e. from f/8 to f/11), the amount of light reaching the sensor is cut in half (divided by 2) and the exposure time required to obtain the same photographic exposure is multiplied by 2. The aperture effectively dictates the light transmitting ability of an imaging system.

Recall that we explored depth of field and bokeh in Chapter 2. Selecting an f-number when determining camera exposure impacts the visual characteristics of the resulting capture. As the aperture gets smaller (increasing f-number), depth of field increases. Increasing the aperture size (decreasing f-number) decreases depth of field. Figure 4-4 illustrates the effect of shooting the same scene at either end of a lens' available f-number settings.

The amount of in-focus scene content (that which falls within the depth of field) is also codependent on sensor size. Smaller sensors like those found in point-and-shoot and smartphone cameras have some of the smallest sensors used for photography. Photographs made with these sensors have particularly large depth of field, rendering most, if not all, of the scene in sharp focus. This is great for avoiding out-of-focus portraits and not so great when you're going for that classic cinematic look with extremely shallow depth of field. Since this characteristic is inherent to small sensors due to geometric optics principles, clever software workarounds exist to simulate the effect. Artificial blurring of the background is possible either through edge detection (blurring anything that the algorithm thinks is surrounding environment) or advanced computer vision. This approach is called *synthetic depth of field* or *synthetic aperture* effects.

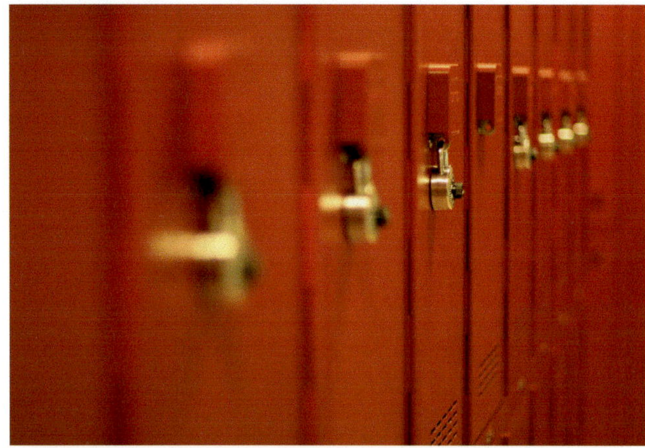

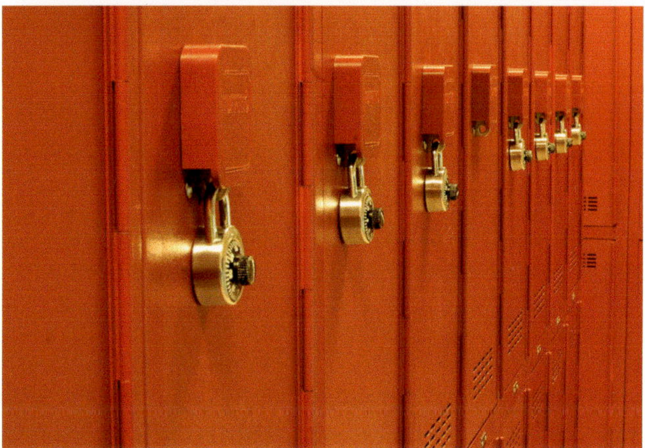

Figure 4-4 The depth of field at f/1.4 (top) compared to f/22 (bottom) with focus position kept constant. Photographs by Rochester Institute of Technology photography alumni Jonathan Damian and Nathan Pallace

Lens Speed

Lastly, a lens' range of available aperture settings is commonly used to describe it with shorthand terminology. Some lenses are described as "fast" and others, "slow." A lens capable of opening wide to an f-number such as f/1.4 or f/2.0 is a fast lens because the wider the opening, the more light available for exposure and the shorter the possible shutter speed. Not all lens designs offer aperture settings this wide, especially as the focal length increases. Zoom lenses often have different maximum aperture widths depending on the variable focal length used. Slow lenses may be limited, for example, to a maximum opening of f/4.0 or f/5.6. This requires slower shutter speeds (multiple stops-worth) to achieve proper exposure. A lens does not need to be fast to be a valuable asset in the photographer's bag, it simply offers additional flexibility for adjusting exposure settings.

Dictating Effective Sensitivity with Gain and ISO

The third parameter for setting exposure is *ISO*, also known as the *sensor speed*. ISO is an acronym for the International Standards Organization, though that's not particularly descriptive in this context. The term speed comes from the characteristic we mentioned describing lens apertures: the "faster" the speed of a sensor, the less time it takes to record a proper photographic exposure. ISO is a standardized industry scale for measuring sensitivity or response to light. This definition might lead to a misunderstanding of camera ISO. Every camera has a *base* or *native* ISO, somewhere between ISO 50 and ISO 200. Thus, ISO is a measure of the sensor's sensitivity to light. So why do cameras have many ISO settings, ranging from 50 to 102,400 and beyond?

Image noise must be better understood before answering this question. There are several types of noise that occur in a camera system. The visual result of all noise is the same: random brightness or color variance in the image. Noise is an image artifact and degrades image quality. The best quality image is one captured when shooting at the camera's base ISO. Chapter 11 unpacks the surprisingly varied forms of image noise. The important takeaway here is that excessive noise should be avoided when setting photographic exposure.

Doubling the ISO or speed increases exposure by one stop. Cameras offer many ISO settings to pick from, ranging from the base ISO (100 or 200) to over 102,400 depending on the model (see Figure 4-5). A common misconception is that changing the ISO alters the sensitivity of the camera to light. This is not the case. Changing the ISO changes the *gain* applied to the electrical signal. The amount of gain dictates the degree of amplification of the original recorded voltages read off of the sensor's photodiodes. This amplification translates to brighter pixel values overall, however, it amplifies any random, non-image forming signal at the same time. Keep in mind that noise is present in all images even when using the sensor's native ISO. Setting a higher ISO to create a desired photographic exposure means adding additional gain to the incoming photon signal. An image may be unusable after a certain degree of signal amplification due to the distracting visual quality of noise.

Some cameras come with "low" or "high" settings that allow for going above or below the native ISO range on the camera, suspiciously forgoing the use of an ISO number. These settings are software simulated speed changes and are likely to result in poor image quality.

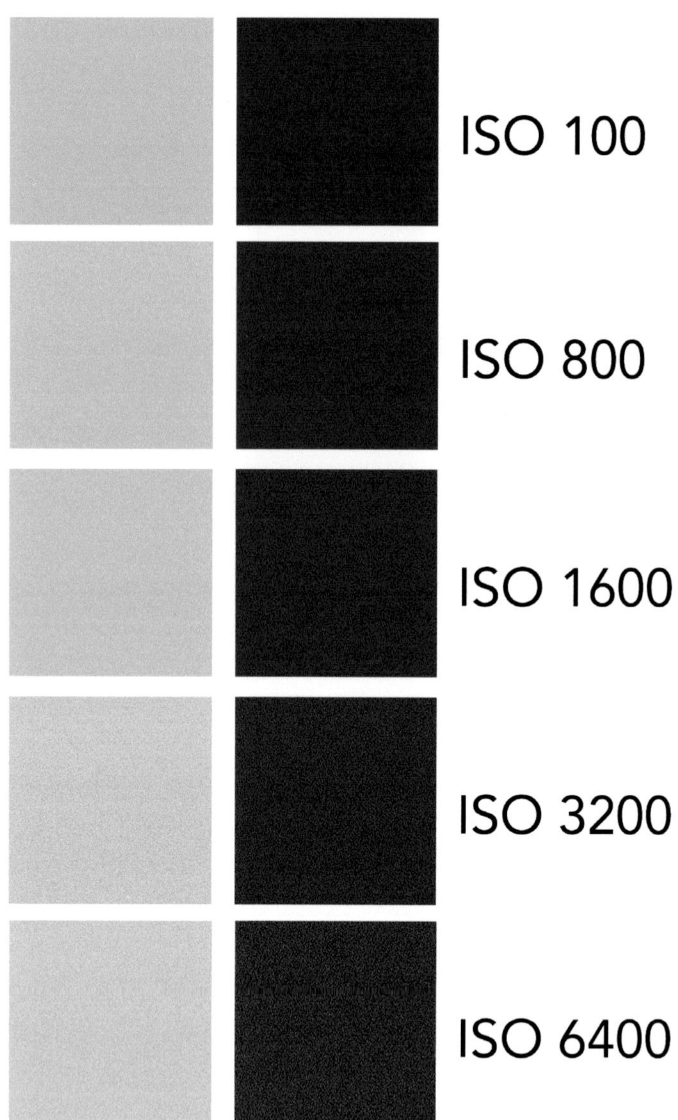

Figure 4-5 A sequence of equivalent exposures of gray and black targets at increasing ISO settings. Image noise increases with higher ISOs, most often becoming visually apparent in dark shadows.

Avoid these settings, as skillful post-processing of an underexposed or overexposed raw file offers superior results.

When possible, use the lowest ISO available. However, ISO is one of the three settings available when setting exposure and should be leveraged when other settings are fixed for one reason or another.

Exposure and Dynamic Range

The term *dynamic range* is used for both capture and output in photography. In this section, we'll stick within the context of photographic exposure. The *sensor dynamic range* is the maximum recordable difference between the brightest and darkest areas of detail. It can be stated as a ratio of light contrast or as the number of stops.

We derive a begrudging appreciation for the range of brightnesses in our world any time we've woken up in the middle of the night to a dark bedroom only to shuffle into the bathroom and flip on the lights. Even though the darkness isn't anywhere near pitch black, nor is the bathroom lighting as extremely bright as the sun, our eyes can't handle the wide range of light values to see in both environments in quick succession. The natural world offers a massive range of luminance from one moment or environment to the next. This is a challenge for photographic exposure because the *scene dynamic range* is potentially greater or wider than the sensor's ability to record in a single instant. While we don't always photograph scenes with dramatically varying brightnesses (also called the *scene luminance ratio*), we need a sensor that keeps up for the times that we do. Sometimes a simple scene leads to lost detail at capture due to bright reflections or dark, light absorbing fabrics. Areas with detail in extreme highlight or extreme shadow are captured as white or black respectively when the scene dynamic range is greater than the sensor's dynamic range.

A sensor photosite's bit depth indicates the range of brightnesses it can record. Consider a photosite like a drinking glass and the photons like drops of water filling it. Once filled, there's no room to hold additional water. A photosite's maximum photon-holding capacity defines the brightest incoming exposure it records before losing detail. This tells us something about the upper limit of the sensor's dynamic range. The lower limit is the *black level* or the darkest possible detail recorded sans noise. Although the sensor photosite's bit depth can indicate the senor's dynamic range it is not always completely accurate. The bit depth does not take into consideration other factors that may further lower a camera's dynamic range such as scene reflections and lens flare.

Dynamic range is described as a ratio such as 1,000:1. Photographers find it useful to measure it in terms of exposure stops since it relates directly to camera settings. The human eye perceives a range of brightnesses upwards of 24 stops. A sensor typically records about 12 stops. It's not a fair fight when you recognize the eye's ability to rapidly modulate incoming light via the pupil and that the retina uses two mechanisms for seeing (one for bright, one for dark scenes) while the camera sensor only has one type of photosite. Sensor technology continues to evolve and perhaps it will someday match the biological evolution of our visual system. For now, a single capture with an image sensor represents a more limited dynamic range recording capability.

We measure scene dynamic range by taking lux readings in the brightest highlight area and the darkest shadows. The difference between the readings, in stops, defines the contrast ratio. We always want our camera's dynamic range to be at least as large as our scene dynamic range so as not to lose detail in either the highlights or shadows. When the scene's dynamic range is larger, we make adjustments such as adding a reflector, fill lighting or using high dynamic range imaging techniques. Alternatively, we choose an exposure that strikes a reasonable balance or prioritizes a subject or scene element over others. Figure 4-6 (overleaf) shows a typical outdoor scene where foreground elements in shade represent different light levels compared to areas of deep shadow and the bright sunny sky. Our eyes concurrently saw clouds with detail and foliage in the dark bushes, yet our camera could not capture the full dynamic range in a single exposed photograph. Capturing a proper exposure for the foreground tree proved the most important given the composition and intent.

When the camera's dynamic range exceeds that of the scene, we're afforded some *exposure latitude*. Exposure latitude is the difference between camera dynamic range and scene dynamic range expressed in stops and it allows for wiggle room in getting capture exposure just right. It is also defined as the range over which the exposure can be increased and decreased from the correct or optimal exposure and still produce acceptable results.

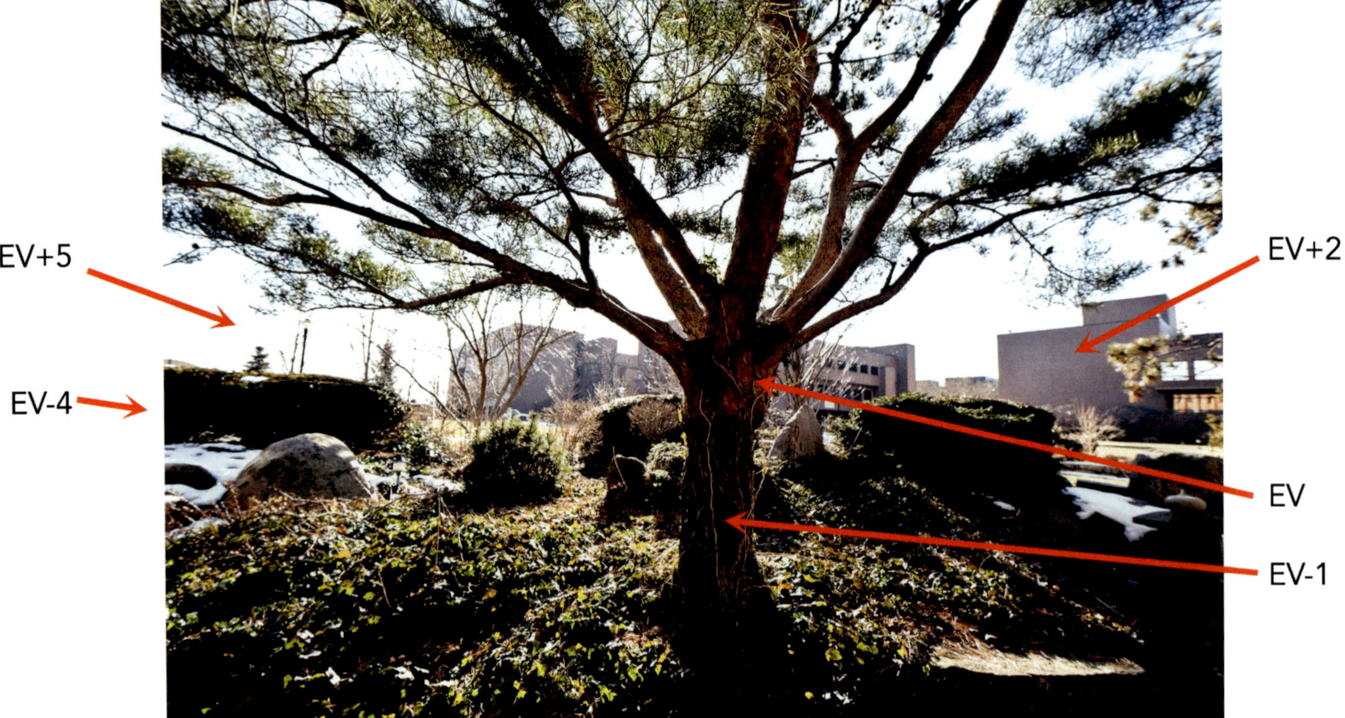

Figure 4-6 Ratios of dark to light in different environments can be extreme, though our eyes are capable of helping us see well in most of them. The camera is more limited in its ability to record such brightness ratios.

As exposure is decreased from the optimum level, called *underexposure*, the darker areas or shadows of the scene first lose contrast and then detail. If we continue to reduce the exposure, detail is lost in progressively lighter areas of the scene and eventually there is no image detail even in the lightest areas or highlights of the scene.

Taking the process in the opposite direction increasing the exposure and *overexposing* the images, the first noticeable change is commonly an increase in shadow contrast (and therefore an increase in overall contrast). Overexposure also produces a decrease in image definition and as we continue to increase exposure, image contrast decreases, first in the highlight areas and then toward progressively darker areas of the scene.

Blooming

Recall that photosites are wells that catch photons and convert them into voltages. Using the analogy of a photosite being akin to a glass filling with water, what happens when the glass fills up before the faucet is turned off? Similar to liquid overflowing, overexposure causes photons to spill out from the photosite well and into neighboring photosites. This is called *blooming* and it occurs when a photosite cannot hold all of the electrical energy it's receiving. Any photons reaching the photosite past this saturation point spills or leaks over. Not only does this mean we're missing out on light information (a fully saturated photosite means clipped highlights), but its effect cascades. When one photosite overflows, the excess spills into its neighbors, who then also overflow more quickly. Blooming occurs most commonly when a particularly bright part of an image (like the sun in the sky) is causing a subset of photosites to overfill. Blooming appears as bright halos on object edges or linear streaks of brightness across

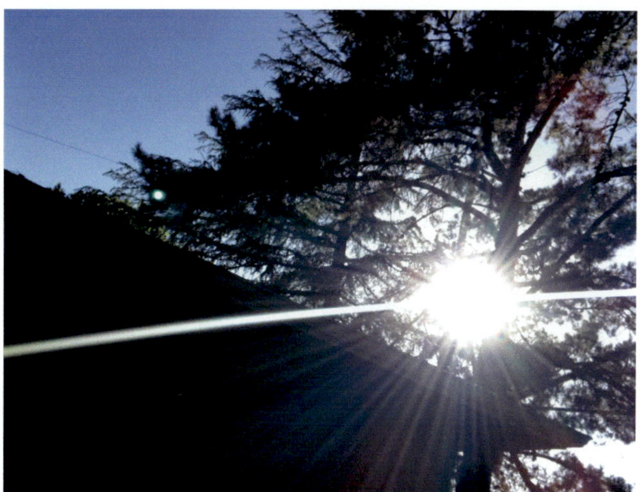

Figure 4-7 Blooming results when photosites receive more photons than they can handle.

the image. Figure 4-7 is an example of blooming mixed with flare from having the sun in the frame.

The Utility of Image Histograms

A *frequency histogram* is a graph that helps visualize the frequency with which some countable quality or event occurs. When listening to a boring lecture, you may idly mark the number of times the speaker says "um," "uh" or "like" in the margins of a notebook. Each time there's an "um," you add a tick mark in that column. At the end of the lecture, you plot the distracting nervous crutches with the x-axis containing all the different filler words and the y-axis indicating how often they were used. This is an example of a frequency histogram. It's also a great way to distract yourself from actually learning something from the lecture (which we do not recommend).

Knowing the frequency of pixel brightnesses in an image is helpful to visualize proper exposure and therefore making a frequency histogram a logical choice for visualizing captured image data. Most digital cameras provide an on-camera histogram so that you don't have to dust off your spreadsheet software. The on-camera histogram is valuable for checking proper exposure immediately after capture and before it's too late to try again. Taking advantage of the histogram plot to perfectly nail exposure requires us to quickly interpret its insights.

An *image histogram* plots the frequency of tones in an image based on scene luminosity. In other words, you're likely to find a *luminosity histogram* unless it's specifically made clear that it's a *color channel histogram* (typically visualized as overlapping red, green and blue channel data). Checking the histogram helps to check that the scene is properly exposed and includes a logical range of brightnesses.

An image histogram is a breakdown of the image's tonal scale and the frequency of pixels at a given tone value (see Figure 4-8). While no two captured

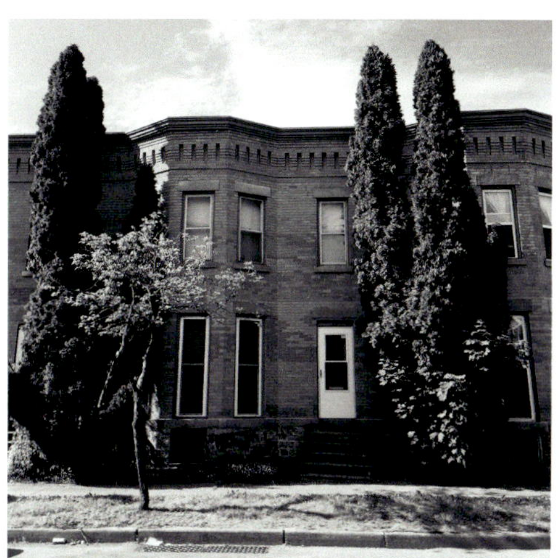

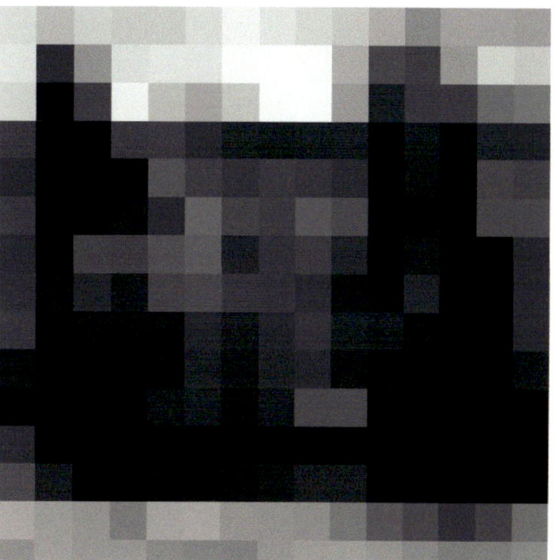

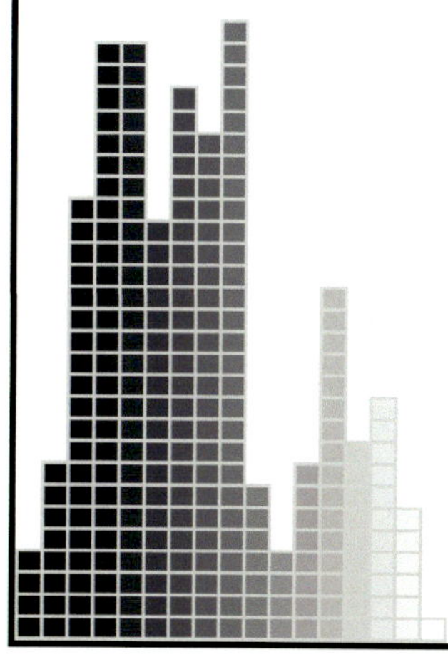

Figure 4-8 A black and white image (left) simplified to a much smaller collection of pixels (middle). Each pixel describes a brightness value. Reorganizing these pixels by brightness and stacking all same-toned pixels yields a basic frequency histogram (right). It's impossible to interpret from the histogram alone that it's an image of a building and trees.

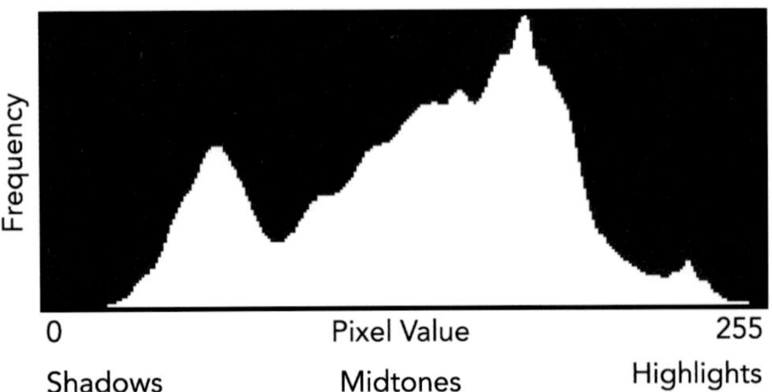

Figure 4-9 A frequency histogram of image pixel values ranging from 0 to 255.

photographs are likely to ever be identical, it is possible to have two images with the same histogram. Think of it like assembling a popular children's toy of interlocking plastic bricks: you can make the model shown on the box with the included pieces or make something entirely different from that same set. Both constructions have, say, 20 red bricks, but they're not going to be used in the same location or in the same arrangement. The same is true for a photograph: it's tempting to think of a histogram like an image's fingerprint, however, its lack of spatial information means it's not a complete encapsulation of the final product.

Let's review the image histogram shown in Figure 4-9. The x-axis plots the brightness levels. This is sometimes labeled *pixel value*, as pixel values are the brightness levels in the image. This particular histogram's x-axis spans from 0 to 255, the range of brightness levels available in an 8-bit JPEG image. All image histograms go from the darkest to the brightest possible pixel values; higher bit depth files see the maximum value increase. The y-axis of a histogram is *frequency*. This is a count of how many pixels exist at each brightness level. It's helpful to consider the histogram in three pieces: the left third represents the shadow information from solid black to a dark gray. The center third represents the midtone information, all middle shades of gray. The right third of the histogram represents highlight information from light gray to pure white. There is no absolute boundary between each of these, as one person's bright shadow tone is another person's dark midtone. Keeping these three general areas in mind makes it easier to interpret photographic exposure.

Taken as a whole, the histogram reveals an image's tonal range. Many photographers characterize the shape of an image's histogram as reminiscent of a mountain range in silhouette (blame those unimaginative landscape photographers).

We can alternatively generate a histogram to show the pixel colors at each brightness level. Figure 4-10 shows an example of such a histogram: the image pixels are rearranged by brightness while retaining their color. We can see how a majority of the green grass pixels are midtones and the blue sky ranges from midtone to bright highlights. Most pixels in the scene are green, second up is blue, followed by some grays and browns in the bench and walking path. Unlike a traditional luminosity histogram, this histogram contains all of the pixels in the original image file. The only difference is their organization.

Histogram Interpretation

A histogram represents a scene's tonal range ranging from black (digital count: 0) to white (digital count: 255) for an 8-bit image. A quick glance at an in-camera histogram easily reveals overexposure or underexposure when we understand that the leftmost edge of the histogram records absolute black, the right side absolute white. Data recorded at these extreme ends has no opportunity for variation or differences considered to be recorded detail. When a histogram shows pixels stacked up against these edges, that suggests its shape (representing the scene's tonal range) would have continued had it not been cut off at value 0 or 255—highlight or shadow details are lost. This characteristic is called *clipping*, where detail is clipped or abruptly cut to the point of being irreversibly lost. Additionally, the term *crushed* specifically refers to underexposure and clipped shadow detail. Camera previews include a clipping warning that overlays a blinking color or alternating black and white pattern to indicate clipped or crushed areas of the scene. Desktop software offers similar visual feedback to easily identify when image edits have introduced clipped highlights or shadows for which some data existed in the original exposure. A small amount of clipping is common and not an automatic

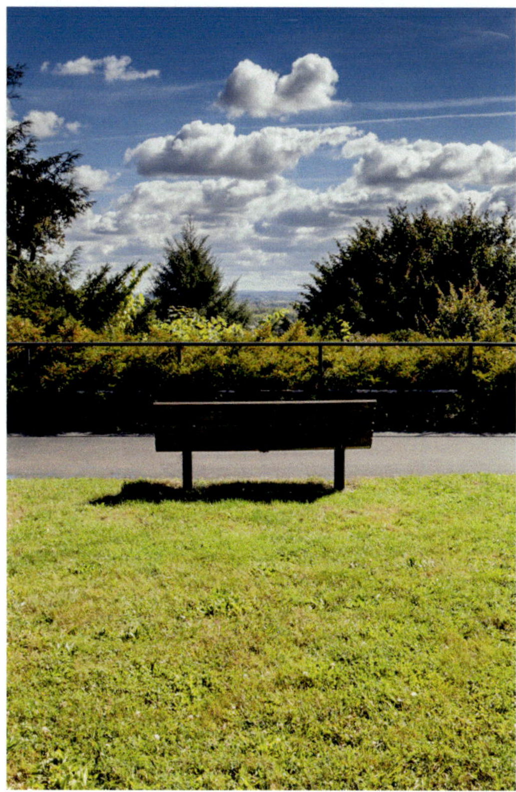
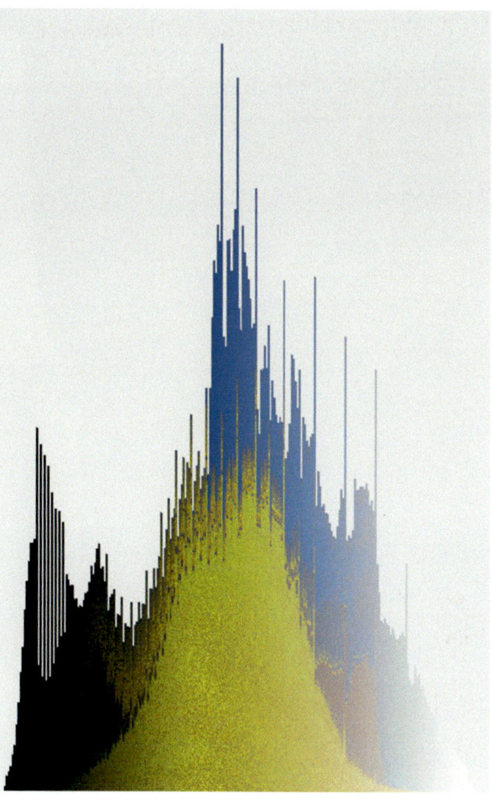

Figure 4-10 A image histogram can be arranged by luminance frequency and plotted using the pixel colors at each of those brightness values. This histogram was generated using a web-based tool called Pixel Chart.[1]

indication of poor camera exposure. A large amount can suggest that a different exposure would capture more scene information.

In addition to overexposure and underexposure, the tonal range plot gives a sense of scene contrast and dynamic range. Figure 4-11 (overleaf) showcases varied examples. We expect that, in an average scene, the histogram clumps toward the center (midtone) region of the plot. Unless it's a high key scene of a white rabbit in the snow, the presence of bright highlights and dark shadows is generally outweighed by middle-gray subject reflectance. A histogram with clumps or peaks at either end of the histogram and a valley in the center is a high contrast scene because it has a relatively large amount of very dark and very bright pixels. A low contrast scene looks like a single pile or peak near the center that tapers off on either end. This indicates that most of its pixels have similar luminances rendered as midtones. A wide histogram with some amount of pixel frequency across the whole range of 0 to 255 indicates a wide dynamic range: a scene containing tones of dark black, bright white and everything in between. A low dynamic range scene appears as a narrow histogram that tapers off well before reaching either end of the plot. While these characteristics may be inherent to the scene, it's useful to identify, for example, if your studio lighting is overly flat and failing to generate intensely bright highlights.

It's valuable to point out that the y-axis of a histogram, representing pixel frequency, is nearly always scaled to the data. This means that two images can show high frequency peaks around the same pixel value—approaching the top edge of the plot—yet have a different number of pixels at that value. The y-axis is scaled depending on the data for readability.

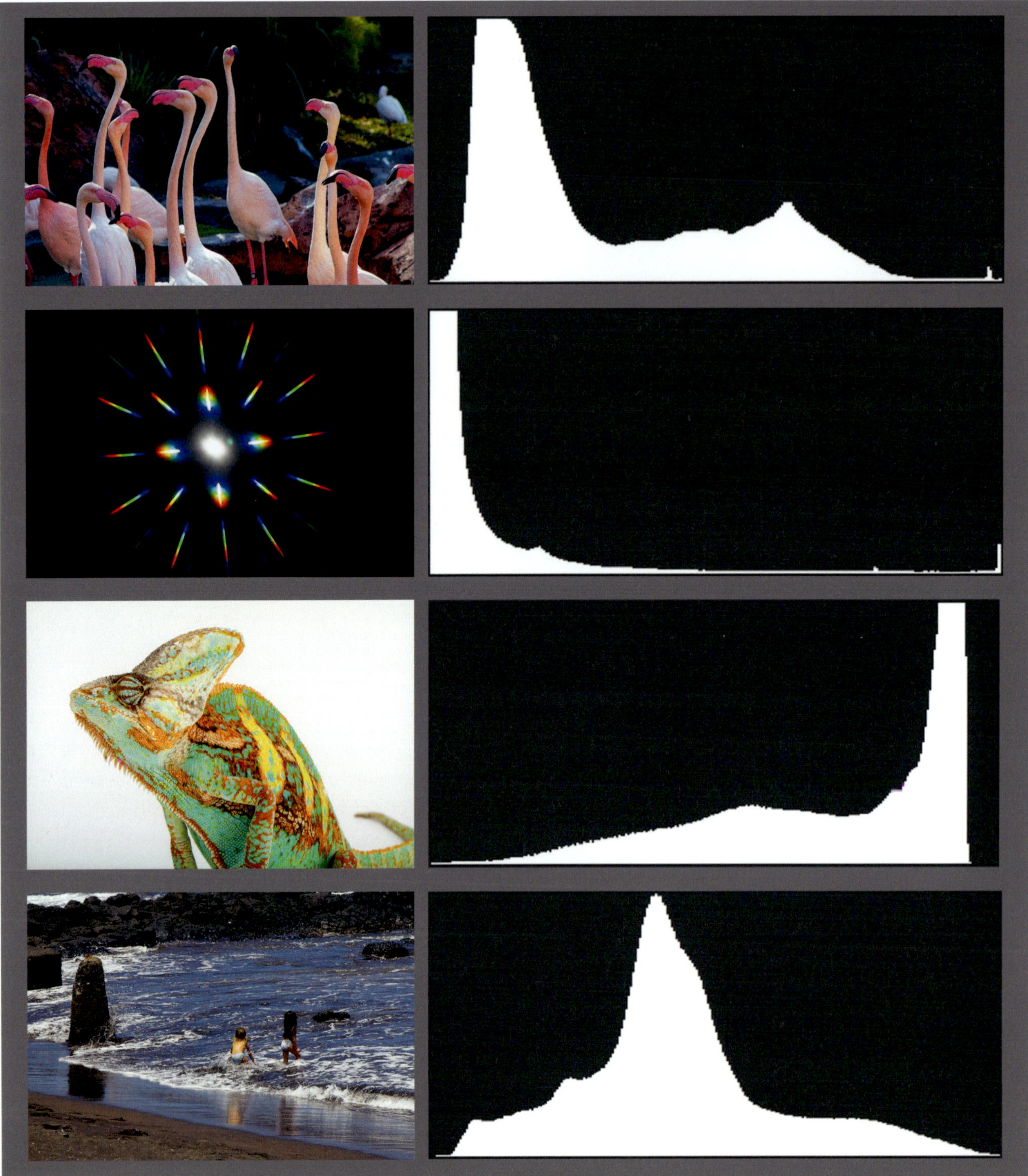

Figure 4-11 Image histograms reflect the range of pixel values that comprise the scene and their shape is dependent on the image content. These images have different histograms that indicate variations in contrast, the range of tones and even the dominant brightness value.

In-Camera versus Desktop Software Histograms

An image histogram can look different when viewed in-camera compared to the histogram generated by Adobe Photoshop or Capture One Pro even when shooting raw. Why does this discrepancy exist? A raw image must be processed through a demosaicing algorithm to produce a full color image. We address demosaicing in Chapter 9; for now, let's accept that there are different algorithms and methods for doing so. The resulting histograms are different due to the different image processing decisions made.

The histogram viewed on the camera is a histogram representing a processed JPEG interpretation of the raw image content. Again, each camera manufacturer uses their own algorithm for this step which is most likely different than the desktop software companies, therefore a difference may exist. The only foolproof way of knowing what your image data histogram consists of requires loading the files into desktop editing software.

Image histograms play a pivotal role in post processing techniques. We revisit them in Chapter 9 to ensure that the hard work of properly exposing at capture is not undermined by haphazard editing decisions.

Exposure Value

Similar to the concept of stops, *exposure value*, or EV, is a measure of exposure that's used as a shorthand when adjusting exposure settings. EV is defined by Equation 4.1 where N is the f-number and t is the shutter speed in seconds.

$$EV = Log_2 \frac{N^2}{t} \qquad \text{(Eq. 4.1)}$$

A camera exposure setting combination of f/11 at 1/15th second yields an EV of 11. The same EV is achieved using f/8 at 1/30th second. Altering the first combination to f/11 at 1/30th second changes the EV to 12. Changing shutter speed from 1/15th to 1/30th second is a one stop change in photographic exposure. The exposure value calculation shows this same change equating to a change in EV of 1.

Exposure value is a useful metric for describing exposure changes that are easily translated to stops. EV is often used in exposure bracketing notation, discussing flash compensation and measuring lighting ratios. Many light and flash meters can measure in EV.

Equivalent Exposure

So far, we've laid out the adjustable parameters for setting photographic exposure and how to evaluate histograms for optimal image capture. Shutter speeds, apertures and ISO are used to gather the necessary amount of light to form a well-exposed photograph. We've elaborated on each of these parameters because there's a great deal of subjective and interpretive control involved in setting them: there's more than one solution to satisfy the goal of optimal photographic exposure. The concept of *equivalent exposure* means recording the same amount of light using different combinations of photographic exposure controls.

Table 4-1 demonstrates how six unique captures of the same scene are made using equivalent exposures. We determined Image A's exposure using a handheld light meter and confirmed optimal exposure by checking the resulting image histogram. This baseline exposure (referred to in shorthand as simply "EV") is 1/60s at f/5.6 and ISO 800. Hypothetically, we're interested in increasing our shutter speed to better freeze motion in the scene. Changing the shutter speed to 1/125s accomplishes this, however, exclusively changing the shutter

Table 4-1 Examples of equivalent exposures using different combinations of camera controls.

Image	ISO	f-number	Shutter Speed
A (EV)	800	5.6	1/60
B	800	4	1/125
C	800	8	1/30
D	1600	8	1/60
E	1600	16	1/15
F	1600	5.6	1/125

speed parameter means underexposing the scene by one full stop (EV-1). This change is compensated or balanced by opening up the aperture one full stop to f/4.0. The resulting exposure of Image B is equivalent to Image A in brightness because we've maintained equivalent photographic exposure. Equivalent exposures are all about balancing the equation of adding and subtracting exposure and is easily managed using stops as the metric.

Looking again at Table 4-1, Images B through F yield photographic exposures with the same overall brightness as our baseline photo, though they differ in other ways. Image E, for example, becomes noisier than Image A as a result of a higher ISO; it shows considerably more depth of field and may require the use of a tripod due to its long shutter speed. Alternatively, Image B is a good option if the subject is on a single focal plane and the background is distracting. It also doesn't require having a tripod handy.

This technique is further extended for considering overexposure or underexposure bracketed frames. Using Image A again as the baseline exposure, imagine that you're looking to capture one frame that's very overexposed (EV+3) and another that's equally underexposed (EV-3) to record highlight and shadow information beyond what the sensor's dynamic range can capture in the baseline exposure. Here, the goal isn't to formulate an equivalent exposure but one that is specifically three full stops over or under relative to Image A. For the overexposed frame, we can increase ISO three stops or perhaps leave ISO the same; opening the aperture one stop and slowing the shutter speed by two stops nets an exposure of EV+3. The key is to consider the starting point and how changes to the three exposure parameters impact exposure relative to it. It's best to alter shutter speed over the other two variables, when possible, as it is less likely to introduce visual differences (noise, differences in depth of field) between the bracketed frames.

The Image Capture/Exposure Sequence

In order to highlight features like autofocus and auto exposure in this chapter, it's helpful to take a bird's eye view of the *image processing pipeline*, the path and processes our photograph undergoes before, during and after pressing the capture button. A generic pipeline looks like this:

1. Clear voltages from photosites
2. Open shutter or turn on photosites
3. Read out voltages
4. Amplify voltages
5. Analog to digital conversion from voltages to bits
6. Store bits in temporary random access memory buffer
7. Transfer and store bits to storage medium.

Note that all of the these events take place in the camera. Photographers use the term *processing* to describe making changes to image data, though they're usually concerned with *post-processing* that happens off-camera (discussed in Sections 2 and 3). Here we're talking about the digital churnings of onboard components to formalize a raw digital image stored to memory.

A camera's image processing pipeline may include additional steps between the analog to digital conversion and storage that introduce post-processing changes. Setting a camera to shoot in JPEG, for example, implicitly appends the image processing pipeline with post-processing adjustments to the raw image to make it aesthetically pleasing. This is because a JPEG is assumed to be a finished, fully cooked image product with enhancements to tone, color and sharpness and other characteristics. Surprisingly, setting a camera to shoot in the raw format does not exempt us from seeing automatic post-processing decisions to our image; the preview on the camera's playback screen is an enhanced JPEG derived from the raw data. It's easier for our cameras to do a little hard work up front in interpreting and enhancing a version of the complex raw data and showing us the fruits of its labor any time thereafter when reviewing what we've shot. This means that we only see a version of what the raw image could look like, subject to the camera's onboard automatic post-processing decisions.

When a camera uses live preview or digital viewfinder, a version of an image processing pipeline happens continuously on the device. This is the case when taking photographs on a smartphone; the display shows a near-instantaneous, processed feed of images as they're recorded (though not permanently saved) by the camera module. Expediting the image processing pipeline to allow for this incredibly fast translation from light detection to processed image is made possible by a *system-on-chip* (SoC) image processor. The SoC lives in the camera or phone hardware and is dedicated to the task of real-time image processing from the image sensor. Feedback about exposure, focus and color balance is generated as the image data works its way through algorithms immediately following their analog to digital conversion. This information is piped back to the sensor controller to make adjustments for the next exposure, over and over until a photograph is taken by the user.

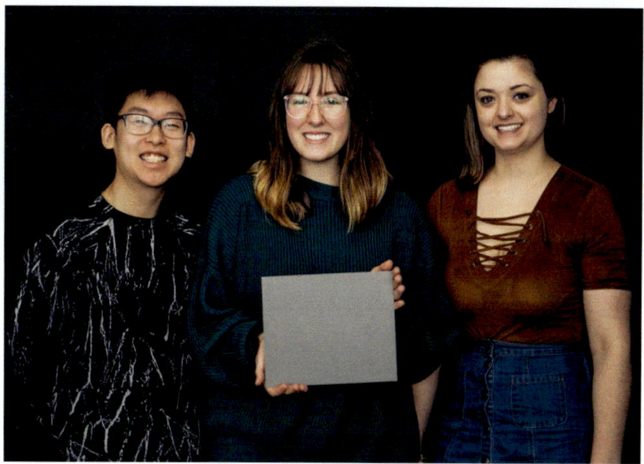

Figure 4-12 Shooting a gray card in the scene as a test frame helps to evaluate exposure at capture. It should not appear clipped (too bright) or approach black (too dark) if it represents the average scene luminance. Photograph by Rochester Institute of Technology photography student Daniel Lemaster

Using a Neutral Reference Target

An *18% gray card* is a uniform target of midtone gray, or a perfect neutral midpoint between black and white. Its *visible light reflectance* is 18%. Achieving a proper exposure is easy using an exposure meter and a normal scene with an average midtone gray tonality, or a reflectance of 18%. The exposure meter is calibrated to this same reflectance and identifies the exposure settings required to record it on the sensor. When a scene's average reflectance is darker or lighter than this, following the exposure meter reading leads to overexposure or underexposure, respectively. A logical strategy, then, is to include a reference target consistent with the exposure meter's calibrated expectations. A neutral target with an 18% reflectance is placed in the scene and metered to avoid exposure errors as demonstrated in Figure 4-12.

The ColorChecker used by photographers includes an 18% gray patch: the fourth patch on the last row. Using a ColorChecker to determine exposure is possible with spot metering and is additionally useful as reference for adjusting white balance in editing software. The target's neutrality makes it valuable for identifying color casts in addition to its light reflectance properties.

In-Camera Exposure Metering

We showed how a camera internally takes light meter readings in the previous chapter. We described the hardware components that make it possible but not the software logic behind its operation. Since the camera is capable of taking multiple readings, continuous readings, or readings from different locations in the frame, it opens up possibilities for many different methods for metering. *Through the lens* (TTL) metering uses a light meter somewhere in the pentaprism or below the mirror assembly in the camera to instantly read the light level entering the camera. This approach is advantageous because it's metering the light after it passed through the camera lens and any filters or optical elements introduced in the imaging path. The result is an accurate measurement of the light near the point where it is detected by the sensor. In short, it provides a meter reading that fully considers the impact of everything between the subject and the sensor. TTL metering is what makes all the fully automatic or partial automatic shooting modes function properly. There are many manufacturer specific variations of TTL metering available, though they are generally one of three basic types: matrix, center-weighted and spot. Figure 4-13

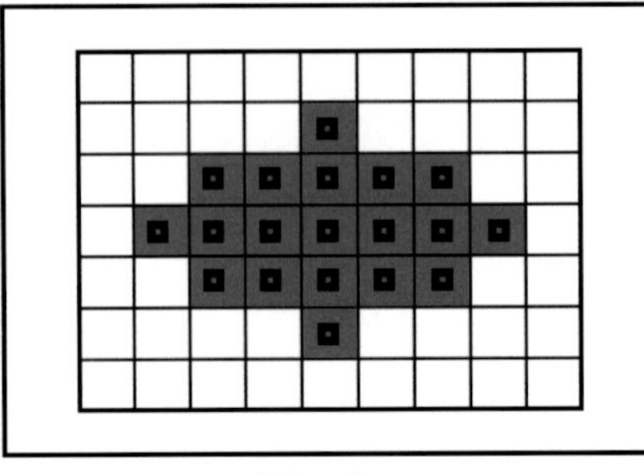

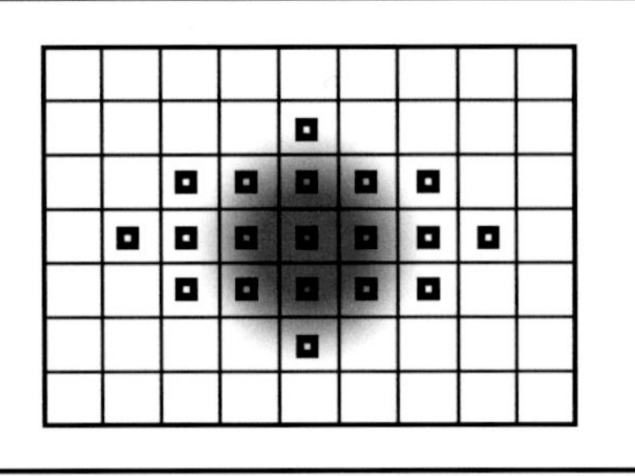

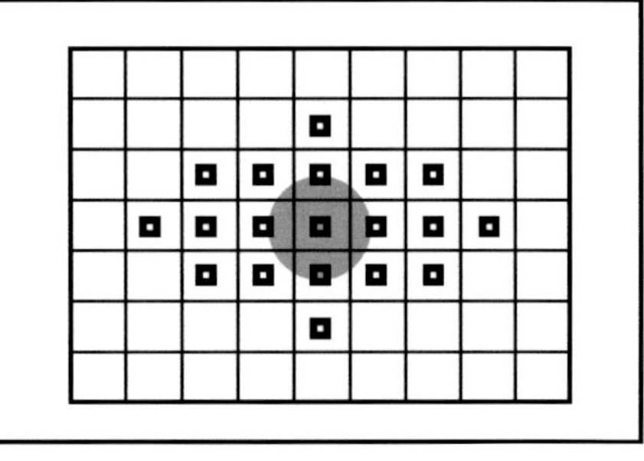

Matrix **Center-weighted** **Spot**

Figure 4-13 Generic in-camera metering patterns: matrix, center-weighted and spot.

illustrates generic in-camera metering patterns. The small boxes represent light measured zones of the image frame and the gray overlay indicates the weight given to those zones.

Matrix or Evaluative Metering

Matrix or *evaluative metering* is most often the default metering mode on SLR cameras. The frame is split into multiple zones. Each zone is then evaluated individually for highlights and shadows. An average of these zones is then determined placing extra weight on the zone where the scene is focused. The exact design, arrangement and prioritization of these zones is unique to the camera model and its programmed firmware.

Center-Weighted Metering

Center-weighted metering measures the entire frame, however, considerably more weight is given to the light requirements of the center of the frame. Some manufacturers ignore the corners or the outer edges of the frame. The success of this metering mode is closely tied with the photographer's compositional strategies and should only be used when the subject is in the center of the frame. Unlike focus that can be set by depressing the shutter button halfway and then recomposing the images, the exposure is set when the image is taken.

Spot Metering

The *spot metering* mode takes a reading from one small point in the frame, with the default position (until defined differently by the photographer) at the center. The size of the spot ranges from 1° to as high as 10°. This conveniently simulates the use of a dedicated handheld spot meter whereby the photographer targets or aims the metering zone at the subject. Spot metering is so narrow in its scope that it is best used to meter and recompose the shot through the viewfinder.

Exposure Compensation

The settings for a good exposure are found using one of the aforementioned strategies. They help us record an image whose histogram avoids clipping at either end whenever possible. There are some scenarios where we want to take the camera's metering results and go one step further. A good exposure is not always the right exposure. Here, *exposure compensation* settings on a camera allow us to inform the camera to expose exactly one half stop, or maybe two full stops, over its normal recommendation. This is useful when a particularly reflective subject may fool the metering into suggesting an overly dark exposure. Or perhaps the photographer has an aesthetic motivation for making a series of portrait exposures brighter than normal.

Automatic Exposure Behaviors

There's no shame in leaning on automatic exposure in a variety of contexts where the photographer's focus and energy might be better spent elsewhere. Its predictable behavior can be piggybacked with intuition or creative intent to achieve the best exposure for the shot. However, automatic exposure is not a perfect tool and it can be fooled. There are four common automatic exposure modes or behaviors on SLR cameras: Full Auto, Aperture Priority, Shutter Priority and Program.

A Full Auto mode selects all exposure settings: shutter speed, aperture and ISO. It may prioritize keeping ISO low or it may use other algorithmic decisions (including motion detection) to find a combination that yields a proper exposure. Aside from exposure compensation, the photographer does not have control over photographic exposure beyond pressing the shutter button to capture. The automatic exposure mode is typically coupled with automatic white balance, flash and other settings to completely minimize the photographer's need for camera setting decision-making.

Aperture and Shutter Priority exposure modes are worthwhile when you want more control of image characteristics without manually juggling all three variables. Aperture Priority allows user-set f-number and ISO to prioritize control of depth of field; the camera automatically sets shutter speed to achieve a proper exposure. In Shutter Priority mode, the user sets shutter speed and ISO to prioritize freezing or blurring motion; the camera sets the appropriate aperture. Program mode is similar to these, sometimes prioritizing ISO, but additionally allowing for user intervention to adjust any of the three variables after initially setting suggested values.

Handheld Light Metering

Take care to avoid metering off of specular highlights on reflective surfaces when spot metering. These areas are best left overexposed and if measured for overall exposure will likely leave the scene underexposed. Specular highlights are significantly brighter than the light reflected off of the rest of a surface, which scatters a percentage of the incident light. Tiny specular highlights like those seen in the eyes of a portrait's model appear most natural when they are rendered as bright and overexposed.

Spot metering is tricky for many photographers. Recall that a meter is calibrated to an 18% reflectance. It takes experience to properly identify an object that is an 18% reflector. We recommend taking a spot meter reading from a calibrated gray card placed in the scene.

Alternative Metering Methods

Smartphone apps offer an interesting alternative to in-camera and dedicated handheld meter equipment. After all, our phones have capable camera apps themselves and are able to take well-exposed photographs with much less hardware than what is found in a photographer's bag. From this, we highlight the humble light meter app: using the smartphone's imaging sensor and some clever software, a poor man's incident light meter is born (see Figure 4-14). Our students have tried several of the available apps and found that they perform relatively well under normal shooting circumstances. This strategy can be further aided by using half of a ping pong ball over the phone camera as an improvised dome diffuser substitute.

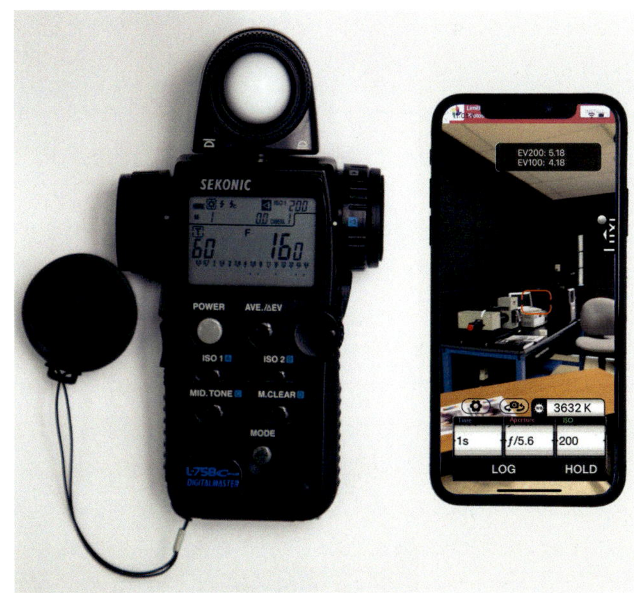

Figure 4-14 A dedicated light meter (left) may offer better accuracy and additional features over a smartphone metering app (right).

Synchronizing Flash and Camera Exposure

Photographic exposure can be accomplished with the assistance of artificial or otherwise controlled lighting in a scene. Adding your own lights means greater control of scene dynamic range, overall scene brightness and light characteristics (low contrast, high contrast, soft, harsh, etc.). Working in the studio with strobe equipment or shooting in the field with handheld flash units requires communication between the camera shutter and flash. The flash trigger is communicated through a camera's hot shoe connector or through a dedicated *PC sync port* when a shutter press initiates an exposure. Some cameras offer built-in radio or infrared transmitters to communicate wirelessly with flash units.

Focal plane shutters necessitate precise flash synchronization in addition to a limited maximum shutter speed to avoid partial frames (illustrated in Chapter 3). The shutter speed must be set such that both the front and rear curtains are out of the sensor's way. This typically happens around 1/125th second and is therefore a functional *sync speed* for flash exposure. Some cameras offer faster sync speeds of 1/250th second.

Flash units can be adjusted in terms of stops, EV or *guide numbers*. Guide numbers are calculated as the subject distance multiplied by the f-number used at ISO 100. This system is not perfectly accurate and assumes that the flash is a point source that behaves according to the inverse square law. Using guide numbers is relatively out of fashion given our reliance on digital camera hardware to estimate subject distance.

In a pinch, there is one workaround that allows for flash exposure without precise synchronization. Keep this idea in your back pocket for the day when your strobe transmitter batteries die or you forget a sync cable: turn out the lights. If you can find a completely light-controlled environment, turn out the lights and set the camera shutter speed to bulb or some multi-second duration. Press the shutter button to start exposure, fire the flash manually and press the shutter button again to end exposure. The lack of synchronization is not a problem as long as the open shutter time before and after the flash firing does not build up any signal on the sensor. This is limiting, of course, because you can no longer see what you're shooting as you stand in the dark.

Rear curtain synchronization is an exposure mode that allows for longer shutter speeds to mix ambient light and flash. Using rear curtain synchronization and setting the shutter speed to 1/4th second, for example, means that the exposure is long enough to build signal from low levels of environmental light that otherwise wouldn't at the traditional 1/125th sync speed. Just before the rear curtain begins its movement to block the sensor from further exposure, the flash is triggered to introduce additional, artificial light to the scene.

Exposing to the Right

Unlike the human eye, camera sensors have a linear response to light. This means that the more energy gathered and output as a voltage by the photosites, the more signal there is to create a properly exposed photograph. A bright area in an image always exhibits less noise than a shadow area; it simply had more light from the scene from which to output an electrical signal. When the signal greatly outweighs the noise, the result appears noise free. When the reverse is true, the noise distracts and obscures detail. It is this behavior that leads us to the *expose to the right* (ETTR) method of photographic exposure.

Exposing to the right means taking the brightest possible exposure that falls just short of clipping highlights. If the traditional method of exposing for the midtones yields a histogram largely clumped at its center, ETTR yields a histogram pushed to the right of the plot. This strategy aims to collect as much photon signal as the scene lighting allows to take advantage of the sensor's high bit depth recording. The image signal is cleaner and more detailed the more light we're able to feed to the sensor (accomplished by maximizing camera exposure).

Many cameras have automatic exposure algorithms that function in accordance with the ETTR rule. With manual exposure, however, we review the in-camera histogram and push it as far to the right as possible without significant clipping. The resulting image may appear slightly overexposed according to the camera's preview screen, however, adjusting the file in post-processing yields an image with good separation in the shadows with minimal noise.

This approach only works with scenes containing primarily dark or middle tones with limited tonal ranges, since any other scene would quickly clip in the highlights. ETTR is more likely to yield better image quality results when accomplished with aperture and shutter speed rather than ISO. Recall that boosting the gain increases noise, which is what ETTR works to minimize.

Bracketing Exposure

Bracketing means taking two or more photographs of the same subject, altering the camera settings between them to capture different exposures of the same scene. This exposure technique is primarily used to ensure proper exposure and is also used for *high dynamic range* (HDR) imaging. Exposure bracketing is not new to digital imaging, as even the earliest wet plate analog photographers took multiple frames and combined them in the darkroom. Digital cameras today have *automatic exposure bracketing* (AEB) modes that take a baseline exposure followed by two more images at a variable stop increment over and under the initial exposure. Bracketing a scene is often successful when altering shutter speed, as altering the f-number changes the depth of field and altering ISO potentially changes the amount of noise. AEB typically defaults to bracketing shutter speed as a result.

HDR bracketing and post-processing are employed when photographing a scene with a dynamic range that is larger than what a camera can capture in a single exposure. Capturing the bright sky and clouds in a landscape scene is likely to underexpose the foreground. Exposing for the foreground overexposes the sky and clips details in the clouds. Bracketing the scene means taking each of these exposures in turn. This might be as few as two frames or as many as five. This ensures that the scene's highlights, midtones and shadows are properly exposed in at least one frame from the sequence as seen in Figure 4-15 (overleaf). Combining information from these exposures is handled by image processing software that looks to minimize clipping and map a wide dynamic range of tones into a range supported by our output media. We can also manually mask and composite multi-exposure brackets for a fully hands-on approach to HDR imaging.

A related exposure strategy is shooting a sequence of frames while keeping all exposure settings the same. This means there's no exposure bracketing going on, however, every one of the sequence's frames will have its unique variation in random noise. A set of six exposures taken one after another, for example, can be leveraged by stacking the image data from all six. This is an option in Adobe Photoshop whereby image layer stacking or blending can function as an extremely effective noise reduction process. The random noise from a single frame is replaced by true image pixel data from a different frame. The more frames the algorithm can look at, the more confident the final output becomes where a larger percentage of pixels are true brightness and color information from the scene. This is a great approach when shooting static scenes on a tripod.

Setting White Balance

The visible light characteristic of color temperature was introduced in Chapter 1. Every light source appears warm, cool or neutral to our eyes. Evaluating the color temperature of the light in a scene was critically important in the analog film days because a particular color positive film was explicitly formulated for a single, primary light source like daylight or tungsten. A photographer loaded their camera with film designed to shoot under the light source present in the scene to achieve accurate, balanced color. If the two were mismatched, the resulting images would exhibit a significant *color cast* where all colors exhibit an obvious tint or skew toward a single color. The other option involved using color correction filters over the lens to compensate. Color negative film lacked this degree of control at capture, opting for a daylight balance and relying on corrections in color print reproduction.

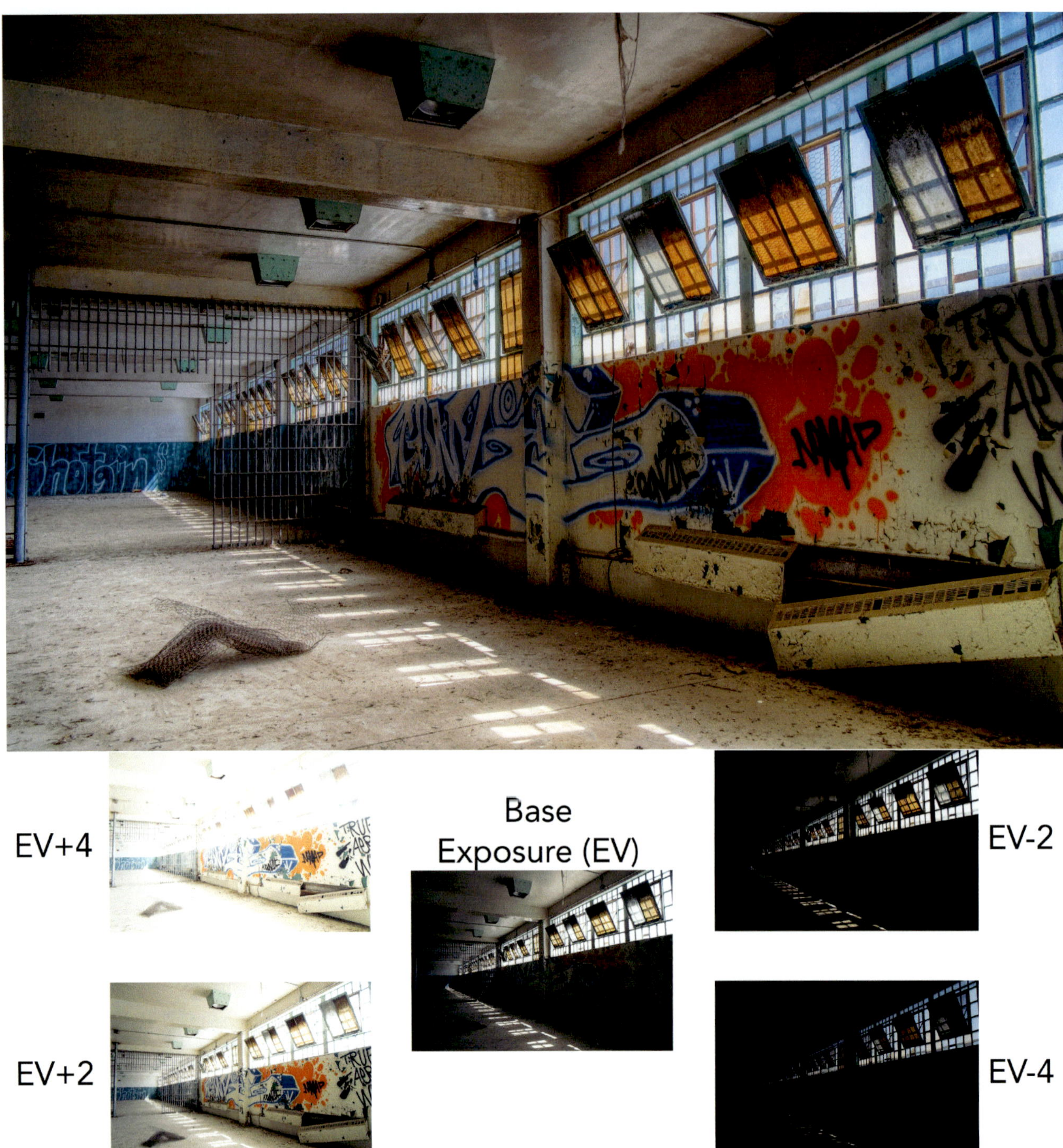

Figure 4-15 Bracketed exposures and the combined HDR composite. Photographs by Rochester Institute of Technology alumnus and Lecturer Dan Hughes

The color temperature of a scene's light is considered in order to find a desirable *white balance* whereby white or neutral objects are rendered as such. Camera sensors are designed to record light regardless of color temperatures, so in this sense, it's not necessary to set a white balance in the camera before taking a picture. The concept still matters because we want the resulting image to show the colors and color relationships as they appeared in person. However, we can set the interpretation of color neutrality in image editing software long after the image is recorded with no ill effect to quality (assuming raw capture). The color of digital images is interpretable in the raw exposure data whereas film chemistry was formulated to record accurate color specific to a tungsten, daylight or fluorescent color temperature.

There are many instances where a scene contains a variety of lights sources, making it impossible to render each one or each area illuminated by those sources perfectly neutral. This is a simple reality, neither good nor bad—we're accustomed to seeing this, since our vision similarly calibrates for a single white point. Figure 4-16 shows an indoor scene containing multiple light sources with different color temperatures. You can quickly determine which white balance setting was used by the photographer by identifying the light most closely approximating a neutral white tone. What is the correct white balance to use? It's a subjective decision, but it's common to see the dominant light source made neutral. It's difficult to get all areas to be neutral with a global correction, but correcting for the dominant light source is a notable improvement. Other times, you may prefer or desire a considerably warmer or cooler cast to the dominant light source to convey a mood or exaggerated interpretation of the scene.

Generally speaking, an improper white balance appears warmer (more yellow-orange), cooler (more blue) or, less commonly, greenish (due to fluorescent light sources). Cameras offer a set of predefined color temperature options that cover most of the bases: incandescent (tungsten), fluorescent, daylight, shade/overcast daylight, flash. Selecting one of these generic options often gets the image preview in the ballpark of where the white balance needs to be in order to produce a neutral white. By virtue of being predefined color temperature categories in a world of infinitely varying light quality, it won't hit the mark every time. There is no single-color temperature for daylight on an overcast day, for example.

Fully automatic white balance functionality is always offered in addition to the generic light source presets. Algorithms work to make the best guess as to the dominant light source by analyzing image pixel data and color distribution. Automatic white balance is a helpful default when shooting

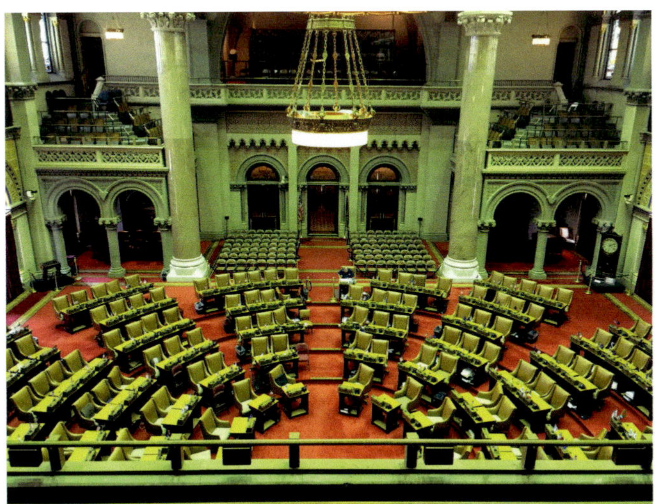

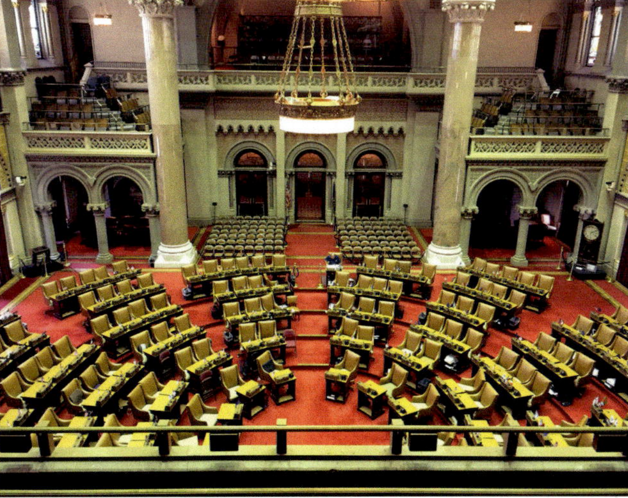

Figure 4-16 An environment with mixed illuminants using the camera's automatic white balance (left) and after a user-defined white balance for fluorescent lights (right).

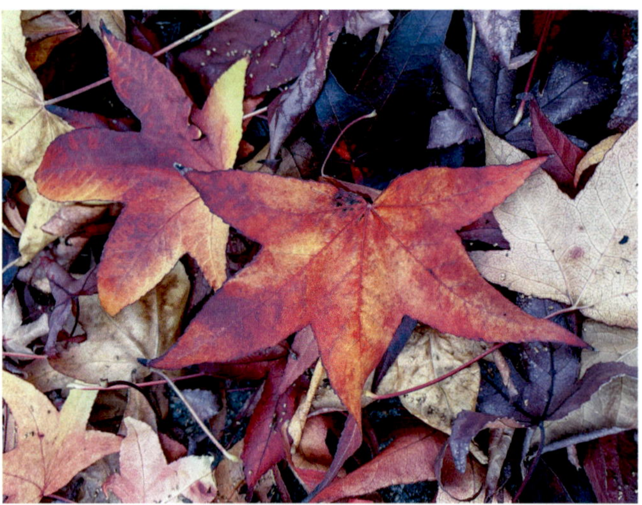
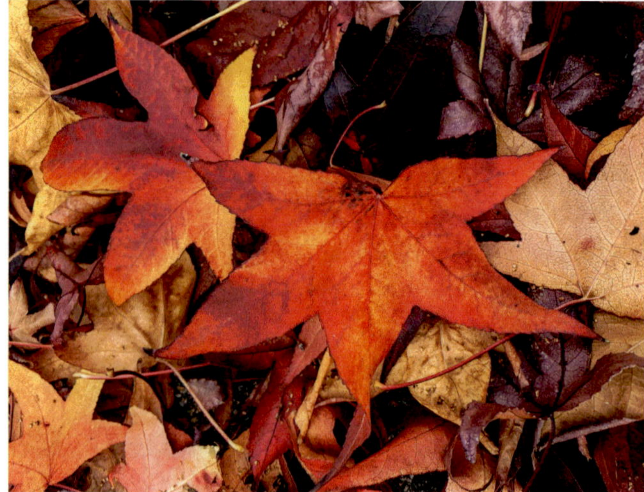

Figure 4-17 An automatic white balance result (left) and its user-corrected rendering (right).

under dynamic shooting conditions when it's often enough work juggling exposure settings, focus and composition. Image editing software additionally offers its own strategies for determining white balance automatically when reviewing and editing raw files. Instances that are likely to trip up automatic white balancing algorithms include:

- extremely skewed dominant light sources (i.e. sodium vapor street lamps);
- when the image frame is filled with a single color (i.e. a pile of red autumn leaves) or the scene does not contain any neutral objects;
- mixed illuminant environments.

Figure 4-17 is an example of a composition dominated by a single color where automatic white balance failed. The lack of a neutral reference and a dominant set of warm hues in the pile of leaves caused the algorithm to overcorrect toward something much cooler. As algorithms become more robust and better implementations trickle down to even the cheapest of cameras, such misfires become less frequent and less egregious.

White balance is a non-destructive parameter that can be changed after the photograph is taken with no negative consequence to image quality or color reproduction. We tend to keep our cameras on auto white balance save for special scenarios and adjust as necessary during post-processing.

Proof of Concept: Optimizing Photographic Exposure with Low Light Shooting

Night photography offers a number of challenges, particularly in regard to lighting and exposure, that aren't present during the day. Nighttime also makes the world a very different looking place compared to when the sun is shining. Photographic exposure is versatile with the right tools, allowing you to make images under incredibly varying conditions. It allows us to create documents of time that extend beyond the immediate, experienced present moment. This is particularly intriguing given our poor low light vision. Use a tripod and your knowledge of camera exposure (shutter speed, aperture and ISO) to explore the world at night.

1. Set the camera to collect raw images. Turn off any in-camera noise reduction.
2. Find and compose an image in a low light environment with the camera mounted to a tripod.
3. Set the camera to its lowest marked ISO. Use the in-camera meter and perhaps some trial and error to get a good exposure (consider what constitutes a good exposure and use the histogram). Be careful: the meter is easily fooled by the challenging lighting conditions of nighttime scenes. If you do not have a cable release, set the camera's self-timer to allow for a delay between the

Table 4-2 Exposure settings for low ISO and high ISO captures.

Image	ISO	Shutter Speed	Aperture
Low ISO Proper Exposure (EV)	100	1s	f/11
Low ISO Under Exposure (EV-2)	100	1/4s	f/11
High ISO Proper Exposure (EV)	6400	1/60s	f/11
High ISO Under Exposure (EV-2)	6400	1/250s	f/11

shutter button press and the shutter opening. Take an image.

4. Take a second image that is two full stops underexposed (EV-2) at the same ISO setting.
5. Change ISO to the highest that your camera offers. Adjust shutter speed to compensate for this increase in sensitivity to create an exposure as close as possible to the original, properly exposed image.
6. Take a second image that is two stops underexposed at the same high ISO setting. Table 4-2 documents the exposures used for our example nighttime scene.
7. Back at your workstation, transfer the images and import them into your image editing software of choice. Figure 4-18 shows one pair of our proper exposure and underexposure frames. Correct the underexposed images using the exposure slider. The exposure slider in Adobe Photoshop Lightroom and Adobe Camera Raw corresponds to changes in EV. Since our images are underexposed by two stops, increasing the exposure slider by +2.0 produces an equivalent brightness correction.

Look at the two ISO exposure pairs side by side and zoom in close to areas of shadow. Consider the following questions:

- What is observable in each ISO pair? Are they comparable in image quality after the underexposed versions are edited to equivalent exposures in post-processing?
- Is an equivalent exposure at capture better or worse than a different exposure at capture made equivalent in post-processing?
- Is there more visible noise in the correct exposures or the underexposure versions? Is this relationship consistent across the ISO settings?
- When shooting at the highest available ISO, does your camera produce an acceptable image?
- What is the downside, if any, to using the lowest available ISO setting?

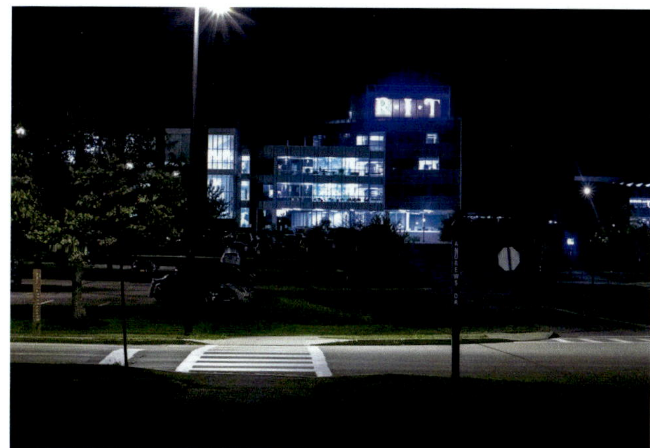

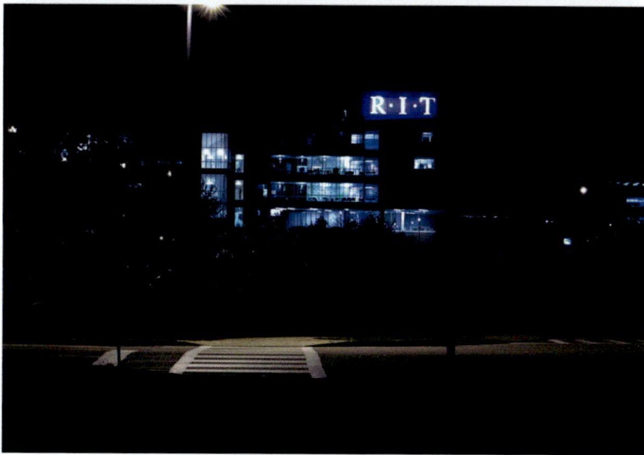

Figure 4-18 A low light, nighttime scene photographed with a proper exposure (top) and underexposed by two stops (bottom). Photographs by Rochester Institute of Technology photography student Matthew Sluka

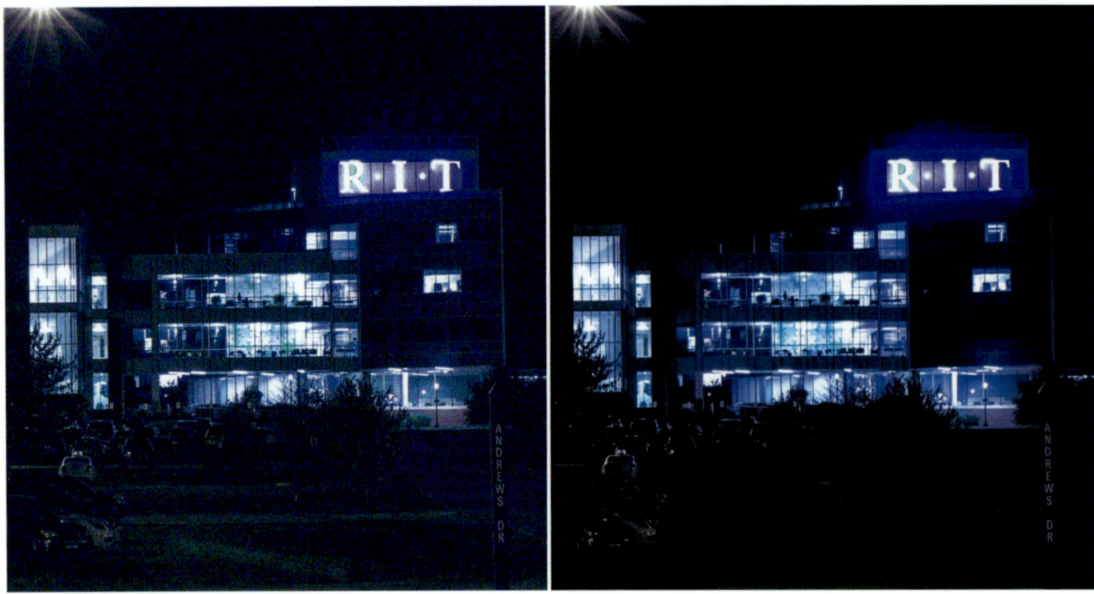

Figure 4-19 Before and after thoughtful noise reduction is applied to our nighttime photograph. Photographs by Rochester Institute of Technology photography student Matthew Sluka

Examine all photographs zoomed to fit the screen as well as at 100%. Look closely at areas of detail and darker tones. Start to get familiar with digital noise: its texture (luminance variability or grain) and its color characteristics. We mitigate the negative visual impact of noise using noise reduction tools in software. Work with the noise reduction options in your image editing software to see how much the high ISO, underexposed frame can be improved without introducing too much smoothing or blurring. Figure 4-19 shows the before and after results of our careful noise reduction choices of a high ISO capture.

Note

1 https://anvaka.github.io/pixchart/

5 Lens Filters

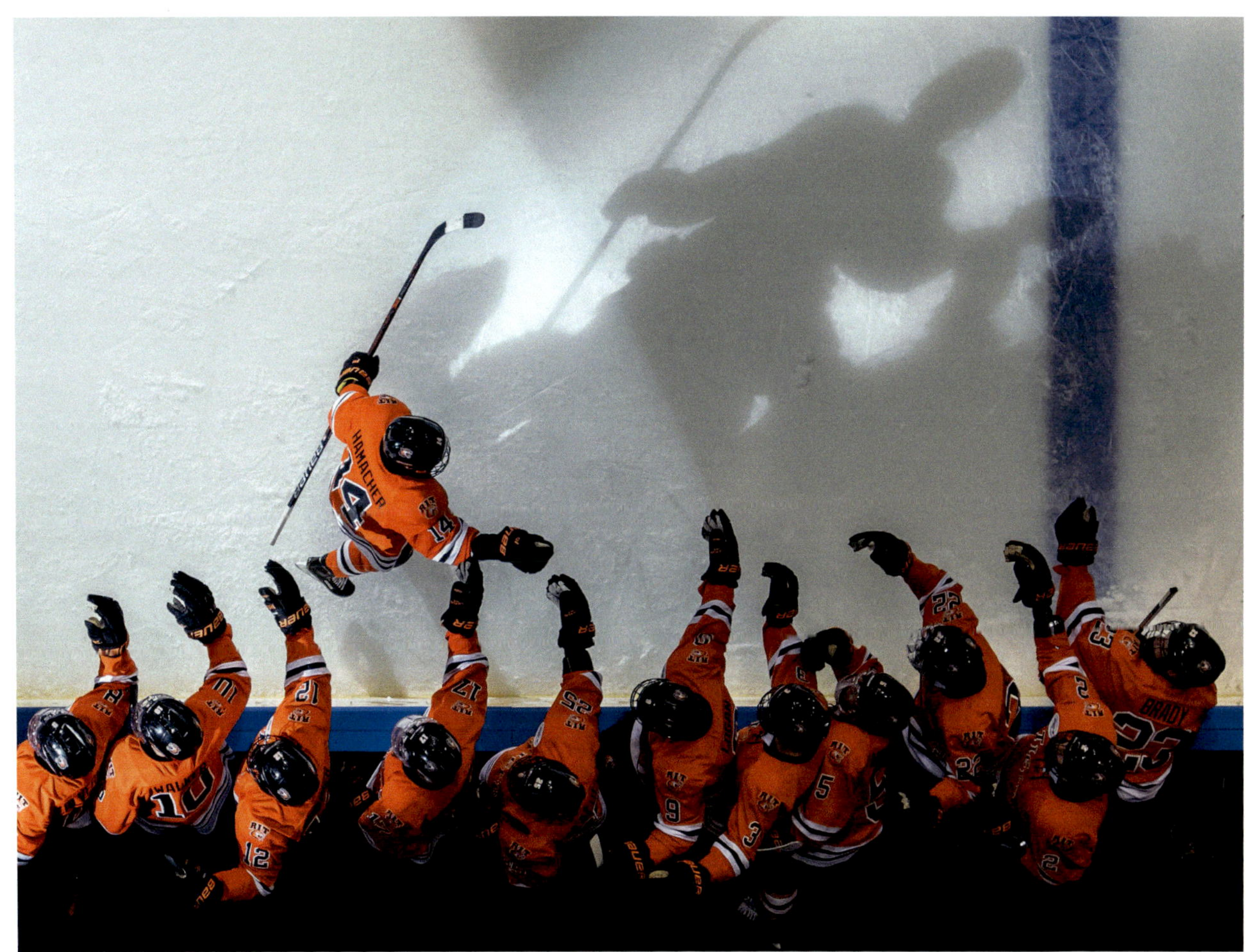

Photograph by Rochester Institute of Technology photography student Eakin Howard

Photographers rely on lenses to form sharply resolved images. Their precision, engineering and materials often necessitate expensive purchases to add lenses to the photographer's toolkit. Filters are accessories that modify or adapt the optics of a camera system and, thankfully, augment our image-making capabilities for cheap. All lens filters change aspects of the light entering the camera. Software processing offers simulations of a subset of lens filters that can be introduced after capture though many filter behaviors cannot be emulated. Our interest in controlling light at the capture stage means considering lens filters as carefully as the camera body, lens focal length and exposure settings. In other words, lens filters are an irreplaceable part of pre-planning and pre-visualization. This chapter explains how light is filtered, how it impacts exposure and the different ways in which filters are used in making photographs. At its end, we take a creative look at reproducing color from monochrome captures with the help of lens filters.

Transmittance, Opacity and Density

All photographic filters reduce the amount of light entering the lens. There are three measurements for quantifying this behavior: transmittance, opacity and density. These measurements apply to light traveling through all materials; here we're interested in light filtration materials in the camera system.

Transmittance describes a material's ability to pass light. It's calculated as the ratio of the light energy falling on a filter to that which is transmitted through it (see Equation 5.1). Put another way, transmittance describes the relationship of how much light we start with and how much we see after it passes through a medium (the filter material).

$$Transmittance\ (T) = \frac{Transmitted\ Light}{Incident\ Light} \quad \text{(Eq. 5.1)}$$

Consider the scenario illustrated in Figure 5-1 where 100 lux of incident light travels through a sample material. Only 50 lux is transmitted from the 100 lux of incident light. Equation 5.1 tells us that the transmittance of the material is 50/100, which equates to 0.50 or 50% transmission. Next, we layer two pieces of that same material, measure the amount of transmitted light from the same 100 lux source and find that 25 lux passes through. The light-stopping ability increases while the transmittance decreases as layers of material are added between the light source and the transmission measurement. Transmittance values get increasingly small as more layers of the sample material are stacked. Even when using percentage to report transmittance, the very small values make it challenging to appreciate the magnitude of change as the light-stopping ability of a material grows.

Opacity is a measure of the lack of transparency and is inversely related to transmittance. Opacity is defined as the ratio of incident light to transmitted light or the reciprocal of the transmittance. It is calculated using the following formula:

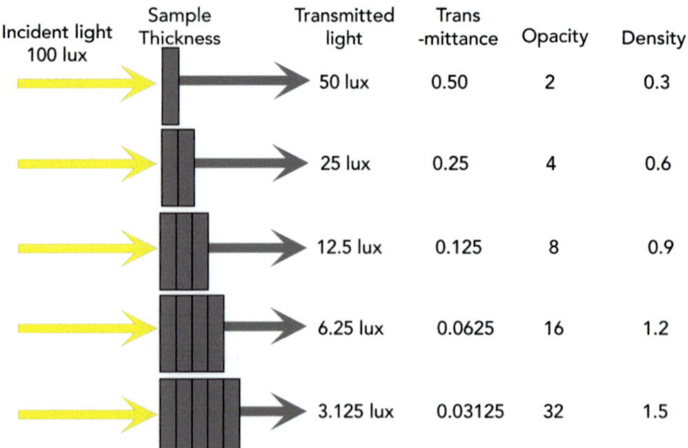

Figure 5-1 The relationship between the sample thickness and transmittance, opacity and density.

$$Opacity\ (O) = \frac{Incident\ Light}{Transmitted\ Light}\ or\ \frac{1}{Transmittance} \quad \text{(Eq. 5.2)}$$

Take another look at Figure 5-1. As sample thickness and light-stopping ability increase, opacity also increases—a more straightforward relationship. Notice that sample thickness increases in equal amounts yet the opacity differences become progressively greater. The opacities form a geometric (or ratio) progression that becomes inconveniently large as the light-stopping ability increases. If we continued the experiment, ten layers of the material would yield an opacity of 1,024. Large numbers can become difficult to deal with, so this might not be the perfect way to keep track of a material's light-stopping ability either.

This brings us to yet another method of measuring light transmission. *Density* is a measure of the extent that a material or medium transmits light. Density is a valuable metric for describing how light travels through a material because it is linear and additive. Density is calculated as the logarithm of opacity:

$$Density\ (D) = log\ (Opacity)\ or\ log \left(\frac{1}{Transmittance}\right) \quad \text{(Eq. 5.3)}$$

Review Figure 5-1 one last time. Density increases as we layer additional material. However, its values increase in equal amounts in a linear fashion, a feature that

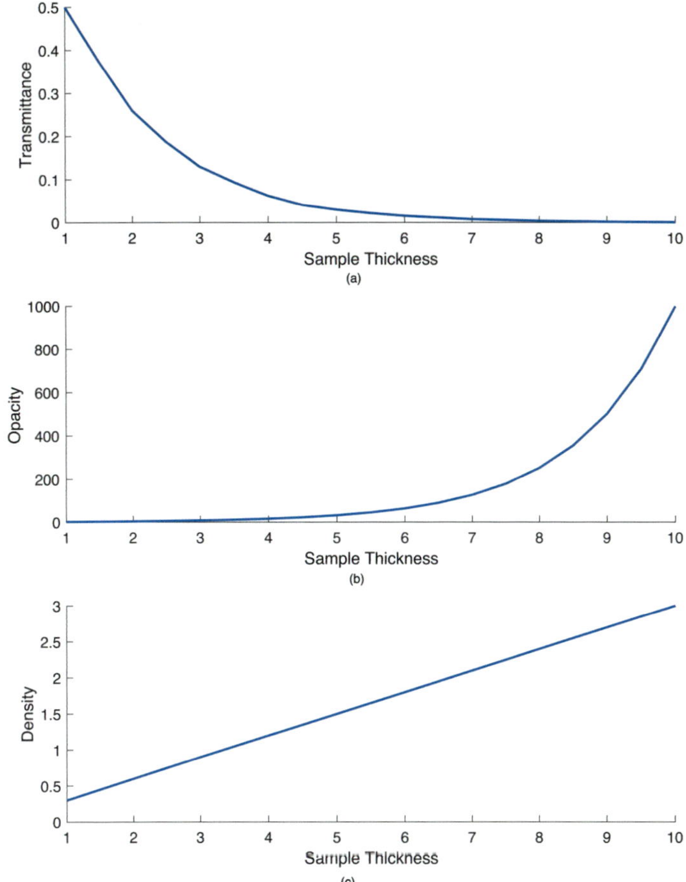

Figure 5-2 Plotting (a) transmittance, (b) opacity and (c) density measurements from layering sample material in front of a light source.

differentiates it from opacity measurements. To summarize: the less light transmitted by a material, the lower its transmittance, the higher its density and opacity. Figure 5-2 illustrates these relationships by plotting the measured values. The density plot shows that density measurements are linear.

How Light is Filtered

Light approaching a filter may scatter before ever reaching its surface. Consider shining a flashlight across a foggy graveyard: some of that light never reaches the rustling bushes you point it toward and instead scatters in the thick, moisture-rich air. If the light does travel to a surface without scattering first, it is then reflected, absorbed or transmitted (or a combination therein) by or through the foliage. Figure 5-3 illustrates the possible light paths as it approaches a

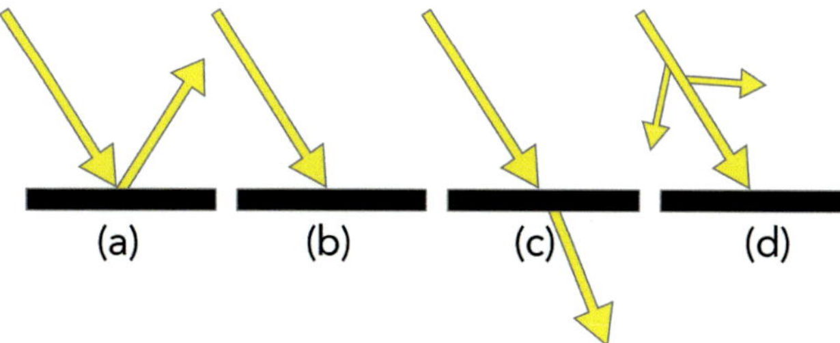

Figure 5-3 Light falling on a surface is (a) reflected, (b) absorbed, (c) transmitted or (d) scattered before reaching the surface.

surface. Common mnemonics for remembering these behaviors are *ARTS* (absorbed, reflected, transmitted, scattered) or *RATS*. Scattered light is the behavior of least concern to photographers other than the fact that it can introduce flare or an inefficiency in our light sources if, say, we have a photoshoot in a foggy graveyard. An object, such as this book, absorbs some of the light striking it while reflecting the rest. A stained glass window, on the other hand, absorbs, transmits and reflects varying amounts of incident light. We don't need to know or observe the exact degree to which these different events occur with the objects we photograph. We do need know the degree to which they occur in materials placed over the camera lens (read: filters). Lens filters help control the types of light passing through our imaging system by leveraging the reflective, transmissive and absorptive characteristics of optical materials.

The perceived color of any object depends on the spectral quality of the reflected or transmitted light by that object. An opaque white object illuminated with white light appears white because the surface reflects a high portion of the incident light at all wavelengths. A black object appears black because it reflects only a small portion of the incident light at all wavelengths. A red object appears red when illuminated with white light because it selectively absorbs most of the blue and green wavelengths striking it while simultaneously reflecting most of the red wavelengths. Here we're grouping wavelengths into large categories, but there are hundreds of possible wavelengths in the visible spectrum that can be reflected or transmitted.

Photographic filters work by removing part of the incident radiation by absorption or reflection such that

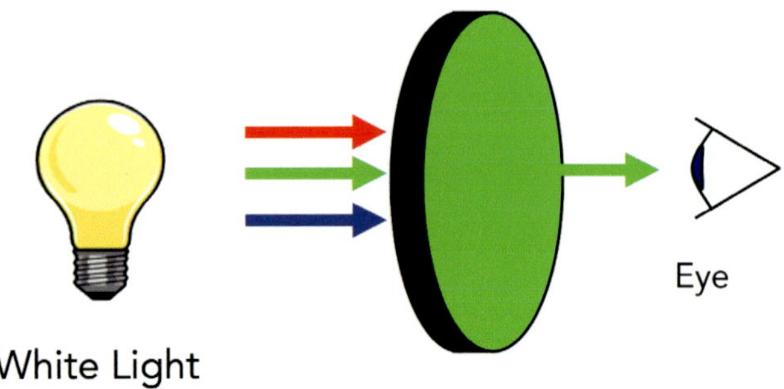

Figure 5-4 A green filter appears green because the filter absorbs the red and blue components of white light and transmits the green.

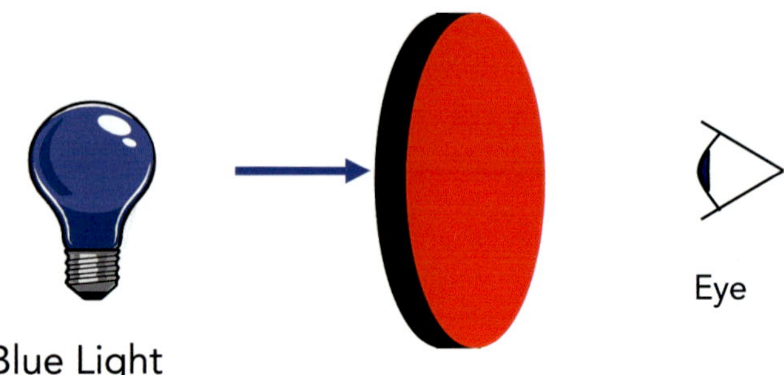

Figure 5-5 Blue light has no red component and therefore using a red filter to transmit only red light yields no visible result.

the transmitted radiation is of the desired spectral quality. Filters cannot add to the incident radiation, only take away from it. A green filter passes green light and absorbs red and blue as seen in Figure 5-4. A red filter cannot transmit red light if there is no red light in the incident light. If a green filter is used when only blue light is present, no light passes through to the sensor or eye (see Figure 5-5).

There are various ways to classify filters. We consider three basic categories defined by their behavior in transmitting incident light. A filter can be:

1. *Selective by wavelength*. These block specific wavelengths or ranges of wavelengths (such as all shades of red). This category is easily represented by color filters that simply transmit a single color; think rose-colored glasses that make everything seem rosy (in appearance, not emotional optimism). It also includes filters that selectively transmit other forms of radiation like infrared.
2. *Non-selective by wavelength*. These reduce the amount of transmitted light equally across wavelengths, effectively acting as darkening filters. The primary examples are neutral density filters, discussed in a section to follow.
3. *Selective by angle of polarization*. These transmit light oriented in a specific direction. Polarizing filters are the primary example and are described in a later section.

The Filter Factor

Any filter placed in front of a lens absorbs light. A notable reduction in light requires a change in camera exposure to compensate else you risk underexposure. The *filter factor* specifies the change in exposure necessary to obtain the same recorded brightness in a neutral subject area with the filter as without. Filter manufacturers often include filter factors on their product packaging to save us the guesswork. Table 5-1 lists common filter factors and the exposure difference rendered by each in stops.

Table 5-1 Filter factors and corresponding number of stops of reduced exposure.

Filter Factor	Number of Stops
1	0
1.3	1/3
1.4	1/2
1.5	2/3
2	1
3	1 2/3
4	2

The relationship between filter factor and the required number of stops by which the exposure must be adjusted is defined in Equation 5.4. For example, we solve the equation for a filter with a filter factor of 16 to determine how many additional stops of exposure are needed:

$$2^{\text{number of stops}} = \text{filter factor} \quad \text{(Eq. 5.4)}$$
$$2^{\text{number of stops}} = 16$$

We then take the natural log (ln) of each side of the equation:

$$number\ of\ stops \times \ln(2) = \ln(16)$$

$$number\ of\ stops = \frac{\ln(16)}{\ln(2)}$$

$$number\ of\ stops = 4$$

An easier method is to divide the logarithm of the filter factor by 0.3 (see Equation 5.5). Recall that 0.3 in neutral density is equivalent to a one stop change in exposure. Continuing from the previous example with a filter factor of 16:

$$number\ of\ stops = \frac{\log(filter\ factor)}{0.3} \quad \text{(Eq. 5.5)}$$

$$number\ of\ stops = \frac{\log(16)}{0.3} = 4$$

If the filter factor adjustment is applied to the exposure time without a filter, the new exposure time is found by multiplying the original exposure by the filter factor. For example, with an initial exposure time of 1/500 second and a filter factor of 16, the new exposure time is 1/500 * 16 = 1/30. If the filter factor is instead applied to the aperture setting and the initial f-stop is f/8, the adjusted f-stop for maintaining equivalent exposure when using the filter is f/2.

The published filter factor may not always produce optimal results. Manufacturers commonly indicate that published filter factors should be modified by the photographer as necessary. Two additional aspects of the photographic process to take into account are the color quality of the illumination and the color sensitivity of the digital sensor. Red filters, for example, have larger filter factors with daylight illumination than with tungsten illumination because they absorb a larger proportion of the bluer daylight illumination. Conversely, blue filters have smaller factors with daylight.

Manufacturers claim that using the through-the-lens light meter inherently compensates for the decrease in the amount of light that reaches the sensor when a filter is added. These claims are valid to the extent that the spectral response of the meter corresponds to the spectral sensitivity of the sensor. Conducting a simple experiment to determine the accuracy of the in-camera meter is accomplished by metering a neutral test target with and without the filter. The difference in exposure readings is compared against the published filter factor and adjusted as necessary.

Color Filters

Color filters are commonly identified by the perceived color of the transmitted light when illuminated by white incident light. In Figure 5-4, the green filter transmits green light and absorbs red and blue light. Color filters differ with respect to a) which part of the visible spectrum is transmitted freely (identified by color hue or peak transmittance wavelength); b) the width of the region transmitted and the sharpness of the cutoff (identified by a general description such as narrow, wide or specific bandpass); c) the degree of absorption of the unwanted colors (identified by general terms such as light yellow and dark yellow, or specific transmittance and density data).

Saturated color filters that almost completely absorb the unwanted colors of light are used in black and white photography to lighten or darken subject colors. Photographers need to predict the effect that such filters have on the tone reproduction of a subject. One method is to look at the subject through the filter and observe which colors are lightened and which are darkened.

The *Maxwell triangle* is a diagram containing the three additive primary colors red, green and blue and the three additive secondary colors cyan, magenta and yellow (see Figure 5-6). The triangle helps predict the effect of color filters on tone assuming that the image is rendered in black

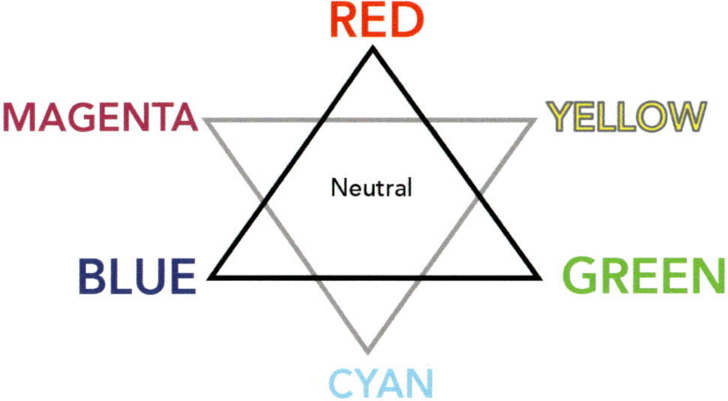

Figure 5-6 The Maxwell triangle is useful for predicting the effect of color filters on subjects in black and white photographs.

and white. We interpret the effect of color filters by understanding the following rules:

1. A filter lightens objects that are the same color as the filter. It also lightens colors adjacent to it on the triangle to a lesser degree.
2. A filter darkens objects that are on the opposite side of the triangle to the filter's color. It also darkens colors adjacent to that opposite color to a lesser degree.

Thus a red filter lightens red, magenta and yellow subject colors while darkening the opposite color, cyan, and its adjacent colors, blue and green. Figure 5-7 shows a scene rendered in full color, converted to black and white with an automatic software filter and using a color filter at capture. The differences in tones and tone contrast can be dramatic when color filters are properly considered. Understanding the color relationships of the Maxwell triangle proves valuable beyond lens filters: we show how they help us to balance color and tone in post-processing in Chapter 10.

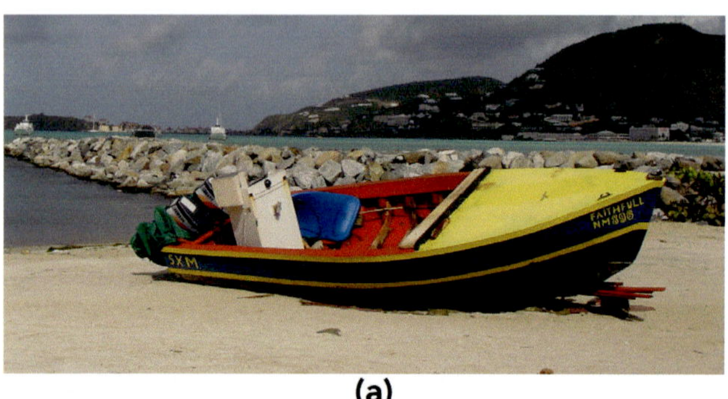

(a)

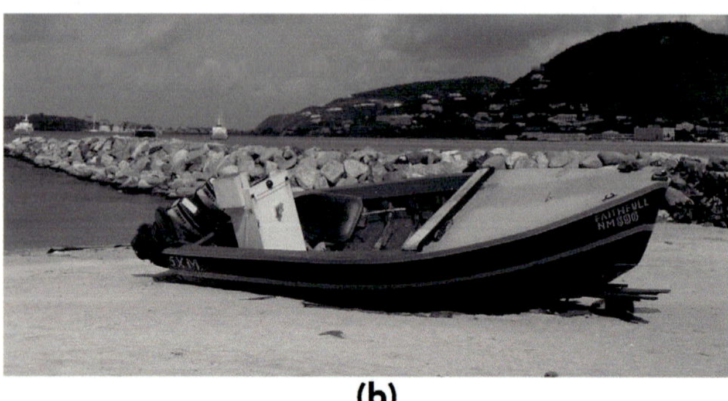

(b)

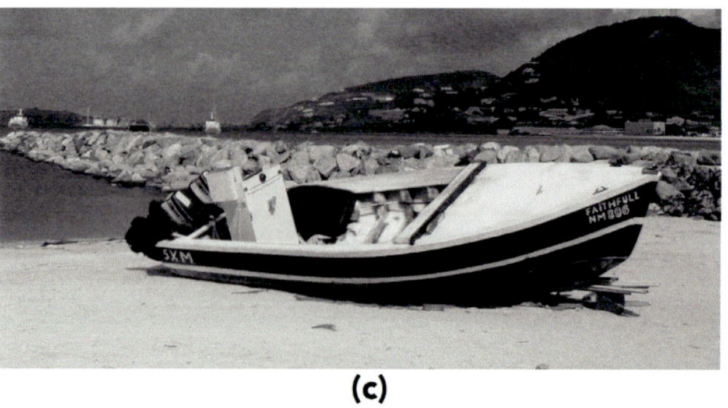

(c)

Figure 5-7 Image B is a black and white version of image A rendered with an automatic conversion filter in image editing software. Image C was photographed using a yellow filter and a monochrome sensor.

Neutral Density Filters

Neutral density (ND) filters reduce the transmitted illuminance by a known factor. ND filters offer an alternative method of controlling exposure when the conventional aperture and shutter controls are inadequate. With highly sensitive photographic materials, a combination of the smallest diaphragm opening and the highest shutter speed may still result in overexposure at high illumination levels. There are also situations in which the diaphragm opening is selected to produce a certain depth of field and the shutter speed is selected for a certain action stopping capability rather than for exposure considerations. The intent is to have the same transmittance for all wavelengths of radiation within specified limits. ND filters are usually calibrated in terms of white light density. A filter with a neutral density of 0.3 has an opacity and filter factor of 2 (the antilog of 0.3) and a transmittance of 0.5 (the reciprocal of the opacity)

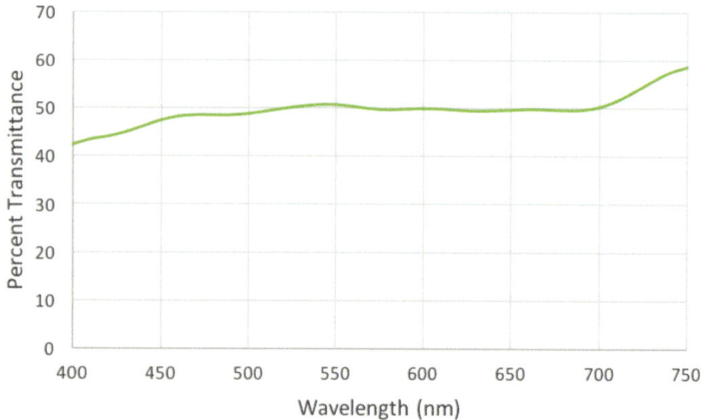

Figure 5-8 The spectral transmittance of 0.3 neutral density filter.

as plotted in Figure 5-8. Some ND filters are calibrated in terms of stops, where each 0.3 in density corresponds to one stop of exposure change. Variable neutral density filters use a rotatable sandwich of filter elements to allow for fine-tuning the degree of light reduction.

Graduated neutral density filters are a special subcategory of particular interest to outdoor and landscape photographers. These filters start out completely transparent on one edge and gradually increase in density until they reach a maximum density (usually 0.3, 0.6 or 0.9) at the opposite edge. This is useful when the brightness range between the sky and the foreground is significant. Often times the dynamic range of an outdoor scene is so large that a single exposure leaves the sky overexposed or the ground underexposed. We can lessen the difference by introducing a graduated neutral density filter and aligning its orientation with the scene horizon. This way, a single shutter speed, aperture and ISO combination captures detail in both the foreground and sky—the area of greatest density on the filter blocks some of that light from the bright sky. The gradual transition makes its presence potentially undetectable to the observer. Since its alignment in front of the camera is dictated by the photographer's composition, square graduated ND filters with filter holders that mount to the lens are an available solution. This way, you have the ability to raise or lower the higher density portion of the filter in relation to your composition.

Polarizing Filters

The phenomenon of polarized light provides photographers with an opportunity to further control light (see Chapter 1 for a refresher). Placing a *polarizing filter* over the lens limits the light recorded by the camera to that which oscillates exclusively in one orientation. This is possible because the filters are manufactured with microscopic crystals aligned a uniform, parallel orientation. There are both *circular* and *linear* polarizing filters, the former more commonly used than the latter as photographic lens attachments. Linear polarizers can cause exposure or focus issues due to their interaction with the camera mirror components. With linear polarizers, if the filter's plane of polarization and the plane of polarization of the light are the same, the maximum amount of light is transmitted. If they are at right angles to each other, no light passes as shown in Figure 5-9. Circular polarizers never align in such a way that completely extinguishes light transmission. Instead, varying amounts of light are transmitted at different rotation angles between the two sandwiched filter elements. In this way, polarizing filters can be thought of as variable neutral density filters. Figure 5-10 demonstrates that rotating a circular polarizing filter alters the total amount of energy transmitted. Note how the filter does not discriminate by wavelength.

If polarizing filters simply reduced the amount of light transmitted, we wouldn't be highlighting them here. Figure 5-10 doesn't tell the whole story of their photographic impact. The unique characteristic of polarizing

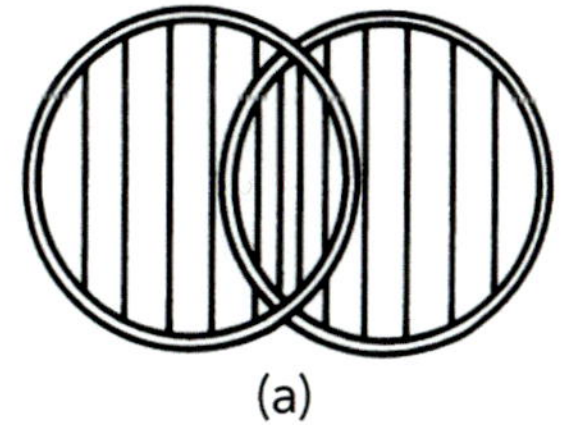

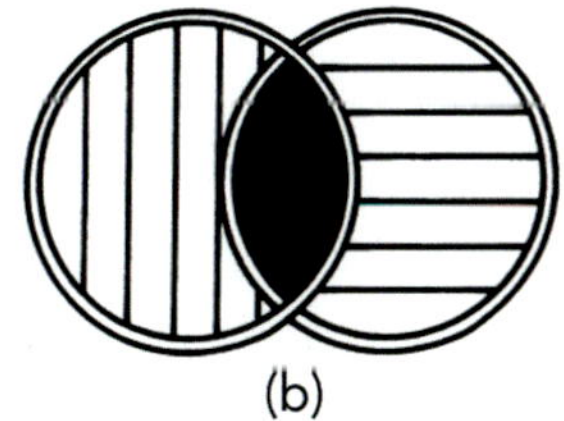

Figure 5-9 When filters are parallel as in (a) polarized light is passed, when they are at right angles (b), no light is passed.

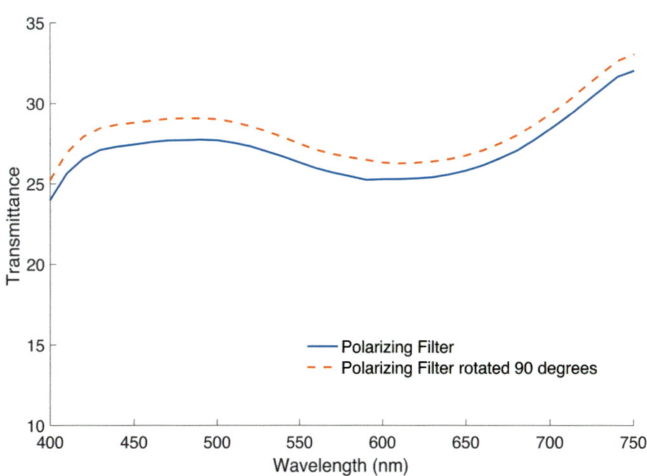

Figure 5-10 Spectral transmittance of a polarizing filter measured at 0° and 90° rotations.

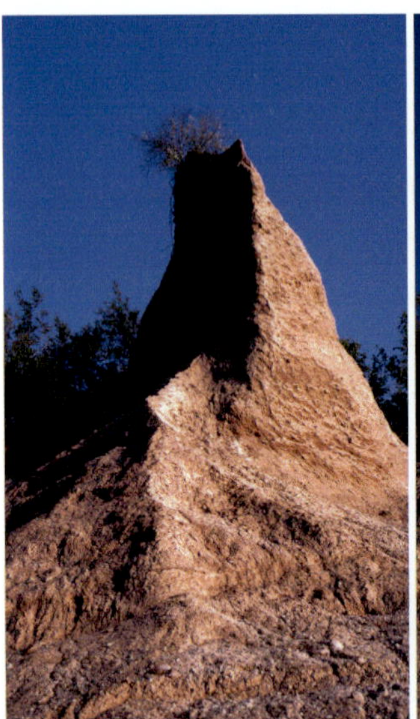

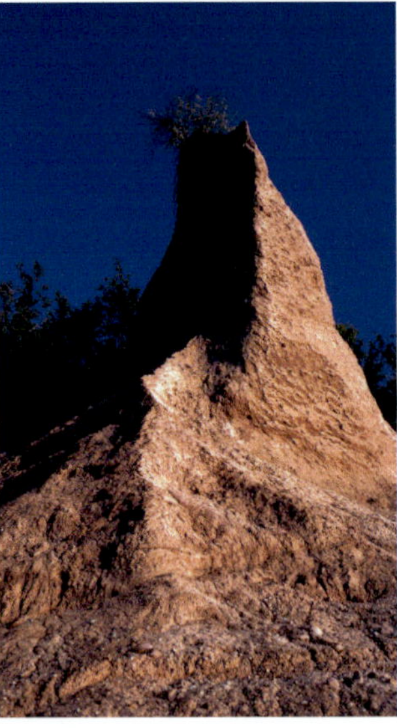

Figure 5-11 An outdoor scene photographed without (left) and with (right) a polarizing filter mounted to the camera lens. Photographs by Stephen J. Diehl

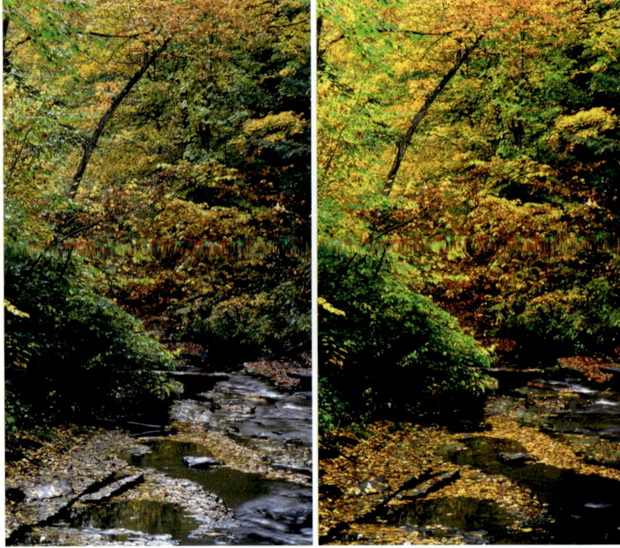

Figure 5-12 An outdoor scene photographed without (left) and with (right) a polarizing filter mounted to the camera lens. The colors in the scene are more saturated thanks to the filter's ability to remove glare. Photographs by Stephen J. Diehl

filters is in how they manipulate an aspect of light that we don't perceive. Light vibrates in all directions but we don't notice any vibration orientation differences. Polarizing filters do, and limiting which light rays get through to the sensor offers the ability to cut down on reflections and haze because their orientations are much more likely to be random and nonuniform.

Figure 5-11 shows a landscape with a blue sky photographed using a polarizing filter. The effect is dramatic: the sky darkens and often becomes a more saturated shade of blue. You've likely experienced a similar result from wearing polarized sunglasses in the summertime. The surfaces of tree leaves reflect light in many directions, resulting in scattering and causing a hazy appearance from a distance. A polarizing filter over the lens reduces this non-image forming light (flare). We know how colorful and vibrant the changing autumn leaves are, yet a standard photograph fails to capture it in part because of this natural haze. A polarizing filter cuts out a lot of the scattered, randomly oriented light waves, leaving an image with more inherent saturation and contrast (Figure 5-12). It comes as no surprise, then, that many outdoor and landscape photographers carry polarizing filters. Clever software tricks may emulate some of the benefits of polarizing filters (like darkening blue skies) but there is no replacement for physically filtering the light before it reaches the sensor—it fundamentally changes the transmitted and therefore recorded light.

Ultraviolet and Infrared Filters

Color filters are defined by their ability to selectively limit the visible light wavelengths transmitted. Ultraviolet and infrared filters behave the same except that they limit the transmission of electromagnetic radiation outside of the visible spectrum.

Ultraviolet (UV) *absorption filters* play an important role in color film photography. The blue-sensitive emulsion layer is also sensitive to ultraviolet radiation (recall that on the electromagnetic spectrum, UV wavelengths precede violet visible light). Placing a UV filter over the lens prevents captured images from having a blue color cast. The need for UV filters with digital sensors is an area of debate, as CMOS chips are fairly insensitive to the UV portion of the spectrum.

Ultraviolet radiation can have a deleterious effect on photographs of some outdoor scenes because short wavelength radiation is scattered much more by the atmosphere than longer-wavelength radiation, creating the appearance of haze. Haze lowers contrast and obscures detail in distant subjects, as discussed in the previous section on polarizing filters. This Rayleigh scattering is inversely proportional to the fourth power of the wavelength of the radiation. A UV filter reduces the appearance of haze due to this atmospheric light scattering. From this, we might conclude that attaching a UV filter is a prerequisite for outdoor shooting. However, many manufacturers incorporate a UV filtering material on the sensor itself, rendering the practice redundant. Still, many feel that using a UV filter is worthwhile if only as additional protection. Camera lenses are expensive; UV filters are not. Photographers like to use UV filters to protect against dust and scratches on the front lens surfaces. After all, we've all used our shirt or sleeve to wipe off a lens and it is cheaper to replace a scratched filter than a scratched lens. The only caveat to this practice: if the UV material is cheap, it can lessen the quality of the image that reaches the sensor. Any time that additional material is added to the optical path, you risk degrading image quality.

Ultraviolet transmission filters are a different story. Instead of blocking UV energy from reaching the sensor, they make sure that nothing *except for* UV gets through. These filters are used by photographers looking to take images exclusively using UV, blocking any visible light present in the scene. Exposures are often much longer than in normal photographs or require significant boosts in ISO because CMOS sensors are not very sensitive in this region.

Infrared (IR) energy, in contrast, is inherently detected by camera sensors. Manufacturers place an *IR cut-off filter* in the sensor to block IR radiation from getting recorded. Such a filter makes it challenging or impractical to shoot IR-exclusive images. IR cut filters are not designed to be removed. However, a quick internet search can direct any enterprising photographer to many sites demonstrating techniques for removing them. Every so often a camera comes to market offering IR photography capabilities by specifically excluding this filter from its design. If you find yourself in possession of such a camera, you'll need an IR transmission filter that, similar to the UV version described earlier, only allows IR energy through.

Spectrophotometric Absorption Curves

The types of filters discussed thus far are usually sufficient to meet the needs of photographers. When more specific information is required for technical and scientific applications, *spectrophotometric curves* showing the absorption characteristics of filters are useful. The spectral transmittance of a filter is measured using a *spectrophotometer*. A spectrophotometer disperses white light to form a spectrum and measures the spectral response, using either transmittance or reflectance, over small wavelength bands. A spectrophotometer typically measures from short wavelength ultraviolet radiation through the visible region to long wavelength infrared radiation. Spectrophotometric curves represent wavelengths on the horizontal axis and transmittance or density values on the vertical axis, with the baseline representing 0% transmittance (or a density of 0).

Curves for blue, green and red color filters are shown in Figure 5-13. The maximum transmittance (or minimum density) is in the wavelength region that identifies the hue of the filter. Notice how the curves do not divide the visible spectrum neatly into thirds. It's impossible to obtain colorants that have perfectly sharp-cutting characteristics at the desired wavelengths. Additionally, most photographic

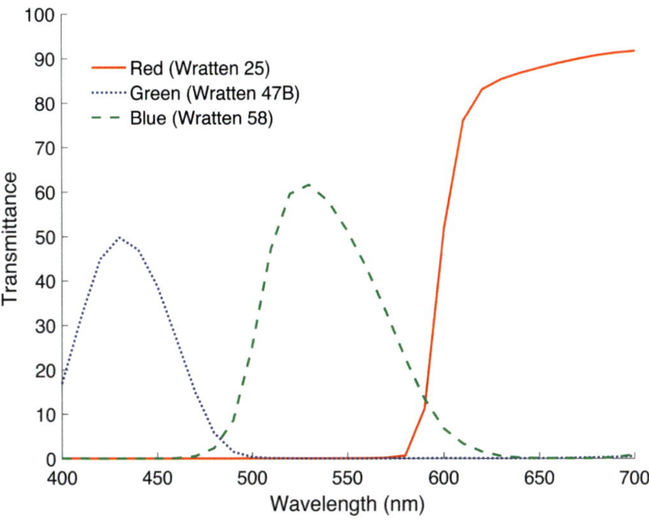

Figure 5-13 Spectrophotometric curves for blue, green and red filters.

filters transmit infrared radiation freely; infrared radiation transmittance is of little consequence because sensor designs include infrared blocking filters.

Proof of Concept: Constructing Color Images Using Color Separations

We can use color filters to make color photographs from three separate images, each exclusively exposing for one additive primary (red, green and blue). This is called shooting *color separations*. James Clerk Maxwell first demonstrated the technique in 1861. It's assumed that a color photograph taken today is captured in a single instant, but it doesn't have to be. Shooting a scene that includes moving elements becomes aesthetically interesting when the frames are combined; the "errors" involved in having a subject move during a sequence of exposures reveals the nature of the process. An outdoor scene with clouds in the sky, trees blowing in the wind or people walking by are all good candidates for color separation shooting.

Use a tripod in order to make the series of photographs. Take three gel filters: red, green and blue to hold in front of the camera lens in turn. Cheap cellophane material designed for placement over studio lights is one way to make such filters. Since they're not specifically calibrated or designed to function as lens filters, we calculated their filter factors by taking density measurements and converting to stops.

1. Set the camera to display a three-color histogram when reviewing images, as it helps to indicate proper exposure of each color separation image.
2. Take a traditional, non-filtered full color exposure first.
3. Determine proper exposure for the three sequential frames. Adjust shutter speed or aperture to obtain equivalent exposures across all three. Varying shutter speed is recommended because varying aperture results in depth of field mismatches.
4. With the red filter covering the lens, take a properly exposed image.
5. With the blue filter covering the lens, take a properly exposed image. Consider waiting 30 seconds or a few minutes to allow for movements or changes in the scene.
6. With the green filter covering the lens, take a properly exposed image. Three example images following these steps are shown in Figure 5-14.

Open the three R, G, B images and the traditional full color image in Adobe Photoshop. Paste the R, G, B images into the full color image document as layers. This is accomplished by dragging-and-dropping them or by copying and pasting. You should have a document with the full color image as the bottom layer and the three R, G or B images as layers above it.

Add a solid black color layer between the RGB separations and the full color version. This is done with a color fill layer: *Layer > New Fill Layer > Solid Color*. This results in the window shown in Figure 5-15. Click OK. Set the R, G and B values to 0 in the color picker to make the Fill Layer black.

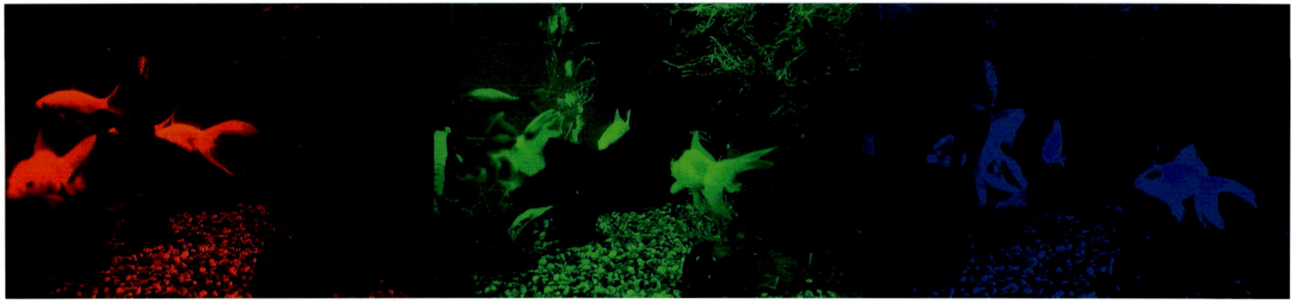

Figure 5-14 Three color separation images photographed sequentially through gel filters. Photographs by Rochester Institute of Technology photography alumni Carissa Hurdstrom and Nicole LeClair

Now you are ready to put the additive color process to work! With the red image layer selected, change the Blend Mode to "Linear Dodge (Add)" as shown in Figure 5-16.

Make this same Blend Mode change for the blue and green layers. If done correctly, the result is a full color image created by three independent exposures, each of which only recorded one of the three additive primary colors at capture. Use the Move tool to line up the three layers if there is poor registration between them.

Any differences in the scene between the three exposures appear as colorful ghosting because moving subject matter was recorded with R, G or B information exclusively at a given location (see Figure 5-17, overleaf). A significant colorcast in the composite is indicative of improper exposure in one or more of the three filtered images and we recommend trying again with more due diligence paid to exposure compensation.

Toggle visibility of the R, G, B layers to compare the composite version to the traditional full color image made in a single capture.

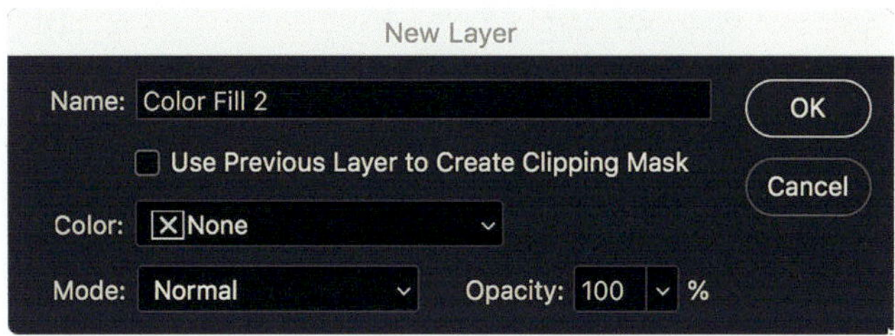

Figure 5-15 The New Fill Layer dialog box.

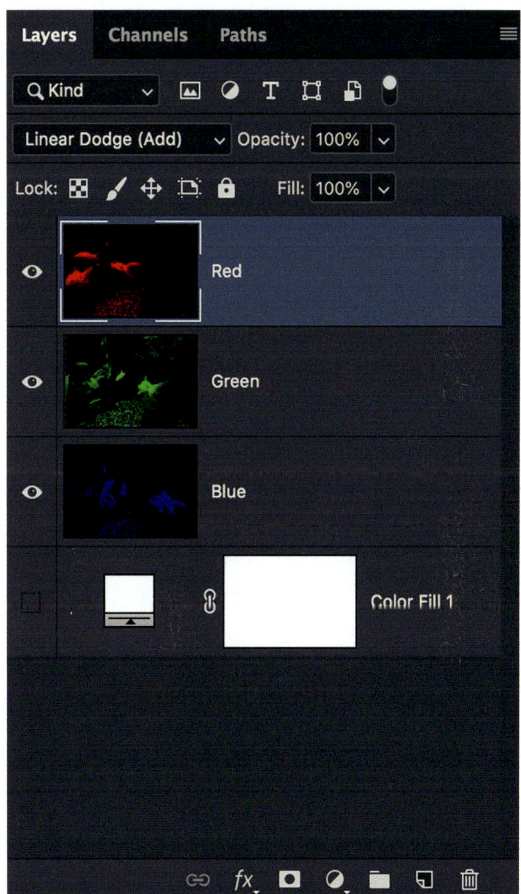

Figure 5-16 The layers palette with all image and color fill layers in place. Set the Blend Mode for red, green and blue separation image layers to Linear Dodge.

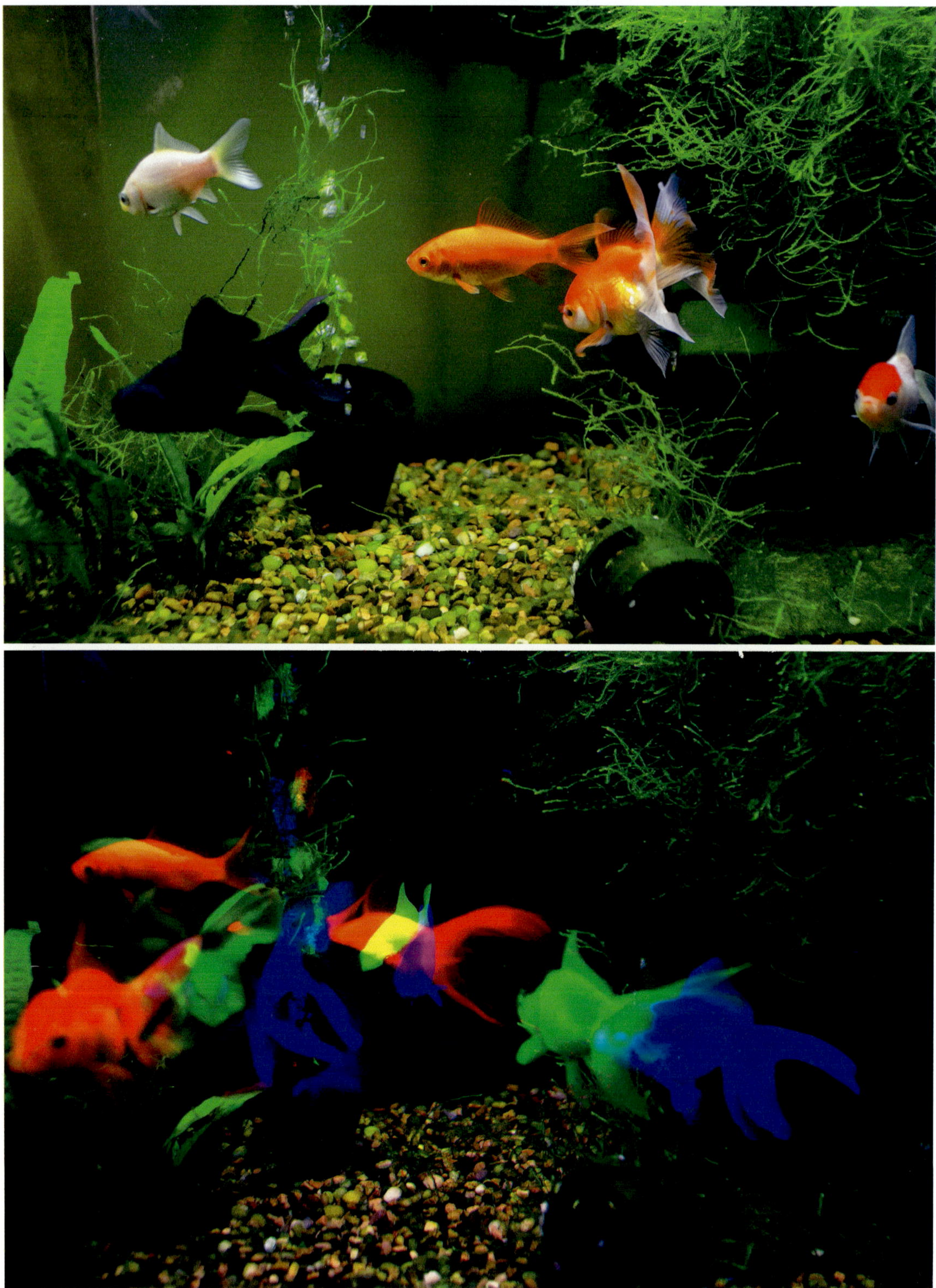

Figure 5-17 A full color image made in a single capture (top) and full color image created using three color separation captures. Photographs by Rochester Institute of Technology photography alumni Carissa Hurdstrom and Nicole LeClair

6 Motion Video Fundamentals

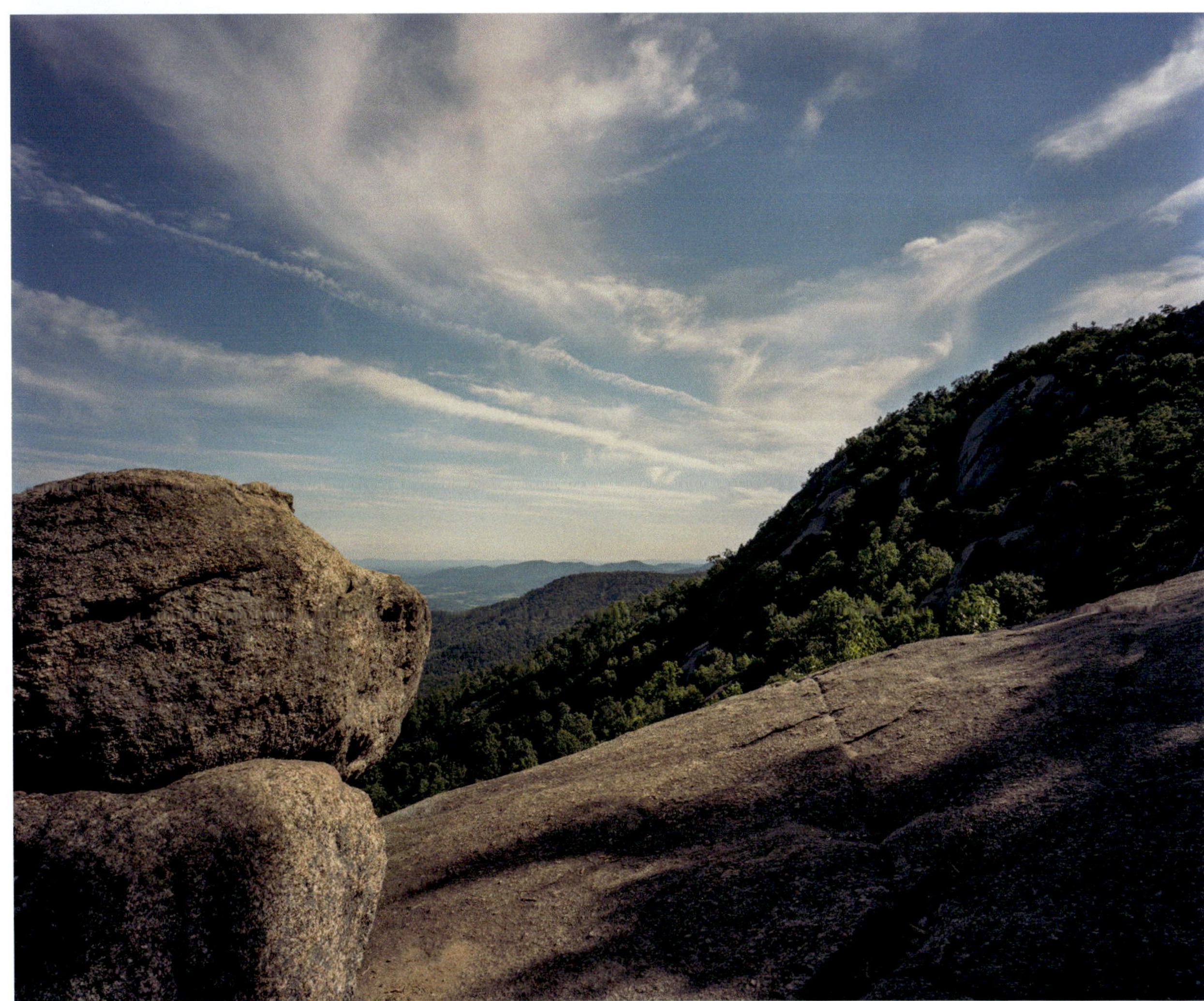

Photograph by Rochester Institute of Technology photography student Justin Scalera

Still photography and motion video share some fundamental mechanics and are often used hand in hand as visual media assets in commercial and personal spheres. The last decade saw a hardware convergence where professional still cameras gained video recording capabilities and professional video cameras gained high resolution still photography capabilities. Each medium continues to retain unique applications and artistic possibilities while the dividing line between photographer and videographer becomes less rigid. The concepts discussed in this chapter are for still photographers that find themselves working with video; to fully detail the materials and technologies of motion picture science requires a book of its own. We'll use our familiarity with photography to inform our discussion of motion video fundamentals: motion perception, video capture parameters, formats, codecs, data rates and video quality artifacts.

Motion Perception and Memory

Some of the light now reaching Earth from distant stars originated millions and even billions of years ago. Celestial events observed through powerful telescopes occurred long ago. The delay between those events and our perception of them is extreme. At smaller distances here on Earth, the delay between light falling on the retina and its perception is extremely short and negligible as it relates to our visual sense. Perceptions that occur after light stops falling on the retina, however, are of considerable importance. Such post-stimulus perceptions include persistent images, afterimages and visual memory. These human visual system responses play an important role in our experience of motion video media.

Persistent Images

Laboratory studies indicate that *persistent images* last an average of one-quarter of a second after the stimulus is removed. Consider an experiment where the letter "A" is projected onto a screen in a darkened room and the presentation time is controlled with a shutter. The presentation time cannot be made so short that the image cannot be seen, provided that luminance is increased proportionally such that the same total amount of light is available to the viewer. Equation 6.1 defines *Bloch's law* which predicts that the visual effect is the same for different combinations of luminance (I) and time (t) as long as the product (k) remains the same. Bloch's law is not valid for very bright and very low light values, however. Perception occurs with short exposure times because the persistent image keeps the image available to the viewer for somewhat longer than the actual presentation time.

$$I \times t = k \qquad \text{(Eq. 6.1)}$$

Additionally, the *apparent motion effect* is observed whereby a static stimulus is shown in a sequence of changing locations at 100 milliseconds or shorter intervals.[1] This presentation is perceived as realistic motion rather than discrete changes in stimuli position. Motion pictures began with film projected in a dark room using a rotating shutter in the projector. Each frame was positioned between the light source and the projection lens while the shutter blocked all light from projection in the time it took to advance the frames. The projection went dark between frames. The persistent image behavior and apparent motion response of our visual system combined with its *flicker fusion* prevented viewers from seeing these dark intervals that would otherwise appear as flickering brightness changes and stilted motion. Early motion pictures were sometimes referred to as *flicks* because they were shown at 16 frames per second and flicker was apparent.

Computer and television displays create the illusion of a constantly changing, smooth motion video by taking advantage of the persistent image effect so that the viewer sees a complete picture. Duration of the persistent image can vary depending upon several factors including the image luminance level and whether removal of the stimulus is followed by darkness or by another image.

It's reasonable to speculate that increasing image luminance produces a stronger effect on the visual system which then increases the duration of the persistent image. The effect is actually the reverse. The increase in persistent image duration with decreasing luminance is explained by comparing the visual effect with capturing an image at low light levels. If the sensor does not receive sufficient exposure at a selected shutter speed and aperture setting, the exposure time must be increased in order to obtain a satisfactory image. The visual system effectively compensates for the lower image luminance by sacrificing temporal resolution and increasing the duration of the persistent image, which is the equivalent of increasing the exposure time.

This effect is illustrated with motion picture film projected onto a screen. If flickering of the intermittent image is just noticeable at a certain luminance level, reducing the luminance increases the duration of the persistent image to include the time when the screen is dark and the flicker disappears. The decrease in luminance can be accomplished by using a smaller projector bulb, increasing the projector-to-screen distance or by viewing the projection through a neutral density filter.

Afterimages

The human visual response produces *afterimages* that are recognized by the viewer as visual anomalies. Afterimages are most evident when the eye is exposed to an intense flash of light. Looking directly at a camera flash usually causes the flashed individual to see a vivid afterimage bright spot for some time. An afterimage can be formed with a stimulus having lower luminance, such as a white X on a black background, by staring at it for a long time and then looking at a uniform surface (see Figure 6-1).

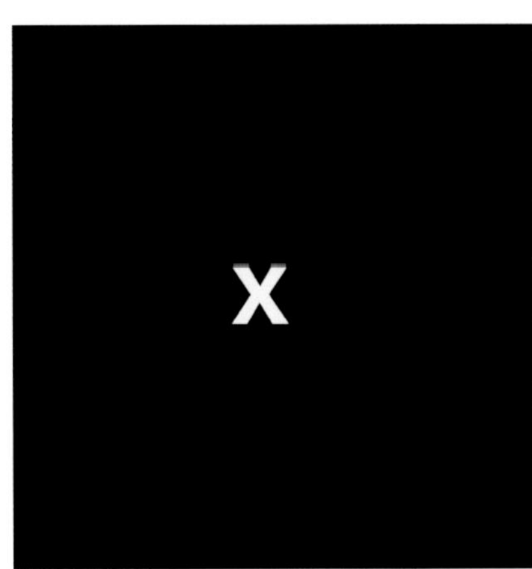

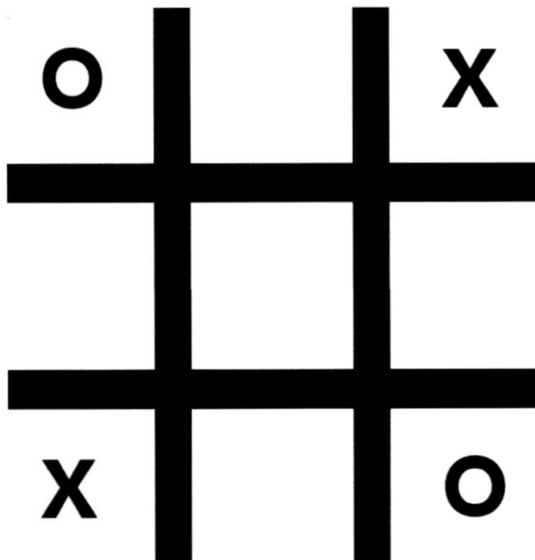

Figure 6-1 An afterimage illusion. Stare at the isolated white X for about 1 minute. Shift your gaze to the middle square in the grid below it and win the game of tic-tac-toe.

Afterimages can be negative or positive. Negative afterimages are attributed to local bleaching of the pigments in the retina's photoreceptors. Positive afterimages are due to the nerve cells continuing to fire signals to the brain. Negative afterimages of colored stimuli tend to be approximately complementary in color: a bright yellow light tends to produce a bluish afterimage, for example.

Visual Memory

Visual memory shares many characteristics with other types of memory but it includes an ability to retain or recall a visual image that is distinct from persistent images and afterimages. Visual memories can be short term or long term. They are exploited heavily by filmmakers to consciously and subconsciously build connections and structure with imagery. Just as a phone number can be remembered long enough to dial it by repeating it and keeping it in the conscious mind, so too can a visual image be remembered for a short time by keeping it in visual memory. Experiments indicate that most people cannot retain more than five to nine independent pieces of information in short-term memory (phone numbers are pushing it, even when breaking them up with cadence).

Furthermore, a viewer should not expect to remember, even for a short time, all of the details in a complex picture. One tends to remember the details that attract the most attention or hold the most interest. Short-term visual memory is used even when scanning a picture and fixating on different parts of the composition. This enables us to create a composite perception of the total picture. Once attention is allowed to go on to other things, long-term memory is required to revive an earlier visual image. Except for simple stimuli such as a circle or a square, visual memory images are generally not facsimile representations of the original scene; they usually contain just the most important details.

The human visual system is designed to detect motion over the entire area of the retina so that moving objects in the periphery of our field of view are detected.

A semi-reflexive eye movement enables the viewer to position the moving object image on the fovea of the retina where visual acuity is highest. Once the object is fixated, the visual system is quite good in tracking its movement unless the speed is very high or the direction of movement is erratic. It is almost impossible to pan the eyes smoothly except when tracking a moving object. Instead, the eyes tend to move in quick jumps called *saccades* that are apparent in high speed video recordings. Skill in tracking rapidly moving objects is important for photographers looking to catch the optimal moment, be it an athlete's action or the perfect timing of everyday activity. Our visual memory weighs these tracked objects heavily and may miss static or surrounding detail as events unfold.

Defining Motion Video and its Parameters

In a world of digital publications, Twitter, messaging apps and streaming television, how do we draw the boundaries between visual media formats? A photograph traditionally meant a single instance captured in an image frame, viewed on a physical output medium like print. A video traditionally meant motion pictures capturing longer durations and viewed on a display or projection screen. Photographs were viewed on a wall or on the page while video was watched in a movie theater or on television. Today's use of photography and videography is decidedly more blended and their output is frequently through mobile and personal computing devices. Still, a baseline set of parameters delineate *motion video* (sometimes colloquially called "film" or simply "video") from photographs. Let's expand on the characteristics that make motion video a unique medium while highlighting what the photographer must consider when working with video parameters.

Frame Rate

A photograph is a single frame. It captures an ephemeral instance of time even with long exposures since they ultimately compress temporal changes into a static visual. Motion video takes the photograph and multiplies it: it's a sequence of image frames shown in rapid succession in a way that our human visual system perceives as similar to our experience of the living, moving world (see Figure 6-2). This perception of motion from sequences of discrete, still pictures is known as the *phi phenomenon*. How many frames are used every second to perceive smooth, natural and real-time motion? Full motion video is generally considered to be at least 15 *frames per second* (fps). Video with this *frame rate*, the number of frames displayed in one second of playback, appears stilted even though it begins to convey a series of instances in sequence. This stilted look is a video quality artifact called *motion jitter*. The number of frames recorded per second is a form of *temporal sampling* similar to how sensor resolution is a form of *spatial sampling*. The greater the sampling rate, the more information recorded over the capture duration and the smoother motion appears.

Early silent film endeavors featured 16–18 fps recordings. This satisfied the fluid motion component but was not enough temporal sampling for natural-sounding audio. A higher frame rate of 24 fps supplanted 18 to accommodate an audio track which settled into a long-standing standard for motion pictures. Our many decades of watching and enjoying films captured at 24 frames per second at a specific shutter angle (described later in this chapter) means that we have a particular familiarity and penchant for its motion characteristics.

Standard capture and playback frame rates for motion video are 24, 29.97, 48 and 59.94 frames per second. Cinema primarily uses 24 fps; consumer recording devices tend to record at 29.97 fps. Professional still cameras including SLRs offer multiple standard recording frame rate options. Anything higher than 30 fps is considered *high frame rate* (HFR). Lower frame rates mean fewer total frames for a given video recording duration and therefore might be considered if storage space is an issue. High frame rate capture and playback is particularly beneficial with fast moving subjects and camera movement like panning shots. Traditional panning shots must be below a certain speed for the viewer to keep track of the scene content at 24 frames per second. High frame rates reduce motion blur and panning smoothness.[2]

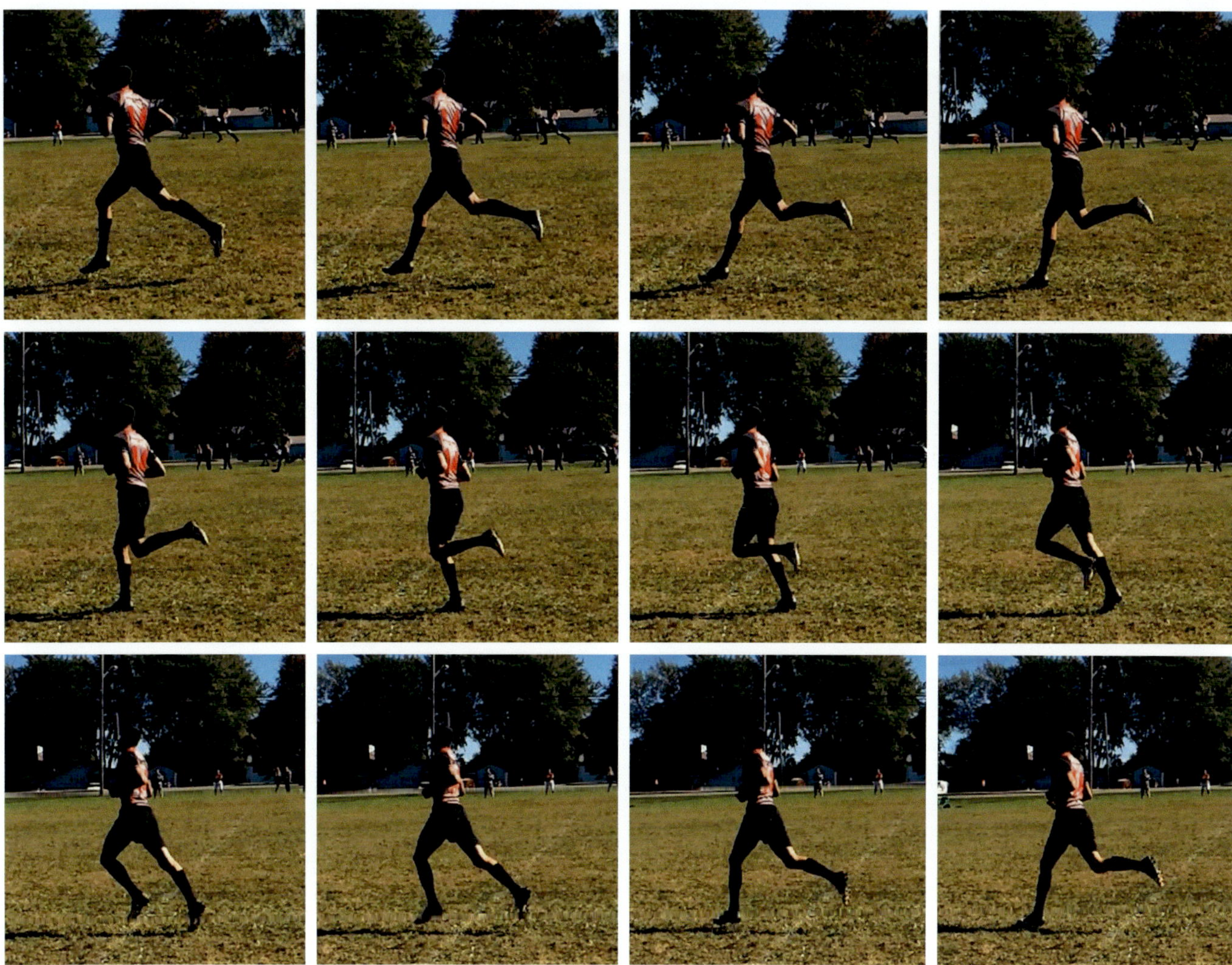

Figure 6-2 A sequence of video frames captured at 30 frames per second.

Capture frame rate and playback frame rate are not always matched. Time-lapse imagery can show a flower bud transitioning into full bloom in a matter of seconds despite recording the event over many hours. On the other end of the scale, recording at frame rates above 48 fps is common practice when the intent is to play those frames back at a standard 24 fps. This is the basis for slow motion video. By sampling many more frames in real time at capture and playing them back at a lesser rate, time is expanded to show brief moments of action over longer durations. Capturing at hundreds or thousands of frames per second is what makes filming extreme slow motion events like explosions or guns firing possible. Recording at 10,000 fps and playing it back at 24 fps, for example, slows down real-time motion to 1/400th of the original speed. Expanding these incredibly fast events to play out over a time scale that our visual system is attuned to reveals a temporal experience of our world that is otherwise inaccessible. Figure 6-3 (overleaf) shows sequential frames from a high speed video recording of a fast event. The motion details and microsecond events that unfold become easily observable in a way that is impossible in real time.

Note that reducing frame rate is a viable form of data compression as it lessens the amount of stored data relative to a higher frame rate original. However, the visual impact of lowering a video's frame rate is often not worth the storage gains. This strategy is also hampered by the

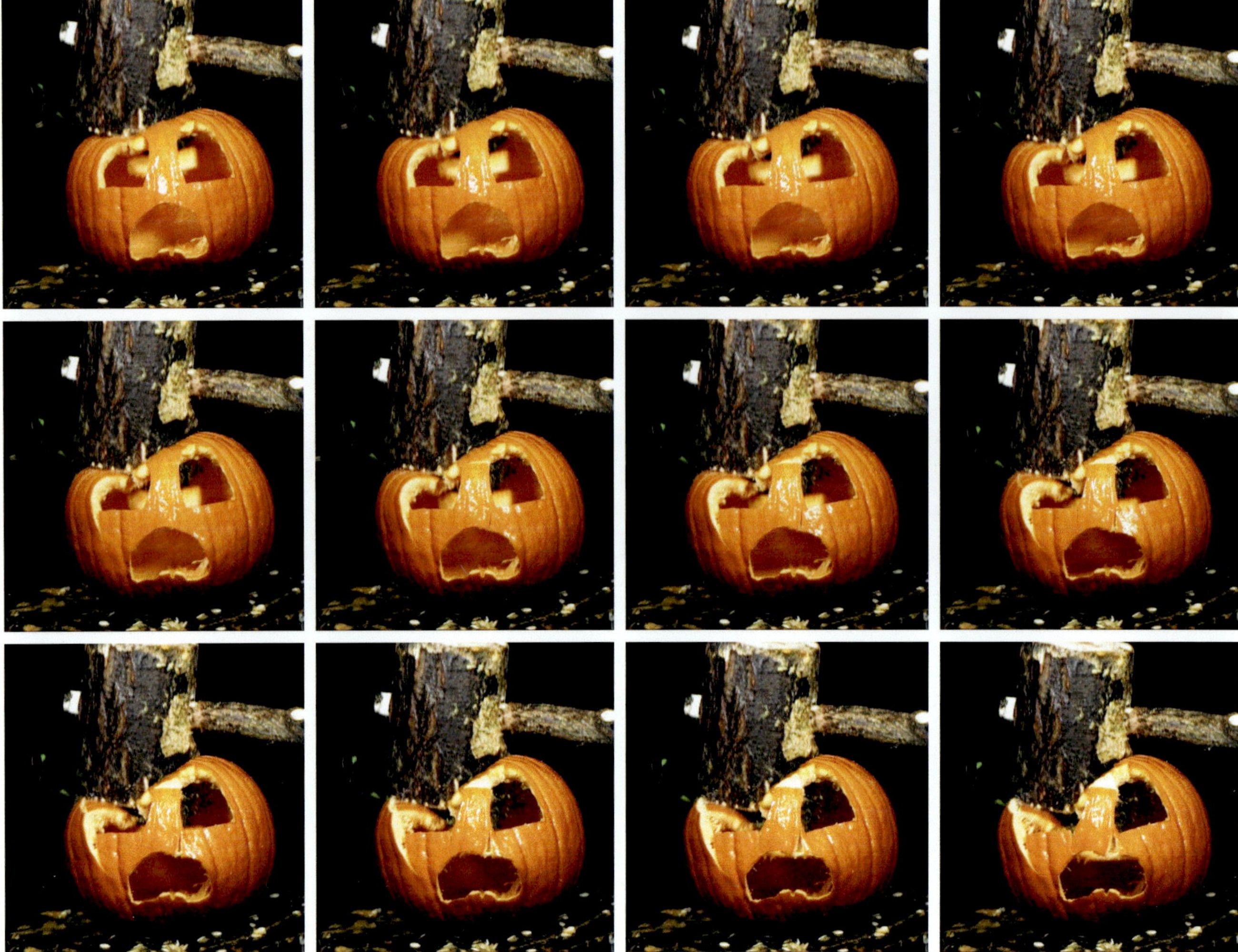

Figure 6-3 A sequence of frames from a high frame rate capture. Playing the frames back at 24 fps creates a slow motion effect that dilates time. Photographs by Rochester Institute of Technology Assistant Professor Ted Kinsman

math of turning 30 fps into 24 fps, as one example, since it involves blending, interpolating or dropping select frames in a specific pattern. It's more common to decrease frame size or data rate to lessen the amount of video data.

Shutter Angle

Photography and videography both start with the act of recording light. However, a single instance frozen in a photograph makes up just a fraction of a second of screen time in a video. This is an area of friction if your photography exposure knowledge is ingrained and you're new to video; the photographer's available range of exposure times is vast compared to that of a videographer. Photographic exposure can integrate many moments of time into one combined image, like in the case of a long exposure of highway traffic at night. The changing positions of car headlights and taillights are never still and the resulting photograph shows long light streaks along the road. Motion video exposure cannot extend or integrate multiple seconds into one frame in quite this way if the goal is recording light over a period of time. Instead, frame exposure is limited in duration based on the frame rate.

Analog motion picture cameras use continuous rolls of photographic film. A gate or rotary shutter moves in front of the film for a fraction of a second to create distinct, separate exposures. Where a still camera's focal plane shutter is a pair of synchronized curtains, a motion picture camera shutter is a circular disc with an angled opening whose size dictates exposure duration. Digital image sensors reproduce the effect of rotary shutters by electronically controlling exposure time and frame readout. As we learned in Chapter 4, longer shutter speeds introduce motion blur as scene motion can occur over a single frame's exposure duration. Thus, one of the biggest departures from still photography exposure variables is the *shutter angle* relative to the frame rate and it is described in degrees. Though digital cameras lack a physical rotary shutter like their analog ancestors, the concept here remains the same and the term persists. A 360° shutter angle is the largest possible setting and means that a single frame is exposed for the entire duration possible while recording at a given frame rate. Calculating video shutter speed is accomplished using the formula in Equation 6.2:

$$\text{Shutter Speed (sec)} = \frac{1}{\frac{\text{Frame Rate (fps)} \times 360\text{ (degrees)}}{\text{Shutter Angle (degrees)}}} \qquad \text{(Eq. 6.2)}$$

A 360° shutter angle when recording at 30 fps equates to a single frame exposure time of 1/30th second. It is impossible to record 30 unique frames in 1 second if a single frame is exposed for longer than 1/30th. A shutter angle of 180° renders an exposure time of 1/60th second at the same frame rate, as it represents a rotary shutter that exposes for exactly half of its rotation. Smaller shutter angles translate to shorter exposure times and less motion blur. A shutter angle of 180° is traditional for motion picture capture and creates the degree of blur we're accustomed to seeing in movies. It also dictates how quickly filmmakers can pan the camera and expect viewers to clearly follow and focus the action. A smaller shutter angle is imperative if there is an expectation of pulling still photographs from high-resolution video: it increases the likelihood that individual frames are sharp with minimal motion blur. Small shutter angles mean fast shutter speeds which translates to crisp, frozen motion. Going too fast in shutter speed is problematic because it leaves temporal gaps at standard frame rates. A shutter speed of 1/500th second at 30 fps, for example, might be great for pulling a still frame but in motion looks choppy and becomes difficult to watch.

Ultimately, video considers shutter speed or shutter angle in the context of the desired frame rate as it limits the upper end of how long a single frame can be exposed. Faster frame rates are more light-hungry in the sense that the available exposure durations are more limited. Both frame rate and shutter speed are time-based characteristics, but frame rate on its own does not define the duration of one frame's exposure.

All of this is important because exposure in video is much more dependent on light manipulation and control to achieve good motion characteristics, desired depth of field (via the aperture), standard frame rates and overall brightness. Better sensor sensitivity helps, though video production is strongly aided by bright, continuous light sources on set and neutral density filters when natural light is not easily controlled.

Resolution

Digital video resolution, the number of pixels that make up the two-dimensional frame, is strictly standardized. There's no technical reason why a video can't be 3000 by 250 pixels but it doesn't make for an enjoyable viewing experience when our displays cannot adapt to unusual shapes or dimensions. Viewers appreciate the consistency of standard video resolutions and that content makes full use of their expensive television's screen real estate.

A single frame of video, until recently, was lower resolution than any digital still image; the difference is that the brain has plenty to process when presented with dozens of images per second. Photographers sometimes describe an image file in terms of megapixels as a shorthand for the number of pixels in height and width. However, aside from bragging, this is not a particularly useful descriptor for still images. Additionally, photographs can be every possible combination of pixel widths and heights. Video has distinct resolutions that tell us a key parameter of the viewing experience. Table 6-1 (overleaf) lists the industry standard video resolutions in pixel dimensions, aspect ratio (the ratio of frame width to height) and the general name for each

Table 6-1 Standard video resolutions and their aspect ratios.

Video Resolution	Pixel Dimensions (Width x Height)	Aspect Ratio (Width:Height)
Standard Definition (SD), "480p"	640x480	4:3 or 1.33:1
High Definition (HD), "720p"	1280x720	16:9 or 1.78:1
High Definition (Full HD), "1080p"	1920x1080	16:9 or 1.78:1
Ultra High Definition (UHD), "4K"	3840x2160	16:9 or 1.78:1
Digital Cinema 4K	4096x2160	1.85:1; 2.35:1
Ultra High Definition (UHD), "8K"	7680x4320	16:9 or 1.78:1

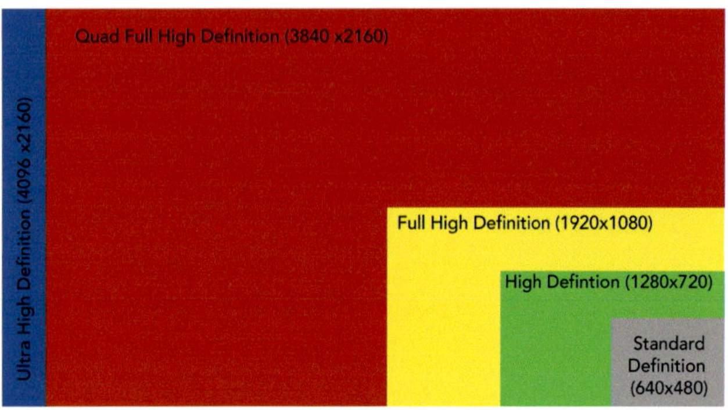

Figure 6-4 Relative frame sizes of standard video resolutions.

tier. Figure 6-4 illustrates the relative frame sizes of the different video resolutions. Note that the higher resolution formats are large enough that single frames are serviceable as reproducible photographs.

It's easy to see the progression: *standard definition* (SD) came first and was superseded by *high definition* (HD). There are two versions of high definition with the larger (and more common) designated as *Full HD*. From there, video started being captured and displayed at *ultra high definitions* or UHD (4K and 8K are both members of this club). We're skimming past the distinction between *interlaced* and *progressive scan* simply because you're unlikely to encounter interlaced video in today's media landscape. However, note that the "p" in "1080p" indicates a video as progressive scan.

It's common for sensors to record at resolutions greater than the intended output, i.e. recording at 2K to produce a 1280x720 video. The additional captured pixels likely won't be used—in the end, 1280x720 pixels are in the final video frame—but it offers the flexibility to crop in from a wider view or digitally pan the composition. This strategy is known as *overscan*. The additional pixels also help for electronic image stabilization processing that employs a form of digital panning to keep subjects at a static position in the video frame. Just like rolling out the dough for covering a pie, it helps to have a little more than what's needed rather than leaving zero margin for error. This is particularly helpful for photographers whose cameras allow for ultra-high-definition video recording resolutions.

Aspect Ratio

Similar to resolution, video requires working with a limited set of aspect ratios to ensure supported and standardized output across displays. The *aspect ratio* is the relationship between the width and height dimensions of a frame or video without a dependency on physical dimensions or pixel counts. A square frame has an aspect ratio of 1:1 as its height and width dimensions are equal. The larger the difference between the two numbers, the more rectangular the shape.

The cinema dictated the early decades of film formats and commonly used aspect ratios went through different eras. The Academy aspect ratio was 1.375:1 until the 1950s while some short-lived formats went as wide as 2.35:1 (CinemaScope).[3] Today, the cinema standard is 1.85:1. High-definition television and computer displays frequently use 1.77:1, also known as 16:9. This was likely picked because it sits comfortably between the 4:3 standard for television that came before it and the 1.85:1 standard for movies and film. An aspect ratio that is wider than it is tall is inherent to motion video due to our vision's larger horizontal field of view. This is different from photographs, which have always allowed portrait and landscape frame orientations in output reproduction.

The only time we accept aspect ratios that differ from our televisions or phone screens is when padding called *letterboxing* (or its sideways equivalent, *pillarboxing*) is used; black bars are added above and below or on either side of the active video area. Even then, we understand that this strategy is not making full use of the total pixels available on the displays.

Consumers buy televisions or hold their phones sideways and expect that the majority of our display is put to good use in playing video content. When there's a mismatch between the aspect ratio of a video and that of the display, playback software has three options:

1. Crop the video in the height or width dimension to fill the screen
2. Add letterboxing (black bars on the top and bottom)
3. Add pillarboxing (black bars on the left and right)

An aspect ratio of 4:3 was the norm in the days of standard definition and is a ratio that photographers find familiar. High-definition formats, including the broadcast television standard, use a 16:9 aspect ratio. This is more of an elongated rectangle compared to 4:3 as shown in Figure 6-5.

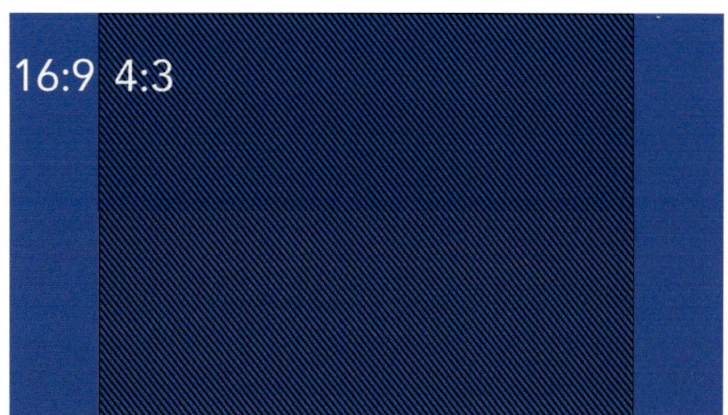

Figure 6-5 The width and height of SD and HD frames, independent of resolution, shows the difference in aspect ratio. High definition often uses a wider 16:9 while standard definition uses the squarer 4:3.

Video Formats and Encoding Strategies

Digital videos are stored in a variety of file formats. In contrast to image file formats, video file formats are containers and do not dictate everything about their contents in the way that a JPEG or TIFF does. A JPEG file describes the format—JPEG has a particular structure to storing metadata and image pixel information—and it also dictates the use of the JPEG compression algorithm. Video coding separates the two elements; both the container format (also called the *wrapper*) and the compression method must be defined and knowing one does not necessarily tell us what the other will be. Video files consist of the video stream, the audio if applicable, metadata and the encoding information encapsulated in a container. Common video container formats include MOV, AVI, MP4, MKV and MPEG with file extensions that match.

If the video container is like the carry-on luggage, the *codec* is how you pack your clothes to travel. A codec is the hardware or software that handles writing and reading video data for storage and playback. The term comes from a concatenation of *compression-decompression* and its role is handling the *encoding* and *decoding* of video data. A video must first be encoded for the data to be organized and stored in a container file. The container likely also contains audio data which requires its own type of encoding. The act of encoding involves applying compression algorithms so that the video is efficiently packaged. This encoded data can be stored to memory or transferred over a network and when it gets to its destination, it is decoded—unpacked, translated—before it can be played back to the viewer. Codecs are the heart of a video file when we want to know how to play it and what to expect in terms of compression and compatibility. At risk of overusing the analogy, video containers are easy to convert between in much the same way that clothes can be moved from one carry-on to another. This does not change the contents or the weird way you fold your socks, only the storage mechanism.

Photographers take for granted that JPEG images are universally and instantaneously decoded by image viewers and photo editing software. Video must be similarly decoded, though it has to happen on a per-frame basis. If it can't be done quickly, we don't get to see seamless full motion video. A piece of software or hardware works in real-time to decode and unpack the video (and audio if present) fast enough to put a frame on screen at just the right moment.

Intraframe and Interframe Encoding

Frames are the building block of a motion video. Recall that a standard 30 fps video has 30 unique images shown over a 1-second duration. The process of encoding video starts with a basic question: how do these frames relate to one another in sequence? It's very likely that, over the course of one single second, some of the content in those 30 frames is shared (Figure 6-6 shows one such example). Put another way, the content remains mostly the same across fractions of seconds of elapsed time. Even within a frame, it's likely that local groups of pixels are similar. Both of these facts help codecs approach compression strategies to great effect.

A single video frame is subdivided into square groups of pixels called *macroblocks* that are treated as single units for compression and motion compensation. A common size for macroblocks is 16x16 pixels. *Intraframe compression* looks at sections of a frame, most often grouped into macroblocks, and independently compresses those sections. The encoder's compression considers only the pixels in that frame similar to JPEG compression on a single photograph. A video player decodes the data one macroblock at a time.

Interframe compression considers the frame information that comes before and after the frame being compressed. This is where the video encoding process takes advantage of the redundancy across a proximate set of frames called *temporal redundancy*. If the information exists in frame 1 and stays the same for frames 2, 3 and 4, frames 2–4 don't need to store that same information. The only pixel

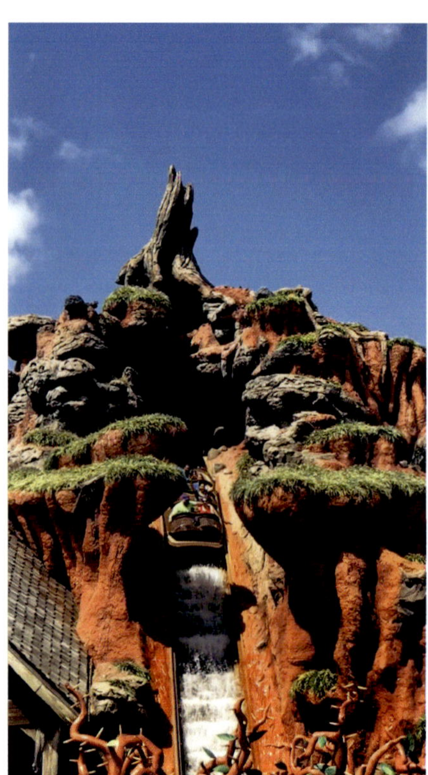
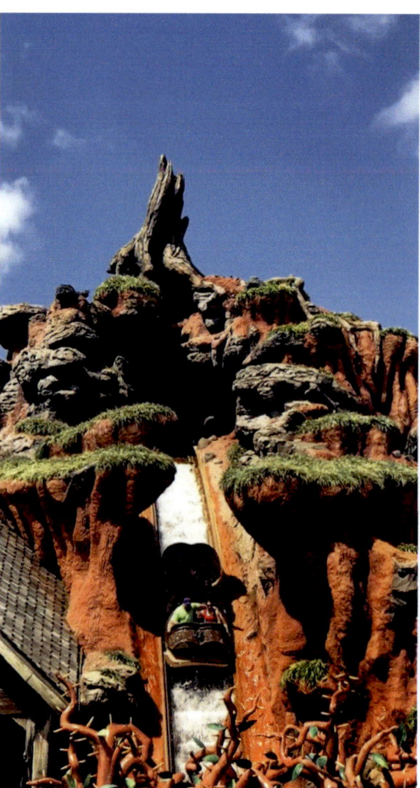
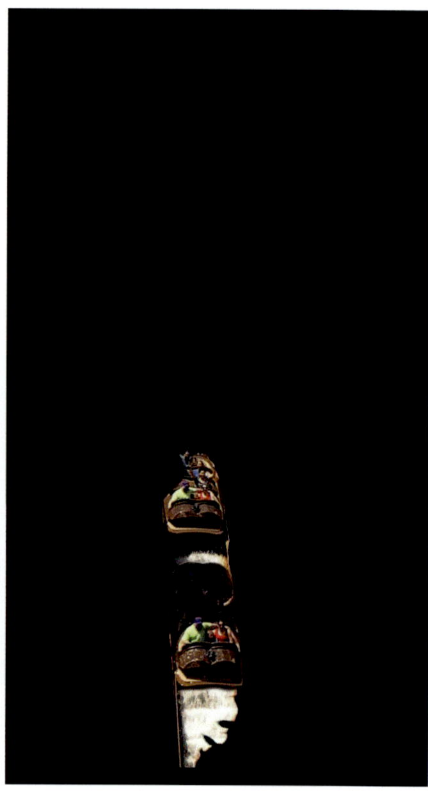

Figure 6-6 Some videos feature relatively static pixel content from one frame to the next with a subset that changes over their duration. Above, the third image shows a frame-differenced view of the areas that see changing content.

information that must be stored in those subsequent frames is that which changes in brightness or color. Thus, video encoded using interframe compression specifies *coded picture frame types* to minimize redundancies and data storage while maintaining image content over its duration.

There are three frame types in interframe encoding. The first is the *intra-coded* or *I-frame* (also known as the key frame). I-frames are completely new, wholly independent pixel content. The macroblocks of the I-frame can be compressed but there is no dependency on the frame that precedes it or the frame that follows. It helps to associate the "I" in I-frame with "independent." Every so often (the exact interval is controlled by the encoder), an encoded video needs an I-frame as a sort of data landmark. These can be one second apart or 20 seconds apart, for example. The easiest video encoding for a decoder to process is a video comprised entirely of I-frames as they are effectively sequential JPEG photographs. The downside to encoding purely I-frames is that the file size becomes gigantic. The increased computational complexity of introducing frame types beyond I-frames is an acceptable compromise in an effort to keep file sizes manageable.

Between I-frames are *predicted* or *P-frames* when a video is encoded with varying coded picture frame types. P-frames rely on information from a preceding I-frame to decode, as they only contain information related to changes that happen in the time elapsed from that last I-frame. They borrow everything else from the referenced frame. They are also referred to as *delta frames* to reflect this behavior. P-frames are smaller in size and are compressed more aggressively to save on space. Since a P-frame is only seen for a fraction of a second, you're not as likely to notice as long as high-quality I-frames appear at a regular interval. P-frames can be very small relative to I-frames assuming that little motion occurs from frame to frame.

Bidirectional or *B-frames* are sometimes used in encoded video between I-frames. The bidirectional characteristic means that they reference pixel information from the preceding frames and the ones that follow. They can be compressed even more than P-frames and are the most efficient frame time as a result since they take advantage of redundant content in either direction. A B-frame only contains pixel content that doesn't exist in the previous or following frame which can translate to a small amount of new data. Encoding and decoding a video with B-frames is more computationally intensive and is sometimes avoided to ensure compatibility with lower-end output devices.

Both B-frames and P-frames use *motion estimation vectors* to identify pixel groups that appear to stay the same while moving in the frame between two I-frames. If the camera is static, motion vectors are effective at storing only the position changes of pixels. A moving camera and a moving subject make this technique less efficient, as much of the frame is rapidly changing from one moment to the next. Motion vectors can cause visual warping or other quality artifacts if there's any data loss or errors when encoding I-frames. Figure 6-7 (overleaf) shows a video frame with a motion vector overlay. Notice how the static surround does not show any but the falling log flume is identified as a subset of image pixels with a downward movement that will continue into succeeding frames.

A few seconds of video may be encoded to consist of all three of these frame types (I, P and B) in an arrangement called a *group of pictures* (GOP) illustrated in Figure 6-8 (overleaf). Video decoding software often requires that playback start at the beginning of a GOP because it needs to establish the first I-frame that is decoded without dependency on other frame data. You may find that video players take a moment or two to start playing back video content, especially when seeking through a timeline: this is related to the software locating the start of a GOP. You may also notice frame quality "breathe" in and out in heavily compressed video: the P-frames and B-frames degrade quickly but the I-frames show the least compression and appear with the least amount of quality artifacts on a recurring basis. For the most part, the perceptual phenomenon of visual memory makes interframe compression extremely effective; we remember details from previous frames and primarily follow pieces in motion.

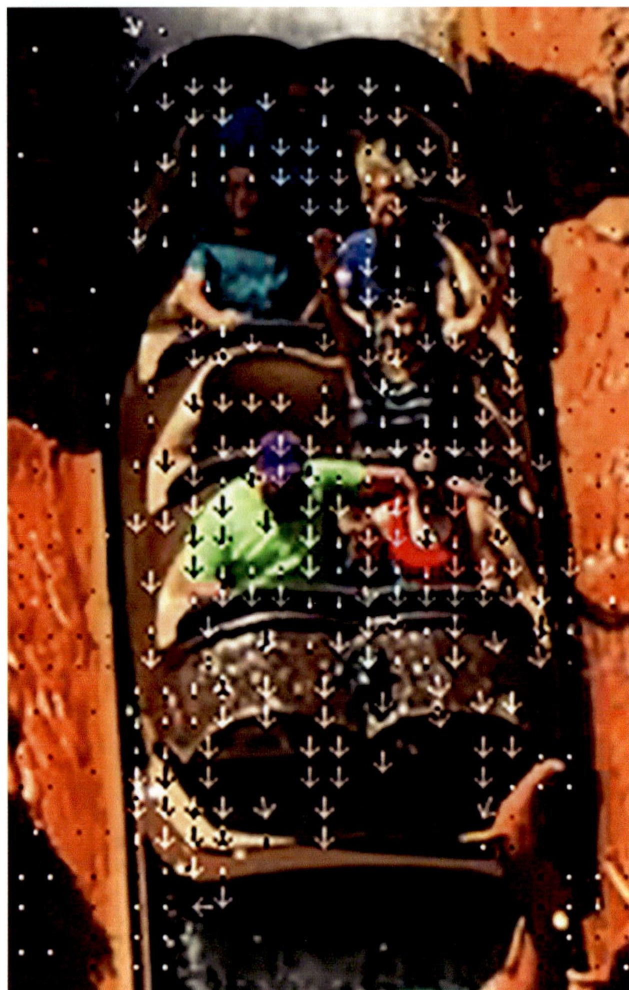

Figure 6-7 A single frame from a video clip with a motion vector overlay. The motion estimation data is used to efficiently encode P-frames and B-frames.

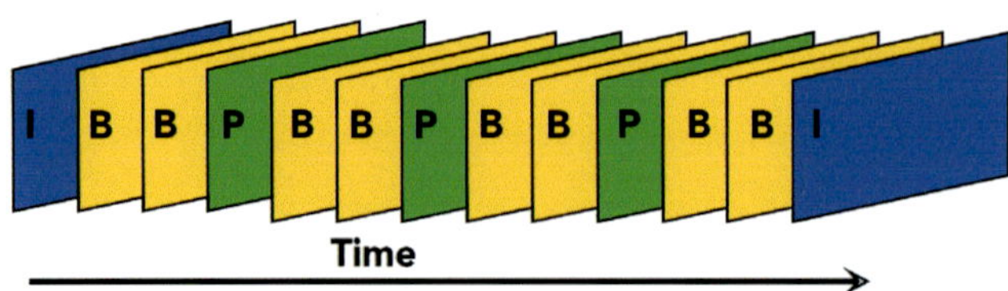

Figure 6-8 A group of pictures structure for sequential video frames using interframe encoding. The GOP is measured from an I-frame up until (but not including) the next I-frame. This illustration shows a GOP size of 12.

Chroma Subsampling

Our outsized sensitivity to luminance means that, particularly when it comes time to keep file sizes small and convenient, color data is simplified or otherwise made a lesser priority. That doesn't necessarily translate to observable quality degradation but it is important to appreciate how effective compression is accomplished. The story is the same for digital motion video: it's costly to store all of the bits to describe every pixel luminance and color and every location when there are tens of frames to store for every second of play time. The forms of video encoding encountered by photographers employ *chroma subsampling* to slim down the amount of information needed to render a full color video. Chroma subsampling is a type of lossy compression. Skipping chroma subsampling is preferred only when the post-processing workflow needs the maximum amount of editing headroom.

The video data is divided into a *luma* (tone) component and two *chrominance* (color) components. Video uses a sampling ratio shorthand to describe exactly how the chrominance information is subsampled that we describe further in Chapter 12.

Video Codecs

Video codecs are responsible for systematically packaging the video data and for its equal and opposite unpacking. They are an outside force that the data relies upon for reading and writing it. The *encoder* part of the codec packs a video into a *bitstream* of compressed data for storage and transmission. The *decoder* unpacks and decompresses the bitstream, often on-the-fly during playback, for viewing.[4] An encoded video takes up less space on disk but requires a decoder to be a playable asset. The goal is always to minimize the data stored and transmitted while maintaining video quality. Codecs are used for videos, videoconferencing and live streaming. The most commonly encountered video codecs are described here. Any time that an encoded video file is re-encoded with different parameters (for example, a lower frame rate or frame size) it's called *transcoding*. Transcoding can compound or exacerbate compression artifacts and must be minimized in a video workflow.

Motion JPEG

The easiest video codec to remember is *Motion JPEG* (or MJPEG) because its name indicates what you're getting. This codec does not use any interframe encoding and instead treats each frame exactly how stand-alone image files are compressed. It is a sequence of JPEGs with each frame compressed independent of one another (intraframe encoding). MJPEG is like having a video that's entirely I-frames (like a favorite childhood breakfast cereal composed exclusively of the marshmallow bits). Motion JPEG is not practical because of its large file sizes, yet we mention it because it's such an easy logic jump from working with JPEG-compressed photographs.

MPEG-4 Advanced Video Coding (H.264)

The most commonly used codec today is *MPEG-4 Advanced Video Coding* (AVC) also known as *H.264*. Its ubiquity is due to its flexibility and performance; AVC is a family of profiles that fit a variety of video needs like minimal disk storage or low bandwidth streaming. The codec compresses frames at the macroblock level and uses motion prediction to efficiently store parts of the image that change while keeping unchanging parts the same. AVC compression is widely supported by browsers, televisions, mobile devices and anything else you find yourself watching video media on. Its compatibility makes it a great choice when sharing through platforms where the content creator doesn't have precise control over the viewer's decoding setup. In constant use for well over a decade, AVC is an excellent default choice for video encoding. The codec is supported by the common video container formats MOV and MP4.

High Efficiency Video Coding (H.265)

The successor to the ubiquitous H.264 codec is *H.265*, formalized in 2013. It has a secondary name, too: *High Efficiency Video Coding* (HEVC). This codec is capable of compressing video to half the size that AVC is able to encode. This means that the same video file requires half of the bandwidth or storage when encoded with HEVC over AVC. Alternatively, it means that we can make a video twice as large (say, through higher resolution) and stream it across the same bandwidth previously used for an AVC video. The 50% efficiency number is touted in marketing despite real-world results yielding closer to 35–40% improvements at comparable quality.[5] This is considerable, though it's always a good idea to test and evaluate compression strategies with your specific content. A 2017 survey of video developers showed that 28% were working with HEVC in their workflows.[6] HEVC is supported by MOV and MP4 containers.

HEVC uses smaller subdivisions than macroblocks for compression (transform blocks, further subdivided into predictive blocks) and forgoes the straightforward macroblock encoding approach for a *coding tree* algorithm. It also offers motion prediction vectors more advanced than AVC encoding. These help to compress more effectively but add encoding and decoding complexity. Early use was limited to desktop computer platforms that guaranteed a level of computing power to decode for smooth playback. Mobile processors have caught up, though, and are now up to the task. HEVC is not the only candidate available for high-quality, high bitrate motion video, though it has increasing support in streaming media applications. AVC is capable of encoding large frame resolutions like 4K and 8K, however, you'll find that these data-heavy formats increasingly opt for HEVC encoding instead. This is to minimize the bandwidth needs as our hunger for larger video grows. HEVC's official successor is already in the works and is tentatively called *Versatile Video Coding* (VVC).[7]

VP9

Concurrent to the development of HEVC, Google created its own video codec for the modern web and beyond called *VP9*. There are eight versions that precede it, many of them developed by On2 Technologies (which was bought by Google in 2010). It's an open-source standard in contrast to AVC and HEVC, which require royalty payments from companies that use them to serve up thousands of videos on our phones, televisions and websites. Given that Google owns YouTube, it is not surprising that they have joined the fight to optimize video encoding while avoiding royalties or dependencies on outside parties.

AOMedia Video 1 (AV1)

Very recently finalized, as of this writing, *AOMedia Video 1* or *AV1* was developed by the Alliance for Open Media consortium. The consortium designed AV1 to replace VP9 as a royalty-free, next generation video codec in direct competition for widespread adoption against HEVC. Its specification requires a low computational footprint that is optimized for mobile hardware to produce consistent, high-quality real-time video delivery that's scalable to any bandwidth. AV1's development team expects an approximate 30% improvement over VP9 and HEVC, though current usability is limited due to very long encoding times.

Audio in Video

Sound is digitally recorded *monoscopically* (one microphone, one direction), *stereoscopically* (two microphones for two-channel playback) or *spatially* (surround sound or binaural). Stereo audio begins to emulate our two audio sensors: our ears. However, our sense of space in three dimensions is due in part to our incredibly nuanced ability to sense small differences in volume and direction. The more we can sample audio in all directions and play it back as if it's originating from those many directions, the more immersive and realistic the experience. Professional productions do not rely on built-in microphones because of their relatively poor sound recording quality and because they are fixed to the camera body itself. If the sounds of interest are not near the camera, the recording ability becomes severely limited. Many cameras offer plug-in microphone jack options, at the very least, though serious productions leave the audio recording to completely independent hardware including digital audio recorders. Audio tracks are synchronized and combined with the visuals in post-production.

Similar to video, audio is an analog phenomenon sampled, recorded and converted to a digital signal that must be encoded and decoded. The higher the *sampling rate*, measured as a function of samples per second, the higher the audio fidelity. The higher the sampling rate, the more data generated and stored. Common audio sampling rates are 44.1, 48, 96 and 192 kHz. The digital audio signal can be recorded at different bit depths (8, 12, 16, 24) that dictate the maximum number of bits used to define each sample, similar to image sensors and photographs.

A video file container holds an encoded video bitstream alongside an encoded audio bitstream. This audio stream is compressed and packaged with its own codec that is similarly decoded upon playback; audio also inherently contains redundancy that can be simplified with compression algorithms. The *Free Lossless Audio Codec* (FLAC) is an open source, lossless option. Not all audio playback hardware or software is capable of decoding FLAC data and just like TIFF files in the photo world, FLAC audio can be cumbersome overkill for most end-user applications. *MP3* is a well-known lossy compression codec and file container that stems from the same encoding protocols as AVC. *Advanced Audio Coding* or AAC is MP3's successor. It's a lossy codec that produces higher audio quality with comparable file sizes to MP3. AAC is the default format for some operating systems and web platforms for delivering audio data.

Bitrate and File Size

Video encoding is often tuned for data transmission. After all, people spend hours watching video content streamed over the internet, cellular data connections or cable television. Playing video files from a local storage device is not the primary means of video playback unless we're the content creator. The rate at which data is transmitted is critical: if frames can't be transmitted and decoded quickly enough during real-time, on-demand playback, you're left watching a buffer animation spin at regular intervals. The only alternative is to transmit a video file in its entirety before beginning playback. Reflecting on this, the *bitrate* is a critical number when working with video media and it is measured in megabits or gigabits per second. The more data that must be transmitted by satellite, ethernet or USB cable, the more content producers weigh the amount of compression and the resulting file size of motion video media. The lower the bitrate, the more video quality artifacts are encountered. The higher the bitrate, the greater the potential for excellent video quality with few compromises.

Table 6-2 YouTube's recommended bitrates for given resolutions and frame rates.

Video Size	Bitrate for 24/25/30 fps	Bitrate for 48/50/60 fps[8]
2160p (4K)	35–45 Mb/s	53–68 Mb/s
1440p (2K)	16 Mb/s	24 Mb/s
1080p	8 Mb/s	12 Mb/s
720p	5 Mb/s	7.5 Mb/s

Bitrate must be considered in context: a high-quality 720p clip encoded at a bitrate of 10 Mb/s does not mean that a 1080p or 4K clip encoded with the same bitrate is comparable in quality. Bitrate dictates the amount of data per second, and larger frame sizes or higher frame rates equate to more data generated. Always consider bitrate relative to the data being compressed. Bitrate should increase as video data grows if there's an expectation of consistent quality. Encoding a 4K clip at 10 Mb/s requires compressing the data much more aggressively than a 720p version. Table 6-2 shows YouTube's encoding bitrate recommendations for common video resolutions as of September 2018.

Strategies get more elaborate when considering video delivery over an inconsistent or unreliable variable bandwidth network. Video streaming services use strategies like *adaptive bitrate* streaming that switch out versions of the content encoded at tiered quality levels so that you never stare at a buffering screen even when your internet connection speed fluctuates. This topic extends beyond that which a photographer is likely responsible to consider and we mention it only to garner some appreciation for the technology that makes our modern video consumption habits possible.

Video Quality Artifacts

Motion video shares a host of potential video quality problems with photographs like flare, exposure clipping and loss of sharpness. All of the technical challenges of using optical components, sensors, electronics and post-processing software exist in video as they do in photography. Video also has a unique set of quality artifacts that are subdivided into two groups: temporal and spatial. Artifacts are any noticeable aberrations or defects in the image. A spatial artifact is observable when the video is paused or in motion. Spatial artifacts include ringing, color bleeding, blurring, blocking or repeating patterns.[9] Temporal artifacts span a duration of time in playback and include jerkiness or judder and mosquito noise.[10] You may be more acquainted with video artifacts than you think thanks to years of online video streaming binges. Many artifacts specific to video are the result of quantization errors in the encoding-decoding process inherent to the medium. Let's describe these video quality artifacts in greater detail.

Blocking

Blocking is a spatial artifact that also goes by the names *checkerboard*, *tiling*, *macroblocking* or *pixelating*.[11] Blocking is the result of compression and is usually the first image defect that viewers notice in compressed video. We find blocking in JPEG images at lower-quality settings but their changing appearance from one frame to the next in motion video is more distracting. Recall that a video frame is divided into groups of pixels, macroblocks, and each macroblock is independently quantized. Some detail loss is expected relative to the video feed prior to encoding. We're not likely to stare at a single video frame and note loss of detail, necessarily, though we are quick to notice how macroblock boundaries show abrupt changes or differences. Blocking is particularly apparent in high frequency content areas because the independently coded blocks show artificial, grid-like boundaries where there should be organic, unstructured detail (see Figure 6-9, overleaf). Some video decoders use active deblocking filters that introduce blurring in areas where these compressed block

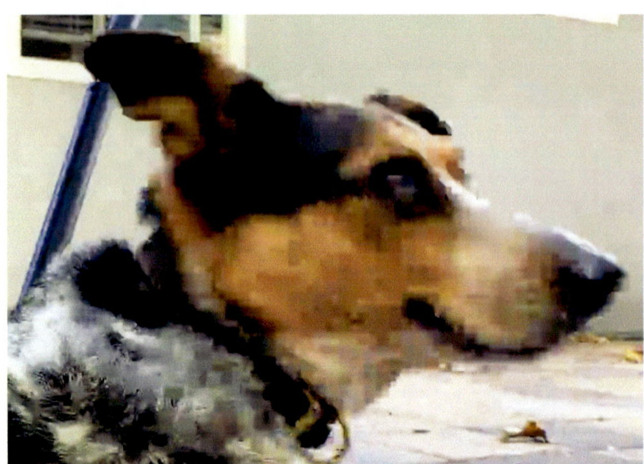

Figure 6-9 Common AVC-encoded blocking artifacts are particularly apparent when using low bitrates, when the video shows fast-moving objects or both.

boundaries do not align with content edges. If such a filter is too aggressive or if the blocking itself is strong, viewers describe the resulting video as blurry or fuzzy. Interframe compression means that I-frames are the least compressed in a group of pictures. If a video is encoded with aggressive settings to keep the file size low, the I-frames can suffer from macroblocking and all P-frames and B-frames that reference them perpetuate the artifacts.

Packet Loss

Blocking can also happen when there's data loss, corruption or interruption whereby some small blocks of image frame information don't make it to the final stage of decoding and playback. This is called *packet loss* or *dropout*. While distinct from normal blocking in the sense that it's lost data, not overly simplified or compressed data, the visual effect can be similar. It appears as small blocks, sometimes clustered together, getting "stuck" or failing to update for one or more frames. Packet loss is occasionally seen during live broadcast digital television. As long as it's a fleeting event and it doesn't happen frequently, most viewers do not consider this artifact to be objectionable. When enough data is lost or dropped either in transmission or because the decoder failed to decode at the correct pace, those small frozen blocks can turn into entire frames. This is called *freezing* where the imagery on screen stops updating until new data arrives and gets decoded. Entire frames failing to record or decode on playback are considered *frame drops*. Frame drops are distracting because they introduce a temporal discontinuity.

Ringing

Ringing spatial artifacts appear as halos or ghost-like rings along subject edges, not unlike oversharpening halos seen in photographs. The ringing halos are relatively static from one frame to the next. These are a consequence of lossy encoding and decoding as the algorithms can overshoot or undershoot edge reconstruction; even high-quality, high bitrate videos can have ringing artifacts.

Mosquito Noise

Mosquito noise is a temporal artifact seen around high frequency details and appears to move and fluctuate. The differing compression characteristics along distinct boundaries causes this artifact to flicker from frame to frame, looking like busyness and noise specific to edges. This occurs when blocks contain some combination of content like an edge and a background; the compression algorithm may waiver from one compressed appearance in a frame to another in an attempt to represent the conflicting content frequency. This is called *quantization error.*[12] Mosquito noise is often mistaken for ringing which is a spatial artifact.

Color Bleeding

The consequence of chroma subsampling, *color bleeding* might remind you of a child's coloring book where the colors don't stay inside the lines. Since color information is sampled at a lower resolution and interpolated up to match that of the luminance data, there can be a mismatch. Sometimes the interpolated color information extends beyond subject edges and looks like the color is leaking or bleeding into other content. If seen at all, this spatial artifact is relatively small in the video frame.

Jerkiness

Jerkiness, also called *judder*, appears as wobbly or inconsistent motion from frame to frame. The main cause is the conversion between 24 frames per second and 30 or 60 frames per second using an interpolation strategy called *3:2 pulldown*. Since neither 30 or 60 divide neatly into 24, straightforward frame duplication or elimination is not possible. The 3:2 pulldown technique creates synthetic frames by combining portions of existing ones. The end result may suffer from jerkiness that disrupts the natural smooth motion appearance expected from video.

Emerging Trends in Motion Video

Motion video is a dynamic medium with a creative and technological momentum from the last decade that parallels still photography. Smartphones, streaming video services and a seemingly exponential growth of screens in our lives means that video is a powerful presence. Here are a few areas where video is evolving or expanding beyond its traditional bounds.

Wide Color Gamut and High Dynamic Range

4K televisions have been logical upgrades for living rooms and are increasingly adopted by consumers. The increased resolution alone doesn't always bring with it a perceived improvement in video quality or clarity due to its dependence on proper viewing distance. Today, displays offer a combination of improvements, of which the increased resolution is just one. *Wide color gamut* (WCG) promises a wider, more saturated and varied color palette that breaks from the color limitations that video has adhered to since the 1990s. *High dynamic range* video capture and display also promises to expand the tonal range to more closely match reality. This necessitates an increased bit depth from the standard 8-bits today up to 10- or 12-bits. The visual impact when these new technologies are combined is exciting and impressive but requires newer equipment and processing to generate content. We expect that motion video will forge ahead with better color, wider dynamic range and higher resolution and never look back.

Short Form or Micro Video

It's impossible to ignore the popularity and "stickiness" of animated GIFs and *micro videos*, that is, video content with very short durations.[13] The video subformat saw success with the now-extinct social media platform Vine (2013–2017). Vine encouraged users to create videos with a maximum run time of 6 seconds. The videos looped indefinitely on playback. Similar features have cropped up in other platforms like Instagram, Snapchat and Facebook. Mobile camera apps include modes to capture "living photographs" that function as assets straddling between photographs and full videos. They tend to be either GIFs or traditional video formats with the latter offering better image quality and compression efficiency.

Short form videos may feature lower than normal frame rates (5–15 fps) to keep their data profile low. The looping characteristic means that very short events can translate to a digestible viewing experience. Once considered a passing trend, micro videos have proven a formidable format in our evolving visual media lexicon. Short form videos or photographic animations can be found in advertising, social media and fine art bodies of work. What started out as a product of technological and bandwidth limitations has now become a unique form of temporal imaging.

Immersive Video

Motion video is always defined as a two-dimensional visual medium viewed on displays and projection screens. This may be changing as accessible technology now allows for video capture rigs that record 180° and 360° field of view scenes in stereo (see Figure 6-10, overleaf). Ultra-wide-angle lenses and action cameras like the GoPro Inc.'s HERO jump-started an era of immersive content and signaled exciting capabilities for taking tiny image sensors to places and perspectives that motion video hadn't yet reached. Depth data for stereoscopic or volumetric video is on the horizon to combine three-dimensional video with computer generated elements. Virtual and augmented reality technologies are blending the ideas of traditional viewing, user experience and interactivity. Immersive video is a dynamic branch of filmmaking that is poised to augment

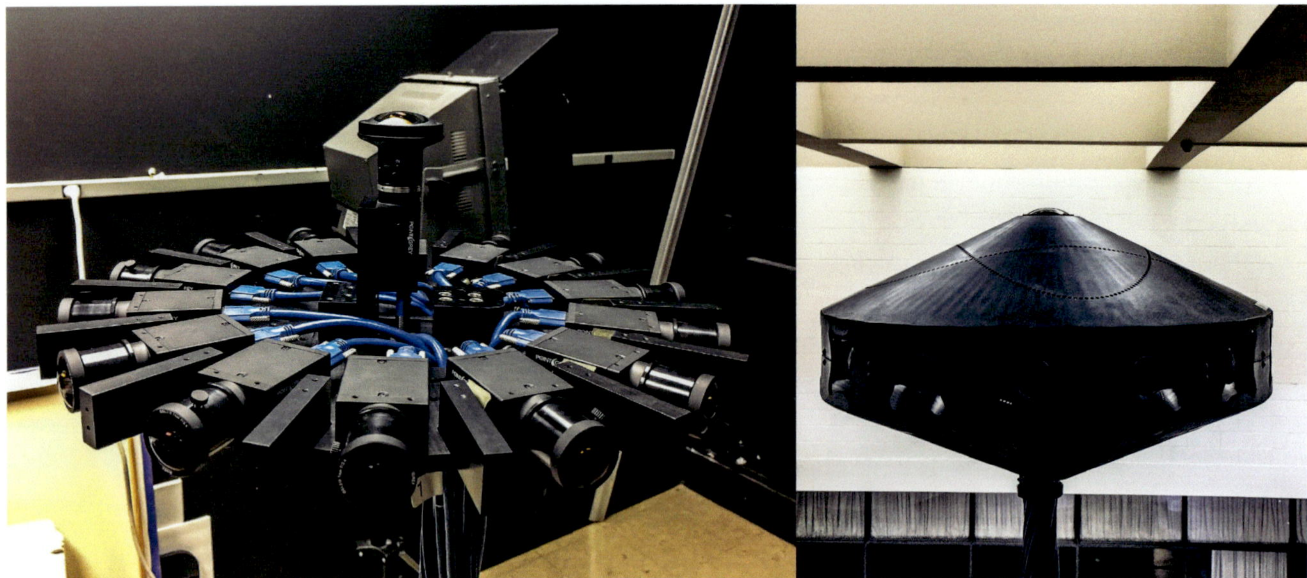

Figure 6-10 A student-built prototype 360° camera based on plans published by Facebook, Inc. called Surround 360.[14] An array of 17 wide-angle video cameras capture simultaneously and the footage is stitched and blended in post-processing. Photographs by Rochester Institute of Technology photography alumnus Nick Franco

and grow our definition of what motion media looks like and how we experience and engage with it.

Notes

1 Phillips, Jonathan B. and Henrik Eliasson. *Camera Image Quality Benchmarking*. John Wiley & Sons, 2018, p. 29.

2 Salmon, Richard, et al. "High frame-rate television – BBC R&D White Paper 169." BBC, Jan. 2008, www.bbc.co.uk/rd/publications/whitepaper169.

3 Raikes, Bob. "Artistic intent and aspect ratios." *DisplayDaily*, vol 24, no. 28, Aug. 1, 2017, www.displaydaily.com/article/display-daily/artistic-intent-and-aspect-ratios.

4 Anil, C.R. and B.R. Krishna. *H.264 Video Coding Artifacts – Measurement and Reduction of Flickering*, www.diva-portal.org/smash/get/diva2:833137/FULLTEXT01.pdf.

5 Ozer, Jan Lee. *Video Encoding by the Numbers: Eliminate the Guesswork from Your Streaming Video*. Doceo Publishing, 2017, p. 212.

6 Vernitsky, Tanya. "2017 video developer report." *Bitmovin*, Sept. 11, 2018, bitmovin.com/2017-video-developer-report/.

7 "Creating a recipe for codec success to please all palates." Edited by Jan Ozer, *Streaming Media Magazine*, Dec. 7, 2018, www.streamingmedia.com/Articles/Editorial/Featured-Articles/Creating-a-Recipe-for-Codec-Success-to-Please-All-Palates-128974.aspx.

8 "Recommended Upload Encoding Settings - YouTube Help." *Google*, Google, support.google.com/youtube/answer/1722171?hl=en.

9 Unterweger, A. "Compression artifacts in modern video coding and state-of-the-art means of compensation." *Multimedia Networking and Coding*, 2012, 28–49. 10.4018/978-1-4666-2660-7.ch002.

10 Urban, John. "Understanding video compression artifacts." *Component*, Biamp.com, Feb. 16, 2017, blog.biamp.com/understanding-video-compression-artifacts/.

11 Punchihewa, Amal and Donald G. Bailey. "Image and vision computing." IVCNZ, *Image and Vision Computing New Zealand: IVCNZ 02*, ser. 197–202, 2002.

12 Unterweger, A. "Compression artifacts in modern video coding and state-of-the-art means of compensation." *Multimedia Networking and Coding*, 2012, 28–49. 10.4018/978-1-4666-2660-7.ch002.

13 Pogue, David. "Why are micro movies so popular these days?" *Scientific American*, May 1, 2013, www.scientificamerican.com/article/why-micro-movies-so-popular-today/.

14 Briggs, Forrest. "Surround 360 is now open source." *Facebook Code*, July 26, 2016, code.fb.com/video-engineering/surround-360-is-now-open-source/.

Section 2
PROCESS

This next section covers the many aspects of image processing that our captured image files undergo, from both a technical and creative viewpoint, before they're ready for output. This continues our exploration of the photographic processes and technologies following our look at image capture. You've made countless decisions leading up to the shutter button press and there are countless more to make for functional and aesthetic objectives at the processing stage.

We start with demosaicing and interpolation: the very first steps of unpacking the digital image information captured by the camera. Photographers are lucky enough to have computer scientists and commercial software products that make downloading and viewing raw image files a seamless experience. It's valuable to understand all of the hard work and image processing that makes this possible, particularly when there are decisions for improving image quality that rely on knowing what happens under the hood.

Practicing photography benefits from an informed and planned workflow called digital asset management. Creating digital data necessitates a degree of literacy in file management, computer hardware and storage solutions. We also review file formats, metadata, image editing software options and computer components.

An image's initial form is not its destiny: it may have its tones redistributed, its content manipulated, sharpened, filtered or compressed (and possibly all of those combined). The original, recorded brightness values at a given pixel location are far from rigid and there is great power in getting the most from our photographic data. A wide world of software filters exist to further modify and expand captured image content: we look at the mechanics of sharpening, blurring and blending operations as well as black and white conversion, special effects and filter masking for compositing and retouching. Software filtering offers a dynamic potential for making photographs that go well beyond traditional capture or objectively faithful reproduction.

Understanding how a camera performs and how we define quality images means describing the imaging pipeline and deconstructing the tasks handled by the camera's image signal processor. We review methods of testing sensor performance and identifying key image quality characteristics like color reproduction, dynamic range and noise. Since the sensor is one player on a team, we also quantify lens quality and interpret lens performance.

Finally, we demystify image compression—a topic that is easily overlooked and underappreciated in its influence on quality, data storage and workflow efficiency. Photographers should understand compression beyond a JPEG quality slider; chapter challenges image-makers to consider forms of data redundancy and our strategies for exploiting them to keep files small. We also review the common image quality artifacts that result from image compression.

7 Demosaicing and Interpolation

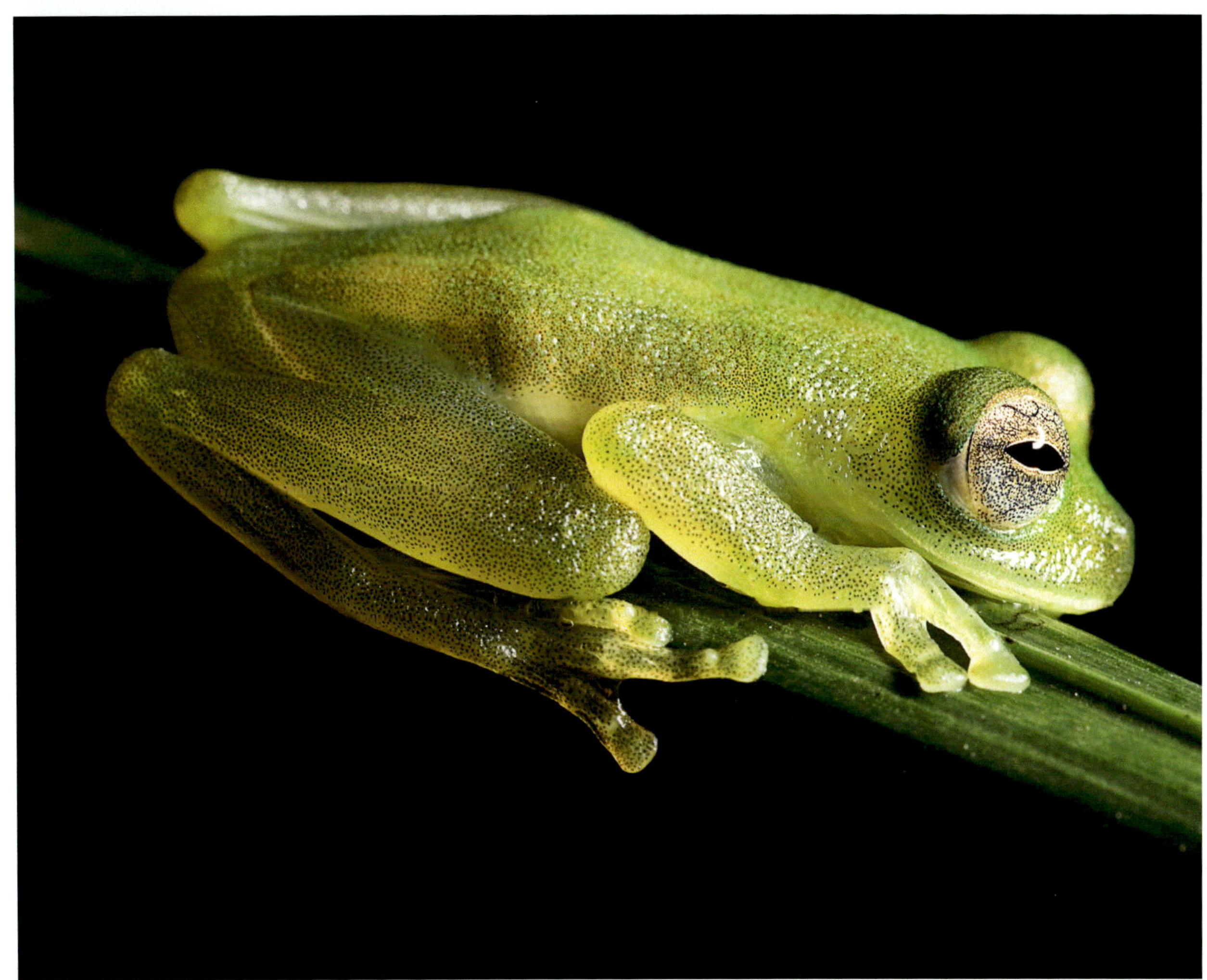

Photograph by Rochester Institute of Technology photography alumnus Josh Shagam

We explored the design of digital sensors including the Bayer pattern color filter array in Chapter 3 and in Chapter 4 we looked at strategies for obtaining perfect photographic exposures. We bring those concepts together here to explore how an image is transformed from sensor signal to a processed image. Getting to the point where our digital image approximates the appearance of the scene as we experienced it takes a considerable number of steps. These steps are often invisible and unknown to photographers since they happen behind the scenes in software processing, yet they're critical to the successful formation of a photograph. Furthermore, the digital information in an image file is modified even going into its final outputs as interpolation is used for upscaling or downscaling pixel data. This chapter dives into the details of a raw file's contents and how they're translated into a functional image file as well as strategies for resampling the data for output.

In the analog realm, pressing the shutter exposes light sensitive film to the scene. An exposure completes when the shutter closes. The resulting image exists as a *latent image* on the film. A chemical change occurs but further events must take place before that image is visible to the eye. These events involve chemistry and development solutions that change the photograph from a latent image to a visible one that can be enlarged, printed and viewed. Despite a difference in materials and technologies, the life of a digital raw image shares some parallels with this translation from potential to realized image data.

Contents of a Raw File

A *raw file* is generically defined as the uncompressed, minimally processed image data and associated metadata captured by the camera. The raw file is not really an image yet; it can't be viewed without special software such as Adobe Camera Raw. A raw image is also inherently grayscale, as shown in Figure 7-1, because the camera sensor detects and records an accumulation of light energy, not color. Raw image files must contain a *header* (the first portion of the file's content) that provides the information necessary to process it into a viewable and editable image. This includes the sensor size, the configuration of the color filter array (CFA) and the color profile. Raw files also host a collection of metadata including all of the camera settings and exposure details. Raw file formats themselves are often proprietary to the camera manufacturer despite sharing these fundamental components.

A raw file's native pixel resolution is established at capture based on the physical number of active photosites on the sensor. For example, a 45.4-megapixel sensor creates a file that's 8256x5504 pixels. Adobe DNG offers an option of reduced-resolution raw files for archiving, however, these simply throw away some of the native pixels. The reality is that the camera dictates the baseline amount of photo information you've got to work with in a raw capture.

Image Interpolation

Data interpolation is a method of creating new data based on known data. Interpolation is used during two different stages in the digital photographic workflow: when converting a raw image file into an editable, viewable photograph and when resizing an image for output or further manipulation. Before describing these use cases, let's establish the basics of image pixel data interpolation.

In the simplest terms, interpolation looks at the existing pixels and uses their values to make an educated guess at the unknown or missing pixel data. Despite sounding straightforward, this is a mathematically complicated operation. Consider just the green pixels in a raw image to start. Recall that the color filter array provides every other green pixel value when capturing the raw photosite data. Once recorded, the missing data in between the green-filtered photosites must be reconstructed. The missing data is represented by question marks in Figure 7-2 (overleaf). Taking each line separately, we could average the pixels on either side to create the missing values. The first line becomes all values of 24 and the second row all values of 36. What about the third row? The first unknown pixel on this row is between pixels with values of 12 and 19. Averaging these two yields 15.5, a problematic number because it's not possible to have non-integer pixel values in an image file. A decision must be made: is this unknown pixel going to have a value of 15 or 16? An alternative approach is to take the average of all four surrounding pixels ([36+12+19+13]/4). This yields a new value of 20 for the unknown pixel, making it brighter than three of the neighbors. This result may be problematic, too.

Now focus on the blue and red pixels: there are even fewer of those to work with. How do we create the pixel values for an entire row of the image when there are no

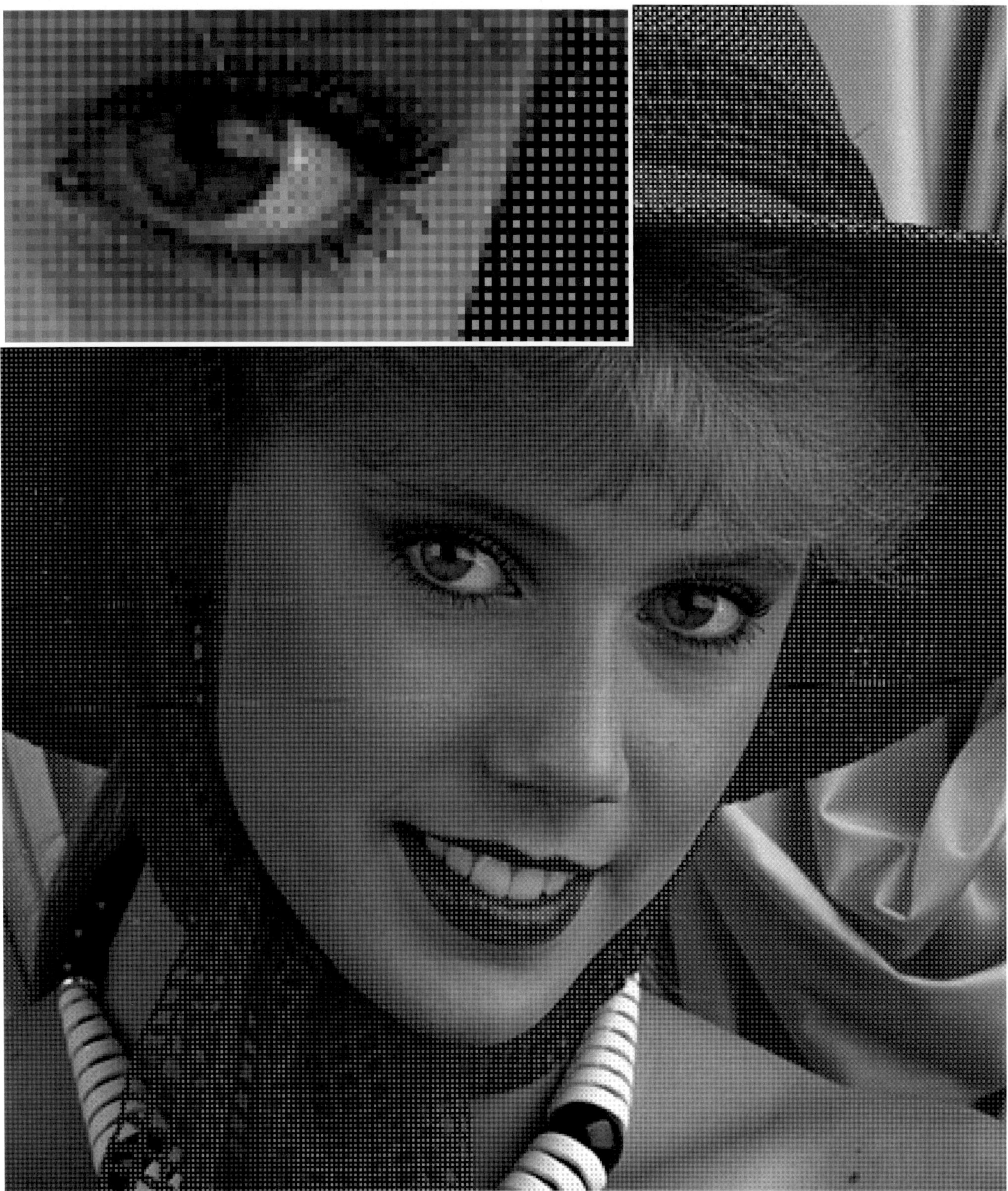

Figure 7-1 A raw Bayer image as it is recorded and stored by the camera.

24	?	24	?	24	?
?	36	?	36	?	36
12	?	19	?	28	?
?	13	?	27	?	30
11	?	12	?	31	?
?	14	?	28	?	32

?	24	?	25	?	24
?	?	?	?	?	?
?	17	?	23	?	32
?	?	?	?	?	?
?	11	?	12	?	32
?	?	?	?	?	?

?	?	?	?	?	?
33	?	24	?	30	?
?	?	?	?	?	?
12	?	20		32	?
?	?	?	?	?	?
12	?	12	?	32	?

Figure 7-2 The pattern of green, red and blue pixels in a raw image. The question marks represent unknown data needed for full color channel resolution.

values from which to average or estimate? This is where interpolation and demosaicing become intertwined. Filling in all of the missing pieces is a complex and nuanced set of operations.

Demosaicing Image Data

A mosaic is a picture or pattern created by placing small color pieces or photographs close together. When viewed at the proper distance, the individual components blend together to reveal a unique image. When we take a photograph through a color filter array, the result is a mosaic comprised of either a red, green or blue pixel value at each sensor photosite location. The process of *demosaicing* a color-filtered raw image creates a red, green and blue pixel value at each location. Demosaicing uses *color interpolation* algorithms to accomplish this task. These algorithms are mathematical approaches to calculating and predicting pixel information. There is no single solution to the problem. Consequently, there is no singular, perfect interpolation algorithm to employ and computer scientists and image scientists continue to develop different approaches in an effort to improve results. Some algorithms actively look to preserve edge detail and look for other patterns in tone or color that may indicate content such as faces or fabric.

Photographers don't need to dive into the math of these algorithms, so we instead cover the key aspects of images that demosaicing and interpolation algorithms depend on. Also keep in mind that there are times when a color filter array is not used to capture an image, negating the need for demosaicing. For those wanting a deeper explanation of the mathematics and sampling theory involved, consider available texts such as *Digital Image Compression Techniques* (1991) by Majid Rabbani or *Introduction to Data Compression* (1996) by Khalid Sayood.

We are much more sensitive to changes in luminance (brightness) than we are to color. We are also more sensitive to green than red or blue. This is a helpful starting point for a demosaicing strategy, so most algorithms start with the information recorded by the green-filtered photosites known as the *green channel* in the image file. The data in this channel is analyzed for subject edges and brightness trends usually through the use of *variance calculations*. Variance is a measure of how different the data is within a small area around the missing pixel data. Depending on the results, the algorithm makes a decision on how to interpolate groups of pixels. A low degree of variance in either the horizontal or vertical direction indicates the presence of an edge. The unknown pixel information is calculated using only the vertical or horizontal surround pixels along that edge. If the variance calculations indicate a gradient, a combination of surrounding pixel values is used to interpolate the unknown pixels to closely approximate the likely values at these locations.

Next up: the green channel information is combined with the red-filtered pixels to fill in the red channel. The reconstructed green channel is used to find edges and gradients in the image to make decisions to recreate the missing red pixels. The blue channel is typically left for last because our camera sensors lack sensitivity in this region of the visible light spectrum. The raw exposure information from blue-filtered photosites tends to have the most noise due to this insensitivity and using noisy data to make variance calculation decisions proves difficult. The end result is a digital image file with a red, green and blue channel brightness pixel value at every location.

The demosaicing process may also include color correction to compensate for the differing sensitivity of the three color channels. This is due both to the sensitivity of the silicon and the unique spectral characteristics of the color filters used in a Bayer filter array. A *color correction matrix* (CCM) corrects for this inconsistency and maps the image to a selected color space.

Demosaicing is one of the most computationally complex steps in the image processing pipeline. A highly optimized version of demosaicing happens after capture, on the camera, in order to render a preview image. Still, we rely on our more powerful desktop computer processors to attend to the task in earnest when we're back in the studio or home office.

Processing Steps Following Demosaicing

Demosaicing the color-filtered photosite data is an initial step in processing the raw image into something viewable. Additional steps may include adjusting any or all of the following: exposure, color translation, white balance, contrast, sharpness and noise reduction (both luminance and color).

Exposure Adjustment

Exposing your photograph correctly at capture always provides the best results for the final image. However, there is still hope if you failed to capture the perfect exposure. Exposure (in the form of redistributing pixel brightnesses) can be adjusted somewhat during the ingestion process with most software packages. There are two general methods for achieving this. The first method uses a simple multiplication of all the pixel values in the image, effectively shifting the histogram to the left toward brighter values overall. This can have negative effects on the image appearance as the shadow areas are mapped into the midtones and noise can become more visually apparent. The second method is to treat the shadows, midtones and highlight areas separately to minimize the amplification of the noise in the shadows and prevent clipping in the highlights. On-camera processing following demosaicing may include some targeted exposure adjustments to satisfy a preset "look and feel" like a high contrast profile.

Color Space Mapping

What's the right color space to set for camera capture? First, we need to establish the concepts of color spaces. A *color space*, in terms of a digital photograph, is the pool of colors available to represent the original scene. Cameras typically offer two choices: *sRGB* and *Adobe RGB*. *ProPhoto RGB* is a third color space used in photography more commonly seen in desktop editing rather than with on-camera capture settings. Figure 7-3 shows all three color spaces as a function of their color gamuts plotted on the CIE

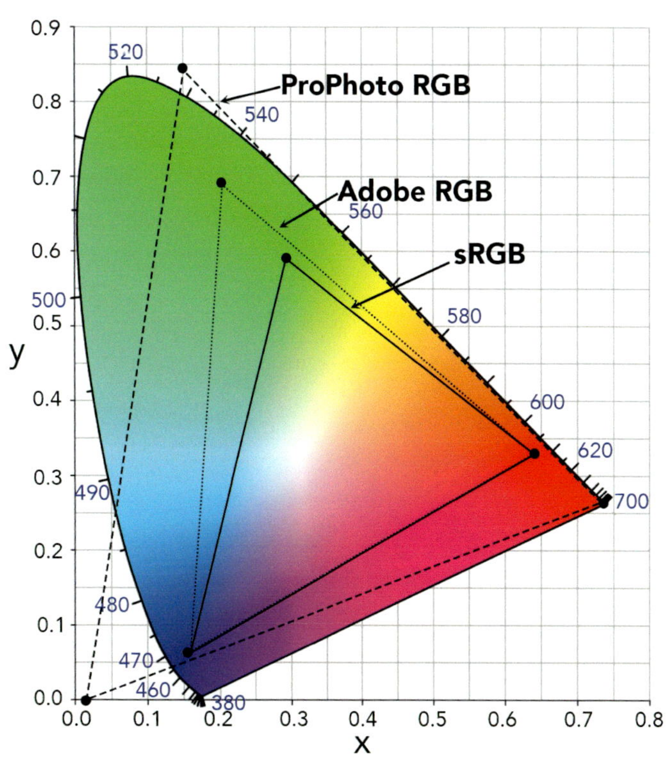

Figure 7-3 ProPhoto RGB, Adobe RGB and sRGB color spaces plotted on a chromaticity diagram.

chromaticity diagram representing the gamut of human vision.

The sRGB color space was developed in 1996 by Hewlett-Packard and Microsoft Corporation for use with digital images. It is smaller than the Adobe RGB color space but is the best choice if the intended output is display and web use—for decades, most displays were only capable of reproducing the sRGB color space and it is a reliable lowest-common-denominator assumption. The Adobe RGB color space was created by Adobe in 1998 to encompass all of the possible colors reproducible using commercial printers. The Adobe RGB color space is approximately 35% larger than the sRGB. The ProPhoto RGB color space was developed by Kodak and is by far the largest of the three color spaces. This space exceeds the bounds of the chromaticity diagram. It is favored by some when editing images because of its extra overhead, even though no output device is capable of reproducing data that sits outside of an output device's reproducible color gamut.

Color spaces come into play more when we get into editing and output, yet it can be important to establish the right choice at capture. With a raw file, the color space is specified during the demosaic process. Choosing the color space setting when shooting raw offers a risk-free option of reprocessing in a different space if desired. Capturing in JPEG means that the camera's output bakes the color space into the file with no way to go back to a larger one. In other words, forcing the decision to restrict a JPEG to sRGB means limiting its potential color gamut from its earliest stages of life.

Gamma Correction

Gamma correction defines the relationship between the numerical pixel values in the image to the actual luminance. There are two gamma operations involved. The first is when the image data is processed in-camera and is called *gamma encoding*. The camera sensor's linear response means that when a pixel receives twice the amount of photons, it produces twice the amount of signal. The relationship between photons and recorded signal is linear. This is great if the sensor is used as a measurement device for scientific research but it is not as useful on its own for making photographic images. Viewing a photograph with a linear luminance mapping looks odd and incorrect to us due to the human visual system's nonlinear response to light. Left unaltered, a properly exposed raw image looks dark and low in contrast relative to our visual experience of the scene. Therefore, a *gamma correction* is applied to an image when it is processed using Equation 7.1.

$$V_{out} = V_{in}^{\,gamma} \qquad \text{(Eq. 7.1)}$$

Where

V_{out} = output luminance value

V_{in} = input luminance value

This second gamma operation happens when the image is displayed on a monitor or projector. The industry standard for monitor gamma is 2.2. The gamma correction is conducted automatically by the computer's operating system based on the display profile configuration.

Noise Reduction

Noise, or random fluctuations of luminance and color, is always present in photographs. Noise often negatively impacts the reproduction of detail and can decrease contrast. Excessive noise can also cause trouble with some interpolation algorithms that use edge detection during the demosaicing process as it can lead to incorrectly identifying edges. There are many different methods available to remove noise such as convolution with a low pass filter, gaussian filter or a bilateral filter. The explanation of the statistics of these methods is beyond the scope of this text.

Noise reduction is a give-and-take operation, presenting a tradespace between the degree of retained detail and the amount of noise present in the final result. Too much noise reduction softens the image by smoothing and averaging pixel variance that previously described true detail. Not enough noise reduction can leave a distracting amount of noise. Noise reduction processes are often done prior to CFA interpolation to prevent the propagation of noise into the demosaicing stage. If left until after demosaicing, noise may be inadvertently exaggerated or amplified.

Anti-Aliasing Filter

Most cameras using a CFA also use an anti-aliasing filter, called an *optical low-pass filter* (OLPF), on top of the imaging sensor. We sample the scene at discrete points when capturing an image. This is a functional approach for much of a scene, however, when we approach an edge or a repeating pattern, the sampling rate (the number of pixels on the sensor) may not be enough to recreate the original details.

This sampling rate failure can result in moiré artifacts or what some call "jaggies" along edges and fine patterns. These artifacts occur because the frequency of these objects in the scene exceeds the Nyquist limit of the sensor. The Nyquist limit is the highest frequency continuous signal that can be recreated by a discrete or sampled signal. The OLPF effectively blurs the signal to smooth the artifact, leaving us with image data in need of baseline sharpening.

Sharpening

A degree of *capture sharpening* is applied to the image following the demosaicing process. The amount is determined by a default preset in most desktop software but is typically adjustable on a per-image basis. It is a global image adjustment that considers all pixels in the image frame. Sharpening is required due to the blurring that occurs in the optical system at multiple stages of image formation: the lens, the IR-blocking filter and the optical low-pass filter. This type of sharpening is broadly categorized as capture sharpening and is just the first of multiple potential processing filters that aim to enhance the appearance of sharpness in the final product.

Reinterpreting Raw with New Algorithms

Recall that working with raw image files is part of a nondestructive workflow whereby any adjustments introduced are instructions that can be changed or reset. Demosaicing is the very first non-destructive decision made to raw files. As such, an old raw file can be taught new tricks if passed through a newer or more advanced demosaicing algorithm. An overly noisy photograph from today could look much better five years from now as long as you hold on to the raw, unprocessed data (though don't expect miracles). Applying interpretation algorithms to raw files allows us the flexibility of reprocessing an image when algorithms change or to try an altogether different algorithm if we aren't happy with the initial results.

Resampling an Image

In addition to demosaicing, interpolation is employed for *resampling* or resizing an image: either enlarging it (upscaling) or making it smaller (downscaling). We stated earlier in this chapter that the native resolution of a raw file is set at the moment of capture and dictated by the sensor. There is no way to generate true image content beyond what was originally recorded. All we can hope to do is interpolate and estimate additional pixels—which, while not "true" information, is often just as good or is unnoticeable to the eye. An 8256x5504 pixel photograph is not destined to exist exclusively at this size because we can upscale or downscale the data using interpolation.

Figure 7-4 (overleaf) illustrates *linear interpolation*. The plot on the left illustrates a simple linear regression and is an example of data that forms a perfect line. A linear regression fits an equation to the data in the format of $y = mx + b$. In this case, we wanted to find the value of y when x was known and the result is a perfect fit. In contrast, the right plot in Figure 7-4 shows a line fitted to data that is not linear that serves as a realistic representation of pixel values in an image. Linear interpolation does a poor job here, showing that we need to use a more complex interpolation method to correctly predict pixel values when upscaling image content.

Upscaling is primarily useful when sending photographs to physical print media output. To enlarge or upscale an image file, we're effectively looking to create additional pixels using the ones we already have. It's assumed that the raw data is demosaiced and that red, green and blue pixel

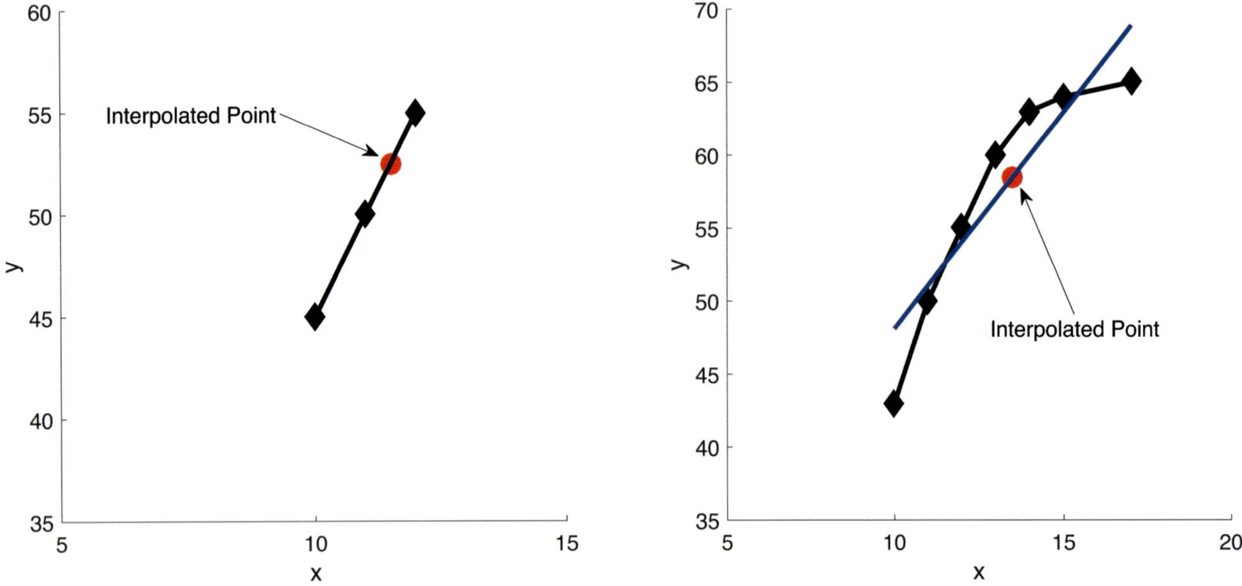

Figure 7-4 Interpolating data offers varying degrees of success based on the original data interpolated and the interpolation method used.

values exist at all locations. Increasing the pixel resolution of the image means creating additional pixel data. The same principles apply as with demosaicing, although the algorithms can be tailored to create smooth gradients or preserve details depending on your need.

Enlarging an image using interpolation is marginally useful for on-screen output applications. We're quick to notice pixelation in image enlargements and unless you're starting from a source that was already created as a final output product (like a thumbnail icon taken from a website), you likely have plenty of pixels in your photograph to display on the web. Enlarging for print is a different story involving viewing distance, discussed further in Chapter 16.

On-the-fly pixel resampling is possible though not ideal for photographic content or any time where you want to assert quality control over the viewing experience. Modern web design uses scaling and elastic layout behaviors (sometimes called *fluid design*) to accommodate the wide variety of device sizes and user interaction models. If left up to web developers, our images might get interpolated and resized freely, prioritizing layout and fit over image fidelity. It's better to stock a family of prepared images on a server at predetermined sizes (think Small, Medium and Large like you're ordering fast food) whereby the dynamic web design serves the best-fit option. This also helps to ensure that someone browsing an image gallery on a smartphone screen isn't wasting data downloading ultra-high-resolution images intended for display on large screen televisions. We prepare the image file variants using the interpolation methods described later that yield the best looking results and let the web browser request the appropriate version. The photographer can pick the interpolation method and degree of compression for each image size in the set, watching for unwanted compromises to image quality. It's a bit more preparation work for the photographer but it improves user experience and it keeps control over reproduction in the hands of the image maker instead of the web designer.

Nearest Neighbor Interpolation

One straightforward method for increasing image resolution is pixel replication. This is called *nearest neighbor interpolation*. If the image needs to be twice its original size, replication takes each existing pixel and duplicates it in an adjacent position. Each new pixel is the same value as its nearest neighbor. This method works well for graphic design elements or text because of their well-defined and

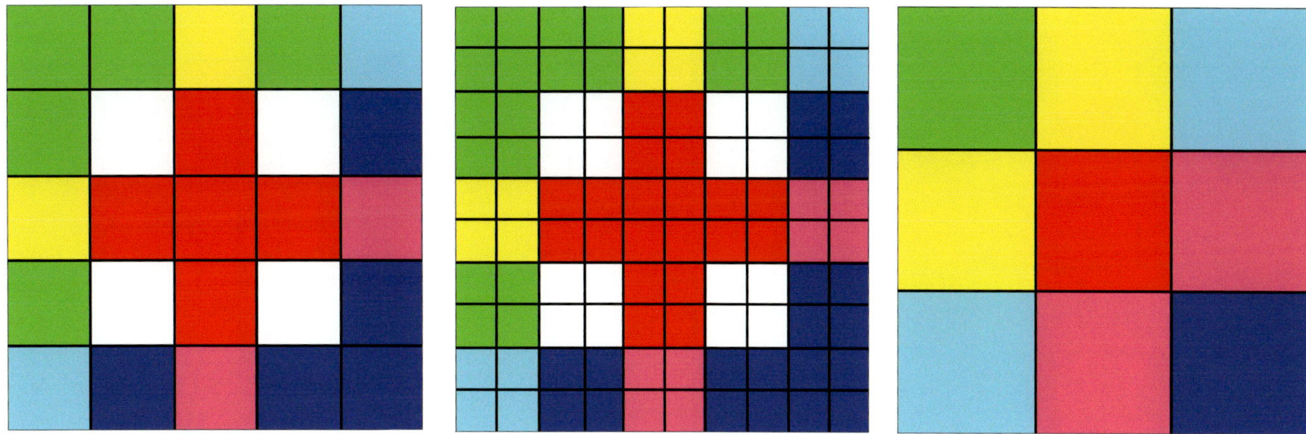

Figure 7-5 The original image data (left), upscaled to twice the pixel resolution (center) and downscaled to half the pixel resolution (right) using nearest neighbor interpolation.

geometric edges. Enlarging photographs with nearest neighbor interpolation, though, leads to an increasingly pixelated appearance due to the visual effect of enlarging the pixels. Note that it only appears this way because pixel data is duplicated without new or unique image content; pixels themselves never change size. One original pixel becomes represented by two identical pixels. Subject edges appear more jagged and small areas of detail appear blocky as a consequence of this approach. Nearest neighbor interpolation is the quickest method, computationally speaking, for upscaling a file. It is not subjectively desirable for photographic content.

This method can also be used for reducing an image size. Instead of replicating pixels, nearest neighbor interpolation for downscaling simply removes every other row and column of pixel data. Figure 7-5 is an example of both upscaling and downscaling. The original and resulting images are rendered at the same size for illustrative purposes. The center version doubles the size in both the width and height relative to the original, increasing the image size from 5x5 to 10x10, by duplicating the rows and columns. This works well due to the simple and graphic nature of the original data. The third image in Figure 7-5 shows a reduction or downscaling of the original. The nearest neighbor algorithm removes rows 2 and 4 and column 2 and 4. The result is missing information present in the original and significantly changes the image's appearance.

Bilinear Interpolation

Bilinear interpolation is a middle-of-the-road algorithm that often produces better results than a nearest neighbor approach. It uses the four neighboring pixels on the left, right, above and below an original pixel value to calculate the new pixel values. Another way to describe its approach is *double linear interpolation* because the algorithm performs a linear interpolation in the x-direction and then again in the y-direction to produce the new values. Bilinear interpolation can lead to a reduction in overall contrast which in turn can make the image appear less sharp to the viewer. Although this method may produce acceptable results with continuous tone photographs, it should not be used with line art or graphics.

Bicubic Interpolation

Bicubic interpolation produces high-quality results with minimal artifacts. Bicubic interpolation uses a 4x4 grid, the 16 pixels surrounding the original, in its calculations to fit a surface and find the new value. It weighs the nearer pixels heavier than the farther pixels to produce a much sharper image than nearest neighbor or bilinear interpolation methods. There are more calculations involved compared to other methods, so it does take longer to run. However, its high-quality result makes it the favored and default choice by many image editing applications.

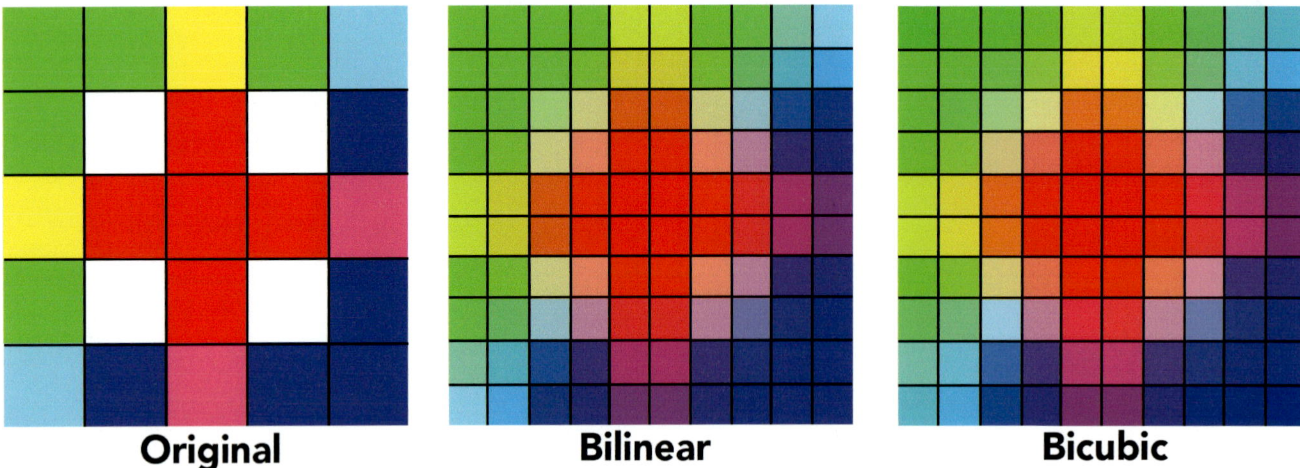

Figure 7-6 The original image data (left), upscaled to twice the pixel resolution using bilinear interpolation (center) and with bicubic interpolation (right).

Figure 7-6 uses our same starting sample target to create an enlargement using bilinear and bicubic interpolation. Here again, the original and resulting images are rendered at the same size for illustrative purposes. Both methods provide improvements over nearest neighbor, however the detail of the white pixels is lost in both. These pixels perhaps represent specular highlights in a photographic image: small but important details that can be lost in the process of interpolating pixel data. Bicubic interpolation produces the smoothest transitions between colors, making it a good choice for photographic content and problematic for graphics with crisp edges and color boundaries.

The Life Cycle of Image Pixel Data

There are many similarities between analog and digital photography; the processes of demosaicing and image interpolation are not among them. The idea of using a Bayer CFA and creating an image with two-thirds of the input data missing seems like it's destined to fail. Instead, demosaicing algorithms have evolved and the number of pixels on our sensors has grown to the point where it is difficult to find artifacts in the resulting images. Making color photographs with CFAs and brightness-detecting photosites is the primary method of capturing digital images with the robustness and high-quality results generated by demosaicing software.

Using interpolation to upscale an image is where caution is required to avoid potential image quality degradation. With a silver-halide-based film negative, it seemed that enlarging was limited only by the size of your darkroom enlarger (in reality, there is a degree of magnification that results in objectionable grain). Upscaling digital image information, effectively creating data that is not in the original capture, can be necessary for making particularly large prints and it's helpful for photographers to understand the available options for making it happen. Using interpolation to downscale an image, effectively removing detail relative to the original capture, is also likely in the life of a photograph as we look to varying platforms, screen sizes and applications on which our work is viewed. Creating output assets specifically prepared for these different outlets can help in maintaining the best possible image quality.

Demosaicing is the critical first stage of image data maturation, though it is hardly the last. Thanks to well-developed image science and computer science, photographers have an array of interpolation tools to translate, scale and generally manipulate digital image files. A given raw capture may be demosaiced and interpolated a number of times over the course if its life.

8 Digital Asset Management

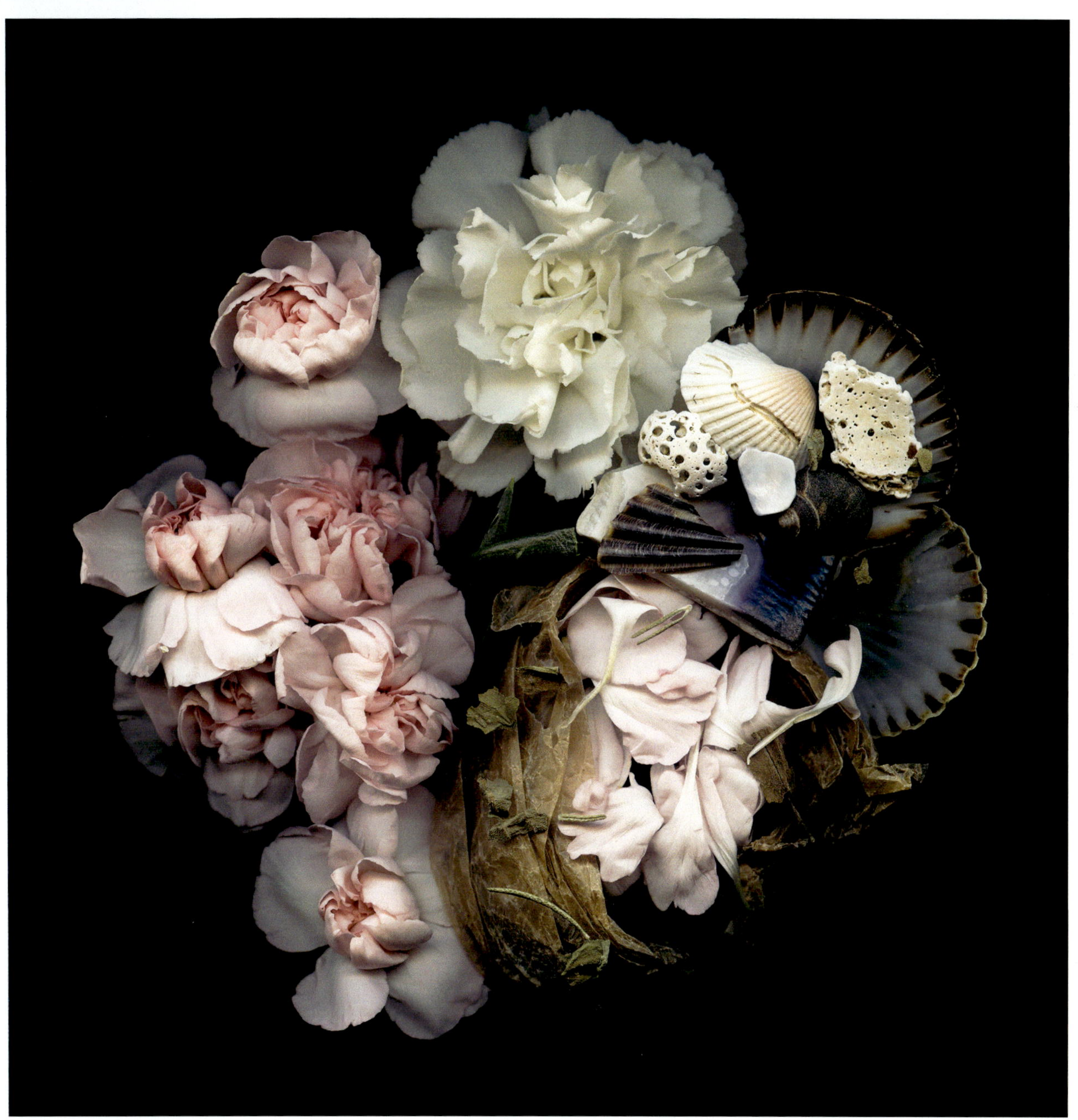

Photograph by Rochester Institute of Technology photography student Svea Elisha

Digital asset management (DAM) is a repeatable and sustainable methodology for storing, sorting and working with digital assets. In photography, this involves downloading and saving images, naming files, organizing, rating and adding metadata. Photographs are what we often think of as the most important digital assets though they are not the only ones. Complete digital asset management includes all files related to your workflow such as editing presets, catalog files, software user configurations, storage media and even invoices and emails. Properly managing all incoming and outgoing assets is fundamental to a professional workflow. It also requires careful planning for backups and fail-safes. Digital assets are valuable but vulnerable; hardware and software can (and frequently do) fail. Digital asset management starts with understanding the data and conceiving strategies for using and managing it while minimizing the chances of mismanagement or catastrophic data loss.

The best DAM workflows are thoughtfully built around the specific requirements of an image-making practice, be it personal or commercial. All require solutions for handling an ever-increasing torrent of digital data. We detail file formats, ingestion workflow, data transfer, storage and computer hardware in the sections that follow.

Defining Image Data

We handle all manner of digital data on a daily basis, so what specifically defines image files? Photographs are always a type of *bitmap*. Bitmaps are strings of bits (the building blocks of digital information) that describe discrete color and brightness values of each pixel along with a series of instructions (the map) that explains where each of those pixels resides in a two-dimensional array. A photograph can have every single one of its many millions of pixels be a unique brightness, color or both. The world we photograph is highly detailed, complex and even random. Bitmapped data is fundamental to image files because of this degree of specificity. Another term for storing pixel-specific image data is *raster graphics*. Graphic designers, in contrast, often use *vector* formats that store visual information in a more mathematically descriptive way. Vector objects are defined by equations rather than discrete pixel samples. Vector files allow for printing graphics at any size or scale and are not limited by pixel resolution. Photographers may find themselves working with vector files when collaborating with designers for publication layouts or advertisements. Vectors are also employed when creating certain layer masks or text in image editing software. Powerful in their own right, vectors are not suited to storing truly photorealistic image data and thus serve a secondary role in the world of photographic assets.

Image Data and Quality

Captured photographs begin as raw digital counts stored in image file containers. The information is untouched by post-capture image processing decisions and adjustments. These *raw files* contain uncompressed data and are the starting point for a potentially long journey of optimization, artistic interpretation and delivery to an output medium. Raw files are large because each pixel in an array of millions has its brightness information recorded and the possible values are numerous. Smaller and more universally compatible image formats are employed for showing photographs on the web and to simplify the amount of stored information. Raw files are the purest archival format for storing the data as it was originally captured. Raw interpreters or editors use this data to generate derivative working image files without permanently altering it.

Image data stored in image file containers is further characterized by the type of *data compression* used to pack it into the smallest storage footprint. *Uncompressed* data does not receive any type of optimization or size reduction and is the least space-efficient way to store digital information. *Lossless compression* means algorithms are employed to lessen file size with no permanent loss of the original image data; it is a reversible process to compress and uncompress. *Lossy compression* means that some image data is discarded or simplified in a way that is irreversible. This may have negative image quality implications or it may be visually unnoticeable with the benefit of smaller files. The goal of both compression approaches is optimizing storage and delivery of image data. We would constantly need to buy additional hard drives and spend our work days watching loading bars without compression. Uncompressed data has a place in a photographic workflow, particularly in video production, if decisions regarding compression or post-processing efforts must be deferred until some point after capture.

Chapter 12 elaborates on how lossless and lossy compression algorithms accomplish their goals. For now, we simply appreciate that decisions in our digital asset management workflow are influenced by our desire to retain the best possible quality images between capture and output. To that end, we employ specific image file formats based on the tradeoffs between maximum quality, minimal storage space and bandwidth requirements.

Table 8-1 Common raw file formats with the camera manufacturers that create and support them.

Raw Format	Manufacturer
CR3, CR2	Canon
NEF	Nikon
ARW	Sony
IIQ	Phase One
3FR	Hasselblad
RAF	Fujifilm
ORF	Olympus
MEF	Mamiya
X3F	Sigma

Image File Formats

Each image file format has its utility and drawbacks for storing and displaying image content. Photographers frequently juggle all of the formats outlined here and consider the right time and place for each. All image files have *header* substructures that precede the *body* or *payload* sections (where the image data resides) containing supplemental information. Headers include descriptors like bit depth and pixel dimensions that are frequently needed at a glance by both users and software. The payload comprises the bulk of the total data in an image file. Let's define the relevant formats: raw, DNG, JPEG, TIFF, BMP, GIF, PNG and HEIF.

Raw

The *raw image format* is generically defined as the uncompressed, minimally processed image data and associated metadata recorded by the camera. Despite the name, raw files are not completely unprepped. Think of it like buying chicken breasts from the grocery store as starting with raw ingredients even though there was some gruesome preparation involved before making it to the shelf. We like to think that we've made dinner from scratch while glossing over some preceding steps that are too messy and cumbersome to deal with. Cameras neatly package the digitally converted light signals and additional metadata as raw files. They are the closest thing to the sensor signal that we wish to handle. Raw images are not intended to be final, deliverable assets as they are large (uncompressed) and incompatible with the average viewer's software.

There is no single file container or extension associated with raw files. Instead, it's a category of a file format similar to how a hatchback describes a type of car but not a specific manufacturer or model. Table 8-1 highlights common raw formats. Camera manufacturers use proprietary file types that often necessitate proprietary software to read and edit them. All support 12-bit or 14-bit image data. Some include encrypted information that helps their associated software yield better looking interpretations of the image data. Luckily, popular image editing software for photographers translates and works with a variety of raw file formats.

Along with the image data from the sensor, a raw file's header section includes *byte-ordering information*, an identifier and the offset that indicates where the data is located in the file structure. It also contains camera metadata to provide cataloging software with the image sensor size, color filter array information and capture metadata like exposure settings, camera model and lens model. Additionally, raw files often house a reduced-resolution JPEG to preview the raw contents without the heavy computational lift of interpreting them. This preview version is like the picture of a cake on a box of cake mix; it's one possible outcome of working with the box contents but it does not directly represent the contents as they exist.

All raw formats have similarities and yet there is no guarantee that software like Adobe Photoshop or Capture One can interpret their contents. It's up to the software developers to devise methods of decoding the packaged raw data. This process can take time and resources. You may have the experience of buying a new camera when it first goes on sale and discover that your photo software cannot open the files until an update is released. To complicate matters, some manufacturers started offering raw format variants like *CRAW*, *mRaw* and *sRaw* that aim to be a middle-ground between quality and file size. These variants are compressed using lossy compression, reduced resolution or both while maintaining characteristics of true raw files like higher bit depths and non-destructive editing support.

DNG

The *digital negative* or DNG is a raw image file format developed by Adobe, first released in 2004. The DNG is an open source standard that can be used free of charge by camera companies. It supports lossless and lossy compression options. Though it is not universally used by cameras, many proprietary raw formats can be converted to DNG using Adobe software. Doing so offers some reduction to file size and uniformity for photographers that work with more than one type of camera (and thus face juggling multiple raw formats). The U.S. Library of Congress-funded *Digital Photography Best Practices and Workflow* project states that "DNG files have proven to be significantly more useful than the proprietary raw files in our workflow."[1] There is no future-proof format for photographs; however, DNG continues to be in the running for long-term support and adoption.

A DNG contains all of the same image data as a raw file from a particular camera manufacturer. The JPEG preview image stored within is updated whenever the file is used in editing software to reflect edits made by the photographer, rather than being a static preview generated by the camera.

The DNG format recently gained an additional ability to use lossy compression and/or reduced resolution image data. This reduces the storage stresses of otherwise large raw files while retaining a version of the image that is untouched by post-processing adjustments. DNG is a popular format for smartphone cameras with raw capture support.

JPEG

The JPEG is undoubtedly the most ubiquitous image file format. It is a name known by even the most casual computer users due to the highly image-dependent nature of the internet and visual media at large. Its name comes from the acronym describing the standards body that created it: the *Joint Photographic Experts Group*. JPEG describes both the lossy compression standard and its file extension. JPEGs support 8-bit image channel data and embedded color profiles. They offer a practical balance of image quality and file size, functioning as an end-product asset: great for emailing to a client or embedding in a website. JPEG compression offers compression levels of up to 1:100. Variations of the JPEG including *JPEG-LS* (featuring lossless compression) and *JPEG2000* exist with some software support, though the baseline JPEG remains the most widely adopted and used.

Photographers don't use JPEGs exclusively because they come with a major caveat. In order for a camera to output JPEGs, it captures the raw sensor data, converts it to a digital signal and sends it through image processing algorithms. Decisions about white balance, sharpness, saturation and contrast are made before a JPEG file is generated. When this produces results that we like, there's no problem. It's when we think that we can do better than the onboard processing, or simply wish to have the flexibility to try multiple approaches at interpreting the data, that the utility of the JPEG format falls short. It's the difference between buying flour, eggs and sugar at the grocery store and buying a cake at the bakery.

JPEG files store image pixel data using lossy compression techniques, helping to keep file sizes relatively small for fast transmission. They degrade in quality each time they are re-saved, often referred to as *generation loss*. This

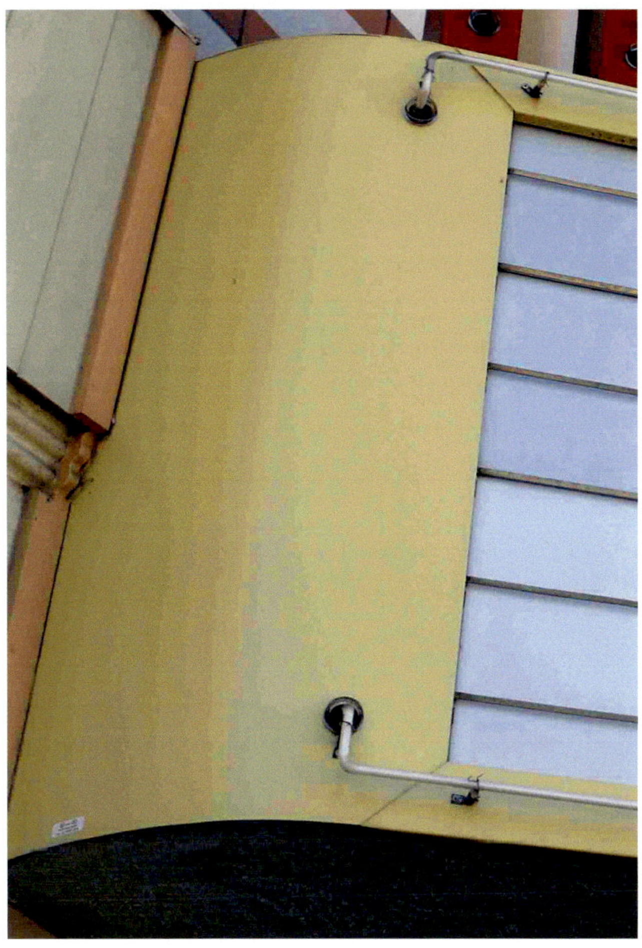

Figure 8-1 Noticeable JPEG artifacts due to lossy compression algorithms.

makes them great as end-of-the-line deliverables but poor as working assets. You don't want to save a JPEG, go back for additional edits, save it again and repeat. JPEG compression artifacts can be distracting and undesirable (see Figure 8-1). The majority of image editing software allows for a sliding scale of JPEG compression, sometimes labeled as a "quality setting," when saving a JPEG. The less aggressive the compression, the better the quality of the resulting image. The downside is the lessened capacity for reducing file size.

There are logical scenarios for shooting/capturing in JPEG over raw:

- Event photography that only requires basic image adjustments;
- Working for photojournalism institutions that expressly require straight-from-the-camera JPEGs for publication;
- When output is direct to a web-based platform and in-camera presets are dialed-in to one's liking.

TIFF

The *Tagged Image File Format* or TIFF is a popular and versatile format created by the Aldus Corporation in 1986. Aldus merged with Adobe in 1994, who now owns the copyright to the TIFF format. It was originally designed for storing black and white image data from scanners; subsequent revisions of the format added support for color, additional bit depth and compression.

TIFF is a bitmap image file format that supports CMYK, RGB, Lab, indexed color and grayscale; 8, 16 or 32 bits per channel are supported bit depths. The maximum size for a TIFF file is 4 GB. The format provides support for tags, multiple image layers, transparency and alpha channels. These additional data components are compatible with Adobe Photoshop layers, making them a convenient choice for working copies that retain a degree of adjustability to post-processing work. Layers in TIFFs appear flattened in non-Adobe software. The TIFF format supports both lossy and lossless compression using JPEG and Lempel–Ziv–Welch (LZW) algorithms respectively. A JPEG and TIFF of the same photograph are visually indistinguishable assuming both are compressed by the same amount, so the benefits of choosing one over the other are dictated by how you intend to use the files. A TIFF is the better option for additional editing or print output at the expense of having to store, transfer or share a larger file.

TIFF's extensibility and wide support across image editing software make it an effective choice for scientific applications. The *Geostationary Earth Orbit Tagged Image File Format*, or GeoTIFF and BigTIFF, are specialized variants for fields with specific needs not addressed by the traditional TIFF. GeoTIFF supports georeferenced and geocoding information for use in Geographic Information Systems (GIS). BigTIFF supports 64-bit and image sizes up to 18,000 petabytes (PB). It is used by GIS and medical fields where scanners and cameras produce incredibly large amounts of data.

BMP

The BMP format is also referred to as *bitmap image file* or a *device independent bitmap* (DIB) and uses the file extensions .BMP or .DIB, respectively. The BMP is a raster graphic format that stores a two-dimensional image. A BMP supports bit depths ranging from 1 to 32 bits per channel, alpha channels and color profiles. It can be uncompressed or compressed, however a compressed BMP is often much larger than an equivalent JPEG. The BMP format is not commonly used by photographers.

GIF

The *Graphics Interchange Format*, or GIF, is a variant of the bitmap. GIFs use LZW compression. Originally designed in 1987 for transmitting image content over limited bandwidth internet connections, the format has a palette restricted to 256 colors (or 8-bits in a single channel). This makes it a poor choice for full color photographs but a viable option for some graphics or illustrations on the web. The 256 colors are variable depending on image content, meaning one GIF might contain 256 unique colors from another GIF, but the total range within a single file remains limited. This limitation is what helps keep file sizes to a minimum. The GIF's utility as a photorealistic, small file format is diminished given the prevalence of high bandwidth internet connections today. The format persists because of its support for multi-frame animations—a trick that JPEG can't offer. The animation capabilities of GIFs are crude in terms of frame rate and yet social media and messaging trends have kept the format relevant.

The desire for an image format that supports animations or short, looping videos (sans audio) spawned alternatives to GIFs that forgo the limited color palette restriction. There is no unified standard; the popular options are typically built on an HTML5 video format. The best image format for video-like content is a video format. GIPHY and GIFV are examples of HTML5-based GIF alternatives that are readable by modern desktop and mobile operating system (OS) web browsers.

PNG

The *Portable Network Graphics* (PNG) file is a raster graphics file format created as a replacement for GIF. In some ways, the PNG offers a middle ground between GIF and JPEG. It offers lossless compression but does not support animation. PNG-8 can only store 256 colors in its palette similar to the GIF limitation. The PNG-24 variant allows for true color images with support for transparency. PNGs are used by both MacOS and Ubuntu operating systems as the default file type for screenshots and are widely used for web design elements. The PNG format is not typically used for photographic images.

HEIF

The *High Efficiency Image File Format* (HEIF) is a newcomer in a long line of attempts to dethrone the JPEG. HEIF was developed by the Moving Picture Experts Group (MPEG) with its specification finalized in 2015. HEIF is based on the High Efficiency Video Coding (HEVC) video compression standard. The storage structure is based on the widely used ISO Base Media File Format (ISOBMFF).

HEIF is better described as a container for both image and audio data instead of a monolithic file format. One container can contain a single image or a series of images. The format borrows tricks from video formats like inter-frame compression to efficiently store similar images from burst-fire or exposure-bracketed sequences. Image sequences saved in this format are, on average, half the size of JPEGs with equivalent or better quality.[2] This type of storage efficiency is increasingly critical as the world moves to storing and sharing visual media on mobile devices with limited memory and transmission bandwidth. The format also supports a strategy for dividing a large image into tiles that are compressed and accessed separately, allowing for high performance viewing of high-resolution panoramic photos, for example. HEIF additionally supports storage of auxiliary data like audio, text, metadata and depth or disparity information for 3D imaging systems. It can potentially replace GIF for animations without quality loss and supports image transparency. HEIF is an intriguing media format because it accommodates many of the visual media products generated by smartphones and offers extensibility for future imaging applications.

HEIF also mimics the raw file model of storing the original image and all subsequent edits as non-destructive instructions. HEIF, like TIFF, supports either lossy or lossless compression and bit depths up to 16-bits. This allows for storage of images from 10-bit sensors without image degradation. The file extension used by HEIF images is .HEIC.

The HEIF format is not yet the de facto image file at the time of writing. Apple, Inc. adopted HEIF for image media storage on iOS in 2017. Even Apple's decision to embrace the format, however, is constrained by the reality that sharing with other devices and platforms offers uncertain compatibility. HEIFs are converted to JPEG for exporting or sharing with others. Popular web browsers do not yet natively display HEIF media.

Proprietary Editing Software Formats

We accept that cameras are likely to generate their own flavor of raw file at capture. We also have to consider proprietary formats that specific software applications generate as by-products of editing and output. These formats can be problematic because of their dependency on the software that creates them. This sometimes translates to software-subscription-ransoms (i.e. if you stop paying for access, you can't work with your images) or a greater threat of obsolescence (the software company stops supporting their product or its development ceases at a certain point for an operating system). On the other hand, these formats allow software developers to build in all sorts of instructions and assets used by their program to accompany the traditional image data. Proprietary editing file formats are a necessary evil unless the industry rallies behind a universal format; the best we can do is mitigate the risk and store TIFF formats for long-term safe-keeping.

A common, proprietary format is the *Photoshop Document* (PSD) generated and used by Adobe Photoshop. The PSD takes full advantage of Adobe Photoshop's image editing capabilities, particularly those that are modifiable, including image layers, layer masks, adjustment layers, vector and alpha channels. Editing with these features allows for non-destructive editing even across multiple sessions where the file is saved and reopened, avoiding permanent image quality loss. Adobe Photoshop provides the option to flatten all of the layers in order to save the image as JPEG or TIFF as needed. A PSD can be as large as 30,000x30,000 pixels, 16-bits and 2 GB in file size. Image documents larger than this can be saved in the *Photoshop Large Document* or *Photoshop Big* format (PSB). This format extends the potential image size to 300,000x300,000 pixels with supported file sizes up to 4 exabytes (4 billion GB). There are several other software packages such as CorelDraw, Paintshop Pro and GIMP that read Adobe Photoshop formats.

Why Raw Works for Digital Asset Management

Now that you're familiar with the options, why does the raw format come out on top for photographers? JPEGs offer excellent, expedient deliverables that don't put heavy stress on memory cards or bandwidth. Most SLRs allow us to adjust contrast, saturation and sharpening preferences to be applied immediately after an exposure to saved JPEGs. Still, there are many advantages to the raw format for a complete photographic workflow.

Setting a camera to record both JPEG and raw, we captured a properly exposed test target image. Figure 8-2 (overleaf) shows the output with no adjustments made to the raw version. The raw image is less sharp and looks low in contrast compared to the out-of-camera JPEG. The target looks better and ready for prime time in the JPEG image because it has the contrast and sharpness we'd expect of a final image. However, not all images should be processed the same and any other scene is likely to have characteristics that we want to fine-tune and adjust using the raw image data.

A raw image lacks any processing for sharpness, contrast or color and contains the maximum dynamic range as dictated by the sensor's capabilities. A JPEG is an 8-bit image, storing 256 possible brightness levels per channel. A raw image holds 12–14 bits of brightness data. This additional headroom means that some overexposed or

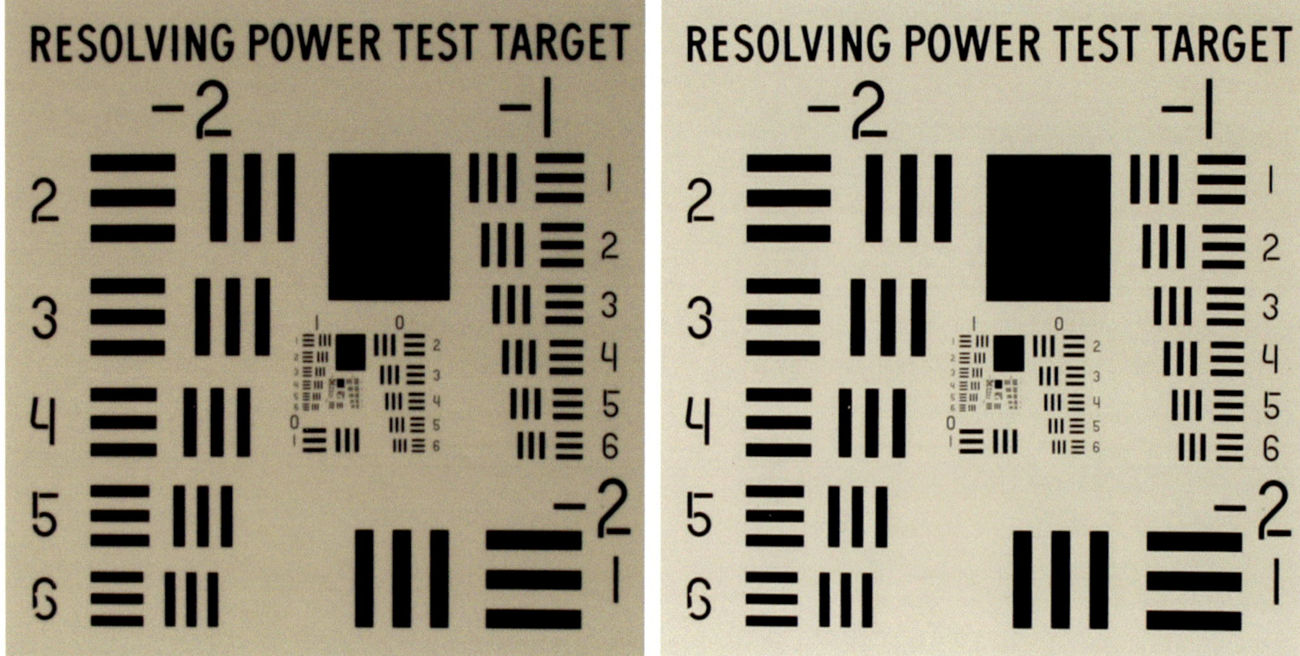

Figure 8-2 The unedited raw (left) and JPEG (right) images straight from the camera.

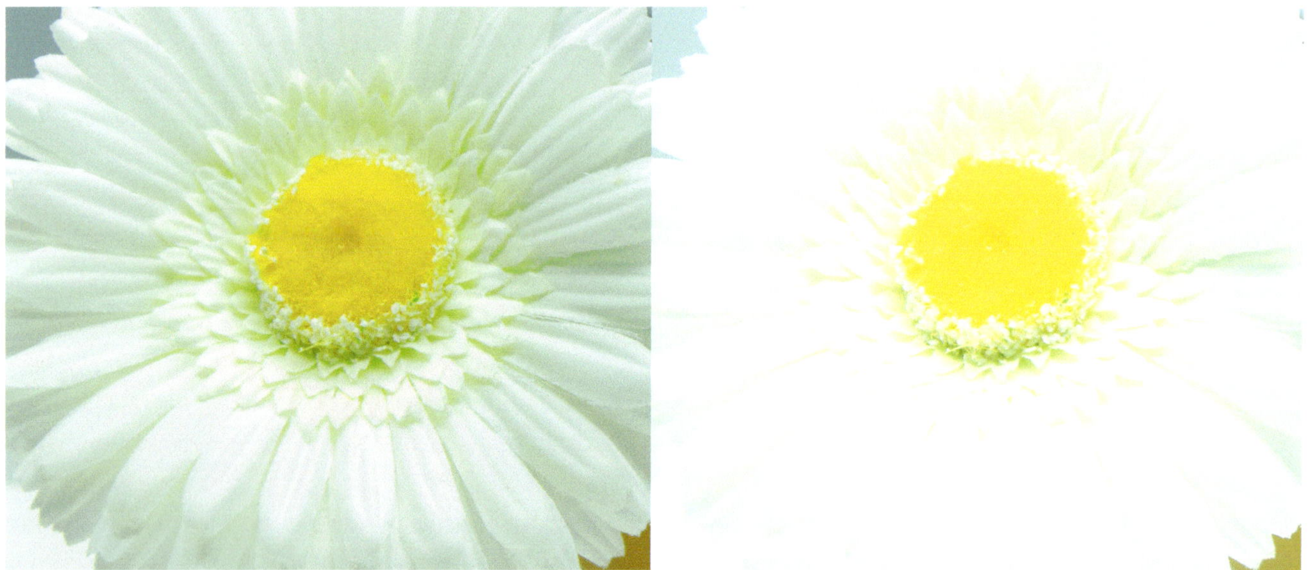

Figure 8-3 Highlight recovery of slightly overexposed image captured as a raw file (left) and as a JPEG (right). Only the raw file's bit depth retained enough brightness headroom to recover detail.

underexposed raw captures can be largely recovered with post-processing as demonstrated in Figure 8-3. A JPEG of comparably poor exposure yields exactly the detail it shows straight off of the camera; software exposure recovery cannot bring back tone information that failed to write to the file format's limited bit depth. Raw captures are ideal for a photographic workflow because they are the least compromised assets we have. They do not degrade over time or over repeated editing sessions and always allow us to return to their just-after-capture state.

If a raw file's captured image data is the star of the show, best supporting role goes to the non-destructive image editing instructions. This data is sometimes stored in the raw file container or it may be written to a separate, companion asset stored in the same location called a *sidecar file*. This sidecar data comes in the form of an *Extensible Metadata Platform* (XMP) file. XMP is an ISO standard (16684-1:2012) created by Adobe in an effort to uphold compatibility and interpretability of metadata while allowing for additional fields or pieces of information to be added. Image editing software uses XMP-stored editing instructions to create an interpreted version of the raw image data, described later in this chapter.

The Photographic Workflow

One's workflow is the system of managing digital assets from capture to output. A generic workflow following image capture consists of:

1. Copying the files to a primary workstation computer
2. Ingesting them into cataloging software (can happen concurrently with the previous step)
3. Making initial selections, rating the stand-out frames from a shooting session
4. Making basic adjustments on those selections
5. Advanced image processing, compositing and cleanup on a subset of selections
6. Outputting edited, derivative files for print or digital distribution
7. Backing up all ingested and derived assets to local storage
8. Archiving all assets to long-term storage solutions, offline and remote

Image Ingestion

The act of transferring images from a memory card to a desktop storage drive can be a simple copy-and-paste operation. We perform this action all the time with text or with miscellaneous files on our computing devices. *Image ingestion* goes a step further in thoughtfully organizing and reviewing the data. Basic copy-and-paste operations are heavily dependent on manual handling and lack a robust strategy for long-term image maintenance. Let's first review the broad strokes and dive into the details in the sections that follow.

We start by establishing a high-level directory for all image assets. All ingested files will be sorted into subdirectories therein. A generic approach from here is to organize subdirectories by year and then calendar date (YYYYMMDD format). Organizing files by capture time makes it easy to track down work through invoices, email correspondence or your memory. This approach lacks content visibility—just because you've got photos from January 9, 2005, it doesn't mean you know what happened that day—we rely on catalog software to assist with that. Some photographers may prefer to use a single, temporary dropbox directory for all incoming media that gets sorted by software in a later step. Alternatively, a more descriptive folder naming system might work better for your professional workflow. Consistency and long-term flexibility are key considerations for your approach.

Downloading files from a memory card can be accomplished with drag-and-drop copying in an operating system's file browser. This approach may not catch problems like corruption or failed transfers. Instead, software like ImageIngester Pro or Adobe Photoshop Lightroom handles the transfer process with greater assurance of proper data handling and consistent organization. They can also be configured to convert proprietary raw files to DNGs or create backup copies to secondary locations. Using a dedicated memory card reader is recommended for image transfer. Connecting the camera via cable invites the possibility of file damage if the camera battery dies. Card readers offer potentially greater transfer speeds because they skip the middleman of the camera's firmware. It's also more likely that you have a card reader and cable supporting the fastest available connection protocol.

Renaming files comes next. This is best done as a batch operation, as no one wants to manually name files one at a time. Basic metadata tagging is helpful to conduct as files are named and stored. This includes the photographer's contact information and usage rights. Descriptors for the entire image set, such as client name, location and a few basic subject keywords, are valuable to introduce here. We'll detail types of metadata later in this chapter and recommend the Digital Photography Best Practices and Workflow project as an additional resource.[3]

Additional processing instructions can be applied as images are ingested into cataloging software. General editing decisions can be made to all ingested files if it speeds up the process of preview, rating and selection. It's not meant to replace the forthcoming step of hands-on editing decisions. If you conduct a photoshoot for a client that intends to print the final images in black and white, it's helpful to set all ingested files to a basic black and white adjustment. This offers quick visual feedback for an entire image set before committing to specific selections and edits.

Once files are transferred, renamed and injected with an initial round of metadata, it's wise to back it all up. We often think that backing up files comes way later in the process, yet immediately following ingestion is one of the best times to do it. Backups of captured images lessen the risk of losing irreplaceable or unrepeatable photo shoots; we'd rather lose a few hours of editing work than lose the sole set of raw files from a one-time shoot. Generating a primary and backup copy of images downloaded from a memory card allows you to erase the card or otherwise write over its stored files on future shoots without hesitation.

Culling and rating images is a helpful follow-up step. We delete very poor-quality images that are unlikely to be of any use. This includes extremely blurry images, missed exposures or catching a model with their eyes closed. We then use a method of flagging or indicating value (a star rating, a color code, etc.) as we quickly review all captures. An initial round of rating and filtering can narrow down the scope of the impending image processing workload; making granular edits on half a dozen frames from a photoshoot containing a few hundred is more realistic than individually editing all of them.

Naming Files

Developing a *file naming convention* is critical for keeping track of images in a file system structure. Cameras use default base filenames like "DSC" or "IMG" with frame numbers at the end (i.e. *IMG_0001.cr2*). After 9999 captures, the counter rolls over to 0001. Alternatively, it's common for photographers to shoot with multiple cameras at the same time, often from the same manufacturer. These scenarios easily lead to duplicate filenames unless actions are taken to make them unique. Even if you are careful to avoid putting identically named files into the same directory, leaving the default filenames is dangerous when sharing images with similarly lazy photographers.

File systems permit filenames as large as 255 characters. Any file naming convention should use numbers, letters and hyphens or underscores (no other symbols or non-Latin characters). Using non-standard symbols or characters invites incompatibility from operating systems and editing software. For example, the "/" indicates a directory separation in many operating systems. The three letter file extension (i.e. ".JPG") must be included at the end of filenames.

It's recommended that file naming templates include your initials or last name, a calendar date and unique numbers (four digits long) that restart for every directory set. You may also wish to use an additional, unique number identifier for invoices or project codes appended to calendar dates. In coordination with your subfolder organization, dates should follow the YYYYMMDD format. Craft a custom naming template with these ideas in mind. As with every step of a DAM workflow, the file naming system must be applied with consistency every time you ingest new work. It's tempting to make directory names descriptive and specific to a job or location. However, your memory is not nearly as capable as a cataloging program is when it's tapped into the numerous data attributes that describe every image file.

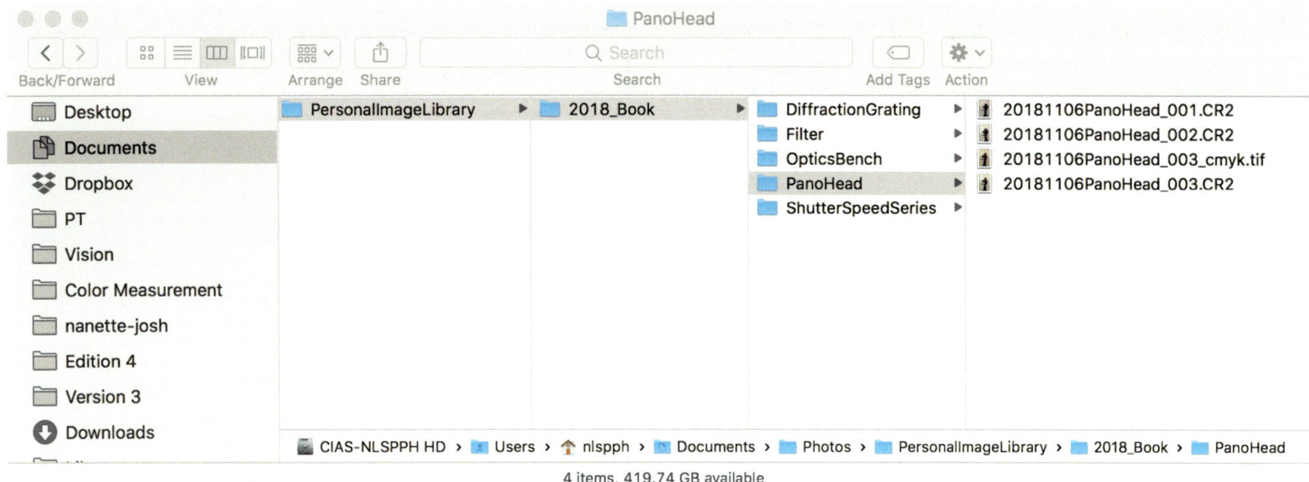

Figure 8-4 Example directory and file naming structure.

The last item to consider is appending filenames with a consistent vocabulary for differentiating between the original and derivative versions. For example, an RGB image converted to CMYK for printing could add the string "_cmyk" to the end of the filename (see Figure 8-4). We did this for every image printed in this book.

Cataloging Software

Software packages such as Adobe Photoshop Lightroom, Capture One Pro, ImageIngester Pro and Canto Cumulus are professional go-to's for cataloging and editing images. These are designed as workflow streamliners and catalog builders. What is an *image catalog* and why is it important to diligently maintain one?

Let's digress for a moment: I had stacks of negatives when I was a photography student in a previous but intentionally unspecified decade. I placed each developed film roll in a negative holder, carefully labelled with their subject and capture date and created a contact sheet. It was relatively easy to find any negative I wanted later by using this system. Digital images changed everything; instead of 36 exposures per roll of film, we capture as many images as our memory card can hold during a given photo shoot. Sorting, labeling and filling every single frame by hand in this new image creation paradigm would take so much time as to eliminate all the time we otherwise enjoy going out and taking the photographs.

A catalog provides the ability to organize, label and locate every image. If image directories are like chapters in a book, the catalog acts as the index. It documents the locations of all ingested media files and their metadata such that your entire photography library can be searched by many dozens of attributes. It can be an overwhelming task when first establishing such an important organizational backbone but it gets easier to maintain once it is incorporated into your workflow. The cataloging software can take the reins on image ingestion to ensure automated, consistent treatment as new content comes in.

The catalog contains supporting information like the star ratings or color coding mentioned earlier. It also includes tools for descriptive keyword tagging that become searchable criteria for future referencing. Keywords and ratings are leveraged by filter queries to find exactly what you need, even if the thing you need is not reinforced by your file directories or naming conventions. For example: the highest rated images of Mary Smith, a regular model of yours, taken over the last five years is easily found in an image catalog system.

Cataloging software typically requires a single, dedicated catalog file that describes and documents access to the image data. The catalog assets store critical documentation for your library's contents and where to find them across any number of directories and storage drives. If the folders or files stored within are moved or deleted, the catalog software loses its link to the data. If the drives are offline, the software continues to index their existence. Conveniently, cataloging software creates previews upon ingesting the full raw images. This allows for viewing a version of the image even if the full resolution file is on an unavailable or disconnected drive. This is very different from accessing files via the operating system's file browser, which can only present data it sees connected in that moment.

The image catalog is vital to asset organization and it should be backed up just as often as your images. We have witnessed students losing their catalogs on too many occasions to shake the paranoia; it's not a pleasant experience to start the whole process over from scratch.

Trends in cataloging and editing software point to a move to the cloud. This provides businesses, large or small, to easily share data across the internet and synchronize all ingested and edited content. In addition, *software as a service* (SaaS) systems provide editing software as well as DAM options, allowing employees access to assets from anywhere including mobile platforms.

Image Editing

It is seldom that a photograph goes completely unedited between capture and output. Whether it is removing a small piece of dust or completely altering the look and feel, image editing is an inevitable stage in a photograph's development. There are two overarching but fundamentally different approaches to image edits: *pixel editing* and the previously mentioned *parametric image editing*.

Pixel editing modifies the original pixel values in an image. The edits are permanent once the file is saved. This is often referred to as "baked in" edits. If you save the edited image using the original filename, effectively writing over the data, the unedited version cannot be retrieved. Consider the following scenario using a pixel editing approach. You make an exposure adjustment that darkens all pixels. You save the image, figuring that the change was for the better and worth preserving. Upon printing, you notice that the shadows are blocked up and detail-less where there was previously tone variation and texture. The exposure adjustment made before printing cannot be undone—the shadow detail is lost forever. If you insist on using pixel editing, archive the original image files and work exclusively with derivative, working copy versions. This way, though your editing is irreversible from a given editing session, you can always fall back to the unedited original capture and start over. Adobe Photoshop is a pixel editing software, though advanced users leverage layers and other special functionality to allow for much more malleable and reversible edits in a working document.

Parametric image editing does not alter the original data. Every edit made to the photograph, from cropping to exposure adjustments and color balance, is recorded as an individual instruction or parameter value in metadata. The software knows how to adjust contrast, for example, it just needs to know by how much. We edit by specifying new values for different image adjustments like saturation, sharpness and brightness. In addition to global changes, advanced instructions can specify pixel locations for local adjustments to portions of an image. Software generates a temporary preview of those adjustments as we edit yet the raw data is preserved. In the future when software and our editing skills improve (or our aesthetic tastes shift), the changes can be undone and new editing decisions applied to the original image data. Parametric image editing software writes these instructions to its own documentation or to XMP sidecar files written alongside the images. We primarily use this technique with raw images yet JPEG and TIFF files can be parametrically edited since the instructions are written independently from the source file.

A great capability of parametric editing is in storing multiple, unique editing sets for a single raw image. Similar to how every grandmother has her own apple pie recipe despite the same standard starting ingredients, a photo can have unique parametric editing instruction sets applied to create different interpretations (see Figure 8-5). One simple use case: keeping both a color and black and white rendering of a photograph. Instead of duplicating the image and doubling the storage burden, parametric image editing software simply writes two recipes and keeps them with the raw file. It's only when we export a version that the software generates a new, derivative and "baked in" image with the editing instructions applied.

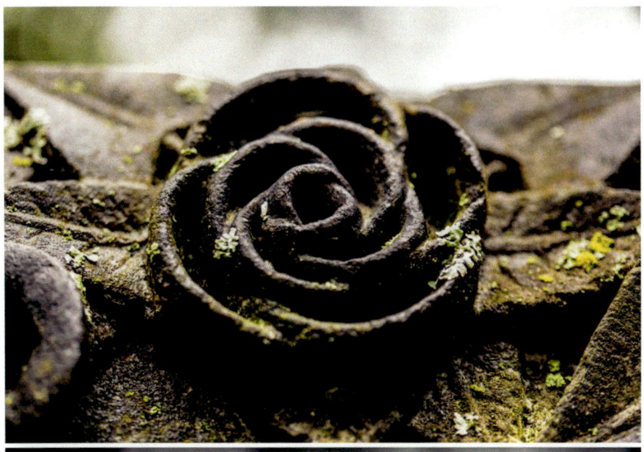
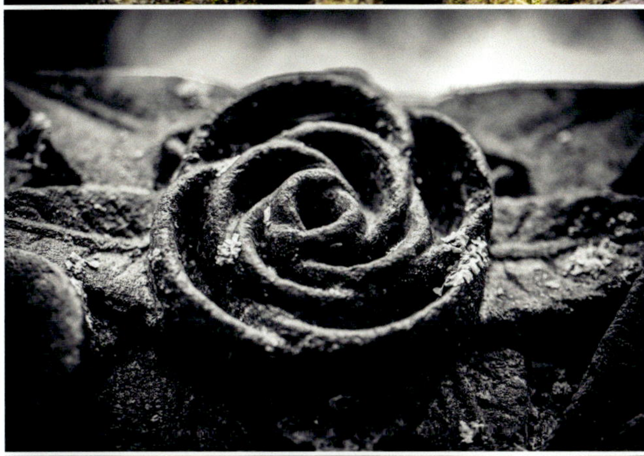
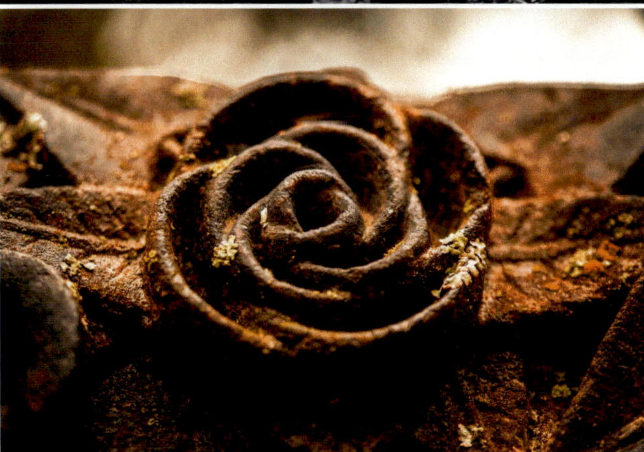

Figure 8-5 Three unique edits of the same raw file. The raw image is stored once with three unique instruction sets when working in parametric image editing software. It's only upon export that new, full resolution image files are generated.

Metadata and Keywords

Metadata is simply data about other data. Photography metadata is information about your images. It can be stored in the image itself and can therefore be available to you or another user whenever the image is available. It may also reside in a sidecar file. Image metadata can be organized into four categories: technical, administrative, descriptive and processing.

Technical metadata is the capture information and gets stored in the *Exchangeable Image File Format* (EXIF) portion of an image file. While raw formats lack standardization, EXIF metadata is consistently used by raw files to record details such as the date and time the photograph was captured, GPS coordinates, shutter speed, aperture setting, ISO, if the flash fired, the camera make, model, serial number and the lens used. The bulk of this is generated automatically and we leverage it for cataloging, filtering and documentation purposes. We typically don't need or have a reason to modify EXIF metadata. EXIF information is also supported and stored by the JPEG format.

Administrative metadata includes International Press Telecommunications Council (IPTC) fields. This set of fields is typically entered after capture with desktop software, though some cameras can be configured to automatically add it to every capture. Here is where contact information is entered, such as name, address, phone number and email address. It's a good idea to populate the "Usage" IPTC field with a statement such as "No usage without express and prior written permission. All rights reserved." This tells others that they don't have free reign to use the photos. IPTC metadata also includes fields for the year of copyright and the copyright holder's name. However, simply having something stored in this part of an image's metadata does not make the copyright official. For that, you must register the work with the Library of Congress. Administrative metadata is easily added en masse to files as they are ingested into a catalog since the information is applicable to entire photo shoots or events.

Descriptive metadata is added by hand after ingest and it's where we add image content descriptions. This can include the title or caption, the concept, the location (an actual name rather than GPS coordinates) and keywords.

Keywords are specific words that help to locate photographs within your library or when included in any sort of large, searchable image database. Example keywords include a client's name or a specific product shoot. Software tools exist to aid in crafting keywords for optimizing search engine results. Google's *Adwords* is one example of a keyword optimization tool. Rating systems, like stars or thumbs up/down indicators, are also descriptive metadata concepts that function like circling frames on a contact sheet as used to be done with darkroom development. They are useful when tagged and reviewed by a single user, perhaps less so when attempting to communicate nuanced opinions or sorting ideas with others.

Descriptive metadata is the most granular and image-specific form of metadata. Descriptive keywords can be generic terms like "landscape" or as specific as is needed, such as "Mary Smith" to tag a model. *Parent* and *child* keywords describe hierarchical keyword groupings where "Rochester, NY" is a child keyword for "New York" which itself sits nested under the parent keyword of "Places." Sometimes it makes sense to use hyper-specific child keywords while other times it's reasonable to stick to higher-level ones. Ideally, descriptive keywords should make thoughtful use of a *controlled vocabulary* such that you consistently use "architecture" instead of haphazardly using "buildings" one day or "manmade structures" another.[4] Machine learning is increasingly leveraged by digital photo album software and social media networks to determine descriptive keywords (including facial recognition) without human input.

Finally, processing metadata is parametric image edit information. This information can be things like instructions for cropping, color correction or contrast adjustments. The specific controls and values for such editing adjustments may be specific to a particular platform or software; one program might understand "exposure: +1.0" while another requires "exp val 15." Such variation is supported because XMP is an extensible metadata structure.

Image Data and File Sizes

The pixel is the smallest and most basic visual building block of a photograph. A pixel is a type of digital information with its own building blocks: binary digits (ones and zeroes). All digital data, from photographs to music to text, boils down to binary information read and stored by a computer. The amount of binary digits needed to describe even a single pixel of a photograph is so large that it's not practical to directly count them. We use units of higher orders instead. For every eight binary digits (or *bits*) there is one *byte*. The conversions between units to quantify file size are shown in Table 8-2.

Table 8-2 File size unit conversions.

Unit	Symbol	Number of Bytes	Binary
Byte	B	1	2
Kilobyte	KB	1,024	210
Megabyte	MB	1,048,576	220
Gigabyte	GB	1,073,741,824	230
Terabyte	TB	1,099,511,627,776	240
Petabyte	PB	1,125,899,906,842,624	250

The practical units relevant to photographers are *kilobytes* (KB), *megabytes* (MB), *gigabytes* (GB) and *terabytes* (TB). Sidecar XMP files and small JPEGs are a few dozen to a few hundred kilobytes a piece. Single raw image files are tens of megabytes. Collections of image assets like those from a single photo shoot can be multiple gigabytes. A photographer's catalog of photoshoots, composite files and exported JPEGs or TIFFs tends to be on the scale of terabytes (and this is where the panic sets in as we price out storage solutions). The more photographic information we want—more layers, channels, reproducible tones, versions—the more the files grow in size. Digital image file sizes are calculated with the following steps:

1. Calculate the total number of pixels.

Total pixels = number of vertical pixels x number of horizontal pixels

2. Determine the number of bits needed.

   Total number of bits = total pixels x bit depth

3. Divide the total number of bits by 8 to determine the number of bytes.

$$\textit{File size (in bytes)} = \frac{\textit{total number of bits}}{\textit{8 bits/byte}}$$

4. Divide the file size in bytes by 1,024 to determine the file size in kilobytes.

$$\textit{File size (in kilobytes)} = \frac{\textit{File size (in bytes)}}{\textit{1,024 bytes/kilobyte}}$$

5. Divide the file size (in kilobytes) by 1,024 to determine the file size in megabytes.

$$\textit{File size (in megabytes)} = \frac{\textit{File size (in kilobytes)}}{\textit{1,024 kilobytes/megabytes}}$$

These steps are summarized into Equation 8.1:

$$\textit{File size (MB)} = \frac{\left(\frac{\frac{[(\textit{Total number of pixels}) \times (\textit{Bit depth})]}{8}}{2{,}048}\right)}{2{,}048} \qquad \text{(Eq. 8.1)}$$

This formula is true for the raw data in an image file and does not consider compression applied or any embedded metadata. The greater the number of pixels and/or the greater the bit depth, the larger the resulting file size. We estimate the size of a raw file from a 42.5MP sensor using the number of pixels (8,000x5,320) and the sensor bit depth (14-bit) following the previous steps, as summarized in Equation 8.2:

$$\frac{((8{,}000 \times 5{,}320) \times 14)}{8} = 74{,}480{,}000 \textit{ bytes} = 71.03 \textit{ megabytes} \qquad \text{(Eq. 8.2)}$$

The raw file may be slightly larger than 71 MB once additional pieces of information are added alongside the image data like proprietary processing metadata. Note that the raw image has a bit depth of 14 as it is brightness information for every photosite location. It is not yet a full color image and undergoes a process of interpretation that generates three channels (R, G, B) of bit depth information. Consider the same photograph after a raw engine demosaiced it and saved a full color, 16-bit TIFF file, calculated in Equation 8.3:

$$\frac{((8{,}000 \times 5{,}320) \times (16 \times 3))}{8} = 255{,}360{,}000 \textit{ bytes or } 243.53 \textit{ megabytes} \qquad \text{(Eq. 8.3)}$$

The TIFF version of the image is much larger now that there are three color channels, each of which contains up to 16 bits of information. One takeaway from Equation 8.3 is that storing raw files over unedited TIFFs is noticeably more space-efficient despite the comparable lossless characteristic. The catch is that the raw data requires the appropriate decoding software (the raw engine) to turn it into a workable photograph. Conversely, the file size of an 8-bit JPEG derived from the raw file is calculated in Equation 8.4:

$$\frac{((8{,}000 \times 5{,}320) \times 8)}{8} = 42{,}560{,}000 \textit{ bytes or } 40.59 \textit{ megabytes} \qquad \text{(Eq. 8.4)}$$

It's even smaller in practice because JPEG introduces size reduction via lossy compression not accounted for in our calculation. Estimating a file size with this consideration is more difficult due to the content-dependent nature of JPEG compression efficiency.

File Storage Options

We reviewed the options for camera capture storage in Chapter 3. Never rely on files stored on capture media for anything other than short-term storage between capture and ingestion. We strongly recommend formatting camera storage cards through the camera's firmware before every new shooting session. Memory cards write to a *File Allocation Table* (FAT) that acts like an address book for where the data resides on the card. Selecting "delete" in a camera's firmware menu typically deletes this table without deleting the image data itself. The image data is only truly deleted when the card runs out of space and writes over it with new data or when you format its contents. This is good news for recovering accidentally deleted data—there's a chance it's on there—but bad news for the stability and health of the capture storage medium. Errors or corruption can occur when data is written over other data.

Once you're safely back in the studio or starving artist studio apartment, it's time to offload all those photos. This means transferring the images from memory cards to your laptop or desktop computer. How safe is that data once it resides on your laptop hard drive, the laptop that has taken more than a few spills off of coffee shop tables and couch cushions? When your digital assets have high monetary and artistic value, you must get serious about storing them. The main options are optical disks, disk drives and offsite cloud storage.

Optical Disc Media

Optical disc media storage includes *Compact Discs* (CDs), *Digital Versatile Discs* (DVDs) and *Blu-ray Discs* (BDs). They store binary information by laser-cutting microscopic pits into the surface of an alloy material. The information is written in a circular, spiral pattern from the center of the disc outwards. An optical disc drive laser reads these pits and lands (the raised or level areas) as the disc spins at high speeds. CDs are an earlier generation optical disc format, followed by DVD and most recently, Blu-ray. Each has increased storage capacity in turn by finding ways to write smaller on the disc surface or by writing at different depths in the material.

Optical disc media can be *write-once-read-many* (WORM) or *rewritable* (RW). Rewritable discs made sense for transferring files back and forth by reusing a single disc but flash drives quickly surpassed this option in speed and convenience. Storage capacities of optical discs are listed in Table 8-3.

Table 8-3 Optical disc media and their storage capacities.

Media Type	Storage Capacity
Compact Disc (CD)	725 MB
Digital Versatile Disc (DVD)	1.8 GB
Dual Layer DVD	3.6 GB
Blu-ray Disc (BD)	25 GB
Dual Layer BD	50 GB

We rarely use optical discs for listening to music or transporting assets between computers anymore. Computer hardware, particularly laptops, increasingly forgoes optical disc drives altogether and thus requires an external peripheral to read and write to disc. Still, the technology offers a cheap backup storage solution for media files. Discs can be scratched and damaged when handled, so cases or disc sleeves are necessary for anything more than short-term transfers. Scratched discs mean an impaired ability to read the data previously written to them. CDs have an estimated lifetime of approximately 100 years under moderate storage conditions.[5]

Hard Disk Drives

A *hard disk drive* (HDD) stores information on a rotating, magnetic platter. A mechanical read/write head sits just above the platter's surface and detects changes in magnetic polarity. Though visually reminiscent of a needle and record on a turntable, these components do not touch. The faster the platter spins, the faster information stored on the platter can be read and written to. Blunt force, especially when the disk is spinning, can irrecoverably damage the platter. This is a particular risk for laptop hard disk drives and external, portable hard drives. Exposure to strong earth magnets can also damage the platter.

The two primary specifications for an HDD are speed (number of revolutions per minute or RPM) and size, in gigabytes or terabytes. Common hard disk drive speeds are 3200 RPM (found in some laptops and all-in-one desktops), 5400 RPM and 7200 RPM (the best option for desktop computers). An HDD that tops out at 3200 RPM is reasonable for a web-browsing machine but insufficient for heavy image or video editing work. Some specialized HDDs used for data servers offer speeds of 15,000 RPM. HDDs come in standard sizes of 2.5" and 3.5" and top out in capacity at 10 TB.

Even extremely fast rotation speeds can't change the physical reality that the read/write head can only be at one place at a time. Accessing information that resides across multiple locations on the platter is time-consuming for the drive. This limitation leads to the recommendation that a computer's operating system and program files should reside on one drive while all working media assets should be stored on a separate drive.

Solid State Drives

Solid state drives (SSDs) are like grown-up USB flash drives or memory cards; the same microchip technology is used to store digital data with non-moving parts. This technology is called *NAND-based flash memory* and it is managed by an onboard processor called a *controller*.

SSDs historically demanded a significant premium in price-per-megabyte compared to HDDs, though recent years have seen prices drop. Solid state drives range in size from 64 GB up to 10 TB (though this upper end capacity rises every year). Since all of the data is stored on flash memory, it doesn't have the physical limitations of an HDD's head and platter movement. On the other hand, flash memory isn't great at reading and writing many tiny files at a time. Additionally, flash memory can degrade. All drives, as a result, are built with more storage than listed and write to new areas as old ones wear out. Shooting video is a great use case for choosing an SSD over an HDD: the volume of data and large file sizes combined with the need to load and view it all quickly make SSDs the superior storage choice.

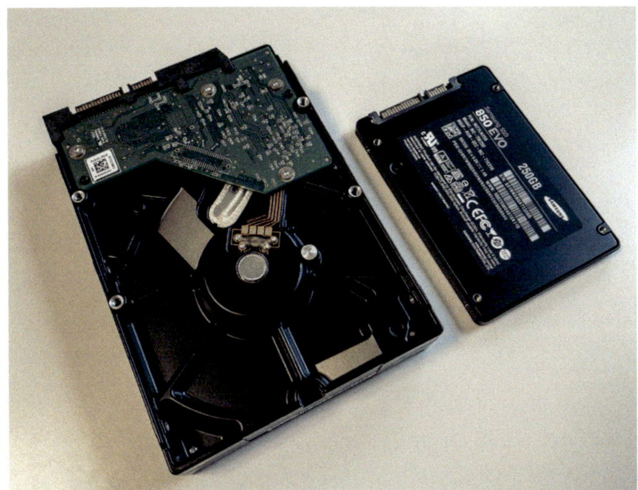

Figure 8-6 A 3.5" hard disk drive next to a 2.5" solid state drive.

Solid state drives come in standard sizes: 1.8", 2.5" and 3.5". Figure 8-6 shows an SSD alongside an HDD. Smaller form factors are used in laptops when space is at a premium, though they can be more expensive. Internal SSDs communicate with the motherboard via Serial Advanced Technology Attachment (SATA) or mini-SATA (mSATA) connections.

Disk Configurations

Data storage can be a nightmare. As your career progresses, the number of photographic assets you need to store grows at an incredible rate. It's unlikely to shrink, save for a major data loss! There are two configuration approaches for data storage on disk drives.

The first is JBOD, short for *just a bunch of disks*. This configuration allows you to attach a collection of disk drives to your computer. A low-tech implementation of JBOD stops here—if you have spare ports, you can plug in more drives—though this is not a sustainable practice. Each disk appears as an independent storage drive to the operating system, necessitating manual data management. A fully realized JBOD system, on the other hand, adds a layer of software that does this management for you. This software groups the collection of storage disks to appear as a single drive. Such mediation may solve the question of "which drive did I put that image on?" but it does not provide any redundancy for your data storage. If a sector or a drive fails, all is lost. That data exists in a singular location that is susceptible to hardware failure and user error. JBOD systems are appealing because they can make use of old or differently sized hard drives that tend to pile up or collect dust in a closet. Still, they threaten to monopolize desk space and are vulnerable to data loss.

The second configuration approach is a *redundant array of independent disks* or RAID. A RAID also uses multiple disks and adds intermediary software to appear as a single drive to the computer. The major departure from JBOD is in its ability to add data storage redundancy. In a redundant configuration, files are written in several different locations across the array of disks. This way, if there is a sector or a disk failure, all the data is preserved and recoverable from one or more of the healthy siblings. There are seven standard levels of RAID configuration: RAID 0 through RAID 6. RAID 0 is essentially a JBOD system that offers no redundancy with unique data existing in a single location on a single disk (confusingly, you can have a RAID configuration that is simultaneously a JBOD). Data redundancy starts at RAID level 1, a mirroring of the data in one additional location. Above level 1, bit- and byte-level striping and parity are used. These increasingly complex mechanisms offer additional data protection. With each ascending RAID level, the amount of available storage space decreases relative to the total amount of disk storage in the array. A RAID 1 configuration, for example, might have two 2 TB drives. Only 2 TB is available to storage data so that it all exists on one physical disk drive and can be mirrored (duplicated) on the second.

Network-attached storage (NAS) hardware is used by photographers to house and manage RAID-configured drives (one of ours is shown in Figure 8-7). NAS units reside on a desktop or they can be connected to the local area network; they function as file storage servers. Network-attached storage solutions range in size based on the number of disks they hold. They often include automated backup and drive health monitoring software that is accessed through a browser-based interface on a desktop computer. RAID-configured storage solutions like NAS are a valuable DAM investment. They can stick with you for years by periodically upgrading the disk drives to larger capacities as your asset library grows.

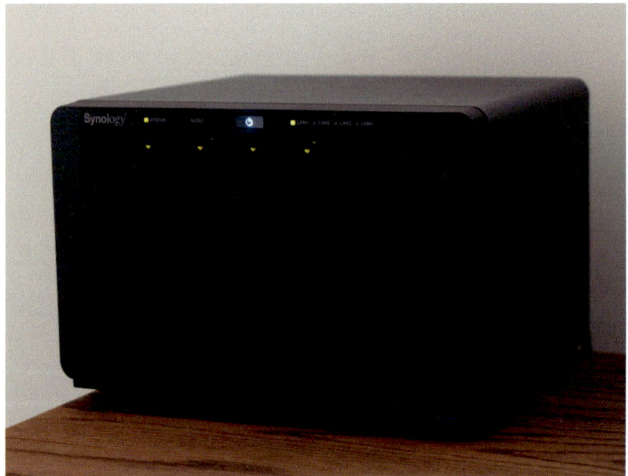

Figure 8-7 A network-attached storage solution with multiple drive bays.

Backup Solutions

A popular idea in backup solutions is the 3-2-1 rule: three copies of your data on two different media with one stored at an alternate location.[6] You want one copy of your image data available to work on and a second copy close at hand in case you accidently delete a file or encounter an unrecoverable file error. The third copy resides at a different physical location—a beach house, perhaps, if your photography career is a lucrative one. Keeping a copy somewhere else protects the data against natural disasters, break-ins or other unforeseeable events that can wipe out all electronics residing at a location (one of the author's homes was struck by lightning, damaging a computer). Using two forms of storage media hedges your bets as every type of media has a different likelihood of failure and degree of future-compatibility-proofing.

Maintaining these copies of your work is a full time job without the help of backup software solutions. Two such solutions are ChronoSync or Carbon Copy Cloner, though there are many options.[7,8] Operating systems and photo cataloging software also offer a degree of automated backup behaviors to make the process painless. Cataloging software may offer the option to immediately make duplicates and store them on a separate drive upon ingestion. Otherwise, scheduled automatic backups of entire drives makes backup plans something to establish once. After that, the systems should remain in place to regularly write new data to all secondary storage drives.

The last piece of the puzzle is knowing the difference between a backup and an archive. A *backup* is meant for assets that you are currently working on. The backup is what you turn to if you accidently delete a file or the file becomes corrupted. The backup must be easily accessible so that valuable work time is not lost. An *archive* means storing files offline for long-term safe-keeping. These are files that are no longer changing, like in the case of finished client assignments, and it's unlikely that you need to access them again in the near future. The files are accessible with some effort and transferred to a convenient, local working environment if they're needed in the future.

There's no such thing as a truly archival format or strategy for digital media. Generations of societies, archivists and librarians have found ways to maintain and preserve all sorts of physical media: paintings, sculpture, text. The medium of photography (starting with analog processes), in the context of humanity's timeline, is brand new. Digital technology is an even more nascent phenomenon whose long-term storage and archiving solutions are in the earliest stages of development. You may not be thinking about your photographs as the next Mona Lisa—though we believe that photography exists amongst the halls of traditional art—but you would like to believe that work from the early days of your career survives ten, 20 and even 40 years down the line. Archiving of digital media is an effort requiring regular tending, moving or updating files to new storage solutions, formats and computer hardware to ensure readability and compatibility. Backup and archive solutions must be regularly revisited and maintained.

Remote Server File Hosting and Storage Services

An increasingly prevalent option for managing digital assets is *cloud-based storage*. Cloud storage and services put all the cost of hardware purchase and maintenance and computer knowledge for setup into someone else's hands (the service provider). The user pays to effectively rent the offsite storage space that is accessible with an internet connection. The provider is responsible for maintaining your data, making it available, and providing backup and recovery. Cloud storage can be used as a primary backup, an archive or as an offsite copy in case of disaster. There is a monthly cost that may outweigh the expense of investing in additional storage on-site in a home or studio. It's also not susceptible to your cat knocking the drive array off your desk. The biggest limitation of cloud-based storage is transfer speed as a function of your internet service provider (ISP). Leaving files to upload overnight is convenient for backups; downloading dozens of images you needed 5 minutes ago is not a viable workflow. Cloud-based storage is best leveraged for asynchronous activities.

File hosting services are a great option for delivering data to a client. Such services enable you to upload files to server-based storage through which clients are granted access to download. There are many options available with either controlled access or access to anyone on the web. File hosting can be read-only specified if needed. Many cloud-based storage sites also have file hosting capabilities.

Data Recovery

You will lose photographs. It happens to everyone. Memory cards get corrupted and you find yourself desperate to recover photographs you've taken but didn't yet transfer to a computer. A hard disk drive sputters and fails to start up one day. Hope is not lost! There are scenarios where the photo data is on the storage device, inaccessible but unharmed. This is where software solutions like Photo Rescue or Disk Warrior can dig through the rubble of your memory card or hard drive disaster. Sometimes it's the storage drive's index that gets garbled, not the data itself, in which case clever software can recover some or all of a drive's data. Best practices to minimize the chance of data loss include minimizing movement or transportation, avoiding extreme temperatures or moisture in storage and ensuring good air circulation around disk drives. Memory cards are particularly susceptible to dust and debris on their contacts, as they are easily pocketable items and are moved between devices on a regular basis.

Avenues for Data Transfer

Bandwidth describes the maximum data transfer rate of a network or connection protocol. It's commonly measured in bits per second (remember: 8-bits is 1 byte of digital data) and gives us a sense of how much digital information can be moved from one place to another, be it two computers, two drives within one computer or from a local network to the internet. Data transfer rates fluctuate based on a host of variables including the number of files and signal stability. For example, a large number of very small files takes longer to transfer than one large PSD file containing the same total number of bits. Additionally, a storage medium is usually only accessible one sector or area at a time. Different connection standards are available for data transfer, independent of where it's headed or what the data payload looks like.

Data Transfer Connection Standards

Here we offer a rundown of available connection standards. Our intention is to make you familiar with each without dipping into the electrical engineering or standards documentation. Just like with every other commercial technology, standards and protocols ensure compatibility and versatility in our image-making toolbox; cables and connection ports are a tangled reality of our digital ecosystems. Connection standards vary in their potential bandwidth and present potential bottlenecks in data transfer, be it moving raw files from camera to computer or from internal storage to an external NAS. Photographers find themselves in variable environments from field shooting, studio work, editing in transit or remotely reviewing photo sets from mobile devices. In short, there isn't a single, neatly determined setup for your gear. The best bet is taking advantage of the best technology available for the photographic workflow task at hand. Table 8-4 lists data transfer protocols and their bandwidth potential. There are more variants than the ones included here and standards are regularly updated with backwards compatibility (at the slower speeds). We've put network connections alongside peripheral connections to appreciate the relative speeds despite their different usage.

Table 8-4 Data connection types and their potential bandwidth for data transfer.

Data Connection Type	Maximum Data Rates[9]
Gigabit Ethernet (1000BASE-T)	1,000 Mb/s
10-Gigabit Ethernet (10GBASE-T)	10 Gb/s
WiFi IEEE 802.11b/g	11 Mb/s, 54 Mb/s
WiFi IEEE 802.11n	600 Mb/s
Bluetooth 4.0/5.0	25 Mb/s, 50 Mb/s
eSATA	3 Gb/s, 6 Gb/s
FireWire 400/800	400 Mb/s, 800 Mb/s
USB 1.0	12 Mb/s
USB 2.0	480 Mb/s
USB 3.0/3.1	5 Gb/s, 10 Gb/s
Thunderbolt 1.0	10 Gb/s (x2 channels)
Thunderbolt 2.0	20 Gb/s
Thunderbolt 3.0	40 Gb/s
DVI Single/Dual	5 Gb/s, 10 Gb/s
DisplayPort 1.0/1.3	10.8 Gb/s, 32 Gb/s
HDMI 1.0/2.1	5 Gb/s, 48 Gb/s

Internal storage drives communicate with other computer components using SATA cables. This connection offers high transfer rates. *External serial advanced technology attachment*, or eSATA, connections use this high-speed bus in service of connecting drives external to the computer motherboard (i.e. an external drive used with a laptop). The connection requires a *peripheral component interconnect express*, or PCIe, card to make the connection possible though these cards are more common on PC machines than Macs and may need to be installed separately.

Ethernet is used for local area networks (LANs), a protocol originally developed by Xerox Corporation and standardized in the early 1980s.[10] We use ethernet connections to hardwire our desktop and sometimes laptop computers to a local network (a router or modem). Ethernet connections are fast and reliable for large data transfers as they are not subject to environmental interference in the way that wireless protocols are. Studio photographers benefit from shooting with high-end SLRs or medium format cameras that offer ethernet ports built into their bodies. This setup is called *shooting tethered* because there's a cabled connection between the camera and a computer workstation. Large raw images can be transferred as they're captured to a storage medium and into cataloging or tethering software that displays immediate previews. Using ethernet in this scenario is the fastest way to move the image data off camera. The niche use case means that ethernet ports are only offered on high-end professional equipment.

WiFi is a wireless network connection protocol that transmits information through radio frequencies. Wireless communications are critical for network connectivity with our many portable devices and we often expect non-wired information transfers. Their ubiquity stems from convenience, not superior speed. We highlight this to stress consideration of the right tools for the job. When a client is waiting on images from your laptop set to go to print on short notice, the right course of action is plugging into an ethernet cable—not transferring over potentially slow WiFi. WiFi standards have increased potential bandwidth capabilities over time. The IEEE standard for WiFi, 802.11, has *a*, *b*, *g* and *n* variants.

One of the most commonly known and encountered connections is the *Universal Serial Bus*, or USB, protocol. USB is used for connecting a wide variety of peripherals to computers and has been around for decades. Its standard connector shape (USB Type A or Standard-A) is a small rectangle; as devices grow smaller and thinner, compact variants like miniUSB, microUSB and others have created a world where our friends never seem to have the exact right connector to charge our phones. USB Type-B, the often overlooked connector, is found on printers. The USB 2.0 standard was published in 2000 and touts speeds up to 480 Mb/s. USB 3.0 "Super Speed," published in 2008, promises up to 5 Gb/s. USB connections can be used to shoot tethered to a workstation or laptop but the transfer speeds lag behind ethernet tethering. As of this writing, USB-C (a form of USB 3.0) is gaining in popularity for a range of portable devices, particularly mobile phones, laptops and tablets. It provides power to directly charge connected devices, supports display output signals and features a symmetrical connector design. This last point is critical for user sanity: It eradicates the all-too-familiar frustration of incorrectly guessing the orientation of a traditional USB-A cable when attempting to plug it in.

Thunderbolt is a protocol developed by Intel and Apple that functions similar to eSATA with a PCIe connection, offering direct and fast access to the motherboard. Thunderbolt 1.0 and 2.0 used a Mini DisplayPort connector; Thunderbolt 3.0 uses a flavor of USB-C. Thunderbolt offers the ability to daisy-chain devices together, something that USB cannot do. Identifying the difference between a Thunderbolt and USB 3.0 port can be difficult since they both use the USB Type-C style connector despite internal differences. Thunderbolt is primarily found on Apple hardware and external hard drive model variants.

We'll mention USB 1.0 and FireWire if photographers find themselves inheriting older hardware, though both standards are superseded by newer and faster ones. USB 1.0 offered slow transfer speeds compared to the latest versions, of course, though its connector design retains compatibility with newer ports and cables. FireWire is a serial bus interface developed by Apple that provided very fast speeds relative to USB in the 1990s and early 2000s. It came in two bandwidth variants: 400 Mb/s and 800 Mb/s (named FireWire 400 and Firewire 800, respectively). FireWire is no longer supported and has no direct or backwards compatible descendant.

A wireless technology standard designed for transferring data over short distances, *Bluetooth*, was invented by Jaap Haartsen in 1994 and it uses radio waves to transmit a signal.[11] Its appeal is a low power draw, making consumer products like wireless cellphone earpieces possible despite the devices' small batteries. Bluetooth has never been particularly useful for data transfer of the scale required for photo or video files, but that could change. The protocol's increasing bandwidth, reliability and accompanying software to pair communication between devices led to its use in dozens of household electronics like wireless speakers, headphones and tablet computers. Bluetooth is categorized by class with available classes of 1–4 in order from greatest power draw to least. At the same time, each successive class decreases the potential signal range of the connection. Class 2 Bluetooth is often found in mobile phones, though some have started using Class 4 for the lower power consumption benefits.

Separate yet related connection standards, *Digital Visual Interface* (DVI), *DisplayPort* and *High-Definition Multimedia Interface* (HDMI) are designed for digital video data transfer to computer monitors and other external displays. Displays are output hardware that require some form of digital video signal; you won't find HDMI ports on external hard drives, for example. Displays have seen similar evolution over the years in increasing throughput needs: a computer sending a 640x480 video stream to a desktop monitor has lower bandwidth requirements than a computer sending 4K video with surround sound to an OLED television. The former is possible with a DVI connection, the latter an HDMI 2.1 connection.

Computer Workstation Hardware

Despite computers saturating every aspect of our lives, the inner-workings and specifications of computer hardware are not necessarily well known to its users. Let's briefly describe the major components considered in relation to image editing and storage. We'll limit mentioning specific numbers because they never age well in printed textbooks. We'd rather not have readers from the distant future laughing at how quaint our computer processing capabilities seem to them.

The backbone of every computer workstation is the motherboard, a circuit board that pumps digital information through the many subcomponents that read, process and store it. It offers connections and ports for expanding input and output capabilities. The motherboard also contains the memory slots that provide *random access memory* (RAM) that all software needs to efficiently operate.

Central Processing Unit

The *central processing unit* (CPU) is the brain of a computer in that it handles the bulk of the computations related to running the operating system and any software therein. When buying a computer intended for image and/or video editing, the specifications of its CPU (clock speed, number of cores) are of primary importance. Each CPU core functions as a unique processing unit, leaving it up to software optimization to split up tasks and computations across available cores. The more cores the better, assuming that the software is written to take advantage of them. *Clock speed* or clock rate is measured in gigahertz (GHz) and describes the frequency at which the CPU core operates. While a faster clock rate is theoretically better for computing performance, it's difficult to pin it on this number exclusively. CPUs generate heat and often require heatsinks and fans in their immediate surroundings. This explains why your computer can get either very hot to the touch or loud during editing sessions when the CPU is taxed more than casual web browsing usage might. The main CPU manufacturers are Intel and AMD.

Graphics Processing Unit

The *graphics processing unit* (GPU) is a processing chip similar to the CPU specifically designated for graphics-related computations like rendering on-screen video, video game engines and image processing calculations. Dedicated GPUs and software that directs tasks to the GPU instead of the CPU are increasingly common. GPU capabilities are often lesser on laptop hardware than desktop hardware due to size and power requirements. GPUs are particularly good at running computations in parallel. Image editing software can see improved performance and speed when configured to leverage a GPU.

Desktop computers support installation of video cards consisting of GPUs with their own, dedicated RAM. This memory is loaded with the relevant data (an image layer in a Photoshop document, for example) so that it can be passed immediately to the GPU for calculating a transformation or filter on that data. The speed and amount of onboard RAM of a computer's GPU are important specifications for photographers because complex image processing tasks demand significant computational power. If you want to open a gigapixel panorama with three dozen adjustment layers at 100% while expecting buttery-smooth scrolling, you'll need a dedicated GPU with a lot of RAM to match your performance expectations.

Random Access Memory

Random access memory can be thought of like the human brain's short-term memory. You keep things readily available for use at a moment's notice, but may move certain information into long-term storage when it's not needed right away. Your brain might keep names and relationships handy at a social gathering, but not the particular details of how a car engine is built. RAM is how the computer keeps track of the different images, the different programs and the endless number of browser tabs you leave open. It's a form of flash storage housed on removable circuit board chips connected to the motherboard. Just like any other storage medium, an important number to know is how much storage it can handle; RAM is commonly described as a function of gigabytes. Unsurprisingly, then, the more RAM a machine has to store this information, the less time you spend watching it think and search for what it was doing. RAM is a computer component that indirectly impacts performance: adding RAM can result in a snappier, more responsive experience when editing photos. It's a relatively inexpensive hardware upgrade that can keep an aging computer on pace with your workflow.

RAM is most effective when it is added in matched pairs (i.e. installing two sticks of 16 GB RAM for a total of 32 GB). We recommend setting Adobe Photoshop's preferences to allocate up to 70% of available RAM to its processes. When Photoshop uses all of the allocated RAM to do its calculations on complex image transforms or filters, it uses empty hard drive space as temporary RAM called *scratch disk space*. This can also be specifically allocated in its preferences. Some photographers take unused drives (after an upgrade to larger ones, for example) and use them as dedicated scratch disks. All of these strategies aim to increase efficiency when editing large images.

Storage Drives

Computer drives store everything: the operating system, user files, software data and everything else you can think of. Without a place to store the information the computer needs to operate, we'd be stuck temporarily loading information in every time we turn it on.

Ideally, a workstation has a dedicated drive for the operating system, a dedicated drive for media assets and possibly a third drive as an internal backup of the second. An operating system reads program information from the drive it's installed on. A program reads and writes information from the drive that contains the image assets. Having these read/write actions spread out over multiple drives means that there are fewer bottlenecks in getting information when it's needed. Using a solid state drive for the operating system is ideal because its faster speeds afford quick boot-up and general performance boosts. Hard disk drives are better suited to large storage archives or backup drives because they can be cheaply stockpiled.

Photographers often use external or portable drives for media storage. These can be HDD or SSD and come in a variety of form factors. A portable drive is plugged into a laptop or desktop computer through a port (USB being the most common). We trade portability and convenience for speed; an internal drive can read and write data faster than on a plugged-in external drive. External drives can be powered through the data connection or using a second cable connected to a power source. Because of the increased power demand of operating at higher speeds, USB-only portable drives tend to have slower read/write speeds compared to externally powered units. Portable drives allow us to transport images from one location to another easily without requiring that we lug an entire computer along with them.

It takes more than the previously mentioned components to build a modern computer workstation. However, most of us aren't looking to assemble one from scratch. Instead, we should look at key specifications like CPU, GPU, RAM and storage capacity to make informed purchase decisions of off-the-shelf machines. Always buy the best machine that you can afford and make that purchase last by planning for incremental hardware upgrades. Consider peripherals for extensive editing sessions like ergonomic mice, drawing tablets and customizable MIDI boards to help with comfort and workflow efficiency.

Proof of Concept: Considering File Types and Image Content

Let's build an appreciation for image file types and their digital asset storage footprint. This exercise highlights what photographers juggle after capturing a great raw photo: how will it be stored long term? How can it be shared over email or the web without compromising image quality? After all the derivative versions are saved, how much data does a single photograph generate?

1. Find a raw image that contains a lot of texture or detail. Consider this Image A. Find another raw capture that is simpler and minimal in detail, like a smooth subject against a plain background. Consider this Photo B (see Figure 8-8, overleaf).
2. Open Photo A in the raw image editing software of your choice. Save a derivative version as DNG (lossless).

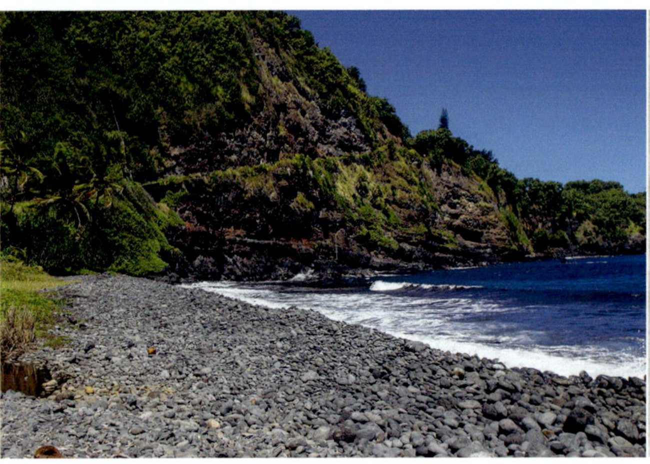
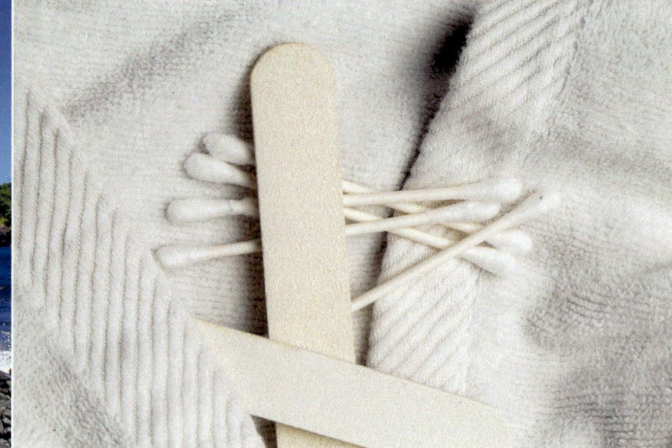

Figure 8-8 Photo A (left) and Photo B (right).

3. From the same editor, save a 16-bit TIFF version with LZW compression.
4. Save an 8-bit JPEG version at the highest-quality setting: usually the top end of a 0–100 or 1–10 scale.
5. Save a series of 8-bit JPEGs, changing the JPEG quality setting by an interval of your choice, stepping down until you reach the lowest setting available. Append the filenames with the selected quality setting for easy reference.
6. Repeat steps 2–5 for Photo B. You should have a set of files for each scene: the original raw, a DNG raw, a TIFF and a series of JPEGs.
7. Record the data size of each file in the sets for Photos A and B using your operating system's file property window. Plot them in spreadsheet software to visualize the relative sizes.

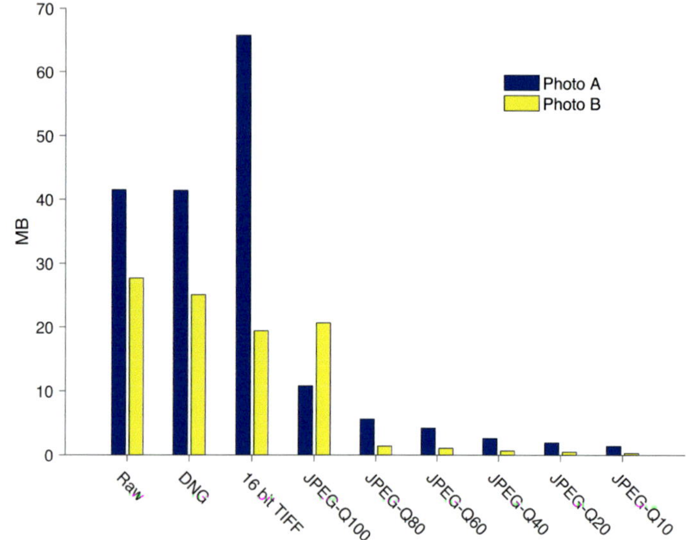

Figure 8-9 File sizes (in megabytes) for different image formats saved from the raw versions of Photo A and Photo B.

Figure 8-8 shows our example photographs. Photo A is a beach landscape with considerable detail in the foreground rocks and background foliage. Photo B is a simple, monochrome still life of cosmetic supplies. Both images started out as proprietary format raw captures before being saved as DNG, TIFF and JPEG. We've plotted our recorded file sizes for both sets in Figure 8-9.

Looking at Figure 8-9, we draw initial conclusions about saving images in different formats. Writing raw image data to DNG sometimes yields a smaller file, but not always (Photo A remained nearly the same size, Photo B slightly shrunk). DNGs offer a small space-saving benefit if we generate them and delete the originals while retaining their non-destructive editability. The TIFF of Photo A is much larger than the raw. Where the raw file stores mosaicked, 14-bit brightness data, the TIFF now houses the demosaiced, three-channel (full color) image and grows in size as a result. Photo B's relative content simplicity and lack of color means that its TIFF doesn't follow suit and is actually somewhat smaller than the raw. The 8-bit JPEGs decrease in size as increasingly aggressive compression is applied. These are useful end-product assets but lose the editing flexibility of the raws, so they're well-positioned as a secondary asset options.

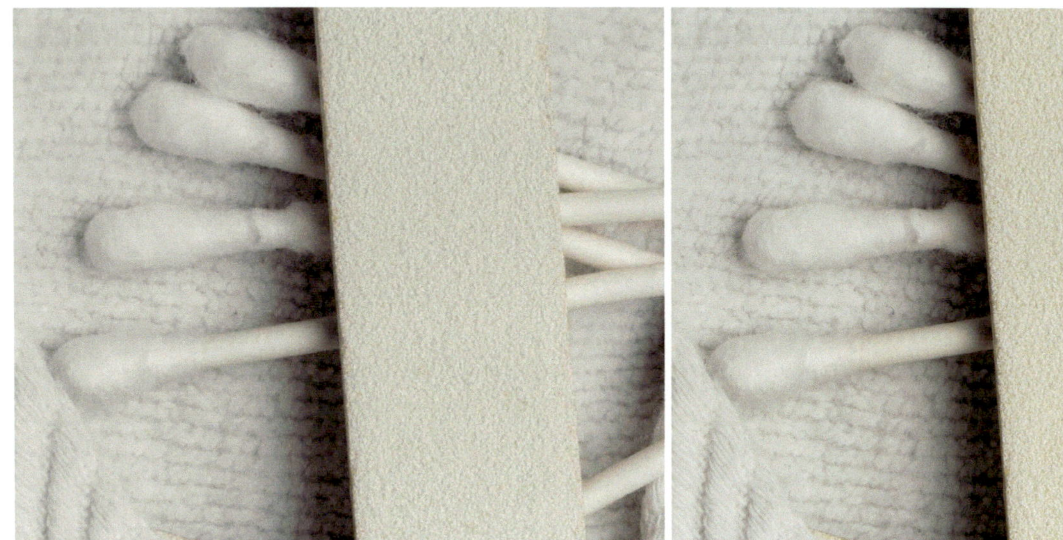

Figure 8-10 A close crop of Photo B as it appears in its native raw capture format (interpreted by a raw engine) and as the lowest-quality JPEG.

Chapter 12 dives deeper into image data compression, its methods and shortcomings. For now, evaluate the different versions of your two photographs up close. Figure 8-10 is a close crop of Photo B. The difference between the original raw and the lowest-quality JPEG are surprisingly minimal from a visual standpoint. Of course, we understand that the utility between the two is vastly different: one is the purest form of a digital image from which to edit, where the other is a fully baked, final output version.

Questions to consider in your digital-asset-managed workflow based on your findings:

- Is it worth it to evaluate JPEG compression settings on a per-image basis or default to a lesser setting at the cost of file size?
- Is the highest compression setting (lowest "quality" number) a visually acceptable output for the images used in this exercise? Determine the quality level at which the compression artifacts become objectionable.
- What real-world use-cases would you use each of these formats for? How do you organize derivative versions of the same photograph as you create different versions?

Notes

1 Anderson, Richard. "Raw file formats." *File Management Overview | DpBestflow*, Sept. 22, 2015, www.dpbestflow.org/node/305.

2 "Technical information." *HEIF Technical Information – High Efficiency Image File Format*, nokiatech.github.io/heif/technical.html.

3 Krogh, Peter. "Metadata overview." *File Management Overview | DpBestflow*, Sept. 22, 2015, www.dpbestflow.org/node/298.

4 "What is a controlled vocabulary, and how is it useful?" *Controlled Vocabulary*, www.controlledvocabulary.com/.

5 Allen, Elizabeth and Sophie Triantaphillidou. *The Manual of Photography*. Elsevier/Focal Press, 2017, p. 341.

6 Russotti, Patti and Richard Anderson. *Digital Photography Best Practices and Workflow Handbook: A Guide to Staying Ahead of the Workflow Curve*. Focal Press, 2009.

7 "Synchronize. Backup. Bootable Backup." *Welcome to Econ Technologies' Store*, www.econtechnologies.com/chronosync/overview.html.

8 "Mac backup software." *Mac Backup Software | Carbon Copy Cloner | Bombich Software*, bombich.com/.

9 "List of Interface Bit Rates." *Wikipedia*, Wikimedia Foundation, 2 Feb. 2019, en.wikipedia.org/wiki/List_of_interface_bit_rates.

10 Roberts, Gideon. "The history of ethernet." *YouTube*, Dec. 14, 2006, www.youtube.com/watch?v=g5MezxMcRmk.

11 "High tech traveler." *Web Archive* , Verizon Wireless, 2011, web.archive.org/web/20110111075514/http://www.hoovers.com/business-information/--pageid__13751--/global-hoov-index.xhtml.

9 Digital Tone Reproduction

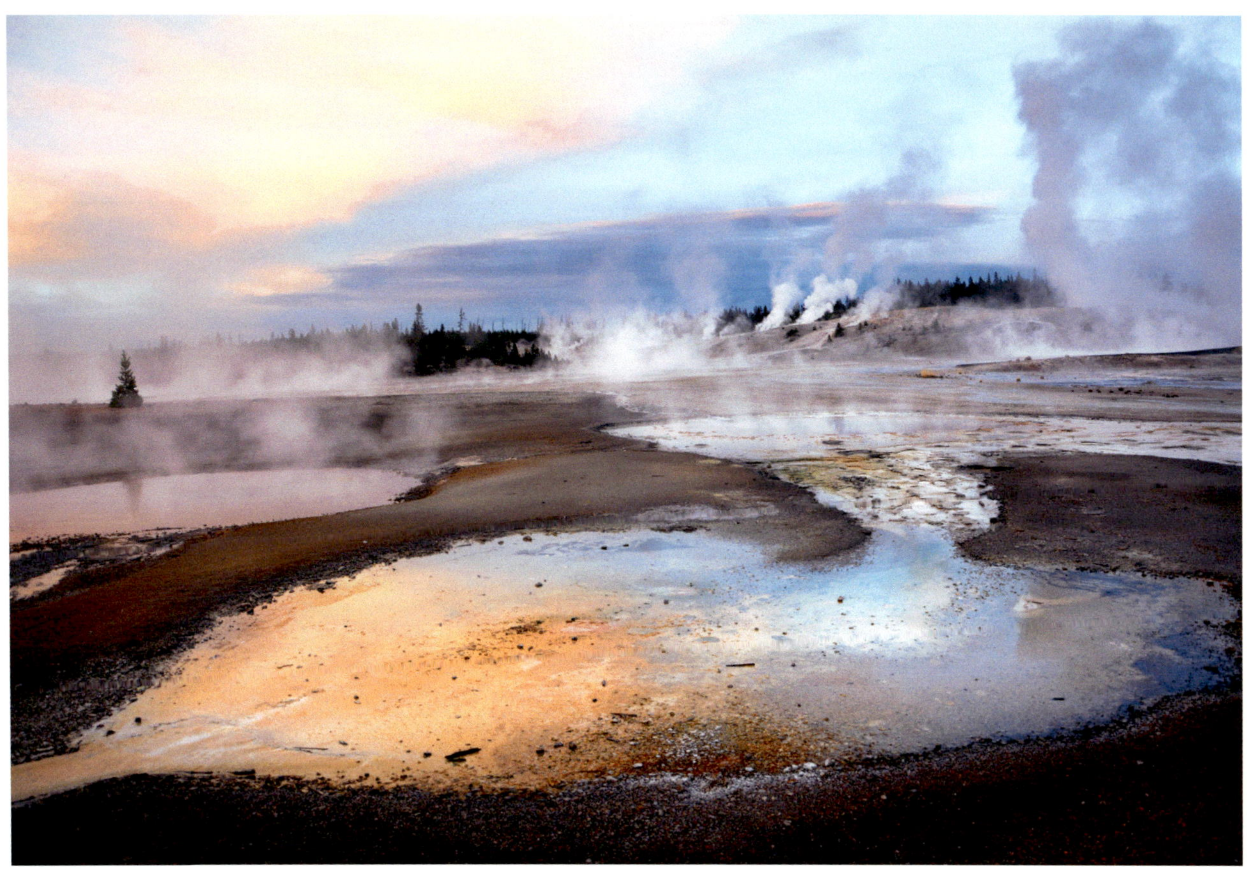

Photograph by John Compton

It's exceedingly rare that the raw capture as it is rendered in-camera conveys the range and interplay of tones, colors and details present in the scene or in our creative vision for that scene. We believe strongly in the power of craft that all photographers should seek to perfect when shooting yet even the best exposed frames are just the starting point for image editing and enhancements. Optimizing digital tone reproduction is a necessary and core tenet of image adjustments that goes a long way in making that great capture into a great print or digital file.

It's an informative exercise to study the relationship between the tones in the original scene and the corresponding tones in the reproduction, even when the final product is intended to bear little resemblance to the original. By studying the factors that influence and the tools that control the reproduction of tone, we can create images that satisfy both technical and creative requirements.

A photograph is a reproduction of recorded light first experienced in-person by the photographer. This original experience is made possible by the human visual system, as is the experience of viewing a photograph in reproduction. With this in mind, perceptual phenomena including brightness adaptation play a significant role. The determination of the objective tone reproduction properties required in a photograph of excellent quality is related to the perceptual conditions at work when the image is viewed. The final image showcases the cumulative tone reproduction characteristics of the camera's sensor, its optics, image processing decisions and the output medium (print or screen).

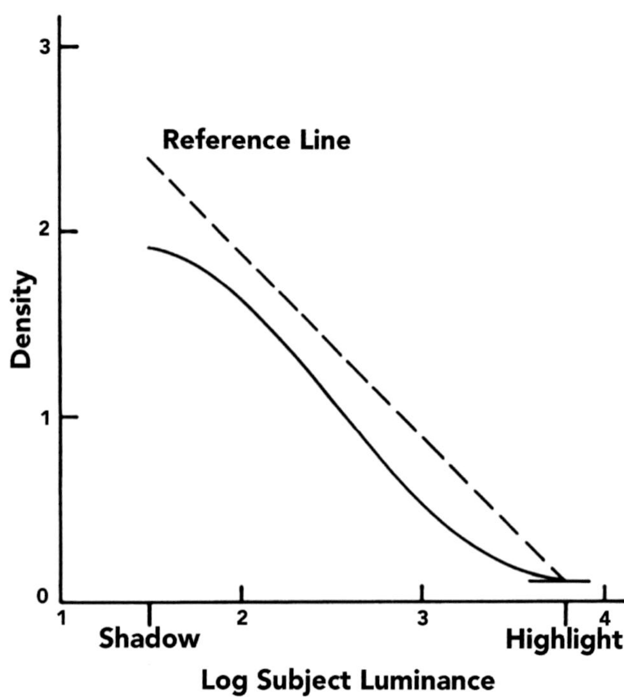

Figure 9-1 An objective tone reproduction curve for a reflective print.

Objective and Subjective Tone Reproduction

There are objective and subjective aspects to consider when determining the tone reproduction properties of the photographic system. In the objective phase, measurements of light reflected from the subject are compared to measurements of light reflected or transmitted by the photographic reproduction or light emitted from a display. These reflected-light readings from the subject are called *luminances* and are accurately measured with a photometer with a relative spectral response equivalent to that of the average human eye. The logarithms of these luminances are plotted against the corresponding reflection or transmission densities in the photographic reproduction and the resulting plot is the *objective tone reproduction curve* as shown in Figure 9-1.

The perception of the lightness of a subject or image area corresponds roughly to its luminance. However, unlike luminance, lightness cannot be directly measured. The perception of lightness involves physiological as well as psychological factors. An area of constant luminance may appear to change in lightness for various reasons, including whether the viewer is adapted to a high or a low light level. Psychological scaling procedures are used to determine the effect of viewing conditions on the perception of lightness and contrast. It's an established fact, for example, that a photograph appears lighter when viewed against a dark background than when viewed against a light background. Similarly, the contrast of a photograph appears lower when viewed with a dark surround than when viewed with a light surround. Understanding these psychological realities can help you decide on things like frame colors and website backgrounds. This is explored more deeply in Chapter 13's section titled *The Roles of Light and Color on Perception and Perspective*.

The subjective tone reproduction curve plots the relationship between the perceived lightnesses of image areas and the measured luminances of those corresponding areas. Since the perception of a photograph's tonal qualities can vary with the viewing conditions, the American National Standards Institute and the International Standards Organization have published ISO 3664:2009 Graphic Technology and Photography – Viewing Conditions, the standard for the viewing conditions under which photographs should be produced, judged and displayed. The influence of viewing conditions should not be underestimated when considering the specifications for optimum tone reproduction.

The Evolution of Tone Reproduction

For those that have been involved with photography from the days of film, tone reproduction reminds us of the classic four quadrant plot that tracks light through the entire imaging pipeline in log space. Quadrant I started with the subject's luminances and took flare and lens transmission into account, resulting in the image luminance values at the film plane. Quadrant II was the negative material, using the image luminance values and the characteristic curve of the film to determine the densities that resulted on the film. The film densities were used in Quadrant III along with the characteristic curve of the photographic paper used to create the print. This resulted in the relationship of the tones on the final print to the original scene luminances. Just writing about it brings back memories of hours spent

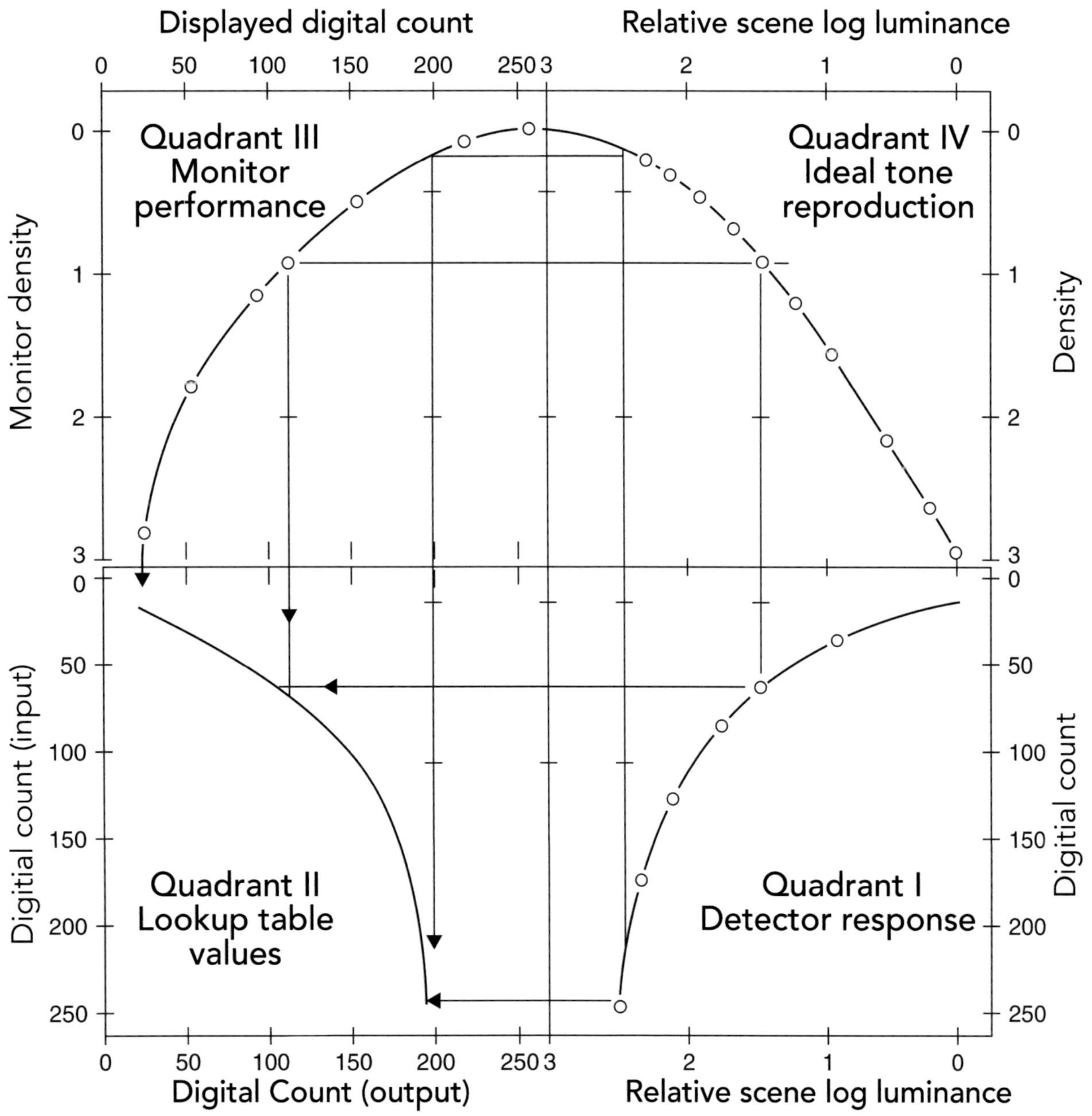

Figure 9-2 Four quadrant plot for a digital tone reproduction study.

in a darkroom with a sensitometer followed by hours with a densitometer and a French curve.

This classic method of tone reproduction analysis has perhaps gone away in the digital world, yet the four quadrant plot concept retains utility. The four quadrant tone reproduction plot can still be used to study a digital system; however, the quadrants take on a different look. Studying a digital tone reproduction system means understanding the scene brightness characteristics, the response of the imaging sensor, the performance of the display used for editing and the output paper characteristics (see Figure 9-2).

In a digital tone reproduction study, Quadrant I shows the tonal transfer between the subject log luminances and the resulting digital counts, often referred to as the *detector response*. An image sensor, either CCD or CMOS, exhibits a more linear relationship to the subject luminances than to the log luminance. As a result, Quadrant I provides the same input-output relationship that a film system once did, only now the output values are digital counts.

Quadrant II represents the ability to alter the image characteristics after the image is captured; with digital data this means processing or altering digital counts. There are many possible alterations, such as adjusting the contrast, color balance or sharpening. Although these operations are done with complex math, all of the operations can be combined into one *lookup table* or LUT. An LUT provides a new output digital value for each input digital count. Quadrant II, then, is represented as an LUT to apply tonal alterations. Quadrant II is plotted as a straight line if no modifications to the image take place: the input digital count values are equal to the output digital count values.

It's reasonable to assume that an image is viewed on a display like a monitor prior to printing. This is where the tone reproduction study ends for some use-cases, as a final print may not be required. Quadrant III illustrates the characteristics of the display device upon which the image is viewed. The input values are digital counts that resulted from the application of the LUT in Quadrant II. The output values describe *monitor density* as defined in Equation 9.1. Several factors affect this quadrant and the measurement of the luminance on the display such as the settings for brightness and contrast.

$$\textit{Monitor Density} = \frac{\textit{Luminance for Digital Count Maximum Brightness}}{\textit{Luminance for Displayed Digital Count}} \quad \text{(Eq. 9.1)}$$

Quadrant IV provides the relationship between the final print made from the image on screen and the original scene luminances. The final print densities can be obtained using a reflection densitometer.

For all practical purposes, the response of our digital sensor in Quadrant I cannot be changed. We can only work to properly expose our images. In contrast, all aspects of our digital image data can be edited on a properly profiled display. The rest of this chapter concentrates on the ways that we modify and change the digital tone values to produce a desired output result.

Revisiting the Image Histogram

Recall that an image histogram is a breakdown of the frequency of pixels at a given tone value and a representation of an image's tonal range. Every element of a digital image channel (of which there are three) is a discrete brightness value. We first encountered histograms in the context of photographic exposure. Histograms are great for evaluating exposure settings and getting a sense of the scene's tone characteristics. Interaction with the histogram at the capture stage is limited to adjusting exposure settings to ensure that the scene's tones are recorded effectively; it's a passive feedback mechanism.

Histograms work double duty as tools for tone reproduction efforts during post-processing, this time as an interactive and malleable representation of changes made to tone, contrast and color. The concepts of *luminosity histograms* and *color channel histograms* were introduced in Chapter 4. Let's unpack those further now that we're taking a close look at how this visualization helps in post-processing edits.

Generally speaking, the range of brightnesses in an image is the *tonal range*. The darkest tone is black, the brightest is white and the tone perfectly between those two is midtone gray. These points along the tonal range also help us divide histograms into three sections: highlights, midtones and shadows. A luminosity histogram better represents the distribution of perceived brightnesses

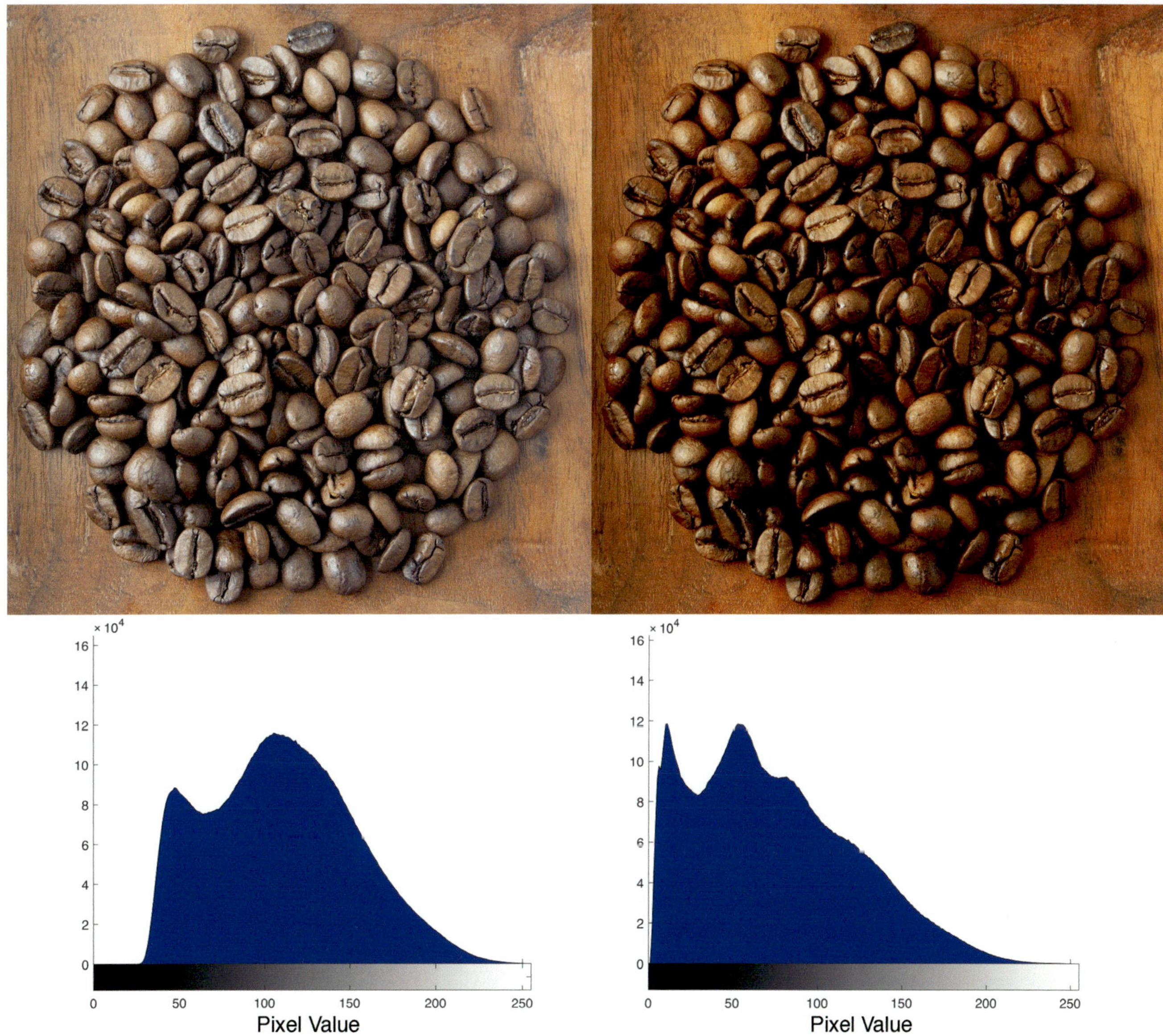

Figure 9-3 Many of the midtone values from the raw file (left) can be reassigned to dark shadow values to create a rich, contrasty final product with a strong visual impact (right). The histogram's changed appearance echoes the visual changes in the photo.

when all three color channels are combined. It gives more weight to the green channel in correspondence with our visual system sensitivity rather than being an additive version of the three channels of data. If you prefer to view the image information as additive RGB channels, use an *RGB histogram*. This is what the camera firmware typically uses to preview captured exposure information. Luminosity histograms do not necessarily show specific color channel clipping, particularly in the blue channel as it is weighted the least.

Watching the histogram when editing helps to spot a number of potentially detrimental changes and we recommend having a histogram window or panel open at all times. The first of those changes is clipped highlight or shadow detail. Clipped tones are indicated by sharp cut-offs at either end of the histogram where it appears that the data would continue if it wasn't abruptly ended. Some small amount of clipped highlights is usually acceptable depending on the scene just as crushing some shadow areas to solid black is not objectionable. It's usually

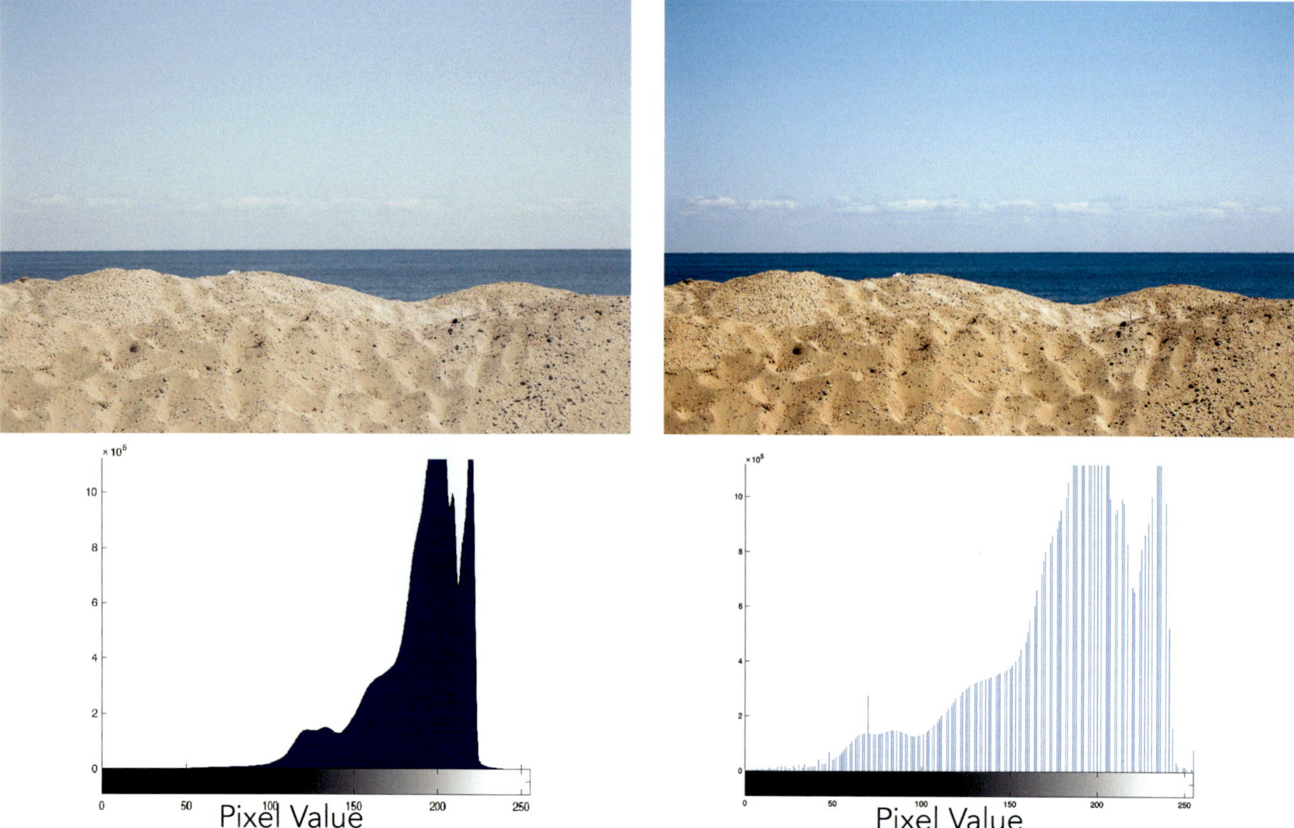

Figure 9-4 A low contrast scene and its histogram (left) and the same scene after a contrast adjustment (right). Notice how the post-edit histogram shows pixel values spanning a broader tonal range with small gaps throughout.

desirable to maintain all the descriptive image data in the edited file after working hard to avoid clipping at capture. In addition to keeping a watchful eye on the histogram, image editing software provides overlays or warnings to show where parts of the image are clipped. Figure 9-3 shows a well-exposed image with a reasonable starting histogram. Introducing a darker black point means adding some much needed tone contrast, moving the shadow tones to even darker values with a small amount of shadow clipping. The minor loss of shadow detail is unlikely to be noticeable. Though the raw image version may accurately represent the scene as it appeared in person, modifying its tone reproduction provides a visual punch, commanding attention and making the subject more appealing. Always keep in mind that tone reproduction is not strictly concerned with objective or numeric optimization. Subjective and thoughtful consideration for how an image should look largely drives this process.

A photograph with very little range of tones is considered flat or low contrast. A black cat sitting on a pile of coal is one inherently low contrast scenario. Adding contrast can help emphasize texture, tonality and the appearance of sharpness. Contrast adjustments are like the caffeine of image edits: it's easy to get hooked and start thinking that every situation calls for more. You eventually overdo it and learn that there's an effective time and place for adding contrast. *Combing* in a histogram occurs when an image that has already been processed is adjusted again or when a low dynamic range image is stretched to adjust contrast. Pushing a flat scene far beyond its available tones leads to combing. The name stems from the histogram's appearance after such a drastic change: instead of a full mountain range of tones, the histogram shows frequent gaps similar to a hair comb (see Figure 9-4). This happens because the additional processing leaves some pixel values empty and can signal visible posterization in the edited image. Shooting in raw and saving images to an uncompressed file format during editing helps avoid combing.

Interpreting the Tone Curve

A transfer curve shows the mapping of input data to output data. A *tone curve* is a transfer curve specific to image pixel values representing photographic tones. During camera capture, the tone curve maps the input scene luminances to the recorded digital counts. At the editing stage, the tone curve represents the starting digital counts mapped to the final digital counts after post-processing adjustments. Figure 9-5 shows a tone curve as seen in Adobe Photoshop Lightroom. The 45° line is the default mapping prior to any adjustments such that the input and output values are equivalent. Any change made to this line, either with an editing preset or through targeted edits, is a form of *tone mapping*. This term is also used in the context of High Dynamic Range imaging when the input data consists of many more discrete tone values than can be reproduced on screen or in print. Here we use the term to describe any instance of reassigning pixel values.

The x-axis in Figure 9-5 represents the input digital counts as they exist in the unedited image. The y-axis represents the digital counts after editing. The image histogram is underlaid for reference with the 0 digital count representing black on the left and the digital count 255 representing white on the right.

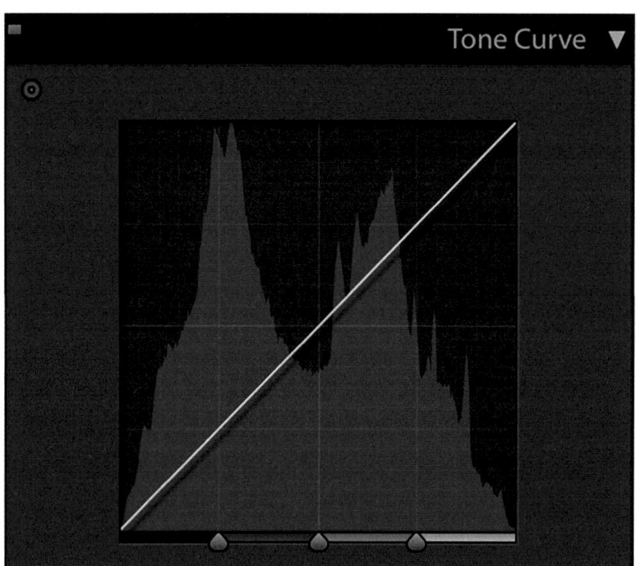

Figure 9-5 An example image tone curve with a histogram reference behind it.

Figure 9-5 is example is an implementation of a user-controllable tone transfer curve. There is also the option of using *tone transfer compensation* (TTC) profiles to automatically edit files if the workflow is highly controlled (scanning film from a specific camera and lighting setup, for example). TTC is a method of selectively expanding or compressing specific portions of an image's tonal range using lookup tables to remap each input pixel to a new output value.

Using the Curves Tool to Modify Tones

Tone reproduction can be controlled with the *Curves tool*, an intimidating but valuable software interface for editing the image pixel values. By default, the tool offers a plot of input–output values and is not a curve at all—it's a straight diagonal line from left to right as shown in Figure 9-6 (overleaf). This line indicates that any pixel with a value of 0 before the user changes it is a value of 0 afterwards (and so on through all available tones). Put another way, there is a perfect 1:1 relationship between input and output. The Curves tool remaps tones based on changes made to this diagonal line so that the output is changed from the input. Any abrupt or erratic jumps within small tone ranges (say, dark gray to slightly lighter gray) are unnatural in a continuous tone photograph and as such the curve behaves more like a tightrope than a zig-zagging rigid line. This is to encourage a natural ramping or gradation between user-introduced tone changes. A tightrope is also an appropriate metaphor that serves as a reminder to use Curves adjustments cautiously and with forethought to the destination.

Modifying the diagonal line to form a slanted "S" shape is a common Curves tool adjustment and is accomplished by adding pivot points as shown in Figure 9-6. An *S-curve* darkens the shadows, lightens the highlights and impacts the midtones very little. It also avoids clipping on either end by virtue of ramping down or dampening the changes at the extreme ends of the tone range. This tool allows fine control over gray-level distribution; we can add multiple pivot points that

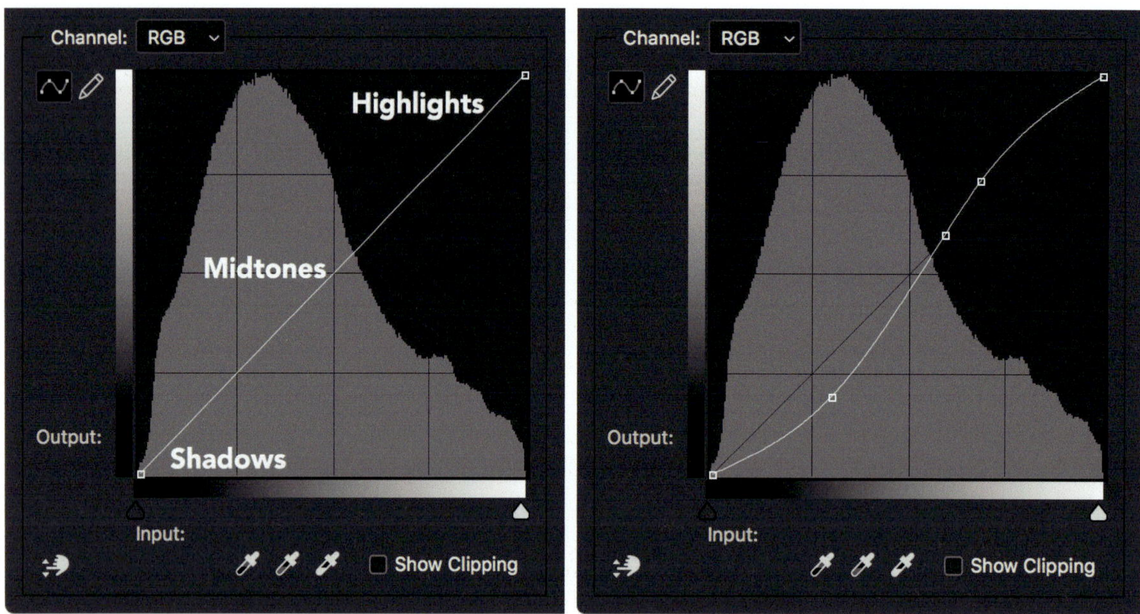

Figure 9-6 The Curve tool's tone reproduction plot with a 1:1 reproduction line (left) that has no impact on the image compared to an S-curve (right) that darkens the shadows and lightens the highlights.

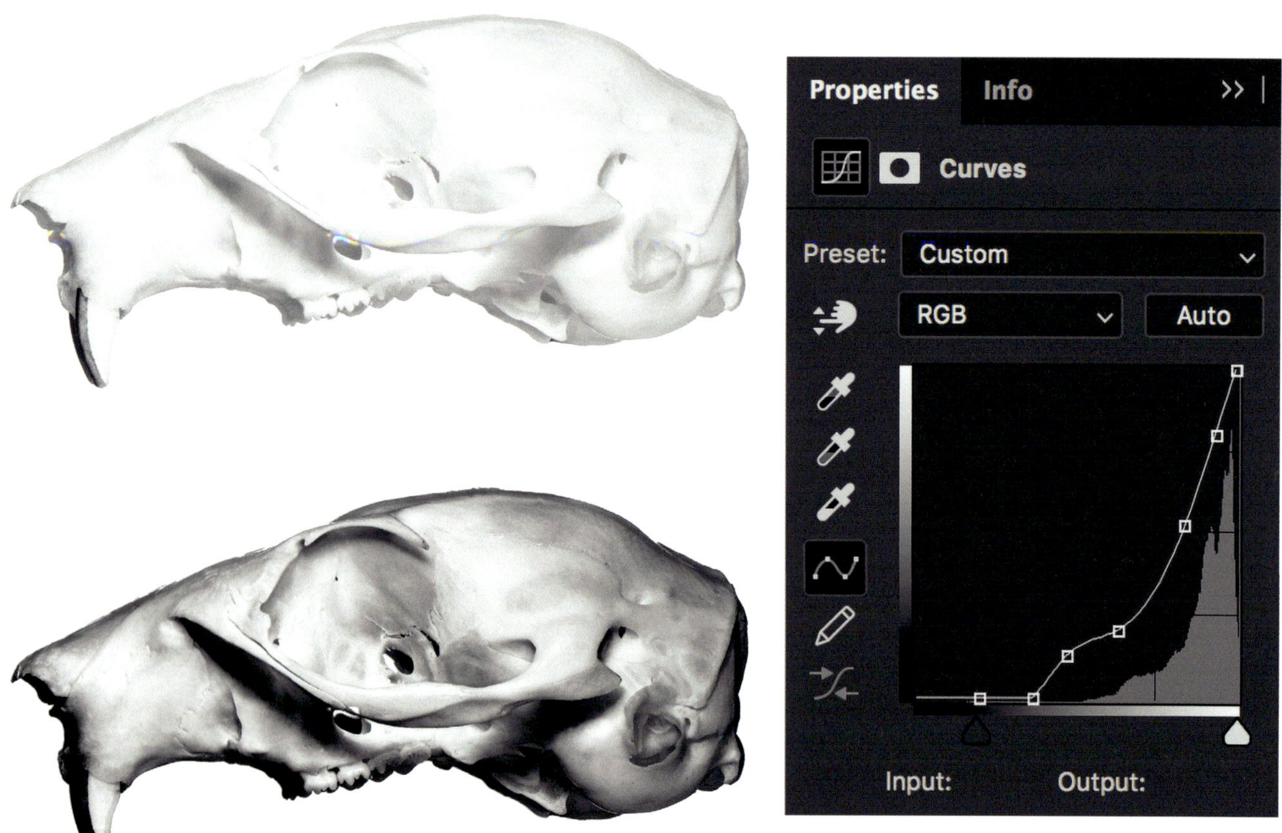

Figure 9-7 Curves tool adjustments go beyond s-curves. Here, the original image is very high key and flat. A tone adjustment pulls down deeper shadows and introduces contrast overall.

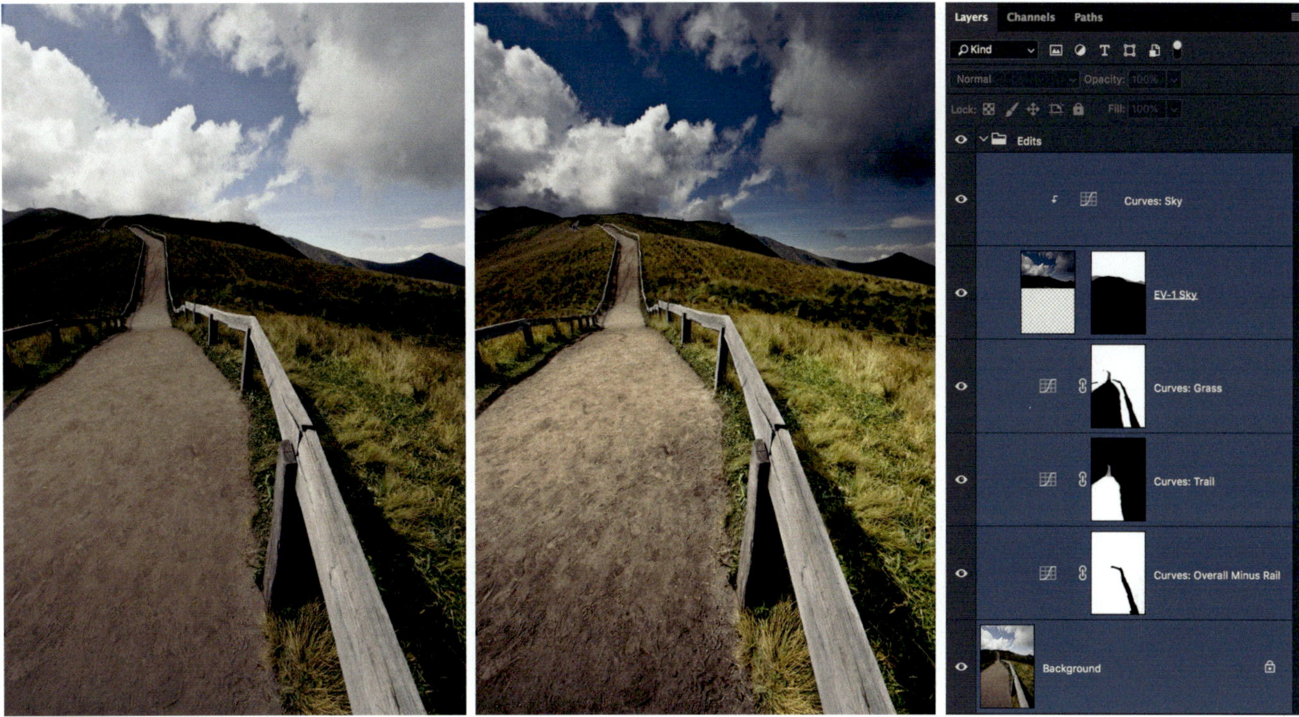

Figure 9-8 The original image (left) and the tone-optimized version (middle). Targeted tone corrections bring out the best of varied scene content. The layers panel (right) shows how different tone changes are isolated to the trail, the grass and the sky.

impact the contrast of pixel tones on either side of each point like in Figure 9-7. Adding and moving pivot points on the Curves plot can take some getting used to, as it has a rubber-band-like behavior where pulling on one area makes changes to another. It's tempting to add lots of points to isolate affected areas. This invites unintended or unwieldy changes that are hard to manage. The Curves tool is often considered to be one of the most powerful and most difficult to master tools in tone reproduction editing. Consequently, the tool includes presets for assisting the novice user or to provide a convenient starting point.

Curves adjustments can be treated as global image edits in that the rules and changes they establish apply to every pixel in the file. Global tone adjustments are often necessary yet are unlikely to be the one-stop solution for tone reproduction in a photographer's workflow. Instead, treating Curves modifications as separate layers (called "adjustment layers" in Adobe Photoshop) is most flexible when combined with layer masking. Masking tone adjustments to specific parts of the frame or subjects like the ones shown in Figure 9-8 is the modern equivalent of darkroom dodging and burning and offers the greatest amount of nuance and control of the final product.

Inverting Tones for Negative Film Scans

Complement mapping inverts all values in the image: black becomes white, white becomes black and gray values are mapped to their complementary tones above and below a middle gray. This is accomplished with a diagonal line in the Curves tool that starts at the top left and travels down to the bottom right (the exact opposite of its default form). There aren't many scenarios where this approach to pixel remapping is valuable yet we include it here because you might scan film negatives at some point. A complement mapping turns scanned negatives into positive images as shown in Figure 9-9 (overleaf).

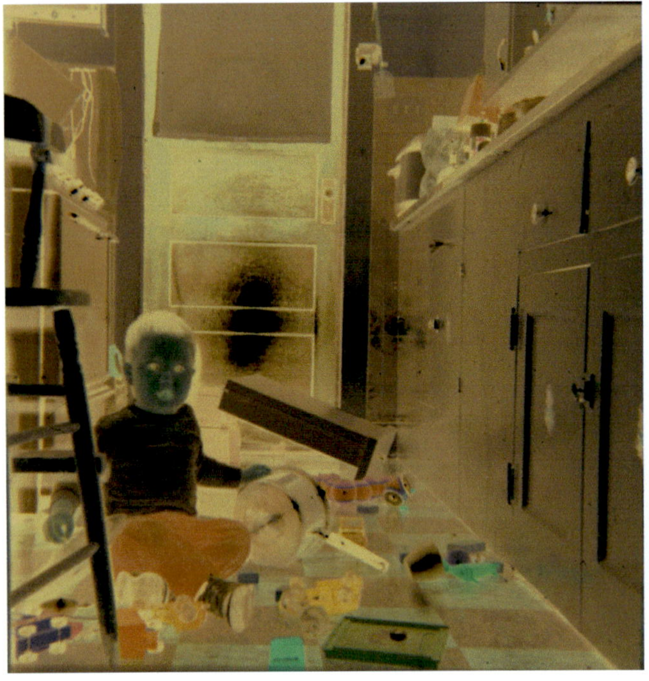

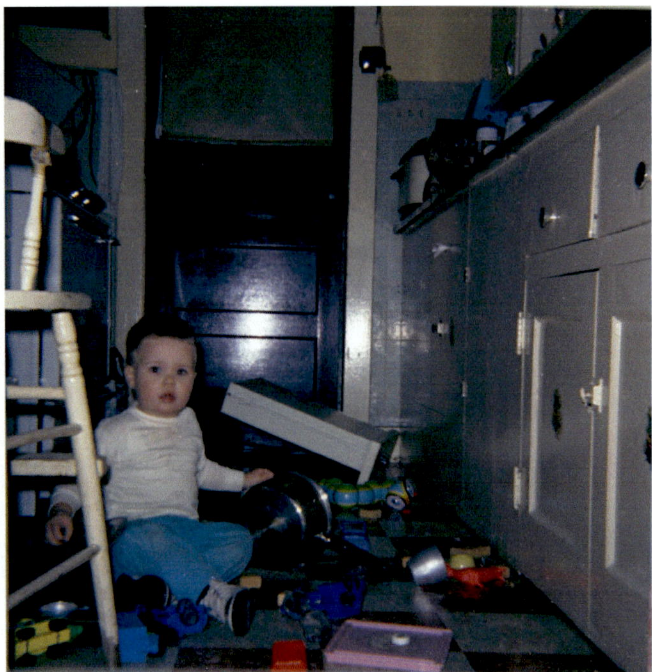

Figure 9-9 Complimentary mapping applied to a color negative film scan.

The Zero-Sum Game of Tone Reproduction

Tone-remapping editing is a zero-sum game when it comes to the pixel data. We're redistributing contrast across different portions of the tone curve and there's risk in spending more than what you start with. We always hope that there's enough data to achieve our aesthetic objectives for the final product. However, going too far with the adjustments or starting out with a sub-par set of data—like having an underexposed raw image and attempting to show beautiful shadow detail in the edited version—reminds us that digital tone reproduction is not magic. Capturing at higher bit depths and preserving it throughout your workflow make this a less risky endeavor when working to maintaining image quality.

Here's an analogy to bolster an appreciation of bit depth in tone reproduction. You've got a pair of dress pants that just barely fit and a pair of sweatpants with an elastic waistband. You gain a few pounds around the waist after the winter holiday festivities. The dress pants that fit snuggly before all of the holiday cookies are no longer an option; the sweatpants provide a much-welcome flexibility to accommodate your newfound love handles. The only problem is convincing your boss that your "binge-watching uniform" meets the workplace dress code. The difference between an 8-bit photograph and a 16-bit photograph that exhibits a similar dynamic: 8-bits are enough but there's no room for adjusting tone or contrast without potential quality degradations; 16-bits works equally well if no adjustments are needed and really save the day when image processing is introduced to tweak tones.

In the motion video world, we're quickly entering a shift from 8-bit to 10-bit video capture, editing and playback. Professional video production teams have been shooting high bit depth capture footage for years for the same reason that still photographers shoot raw and edit 16-bit files. The bigger change is that High Dynamic Range and Wide Color Gamut video standards require at least 10-bits of tone storage to deliver the improved image quality experience to home viewers. Televisions, combined with streaming media services, are increasingly offering 10-bit video content that promises better tone reproduction.

Using the Levels Tool to Modify Tones

Pixel point processing uses a mathematical function to map the original pixel values to new output values, lightening, darkening or changing the contrast of an image. The simplest form of remapping values is *slide mapping*. Adding or subtracting a constant value to all pixels in the image alters its overall brightness. This has the effect of moving all of the pixel values in the histogram to the right or to the left (brighter or darker, respectively). The drawback to slide mapping is the ease with which one can clip highlights or shadows. For example, adding 50 to all pixel values means that all the pixels whose values are 205 or higher become 255. Slide mapping is a blunt approach previously found in Adobe Photoshop's "Brightness/Contrast" legacy tool from the early days of digital tone reproduction and editing.

A constant value applied to only one of the color channel levels changes the overall color balance of the scene. Adobe Photoshop's color balance tool takes the slide mapping approach while weighing the constant value, applying it more heavily toward the shadows, midtones or highlights. Alternatively, our knowledge of the Maxwell triangle takes the guesswork out of manual color correction: determine the starting color cast, find its opposite on the triangle, and either decrease the color of the cast or increase its opposite. An image with a blue cast, for example, can be neutrally balanced by introducing more yellow.

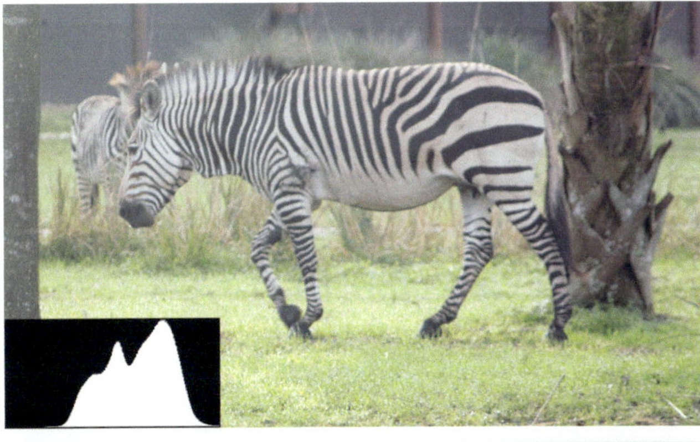

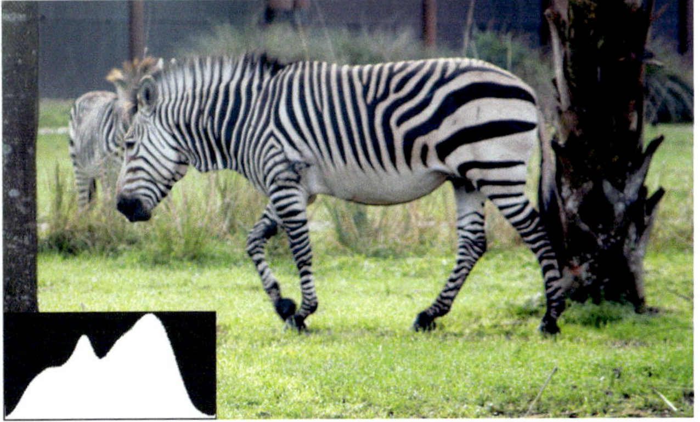

Figure 9-10 An example of stretch mapping.

Another approach to pixel remapping is *stretch mapping*. Stretch mapping uses multiplication or division by a constant value to stretch or contract the tonal values over the histogram. This can be used to stretch a low contrast image over the full range of values to produce normal contrast as shown in Figure 9-10.

The *Levels tool*, as it is called in Adobe Photoshop (similarly available in other software), is like a direct histogram editor. If the histogram is like a sandbox filled with our image pixels, the Levels tool is like handing photographers toy shovels and rakes to use in that sandbox. Our zero-sum observation still applies: there's no adding sand to the sandbox, only redistributing what's there at the start. Working with Levels means using the feedback provided by the histogram to distribute or reassign pixel tones. A single luminance histogram is available for modification as well as the separate red, green and blue color channel histograms.

On either end of the Levels histogram are black and white points or anchors. The position of each dictates which part of the starting histogram is assigned to values of 0 and 255. Just like the tone curve plot, the adjusted positions of these anchor points dictate the remapping of pixel values between input and output (before and after the change). The middle-gray point adjusts gamma. It impacts the midtones while leaving the white and black points untouched. Instead of applying a constant value, the midtones are changed using a Gaussian (normal) distribution, with greater amounts of change in the middle values and decreasing amounts toward the highlights and shadows. Moving the middle-gray point to the left lightens midtones and moving it to the right darkens them. Figure 9-11 (overleaf) demonstrates using only the middle-gray point adjustment to improve the overall contrast of an image. While the Curves tool allows users to create an anchor point anywhere along the tonal range, Levels only offers the white, midtone and black points as adjustable anchors.

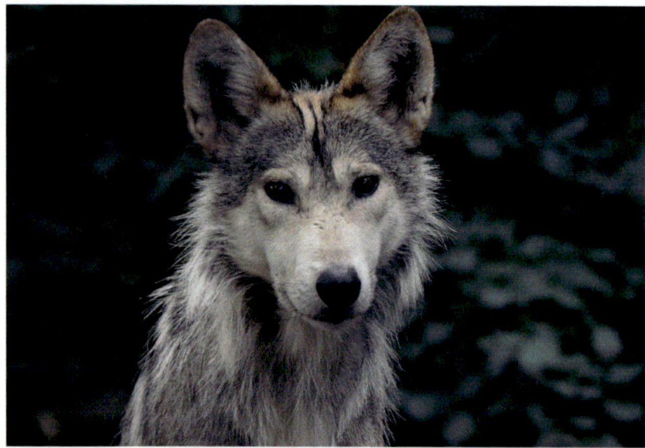

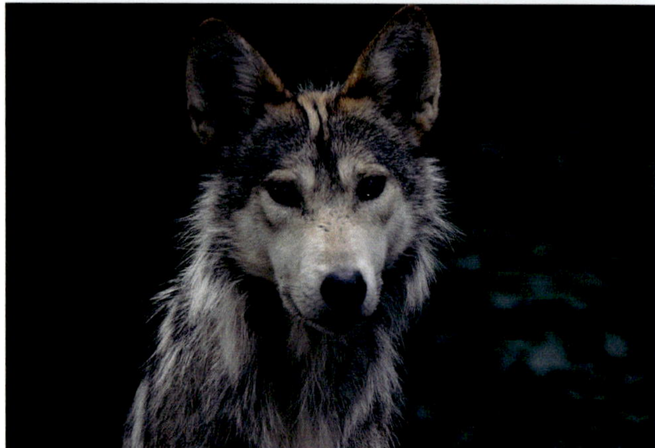

Figure 9-11 An image before (top) and after (bottom) a tone change using only the middle-gray point adjustment of the Levels tool.

Common Tone Reproduction Software Controls

Levels and Curves are great tools once photographers develop an intuitive sense of how they can be controlled to improve photographs. After all, we're visual people and the idea of using graphs and numbers can be a confusing intermediary between what we want to do and what we see. While mastering both tools is recommended, there are also times where such deep-tissue pixel massaging is too time consuming or unnecessary. This is particularly true when a set of images needs the same sort of treatment and it needs to happen quickly such as portrait sessions or event series. Spending minutes or hours on one image file is unrealistic in these circumstances. For the quick-and-easy shoulder-rub of pixel remapping, we turn to image editing controls (often taking the form of adjustment sliders). The commonly encountered ones are described here. Try each control in your software of choice while watching the histogram as it often reveals the tool's underlying behavior.

The *Exposure* or *Brightness* slider targets the brightest areas of the image. It's useful when looking at the overall lightness or darkness of the scene. Even with an adequate capture exposure, minor changes to the brightness are often desirable. Using this adjustment tool can compress or expand the highlights. Clipping is easy to introduce here, so consider taking advantage of any clipping warning overlays available.

The *Highlights/Shadows* slider avoids the midtones entirely and instead looks to remap the brighter highlight or darker shadow portions of the image histogram. This is equivalent to pulling up or pushing down a small area on a Curve plot with the intention of modifying just the small range of tones considered to be highlights or shadows. Concurrently brightening the highlights and darkening the shadows effectively introduces additional image contrast.

The *Whites and Blacks* sliders adjust the white and black points. Whereas the Exposure slider stretches the histogram toward the highlights (altering the entire histogram), the whites slider moves the white point while generally maintaining the overall shape of the histogram. The black slider performs the same way for the other end of the tonal range.

Applying a positive *Contrast adjustment* to an image darkens the darker midtones and lightens the brighter midtones. It also widens the entire histogram in the process. Adding contrast can be easily overdone. Alternatively, negative contrast flattens the tonal range and begins to make a potentially wide range of shadows and highlights into similar midtones. Controls called *clarity* or *texture* are contrast controls for a narrow set of midtones rather than the wider range of highlights and shadows. These tools impact local contrast but do not add or remove global contrast in the same way that a traditional contrast control does.

Finally, *dehaze* or *aerial haze adjustment* sliders reintroduce contrast in areas where aerial haze inherently lessens it. Aerial haze is most apparent in landscapes with objects that extend out to the horizon; the farther

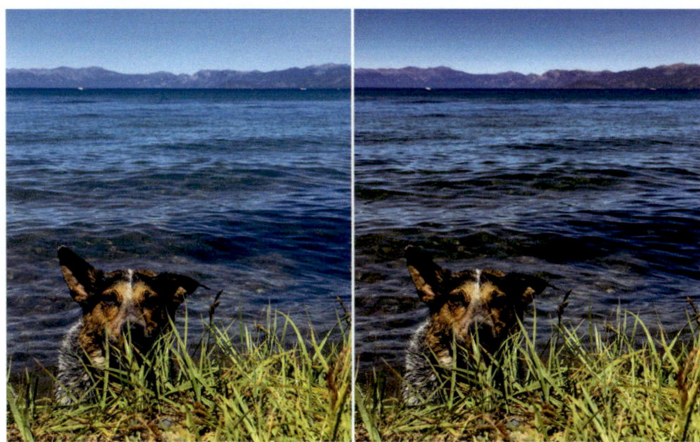

Figure 9-12 An outdoor landscape often exhibits reduced contrast to distant elements due to aerial haze (left). A dehaze tool can reintroduce contrast to these elements (right).

away things are, the more that the atmosphere scatters light and reduces tone contrast. Dehaze tools attempt to add contrast back in these parts of the scene and they require some knowledge or educated guess regarding scene depth to do so. This is accomplished with context-sensitive estimation algorithms (taking factors into consideration like focal length and local contrast in the original image) or with the help of depth maps generated from dual camera systems. Software can reintroduce contrast to groups of pixels that it believes are farther from the camera. Such tools may also introduce saturation or color shift changes. Figure 9-12 shows a before and after dehaze adjustment example where the distant mountains see a tone improvement. A dehaze slider may be adjustable in the negative or inverse direction to intentionally add a haze effect if desired.

Color Correction and the ColorChecker

The ColorChecker was invented in 1976 and was designed for use with analog film.[1] The goal was to have an object that could easily be compared with its image either visually or through objective measurements to ensure proper color reproduction. The ColorChecker target design features 24 unique patches proportioned to fill the frame of a 35mm frame (see Figure 9-13). This is, conveniently, the same aspect ratio as full frame DSLR cameras. The target design includes evenly spaced neutral patches between white and black and the additive and subtractive primaries. Four patches represent common objects (light skin, dark skin, blue sky, foliage) that color scientists deemed critical for evaluating tone and color reproduction. The other patches represent colors that were particularly challenging to reproduce on film (such as a specific blue flower). These colors do not necessarily pose the same challenges for digital sensors or modern photographic output but tradition and general utility have meant that use of the classic ColorChecker patches persists. Modern updates like the Digital ColorChecker SG supplement the classic set with a large number of new color patches attuned to sensor characteristics and to provide additional data points for automated software evaluation.

Setting the proper white balance when shooting is always the best practice and is easily done with an X-Rite ColorChecker. Or, if circumstances don't allow for the time it takes to set a custom white balance, a photograph of the reference target can be used at the editing stage with equal effectiveness. These uses make the ColorChecker a staple piece of equipment for every photographer. X-Rite also makes a smaller version, the ColorChecker Passport, that comes in a hard case to toss into an equipment bag without fear of damage. Using the target for accurate color balancing starts by taking a reference photograph during a photo shoot like we did in Figure 9-14 (overleaf).

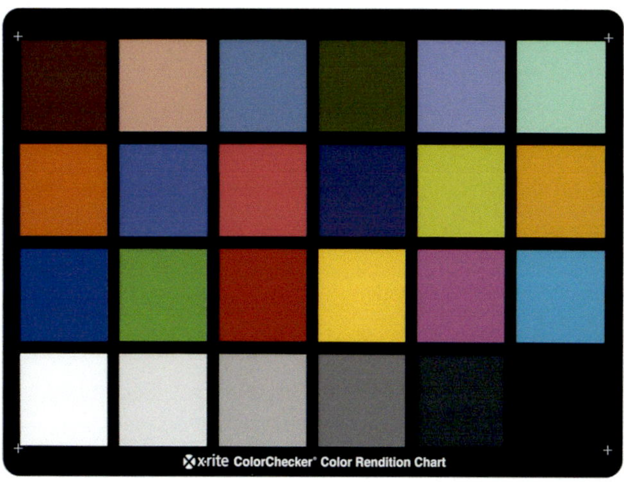

Figure 9-13 The X-Rite ColorChecker.

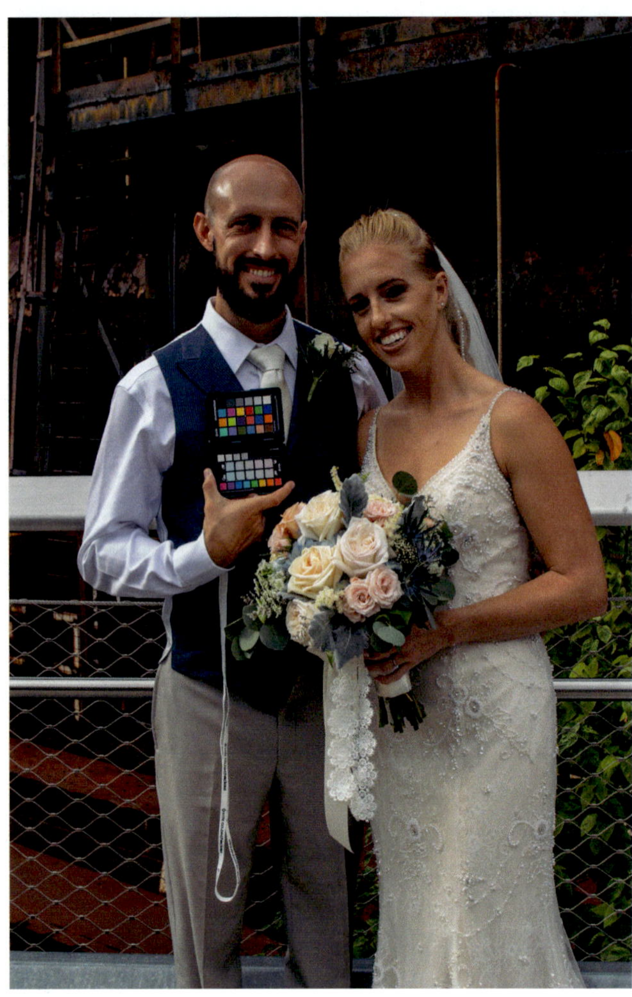

Figure 9-14 Having a ColorChecker Passport handy in never-to-be-repeated scenarios can be a color correction lifesaver when it comes time to edit.

Camera firmware typically includes an option to set custom white balance during a shoot. This is helpful if the lighting is unusual and previewing color is important as the shoot progresses. The firmware requires a captured, reference photograph containing a neutral object. Going this route is convenient but not altogether necessary, as a similar set of steps can be done at the post-processing stage.

Automatic color balancing tools are found in almost all image editing software. These algorithms are proprietary but use one of two methods to establish color balance. They either assume that the scene, when averaged, produces a mid-level gray or they find the brightest areas of the scene, like bright specular highlights, and assume that they should be neutral. The algorithms are not always right, regardless of the method used. The ColorChecker includes neutral patches to leverage with eyedropper-style color correction tools. Such tools tell software that a small group of pixels identified by the user should be neutral. Any color cast exhibit by these pixels is counteracted with a global change that impacts all pixels. The neutral patches on the ColorChecker are great to lean on for this task since we always know that the pixels recorded at these patches should be neutral in the processed image. It's conceivable to use a random subject or scene area with an eyedropper tool to establish a neutral point, however, a truly neutral surface is not always available. Worse, you might incorrectly recall a subject or scene element to be neutral when it was not.

Clients are unlikely to be interested in photographs of a color patch target. Instead, the suggested workflow involves shooting reference images with the ColorChecker in every new lighting environment. These images are white balanced and their color corrections are copied or replicated on all related captures from a shoot. This is particularly effective in a parametric image editing workflow where such corrections are efficient, metadata-based instructions that can be quickly applied to dozens or even hundreds of frames at once.

The ColorChecker patches are also valuable as references when a specific color cast or color treatment is desired. If the intent is to create an aesthetically pleasing, warm color tone, for example, then watching the known color patches and memory colors shift is like having a visual landmark. Knowing where you have been is just as constructive as knowing where you are going with creative color reproduction.

Color Balancing Using Color Channel Curves

The absence of a neutral target or a neutral object in the scene doesn't mean that color balancing is impossible. We can turn to the image channel data to clue us into a color imbalance between the red, green and blue channel data. Keep in mind that neutral tones are represented by

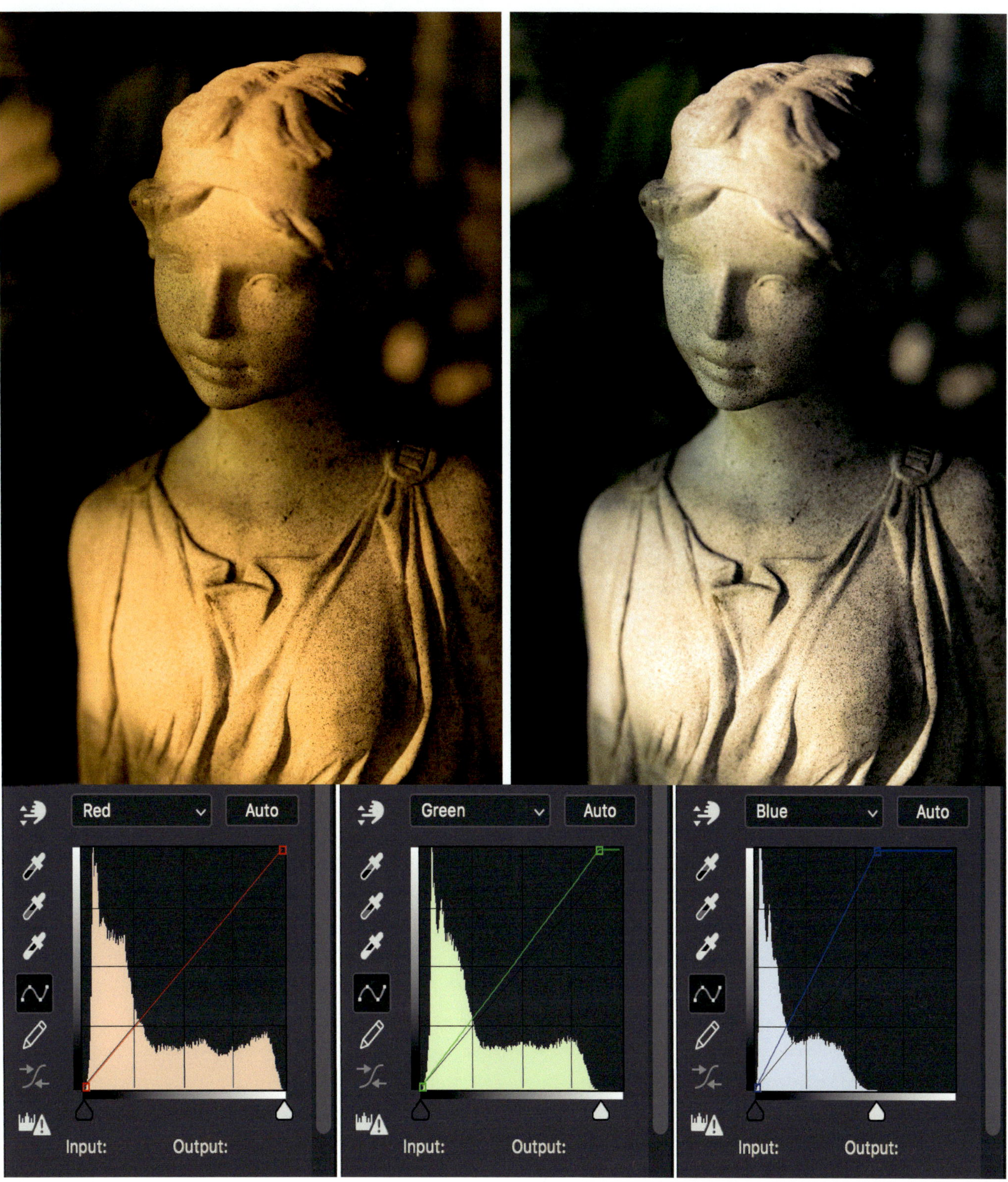

Figure 9-15 Adjusting the red, green and blue channel curves independently to maximize the tonal range in each helps to color balance.

equal amounts of red, green and blue pixel brightnesses. Any deviation from this relationship creates a non-neutral color.

Throughout this chapter thus far, we stuck to the single luminance curve that represents the combination of all three color channels in a color image. Once you're comfortable manipulating the luminance curve, the next place to hone your skills is by working independently with the red, green and blue channel tone curves. For the task of color balancing, we recommend setting a Curves adjustment to a "Color" blend mode in Adobe Photoshop to ensure that the changes impact color separately from luminance.

Figure 9-15 shows a starting image, a low light long exposure and the adjustments made to each of its three channels with the Curves tool to produce a color balanced version (shown to the right of the original). The blue channel histogram is the smallest, indicating that there's less blue overall and confirming the original image's visibly yellowish cast (recall the Maxwell triangle to appreciate the relationship that makes this true). We start by adjusting the black and white points of each channel histogram in order to stretch each one to maximize the available tone information recorded. This often gets us close to a desired final product as it makes it so that pixels representing neutral content have equivalent or very similar amounts of brightness across all three channels. Be aware that this can reveal noise that wasn't as visible before such changes. From here, we pull up or push down each curve from its midpoint to add that color or its complement, respectively. We pull the blue and green channel curves down a touch and leave the red channel mostly as-is in our example. The color-corrected version shows the concrete statue with a more realistic, neutral appearance compared to the warm tungsten cast in the original.

The Curves tool is alternatively accommodating in those instances where we do have a neutral reference patch or target, offering "eyedropper" functionality to automatically set black, white and midpoints on an image histogram. We can perform this tone mapping to either the combined RGB luminosity histogram or the separate channels.

Split Toning

The same strategy of independently modifying channel curves is useful for introducing *split toning* to an image. Split toning introduces color casts to shadows and highlights independently and does not modify luminance. The goal is to add a color cast (or two) rather than removing one. Split toning can be applied to color or black and white photographs. A popular combination sees the shadows made cooler and blue and the highlights a warmer yellow as shown in Figure 9-16. We include a black-to-white gradient below the images to better show the toning change, independent of subject content. This yellow/blue combination contributes to our innate association of light and warmth and its absence as cooler in temperature. Subtle toning of shadows and highlights is a purely subjective practice.

Proof of Concept: Color Correcting Film Scans using Curves

There are three approaches to color correcting an image: going strictly by-the-numbers with RGB pixel values and attempt to make the image neutral; using educated trial-and-error and visual subjectivity; embracing the lack of color correction and create an intentionally unnatural or inaccurate aesthetic choice. These methods can co-exist in your editing toolkit. We use a mix of the first and second approaches in this exercise.

Color film scans are great subjects on which to practice color correction techniques. Unlike raw digital captures, color film frames can have significant color casts that don't have an easy toggle to alternate through white balance settings. Older film can also show color degradation due to natural fading and exposure to the elements. We dug up the Kodachrome slide shown in Figure 9-17 from an old family photo collection. Despite being taken in the 1960s, the act of taking one's cat for a walk on a leash is forever fashionable. Follow along with our example or use your own scanned image.

1. Set your Adobe Photoshop workspace surrounding color to a neutral, midtone gray by right-clicking it and

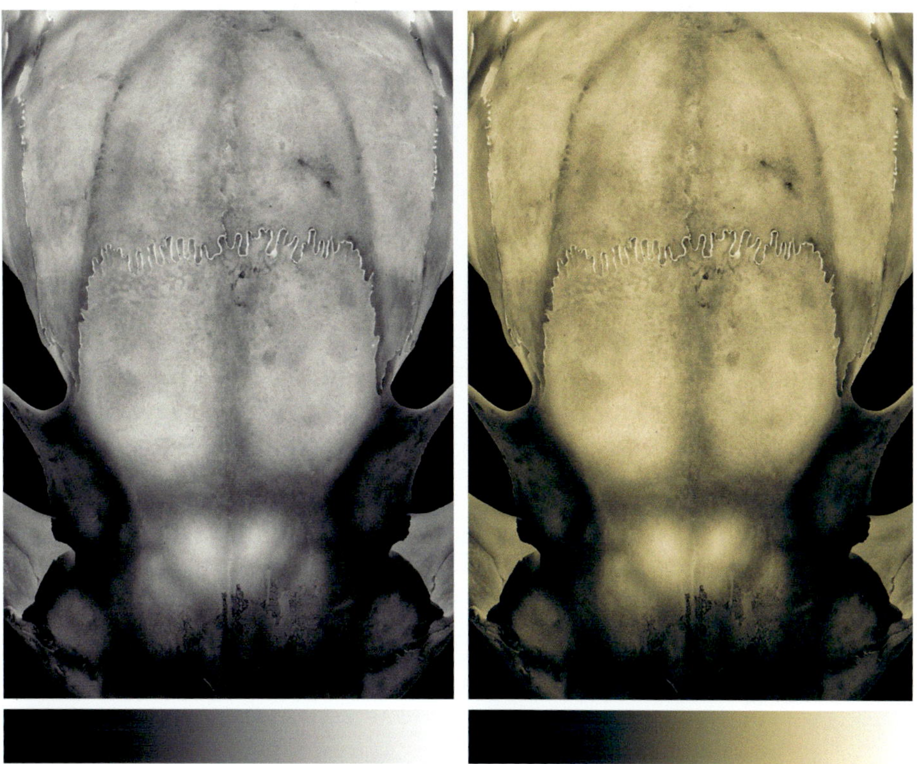

Figure 9-16 Split toning an image is a subjective practice that serves aesthetics over objective accuracy. Here, the shadows are rendered with a blue cast and the highlights with a yellow cast.

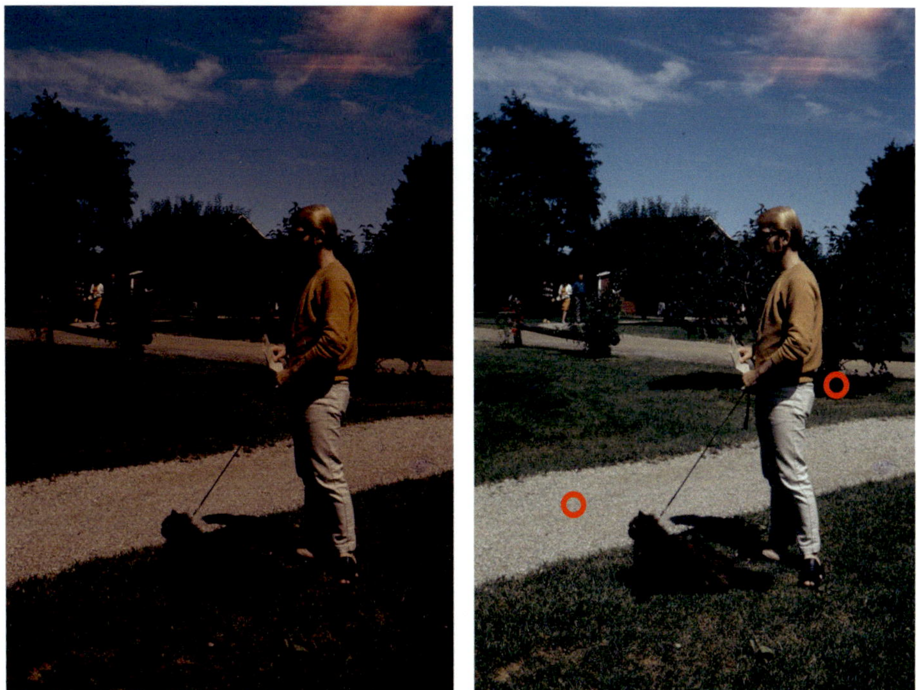

Figure 9-17 The color and tones are an unedited rendering from a film scanner (left). The color-corrected version (right) is improved thanks to modifying the tone distribution of the separate color channels.

Table 9-1 Highlight and shadow pixel values from sampled areas.

Sampled Points	L*	a*	b*	R	G	B
Sampled Highlight Before Color Correction	56	0	0	147	125	117
Sampled Highlight After Color Correction	73	0	0	179	179	178
Sampled Shadow Before Color Correction	13	5	-1	43	37	30
Sampled Shadow After Color Correction	25	-2	-5	59	63	68

selecting *Select Custom Color.* Set R, G and B fields to 128. This is critical as a neutral reference point for our eyes to make accurate color assessments.

2. Use the Color Sampler tool to define two points of interest: one in a highlight area and another in a shadow area. Try to find areas in the scene that should be neutral like white walls, concrete pavement or clothing details. The Color Sampler tool holds the selected pixel areas and displays their CIELAB and RGB values in the Info panel. The red circles in Figure 9-17 indicate where we measured the pixel values in our image.
3. Observe the sample points' CIELAB and RGB values (ours are recorded in Table 9-1). Consider that any truly neutral area in an image has near-identical R, G and B values once it is color corrected. Alternatively, neutral areas have near-zero a* and b* values.
4. Add a Curves Adjustment layer. Use the dropdown menu to switch to the Red channel histogram and curve.
5. There is tone information (the histogram peaks) in the red channel yet the black and white points may not be matched with the dynamic range of the image. Adjust the black point to the location where the darkest pixel information exists to introduce stretch mapping to the channel data. Do the same with the white point.
6. Repeat this process with the Green and Blue channels.
7. Cycle through the channel curves again. In each, click on the diagonal line and drag the curve up to add more of that channel color; pull it down to subtract it. Adding multiple points to a curve allows for independent adjustment of shadows, midtones and highlights within a color channel, i.e. adding green to the shadows while taking away green in the highlights.
8. Watch the Info panel where the highlight and shadow samples' RGB values are displayed. Try to match the R, G and B values for both samples while visually evaluating the changing appearance of the overall image. Always keep in mind that your subjective opinion on color reproduction holds weight alongside any numeric balance. Our finished Curves adjustment is shown in Figure 9-18.

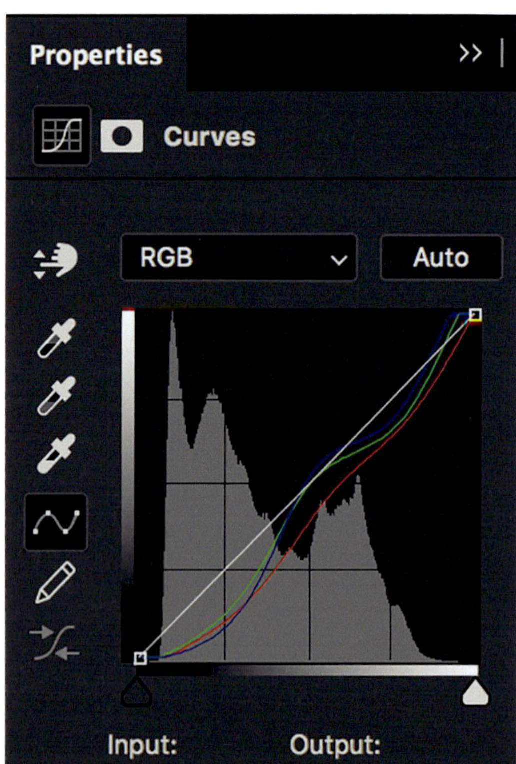

Figure 9-18 The resulting Curves tool adjustment made to our Kodachrome film scan.

Compare the color-corrected version against the original. Leaving the adjustment layers set to a Normal blend mode means that the changes affect both color and tone. The original and final versions should show notably improved color and tone reproduction. Working with raw image data is often easier than film scans but can be equally challenging when scenes contain multiple light sources or brightly colored and reflective surfaces. It's here that using Curves adjustments and carefully considering shadows, midtones and highlights independent of one another that the best results can be achieved. Of course, having a ColorChecker in the scene from which to set sample points is the ideal scenario to aid in manual color correction.

Note

1 McCamy, C.S., H. Marcus and J.G. Davidson. "A color rendition chart." *Journal of Applied Photographic Engineering*, vol. 2, no. 3, 1976.

10 Software Filters

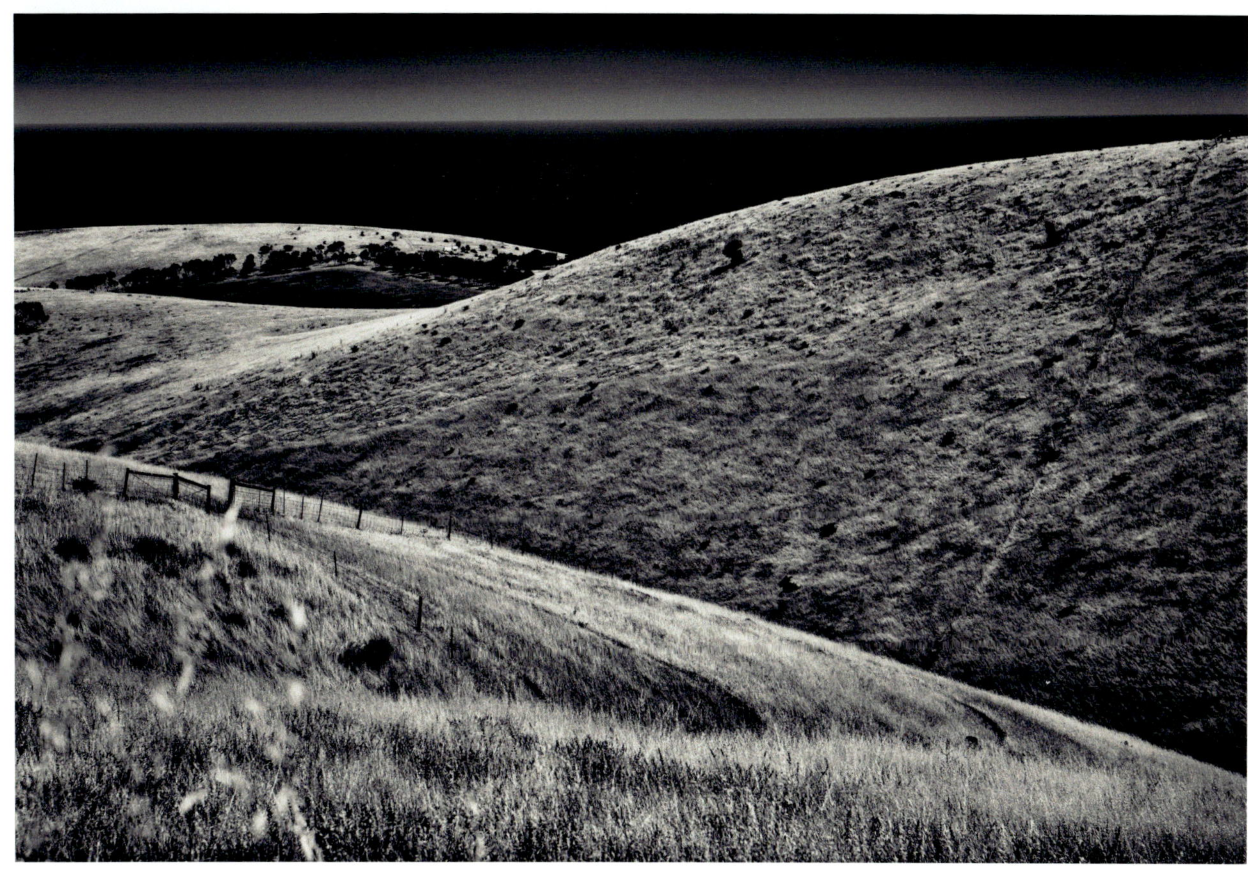

Photograph by Rochester Institute of Technology alumnus and Lecturer Dan Hughes

This chapter is an overview of the digital filters we apply to images after capture, during our post-processing workflow. In Chapter 5, we discussed using optical filters like neutral density and UV filters placed in front of our lens when capturing an image. Optical filters dictate characteristics of the image recorded relative to the scene itself. *Software filters* take the digital information recorded and work to modify its characteristics for different visual effects. Software filters allow photographers to express their creativity in ways never possible with film, offering opportunities to enhance the raw image data in both broad strokes and with extreme, pixel-level precision when desired. Thoughtful and skillful use of filters on image files elevates a photographer with a good eye to a photographer that produces amazing photographs. The software filters or image processing filter techniques discussed are sharpening, blurring, blending and black and white conversion. We'll conduct some applied sleuthing at the end of the chapter to reverse-engineer a combination of edits made by a mobile app image processing filter.

Sharpening an Image

Sharpening filters enhance the appearance of sharpness or clarity in images. That is, they improve *acutance* or how quickly the edges in an image transition from one contrasting tone to another. Before you get the idea that sharpening filters are miracle workers, know that no amount of post-processing sharpening will save a blurry or out-of-focus capture. Excessively blurry or out-of-focus frames are not restorable despite what crime scene investigation television shows may have us believe. A subject edge recorded as a blurry smear cannot be reconstructed as an edge. Additionally, we closely associate sharpness with optical resolution whereby the camera resolved fine detail. No post-processing filter exists that can restore a combined lack of resolved detail and acutance.

Sharpening filters follow mathematical rules and behaviors. Don't let that lull you into a false sense of security. Both under- and oversharpening are very real possibilities in post-processing and being at either end of this spectrum is detrimental to the perceived quality of your images. Knowing when, where and by how much to sharpen is an acquired skill empowered by a strong understanding of the way in which sharpening filters work.

Sharpening software filters locate the edges in your scene and increase the contrast along those edges to create the illusion of additional image sharpness. We use the term "illusion" carefully as not to imply falsehood or trickery: sharpening plays to the behavior of our visual system. You're going to really stress your good qualities during a job interview while glossing over the dubious details of your work history. It's not inherently malicious or misleading, it's making the best of what you've got. The same is true for sharpening image data. We perceive sharpness and detail when we have local contrast to delineate where one structure begins and another ends. The delineation between a building edge and the blue sky behind it should be clear-cut and distinct: the pixels representing the building are one tone and color while the blue sky pixels are another (see Figure 10-1). There shouldn't be blue pixels breaching that building edge if the image is sharply resolved.

Sometimes even a well-recorded edge isn't enough to appear as sharp as we'd like in the final, edited version. Here we have the option to exaggerate edges by creating extra contrast, well beyond what is recorded by the sensor. Figure 10-1 shows what this looks like in practice. We *overshoot* edges by artificially darkening a darker edge and lightening the lighter side of the edge. The transitions become more extreme or abrupt as a result. Despite it looking exaggerated and unnatural up close, this strategy can contribute to a sense of sharpness at the proper viewing distance. The risk of overshooting edge contrast is in creating *halo* artifacts. Like the name implies, this image quality degradation looks like bright rings or outlines around subject edges. Avoid sharpening to the point where obvious haloing appears.

There are three points in a photographic workflow where sharpening should occur: directly following camera capture, during creative enhancement and immediately preceding print or screen output.

Figure 10-1 A simplified illustration of a building edge against a blue sky. On the right, the image is sharply focused and the boundaries are distinct. The center image is blurred and the building edges appear to transition from the sky over multiple pixels. In the left image, the building is oversharpened to show overshoot.

Capture sharpening happens right after capturing the image or as the initial phase of demosaicing and processing. The need for capture sharpening is a result of the anti-aliasing filter placed in front of the digital sensor to help reduce the appearance of stair-stepping along object edges and avoid moiré artifacts. The anti-aliasing filter reduces overall image sharpness at capture, an acceptable compromise. Capture sharpening is applied in-camera when shooting directly to JPEG and is destructive (meaning that it cannot be reversed). Some camera firmware allows for user adjustments to the amount of JPEG capture sharpening, others do not. Capture sharpening for raw images is available in image processing software and should be applied at an early stage of image ingestion or basic adjustments. As with all raw editing adjustments, it is non-destructive. It's common for raw image editors to default to a preset for capture sharpening because we expect that the raw image data needs sharpness enhancement right out of the gate. You may find that modifying this default capture sharpening filter brings your images up to a good baseline level of sharpness before moving on to other filters and adjustments in your workflow. An example of capture sharpening settings is shown in Figure 10-2.

Capture sharpening is a *global enhancement*. Global enhancements, such as sharpening, are applied to the entire image: every pixel is evaluated and modified with the same rules. This does not mean that every pixel is affected the same way, only that the entirety of pixels is considered. Since the anti-aliasing filter is installed over the entire area of the digital sensor on most cameras, global capture sharpening is necessary.

Creative sharpening is a subjective strategy of enhancing specific parts of the scene for emphasis. For example, it is quite common to apply some creative sharpening to the eyes in portrait photographs. The eyes may be just as objectively sharp as every other detail in the image after capture, yet we want to further sculpt and direct the attention of the viewer. Creative sharpening is employed as a *local enhancement* for this reason. A subset of pixels are targeted and filtered with specific intent and control. All other pixels are left unmodified by the software filtering. Creative sharpening is key to achieving the aesthetic you want for your image. There are no exact rules or instructions to dictate the most effective use of this processing stage as it is heavily context dependent and creatively open-ended.

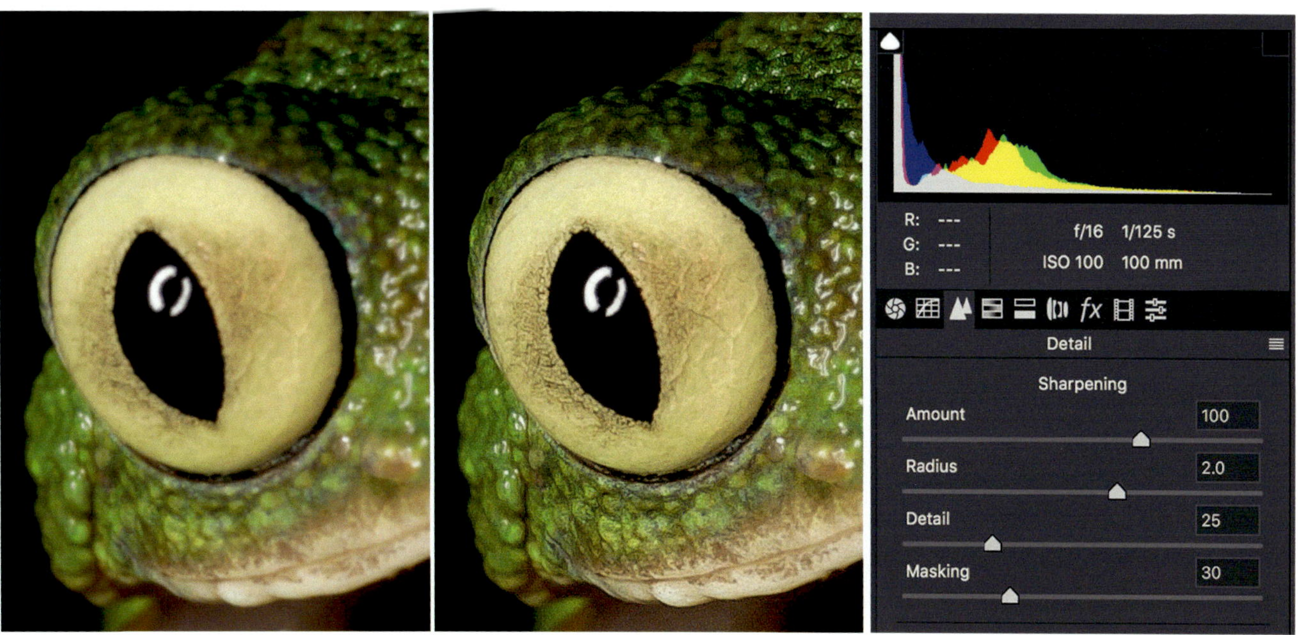

Figure 10-2 Capture sharpening controls in Adobe Camera Raw introduce a base level of sharpness that is inherently lost at capture and demosaicing.

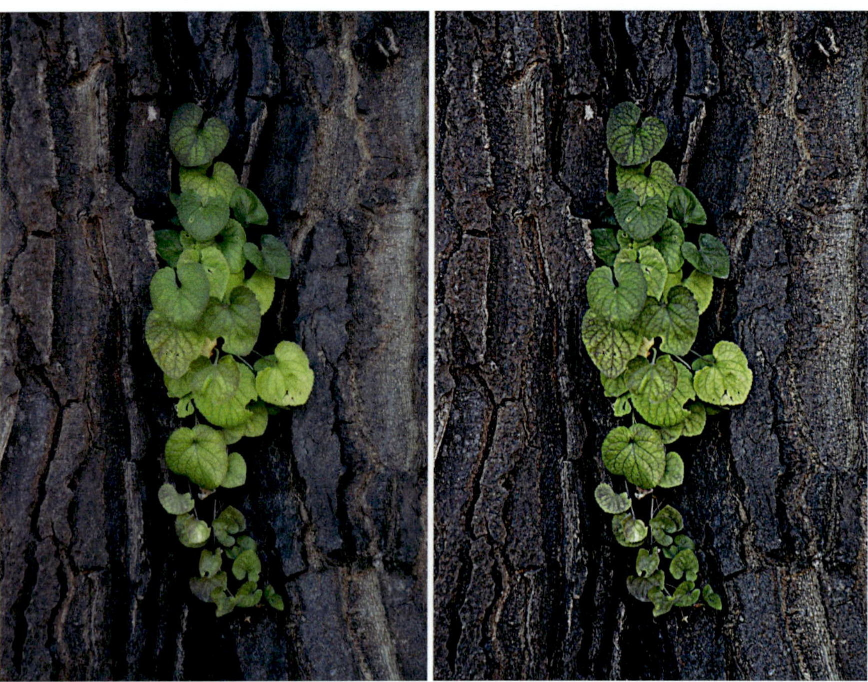

Figure 10-3 Unsharp mask sharpening applied to an image without care to adjusting its parameters can lead to extreme, exaggerated sharpening effects.

Let's highlight three types of creative sharpening via software filters, though there are many others: unsharp masking, smart sharpening and high pass sharpening. All three are strong options for creative sharpening, however, they can alternatively be used as global enhancements for output sharpening.

Unsharp masking holds many bad memories for anyone who studied film photography. The name comes from creating an unsharp or blurry film negative to mask the original image in the darkroom. It was a difficult and frustrating process. Unsharp masking in the digital world is, thankfully, much easier, though based on the same idea. Taking a blurred (or "unsharp") version of an image file and subtracting its pixel values from the original leaves behind the photograph's edges. This subtracted, edges-only product is used as a mask or guide to dictate where the edge contrast enhancement takes effect.

The unsharp mask filter commonly offers three adjustment parameters. The *Amount* parameter controls how much contrast is increased between adjacent pixels. It is closely tied to the overall perception of sharpening; it has a direct and coarse relationship to how sharp the image becomes. The *Radius* parameter controls how many of the neighboring pixels are affected. A larger radius means that the amount of sharpening extends to pixels farther away from the edge. A smaller radius enhances small details; a large radius impacts all details and possible edges. The radius and amount settings affect each other: if we increase the radius, the amount should be decreased to avoid gross oversharpening. The third adjustable parameter of unsharp mask filtering is the *Threshold* value. The threshold dictates how different the adjacent pixel values must be in order to be sharpened. Setting the threshold to 0 sharpens the entire image with no distinction between edge pixels and non-edge pixels, making this a global adjustment (see Figure 10-3). This tends to over-emphasize image noise. Increasing the threshold will leave low contrast areas (which are likely to be non-edge content) alone. We typically adjust the radius first to get a sense of which areas are going to receive the sharpening, dial in the amount and finally tweak the threshold to minimize oversharpening in areas where we don't want it.

Smart sharpening offers more control than unsharp masking. The options are similar, however smart sharpen

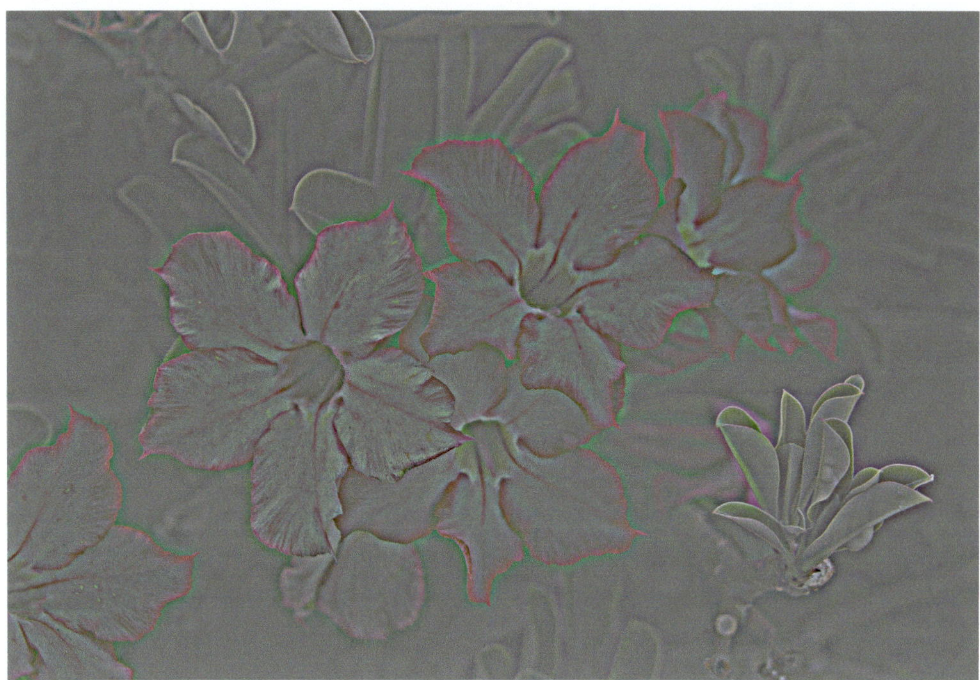

Figure 10-4 The result of a high pass filtered image. This can be blended or overlaid with the original to introduce edge sharpening.

allows the sharpening to be reduced or faded in the shadows and highlights. This reduces halos and deemphasizes noise that is always present in the shadows. Smart sharpen has options to correct blur, motion, lens or Gaussian blur (we define Gaussian later in this chapter). Unsharp masking can only correct Gaussian blur. Lastly, if you are using smart sharpen in Photoshop, the settings can be saved as a preset, which can speed up workflow in the future.

The last method we'll cover is *high pass filtering*. While it is not inherently a sharpening filter, many photographers find that employing it as such is one of the most effective sharpening strategies. Recall that we create the illusion of sharpness by increasing the contrast along the edges. Successful sharpening affects the edges only, leaving all other areas in the image untouched. The high pass filter is an edge detection filter and its output is shown in Figure 10-4. When using Adobe Photoshop, high pass filter results are combined with the image using the luminosity blend mode to sharpen edges without negatively affecting the rest of the image. The luminosity blend mode helps avoid color shifts that can otherwise arise with the high pass sharpening method.

Let's mention a bonus software filter to round out our creative sharpening options. *Midtone sharpening* also goes by names like *clarity* and *structure* depending on the image processing software used. This method targets midtone pixel edges exclusively rather than going after all edges across the shadows, midtones or highlights of the scene. Midtone sharpening tools may use the same types of adjustable parameters (amount, radius, threshold) as the previously described filters. Content in the midtones is likely to be fine texture or small details that get a boost when their edges receive additional contrast. Instead of emphasizing building edges or large object boundaries, midtone edge contrast enhances the perceived sharpness of elements like skin and hair. This gives scenes a pop of perceived detail or clarity and can be combined with additional, global sharpening.

Output sharpening is necessary because the final destinations and output processes for your photographs affect their appearance. When printing, paper surfaces accept ink differently. Newsprint, as an example medium, absorbs ink. An ink applied to newsprint spreads out as it is absorbed into the material. This spreading means that distinct edges begin to blur. If your photograph's output destination is newsprint, the file must be prepared with significant amounts of sharpening before it is printed. Photographic papers, on the other hand, are designed so that the ink does not spread significantly when absorbed into the paper. Output sharpening strategies for printing on photo paper are driven by the paper surfaces, such as matte or glossy, and the anticipated viewing distance (as a function of print size and venue). A highly reflective glossy paper requires less sharpening than a diffuse reflecting surface such as matte paper. If your final destination is display, you may not need any additional sharpening at all.

Output sharpening is not tied to a specific filter or approach, so the previously mentioned sharpening tools are valuable here. The difference is that output sharpening is only intended as processing in anticipation of the image's final presentation on a medium with sharpness considerations. Output sharpening is primarily global in nature. Image processing software typically includes the option to sharpen for output in the stages immediately preceding printing. This means that we don't necessarily save the output-sharpened result for later; it's treated as a temporary, as-needed and in-context software filter. Also note that camera firmware offers sharpening options when shooting directly to JPEG, typically only in vague scales like "low, medium, high" as the presumption is that these JPEGs are skipping most of the processing pipeline. These JPEGs are suitable for printing, though the lack of fine control over the sharpening approach (and every other aspect of the image's appearance) makes this a blunt and limiting strategy. Chapter 16 covers print media and the appropriate considerations for optimal photographic quality. Output sharpening takes practice and a familiarity with your equipment to get great results.

Blurring an Image

The use of blur in a photograph starts with decisions at capture. Blurring strategies include using aperture settings to limit depth of field and panning on a moving object to blur the background. Introducing blur in post-processing is another approach, either in combination with or completely independent from capture decisions. Maybe we want to minimize the visual weight of a distracting object or simply blur the entire image to use it as a background. Blur can also imply motion or a feeling of uncertainty and ambiguity.

There are three common *low pass filter* approaches for creating blur with software processing: a mean filter, a weighted average filter or a Gaussian filter. The *mean filter* is the simplest of the three. It takes a sliding window (typically 3x3 pixels) passed over the image and replaces the center pixel with the average of all the pixels in that window. Expanding the window to 5x5 pixels or larger introduces even more blurring. A mean filter can be applied to the entire image or a locally masked area such as the scene background. An example of a 3x3 average filter is shown in

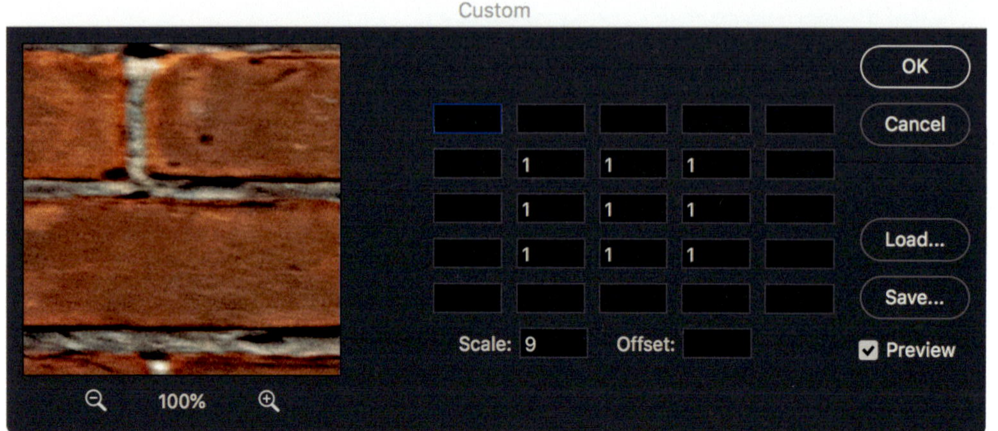

1	1	1
1	1	1
1	1	1

Figure 10-5 A sample averaging filter.

Figure 10-5. A mean filter must be odd ordered (3x3, 5x5, 9x9 and so on), all of the filter elements must be the same and sum to 1. To have the elements sum to 1 using the custom filter tool in Adobe Photoshop, we need a scale value equal to the sum of the filter elements. In Figure 10-5, the sum of the elements is 9, so we have to divide our filter by 1/9. This means using a scale factor of 9.

The *weighted average filter* places greater importance on the center pixel value relative to the surrounding pixels. This blurring technique offers more control over the amount of blur introduced. A weighted average filter must meet three conditions. The filter must be odd-ordered (3x3, 5x5, 9x9), all filter elements surrounding the center must be 1 and the center value must be larger than 1 which gives it the weight or greater influence on the image. In order for the elements to sum to 1 using Adobe Photoshop's custom filter tool, we need a scale factor equal to the sum of all the elements. The sum of the elements in Figure 10-6 is 13, so we divide our filter by 1/13. In Photoshop, this makes our scale factor 13.

Lastly, we have the *Gaussian blur filter*, also referred to as *Gaussian smoothing*. Recall from math class that a Gaussian distribution is a normal or bell-shaped curve. Jogging your memory further, a normal curve can have different widths or standard deviations. A Gaussian blur filter takes on the shape of a two-dimensional gaussian curve; it's used to reduce the presence of noise and smooth details. The larger the kernel, the larger the deviation of pixels blurred in the filtered image.

Blending Images

Blending pixels from two or more sources is commonplace in photographic compositing and retouching. Consider image files as two-dimensional arrays of pixel data that can be stacked or layered together. The next step in working with these layers is deciding on the rules dictating their interactions. Simply placing one image on top of another will completely obscure the bottom-most image like milk foam layered on top of a cappuccino. We blend elements of both image layers to achieve some constructive creative output from the exercise, otherwise we simply see the top-most image. *Blend modes* or *blending interaction rules* use the numeric representation of pixels—their luminance values between 0 and 255 (across three color channels)—to establish predictable outcomes from their combination. Common blend interaction rules are as follows[1]:

1. Darkening
   A *darkening blend mode* always prioritizes the darkest pixel at a location of the blended (or active) image layer over pixels on layers below. Simply stated, this blend behavior takes the darkest (lowest luminance value) pixel at a given X,Y coordinate and has the effect of darkening at least part of the image relative to where it started. Some forms of darkening blending multiply pixel values of the blended layers to create new pixel values. See Figure 10-7 (overleaf) for an example of blending using a darkening interaction rule; notice how

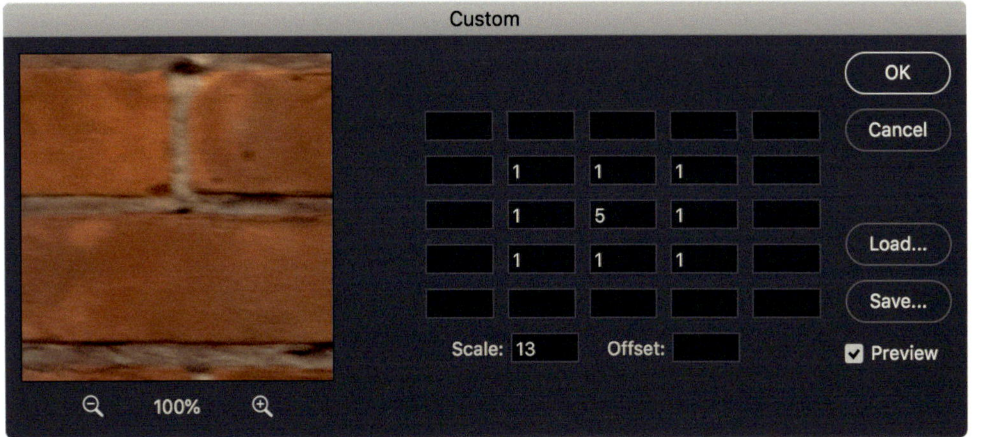

1	1	1
1	5	1
1	1	1

Figure 10-6 A sample weighted averaging filter.

the white background of the plant image is treated differently based on the blending strategy.

2. Lightening

   A *lightening blend mode* is the opposite of a darkening blend mode whereby the brightest pixel (highest luminance value) across stacked image layers is used. Some forms of lightening multiply pixel values of the blended layers to create new pixel values. Figure 10-7 also shows an example of this interaction.

3. Contrast

   A *contrast blend mode* is a mix of both the darkening and lightening blend modes that introduces additional contrast by examining each pixel. If the pixel is brighter than 50% or midtone gray, it is lightened. Conversely, if it is darker than midtone gray, the pixel is darkened.

4. Compare

   Comparison blend modes compares pixel values between active and inactive image layers and performs different mathematical evaluations like subtraction or division to derive new pixel values. These blend modes are particularly difficult to anticipate or previsualize because the behavior is not as visually intuitive as lighten or darken blend modes.

5. Component

   Component blend modes separately change hue, saturation, color and/or luminosity. A saturation blend mode, for example, takes the saturation component of the active layer pixels and applies it to the luminance and hue of the image layer beneath.

We've framed the concepts of blending filters in terms of two unique image layers. This is just one of many possible ways to employ blend modes or filters; entire groups of image layers (and non-photo pixels, like design elements) or small subsets of images can be combined when doing heavy photographic compositing. Blending pixels from two image layers is just the tip of the iceberg. The previous list covers the five categories for blend mode interactions—there are often multiple variations within these categories. Finally, working with degrees of image layer opacity adds additional complexity to pixel interactions. Blending image elements is both an art and a science and we're often encouraged by the results of experimenting. Naturally, Adobe Photoshop professionals have considerable documentation and insight on this topic and we point you to them for further information.[2]

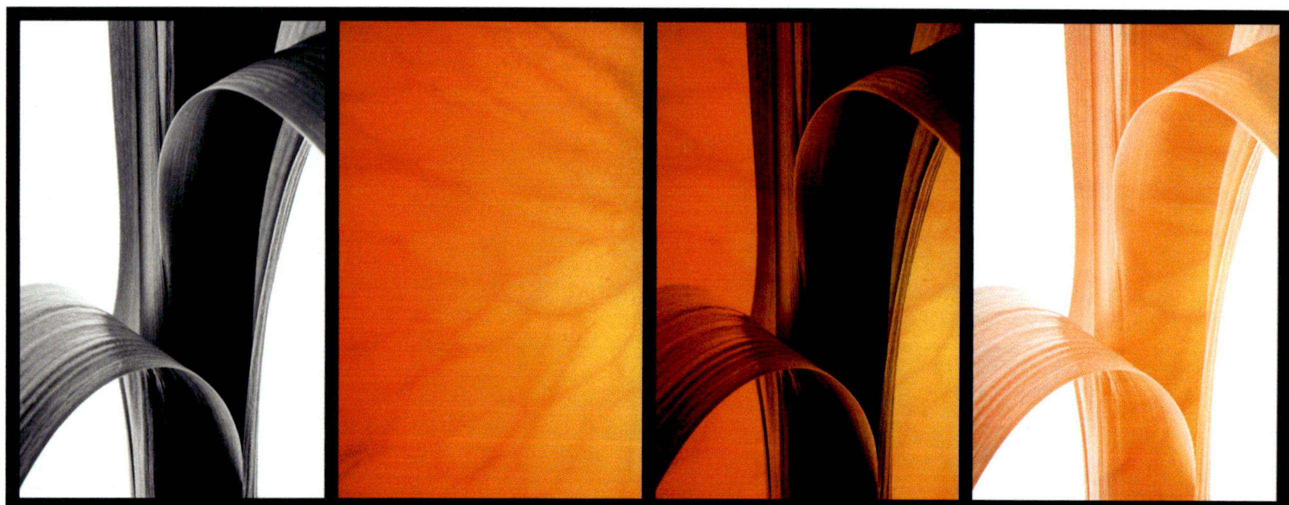

Figure 10-7 The left two images are stacked and blended using a darkening blend mode to create the next image. The rightmost image is blended using a lightening blend mode.

Black and White Conversion

One might say that we are returning to our roots where photography began by taking color images and converting them to black and white. There are three options for creating black and white images in the digital era. The first option is to set your camera to monochrome mode, available in many DSLRs' camera firmware, though this only applies to JPEG shooting. Raw image files will always retain all of the color information even if the camera generates a black and white preview. A second option is to convert the digital color image to black and white after capture with software filters. The third option, which we won't expound on here, is using a dedicated, feature-built monochrome-only camera. Such cameras are offered sans color filter array for shooting exclusively in black and white. Their niche functionality tends to make them expensive and uncommon equipment.

Let's refresh our memory regarding color filters and their functions. A color filter is named for the color it passes, for example a red filter passes red light and to a lesser extent yellow and magenta while blocking cyan, green and blue. Analog photographers routinely use color filters when

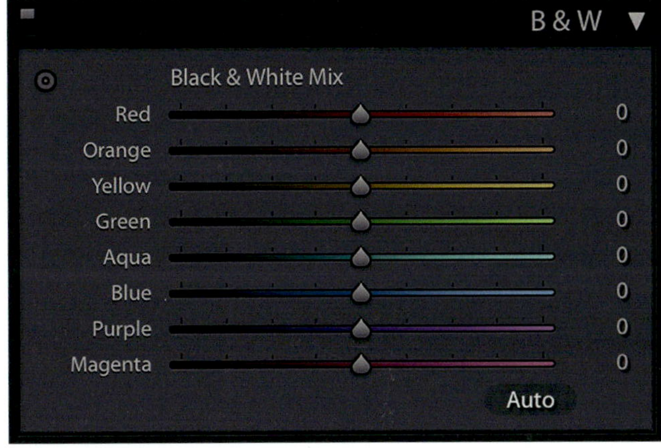

Figure 10-8 Black and white conversion controls in Adobe Photoshop Lightroom.

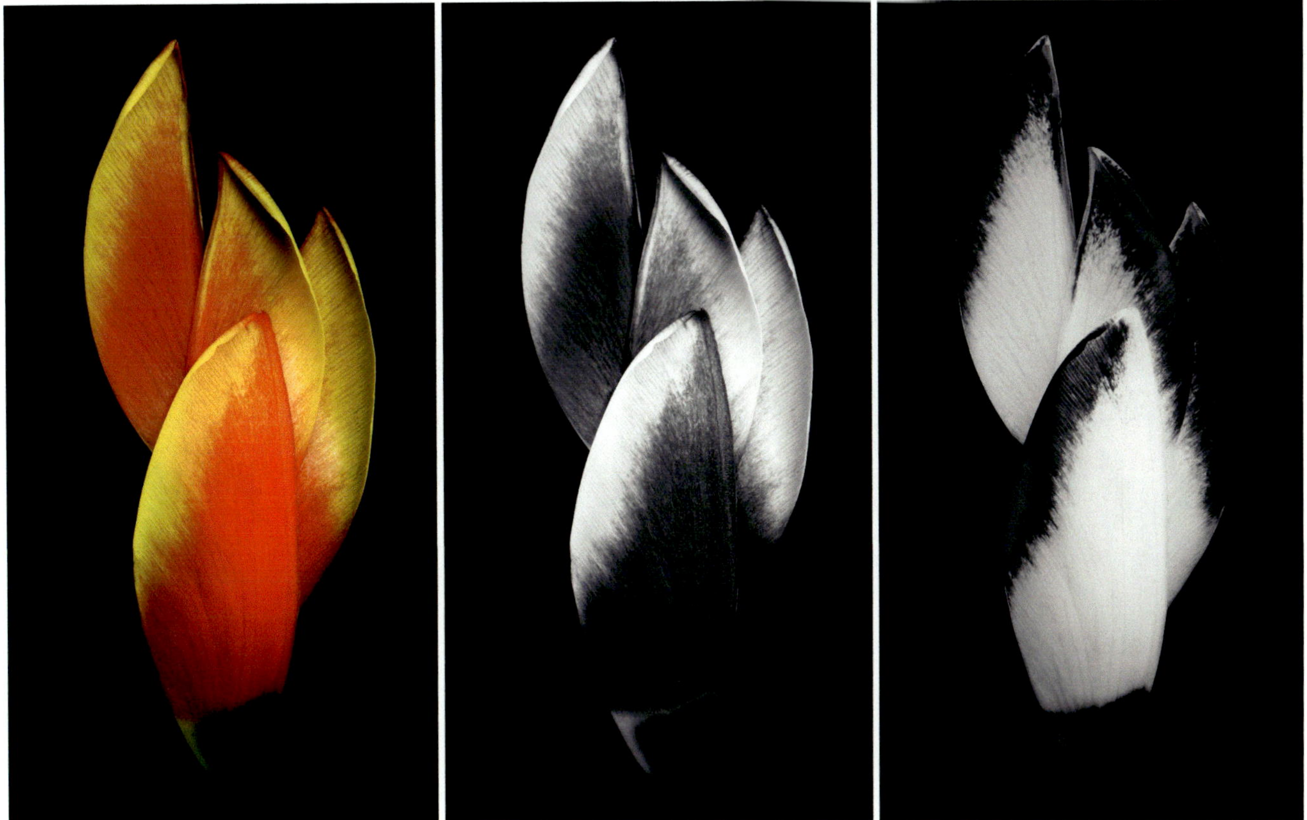

Figure 10-9 A color image and two unique black and white conversions made by independently adjusting the brightnesses of yellows and reds.

shooting with black and white film. Landscape photography using black and white film benefits from using a yellow filter to darken bright skies, enhancing the separation between the sky and white clouds. On-camera black and white modes simulate this use of color filters. Removing color from the process allows the artist to concentrate on composition and lighting. For complete control of the tonality rendered in a black and white image, most professionals and experienced editors opt for conversion later in post-processing.

Converting a color image to black and white in editing software allows for much more creativity and flexibility. Editing software provides preset options as well as the ability to adjust individual color brightnesses as shown in Figure 10-8. This provides endless options for black and white conversion from a full color image. Figure 10-9 highlights an example of two very different black and white interpretations relative to the original by increasing the tone brightness of some color pixels and darkening others.

Digital Filtering for Special Effect

With the ever-increasing processing power of chips in all cameras, from smartphones to high-end DSLRs, comes the ability to introduce in-camera digital filtering. These filters include special effects like grainy black and white, soft focus, fish-eye distortion, watercolor painting and miniaturization. All of these can be applied directly to images as they are captured or when reviewing them on the camera's preview screen. They require no extra training or separate, off-camera software. The effects can range from a simple black and white conversion to abstracted interpretations.

Moving to desktop software offers additional creative options; special effect filters available in Adobe Photoshop or DxO's Nik Collection are seemingly endless. It's possible to add a realistic soft-focus like the one shown in Figure 10-10 or simulate different media ranging from charcoal drawings to stained glass (see Figure 10-11). Some special effect filters offer a host of tweakable sliders and settings to finely tune the outcome. Some are kitschy, one-trick-pony affairs while others are valuable aesthetic options when used in the right context.

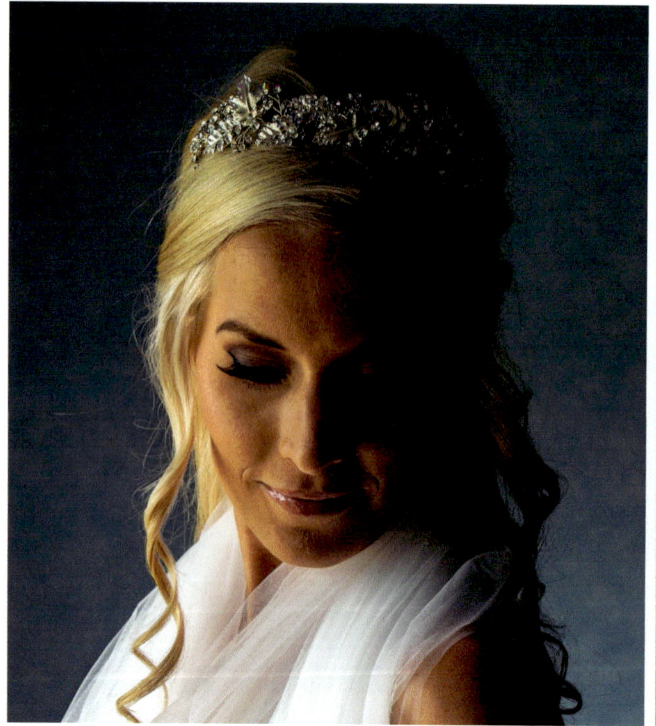

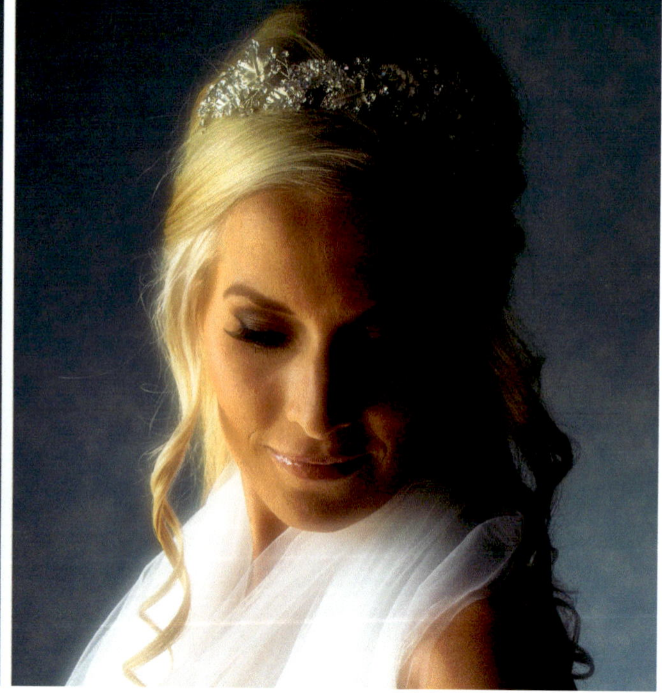

Figure 10-10 DxO's Nik Collection soft focus filter.

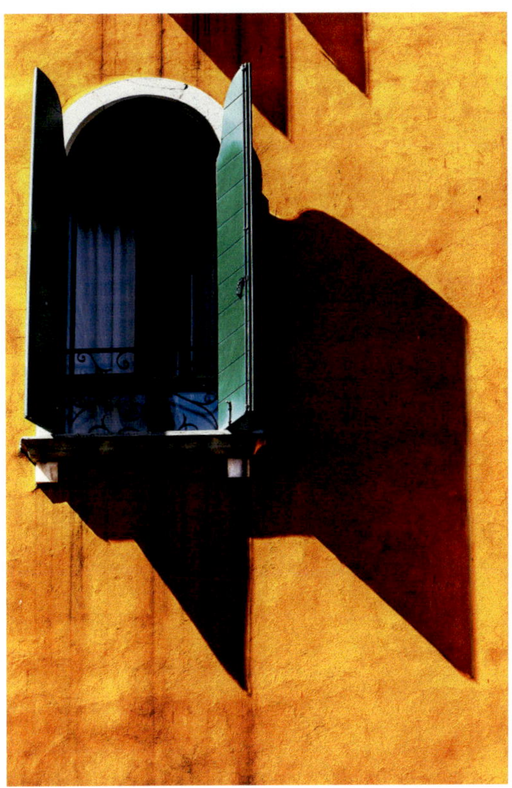
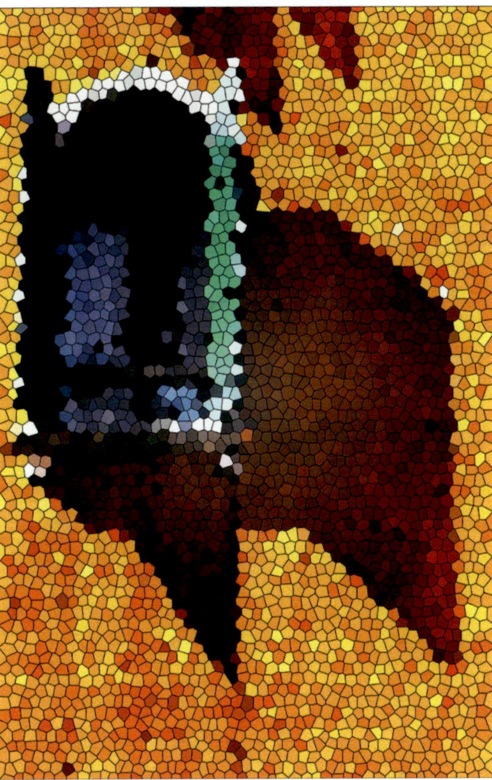

Figure 10-11 Adobe Photoshop's stained glass filter.

Filter Masking

We described the difference between global and local enhancements earlier in this chapter. Global enhancements are easy to explain because we can increase the brightness value of every single pixel in an image, as one example. There are no coordinates or other complex instructions needed to grasp which pixels change when applying the adjustment or filter. Local adjustments do require this specificity, so how can we define selections of pixels with minimal impact to file size, processing requirements and do so in a non-destructive manner?

Making selections in software such as Photoshop is a dense topic because it offers a variety of ways to do so. Some selections are temporary while others can be recorded and called up at any time, even in a later editing session. Under the hood, though, all local selections use the same central programming concept: the selections are grayscale bitmap or vector files used to designate active and inactive areas of the image frame. A temporary selection tool identifies a local set of pixels for filtering or other modifications; we never see the reference grayscale file used to define them and the software stores it in temporary memory only.

A robust selection strategy for local filtering and processing includes using an alpha channel layer called a *layer mask*. Photoshop displays this mask as a black and white layer of pixels, though it is not a visible set of pixels in the final image. Instead, the mask information dictates the degree of "on" or "off" a filter or adjustment exhibits on the image pixels. Think of a layer mask like a dimmer switch controlling a lamp. In addition to being switched off, the dimmer allows for a set of increasingly brighter settings before reaching maximum brightness. Working with a layer mask means modifying a grayscale file that defines active and inactive areas for local image adjustments. On one end of the grayscale, black pixels indicate completely inactive areas. Combined with a filter or adjustment, these are considered "off" and the original image pixels are unaffected. White pixels, on the other end of the grayscale, are fully

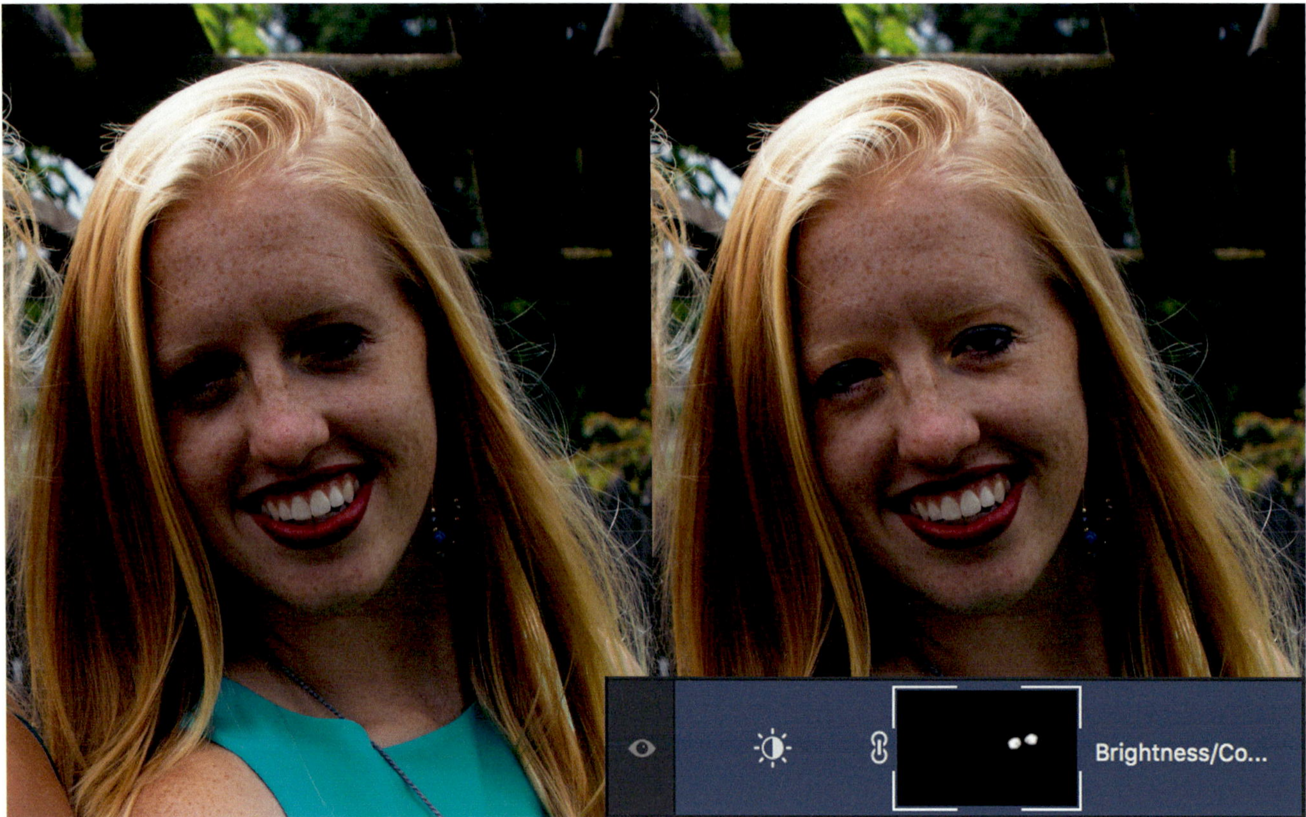

Figure 10-12 Masking image adjustments non-destructively is accomplished with an overlaid but invisible mapping of which pixels are and which are not modified by the filter.

"on" and these areas receive the filter or adjustment at full strength. Everything in between represents a gradient of strength or influence that a local adjustment has over the underlying image pixels.

Since Adobe Photoshop and similar software offerings use this method of local selections, expert-level image editors take full advantage of their tools by treating layer masks as if they are the images themselves. The grayscale mask histogram can be modified to add contrast, its overall definition can be blurred or sharpened and local changes can be made with paintbrush tools. Furthermore, a photograph can be converted to grayscale and made into a layer mask itself—a powerful strategy for complex selections, especially when the image has color or brightness contrast along subject edges.

Layer masking is ideal for software filters and any image adjustment in general. Our intention in Figure 10-12 is to lighten the eyes in a portrait. The filter mask we defined acts as instructions: only the pixel positions indicated by white areas of the mask will receive the brightness adjustment. All areas in black will remain the original brightness. The mask's instructions at specific pixel locations are a form of *pixel addressing* using X,Y coordinates in our two-dimensional image frame. Pixel addressing is a software filter strategy that allows for local, isolated pixel changes.

Alpha channel masks do add to file size. They're like additional image layers, only in shades of gray and often with less detail than a continuous tone photograph. They can be either 8-bit or 16-bits, the latter offering much more granular control over mask opacity via the extended grayscale palette. Expect them to add to your overall file sizes when saving working-copy documents like PSDs. Leveraging editable selections for future use makes masking a flexible post-processing skill.

Proof of Concept: Reproducing an Aesthetic Filter Process

Effective implementations of software filters for quick and effective image processing can be found in popular social media apps like Snapchat and Instagram. Catering to a different audience, perhaps, their mobile apps include advanced image processing filters that turn a standard image into something with serious visual punch without requiring users' time or expertise. The challenge with apps' look-and-feel filters is that their inner workings are locked away in proprietary, special sauce source code. Photographers may enjoy using a particular filter without knowing how to reproduce it with traditional image processing tools on the desktop. We set out to explore a method of deconstructing and emulating existing filters so that they can become a regular part of our photographic workflow.

Extensive research and computer scientists are regularly finding new ways to truly reverse-engineer image processing steps with nothing more than the final result using deep convolutional neural networks.[3] Our approach here is relatively simple: take a known input image, feed it through the app processing of our choosing and compare it to the output (see Figure 10-13). This renders a processed version of the original that we like and would love to have as an image processing preset in Adobe Photoshop Lightroom for future use.

Ending our investigation here provides limited insight. What does this filter do with colors and tones not present in this single example image? It's best to use an image target with known colors and tones that cover all possible subject content. Our deduction skills are greatly aided by an ability to directly compare and contrast, so we build a reference target and a Photoshop document to drop in the before and after versions (see Figures 10-14 and 10-15, overleaf).

Our target includes useful patches including skin tones and highly saturated colors. It also uses a tone gradient to help identify contrast and adjustments like white point or black point changes. We encourage you to make a custom target to your liking that includes similar elements to make the reverse-engineering easier. The comparison tool is simply an Adobe Photoshop document with the baseline, unprocessed target image and a layer mask that cuts out

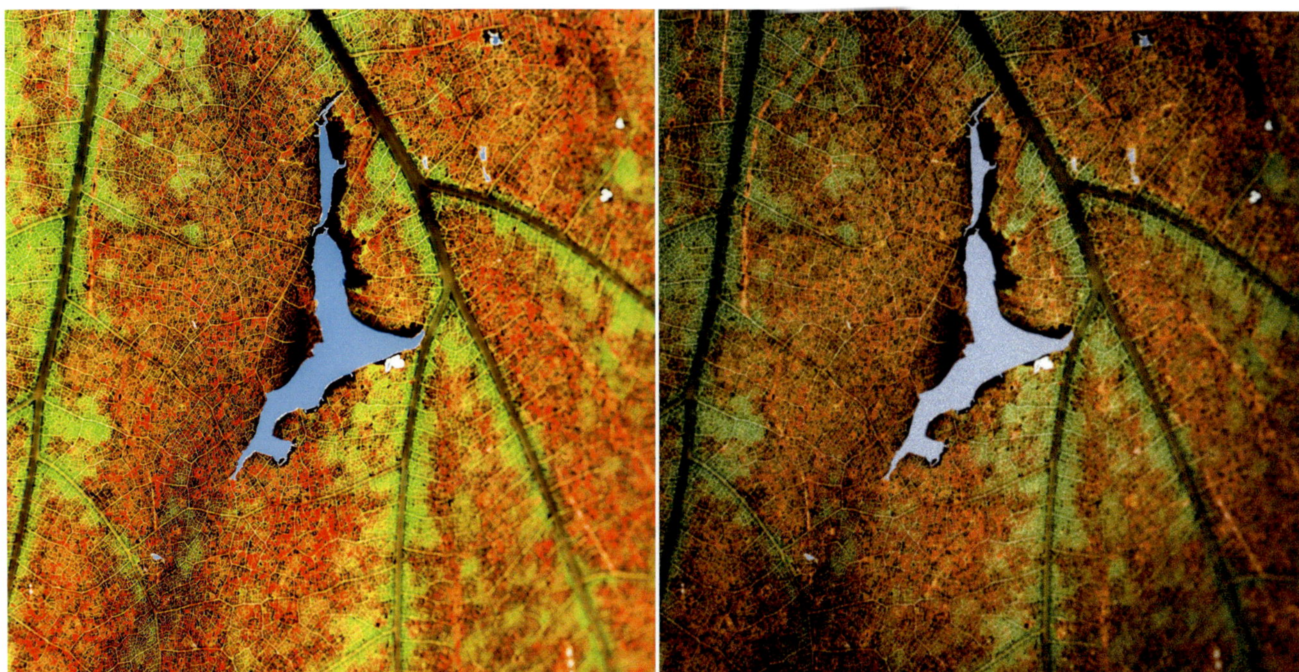

Figure 10-13 A photograph before and after the mobile app processing. We like the overall effect and recognize a few key trends in what was done, but the more precise we can reproduce it, the better.

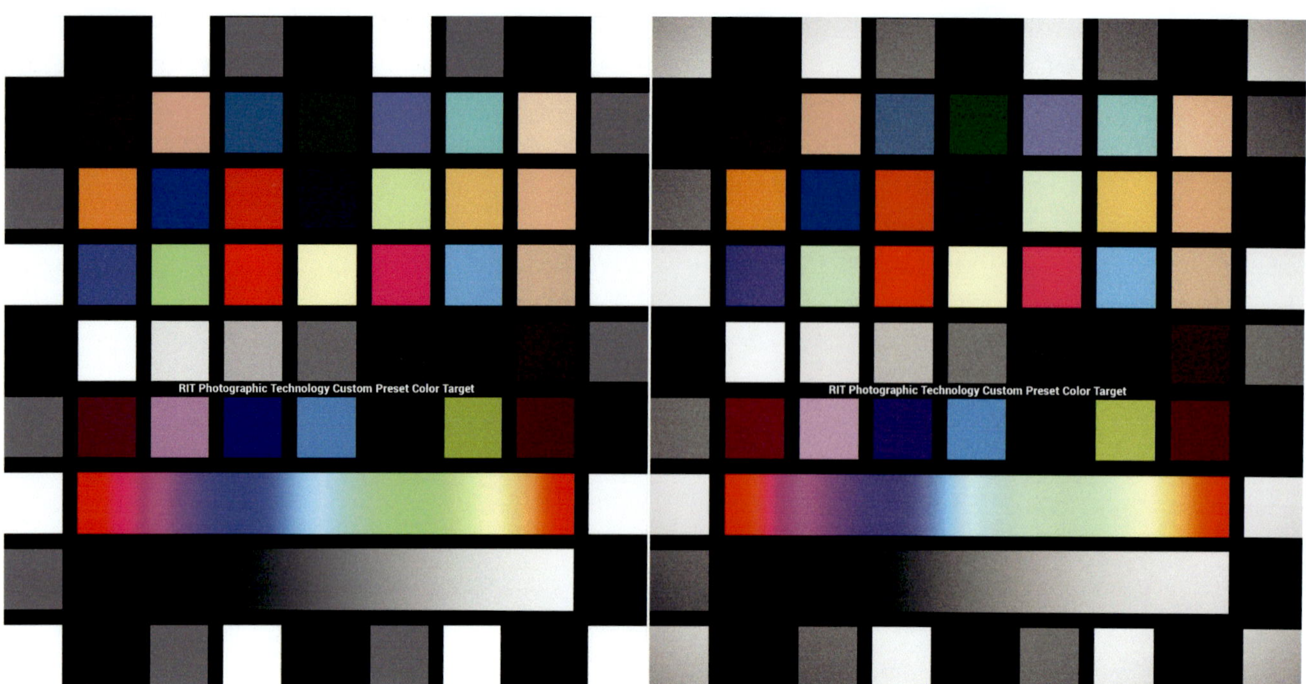

Figure 10-14 A custom reference target before and after the smartphone app filter.

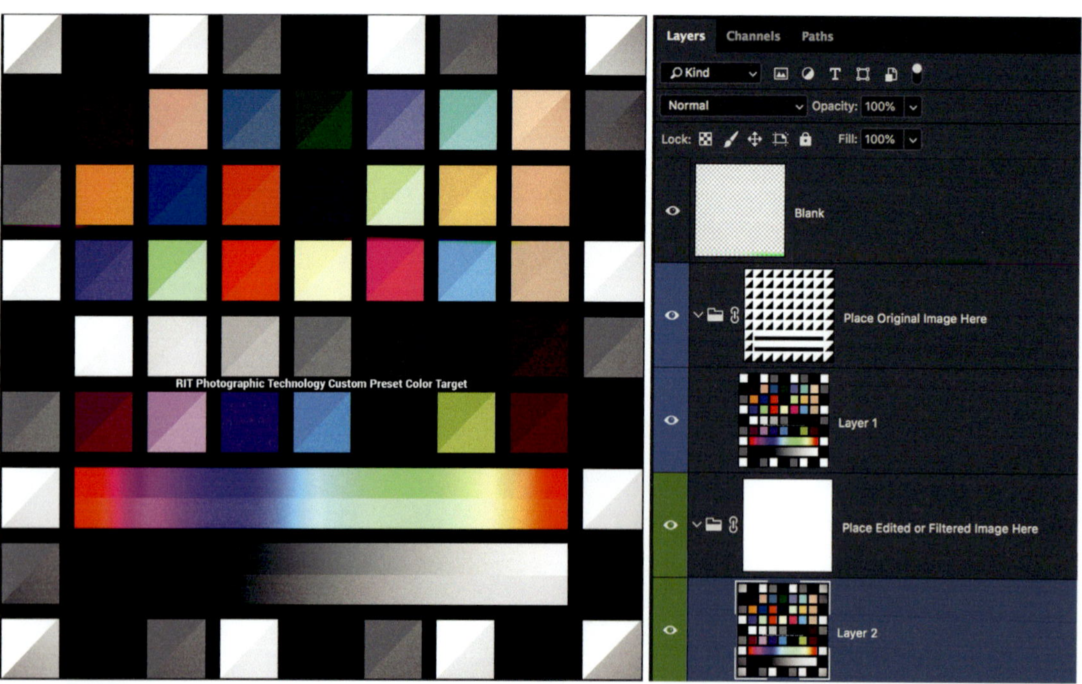

Figure 10-15 A layer mask applied to the original target image allows us to insert the processed version as a layer underneath. The mask allows the patches from both versions to appear side by side for easy comparison.

half of every patch. The layer mask hides half of the patch and leaves a transparency under which we insert the processed version of the target as its own layer. This offers a split before and after comparison of the filter effects.

Notice how Figure 10-15 reveals key characteristics of the app filter right away. The white patches in the corners get much darker and yet the lighter neutral patches near the center do not darken to the same degree, indicating a vignetting effect was introduced. The solid tone patches now show a textured noise, almost like film grain, where they were previously uniform. Color and saturation get trickier. However, using the Eyedropper tool reveals RGB and L*a*b* pixel values that Chapter 13 helps make sense of. Overall saturation appears lower and the greens and blues in particular are almost completely blanched. Pay close attention to trends in brightness as well as changes to shadows relative to highlights (like different color casts).

Try creating an Adobe Lightroom Edit preset that closely emulates the app filter effect on a photograph to see how close you can get using the raw image editing tools. These filters tend to make global adjustments to tone and contrast but very specific tweaks to color. Periodically take a version and drop it into the Photoshop comparison document. Swap out the original, unprocessed target with the app filtered image and compare it against your Adobe Lightroom interpretation. As long as we've got the ability to send an original through the black box image processing, we have this capability to compare and match results.

Strategies and tips:

- Use a comparison PSD file tool. The top half of each patch shows the "original" and the bottom half is the "processed." Look closely for changes in tone, color and texture.
- Create your preset using the color target before trying it with an example photograph, as the target patches provide a much clearer picture as to the types of changes going on.
- Do you see evidence of global or selective sharpening? What about blurring? How might you replicate these types of edits?
- Spend time in the HSL panel using the Targeted Adjustment Tool to select specific color patches and shift their hue, saturation, luminance or any combination therein. Some of these filters make extremely targeted processing adjustments.
- Make use of the Compare view mode in the Library module of Adobe Photoshop Lightroom to put your preset head to head with the real app filtered version.

Notes

1 Eismann, Katrin, et al. *Photoshop Masking & Compositing*. 2nd ed., New Riders, 2013.

2 Kost, Julieanne. "Adobe Photoshop CS blend mode magic." *Julieanne Kost Principle Digital Imaging Evangelist, Adobe*, jkost.com/pdf/photoshop/past_events/Blendmodemagic.pdf.

3 Hu, Yuanming, et al. "Exposure." *ACM Transactions on Graphics*, vol. 37, no. 2, 2018, pp. 1–17., doi:10.1145/3181974.

11 Camera Characterization and Image Quality

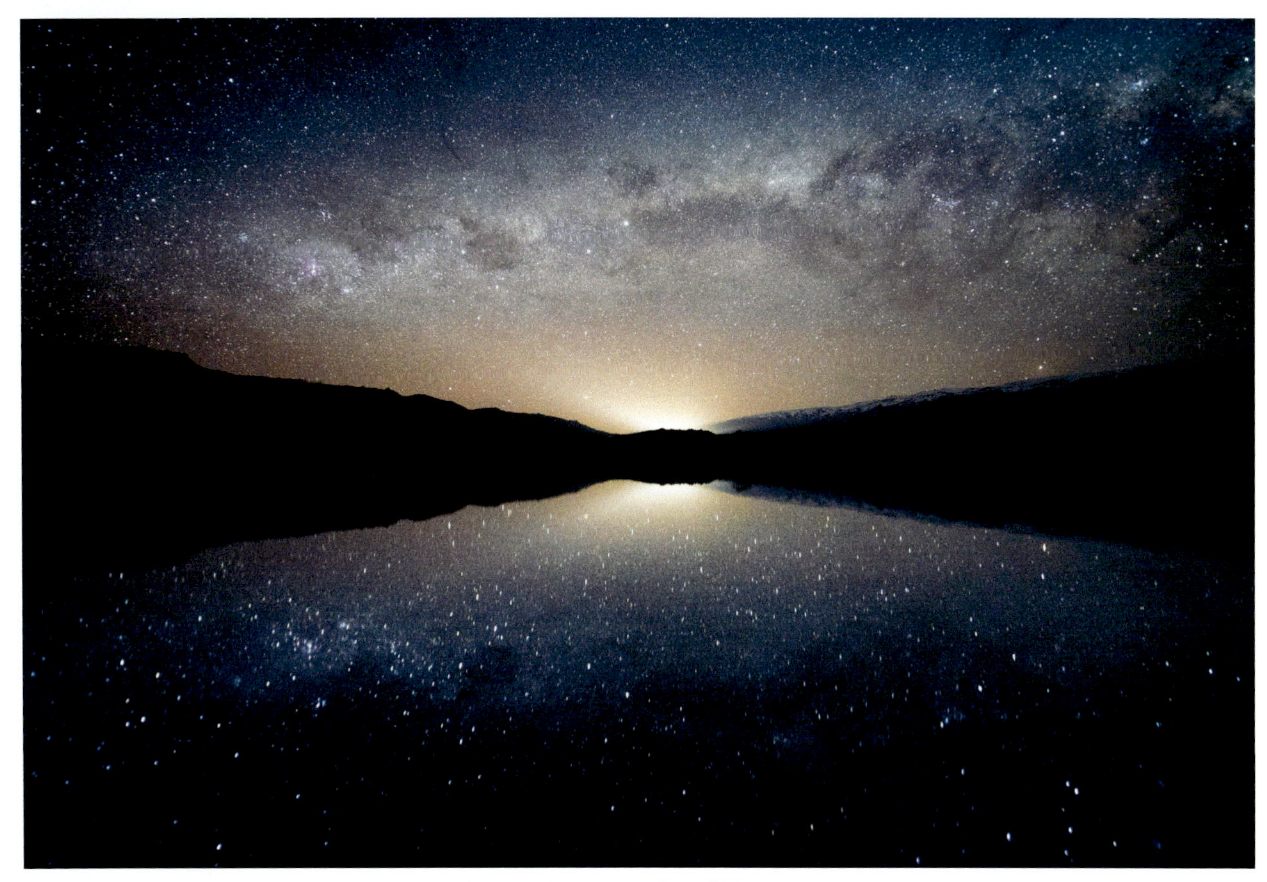

Photograph by Rochester Institute of Technology photography alumnus Dave Kelby

Image quality matters to every photographer. This chapter reviews the pillars of image quality and camera characterization to better understand the results that we get—or fail to get, as the case may be—from a camera. The state of high-quality photographic equipment today is one of abundance, yet every photographer has moments of frustration or disappointment when they see a flawed image on their screen. Characterizing an imaging system is a means of identifying its capabilities as well as its shortcomings. We start by providing an overview of an imaging system pipeline and then head straight into the many facets of quality as a function of appearance, technical accuracy and usability for photographers' image-making practices. These facets include noise, dynamic range, non-uniformities, sharpness and color.

Jonathan B. Phillips and Henrik Eliasson define image quality in their book, *Camera Image Quality Benchmarking* as "the perceived quality of an image under a particular viewing condition as determined by the settings and properties of the input and output imaging systems that ultimately influences a person's value judgement of the image."[1] We are partial to this definition because it encapsulates the many variables that impact our criteria for good image quality. It ultimately comes down to an individual's assessment and the standards set by one's use of the imagery. The judgment of both the photographer and the viewer are critical but not necessarily based on objective metrics. Modern photographers must keep one foot in the technical realm and the other in the subjective art of recording light.

The Imaging Pipeline

The earliest stages of a digital photograph's life include critical decisions, calculations and conversions in the *imaging pipeline* that dictate aspects of image captures before and after they're made. The *image signal processor* (ISP) is a dedicated computer chip in a camera that processes live preview video feeds, handles autofocus, exposure and other essential tasks. It is sometimes alternatively termed the *digital signal processor* or *image processing engine*. It takes the raw light signal detected by the sensor as input and creates a usable photographic image or video file as output. The ISP can be a dedicated piece of hardware known as a *system on a chip* or SoC. The path from light to image file displayed flows from scene to optics to ISP to storage. The pipeline includes the following steps (with variations depending on camera hardware, shooting mode and user settings):

- Automatic exposure
- Automatic focus (including face or object recognition)
- Automatic white balance
- Correcting sensor defects such as stuck pixels and non-uniformity
- Noise reduction
- Demosaicing
- Gamma correction
- Correcting lens imperfections such as vignetting or distortions
- Bracketed exposure HDR processing
- Filter effects or image processing styles
- Global and local tone reproduction adjustments
- Color space conversion
- Compression, encoding and storage

Figure 11-1 maps out a generic flow diagram for an imaging pipeline. There are some steps that circuitously repeat during capture such as auto focus; other steps may be omitted based on how the imaging system is setup before capture. Notice how the raw image bypasses many of the steps that interpret and potentially improve image quality shortcomings. These steps are instead offloaded to the post-processing stage of a photographer's workflow and are typically conducted by raw image editor software.

The Many Tasks of the Image Signal Processor

The ISP's primary jobs are demosaicing the data and managing the automatic features that work in a feedback loop to set sharp focus, proper exposure and accurate color. These are known as the *3A's*: auto focus, auto exposure and auto white balance (AF, AE and AWB). These are highly

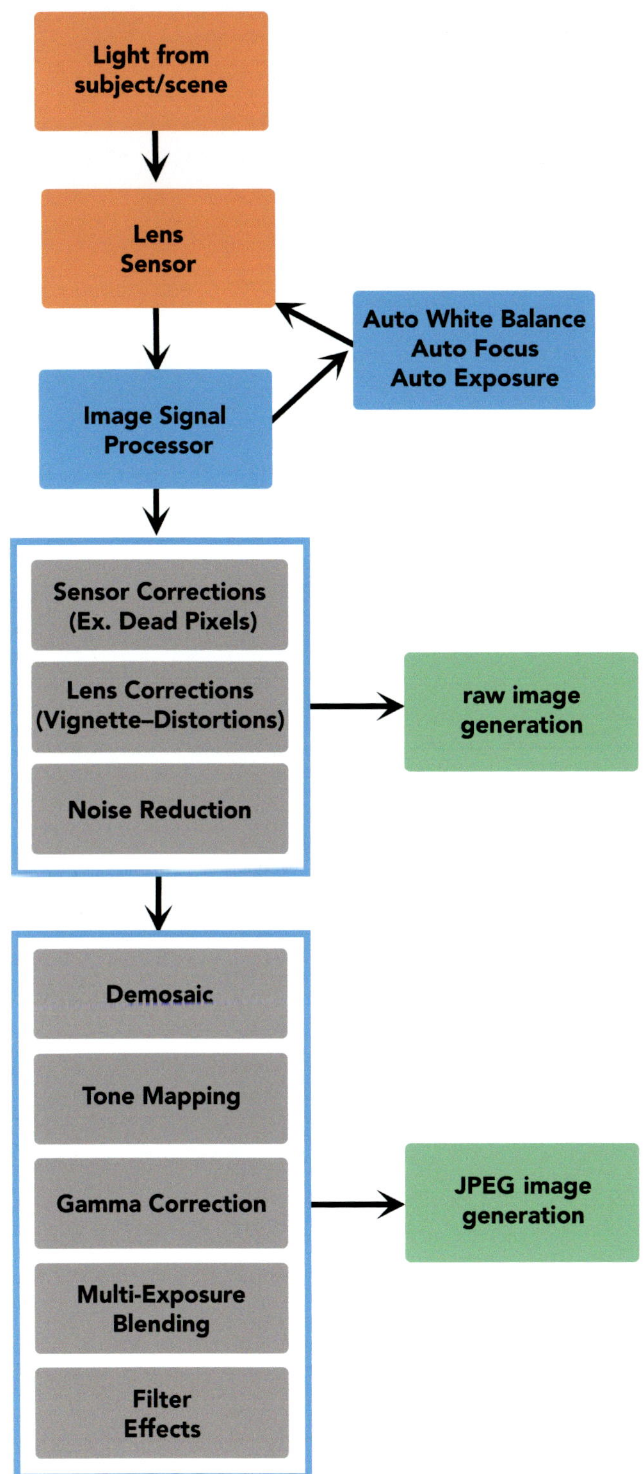

Figure 11-1 The imaging pipeline from scene to image file.

active behaviors, particularly when photographing events or environments with rapidly changing lighting, subject distance and camera movement. In smartphone camera systems where automatic functions and ready-to-share image assets are desired immediately after capture, the ISP can be additionally responsible for face detection, red-eye reduction and other output processing steps. The ISP constantly calculates statistics from the incoming signal to compute informative information about brightness, color and sharpness just to name a few.

Photographers generally consider the raw file to be the purest, no-processing-added form of image data in the life of a photograph. This is true from a post-processing perspective because raw files stop short of making permanent, irreversible editing decisions. However, raw files are truly minimally processed image data given that some decisions are made by the ISP before saving out the data to file. Decisions at the earliest stages of a digital image's life must be made immediately, including signal amplification, analog to digital conversion and automatic estimations for white balance. Truthfully, most photographers shouldn't get in the weeds with this degree of signal processing and are better off picking up where the basic image processing pipeline ends: when we've got a viewable, full color expression of minimally processed data.

The ISP has work to do following image capture even if the output is a raw image. A raw file includes an embedded, processed JPEG for on-camera preview and for desktop file browsers. The details of the JPEG processing chain depend on the camera and any previously established user settings (compression quality, noise reduction, sharpening, filter effects). Pipelines designed for consumer and professional cameras alike aim to match human perception.

ISP Task: Auto White Balance

Automatic white balancing algorithms additionally evaluate the signal strength of each channel and apply analog signal gain to the signals that it deems necessary to boost. If it assumes a *gray-world*, that is, that every scene has an average midtone reflectance, then its job is simply to apply a fixed gain to the channels. Complex automatic white balancing algorithms rely on deeper data analysis or estimated guesses about subject content and lighting conditions from which to draw conclusions about the most accurate relationships between red, green and blue signals. This can be done prior to the analog to digital conversion to minimize noise but is frequently also adjusted following A/D conversion.

ISP Task: Black Level Subtraction

A form of noise reduction also happens prior to demosaicing. Here the image black point is set. *Black level subtraction* determines an offset for every photosite so that when zero light is received, zero signal is recorded. Noise reduction is then applied. Aggressive noise reduction can reduce image sharpness and detail rendered by the optics. Noise will always be present in every image due to the nature of electronics and its forms are discussed later in this chapter. The system risks perpetuating and potentially exacerbating noise if noise reduction is left until after demosaicing.

ISP Task: Stuck Pixels

Just like with television or phone screens, it's not uncommon for the occasional photosite in an array of many millions to get "stuck" or suffer from manufacturing defects. In a screen, this appears as a *stuck* or *dead pixel*. In a photograph, a sensor's equivalent is a single pixel with a stuck value that never changes from image to image (it is not necessarily black). This is a sensor defect. Fortunately, cameras can evaluate their sensors for these shortcoming and mask or hide them before writing photosite data to the raw file. Another solution is to map and document the coordinates of these photosites as instructions for the demosaic algorithms to specifically interpolate from neighboring pixels so as not to perpetuate the junk pixel data. The larger the image sensor, the more opportunities for flaws during manufacturing, which in part contributes to higher price tags for larger sensors.

ISP Task: Demosaicing

Demosaicing occurs next and then global adjustments can be made. We outlined the process of demosaicing and interpolation in Chapter 7. Many DSLR cameras offer some control over key parameters such as sharpness, contrast, saturation and color tone. These adjustments are applied to the image prior to saving the JPEG image. If the camera has picture style presets to choose from such as landscape, portrait, neutral or faithful, the selected style adjustments are applied at this stage. These interpretations of the raw image data are non-destructive and reversible on the raw file but baked into its preview JPEG until a new one is rendered and saved by desktop software. Demosaicing may also leverage insight into stuck pixels to interpolate around them.

ISP Task: Compressing and Saving

When a capture is made and the earlier tasks are completed, it follows that the image data must be saved to memory. Raw files are created and written to solid state storage or sent over a data connection to another form of storage; they contain the mosaiced image data along with metadata from camera firmware and the ISP. This includes exposure information and timestamps. Writing JPEG image files requires applying a JPEG compression algorithm and output sharpening. JPEG quality must be set prior to capture in the camera firmware. More recently, cameras offer raw file variants that feature lossy compression or reduced spatial resolution. Data corruption or loss is likely if this step is interrupted or the RAM buffer fills before the images can be permanently saved. The processor speed combined with the available RAM buffer can dictate the volume and duration of rapid-fire burst exposures it can sustainably process and store.

ISP Task: Video Recording

The ISP also handles video capture in imaging systems that support it. Video capture is a computationally and memory intensive task to maintain throughput at frame rates of 24 frames per second or higher. The ISP will typically subsample the image sensor to determine the 3A's and to provide the user with a live preview stream. The ISP can also handle video stabilization and compressing the video stream with a specified codec, though encoding may be handled by a dedicated graphics processing unit (GPU) once handed off by the ISP.

Characterizing a Camera

Understanding the flow of light information and the many tasks handled by the ISP fosters an appreciation for how many facets of hardware and software work together to function as an imaging system. Characterizing a camera means different things to different people; here, we are interested in determining the performance of an imaging system as identified through testing. This can be done with expensive targets, lighting and software, or, alternatively, with a ColorChecker, some affordable or printed-out targets and your image editing software of choice. Characterizing is about knowing the capabilities and limits of your equipment so that you know what to use when and to pave the way for effective post-processing. The rest of this chapter highlights key areas of camera performance that photographers should explore with their hardware.

Testing Sensor Linearity

CCD and CMOS image sensors provide a linear output. Simply put, this means that doubling the number of photons collected by a photosite also doubles the output pixel brightness values. This characteristic is invaluable when using a sensor for scientific, quantitative purposes. It also allows for combining multiple exposures to extend the dynamic range of a sensor for high dynamic range scenes. However, the linear response of our image sensors does not match the human visual system's detection and perception of light intensity.

Notably, the linearity of a sensor cannot hold at low light levels where the signal can be overtaken by the noise present in the camera electronics. This is further complicated in low light situations when higher ISO settings are used. The increase in gain amplifies both the signal and the noise.

A photographic image with a linear response would appear unnatural. Gamma correction is applied to all photographic images in the processing pipeline as a result. The image data may be converted to a different color space such at CIELAB before gamma correction. Around the same time as linearization is some form of tone mapping to optimize the image data in a subjectively pleasing way. The tone mapping is designed primarily for JPEG assets as they are considered a final output version. Tone mapping and tone reproduction at both the global and local levels were discussed in Chapter 9.

The result of one method for testing sensor linearity is shown in Figure 11-2. Gamma correction must be turned off. Begin by setting up a ColorChecker target with even illumination. Focus and frame to fill the camera field of view with the target. Capture a raw exposure series from very underexposed to very overexposed to obtain the entire range of digital counts. DCRaw is free software that can convert the raw files to 16-bit linear TIFFs. Record and plot the pixel values for the white, midtone gray and black patches against the captured exposure times. These plots help to indicate if the sensor behaves in a linear fashion: changes in exposure time should closely match the change in recorded pixel values. A linear regression was fitted to

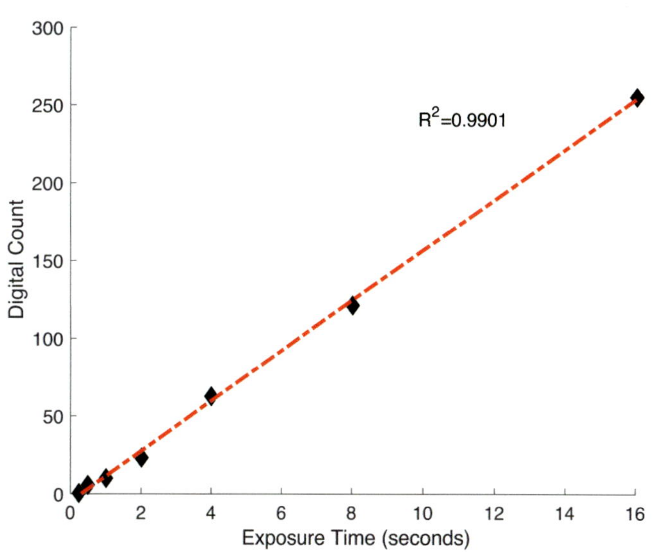

Figure 11-2 A linearity check for the red channel. The data is taken from the midtone gray patch on a ColorChecker. Each channel should be examined separately.

the data so the R^2, goodness of fit value, helps to determine if the camera is performing linearly.

Evaluating Bright and Low Light Performance

DSLRs and other technically inclined cameras offer a range of selectable ISOs. They commonly range from ISO 100 or 200 up to 6400, with most offering extended sensitivities as low as 50 and as high as 409,600. Keep in mind that even though those numbers seem incomprehensibly huge, each doubling of the ISO value equates to a single stop of sensitivity, therefore ISO 50 to 409,600 is a 14-stop range. The *native ISO range* tends to be around the 100–6400 bracket; this range is where the manufacturer tested and evaluated image quality to be very good with minimal offensive noise characteristics. The extended ISO settings are available for more extreme lighting scenarios and photographic exposure flexibility. They also come with the caveat that the results exchange increasing sensitivity for decreasing image quality.

Chapter 4 established that ISO is a function of signal amplification because the true, native sensitivity of an image sensor is fixed. Though a range of 100–6400 is standard, the sensor's inherent sensitivity likely falls somewhere around ISO 100, give or take a stop. It is this native sensitivity that theoretically offers some of the best performance of the camera sensor. Evaluating performance here means shooting in bright light conditions, either natural or with artificial sources, and confirming proper exposure. Bright light conditions represent a best-case scenario and allow for setting lenses to moderate aperture openings and relatively fast shutter speeds.

Offering a lower-than-native ISO setting like ISO 50 requires some engineering creativity. When used, the camera intentionally overexposes and pulls the exposure back in firmware. The consequence is decreased dynamic range with less perceptible noise in shadows regions relative to the native ISO exposure equivalent because the tones are brought down.

On the other end, extending the ISO is achieved by pushing the camera sensor to the high end of its signal gain capabilities and then extrapolating the data to higher ISOs. This often causes quality-degrading levels of noise, though it may be acceptable when the alternative is entirely missing the shot. Some cameras only offer extended ISO settings when shooting JPEGs due to the additional firmware processing the image undergoes in-camera. A good rule of thumb is to only resort to the extended ISO range when there is no other option (a noisy photo may be better than none at all). Extended ISO modes can also affect contrast, dynamic range, sharpness or resolution.

Evaluating the performance of both bright and low light performance of an imaging system means shooting across the range of available ISO settings and lighting conditions while keeping a close eye on accurate exposure, sharpness and image noise.

Categorizing Image Noise

It's easy to bring to mind what noise sounds like when referring to audio: it's not something pleasant, desirable or constructive. The same applies to photography's flavor of noise; the less the better. Visually, *image noise* appears as static-like pixel values that speckle areas that should be smooth, continuous tones and colors. A basic form of image noise can be described as "salt and pepper" in appearance. Any variation from the signal we intend to capture is a form of noise. Recall that most image sensors employ red, green and blue filters over individual photosites to record light. The image file that results after capture and demosaicing contains luminance data across three color channels corresponding to this same red, green and blue set. The materials used to make the color filter array over each photosite, combined with the inherent sensitivity of the photosites themselves, mean that the red, green and blue signals are not equal when recording a scene illuminated by white light even if it's a perfectly gray scene. This is accounted for in the analog to digital conversion process whereby the photosites with lesser sensitivity (i.e. the blue filtered photosites) are amplified more than the green filtered photosites. This is in an effort to reduce a color bias or color cast in the full color image. The lesser

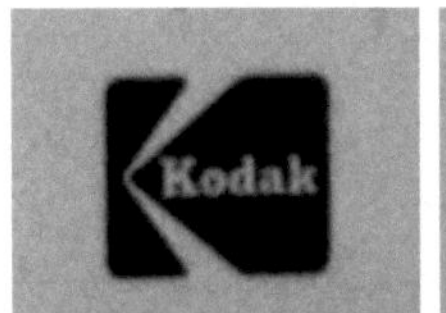

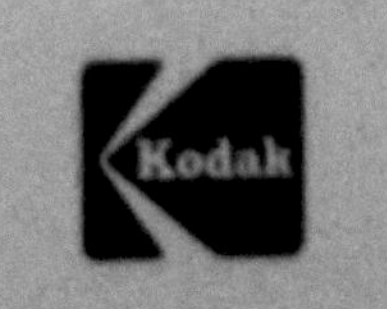

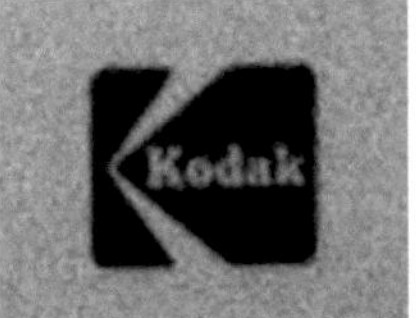

Figure 11-3 Luminance noise differences between red, green and blue channels. The surround is a midtone gray, meaning that the subject reflected equivalent amounts of light across the three wavelength bands.

sensitivity, followed by the signal's relatively increased amplification mean that the blue channel in a photograph can exhibit a greater amount of noise than the other two (seen in Figure 11-3).

It's convenient to talk about noise as a singular, visual artifact in our photographs. However, that generalizes a collection of activities happening in our imaging system. There are different types: fixed pattern, dark, read and photon noise. Visual noise shows variations in luminance (brightness) and variations in chroma (color).

Fixed Pattern Noise

Fixed pattern noise is named for the way that it appears in an image: as an ordered, structured pattern along rows or columns in the image array (see Figure 11-4). If we photograph a uniform source where each photosite receives the same amount of light, the resulting image should have the same pixel value everywhere. That is not the case when fixed pattern noise is present. There are two causes of fixed pattern noise, *dark signal non-uniformity* (DSNU) and *pixel response non-uniformity* (PRNU).

DSNU is seen when taking an image in total darkness (or with the lens cap on). We expect every pixel value to be

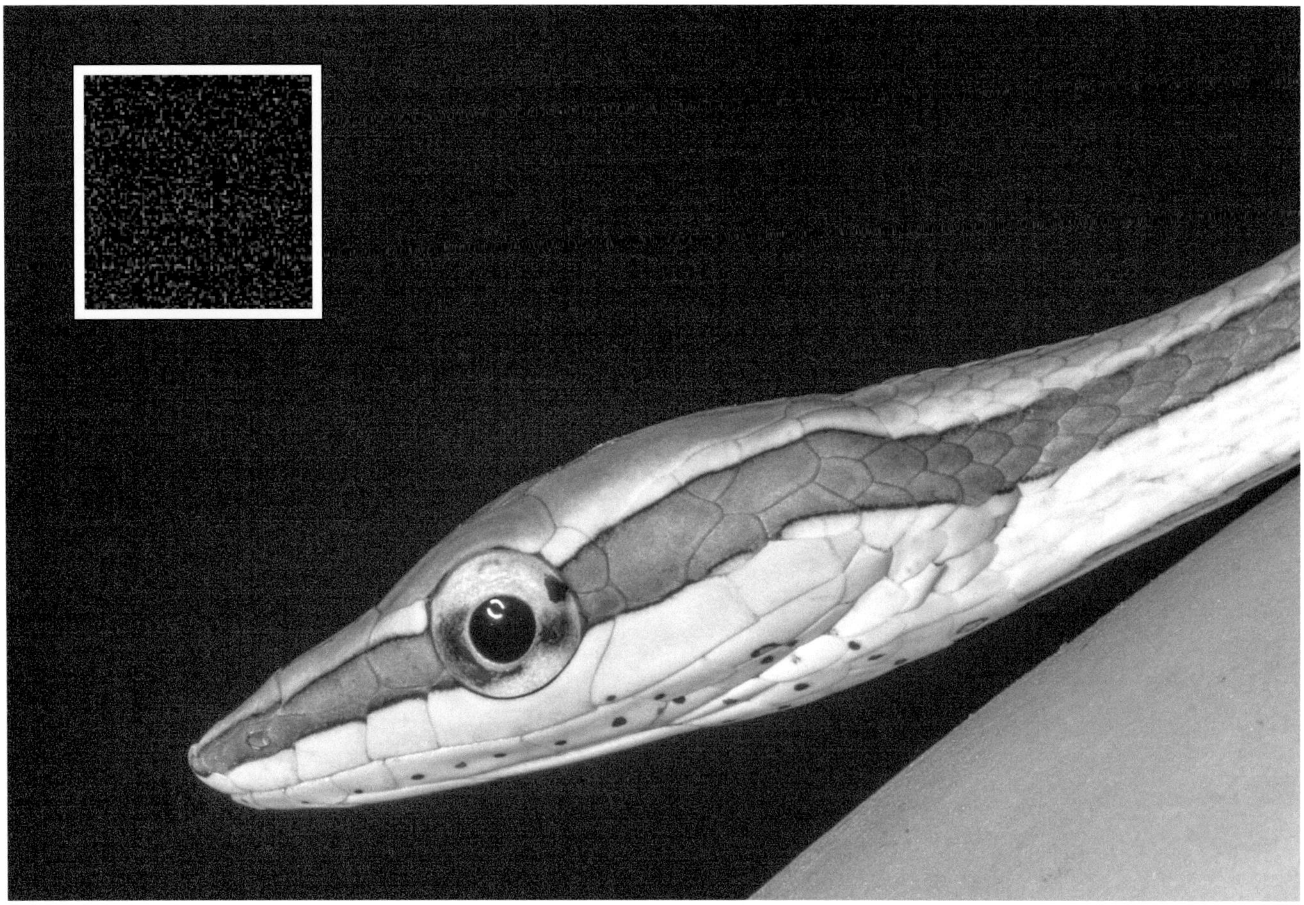

Figure 11-4 Fixed pattern noise seen in underexposed areas of an image. This photograph's shadows are boosted to show the noise characteristics.

zero, however, DSNU presents as an offset between zero and the actual pixel value. DSNU noise can be removed by subtracting a dark image (one taken in total darkness with the shutter closed) from the captured image. A dark image may be taken in a fraction of a second before the true exposure in order to provide the ISP with a baseline reference point. Causes of dark noise are discussed in the next section.

PRNU is due to each photosite's slight variation in response to the same amount of light. We expect each photosite to detect and record the same digital count when exposed to an equal number of photons, yet the reality is not so exact. The variations that occur between photosites is due to an inherent heterogeneity in sensor manufacturing; it can be corrected by applying an offset and gain to each pixel.

Dark Noise

Dark noise (also called *thermal noise*) is the variation in digital count resulting from thermally generated electrons within a pixel. Electrons accumulate over time and are recorded as signal by the photosite, ultimately introducing noise in the image. The amount of dark noise present is dependent on temperature: the lower the temperature, the lesser the thermal noise. Some digital backs feature fans to keep sensor temperatures low. In scientific applications where low light levels are an issue, such as astrophotography or microscopy, there are multiple techniques used to lower the sensor temperature to minimize dark noise including heatsinks and liquid cooling. Longer exposure times causes dark noise to become more prominent as the camera electronics heat up.

Read Noise

Read noise is the most prevalent noise in our camera systems. It is generated by the camera's electronics, particularly the analog to digital (A/D) converter. This noise is introduced into the image signal during the readout processes. Read noise is highly amplified when shooting at high ISOs and is therefore the type we often see when shooting. It can appear as chroma noise, or random variations in color, as well as luminance because the filtered photosites are demosaiced and it's difficult to identify the true color signals that failed to record clearly. Read noise affects the dynamic range of a camera; reducing the read noise lowers the minimum number of photons needed to detect a signal. This results in higher dynamic range in the captured image. Special designs of the electronics can minimize read noise for low light imaging applications.

Photon Noise

Photon noise (also called *shot noise*) is brightness variations recorded due to the randomness of photons hitting the photosites. Imagine setting up four buckets side by side and dropping 100 ping-pong balls above them. A perfect distribution of ping-pong balls would have 25 land in each bucket. That is not likely to occur in reality, though. There may be 24 balls in one bucket, 26 in another and 25 in the remaining two. Photons and the photosites detecting them exhibit this same characteristic. The flow of photons from a light source over time follows a Poisson distribution. This fluctuation of photons results in random variance noise in the image. There is no direct method for correcting this image quality artifact beyond averaging pixel values in uniform areas.

Signal to Noise Ratio

There is always going to be a degree of noise, both luminance and chroma, in a photograph. Instead of considering noise in isolation, it's measured based on the *signal to noise ratio* (SNR), that is, the amount of noise present relative to the amount of signal. The measurement does not delineate between the types or sources of noise as outlined earlier, it simply provides a measure of variance. Noise becomes less visually apparent and distracting with a very strong signal. A high value for SNR means there's a lot of good image information relative to the noise, while a low SNR value means the opposite: any useful signal recorded by the camera is getting drowned out by random noise, obscuring our subject. The base or native ISO of a camera sensor is set by most manufacturers such that the black level is

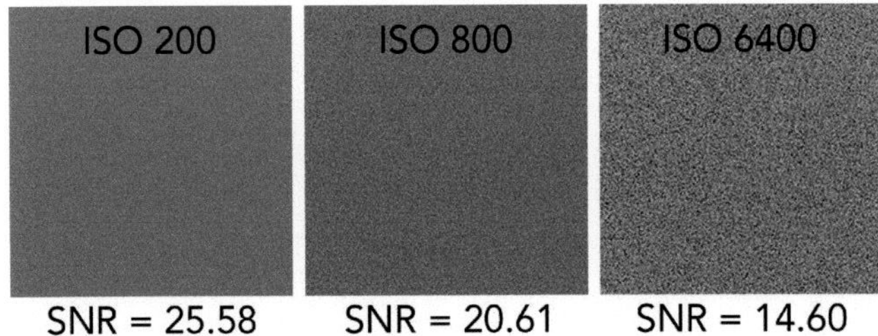

Figure 11-5 The amount of noise in a raw image file as ISO increases, sans noise reduction.

just above the point where noise becomes objectionable. The signal to noise ratio is measured in *decibels* (db) as it describes a form of noise power. The SNR of an image cannot be improved after capture (if "signal" is defined as the original signal we hoped to record), only made worse. Noise reduction algorithms are a valuable means of minimizing the visual appearance of noise, though they are effectively introducing blurring or interpolation to the image data. In this way, noise reduction filters or processing can further degrade detail if aggressively applied. Equation 11.1 offers a basic SNR calculation assuming we can measure the mean pixel values and the standard deviation in a uniform portion of an image:

$$Signal\ to\ Noise\ Ratio = 20\,x\,log\left(\frac{Mean}{Standard\ Deviation}\right) \quad \text{(Eq. 11.1)}$$

Figure 11-5 shows the quality and appearance of noise at three ISO settings when photographing a gray card. The SNR values are calculated below the samples. Note that larger SNR values mean higher signal and therefore lower noise. There are other approaches to calculating signal to noise ratio taking other variables into account. We tend to use this simple equation to get a general sense of pixel variance in our images.

Delineating Noise from Graininess

The terms *noise* and *grain* are often used interchangeably in describing image characteristics. This stems from analog film's equivalent to digital photography's image noise, though they are not the same. All films have grain. *Graininess* occurs because film's light recording abilities come from microscopic, light-sensitive crystals suspended in an emulsion. The crystals are the image building elements of a photograph just like photosites are for a digital sensor, however, the crystals are randomly distributed. The appearance of grain increases with higher ISO film because the crystals are made larger for better low light sensitivity. These larger crystals are more visually apparent and resolved to the human eye at normal viewing distances and look like static, speckled variations of tone. Your eyes notice the texture just like you can feel the difference between ultra-fine powdered sugar on funnel cake and coarse, granular sugar crystals sprinkled on a muffin. Film grain truly is the observable grains of silver halide crystals. Digital imaging, on the other hand, develops different types of noise as the gain or sensitivity increases. It is different because it is not a reflection of any changes to the photosites and it is a uniquely digital artifact.

There are post-processing algorithms available to minimize digital noise. Figure 11-6 (overleaf) shows a high ISO capture with considerable luminance and chroma noise visible upon zooming in. Software controls for lessening the appearance of both offer sliders dictating noise reduction strength, thresholds or tolerances for how much variation is considered noise and even edge-preserving filtering. The background area is greatly improved from a noise reduction standpoint, though aggressive reduction can easily smooth out true high frequency detail and leave the subject looking overly soft and featureless.

There are occasions where digital image noise is preferred, even if it's not entirely desirable. Random variations in color and luminance help to disguise posterization in smooth-toned areas like the sky at sunset. Posterization is visually distracting, as the discrete jumps in color or tone are distracting when the transition should be gradual and imperceptible. Adding a bit of noise (or restraining from applying noise reduction) makes posterization artifacts less obvious or degrading to the perceived image quality. We can avoid the possibility of posterization by capturing and editing image data at higher bit depths.

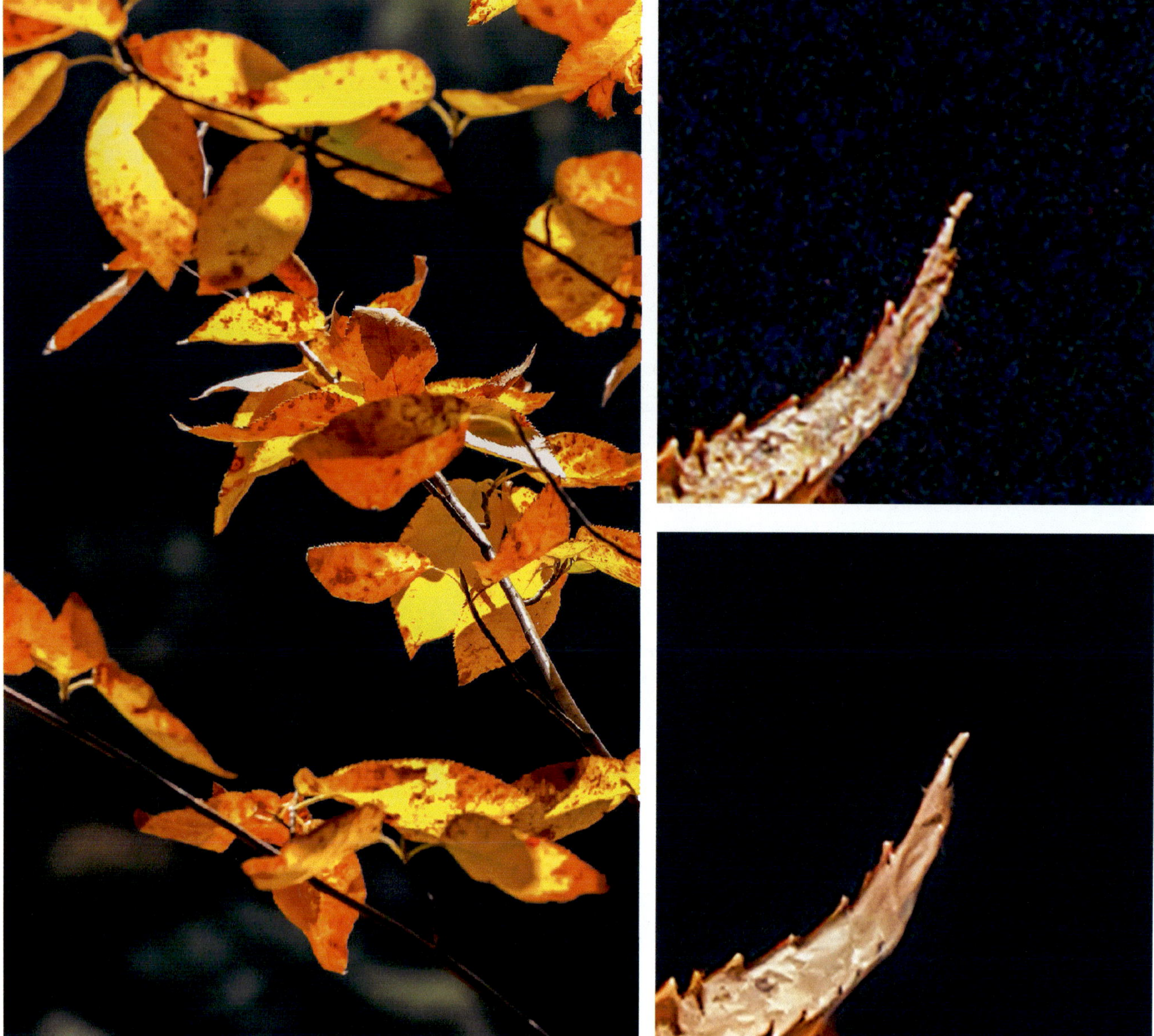

Figure 11-6 A photograph captured at ISO 12800. The close crops show before (top right) and after (bottom right) luminance and chroma noise reduction.

Considering Sensor Dynamic Range

Recall that bit depth dictates how many distinct tones are available to describe brightness. Bit depth and dynamic range go hand in hand even though they are not precisely equivalent characteristics of a camera system. Scene dynamic range is the range of brightnesses present, from the deepest shadow to the brightest highlight with detail, that we aim to record. *Sensor dynamic range* is the range of tones from a scene that the camera actually records. Sensor dynamic range is largely dependent on a sensor's bit depth—its ability to delineate and record a wide range of photon signals and then convert that to digital values. A sensor with a small or limited bit depth is unable to record a scene image with a large tonal range of incoming signal. Therefore, we practically consider that bit depth dictates the potential dynamic range of a sensor.

The camera manufacturer states a sensor's dynamic range performance in an ideal situation and can therefore be misleading. In real-world use, the lens adds flare, the IR-blocking and anti-aliasing filters add blur and noise is always present. These elements lessen the overall dynamic range of the image formed on the sensor which effectively lowers the recorded bit depth. Sensor dynamic range is also a function of sensor design and sensitivity: a sensor that can successfully record unique values for 150 photons versus 160 photons, for example, can exhibit better low light recording capabilities. We've made up these numbers but consider the principle; a sensor that is finely attuned to low amounts of signal but that can also handle huge deluges of photons in bright light makes for a wide dynamic range recording instrument.

Note the distinction between potential recorded bit depth and file bit depth. Like a bag of potato chips, the bit depth supported by the file is not necessarily maximized by the data stored within it. A bag of chips might be twice the size relative to the volume of chips, a disappointing but necessary design that gives the fragile food an air buffer for transport. File bit depth simply tells us the supported range of tones that could be stored if they exist in the scene. Otherwise, that extra space is padded. Unlike a bag of potato chips, we have the power to fill our image file when needed.

Raw image files use between 12 and 16 bits to store capture data (purely brightness information, not yet demosaiced into color channels). It's impossible to distinguish between a 12-bit or 16-bit file by eye, so we rely on software to tell us exactly what data we've got. An image with 12–16 bits of information equates to somewhere between 68.68 billion and 281 trillion possible colors. It is estimated that humans can see approximately 10 million colors.[2] The additional headroom is critical for editing and processing decisions to prevent artifacts like posterization and banding. A numeric representation of brightness and color, even if it's too granular for our eyes to see, has implications for the mathematical operations applied to that information. The characteristic of bit depth by itself does not inherently indicate any measure of quality. On the

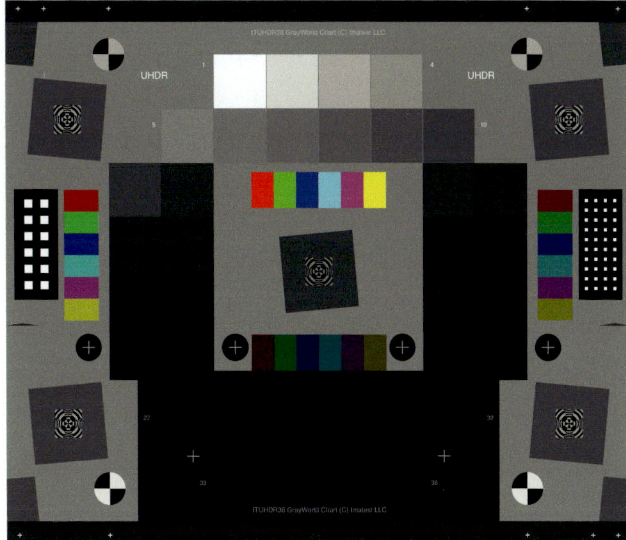

Figure 11-7 A standard test chart from ISO 12233. (Image courtesy of Imatest LLC)

other hand, image quality is more likely to be maintained or maximized through the image processing workflow if higher bit depth information is preserved throughout. This is particularly true any time that tone changes or remappings are introduced.

Testing dynamic range is challenging. In a laboratory setting, a calibrated step wedge such as the ISO 12233 standard test chart shown in Figure 11-7 can be used. It features a set of neutral tone patches spanning a wide tonal range. A measured system dynamic range is specific to a single lens, sensor and ISO setting combination and the dynamic range achieved in a laboratory is nearly always larger than what is achieved in the real world. Real-world testing can involve a wide dynamic range scene and a spot meter to calculate the range (in stops) of light levels successfully recorded with detail.

Identifying Non-Uniformities

There are multiple types of non-uniformity in an imaging system and all have potential mitigations to minimize degradations to image quality. Pixel response non-uniformity is a form of noise described earlier due to the variation from photosite to photosite in its response to incoming photons. We ideally want all of the photosites to exhibit near-identical responses and recordings of light across the sensor array. *Focus non-uniformity* is any inconsistency in how the optics form an image on the image plane (look back to Figure 2-42 for one example). We typically desire an optical system that provides a sharply resolved image at the center as well as at the corners and everywhere in between. Measuring a lens, described later in this chapter, helps to identify focus non-uniformity. *Luminance non-uniformity* is an inconsistent light level across the image plane due to one or more types of vignetting. Here again, we ideally want to have an even rendering of a flat field. Finally, *color non-uniformity* is an inconsistency in color recording across the image area and is most commonly the result of filtering and oblique angle light.

Optical vignetting is a result of light bending around the aperture in the lens. The result is less light reaching the far edges of the image plane. The degree of optical vignetting is lessened when the aperture is wide open relative to when it is stopped down. The smaller aperture opening causes the light to bend more severely, introducing more light fall-off. Mechanical vignetting is the result of a physical obstruction in the light path such as a lens hood or a filter that is not large enough for the lens. Pixel vignetting is caused by the physical depth of each photosite. It is more difficult for the light to reach the photosites at the edge of the sensor. This image quality artifact is often compensated for by the ISP by boosting the signal in local areas of the frame.

Both optical and pixel vignetting can be modeled by imaging a flat field (a subject with uniform reflectance). This provides software with a roadmap of brightness non-uniformity from which to counteract. Once the effect is modeled, it can be digitally corrected. This must be done for every lens used with a given camera and at every aperture setting.

Non-uniformity in color is another potential image quality problem in an imaging system. Color non-uniformity is also called *lens cast* or *color shading* (see Figure 11-8). Lens cast appears as green in one corner of the image and ends as a magenta shade in the opposite corner. This results from light entering the lens and/or the color filters atop the photosites at sharp angles. This can be corrected in the same manner as vignetting in the ISP or in post-processing software assuming it has a calibration database or can dynamically detect the artifact. An image made with a white translucent material over the lens produces an image that can be used as a reference for correction.

Figure 11-8 Lens vignetting with a 50mm prime lens at f/1.2 (top). A simulation of color shading (bottom).

A related artifact can be introduced by inaccurate or overcorrection by the ISP. This can show color shading, either non-uniform or radial from the center of the frame outward. Such an artifact is effectively an image processing error attempting to resolve an optical artifact; it can be considered an inverse-color shading artifact.

Evaluating Lens Quality: Sharpness and Detail

Photographic optics are a complex network of engineering, tradeoffs and use-case considerations. Photographers may not find themselves designing a camera lens for themselves but they are likely to be critical consumers and craftsmen in search of the best tools. The following sections outline how to evaluate lenses coupled with image sensors for their image-making capabilities.

Modulation Transfer Function

The most common method of evaluating lens quality is measuring its *modulation transfer function* or MTF. The first time MTF was explained to us, the professor said that you measure MTF to determine if you paid too much for your lens! MTF measures the performance of a lens by its sharpness and contrast reproduction ability. In other words, it measures the amount of detail reproduced by a lens. Let's unpack exactly what that means in optical terms.

Optical systems including our cameras use *spatial frequency* to evaluate and report quality, telling us how many *cycles per millimeter* a lens or the system can reproduce. These cycles are alternating white and black lines whereby an image of such a pattern theoretically cycles between maximum and minimum brightnesses (i.e. white and black). A pattern of 10 lines per millimeter is used to judge contrast performance and 30 lines per millimeter is used to judge resolution.

We start by passing a perfect pattern through the system and record the output. If the recorded pattern is an exact replica, the system exhibits a perfect 1:1 contrast reproduction. If you ever buy a lens that performs this well, any amount spent is worth it. No lens is perfect in the real world, though. The reproduced pattern image has a different modulation and can be shifted.

Seems simple enough, however there are many frequencies present in an image. Low frequency information, the details in a scene, may show very little or no degradation. High frequency information, the fine details, may be severely impacted or not reproduced at all. To further complicate the issue, camera manufacturers often provide MTF performance data at both 10 lines/mm and 30 lines/mm. Published manufacturer information also includes *sagittal* and *meridional* MTF data. Measuring along these planes of an optical system identifies if it suffers from *astigmatism*, an asymmetrical blurring due to misshapen lens elements. The term is familiar to those of us with prescription glasses as our eyes can also be astigmatic. The further apart the sagittal and meridional MTF curves are, the more astigmatism present in the lens.

The obvious question remains: what is a good modulation transfer function for a digital camera and lens combination? The MTF at 10 lines/mm is usually better than the 30 lines/mm, meaning that a lens exhibits better contrast reproduction than sharpness performance. Contrast measurements are generally broken up into categories of excellent (greater than 0.9), very good (0.7–0.9) and average (0.5–0.7). A value less than 0.5 indicates a soft lens. The scale for resolution is subjective and based on how the lens is used.

Interpreting an MTF Plot

Once targets are photographed, the results of an MTF test are commonly presented in the form of *modulation transfer function curves* in which the input spatial frequency is plotted as cycles per millimeter on the horizontal axis against output contrast as percent modulation on the vertical axis. A perfect reproduction would have image contrast equal to target contrast at all frequencies. This would look like a straight horizontal line at 1.0 on an MTF plot. In practice, the lines always slope downward to the right, since image contrast decreases as the spatial frequency increases. Eventually the lines reach the baseline, representing zero contrast, when the imaging system is no longer able to detect the luminance variations in the test target. The advantage of modulation transfer functions is that they provide information about image quality over a range of frequencies rather than just at the limiting frequency as does resolving power; there are also disadvantages. For example, photographers cannot easily prepare their own modulation transfer functions and the curves are more difficult to interpret than a single resolving-power number. MTFs are most useful for comparison purposes.

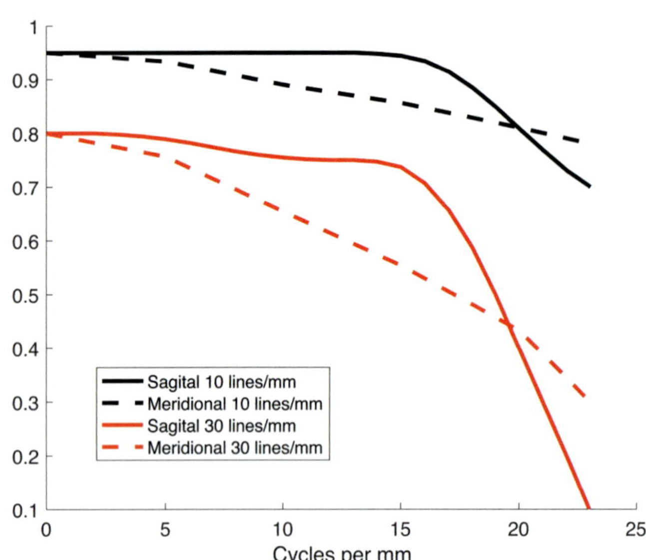

Figure 11-9 An MTF plot of a lens at f/16.

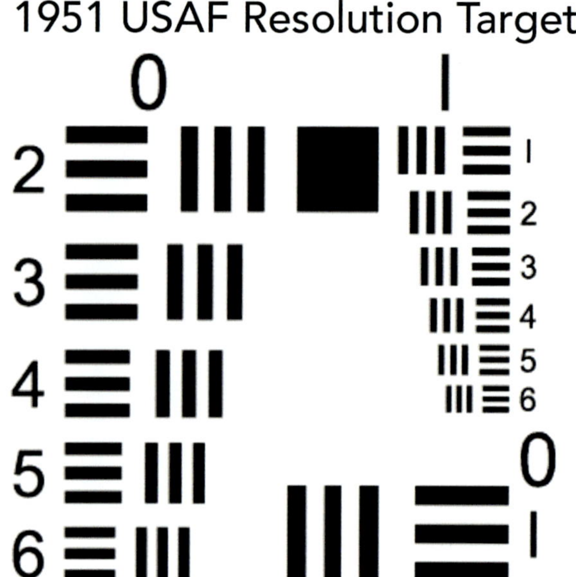

Figure 11-10 A United States Air Force (USAF) Resolution Target.

Representative curves for a single lens and camera at ISO 100 are shown in Figure 11-9. These MTF curves show that the lens tests exhibit some astigmatism as the sagittal and meridional curves diverge away from the center of the lens. Recall that the 10 lines/millimeter data represents contrast performance and 30 lines/millimeter data represents resolution.

Furthermore, *resolving power* is not a reliable indicator of the appearance of sharpness of photographic images. Resolving power is a widely used yet controversial method of checking image definition. The testing procedure is simple. The lens is focused on a row of a resolution target placed at a specified distance from the lens featuring alternating light and dark stripes as shown in Figure 11-10. The separate targets are arranged so that the images fall on a diagonal line on the sensor plane with the center target on the lens axis and oriented so that the mutually perpendicular sets of stripes constitute radial and tangential lines. Resolving power is measured as the maximum number of light-dark line pairs per millimeter that can be resolved.

Critics of the resolving power metric note that different observers may not agree on which is the smallest set of stripes that can be resolved and that in comparing two lenses, photographs made with the higher resolving power of the two sometimes appears less sharp. In defense of resolving power, studies show that observers can be quite consistent even if they don't agree with other observers. Consistency makes their judgments valid on a comparative basis such as between on-axis and off-axis images, images at two different f-numbers and images formed with two different lenses. It's appropriate to make comparisons between lenses on the basis of resolving power as long as it's understood that resolving power relates to the ability of the lens to image fine detail rather than the overall quality of the image.

Shooting to Evaluate Image Definition

Testing image definition requires the following:

1. The subject must conform to a flat surface that is perpendicular to the lens axis and parallel to the sensor plane.
2. The subject must exhibit good detail with local contrast as high as is likely to be encountered and contain a variety of colors.
3. The subject must be large enough to cover the angle of view of the camera and lens combination at an average object distance.

4. The subject must also be photographed at the closest object distance.
5. Photographs must be made at the maximum, minimum and at least one intermediate aperture opening.
6. Care must be taken to place the optimal image focus at the sensor plane, which may require bracketing focus.
7. Care must be taken to avoid camera movement, noting that mirror action in SLR cameras can cause blurring especially with small object distances or long focal length lenses.

If the same subject is used to test for image shape, it must have straight parallel lines imaged near the edges of the sensor to reveal pincushion or barrel distortion. If it's also to be used to test for uniformity of illumination at the sensor plane, it must contain areas of uniform luminance from center to edge. Tests for flare and ghost images require other subject attributes. A practical test cannot be overly simple if it's going to provide useful information about the lens. Evaluation of the results is easier and more meaningful if a parallel test is conducted on a lens of known quality for comparison.

Practical tests such as these are not truly lens tests. Instead they are systems tests that include subject, lens, camera, sensor, exposure, onboard processing and the output medium (display or print). The advantage that such tests have of being realistic must be weighed against the disadvantage that tests of a system reduce the effect of variations of one component, such as the lens, even if all the other factors remain exactly the same.

Assessing Color Accuracy

Reproducing color accurately is a complex issue. A display and a printer can be profiled and calibrated to ensure that the system is doing the best it can do to match what we see on the screen to what we see on the print. So what part does the camera play? Veteran shooters often talk about one brand or model rendering colors to their tastes more than a competitor, though this is highly subjective and largely anecdotal. Cameras are not typically profiled, as we would need a profile specific to every camera sensor, lens, ISO and light source combination. In other words, a camera profile is needed for every unique configuration and shooting scenario. This is a realistic option for studio photographers with a highly consistent setup—shooting product shots with the same lens and lights everyday—and lens profiling software exists to serve this niche. Lens profiling can mitigate color inaccuracies as well as non-uniformities and optical distortions.

Calculating Color Difference

Those of us with a fleet of lenses, multiple camera bodies, varying subject matter and organic lighting scenarios need another option. We lean on our trusty ColorChecker to evaluate color differences between a subject and its reproduction. Setting up the ColorChecker with uniform illumination, setting a custom white balance and shooting a perfectly exposed image in both raw and JPEG formats provides us the opportunity to evaluate how a camera system reproduces color. The ColorChecker patches have known, published CIELAB values though we can also measure them ourselves with a spectrophotometer. Using these and reading the color patch CIELAB pixel values from the raw image file allow us to calculate *Delta* E_{ab} (or ΔE_{ab}) differences. Delta E_{ab} is a measurement of the difference between two samples (see Equation 11.2). A value of approximately 2.3 is considered a just noticeable difference when using this metric.[3] We can do the same with the captured JPEG to observe the color reproduction choices made by the camera ISP's JPEG processing. From this exercise we can work to correct major color inaccuracies if present.

$$\Delta E_{ab} = \sqrt{(L_R - L_O)^2 + (a_R - a_O)^2 + (b_R - b_O)^2} \qquad \text{(Eq. 11.2)}$$

Where

L_O, a_O and b_O are the CIELAB values of the original target patches

L_R, a_R and b_R are the CIELAB values of the image reproduction

The ΔE_{ab} metric presented here is just one possible ΔE measurement to consider depending on the intent of your color accuracy assessment. Delta E_{ab} is a simple distance measurement in the three-dimensional CIELAB color space. The CIE recommends a ΔE_{00} (Delta E 2000) which is much more computationally rigorous and places heavier weight on luminance over chroma and hue values.

White Balance Accuracy

Chapter 4's overview of photographic exposure parameters included the role of white balance. Consciously setting the white balance before capture can help in accurately recording and representing color. Doing so means estimating or correctly determining the dominant light source type in the scene, a degree of human insight, logic and context that camera software alone cannot reproduce. Our visual system also benefits from color constancy where colors appear correct no matter the light source. Automatic white balance (AWB) algorithms leverage the incoming light information detected by the sensor photosites. One software strategy employs a *gray world assumption*, the premise that all scenes and subjects are neutral and should reflect or absorb light by the same amount. If this premise is true, then there should be equal signal received across all three channels of color image data (red, green and blue). If one of these channels records less light, signal gain is introduced to boost it up to the level of the other two. This behavior is true for all three channels; the goal of the algorithm is to end up with the same signal strength in all three. Figure 11-11 illustrates this approach in action, starting with an image with an inaccurate white balance. Taking an average of all pixels shows a decidedly blue color cast that is corrected to a neutral gray by changing the color channel's tone reproduction.[4] Making this same adjustment to the image results in a properly white balanced scene. Try this with your own images to learn that this works in some instances but does not work in many others.

Another strategy is to identify common patterns like the distribution of tones in a classic landscape composition and use an internal database to find the closest match. Building this database can be the difference between a good AWB algorithm and one that regularly fails. Machine learning and object recognition software is increasingly leveraged to make decisions on white balance. For example, face detection can send automatic image processing and color reproduction down a path of prioritizing the accurate reproduction of skin tones. Consider how such artificial intelligence insights that mimic those conscious and contextual decisions made by photographers might improve AWB performance. A photograph featuring a close-up of red autumn leaves causes an over-compensation in cyan when employing a gray world assumption algorithm. A system that interprets pixel patterns and recognizes the shapes and colors as leaves or recognizes the broad strokes of an outdoor landscape, and not simply

Figure 11-11 Averaging all pixels in this image reveals a blue cast. Correcting this averaged version to be neutral provides a channel adjustment applicable to the original image.

a collection of mostly red pixels, might instead choose to settle on a warmer white balance. Shooting ColorChecker target reference images is always an excellent backup plan for challenging lighting environments to ensure accurate color reproduction.

Calibrating Autofocus

Front-focusing or *back-focusing* are problematic behaviors where the camera's autofocus puts the focused image just in front of or behind the sensor plane. If this behavior is observed across different lenses, it's likely a camera problem that is fixable with a simple calibration process. If it's exclusive to one particular lens in your loadout, it might indicate a problem with optical element alignment (maybe from that time you dropped the lens and thought everything was fine) which could require professional repair.

Recall that the primary method of automatic focus on the traditional SLR camera involves a dedicated, phase detection sensor receiving a reflected, secondary image from the primary mirror. Micro-adjustments can be necessary if the phase detection sensor is receiving a slightly different version of the image that reaches the image sensor during capture; they tell the algorithms to bias their findings by a user-determined offset. Mirrorless systems or using contrast autofocus methods are not as likely to require such calibration.

Autofocus micro-adjustments are the solution to the first problem and luckily, professional cameras offer calibration settings in their firmware. Using an alignment tool such as LensAlign can assist in determining if a lens and camera combination is properly focusing. A focus calibration chart features a ruler at a 45° angle relative to the camera; instructions for do-it-yourself, inkjet-printed ones can be found online. We use the one shown in Figure 11-12. Capturing an image of such a target using your camera's single-AF point mode can identify any front-focusing or back-focusing behavior and the ruler offers useful visual landmarks. The camera firmware offers manually-set micro-adjustments in the forwards or backwards direction to compensate for any observed inaccuracy in where the auto focus position lands. Reshooting the target after an adjustment can confirm that the automatic focus is hitting its desired focus distance every time. The steps to identify and correct focusing errors are as follows:

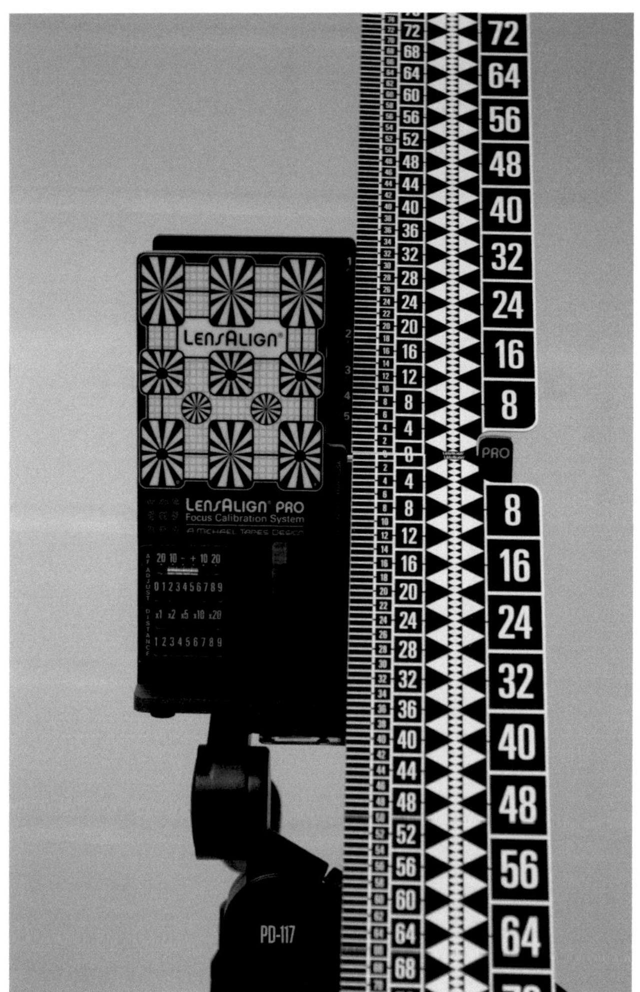

Figure 11-12 A lens alignment chart.

1. Setup camera on a tripod
2. Set the camera AF mode to single point
3. Focus on an evenly illuminated test target positioned at 45° relative to the camera
4. Capture at the widest available aperture
5. Evaluate the image at 100% zoom. Check if focus is in front of, behind or at the center mark on the target
6. Tweak AF micro-adjustment in camera firmware menu (plus or minus)
7. Repeat steps 3–6 until focus discrepancy is resolved

Similar to this method but perhaps a bit more difficult to execute involves using a resolution target mounted perpendicular to the camera. The image of the target can then be examined for sharpness and any focus non-uniformity. This method requires some guesswork to determine in which direction the system is mis-focusing.

Considering Your Imaging Tools

Sensor specifications, lens performance and everything else in this chapter are interesting topics in isolation. There are also additional image quality areas that extend beyond what we've offered here. At the end of the day, what matters is the combination of equipment, settings and image processing that come together in your photographic practice. Most photographers have multiple cameras and knowing which one to use in which situation is key to creating the perfect image in every situation.

Testing tools like Adobe Camera Calibration uses a checkerboard target and accompanying Lens Profiling software can make quick work of identifying image quality shortcomings of your system (focus, distortion, light fall-off, chromatic aberration). This is a great option for the photographer that lacks the resources or time to dive into more exacting measurements. Resources like DxOMark are valuable when looking for new equipment or to generally understand how camera systems can be tested in-depth.[5]

Characterizing your camera system means knowing its low light limits, its focusing accuracy, its detail resolving power and the numerous other image quality aspects described in this chapter. No system is perfect and our take on camera hardware prioritizes facilitating good image makers rather than any purely objective, on-paper performance. We use our cameras every day and always keep perspective that these are artistic tools with deep engineering and technological foundations.

Proof of Concept: Comparing Noise Characteristics of Two Cameras

Evaluating noise characteristics in a camera is a great way to make objective comparisons across sensors while also offering an opportunity for subjective analysis. The following exercise can reveal the upper limits of sensor sensitivity for your personal tastes. Your camera might have a super high ISO setting that isn't worth considering when adjusting exposure variables if it produces a distracting amount of noise. Photographers ought to feel comfortable knowing what sort of quality they can expect from their camera hardware when working in limited light environments:

1. Set the camera to collect raw images. Turn off all in-camera noise reduction. Do not assume that the default settings exclude noise reduction.
2. Place the camera on a tripod. Arrange a scene with a ColorChecker target and any props that are relevant to your shooting practices.
3. Capture a properly exposed image at each available whole stop increment of ISO. We exclude "low" or "high" settings in our example. Adjust shutter speed while varying ISO to create equivalent exposures to keep image brightness the same throughout. Figure 11-13 shows close crops from our sequence.
4. Ingest the captured set and open the raw files into Adobe Photoshop. Navigate to *Window > Histogram*. In the upper right-hand corner of the histogram window is a pull down; select *Expand View*. This shows mean and standard deviation readouts.
5. Use the rectangular marquee selection tool to select a square area within the gray patch of the ColorChecker.
6. Measure and record mean and standard deviation values from the Histogram window. Repeat for the black patch on the ColorChecker and for all raw captures in the set.
7. Calculate the signal to noise ratios for both patches: *SNR = 20*log(mean/standard deviation)*.

We calculated SNR values for our Camera A and Camera B across a range of ISO settings. For example, at ISO 200, Camera A shows a gray patch luminance value mean of

Figure 11-13 A lineup of gray patches from ISO 100–6400 captured by two cameras.

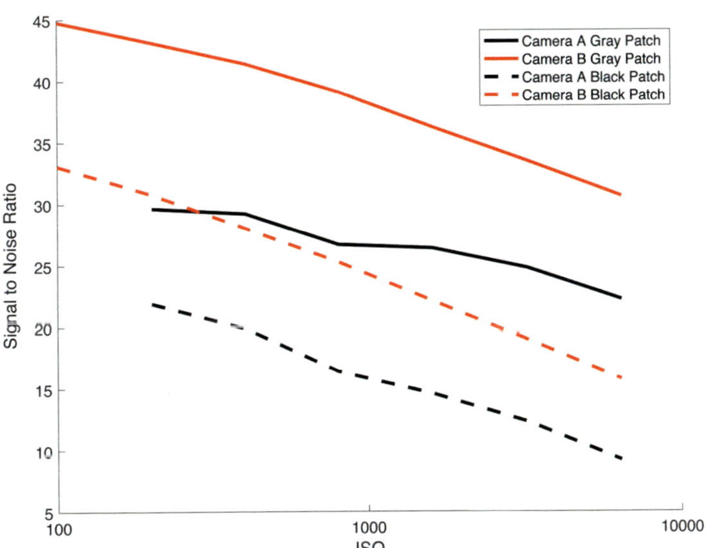

Figure 11-14 Plotting SNR values of Camera A and Camera B for gray and black patches across a range of ISO settings.

176.64 with a standard deviation of 5.82. This calculates to a SNR of 29.64. Setting up a spreadsheet to calculate the set of recorded values considerably speeds up this exercise. Plotting this data with an x-y scatter is visually intuitive (see Figure 11-14).

We observe that Camera A records the neutral patches at consistently higher signal to noise ratios at every ISO compared to Camera B. For example, Camera B at ISO 200 has roughly the same amount of shadow noise as Camera A at ISO 1600. This is consistent with our understanding that larger pixels are generally better at gathering light: Camera A is a full frame, high-end DSLR while Camera B is an older mirrorless crop sensor. Camera B has smaller photosites packed into a small sensor size footprint relative to Camera A and noise performance is a clear area where it serves as a disadvantage.

Visually examine the gray and black patches in your photographs at each ISO and for each camera. Consider the following questions:

- At which ISO does the noise become objectionable? Is luminance or chroma noise more distracting or degrading to image content?
- Do the numbers make sense when comparing the two cameras given their hardware differences?
- Is the relationship between ISO and noise in midtones and shadows linear?
- Are the noise levels the same in the gray patch compared to the black patch?
- How might you capture images to discover fixed pattern noise in a camera?

Notes

1 Phillips, Jonathan B. and Henrik Eliasson. *Camera Image Quality Benchmarking*. John Wiley & Sons, 2018, p. 29.

2 "Color in business, science, and industry." *Color in Business, Science, and Industry*, by Deane Brewster, Judd and Günter Wyszecki, Wiley, 1975, p. 388.

3 Sharma, Gaurav. *Digital Color Imaging Handbook*. CRC Press, 2017.

4 Abell, Mark. "White balance, part 2: The gray world assumption and the Retinex Theory." *The Refracted Light*, Sept. 15, 2011, therefractedlight.blogspot.com/2011/09/white-balance-part-2-gray-world.html.

5 "The reference for image quality." *DxOMark*, www.dxomark.com/.

12 Image Compression

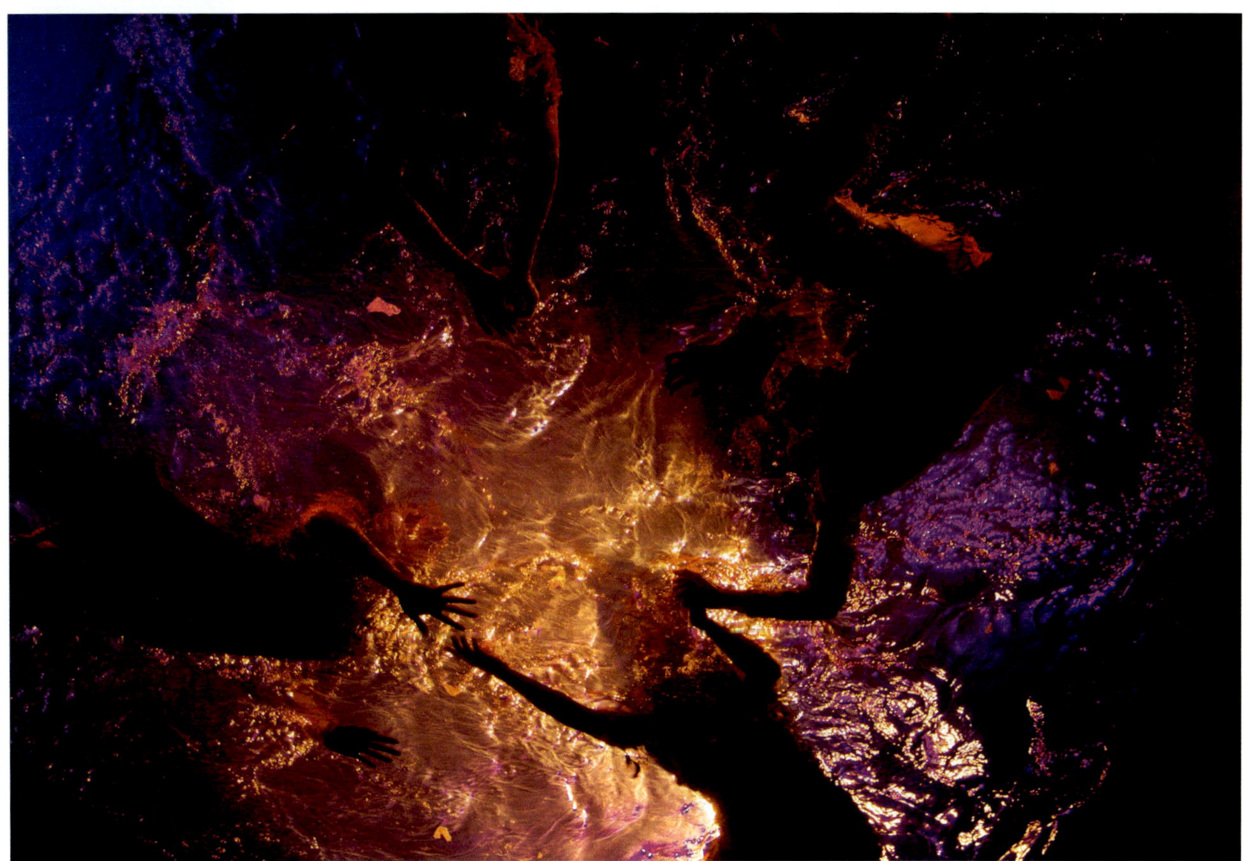

Photograph by Rochester Institute of Technology photography student Caroline Brodt

The growth and maturation of a visual medium happens when creatives are able to create, imagine, make, capture and share new work. Though purely creative types may not think of their creations as boiling down to digital data, the reality is that photographs (along with graphic design, video and audio) are built on the foundational building blocks of ones and zeroes. When we create millions of new pixels, dozens of composite layers or hours of high-definition video, the challenge of storing all of this digital information can't be ignored. This textbook has so far highlighted the hardware used to house this data (see Chapter 8 on the topic of *File Storage*) and approaches to managing it. Still, we'd drown in data if it weren't for compression techniques that help to keep files reasonably sized. Applying compression to photographic data is a key technological necessity in the digital realm. Here, we explore the details of image compression mechanisms by reviewing the concepts of information redundancy, the primary algorithmic approaches to compressing data and the potential image quality artifacts that crop up.

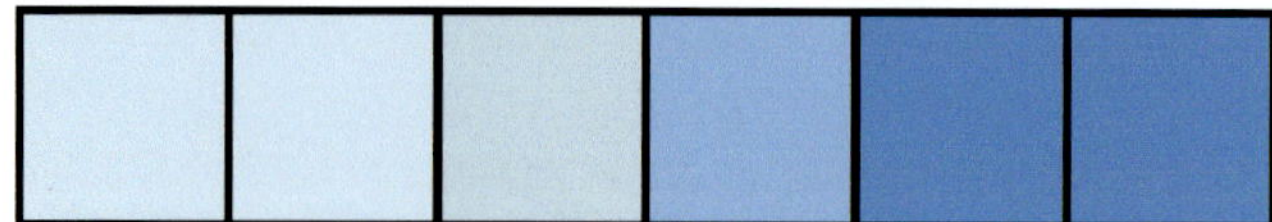

Figure 12-1 A selection of pixels from the sky in a landscape photograph.

Image Compression and Information Theory

Image compression is a little like physical compression. You pile on shirts, socks and other clothing when packing a suitcase for vacation. Sometimes you resort to sitting on the luggage to get it to close: you're compressing your clothes to fit into a container with limited space. When you arrive at your destination and open up the suitcase, all of your clothes are there and return to their original size when you take them out (wrinkled, but an iron can fix that). You just experienced lossless compression! Now imagine the same scenario with smaller, carry-on luggage. No amount of sitting on your outfits compresses them enough to fit, so you start sacrificing pairs of socks and extra shirts. This is lossy compression: you're excluding some previously available material to fulfill a stricter storage requirement. The consequence is that you won't have those abandoned items available when you get to your destination.

This example is a simplified explanation of compression but it begins to convey the challenge and the compromises of the process. Image compression is based on *information theory* which the Encyclopedia Britannica defines as "a mathematical representation of the conditions and parameters affecting the transmission and processing of information."[1] It's important to clarify the difference between *data* and *information*. Data are the binary representations of the pixel values in an image. Information is how the pixel values are arranged in the image frame to represent photographic content. The goal of image compression, then, is to reduce the information by reducing the amount of redundancy in the data used to convey it.

The example of packing a suitcase works because it's possible to maximize the use of a physical space by minimizing the amount of air between objects. We also accept the reversible process of our clothes getting wrinkled because we assume an iron is available at our destination hotel room. Image compression is possible because software algorithms can maximize the amount of data stored by finding redundancies and predictable patterns. It similarly assumes that software on the other end can understand some instructions or coding shorthand to make sense of the stored information. Consider a landscape photograph with a blue sky above the horizon. Zooming in close on the image file, a section of the sky might contain a row of pixels like the ones shown in Figure 12-1.

Each pixel consists of a color and brightness that defines its appearance. Storing the brightness and color information of each pixel can be accomplished in three ways: without compression, using lossless compression and using lossy compression. Imagine being tasked with describing these six pixels over the phone. You can use one of these three approaches:

1. Uncompressed: "Pixel 1 is light blue. Pixel 2 is light blue. Pixel 3 is light blue. Pixel 4 is medium blue. Pixel 5 is dark blue. Pixel 6 is dark blue."
2. Lossless Compressed: "Pixels 1 through 3 are light blue. Pixel 4 is medium blue. Pixels 5 and 6 are dark blue."
3. Lossy Compressed: "Pixels 1 through 6 are light blue."

The uncompressed approach explicitly conveys every pixel with absolute fidelity. The lossless compressed version does the same but with fewer words thanks to the layer of logic applied. The person on the other end of the phone knows that "pixels 1 through 3" describes a redundancy or repetition of light blue. The lossy compressed description simplifies the sky's subtle differences in shades of blue in the interest of brevity. It effectively compresses redundant information as long as we don't mind our sky depicted with the same light blue throughout. It cannot, however, be used to accurately reconstruct the original, varied pixel values if desired.

Image compression algorithms are much more sophisticated than the previous example yet the basic concept holds true. The lossless description mimics a common data storage technique called *run-length encoding* that stores a piece of information once and a count of how many times in a row that information is repeated (i.e. light blue pixel, three instances). The brightness values of two neighboring pixels are more often than not the same or similar, so saving a version of an image that rounds some of these similar, neighboring pixels (called *interpixel redundancy*) reduces the file size with minimal impact to image detail. Additionally, common image compression algorithms separate the luminance and chroma information and approach each with different strategies that have the best chances of minimizing noticeable quality degradation. The delicate balance of compression is in reducing file sizes without introducing noticeable, distracting image quality artifacts.

The Basic Stages of Image Compression

Image data compression exploits redundancies and limitations of the human visual system. Redundancy means excess content or information that can be discarded without it resulting in a noticeable difference to the final product. All digital images contain redundancy at the pixel level. We compress image files without noticeable loss of quality when taking advantage of these redundancies. The limitations of compression are defined by our ability to notice shortcomings or unfaithful reproductions. We could heavily compress every image and have the benefit of small file sizes but at a certain point we're not willing to trade reduced visual fidelity or quality for those gains.

Image compression is a two or three step process. The first step is often referred to as *pre-processing*. Interpixel redundancy reduction occurs during the pre-processing step. This is accomplished through run-length encoding, *differential encoding* or using *discrete cosine transform* (DCT). Run-length encoding and differential encoding are lossless redundancy reduction processes; DCT is lossy. Mapping RGB data to luminance and chrominance channels commonly occurs during this first step. When lossy compression is desired, the next step is the *quantization stage*. This is where information is removed: chrominance information and psychovisual redundancy are often reduced, driven by user input. The *encoding stage* is the last step for both lossless and lossy compression. Variable-length encoding, such as Huffman coding described later, occurs at this stage.

Finding Redundancies in Image Data

Lossless compression is appealing because there is no loss of information between compression and decompression. It is limited in effectiveness, though, because there is only so much that a lossless compression algorithm can do to lessen the file size while preserving the original information.

Spatial or Interpixel Redundancy

The digital counts or brightness values of adjacent pixels are more often than not the same or similar. If we have to guess a missing pixel value, we could do so based on the surrounding pixel values. Knowing this, it's not necessary to keep all of the pixel data to represent the image. Duplicate elements in a structure, such as the same pixel values repeated in a row of an image array, are the definition of *spatial* or *interpixel redundancy*. Greater spatial redundancy offers increased compression effectiveness. Graphic designs tend to have many redundancies since they are simplified tones and colors. Photographs of the real world are much more random and varied in pixel content, meaning that taking advantage of interpixel redundancies happens on relatively local areas rather than across large parts of an image file.

Spatial redundancy is also helpful for removing dead pixels or small dust spots. These outlier pixels are surrounded by valid image data and as such our algorithms borrow or interpolate from their neighbors. This is a highly effective process since there is a good likelihood that the

Table 12-1 The bits used in an uncompressed image compared to a compressed version of the same image.

Pixel Value Range	Bits Used (uncompressed image)	Bits Needed (compressed image)
0–1	8	1
2–3	8	2
4–7	8	3
8–15	8	4
16–31	8	5
32–63	8	6
64–127	8	7
128–256	8	8

adjacent pixels are the same color and brightness. The junk pixels are replaced with the interpolated values.

Coding Redundancy

An uncompressed 8-bit image has a fixed length in which to record each pixel value. A pixel can have a value from 0 (black) to 255 (white) in each color channel. Computers use binary codes to represent all characters. In other words, every pixel in an image array uses 8 bits, each set to either a 1 or a 0, when describing its brightness value. Table 12-1 shows the number of bits used to record different ranges of pixel values. An 8-bit file uses 8 bits for each value whether all of those bits are needed or not. For example: the binary form of a pixel value of 2 is *00000010*. This uses 8-bits to describe the value yet the same thing can be stored using just 2 bits (coded as *10* in binary). Both coding methods describe a pixel value of 2; the latter does so using less disk space. Lossless compression uses this *coding redundancy* to reduce file size.

Psychovisual Redundancy

Taking advantage of the human visual system's shortcomings is the strategy used by *psychovisual redundancy* compression. Our visual system relies more on spatial information than color information and it is more sensitive to lower frequency information than high frequency information. Subtle changes in luminance are more noticeable than the same amount of change in chroma. Some color and brightness differences fall below the threshold of our perception. Compression takes advantage of these scientifically proven insights by treating color information independently from brightness to reduce file sizes. Our greater sensitivity to luminance changes means that the eye is quicker to detect artifacts and image quality

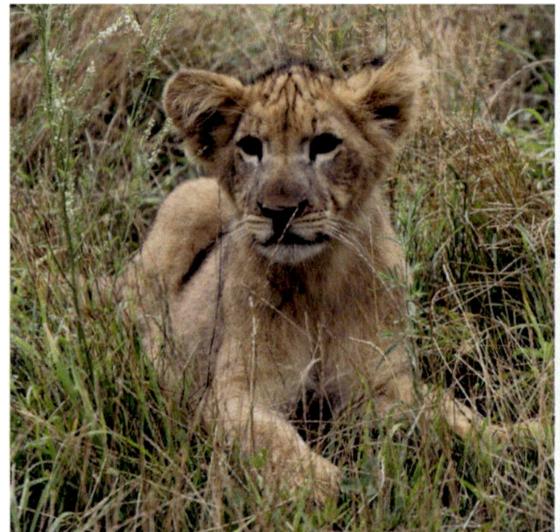
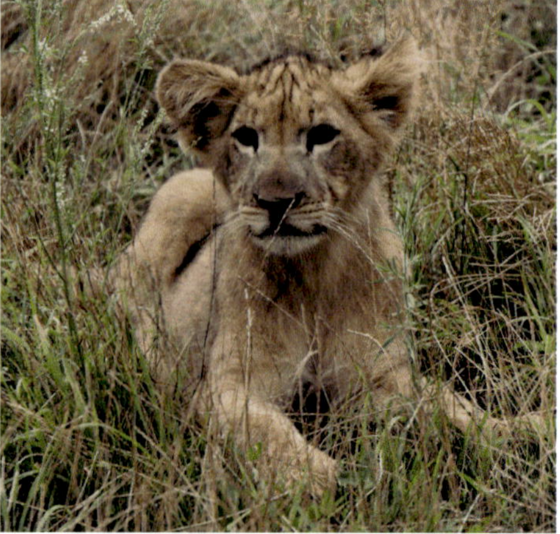

Figure 12-2 An example of psychovisual redundancy. The high frequency image on the left is represented by 8-bits per channel. The image on the right is a 6-bit per channel image. The images appear the same.

degradations if compression algorithms are too aggressive with brightness data. Figure 12-2 is an example of psychovisual redundancy.

Temporal Redundancy

Videos and short animations are comprised of images shown in sequence over a specified duration. Content from one frame to the next is often highly redundant: this is temporal redundancy. A video of a model walking down a runway shows frame after frame of the runway and the surrounding audience. The only changing content is the model's movement. The background pixels exhibit *temporal redundancy*; they are highly similar from one moment to the next and potentially over many dozens of frames or seconds. Compression algorithms take advantage of this repetition across sequential video frames. We explored temporal redundancy under the guise of intraframe compression in Chapter 6.

Compression and Scene Content

Consider two images: one with large areas of high frequency information (like the lion cub image in Figure 12-2) and another with large areas of low frequency information (like the studio still life image in Figure 12-3). Both images are taken with the same camera, saved in the camera's native, uncompressed raw format and are the same approximate file size. The images are then ingested and converted to DNGs with lossless compression. Lossy compressed JPEG versions are also generated. The resulting files from these two scenes end up being very different file sizes. The second scene includes large areas of similar pixel values which both DNG and JPEG compression strategies take advantage of to minimize data storage. The lion cub image does not have significant data redundancy and therefore does not compress well. These examples highlight that the effectiveness of compression is image or scene content dependent: some images are easier to compress than others. Both scenes can be lossy compressed to the same file size if desired, but the lion cub image is more likely to show image quality degradation from that exercise.

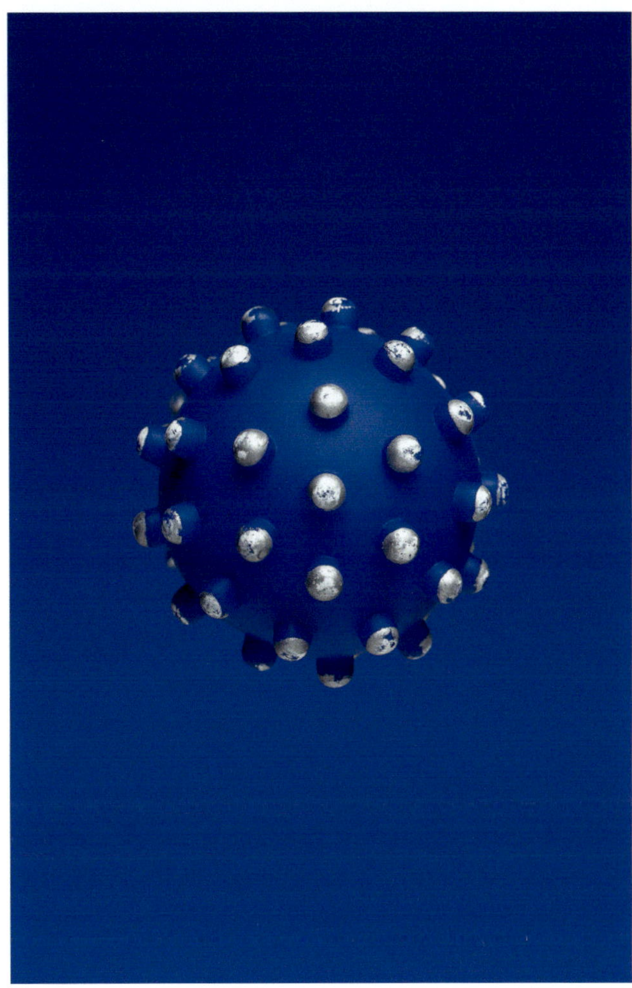

Figure 12-3 A photograph with low frequency areas is easier for a compression algorithm to efficiently compress.

Lossless Compression Approaches for Removing Spatial Redundancy

There are many methods to achieve lossless image compression without losing any original data. Three methods are described here: run-length encoding, differential coding and bit-plane encoding.

Run-Length Encoding

We started to explain run-length encoding (RLE) earlier in this chapter when describing Figure 12-1. RLE is supported by most bitmap file formats and operates under the principle that adjacent image pixels exhibit spatial

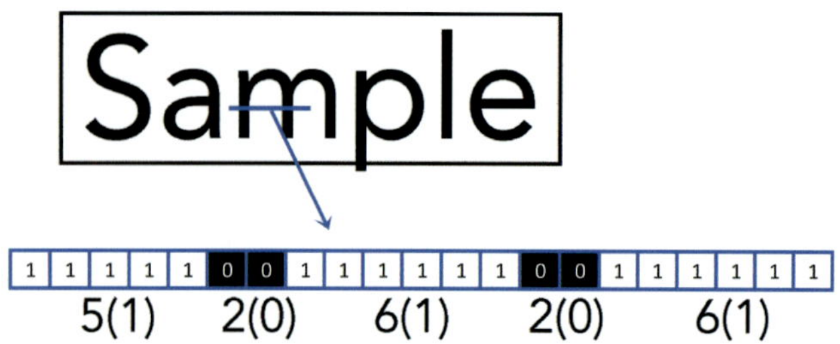

Figure 12-4 The pixel values of the blue area through the letter "m" are represented by the row of black and white squares. This string of ones and zeroes is simplified to the description below it using run-length encoding.

redundancy. This is especially true for images with graphics or text in them. This example contains large areas or runs of white (pixel value 1) with small instances of black (pixel value 0) that represent the letters. The size of the file is greatly reduced by replacing a run, or repeated string, of the same pixel value with a 2-byte representation. The first bit is the *run count* or the number of times that a pixel value occurs. The second byte is the *run value*, the value of the pixel. Figure 12-4 shows how long runs of the pixel value 1 are losslessly replaced using a run-length encoding strategy.

Bit-Plane Encoding

Another approach is *bit-plane encoding* which looks at an image as a stack of eight 1-bit images rather than a single layer comprised of 8-bit data. Recall that every pixel in an image uses 1 byte of memory. One byte is made up of 8-bits or a combination of 8 ones and zeros. Separating each bit into its own plane creates eight binary image planes, planes 0 through 7, as illustrated in Figure 12-5. So how does that help to compress the data?

We need to look back at how information is stored to answer that question. The first digit of our 1-byte number is considered the most significant bit as it contains most of the data. The first bit is 1 for all pixel values above 128 and 0 for all pixels below 128. Table 12-2 shows that the amount of information each bit represents gets smaller as the pixel values decrease. The last bit is considered the least significant bit as it often represents the digital noise in an imaging system.

When each level is reduced to a binary image, the probability that an adjacent pixel is equal translates to higher spatial redundancy. Higher spatial redundancy translates to higher compression rates. Figure 12-5 illustrates a portion of an image separated into eight separate bit planes. The first two pixels have values of

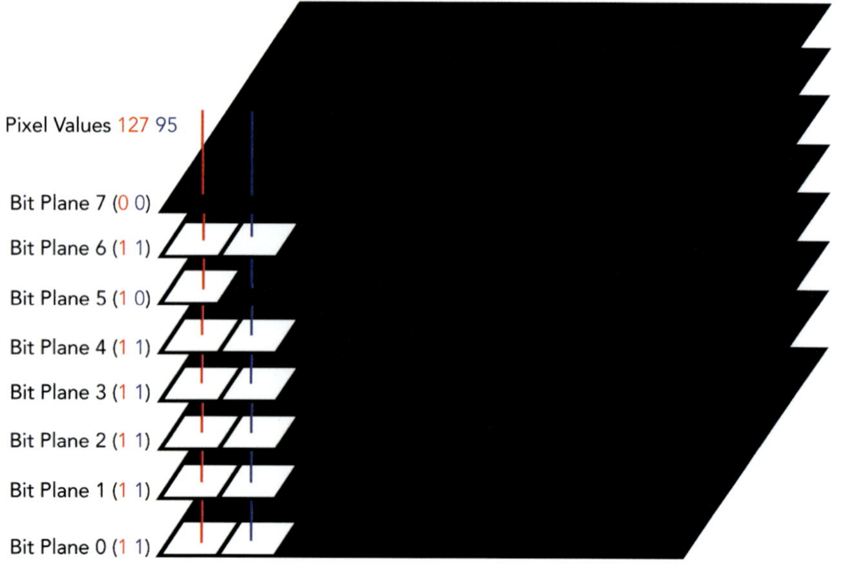

Figure 12-5 An image pixel array separated into eight bit planes. Bit Plane 7 exhibits spatial redundancy across the entire plane.[2]

Table 12-2 Binary representation of pixel values.

Decimal	Binary
128	10000000
64	01000000
32	00100000
16	00010000
8	00001000
4	00000100
2	00000010
1	00000001

127 and 95 and they are not similar in any way. The spatial redundancy becomes apparent when viewed in bit planes: planes 0, 1, 2, 3, 4 and 6 for both pixel values are the same.

Differential Encoding

The last method of reducing spatial redundancy is called *differential redundancy*. It's unlikely to find long runs of identical pixel values even when looking at low frequency areas like a clear blue sky. That said, low frequency areas have minimal variation in those values. Differential encoding takes advantage of this low variance. The first pixel value is recorded and only differences from that pixel are recorded after it. This is conducted in small pixel groups segmented from the entire pixel array. Figure 12-6 is an example of differential encoding applied to a row of six pixels starting with a value of 60. These six pixel values require 48-bits to store them uncompressed. Using differential encoding reduces this to 13-bits, a substantial space saving. High variance makes this approach much less effective since the differential might be just as big or bigger than the native value.

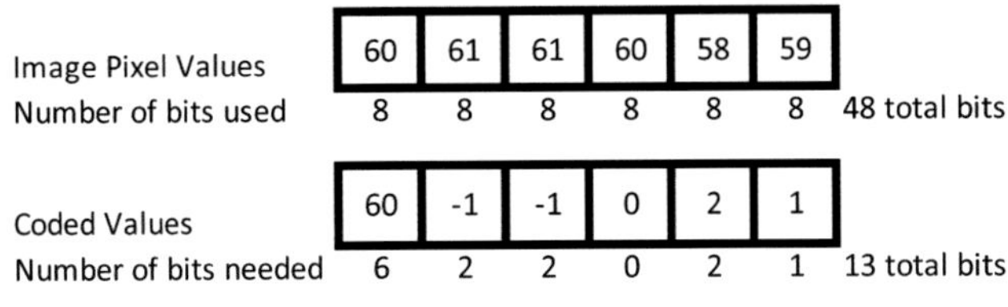

Figure 12-6 Differential encoding stores the first value in a set and then the relative difference of the values that follow. The fifth pixel value, 58, is 2 away from 60. Compared to storing the value of 58, a differential value of 2 requires fewer bits.

Lossless Compression Approaches for Removing Coding Redundancy

There are many techniques for removing coding redundancy. The two techniques commonly used with photographic content are Huffman coding and Lempel–Ziv–Welch (LZW) compression.

Huffman Coding

Huffman coding is a lossless technique that looks for statistical patterns and assigns symbols to each pattern element. This approach is not limited to image data and can be applied to video, audio, text documents and spreadsheets. *Static Huffman coding* can be applied in a single pass if the content of the data is already known. *Dynamic Huffman coding* is a two-pass process. A histogram of pixel values is created on the first pass. Each bin in the histogram is turned into a probability of occurrence called a *leaf node*. Table 12-3 is a frequency count of letters found in alphabet soup and its corresponding leaf nodes.

The second pass encodes the data. Both static and dynamic methods use the same encoding technique to build a *Huffman Tree* like the one shown in Figure 12-7 (overleaf). The algorithm locates the two leaf nodes with

Table 12-3 A frequency tally of letters found in alphabet soup and the corresponding leaf node values calculated for dynamic Huffman coding.

Letter	Tally	Leaf Node Value
a	8	0.08
b	10	0.01
c	12	0.12
d	14	0.14
e	24	0.24
f	32	0.32
Total	100	1

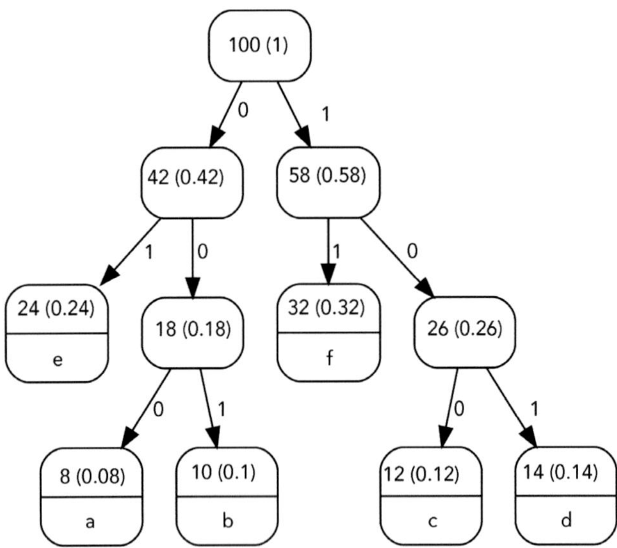

Figure 12-7 A Huffman tree for our alphabet soup data.

the lowest occurrences or probabilities and combines them into a new node. The leaf node with the lower probability prior to combing is assigned a 0. The higher leaf node is assigned a value of 1. The process is repeated until all nodes are combined to create a root with a probability of 1. A code look-up table is created to compress the data. The same table is used in reverse to decipher these symbol assignments when an encoded file is decoded for display. Figure 12-8 shows how the Huffman coding approach reduces the file storage of our alphabet soup data by 88%.

Lempel–Ziv–Welch Compression

The *Lempel–Ziv–Welch lossless compression algorithm* was developed in 1984 by Abraham Lempel, Jacob Ziv and Terry Welch. The algorithm is employed to effectively compress GIF, TIFF and PDF files. LZW compression creates a code table that typically contains 4,096 entries. Compressing an 8-bit image means that the first 256 entries in the code table contain the pixel values 0 through 256 while the other entries are left blank. The algorithm steps through the image data looking for unique strings and adds them to the code table while concurrently compressing it.

Let's step through compressing a string of letters, "ABADABA" in Figure 12-9. The original file size before applying LZW compression is 56-bits. We'll assume that there are only four possible letters in a string: A, B, C and D. The code table for the example string is populated with those letters as codes 0 through 3 and the remainder of the table is left empty. In Step 1, the first character in the original string ("A") is examined to determine if it is in the code table. It is present, so Step 2 takes the next character from the original string and adds it to the current string (making it "AB"). The string "AB" is not in the code table, so the LZW coding adds it as code value 4. The "A" is removed from the front of the "AB" string and encodes it as 0, leaving "B" behind. Step 3 examines "B" and finds it in the coding table. It then takes the next character from the original string and adds it to the current string making it "BA." In Step 4, "BA" is not found in the code table, so it gets added as code value 5. The "B" is then removed from "BA" and encoded as 1. This same process is followed for all of the remaining characters in the original string. When it's complete, the resulting LZW-encoded string is "010340" that can be stored with the coding table in a file size of 10-bits. The code table is used in reverse to decode the data. This method results in a full restoration of the original information with nothing lost or abbreviated while offering a notable storage efficiency improvement.

Letter	Tally	Uncompressed Binary Code	Number of bits uncompressed	Binary Huffman Code	Number of bits compressed
a	8	01100001	64	000	24
b	10	01100010	100	001	30
c	12	01100011	144	100	36
d	14	01100100	196	101	42
e	24	01100101	576	01	48
f	32	01100110	1024	11	64
		Total Bits Used	2104		244
					88% Compression

Figure 12-8 Huffman coding compresses the alphabet soup data by 88%.

Code Table

Code Value	Strings
0	A
1	B
2	C
3	D
4	AB
5	BA
6	AD
7	DA
8	ABA

Original String	"ABADABA"	56 bit file
Encoded String	"010340"	10 bit file

Compression Steps	Current String	Action	Building Encoded Stream
Step 1	A	In Table, Add next character from string	
Step 2	AB	Add "AB" to Table, Encode A and remove from string	A 0
Step 3	B	In Table, Add next character from string	
Step 4	BA	Add "BA" to Table, Encode B and remove from string	A B 0 1
Step 5	A	In Table, Add next character from string	
Step 6	AD	Add "AD" to Table, Encode A and remove from string	A B A 0 1 0
Step 7	D	In Table, Add next character from string	
Step 8	DA	Add "DA" to Table, Encode D and remove from string	A B A D 0 1 0 3
Step 9	A	In Table, Add next character from string	
Step 10	AB	In Table, Add next character from string	
Step 11	ABA	Add "ABA" to Table, Encode AB and remove from string	A B A D AB 0 1 0 3 4
Step 12	A	Last character, Encode	A B A D AB A 0 1 0 3 4 0

Figure 12-9 Construction of an LZW code table.

The YC_bC_r Color Space

Every pixel in a color image is represented by a red, green and blue value. This is great for image display as monitors expect these RGB values. It's not the optimal space in which to operate for image compression, however. Instead, RGB images are converted to a *luma-chrominance color space* where every pixel location is described by three values: luminance (Y), chroma blue (C_b) and chroma red (C_r).

Conversion to the *YC_bC_r color space* is a valuable practice for compression algorithms. Human vision is more sensitive to changes in luminance than to small changes in color. Separating the brightness information from the color information allows algorithms to apply different, independent compression rates for luminance and color

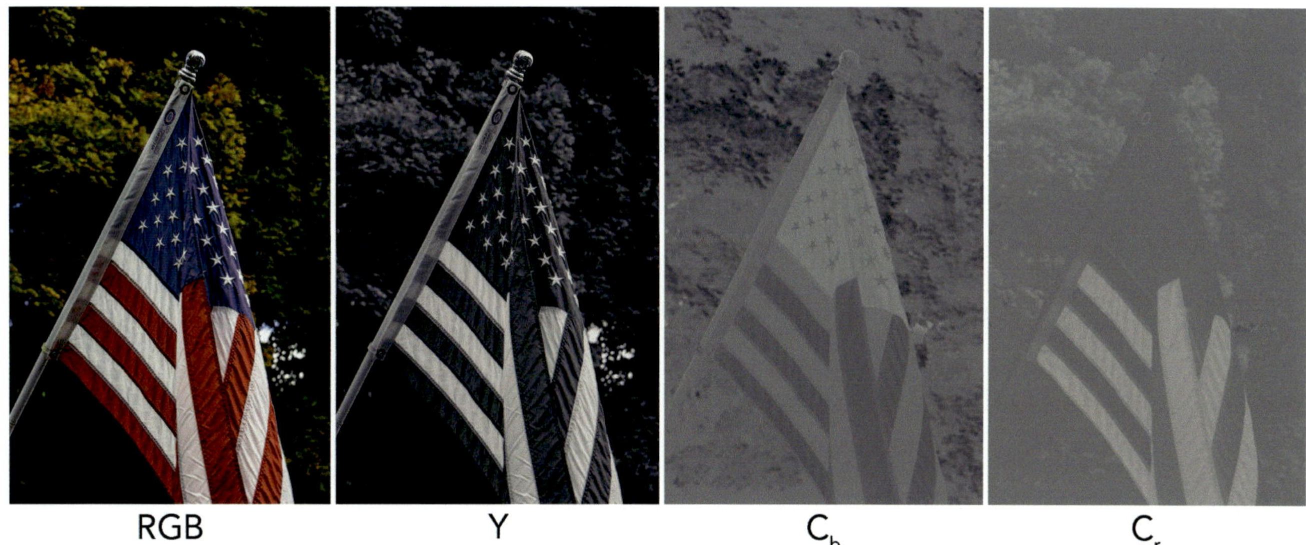

Figure 12-10 The original RGB image (left) and the three YC_bC_r components after conversion to a luma-chrominance color space.

to achieve additional storage efficiency. The conversion from RGB to YC_bC_r is defined for standard definition television in the International Radiocommunication Sector (ITU-R) BT.601 standard. Equations 12.1–12.3 list the conversion equations.

$$Y = 0.299R + 0.587G + 0.114B \quad \text{(Eq. 12.1)}$$

$$C_b = 128 - 0.168736R - 0.331264G + 0.5B \quad \text{(Eq. 12.2)}$$

$$C_r = 128 + 0.5R - 0.418688G - 0.081312B \quad \text{(Eq. 12.3)}$$

Figure 12-10 illustrates an RGB color image file converted to YC_bC_r. It's possible that some information is lost when transforming from RGB to YC_bC_r due to rounding errors.

Compressing Color

Converting image data into the YC_bC_r space means that the color characteristics can be compressed independently from luminance. Applying additional color compression is a strategy used in JPEG compression and it is also particularly effective in video encoding. This is because video compression can take advantage of the combined effects of psychovisual and temporal redundancies by subsampling color in image frames. *Chrominance subsampling* uses the same color values across multiple pixels in an effort to reduce the amount of data; the relative insensitivity of the human visual system suggests that this approach is possible with minimal observable degradation to the imagery. Chroma subsampling was originally invented for color television broadcasting. If an uncompressed image is built from color and luminance layers at full resolution, a chroma subsampled image has a full resolution luminance layer and lower resolution chroma layers (see Figure 12-11).

Chroma subsampling is described with the following notation:

$$A:B:C \quad \text{(Eq. 12.4)}$$

where

A = the number of pixels wide (by 2 pixels in height) that define the sample area

B = the chroma samples in the first row of Ax2

C = the chroma samples in the chroma samples in the second row of Ax2

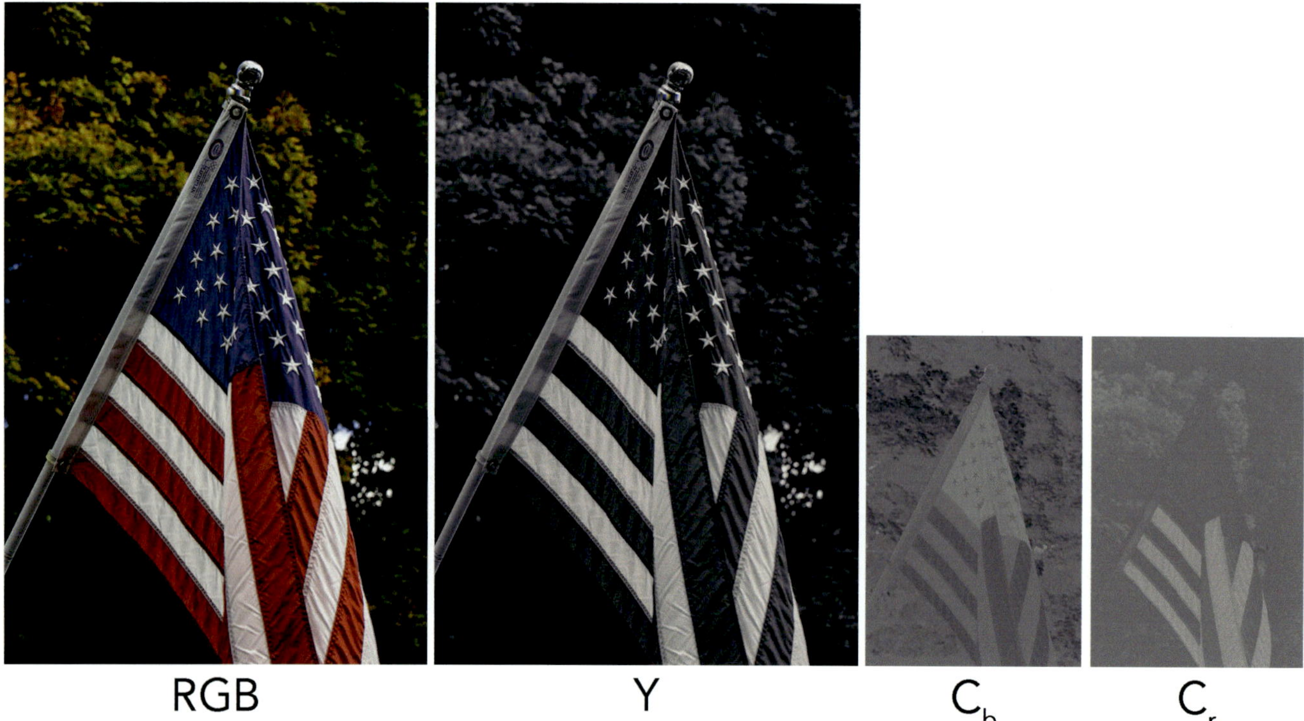

Figure 12-11 Converting an RGB image to YC_bC_r and subsampling the chroma channels.

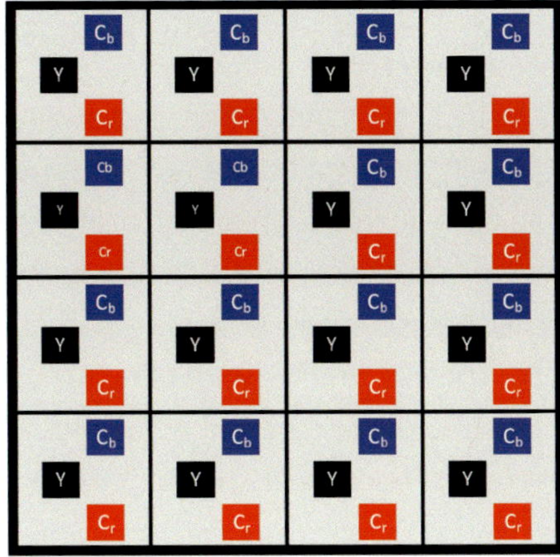

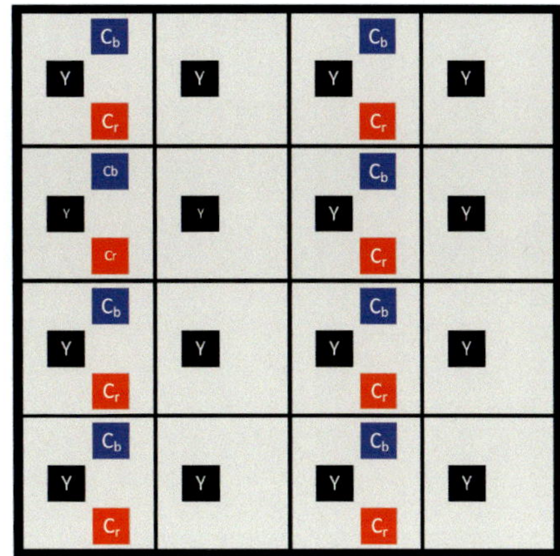

Figure 12-12 The array on the left represents a group of image pixels with full luma and chroma sampling (4:4:4), the array on the right represents a 4:2:2 sampling schema.

An image without chroma subsampling is described as *4:4:4* where a 4x2 pixel section of an image has unique chroma samples for all pixels. Using the same chroma values for every other pixel in a row is called *4:2:2* and effectively halves the chroma resolution (see Figures 12-12 and 12-13). Further sharing the chroma samples from row 1 with row 2 yields *4:2:0* subsampling (also called *2x2*). Using the same chroma values for every fourth pixel (i.e. 1/4 sampling) is *4:1:1*. The more that the chroma data is subsampled, the greater the potential compression ratio relative to the original, uncompressed image or video frame. Video encoders offer this chroma subsampling notation as a tunable parameter (*4:2:0* is common, particularly with cameras designed for still photography). JPEG compression may use chroma subsampling at higher compression levels (lower "quality" levels) to achieve smaller file sizes, though the exact sampling method is decided by the image editing software.

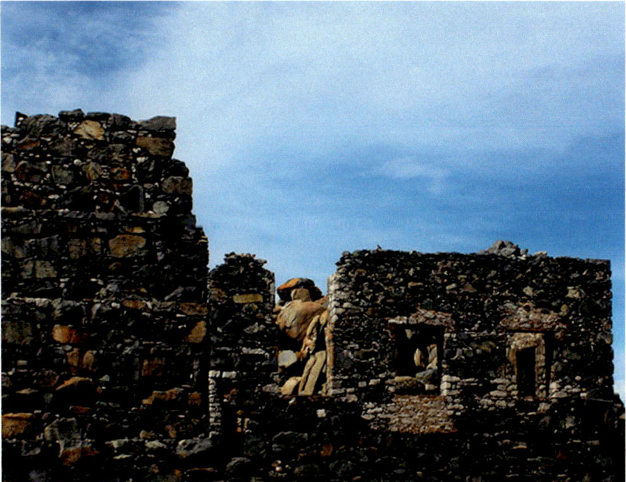

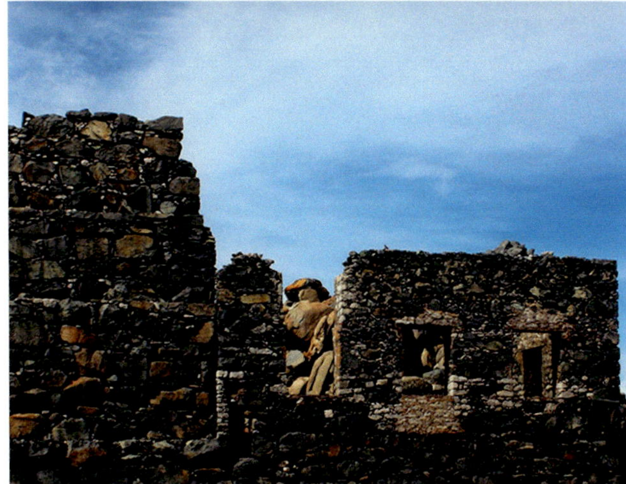

Figure 12-13 An image compressed with 4:4:4 (top) and with 4:2:2 (bottom). Our vision is not as discerning when the color resolution is halved.

Using Discrete Cosine Transforms to Compress

Discrete cosine transforms rely on representing all image content using combinations of cosine waves at different frequencies. Images are broken up into 8x8 pixel blocks or 64 pixel values in total. Any combination or arrangement of pixels in the 8x8 pixel block can be represented

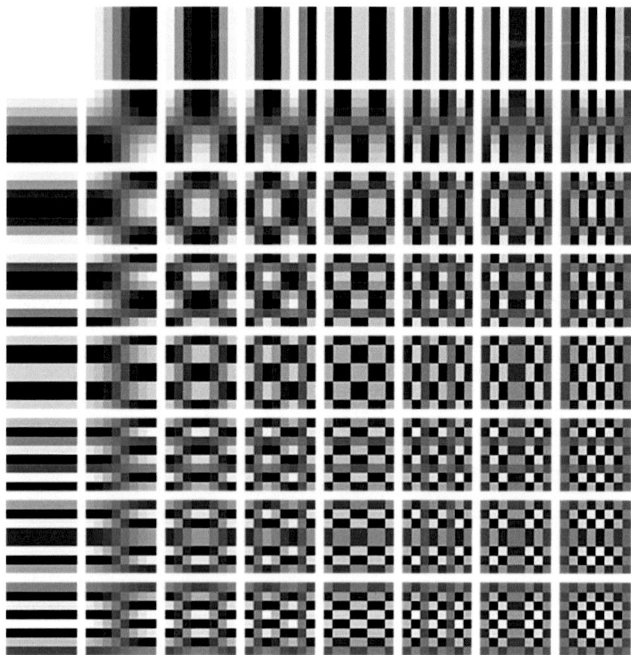

Figure 12-14 The DCT 64 base cosine waves used to replicate any 8x8 image pixel group.

by combining 64 cosine waves of different values. Figure 12-14 shows these combined cosine waves represented in image pixels. The upper leftmost square represents low frequency flat areas. The frequency of the image data increases moving toward the lower rightmost square.

DCT compression starts by segmenting an entire image into 8x8 pixel blocks. Using the 64 base cosine waves shown in Figure 12-14 (also an 8x8 block), a coefficient is assigned for each of the blocks. Each coefficient represents how much that cosine wave pattern contributes to the block. For example, if the coefficient for the upper left-hand cosine wave block of Figure 12-14 is large, it indicates that there is a significant amount of low frequency information in the 8x8 pixel block. The resulting 8x8 array of coefficients will typically have a common arrangement. The upper left square is the *DC coefficient* and it typically stores a very large value. The DC coefficient represents the low frequency information in the 8x8 block. As you traverse the 8x8 block diagonally to the lower right, the coefficients typically become smaller and smaller. In terms of image data, the lower right checkerboard pattern in Figure 12-14 is the high frequency data. We often find that removing high frequency data from an image is unlikely to introduce a noticeable difference in appearance.

The user defines the desired quality level when compressing an image using DCT. The quality level is used to create a quantization table. Recall from Chapter 3 that we quantize the continuous analog light signal into digital bits that represent pixel values in a photograph. The quantization table is used to weight the DCT coefficients which are then rounded to the nearest integer. Many of the DCT coefficients are set to zero when the compression level is set to a low value, for example. This may result in noticeable data loss or image quality degradation.

There are other options beyond DCT, namely using *discrete wavelet transform* (DWT). DWT is used by JPEG 2000 for specialized imaging applications. For a detailed explanation of this, we suggest Chapters 28 and 29 in *The Manual of Photography* by Allen and Triantaphillidou.[3]

JPEG Compression

The JPEG is the go-to format for end-product image files to send to clients or for embedding on websites. Recall that the JPEG name refers to both the file container format and the lossy compression standard it uses to store the image data. A color image undergoes the following steps with JPEG compression algorithms:

1. The image is converted from the RGB space to the YC_bC_r color space.
2. The chrominance channels (C_bC_r) are subsampled, taking advantage of psychovisual redundancy.
3. The image is divided into 8x8 blocks. If the image rows and columns are not perfectly divisible by eight, the bottom row and right column of the image are duplicated to fill the block.
4. A Discrete Cosine Transform is performed to determine compression coefficients.
5. The compression coefficients are quantized according to a user-defined quality factor. The range of this factor is defined by the software package used to create the JPEG.
6. The resulting quantized data is Huffman coded for additional storage efficiency.

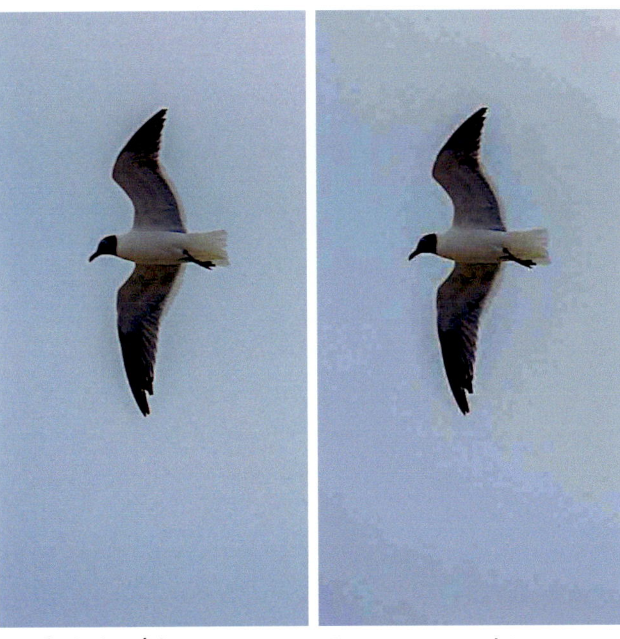

Figure 12-15 The JPEG compression quantization factor was set to an aggressive value that degraded image quality but reduced the file size by more than half. Photograph by Ruben Vargas

7. The compressed image data is saved to a JPEG container file (see Figure 12-15).

The JPEG compression process has two lossy steps. Step 2 subsamples the chrominance channels (C_bC_r). Once the chrominance channel data is subsampled, it cannot be restored faithfully to the original image data. Step 5 introduces additional data loss; the lower the user-defined quality factor, the more data is lost.

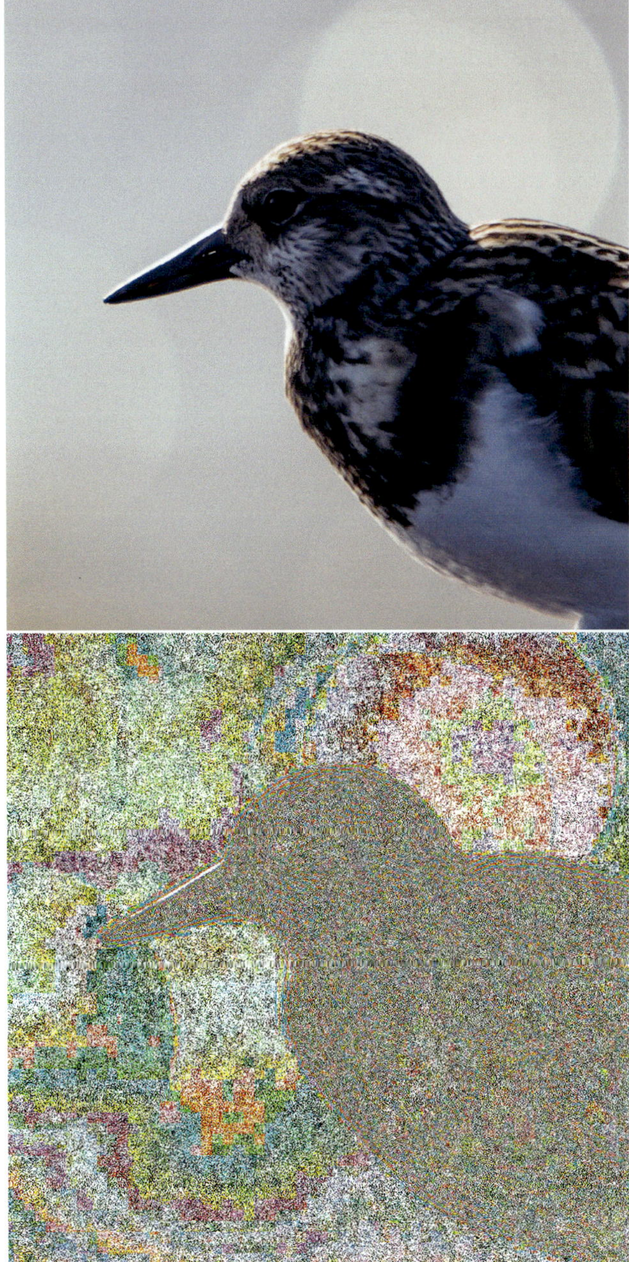

Figure 12-16 A JPEG-compressed image (top) and an image-differenced rendering (bottom) showing pixel changes between the original raw data and the JPEG.

Common Image Compression Artifacts

In a perfect world, lossless compression is computationally cheap, fast and extremely efficient at keeping file sizes small. The real world is one where tradeoffs and compromise are necessary: the smaller the desired file, the more we must accept losses in image fidelity. There is always a balance between minimizing disk space used and image quality loss.

Image degradations resulting from compression algorithms are called *compression artifacts*. Ultimately, choices made regarding compression can boil down to the final product: is the resulting image an acceptable representation of the original content? Navigating and balancing storage space, data transmission and image fidelity hinges on minimizing the presence of compression artifacts. The primary artifacts resulting from JPEG compression—highlighted here because if its ubiquitous use—include blocking, ringing and posterization. Artifacts are rarely exclusive and we encounter combinations of blocking and ringing, for example, in a heavily compressed image. Figure 12-16 shows a close crop of a JPEG-compressed image next to a calculated difference between it and the original raw capture; notice how the compression algorithms grouped similar background tones into uniform blocks. This method of visualization starts to highlight the compression operation and potentially problematic areas of scene content that may show artifacts.

Blocking Artifacts

A commonly spotted image quality artifact resulting from excessive compression, particularly JPEG compression, is *blocking*. One might describe it as "pixelated" or "checkerboard" because the blocks of local compression are apparent (see Figure 12-17). Compression algorithms take small subsets of an image frame and work to simplify their contents on a per-block basis. The problem arises when the compression of one block (for example, an 8x8 pixel array) alters the pixels along that block's edge. If the neighboring block gets the same treatment, there's no guarantee that the shared border where they meet will have a natural transition of color or tone. Our eyes start to suspect something is amiss and a subtle, grid-like abruptness of pixel values becomes apparent along these block borders. Blocking artifacts increase with the increase in target compression ratio.

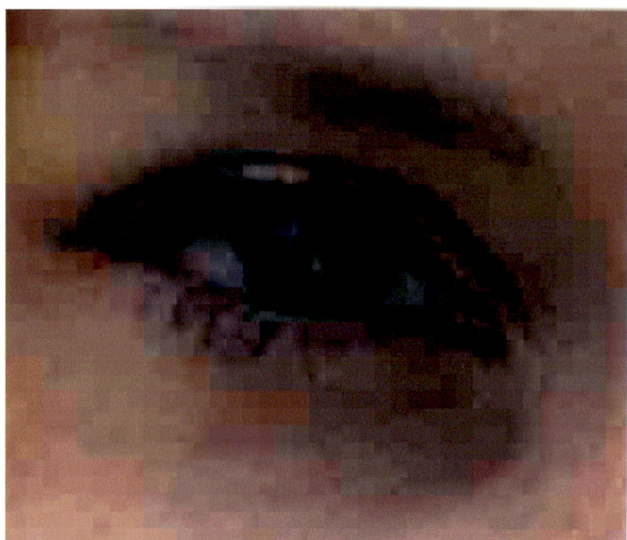

Figure 12-17 The 8x8 pixel blocks become apparent when they are heavily quantized. The abrupt changes in color and tone from one block to the next is far from the continuous, seamless transitions we experience in real life.

Ringing Artifacts

Edges are a critical component to any image as they define the boundaries of subjects and image details. Edge detail must be maintained between the source content and a compressed variant, leading compression algorithms to handle edges differently from other pixels. JPEG compression can introduce halo-like outlines like pond ripples along contrast boundaries called *ringing artifacts*. Recall that JPEG compression segments an image into 8x8 blocks; ringing occurs when an edge spans across multiple adjacent blocks. In addition, most compression algorithms sacrifice high frequency data as we are less sensitive to it. Edges are high frequency information and are therefore nearly always affected by compression algorithms. Ringing artifacts are illustrated in Figure 12-18.

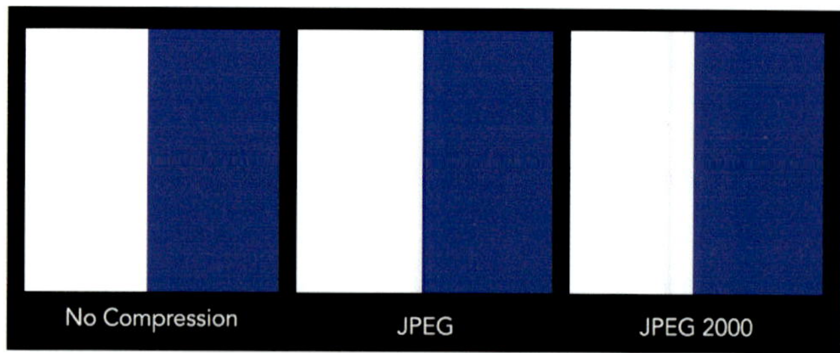

Figure 12-18 Ringing artifacts occur along edges and areas of high contrast when JPEG and JPEG 2000 compression image quality is set very low.

Posterization

Areas of continuous tone or subtle gradation can suffer from *posterization* if they are too heavily compressed. Areas that seem homogenous like skies often have small changes in tone (say, from a darker blue to a lighter blue-cyan). Compression algorithms see a lot of pixels that are similar to their neighbors and generalize them as the same luminance and/or color. This strategy, when applied over

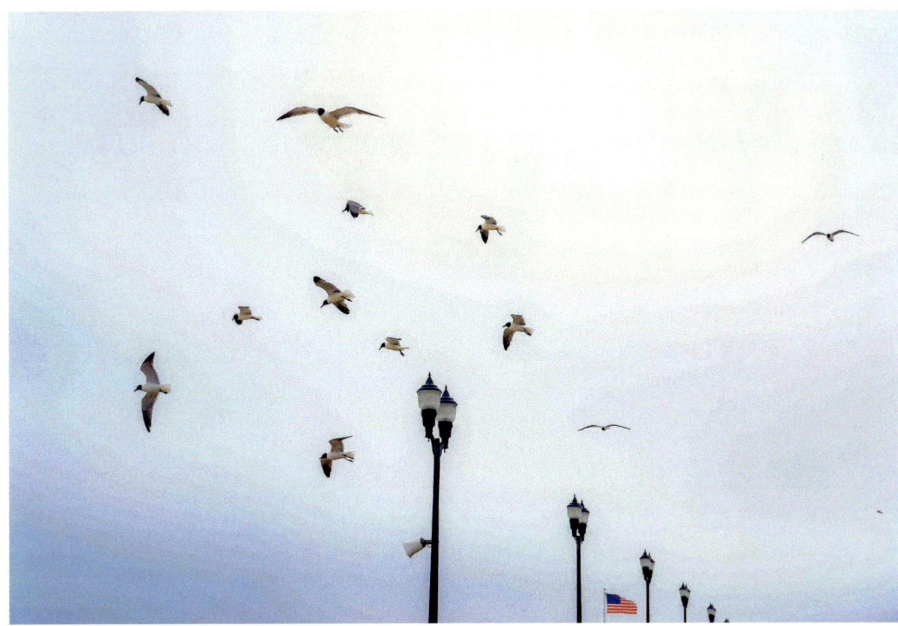

Figure 12-19 Posterization seen in the sky as a result of excessive JPEG compression. Photograph by Ruben Vargas

an area that transitions from one color to a slightly different one, introduces discrete changes. Posterization describes these rough, abrupt transitions where we expect to see a visually seamless, full color gradient. It is also called *banding* because of the distinct bands of color or tone that manifest in areas of gradation (see Figure 12-19).

Color Bleeding

The negative consequence of chroma subsampling is seen as *color bleeding* artifacts where the subsampled colors begin to exceed the boundaries defined by the luminance. Like the name indicates, think of this artifact like watercolor paint: the color boundaries blur and do not necessarily stay within the lines of subject edges in the image.

Generation Loss

If you've spent enough time on social media platforms then you've undoubtedly seen photos, video or graphics that, like leftovers from a once-fresh meal reheated one too many times, show serious signs of wear. *Generation loss* is degradation due to repeated lossy compression and can reveal all of the previously listed artifacts compounded on one another. On social media, this stems from people downloading, saving and uploading content over and over again. Each time that image data is reuploaded or changed and re-saved, the resulting content becomes one generation more distant from its parent source. Photographers can get away with resaving a JPEG a few times in a row without major artifacts appearing. Content on social media, though, is typically hit with high compression ratios to save the host companies money on bandwidth and storage. The effects of generation loss quickly manifest as these heavily compressed files are shared, downloaded and reuploaded and compressed at every iteration.

Notes

1 Markowsky, George. "Information theory." *Encyclopedia Britannica*, Encyclopedia Britannica, Inc., June 16, 2017, www.britannica.com/science/information-theory.

2 Patil, Aditi Y., et al. "Security of grayscale images by VSS with novel method of bit-plane slicing – Semantic Scholar." *Semantic Scholar*, Jan. 1, 1970, www.semanticscholar.org/paper/Security-of-grayscale-images-by-VSS-with-novel-of-Patil-Alexander/68d7294b51b105443fc71d956d1317dae18d114c.

3 Allen, Elizabeth and Sophie Triantaphillidou. *The Manual of Photography*. Elsevier/Focal Press, 2017.

Section 3

OUTPUT

Output is an exciting stage in the life of a photograph because it promises to showcase all of the pre-planning, careful capture and exposure, digital asset management and post-processing editing work. Without delivering your photography, either via print or screen, it's doomed to reside as files on a hard drive. Photographic output is the final leg of the race: just like the earlier stages of capture and processing, it demands an attention to detail and a working understanding of human vision, output technology and technical photographic processes.

This final section of this textbook covers color vision and systems, color management, displays and finally, printing and physical media. We start with color vision to appreciate how our eyes work and how our photographic media simultaneously excel and fall short of satisfying our highly sensitive visual organs. Then we tackle the much-maligned topic of color management that brings together everything we've explored regarding light, digital imaging technology, software and hardware. Once we're comfortable with concepts such as color profiles and rendering intents, we look at the potential output technologies for our photographs: displays and printed media. Showing your photography to the world is like crossing the finish line after the marathon of visual media production (and of reading this book): it should be satisfying, impactful and the culmination of everything you've worked toward. Photographic output is the means by which the world experiences your creative endeavors.

13 Color Vision and Systems

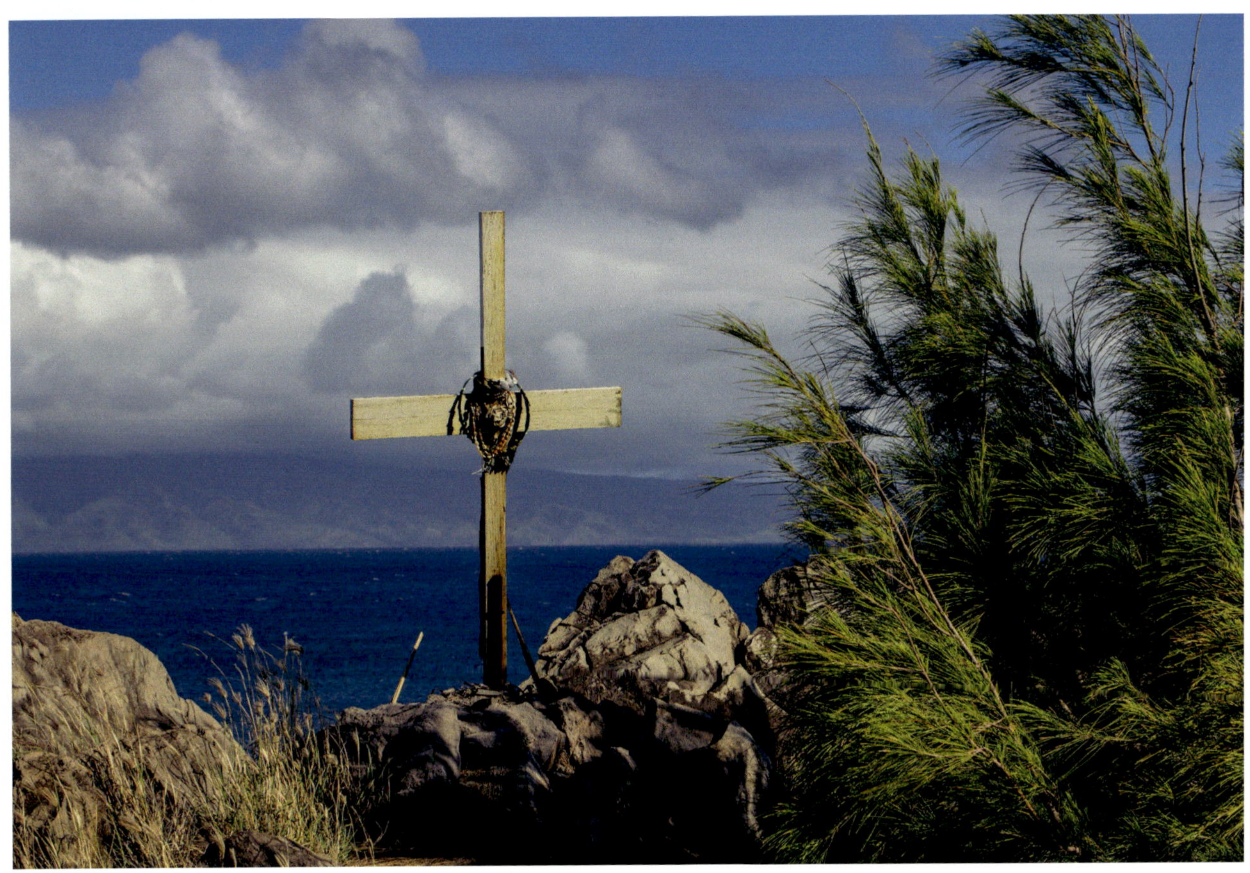

Photograph by Rochester Institute of Technology alumnus and Lecturer Nanette L. Salvaggio

The experience of perceiving color does not depend upon language or numbers, but the communication of information about that experience does. It is important to use an agreed-upon and established vocabulary to talk about color if we are to be successful at communicating it. In the past, various disciplines including photography, painting and the graphic arts have had difficulty communicating with each other due to the absence of a common color language. The Munsell Color System and the CIE System of Color Specification emerged as two of the more successful attempts to organize the variables of color into a universally accepted system. In addition, the Inter-Society Color Council brought together representatives of the various disciplines that use color in an effort to lower the barriers to communication. The stated aims and purposes of the organization are to "stimulate and coordinate the work being done by various societies and associations leading to the standardization, description and specification of color and to promote the practical application of these results to the color problems arising in science, art and industry."[1]

Before examining color systems, however, we have to establish a definition of color. Color is a visual experience. It is a perception, a human physiological and psychological response to light. *Color perception* requires three components: an object, a light source and an eye or visual system. There is no perception of color if any of these components are absent. Color is associated with words like red, green, blue and yellow in everyday language, yet these words refer to only one of three attributes of color: hue. The other attributes are brightness (or lightness) and saturation.

We further clarify our language of describing color by separating the terms referring to the visual perception of an object and those referring to the physical characteristics of that object. For example, one can argue that we shouldn't describe an apple as being red. We perceive it as red because the surface of the apple has physical properties that reflect certain wavelengths and absorb other wavelengths of the white light that illuminates it. When a red object is illuminated with blue light, most of the light is absorbed and the object is perceived as black (see Figure 13-1). When we identify an object as being red, we mean that individuals with normal color vision generally perceive it as being red when viewed under normal viewing conditions and white light illumination.

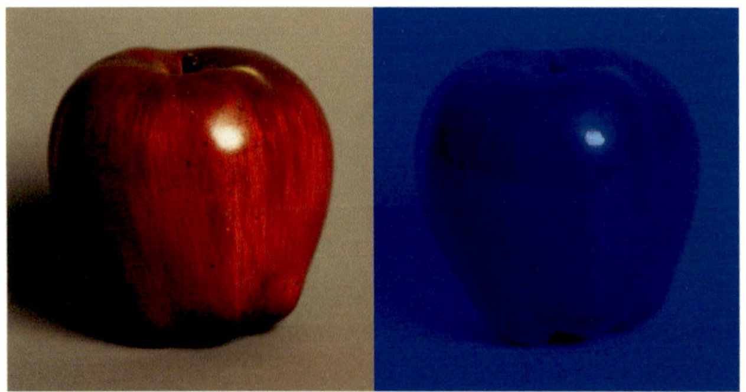

Figure 13-1 A red apple photographed under white light (left) and under blue light (right).

Sensing Light with the Human Eye

The human eye is a complex sensing organ worthy of its own textbook (others have written them) detailing its anatomy and function. Figure 13-2 illustrates the basic anatomy of the eye. The *cornea* is a fixed lens and does the majority of the light-focusing, followed by a flexible crystalline lens suspended by tissue that provides us with some refocusing abilities for close and far subject distances (called *accommodation*). The main cavity of the eye is not empty space despite how it may appear in illustrations. It is occupied by a clear fluid called the *vitreous humor* that functions to maintain the shape of the eye.

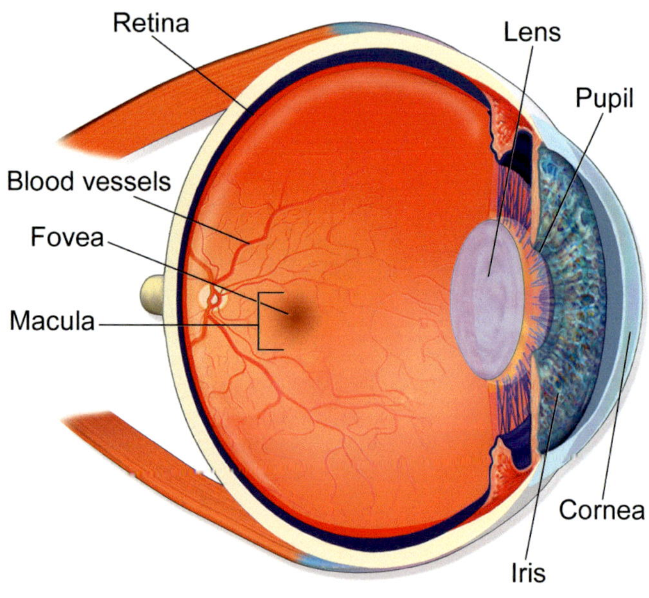

Figure 13-2 Anatomy of the human eye. Our central vision is sensed from the fovea, the illustrated here as the dark region on the retina.

The *retina* is the area at the back of the eye that detects light entering from the opening at the front of the eye (the pupil). The retina contains both *rods* and *cones*, the names given to the types of light receptors residing in the retina. Both get their name from their unique physical shapes. There are approximately 120 million rods in a human eye. Rods provide *scotopic vision* or our ability to see at night in very low light conditions. Rods are only active in the dark, so their use is also described as *dark-adapted vision*. The chemical in the rods, rhodopsin, gives us this ability to see when light is limited. Rhodopsin bleaches and becomes inactive when exposed to bright light. It takes about 30 minutes for the rods to reach maximum sensitivity in a dark environment and due to their inability to distinguish color, we are colorblind when completely dark-adapted.

There are approximately six million cones in the retina. Cones provide us with both the ability to see color and with *photopic vision*, the ability to see in lighted conditions. Your vision is considered to be *light-adapted* when the eyes rely on the cone receptors. There are three types of cones in the retina that are sensitive to different wavelength bands. You may have learned these in grade school as being red, green and blue cones. This is an oversimplification and are correctly referred to as long-wave (red), mid-wave (green) and short wave (blue) cones. Each cone type senses one of those three wavelength ranges, respectively, with an additional degree of overlap.

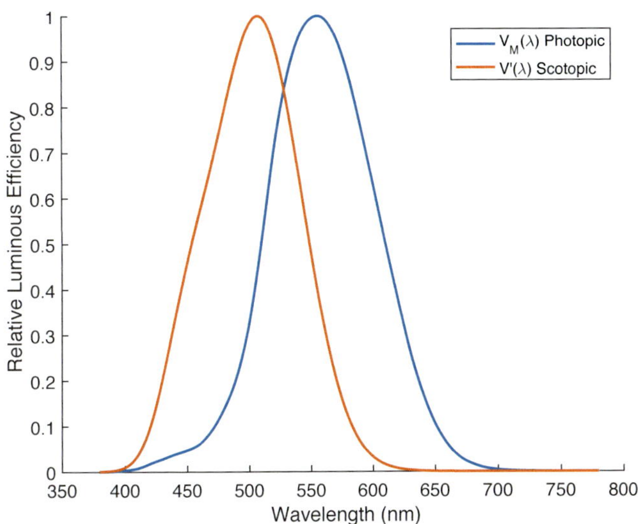

Figure 13-3 V-Lambda curves for photopic and scotopic vision.

Photopic vision is quantified by measuring the sensitivity of cone receptors to white light. The result is a *luminous efficiency function*, $V_M(\lambda)$, describing the average spectral sensitivity of human vision. Figure 13-3 reveals that human vision is most sensitive in the green-yellow wavelengths around 555 nm. The maximum sensitivity shifts when dark-adapted or using scotopic vision to approximately 507 nm. This shift in peak sensitivity is referred to as the *Purkinje shift*.

There is one more type of vision: *mesopic vision*. Mesopic vision is used in low light environments by employing both rods and cones. Such visual perception provides some ability to see colors (though they appear muted). The peak of the luminous efficiency function shifts with mesopic vision, pushing our peak color sensitivity toward a slightly lower wavelength.

Rods and cones are not evenly distributed across the retina. Instead, a high concentration of cones is found at the *fovea*, the area responsible for our central vision. Locking your gaze at text on a page is a collaboration between the body and mind to align the fovea such that your best visual acuity is put to good use. Anything that falls outside of this center portion of our field of view is perceived at a lesser degree of fidelity. We often like to compare the camera sensor to the human eye, but this is one place where the analogy is deceiving. Human vision is a combination of detection and interpretation and its detection mechanisms are not uniform. An image sensor is evenly distributed with photosites and color filters. The pixels at the center of the frame detect and record light exactly as the photosites along the edges do. Our retina lacks this uniformity, making up for it with cognitive processing that keeps us from noticing. Our eyes resolve a fraction of the detail outside of a 20° field of view from our centermost vision and with much less color information at that. Figure 13-4 (overleaf) is an interpretive illustration of the visual information detected by the retina. Our central vision contains the most detail while the surrounding periphery quickly decreases in fidelity and color information moving away from the fovea. This raw input data is masked as something much better thanks to color memory, rapid eye movements and a stage of cognitive processing.

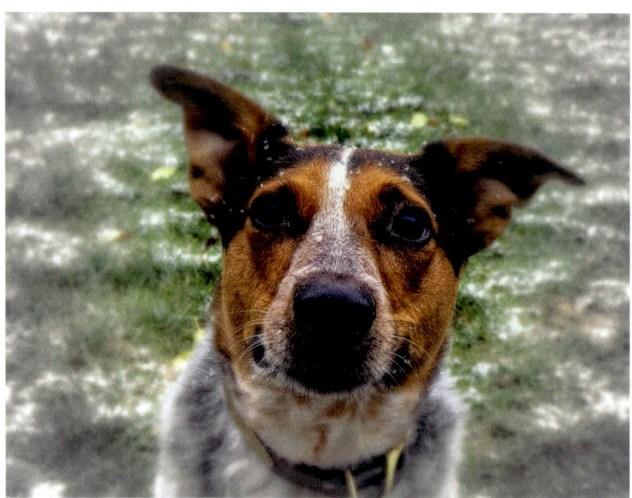

Figure 13-4 An interpretive illustration of what the retina detects, given the high concentration of cones at the fovea and low concentration of rods along the periphery. Adapted from an illustration found in the textbook *Basic Vision*[2]

All of this established, we've so far neglected to point out that we've got *two* of these incredible, complex sensing organs in our heads. *Binocular vision* is the result of having two eyes, spaced apart, perceiving the same scene. Unlike certain animals like chameleons or hammerhead sharks, our perceptual experience of these two eyes is that of a single, fused image. We do not typically see two different feeds or have the ability to control each eye independently (something is medically awry if it does happen). Binocular vision provides the brain with subconsciously interpreted data because we see the same scene from slightly different points of view. This gives us *depth perception*, an understanding of relative object positions and distance, up to about 20 feet in front of us. The brain uses other cues (see the discussion on perspective later in this chapter) to infer depth and distance beyond 20 feet. That 20 feet distance of binocular depth perception could be extended if we could somehow move our eyes farther apart than 2.5 inches, the average person's *interpupillary distance*.

Color Vision Theories

As early as 1666, a 23-year-old instructor at Cambridge University, Sir Isaac Newton, demonstrated that white sunlight is made up of all colors of light. Newton did so by passing sunlight through a prism to reveal a spectrum of colors. This demonstration gave visual evidence that white light can be separated into different colors. It was not until 1704 that Newton put forth a hypothesis to explain the process by which we see these colors. He speculated that the retina contains innumerable light receptors, each of which responds to a specific color stimulus. Thomas Young rejected this idea nearly one hundred years later in 1801. Young hypothesized that there are only three different kinds of light receptors in the retina with each kind responding to one color of light: red, green or blue. His theory was rejected and ignored by his contemporaries. Young's theory was rediscovered by Maxwell and Helmholtz in 1850.

Despite the many theories that attempt to explain our response to color, there remain numerous unanswered questions regarding color vision and the human eye. Some theories are more useful than others. The oldest, most efficient and most persistent theory of color vision is the *Young–Helmholtz theory* of trichromatic color vision. This theory postulates that there are three kinds of receptors in the retina that selectively react. We can think of these as red or long-wave, green or mid-wave and blue or short-wave receptors that combine in our visual system and produce the perception of all possible colors.

Some unanswerable questions have been raised regarding this three-color theory for human vision. For example, the eye distinguishes four fundamental or primary colors—colors that are distinct and have no trace of other colors. These colors are red, yellow, green and blue and are called the *psychological primaries*. The *Hering opponent color theory* takes this into account.

Whereas the Young–Helmholtz theory is based on three-color stimuli, the Hering opponent color theory is based on the response to pairs of color stimuli. It assumes that there are six basic independent colors (red, yellow, green, blue, white and black). Rather than postulating special and separate receptors for the six colors, Hering proposed that the light absorbed by the red, green and blue sensitive receptors in the retina starts a flow of activity in the visual system. Somehow this flow is channeled into three pairs of processes with the two components of each opposing one another. The opposing pairs are blue-yellow, green-red and white-black. For example, a color may look bluish or yellowish, never both at the same time. Blue opposes and cancels yellow and vice versa.

A variation on the Hering theory that provides for quantification is the modern *opponent-colors theory* (also called a *stage theory*). This theory assumes a two-stage process. The first is the excitation stage, occurring in the cones of the retina and consisting of four light-receiving cells that contain combinations of three photochemicals. The second stage is an associated response stage occurring beyond the retina in the visual nerve center. It has three paired-opponent processes: blue-yellow, green-red and white-black. This opponent-response theory represents differences in the neural response to the stimulation that originates when the cones in the retina are excited. A single nerve transmits two different messages by one of the pairs of opponent colors, raising the neural firing rate above the normal rate (excitation) and the other lowering the firing rate below the normal rate (inhibition).

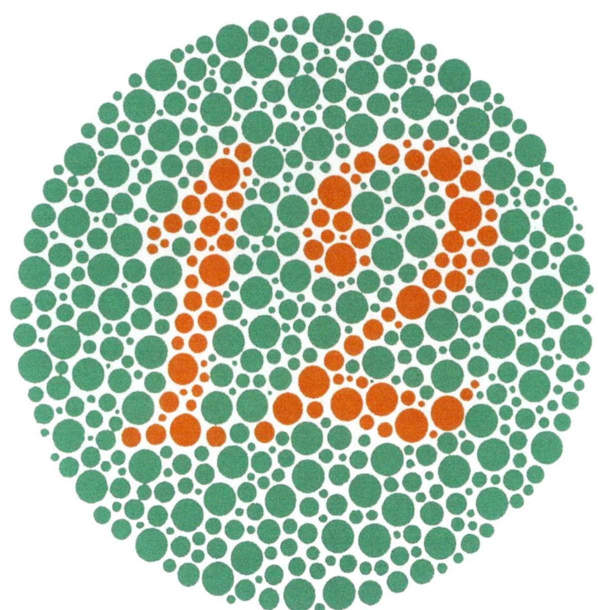

Figure 13-5 An Ishihara test plate containing the number 12.

Testing Color Vision

Take a moment and think about how color plays a role in your day-to-day experiences. Whether it's selecting clothes in the morning that match, picking a ripe banana for breakfast or telling the difference between a red and green traffic light on the drive to work, the functional role of color is undeniable. It's particularly important to photographers. Color vision screening begins as early as 4 or 5 years old when children learn to identify colors.

How do we test our color vision or the possible lack thereof? One common method is the *Ishihara Color Vision Test*, also referred to as *pseudoisochromatic plates*. The test is named after its creator, Dr. Shinobu Ishihara (1879–1963), who published the test in 1917. The Ishihara Color Vision Test screens for red-green color deficiencies. The test contains between 14 and 38 color plates. Each plate is made up of many dots that vary in size, brightness and color arranged in a circle, an example of which is shown in Figure 13-5. The dots are placed in such a way that a person with normal color vision is able to identify the digit number within the circle. A person who is colorblind or has a color deficiency sees either no number or a different number than a person with normal color vision. There are versions of the Ishihara test that use shapes instead of numbers so that young children can trace the figures or identify the shapes.

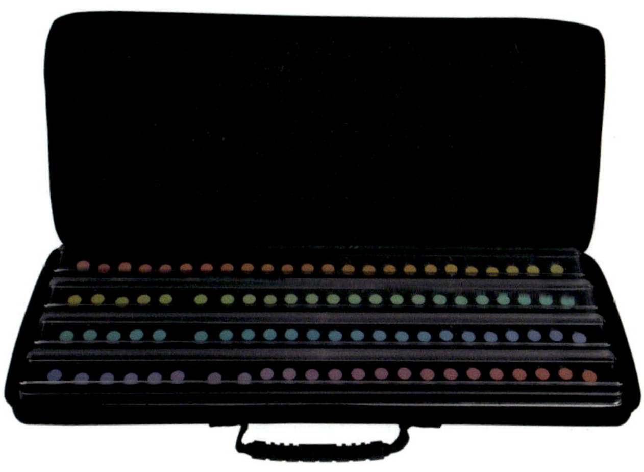

Figure 13-6 The Farnsworth–Munsell 100 Hue test trays.
Image courtesy of © X-Rite Incorporated | www.xrite.com

The *Farnsworth–Munsell 100 Hue Test* (FM-100 Hue Test) is a more extensive method of evaluating color vision and helps to identify all types of color vision issues. The FM-100 Hue Test consists of four separate trays of color caps containing disks of varying hues as shown in Figure 13-6. Each tray contains two disks that are fixed in place.

The test administrator removes the caps from the tray and mixes their order. The test taker is tasked with placing the caps back into the tray in the proper order whereby the color gradually changes from one end of the box to the other. A quantitative score is calculated upon completion of all four boxes that quantifies an individual's level of color discrimination.

Color Vision Deficiencies

Not everyone has normal color vision. Persons with normal color vision are identified as *normal trichromats* based on the three types of cones in the retina. Even then, not all normal trichromats respond to colors in exactly the same way. For this reason, scientific studies of color vision make use of the average response of a number of people with normal color vision.

There are a number of types of defective color vision despite the common catch-all term "colorblind." A person who is missing one of the three types of cone pigments is known as a *dichromat*. *Monochromats* are missing two of the three cone pigments (or possibly have rhodopsin, the rod photopigment, in the cones). Dichromats have difficulty distinguishing between red and green, or more rarely between blue and yellow. There are very few monochromats, but their vision is the equivalent of black and white photography. Figure 13-7 simulates how each of these color vision deficiencies renders the perception of colors.

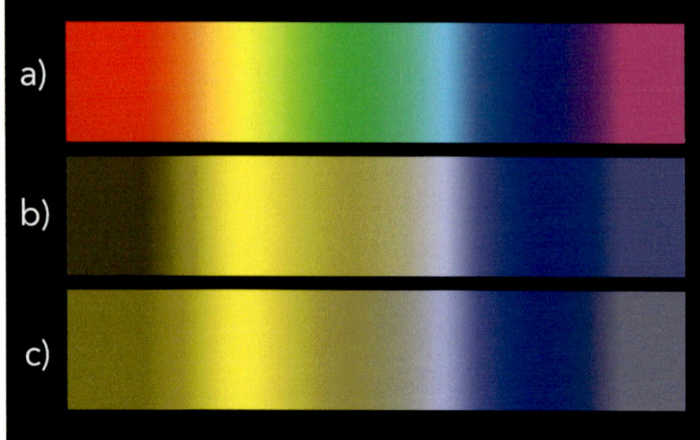

Figure 13-7 Simulations of a) normal color vision, b) protanopia and c) deuteranopia.

The red, green and blue cone sensitivities suggest a simple trichromatic theory of color vision, though much of the experimental evidence supports the opponent theory of color vision whereby information from the red-, green- and blue-sensitive cones is thought to be transmitted in combinations—specifically red-green, blue-yellow and black-white—through three separate channels.

Aside from missing one or two of the three types of cone photopigments, defective color vision can also be associated with reduced sensitivity of one or two of the three cone types or with a shift in sensitivity along the spectrum for one or more of the cone types. People who have all three types of cone photopigments but who do not have normal color vision for either of the reasons cited are referred to as *anomalous trichromats*—as distinct from the conventional trichromats, dichromats and monochromats.

Accurate color identification requires normal color vision, standard viewing conditions and the opportunity to make side-by-side comparisons with standard colors. A person with normal color vision may have inaccurate perception of stimulus colors under certain conditions such as:

- when the image is formed near the periphery of the retina;
- when the light level is very low or very high;
- when the stimulus is small in area;
- when the stimulus is presented for a very short time;
- when the stimulus is illuminated with something other than white light;
- when the viewer is adapted to a different color.

Heredity is responsible for most cases of defective color vision. It may also result from other causes such as the use of certain drugs, excessive use of alcohol and brain damage. About 8% of Caucasian males and 0.4% of females across all ethnicities have some form of defective color vision. There is no cure for congenital defective color vision. Some people whose occupations require being able to discriminate between certain colors have been helped by using color filters over the eyes. Photographers with defective color vision are able to make color prints that are acceptable to themselves, but the prints often do not appear correct to people with normal color vision.

A company called Enchroma® developed a pair of glasses that aid those with red-green color blindness. Those with red-green color blindness have the mid-wave and long-wave cone responses overlap more than normal. Enchroma® glasses have a notch filter that helps the brain separate these two signals. This technique restores some color vision. We have seen several of our students try these glasses and the results have been truly amazing and life-changing for them.

Methods of Creating Color

All color reproduction systems operate on the assumption that the human eye contains three different types of color receptors. Many experiments show that almost all colors can be produced through the appropriate mixture of red, green and blue light. Although many theories of color vision have been proposed, the trichromatic theory offers the most satisfactory explanation of color perception as it relates to color photography. For a color photographic system to be successful, it must be capable of recording and controlling the red, green and blue components of the light being reflected, transmitted or emitted by the subject. There are two basic methods for controlling the color of the light produced in a color reproduction system: additive color mixture, which involves combining red, green and blue light; and subtractive color mixture, which involves colorants that selectively absorb red, green and blue light. Reproducing color captured in photographs on displays and in print is the key to creating breathtaking images. Mastering color reproduction means exploring additive and subtractive color mixing along with how partitive mixing plays a role in both systems.

Additive Mixing

Computer screens and digital image sensors use additive systems to produce a wide variety of colors. They do this by controlling the amounts of red, green and blue light present. *Additive color mixing* is demonstrated by using three identical projectors in a darkened room, each equipped with a different colored filter (red, green and blue) aimed at a projection screen. Equipping each projector with a variable aperture allows the illuminance of each color to be adjusted to create brighter or darker colors. Overlapping the blue and the green lights and altering the illuminance of each of the lights produces a series of blue-green or cyan colors. Adding red light to the system and overlapping it with the blue light results in a series or red-blue or magenta colors. Likewise, overlapping the red light with the green light produces a series of yellow colors.

Figure 13-8 shows the results of such a demonstration. That cyan is formed where the blue and green overlap is not surprising, nor is the formation of magenta from the combination of blue and red light. Visually, the colors produced are consistent with the contributions made by the primary colors. However, for the mixture of red light and green light to appear yellow is an amazing result when yellow does not seem to resemble the red or green light. This phenomenon is a consequence of the three cone sensitivities. To perceive yellow, the M (green) and L (red) cones must be excited. The sensitivity responses of these two cones overlap each other as shown in Figure 13-9 (overleaf). White light results at the spot where all three colored light beams overlap.

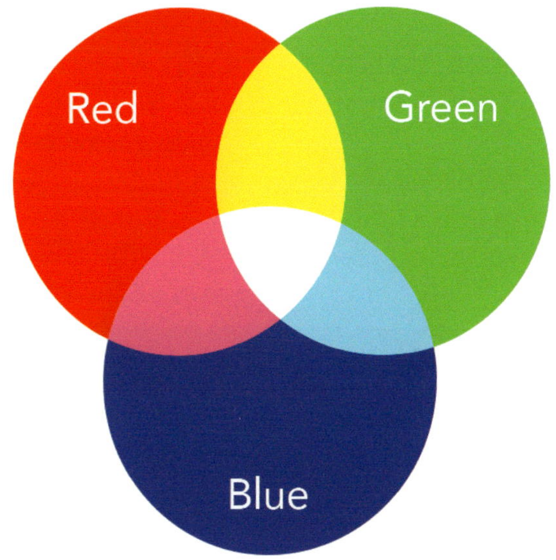

Figure 13-8 The additive color system: red, green and blue.

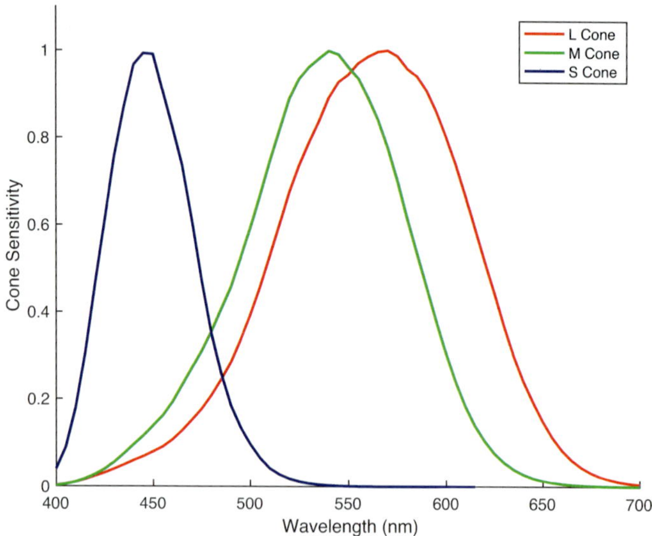

Figure 13-9 Cone sensitivity functions.

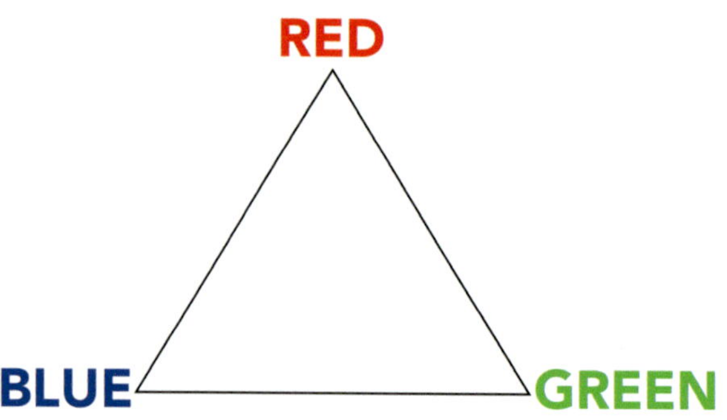

Figure 13-10 The Maxwell triangle.

The term *additive* implies that combinations of colored light produce additional colors. All additive color reproduction systems require the use of the three colors represented in this example: red light, green light and blue light. Consequently, these colors are referred to as the *additive primaries*. Table 13-1 lists the color combinations that result from these additive color primaries.

Practically any color is reproducible by controlling the amount of light coming from each projector. Hue, lightness and saturation can all be adjusted by varying the amounts of red, green and blue light falling on the screen. The only colors that can't be produced are *spectral colors*. These are highly saturated colors that are not easily produced with our projector example.

Recall from Chapter 5 that James Maxwell proposed the concept of the Maxwell triangle in the 1870s. He placed the three additive primaries at the corners of an equilateral triangle and proposed that all possible colors exist at points within the triangle as a result of different primary color mixtures (see Figure 13-10). The Maxwell triangle set the stage for many color systems to follow.

There is another approach that employs the principles of additive color mixing to create a spectrum of colors. A single projector projecting red, green and blue images in rapid succession is perceived as a full color image by our eyes. The rapid switching between each red, green or blue version of the image is not distinguishable by the human visual system and instead appear as one. This perceptual phenomenon is called *persistence of vision* and is the result of *temporal color mixing* since the colors are created with the help of lapsed time. *Digital Light Processing* (DLP) projection systems, sometimes used in movie theaters, use temporal color mixing to produce full color imagery.

Table 13-1 Additive color formation (the mixing of lights).

Lights	Produce
Blue light + green light	Cyan
Blue light + red light	Magenta
Green light + red light	Yellow
Blue light + green light + red light	White
No light	Black

Subtractive Mixing

Printing photographs is unique from displaying them with monitors or projectors because it requires *subtractive color mixing*. Subtractive color mixing is characterized by the mixing of colorants such as inks, dyes, pigments and paints. Although subtractive mixing involves a fundamentally different set of materials compared to additive mixing, the approach is capable of producing nearly the same range of colors. Subtractive mixing colorants control the red, green and blue portions of white light that reflect off of the image surface to render faithful reproductions of our photographs. There are three colorants that meet this requirement: cyan, magenta and yellow. Cyan absorbs red light and reflects or transmits blue and green light, creating its blue-green appearance. Magenta absorbs green light and reflects or transmits blue light and red light, causing its blue-red appearance. Yellow absorbs blue light and reflects or transmits red and green light. These *subtractive primaries* can also be described in terms of what color they subtract from the incident white light:

- cyan = minus red
- magenta = minus green
- yellow = minus blue

Figure 13-11 illustrates the results of mixing of cyan, magenta and yellow colorants. We assume that the receiving substrate (typically paper) is illuminated by white light which contains nearly equal amounts of red, green and blue light. A white sheet of paper should reflect that light and appear white before anything is printed onto it. Where the yellow colorant is mixed with the cyan colorant, the area of overlap produces the color green. The yellow colorant absorbs the blue portion of the white light and the cyan colorant absorbs the red portion of the white light, leaving only the green to reflect back to our eyes. Similarly, where the yellow and magenta colorants overlap, the color red appears. The blue light is absorbed by the yellow colorant and the green light by the magenta colorant, leaving only the red light to be reflected to our eyes. Finally, where the cyan and magenta colorants overlap, the color blue appears. The red light absorption by the cyan colorant and the green light absorption by the magenta leave only the blue light component of the original white light to be reflected to our eyes. A wide variety of hues are reproduced by mixing varying amounts of these three colorants. If all three are mixed in equal amounts, a neutral results. Table 13-2 provides the possible results of mixing colorants.

A fourth colorant is used in many subtractive printing systems: black. These systems are referred to as *CMYK* with *K* representing the black ink (it stands for "Key" and comes from printing press terminology). The use of a black colorant provides two benefits. First, it is difficult to produce a true black using cyan, magenta and yellow inks. When mixed, the resulting color is often a muddy gray-brown instead of a rich, neutral black due to colorant impurities. Second, these three colored inks are expensive, meaning that the practice of using all three to make black is a costly

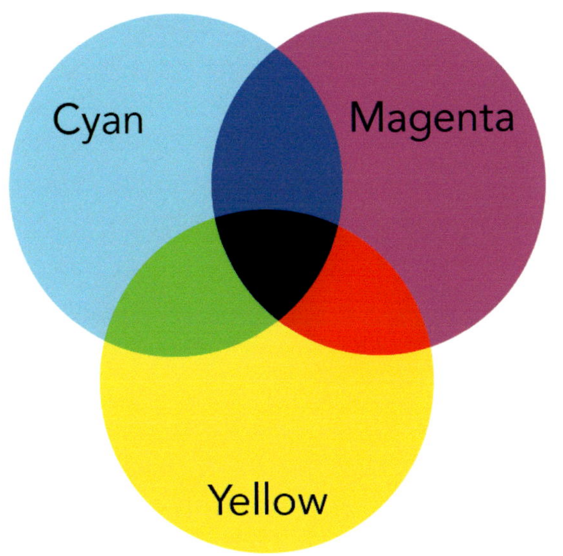

Figure 13-11 The subtractive color system: cyan, magenta and yellow.

Table 13-2 Basic facts of subtractive color formation (mixing of colorants).

Colorant	Absorbs	Produces/Reflects
Cyan	Red	Cyan (blue-green)
Magenta	Green	Magenta (blue-red)
Yellow	Blue	Yellow (green-red)
Cyan + magenta	Red and green	Blue
Cyan + yellow	Red and blue	Green
Magenta + yellow	Green and blue	Red
Cyan + magenta + yellow	Red, green and blue	Black
No colorant	Nothing	White

one. Adding a separate, no-mixing-needed black ink solves both problems. It ensures a pure black and is much less expensive to produce. Some inkjet printers further subdivide the primary colorants to include dedicated cartridges like Light Magenta and Light Cyan.

Metamerism's Role in Color Reproduction

Have you ever bought a shirt and a pair of pants thinking they are a perfect match, only to wear them together and realize that they look completely different in the light of day? This fashion embarrassment occurred because you viewed the clothing under the store's lighting and then later under different illumination. They matched in the first environment and not the second due to *metamerism*. Metamerism is the phenomenon of perceiving two objects as the same color when viewing them under an illuminant even though they have different spectral reflectances. These two objects, in this example the shirt and pair of pants, are *metamers* or a *metameric pair*. Despite being manufactured independently with different fabrics or dyes, the two articles of clothing appeared as the same color in the store. These differences become apparent only when the available light source changes the color reproduction equation. Figure 13-12 shows metameric fabrics next to one another under different illuminants.

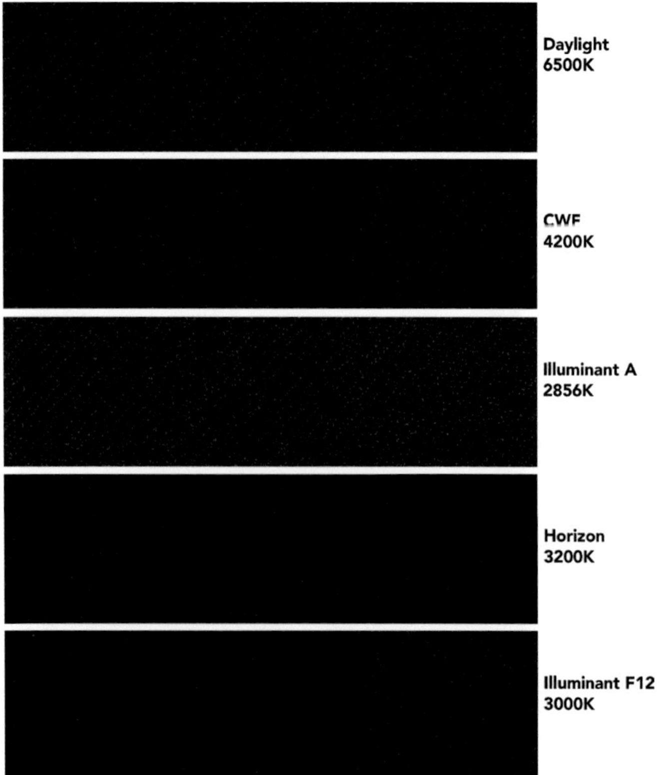

Figure 13-12 Three fabric samples that change appearance under different light sources.

What makes two objects appear to be the same color despite being different materials? The colors we perceive are governed by three components. The first is the object's spectral reflectance: the amount of energy reflected at all visible wavelengths. The second component is the spectral power distribution of the light source under which we view the object. The third component is our vision. As discussed earlier in this chapter, our retinal anatomy includes three cone types (long-wave, mid-wave and short-wave) with overlapping sensitivities. All observed colors are therefore reduced to three sensory quantities, one from each cone. These three quantities integrate together when we perceive color. An object's spectral reflectance and our vision remain the same while the light source can vary. When the spectral power distribution of the dominant light changes and the color we perceive changes with it, two seemingly similar colors may reveal themselves to be otherwise. The example of the shirt and pair of pants describes two materials that do not have the same spectral reflectance yet the store's lighting lead you to perceive them as matching. The change in illuminants when you brought the clothes home revealed the underlying disparity. Measuring the spectral reflectance of objects is accomplished using a spectrophotometer under multiple illuminants with distinct spectral power distributions such as Standard Illuminant A and D65.

Consider how the appearances of Sample 1 and Sample 2 change when the lighting is changed (see Figure 13-13). The spectral reflectance of the samples intertwines up until approximately 620 nm. Beyond that, their reflectance's separate and end up roughly 40% different from each other. When the samples are viewed under daylight illumination (D65), the amount of energy above 620 nm is insufficient to show the sample differences. A lack of red energy means that the samples cannot reflect it by

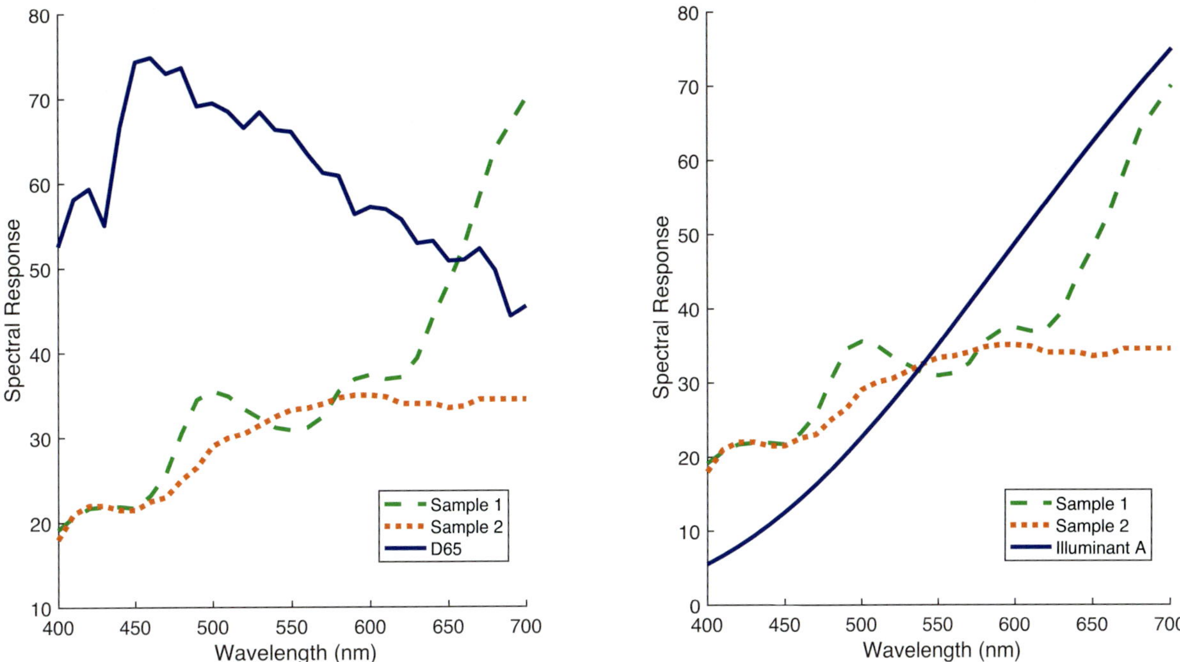

Figure 13-13 The spectral reflectance's of a metameric pair compared under two different illuminants.

different amounts, thus rendering their appearances similar. The amount of energy present around 620 nm is much greater when the samples are viewed under Illuminant A (tungsten). Sample 1's reflectance at this portion of the spectrum means that it appears quite different from Sample 2.

Although metamerism can cause us frustration when trying to match clothes, its role in color photographic output and color management is an essential one. We reproduce recorded colors of our world and display them on monitors, prints, fabrics and various other media with a relative degree of success because metamerism allows us to perceive the same colors through different means. In other words, without metamerism, the use of subtractive mixing and ink colorants does not work to recreate the colors we see when taking photographs. We can photograph and print an image of green grass in a field that appears true to life in its color without needing the grass itself and the sun shining on that print thanks to color mixing and metamerism.

Partitive Mixing

Additive and subtractive mixing rely on *spatial color mixing*, also called *partitive mixing*. In partitive mixing, small amounts of red, green and blue lights or small amounts of cyan, magenta and yellow pigments are placed side by side to form an image. The individual points of light or ink drops are so small that the eye cannot readily distinguish them as distinct colored spots at a normal viewing distance. A classic example of partitive mixing in art history is painter George Seurat's pointillism works.

Partitive mixing is employed in televisions and computer monitors. These displays create images using small pixels filtered to be red, green or blue (the additive primaries). Their intensities are electronically controlled to reproduce a range of perceived colors and tones. The smaller the pixels or the greater the viewing distance, the less likely we are to perceive them as independent points of color. Displays use fixed pixel sizes as they cannot dynamically adjust in size or shape.

For subtractive color, small dots of inks are deposited on paper or other substrates at varying densities. These dots are printed in precise patterns and amounts that appear

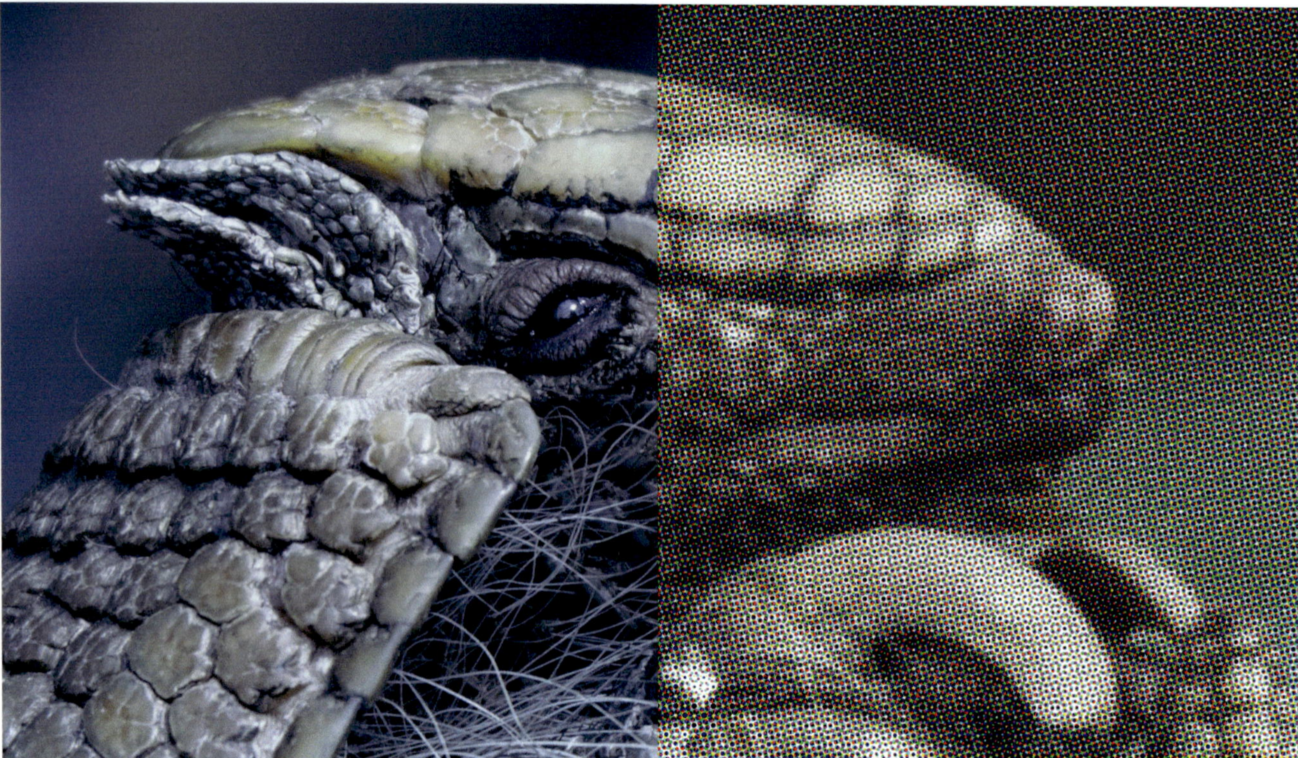

Figure 13-14 A continuous color photograph (left) reproduced with a CMYK ink pattern (right).

as continuous, full color images when viewed from the appropriate distance (magnified for illustration in Figure 13-14). Ink dot sizes can vary in radius depending on the capabilities of the printer and the pigment or dye used. Printing on a substrate like white paper means that any areas not covered with ink influence the perception of color and tone; varying the distances and spaces between dots adds an additional parameter in partitive mixing that is not available in fixed-pixel, additive color displays. Taking a close look at both monitors and printed materials reveals these dense but distinct units of color that form our photographic reproductions.

Defining Color with Color Specification Systems

Color specification systems define *color spaces*, color models with known references and scales. There are three basic systems for describing or specifying a color. The first method is defined by color mixing. This system provides the observer with a discrete set of color sample chips to choose from. When a selection is made, documented information from that chip is used to create that color. That information includes the percentages of different inks, pigments or paints that must be mixed to produce a color to match the selected chip.

The second system for object-color specification is a *color-order system* defined by human perception. Color chips are spaced so that they appear to have uniform intervals or differences in hue, saturation and lightness. This requires judgment by a standard observer under a standard set of viewing conditions. The Munsell Color System is a color-order system that consists of hundreds of samples; it continues to be useful for visual artists, agriculture and food industries and even government standards.

The third system is defined by matching perceptions to a standardized set of lights. An example is the CIE Color System that specifies color in terms of three parameters: *Y*, *x* and *y*. These parameters are calculated based on the visual response of a standard observer, the spectral power distribution of the light source and the spectral reflectance of the sample. The CIE system is used extensively in color management systems and is discussed in greater detail later in this chapter.

The Pantone System of Color Specification

A commonly encountered example of a color mixing system is The Pantone Matching System®. You may be familiar with this approach if you've ever gone to a home improvement store and picked out a sample that is mixed by an employee on the spot. It is a functional system that uses prepared samples and precise recipes that help create the color you pick out every time. The Pantone Matching System® is widely used in the graphic arts and it uses inks as the colorants. Using colorants similar to those used for printing provides a closer match between the colors selected and specified by the client and the colors produced by a printer. The Pantone Matching System® includes a series of books containing thousands of printed color samples and their formulas as shown in Figure 13-15.

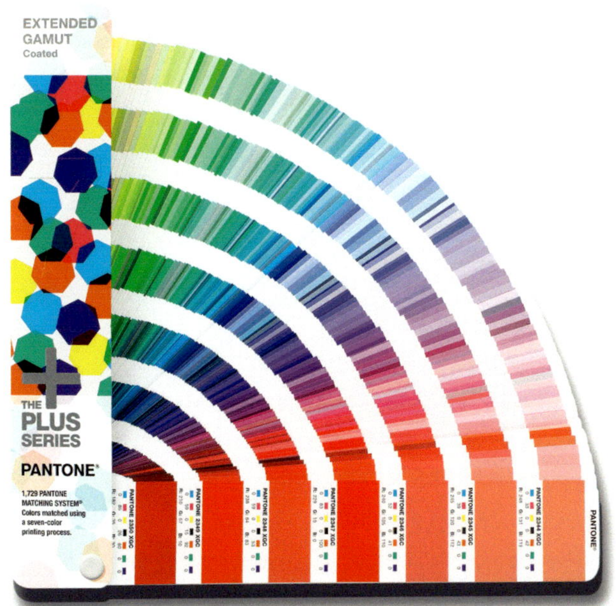

Figure 13-15 An example Pantone color sample book. Image courtesy of © X-Rite Incorporated | www.xrite.com

Some samples are available on several different surfaces and finishes.

The Pantone system is used in printing, plastics, fashion, home and color evaluation industries. It's great for identifying and using specific colors for designs, logos and graphics made from scratch, though we don't have the luxury of hand-selecting colors in quite the same way when photographing real-world objects. One shortfall of the Pantone system is that not all colors are available. Only those found in the Pantone Sample book can be used. As a consequence, it's not possible to make an exact color match if we convert a photographic image to a Pantone color space.

The Munsell System of Color Specification

Albert Henry Munsell was a painter and an art teacher. He found communicating about color with his students to be frustrating and sought a scientific approach to make things easier. The result of his explorations is the *Munsell Color System*. Munsell went on to publish *A Color Notation* in 1905 and the *Atlas of the Munsell Color System* in 1915 based on his explorations of organizing color and describing color. The Munsell System for color identification is one of the earliest attempts to create an accurate system to numerically describe color. One of the Munsell System's strengths is in providing a common notation for color in which a person first identifies a color visually and then uses language to describe it. To accomplish this, Munsell prepared a large variety of painted color chips. Munsell described *hue* as "the name of the color" or "the quality by which we distinguish one color from another, as a red from a yellow, a green, a blue or a purple." He defined *value* as "the light of color" or "the quality by which we distinguish a light color from a dark one." Lastly, he described *chroma* as "the strength of a color" or "that quality by which we distinguish a strong color from a weak one."[3]

Munsell started with a collection of chips spanning a wide range of colors. He first grouped the chips into ten named major hues: red, red-yellow, yellow, yellow-green, green, green-blue, blue, blue-purple, purple and

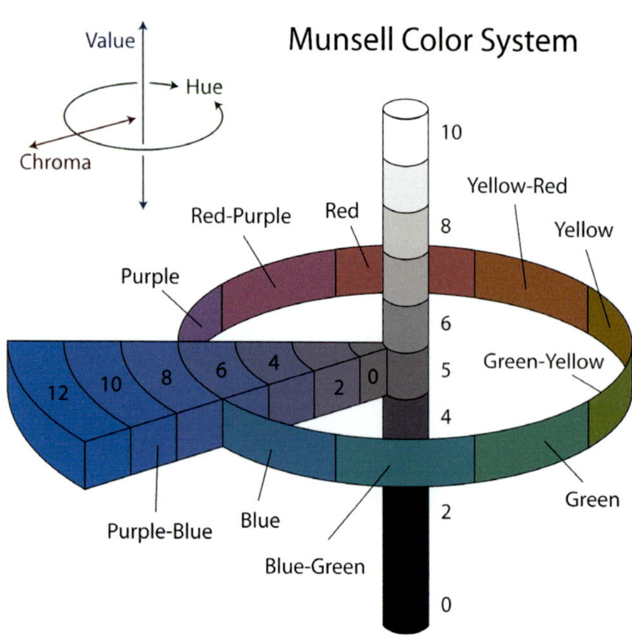

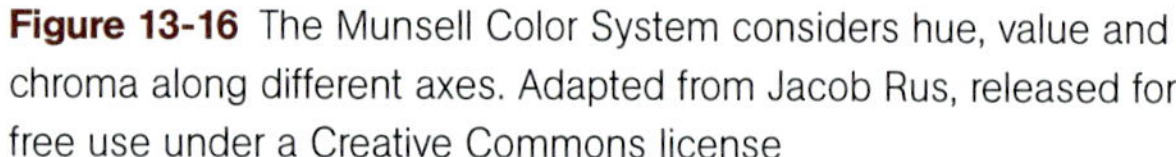
Figure 13-16 The Munsell Color System considers hue, value and chroma along different axes. Adapted from Jacob Rus, released for free use under a Creative Commons license

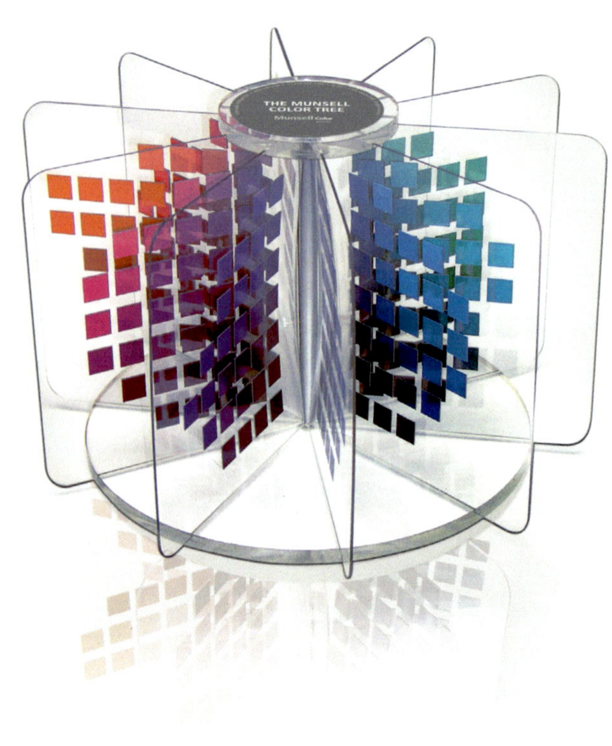

Figure 13-17 The Munsell color tree. Image courtesy of © X-Rite Incorporated | www.xrite.com

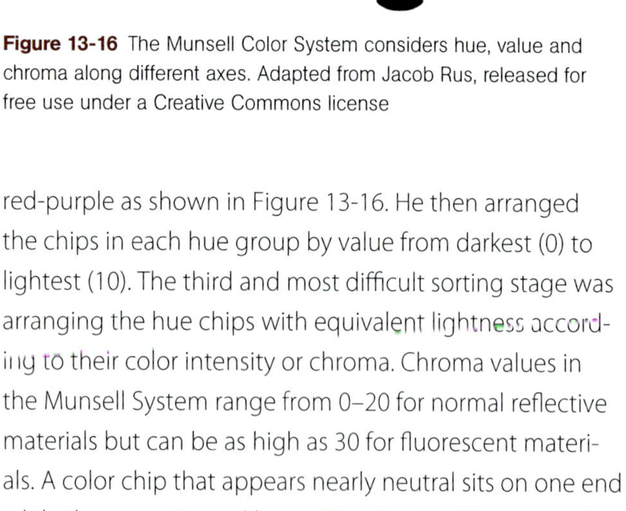
red-purple as shown in Figure 13-16. He then arranged the chips in each hue group by value from darkest (0) to lightest (10). The third and most difficult sorting stage was arranging the hue chips with equivalent lightness according to their color intensity or chroma. Chroma values in the Munsell System range from 0–20 for normal reflective materials but can be as high as 30 for fluorescent materials. A color chip that appears nearly neutral sits on one end while the opposite end has a vibrant or highly saturated instance of a given hue.

Munsell also made one critical refinement from there. He ordered the colored chips so that the interval between adjoining chips was visually equal in hue, value and chroma—a monumental task. With this visual structuring completed, he had to communicate it to others so they could also visualize the arrangement and adopt a common language to describe the colors. The three attributes of color as defined by Munsell (hue, value, chroma) occupy a three-dimensional space or volume. Munsell described this volume in terms of a *color tree* (see Figure 13-17). He wrote: "The color tree . . . carries a scale of value, for the trunk. The branches are at right angles to the trunk . . . carry the scale of chroma . . . branches tell their hue."[4] The hues change as one walks around the tree, the values increase as one climbs up the tree and the chromas increase as one moves out along the branches.

The overall shape of the color volume that Munsell creatively imagined as a tree is not symmetrical. This is because the range of chromas is not the same for all hues. For example, it's possible to have a yellow hue of high value and high chroma but not one of low value and high chroma. Concurrently, a blue hue of high value and high chroma is not attainable. As a result, the blue and yellow portions of the tree do not have the same shape. The three-dimensional, asymmetrical color volume of the modern Munsell color tree represents stable and reproducible colorants available today, excluding fluorescent colors. The Munsell space is expanded as new colorants become available.

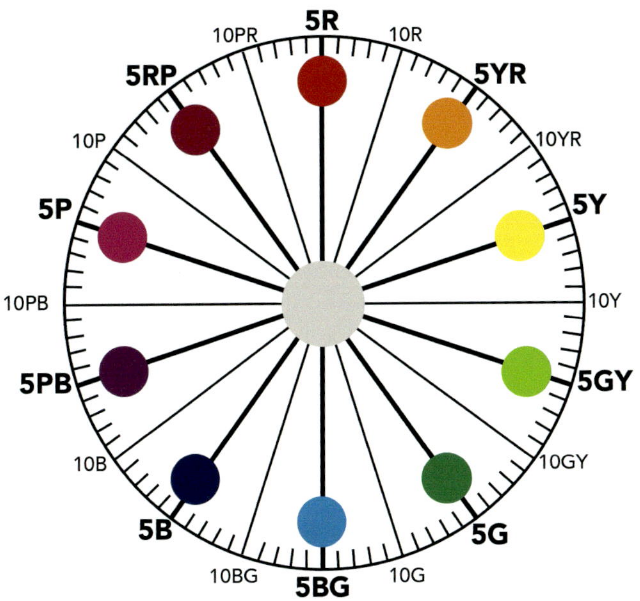

Figure 13-18 A top-down view of Munsell's color tree highlights the radial positions of different hues.

There are 100 unique hue groups represented in the Munsell system though only a select sample of ten are actually shown in the color tree. The unseen hues exist between those ten with the full 100 hues being equally spaced in terms of visual differences, illustrated in Figure 13-18.

Figure 13-18 shows how the ten major hue names are used for qualitative notation. The numbers along the circle provide more precise notation. These numbers make it easy to use the Munsell system for statistical work, cataloging and computer programming. The combination of numerals with hue initials is considered the most descriptive form of designation. This combination is shown in the inner circle: 5R, 7.5R, 10R, 2.5YR, 5YR, 7.5YR, 10YR and so on for a total of 40 named hues called *constant hues*. The Munsell Book of Color provides over 1,600 samples of these 40 constant hues.

The Munsell system specifies colors with the alphanumeric sequence *Hue Value/Chroma* (H V/C). For example, a 5R hue with a value of 8 and a chroma of 4—a light pink—is designated as 5R 8/4 or simply R 8/4. Hues positioned anywhere other than at the 5 position along the hue circle must be explicitly noted, but those at 5 can leave the number off (as it's assumed to be 5R if it's written as R). Another example, R 5/12, translates to a strong red because its value is 5 and its chroma is 12. At the center of the Munsell tree are the neutrals. The notation for a neutral (achromatic) color is written *NV/*; for a middle gray (18% gray) the notation is *N5/*. Since the chroma is zero, it is usually omitted.

Near-neutrals have chromas less than 0.3 and are usually treated as neutrals. If more precision is needed, the format *N V/(H,C)* is used where H is represented by one of the ten select hues. For example, a light gray with a slightly yellowish cast might be noted as N 8/Y,0.2 or, using the regular H V/C form, Y 8/0.2. The form *N V/0* can be reserved for absolute neutrals.

The CIE System of Color Specification

The International Commission on Illumination (CIE, based on the French name *Commission Internationale de l'Eclairage*) *Color Specification System* became an international standard for colorimetry in 1931. Color specification with the CIE system differs from Munsell's in two important ways. First, it uses mixtures of red, green and blue light to match a given sample rather than color chips. Second, the CIE system is based on *stimulus-synthesis* (the additive mixture of three color primaries) whereas the Munsell system is based on appearance. Both systems have advantages and specifying a color sample with one system allows conversion and notation to the other. The obvious advantage of the Munsell system is its simplicity and its directness. The selection of one of the color chips provides a color and color notation directly in terms of hue, value and chroma; it is a physical match easily made and easily understood. The CIE system requires instrumentation and is based on mathematical conventions, making it abstract and more difficult to conceptualize. It has the advantage, however, that any color can be matched, numerically specified and positioned on a CIE diagram or map. The CIE system provides psychophysical measurements of color whereas the Munsell system, based on color appearance, provides psychological or perceptual measures. The CIE color specification system is used exclusively for color management applications.

The CIE color system specifies colors using three parameters: *Y, x, y*. The tristimulus value Y is a luminance value, representing brightness. The x and y terms are *chromaticity coordinates*. Chromaticity coordinates are plotted on a *chromaticity diagram* that offers insight into the chroma and hue qualities of a color sample. Chromaticity coordinates are derived from the *tristimulus values* of the sample described.

There are three tristimulus values: *X, Y* and *Z*. Tristimulus values are derived by integrating three components needed to see a color (see Equation 13.1). The first component is the spectral power distribution (*S*) of the light source used to illuminate the color sample. Spectral power distributions are measured with a spectroradiometer. The CIE defined several standard light sources that are typically used in tristimulus calculations. The second component is the spectral reflectance (*R*) of the color sample. Spectral reflectance is measured with a spectrophotometer. The third component is the observer. The CIE quantified the response of the standard observer through well-documented experiments to produce the CIE color-matching functions used to calculate tristimulus values.

It's worth noting that the CIE provided the illuminant and color-matching function data in one nanometer increments from 360 to 830 nm. Ideally, we want our sample spectral reflectance in the same one nanometer intervals over the same wavelength range. Most spectrophotometers are not designed this way and instead measure from 400 to 700 nm in increments of 10 or 20 nm. The CIE uses a standard method for altering their data to match for the calculation to work when using these spectrophotometers.

$$X = k\Sigma_\lambda S_\lambda R_\lambda \bar{x}_\lambda \Delta\lambda \quad \text{(Eq. 13.1)}$$

$$Y = k\Sigma_\lambda S_\lambda R_\lambda \bar{y}_\lambda \Delta\lambda$$

$$Z = k\Sigma_\lambda S_\lambda R_\lambda \bar{z}_\lambda \Delta\lambda$$

$$k = \frac{100}{\Sigma_\lambda S_\lambda \bar{y}_\lambda \Delta\lambda}$$

Where:

X, Y and *Z* = tristimulus values

S_λ = spectral power distribution of the illuminant

R_λ = object's spectral reflectance

$\bar{x}, \bar{y}, \bar{z}$ = CIE standard observer color-matching functions

$\Delta\lambda$ = measurement wavelength interval

Σ_λ = summing of the products of the multiplications over the wavelengths measured

k = normalizing constant

Chromaticity coordinates are calculated once the tristimulus values are obtained using the formulas in Equation 13.2. Note that $x + y + z$ always evaluates to 1.

$$x = \frac{X}{X+Y+Z} \qquad y = \frac{Y}{X+Y+Z} \qquad z = \frac{Z}{X+Y+Z} \quad \text{(Eq. 13.2)}$$

The CIE Chromaticity Diagram

Chromaticity describes two attributes of color: hue and chroma. These two qualities, called *dominant wavelength* and *purity* in the CIE system, are plotted on a horseshoe-shaped map called a *chromaticity diagram* shown in Figure 13-19. This diagram represents all of the colors visible to the average observer. Around the periphery of the curved section are wavelengths of visible light scaled from 380 to 770 nm. The x- and y-axes are used to plot the position of the chromaticity of a particular color. Importantly, the color is always plotted relative to a specific light source under which it is viewed. In this example, the daylight source is located in the lower middle of the chromaticity diagram. It is located on the *Planckian Locus*, a plotted line representing all light sources that are incandescent blackbody radiators. This serves as a neutral reference point. The farther a color plots from the reference neutral, the greater the purity (chroma). A green sample is identified by the coordinates x = 0.22 and y = 0.52. Not shown is the luminance (brightness) of the green. This value is obtained separately from the data used to calculate the x and y coordinates. The dominant wavelength (hue) is determined by drawing a line from the reference point through the plotted point to the curved wavelength line. The green filter shown has a dominant wavelength of 520 nm.

The chromaticity diagram is also valuable for visualizing *color gamut*. The gamut is the range of reproducible colors for a given system or device and it's most commonly a subset of the perceivable color space (CIE space). The chromaticity diagram as a whole represents the gamut of

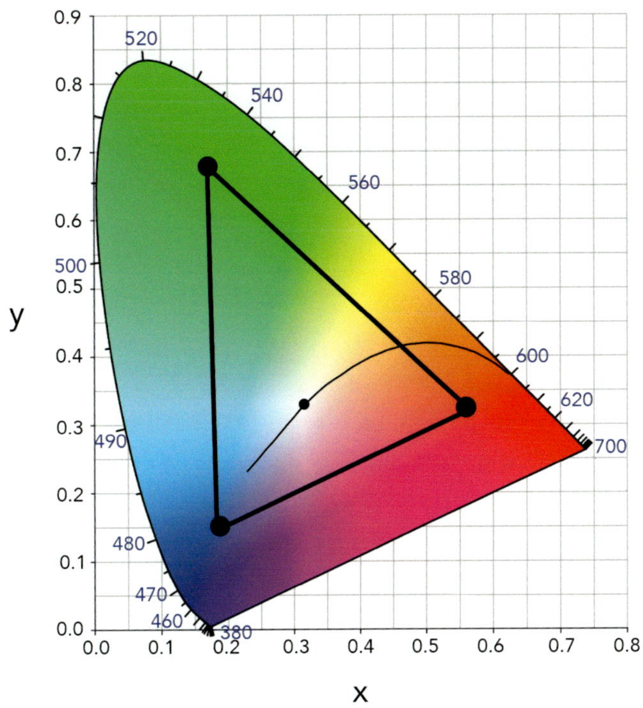

Figure 13-19 A chromaticity diagram. The inset triangle represents a color gamut and the dot in the center represents a light source. The Planckian Locus is the thin line upon which the example light source sits.

human vision. A greater number of colors can be shown with a larger gamut while a small gamut limits the possible colors to a smaller number and range. Mapping the primary colors used by an output device (like a display) on the chromaticity diagram helps to identify its reproducible colors. The inset triangle in Figure 13-19 maps the chromaticities of the red, green and blue pixels of a computer monitor. Drawing straight lines to connect the three additive primary chromaticity points reveals the monitor's color gamut as a two-dimensional area. Any color that sits inside of this triangle can be accurately displayed. Photographs don't always contain a wide range of colors and this gamut may be enough to reproduce all colors in the image. However, you may find that a vibrant red dress doesn't look quite so saturated on screen compared to seeing it in person. In this example, the image content includes reds that fall outside of the monitor's reproducible gamut in the red portion of the color space. We'll explore this further in Chapter 14's look at managing these color reproduction challenges.

CIELAB Space

The CIE 1931 chromaticity diagram in Figure 13-19 provides a convenient mapping space for displaying chromaticity coordinates and color gamuts, however, color differences displayed by these coordinates are not uniformly distributed. Similar color differences between two samples of a reddish or bluish color are compressed, whereas the same visual difference greenish colors appear expanded in the diagram. This non-uniformity of plotted color differences was reported in research done by David MacAdam in 1942. MacAdam used a large number of color difference pairs to determine how much of a color change, in any direction, could be made before an observer perceived a *just noticeable difference* (JND). He found that the variabilities in JNDs were different for each color and that plots of these variability boundaries formed similar elliptical shapes that varied greatly in size from one another. These experimental results helped describe the perceptual non-uniformity of the 1931 CIEXYZ chromaticity diagram and are known as the *MacAdam ellipses*.

The CIE recommended the use of a more uniform color difference formula and related color space in 1976. They designated *CIE L*a*b** (or *CIELAB*) to provide better correlation between visual and measured color differences. The use of CIELAB provided a significant improvement over the non-uniformity of the CIE tristimulus space by deriving metrics that correlate to perceptions of color. CIELAB, based on a simple color vision model, can adjust for changes in the color and amount of illumination, signal compression and opponent signal processing. The CIELAB color space does not have an associated chromaticity diagram because of its exponential non-linear derivation from CIE tristimulus space. However, a three-dimensional color space can be constructed with L* as the vertical axis and a* and b* occupying horizontal planes.

The L* value represents luminance and ranges from 0 (black) to 100 (white). The a* value represents the redness-greenness of the sample. The b* value represents the yellowness-blueness of the sample. There is no numerical limit on a* or b* values and they can be either positive or negative. It is customary to plot only the a* and b* values, resulting in a two-dimensional graph. Color gamut comparisons are easily constructed using the a*

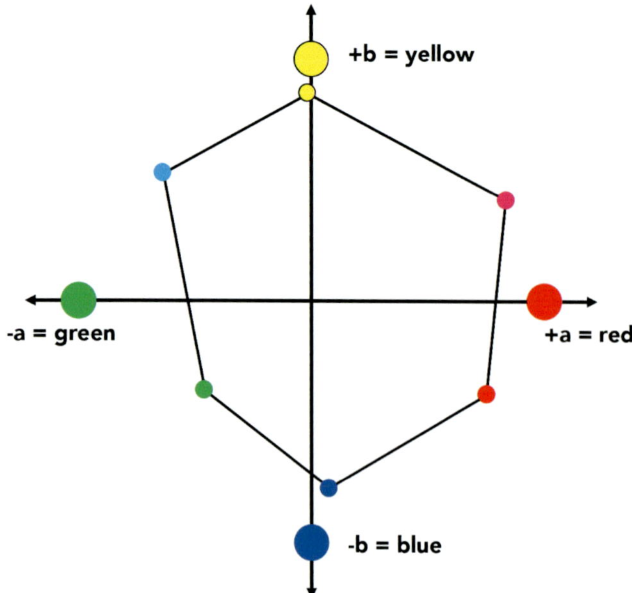

Figure 13-20 An a* versus b* CIELAB plot with a red, green, blue, cyan, magenta and yellow color gamut.

(redness-greenness), and b* (yellowness-blueness) horizontal opponent measurement planes (see Figure 13-20).

Specifying color in terms of CIELAB provides a means for various color specification systems used in photography to communicate with one another across media components. Regardless of the input or output device used—camera, monitor, scanner, printer—and how the colors are being specified, all can feed into a CIELAB based device-independent reference color space. This allows for compatible conversions across all existing components of a digital color reproduction system. CIELAB's L* and a*, b* component performance as a simple color appearance model makes it useful in color management systems. However, due to its still-not-perfect uniformity, some software vendors prefer to implement their own color space configurations based around CIEXYZ tristimulus values.

The Roles of Light and Color on Perception and Perspective

We round out our understanding of vision by outlining how the visual system plays a part in perception and perspective. We described the effect of focal length and object distance on perspective in Chapter 2. Perspective gives us a sense of relative sizes, distances, position and general spatial awareness of three-dimensional scenes. There are additional ways to convey perspective and affect the perception of subject matter in photographs. Light adaptation, linear perspective, color, shape, size, depth of field, overlap, aerial haze and texture all play a role.

Light Adaptation

First, let's explore how our eyes adapt to differences in lighting in ways that affect our perception of objects and potentially make our vision an unreliable instrument. Earlier in this chapter we introduced the functions of photopic, mesopic and scotopic vision for adapting to different light levels. When taking light adaptation into account, the ratio of luminances to which the visual system responds is truly amazing. A white object in sunlight has a luminance approximately 100 million times that of a white object in starlight, yet both objects are easily seen when a person is fully adapted to each light level. A person can detect a flash of light with a luminance 1/100th that of white paper in starlight under optimal adaptation conditions. A person can detect luminance differences up to 1,000 times that of white paper in sunlight when adapted to bright light, though this approaches luminances that can damage the retina. The total response range of the visual system is approximately 10,000,000,000,000:1 (ten trillion to one), or a log luminance difference of 13.

It's important to distinguish between luminance, which is psychophysical and measurable with a light meter, and the perception of brightness, which is influenced by physiological and psychological factors and is not directly measurable. The eye is not a dependable instrument for measuring luminance values. It's difficult to judge whether a black surface in direct sunlight is reflecting more or less light than a white surface illuminated with dim, incandescent indoor light, for example. This difficulty stems from two variables: reflectance of the two surfaces and the amount of light falling on them. The adaptation level of the visual system affects perception in that a surface with a fixed luminance appears lighter when the eye is dark adapted than when it is light adapted. Also, a gray tone

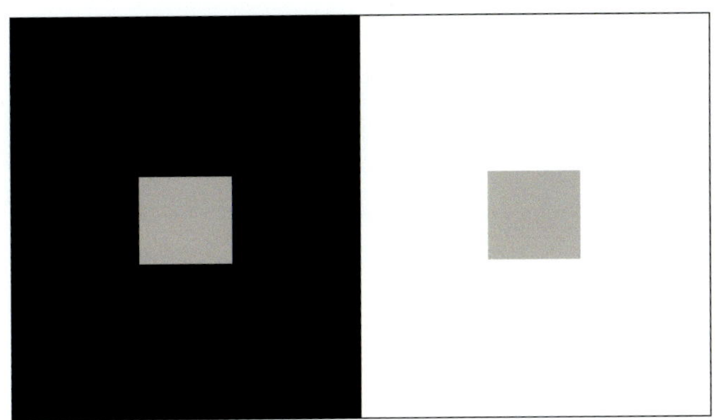

Figure 13-21 Lateral adaptation causes the two boxes, both the same shade of gray, to appear brighter or darker depending on their surround.

appears lighter in front of a black background than in front of a white background, an effect known as *lateral adaptation* or *simultaneous contrast* as shown in Figure 13-21. Simultaneous contrast can impact the appearance of hue, saturation and lightness.

Conversely, the eye is excellent as a null instrument in detecting tiny luminance differences in side-by-side comparisons. Figure 13-22 illustrates an old style of visual densitometer. These devices were quite accurate and took advantage of the side-by-side comparison strength of the human visual system. The measured sample is seen in a circle surrounded by a ring that's adjusted to match the inner circle in brightness.

This method of putting tones next to each other for comparison works well for grayscale objects. It's difficult to match the brightness or lightness of two areas if they differ in hue. If, for example, the inner circle in a visual densitometer is red and the outer ring is blue, the viewer struggles to identify when the two match in brightness. Matching the brightness of differently hued samples requires the use of a *flicker photometer*. This device presents the two samples to the viewer alternately in rapid succession. A flickering is observed when the two are not closely matched in brightness; the flickering ceases when they match.

Color Contrast

Contrast is defined as the difference in luminance between two tones. *Color contrast* is the difference in luminance between two adjacent colors. This applies to overlaid colors as well, such as text on a color background. Colors that are complementary to each other, such as green and magenta shown in Figure 13-23, have a high color contrast when used together. Colors that are adjacent to each other, such as magenta and red, have low contrast. Color contrast influences the use of graphics, computer interfaces, web design and should be considered by photographers for composition and color emphasis when scene and subject content are controllable.

The Web Content Accessibility Guidelines (WCAG) 2.0 provides web designers with guidelines in color contrast for accessible web content.[5] For example, a minimum contrast ratio of 4.5:1 is recommended for text

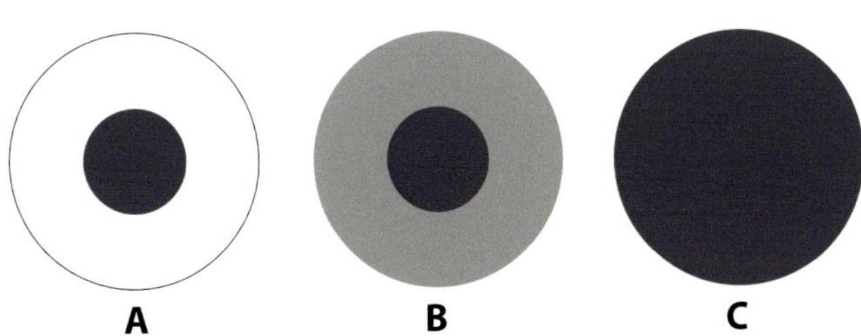

Figure 13-22 Simulated field of view in a visual densitometer. (A) The dark small circle is the unknown sample density. The larger circle is the matching field set at 0 density. (B) The density of the matching field is increased but is insufficient to match the density of the sample. (C) More density is added to the matching field and it now matches the density of the unknown sample. The known density of the matching field is the density of the sample.

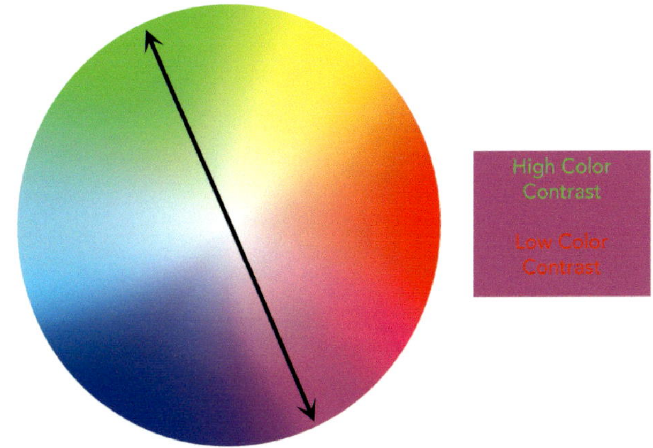

Figure 13-23 Looking to opposite ends of a color wheel finds complimentary colors with high color contrast, like green and magenta.

on a background. Photography doesn't have such clearly defined guidelines but knowledge of color contrast can be used to create more effective images.

Linear Perspective

Linear perspective is used by artists whereby the relative size, shape and position of objects are determined by drawn or imagined lines converging at a point on the horizon. It's a technique of representing a three-dimensional object in a two-dimensional medium. There are three components to creating linear perspective: a horizon line, a vanishing point and orthogonal lines. The horizon line runs across the scene. This is often where the sky appears to meet the ground in an outdoor landscape. The vanishing point is where all parallel lines in the scene appear to converge and sits along the horizon line. The orthogonal lines are visual rays that assist the viewer in connecting all of the edge points in the scene to the vanishing point. Figure 13-24 illustrates linear perspective by identifying these three components. Photographers create photographs with linear perspective, sometimes without realizing it, simply because the medium records a two-dimensional version of a three-dimensional scene. We don't need to worry about drawing any lines or following a vanishing point—thankfully, as some of us aren't the most talented with paper and pencil—but that doesn't mean we can ignore the visual importance of linear perspective. Making careful use of parallel and converging sight lines in a composition goes a long way toward emphasizing or indicating scene depth. The composition of Figure 13-24 places the vanishing point near the center of the image frame, making that a strong focal point. The eye is drawn to the center and the instinct is reinforced by the bright patch far off in the distance.

Linear perspective is bolstered by the size of objects rendered on our retina. The same object, like the trees or the fence posts in Figure 13-24, appears smaller on the retina when it is farther away. We discuss this further in the section on *size* a little later.

If we asked you to precisely describe an object's appearance over the phone, you'd likely break it down in terms of shape, color and size. Different authorities on visual perception often disagree about the critical stimulus attributes for visual perception, the relative importance of each and even the definitions of the terms. For example, the word *form* generally implies different object qualities to artists and photographers. Six attributes are particularly important to photographers: color, shape, depth, size, sharpness and motion.

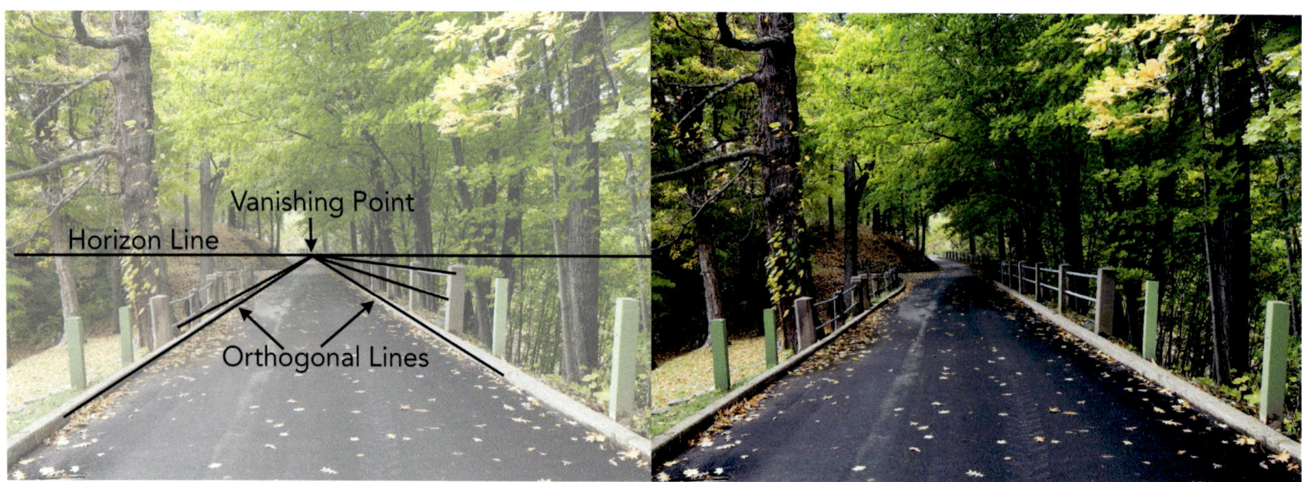

Figure 13-24 This landscape photograph exhibits visual cues of linear perspective (shown in the overlay on the left). The photographer chose a composition that takes advantage of linear perspective to convey depth and to guide the viewer's gaze through the scene.

Color and Perceived Distance

We've established systems for communicating and organizing color, but what happens when our perception of color plays tricks on our understanding of scenes and objects? Warm colors (reds, yellows and oranges) are *approaching colors*. Red objects appear closer to the foreground in an image compared to a cool color such as blue, for example. Cool colors are *receding colors* in how our brain interprets and perceives them. Using both types, approaching and receding, adds exaggerated depth or visual emphasis. Recall that we defined chromatic aberration in lenses in Chapter 2. Your eye also suffers from chromatic aberration. The red wavelengths come into focus behind the retina such that the eye's lens changes shape to bring the image forward. This causes the red object to appear closer. The opposite happens for blue wavelengths that come into focus in front of the retina and have to be refocused backwards. Red is particularly effective at drawing attention and creating a sense of excitement.[6]

Shape and Dimension

An object's shape is a description of its outline. Silhouettes emphasize shape and eliminate or deemphasize other attributes such as color, form and texture. We depend heavily upon the attribute of shape for the identification of many objects. In fact, shape is often the only attribute needed for a viewer to recognize an object in a drawing or photograph.

Three-dimensional objects have many shapes because they are viewable from many different angles. The viewpoint chosen by a photographer to provide the best shape for an object is important even when the object is lit to provide detail. This choice is particularly critical in a silhouette. Silhouettes of people are commonly recognizable only in a full left or right profile view; profile views are used for the images of famous people on coins.

Photographers control the emphasis on object shapes by controlling the separation or contrast between object and background. The term *figure-ground* refers to the subject of a picture and the surrounding area. Figure-ground is an important concept in Gestalt psychology, where the emphasis is on the perception of the whole rather than an analysis of the parts. Experienced photographers have little difficulty separating an object from the background (figure from ground) in a photograph by means of background choice, lighting and depth of field. In contrast, military camouflage conceals the shapes of objects to make them appear to be part of the background and therefore escape detection.

It's not always necessary to see the entire outline shape of a familiar object to identify it and visualize its entire shape. Most people perceive the moon as round when there is a full moon and when there is a half-moon or quarter-moon and the shadow side cannot be separated from the background (see Figure 13-25). One can conduct a simple experiment by looking at objects outdoors through Venetian blinds, starting with the slats in the fully open position and then gradually closing them to determine how small the openings can be before encountering difficulty in identifying the objects. Similarly, a small number of dots arranged in a circular pattern can easily be seen as representing a circle. This effect is known as the *principle of*

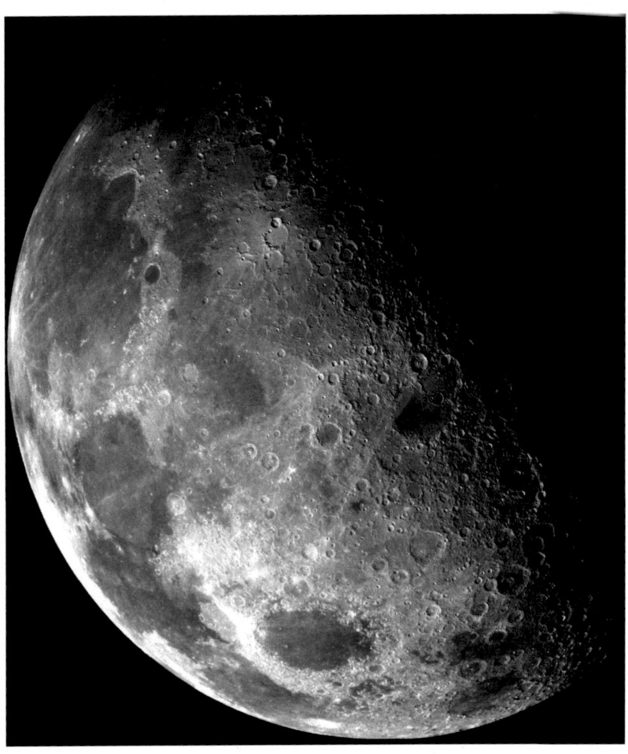

Figure 13-25 View of the moon's north pole assembled from 18 images taken by Galileo's imaging system through a green filter on December 7, 1992. Courtesy of NASA

closure in Gestalt psychology whereby the viewer mentally fills in the spaces between picture elements. A distinction exists between *closure* and *fusion*, where the latter describes when the optical-retinal system in the eye cannot resolve the small discrete elements as in a halftone reproduction or a photographic image at small to moderate magnifications.

Reading printed text is an excellent example of how the mind fills in spaces between fixation points. The area of sharpest vision represented by the fovea of the retina is very small such that when a person fixates one letter in a line of type, only a few letters on each side are clearly seen. It's possible to read rapidly with only two or three fixations per line because the reader recognizes groups of letters as familiar words without examining each letter and understands the meaning of a sentence without examining each word. Printed material containing unfamiliar words and a high concentration of factual information requires more fixations per line. Eye motion studies reveal that viewers rarely scan photographs as thoroughly as they do a printed page; they fixate on a few points while the mind fills in shapes and details between these fixation points.

The accuracy with which we perceive shapes is important in the study of visual perception, but it is not considered as critical in our daily lives as normal color vision and good acuity—which are usually tested before a person obtains a driver's license or is permitted to perform certain occupational tasks. Studies demonstrate that it is easy to deceive a viewer about shape under certain conditions. Figure 13-26 shows how a straight line can be made to appear curved. Under normal conditions, however, we are best able to detect changes in images with simple geometrical shapes such as straight lines, squares, circles and triangles (see Figure 13-27). We are also better at making comparisons with superimposed or side-by-side images than with images separated in time or space that rely on our memory.

Our perception of shapes is complicated by the fact that image shape changes with the angle and distance of the object relative to the eye or camera lens. Parallel subject lines are imaged as converging lines except when viewed or photographed perpendicularly; tilted circles are imaged as ellipses. We learn through experience that the parallel lines and circles do not change shape with a change

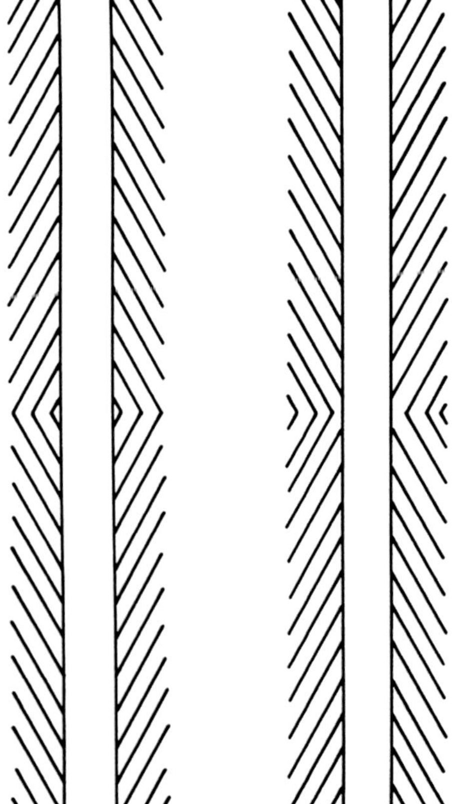

Figure 13-26 Illusory figures. The long straight lines appear curved because of the influence of the diagonal lines.

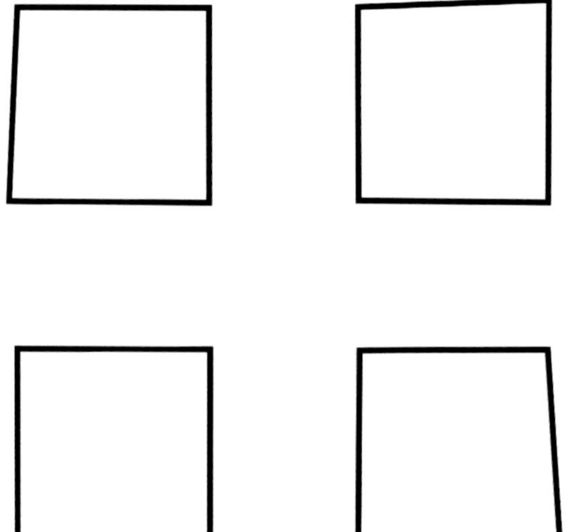

Figure 13-27 Which is the perfect square?

in viewing angle, so we mentally compensate for linear perspective effects. *Shape constancy* refers to this stability of the perceived shape of objects as the viewing or camera angle changes. *Shape generalization* is the tendency to perceive an irregular shape as a simpler shape—obtuse and acute angles seen in perspective may be perceived as right angles, and an ellipse seen in perspective may be perceived as a circle. Memories of perceived shapes can also change with time. The simplification of irregular shapes because of memory is called *leveling*. The exaggeration of a distinctive feature, such as a small gap in an otherwise continuous line, is called *sharpening*.

Size and Relative Size

The perceived size of an object has little relationship to the size of the image on the retina (or the size of the image in a photograph of the object). A car is judged to be approximately the same size when viewed over a wide range of distances as a result of *size constancy*. Experiments demonstrate that the accuracy of judging the size of an abstract shape, such as a circle, depends greatly upon being able to estimate the distance. Accuracy decreases as distance cues are systematically eliminated.

A ruler or other measuring instrument is used for a direct side-by-side comparison when the precise size of

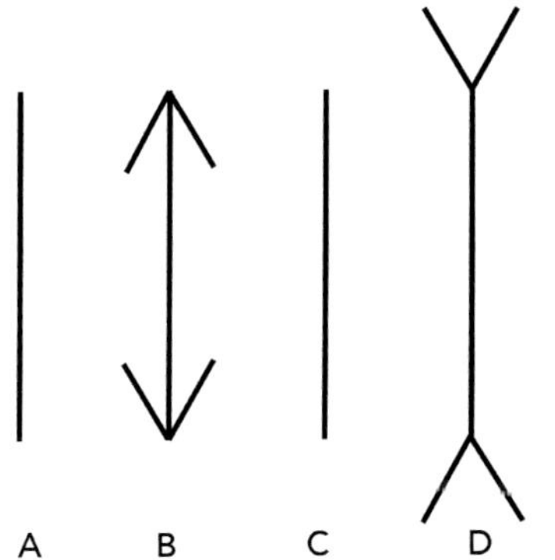

Muller-Lyer Illusion: Vertical lines A, B, C and D are all the same physical length.

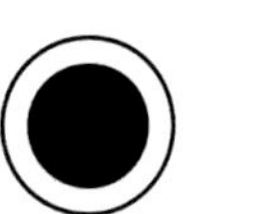
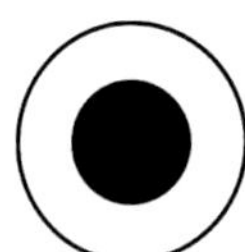

Delboeuf Figure: Both inner circles ar the same physical size.

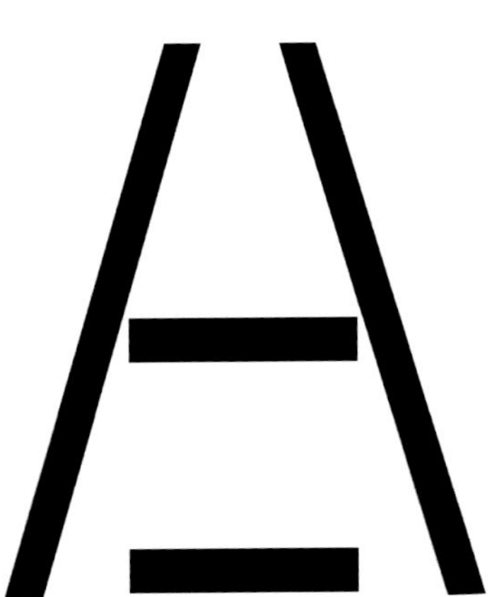

Ponzo Figure: Both horizontal bars are the same physical length.

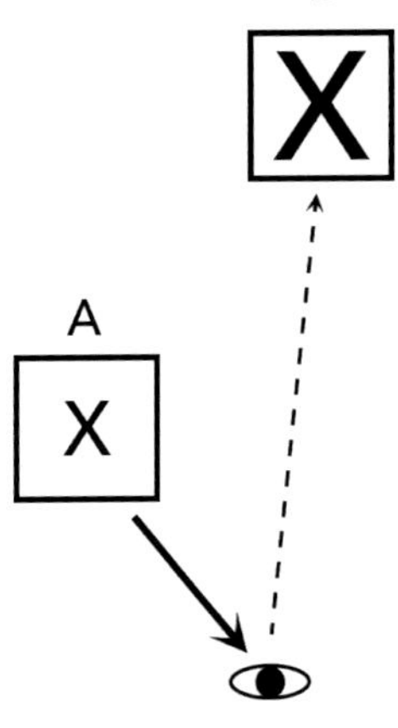

Emmert's Law: The image X is seen projected onto a screen. The afterimage, when "projected"onto a more distant screen appears larger.

Figure 13-28 Size and distance constancy. For familiar objects, size and distance are inseparable. For an object to be the same actual size at a farther distance it must be larger and therefore it appears larger.

an object must be known. As with the perception of other object attributes, the eye is most precise when used as a null instrument in making comparisons between adjacent stimuli. It is sometimes necessary to include a ruler beside an object when size determination is critical, as is often the case in forensic photography. In pictorial photographs it is usually sufficient to include an object of known size with the unfamiliar object and to provide good distance cues.

It's easy to deceive viewers about the size of objects represented in photographs. Use of a short focal length lens tends to make foreground objects appear larger than normal and background objects appear smaller than normal when the photograph is viewed at a comfortable distance. Long focal length lenses have the reverse effect. Line drawings can also cause viewers to misjudge the relative length of lines or size of images. Figure 13-28 illustrates that the Muller–Lyer arrow illusion and the Ponzo railway lines illusion both contain lines of equal length that are perceived as being unequal.

Depth of Field

Depth of field is controlled by the aperture setting and allows photographers to have all the scene in sharp focus or just a portion of it. Use of a limited depth of field, where objects in front of and behind the point of focus in the image are blurred, creates a stronger appearance of depth or perspective than when the entire scene appears sharp.

Lighting

Controlling light is key to successful photography and can affect perception in images. Depth is emphasized with lighting that produces a gradation of tones on curved surfaces, that produces a separation of tones between the planes of box-shaped objects and between objects and backgrounds, and that casts shadows of objects on the foreground or background.

Overlap

Although photographers cannot always control where objects within our image fall, object placement can play an important role. Arranging a scene so that a nearby object obscures part of a distant object provides the viewer with powerful clues as to the relative distances of the objects.

Aerial Haze

There is no controlling the weather, however a hazy day can actually be useful. The scattering of light that occurs in the atmosphere caused by haze makes distant objects appear lighter and less contrasty than nearby objects. Creating thick fog and smoke can create the illusion of depth with relatively small differences in distance.

Texture

Texture refers to the small-scale depth characteristics of a type that might be felt with the fingertips, such as the roughness of a wood file or the smoothness of window glass. Effectively representing texture in two-dimensional photographs depends largely upon using an appropriate scale of reproduction, as well as lighting that produces shadows in the recessed areas and highlights in the raised areas. Photographs made through optical and electron microscopes reveal that many seemingly smooth surfaces, such as writing paper, have a rough texture or heterogeneous form when magnified. Conversely, the craters on the moon appear to have a finger-touching type of texture when photographed from a distance with a small scale of reproduction.

Proof of Concept: Looking Closely at Additive Color Mixing on Displays

This is one of our students' favorite exercises. It ties our knowledge of partitive mixing and additive color mixing together. Figure 13-29 shows a set of color patches with pure red on one end and pure blue on the other. The patches are assigned to an RGB color space: their three channel (red, green and blue) brightness values exist as numeric, digital representations of color interpreted by a display. Of course, you're likely reading this on a printed

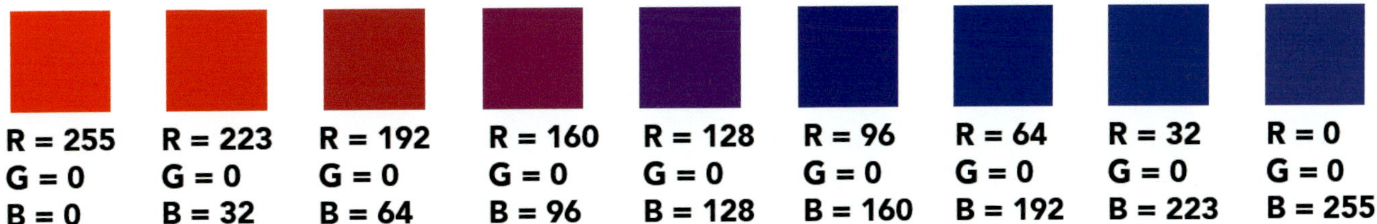

Figure 13-29 Color patches from different combinations of RGB values to create red, blue and the gradient of colors transitioning between them.

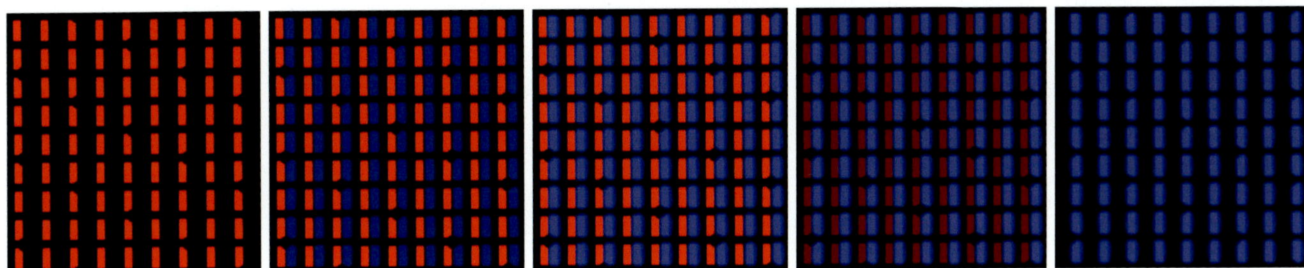

Figure 13-30 Low power microscope views of display showing a red patch (far left), a blue patch (far right) and patches transitioning from one to the other (middle).

page where that information was translated to a subtractive CMY space!

The red patch is made using the brightest possible pixel values in the red channel (255) and the darkest values in the green and blue channel (0). This recipe means that there is truly only red data present in the patch. On the other end of the illustration, the blue patch uses the brightest possible pixel values in the blue channel and the darkest values in the green and red channels. The patches sequenced between red and blue are created by simultaneously increasing the blue channel brightness and decreasing the red channel brightness. The exact middle point in this color mixing exercise creates purple: an even mix of red channel brightness (128) and blue channel brightness (128).

Figure 13-30 illustrates how an LCD monitor takes these RGB pixel value recipes and controls color-filtered liquid crystal element light transmission to display them. On the left is a close-up view of our pure red patch, displayed by turning on all red pixels to maximum brightness while leaving the blue and green pixels off. On the far right is the pure blue patch using a similar strategy. In between them are a few of the color patches transitioning between the red and blue: this is accomplished by mixing different amounts of both. These images are so highly magnified that the partitive mixing effect is lost. The black gaps and individual pixel elements are not visible at the proper viewing distance. Try squinting or backing away from the printed page to confirm that the combinations do create the desired colors.

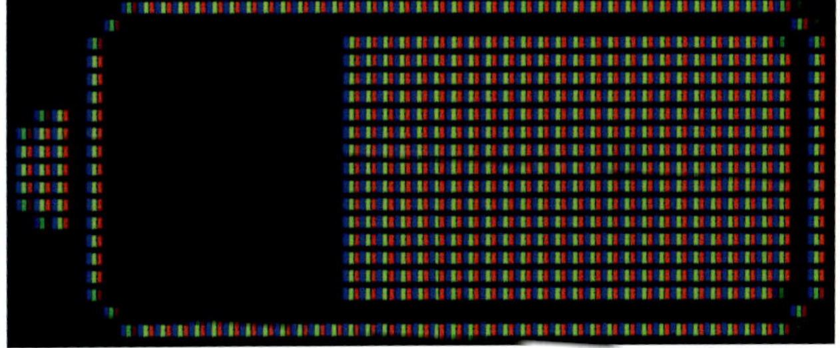

Figure 13-31 A smartphone screen up close, revealing how a white on black user interface icon is rendered on an LCD display. Photograph by Rochester Institute of Technology alumnus Andy Kempchinsky

Recreate our illustration using the illustration software of your choice or make a unique sequence of color patch transitions by modifying R, G and B channel values. Get a close look at your computer monitor using a magnifying glass, a camera with macro lens or your smartphone camera (though it may not be able to focus at such a short working distance). Even with the naked eye, you can discern the separate red, green and blue illuminated pixel elements. Similar to the three color channel digital counts in the illustration patches, the monitor creates every color by varying the brightness of its three additive primaries.

Lastly, Figure 13-31 reveals how a smartphone display creates white: the red, green and blue pixels are turned on at equal brightnesses. The presence of these primary colors is evident in this image but appears as a neutral tone at the proper viewing distance. We encourage you to look at a variety of graphics and photographs rendered on different output media to better understand how color is reproduced and perceived by the human visual system.

Notes

1 "Inter-Society Color Council aims and purposes." *ISCC Aims and Purposes*, Apr. 23, 2013, www.iscc-archive.org/organization/aims.php.

2 Snowden, Robert, et al. *Basic Vision: An Introduction to Visual Perception*. Oxford University Press, 2012.

3 Munsell, Albert H. "A color notation by A. H. Munsell." Free e-book Project Gutenberg, July 14, 2008, www.gutenberg.org/ebooks/26054, pp. 14–15.

4 Munsell, Albert H. "A color Notation by A. H. Munsell." Free e-book Project Gutenberg, July 14, 2008, www.gutenberg.org/ebooks/26054, p. 19.

5 "Web Content Accessibility Guidelines (WCAG) Overview." Edited by Shawn Lawton Henry, *Same Origin Policy - Web Security*, Reuters Limited, June 22, 2018, www.w3.org/WAI/standards-guidelines/wcaq/.

6 Gerald, Gorn, et al. "Effects of color as an executional cue in advertising: They're in the shade." *Operations Research*, June 1996, pubsonline.informs.org/doi/abs/10.1287/mnsc.43.10.1387.

14 Color Management

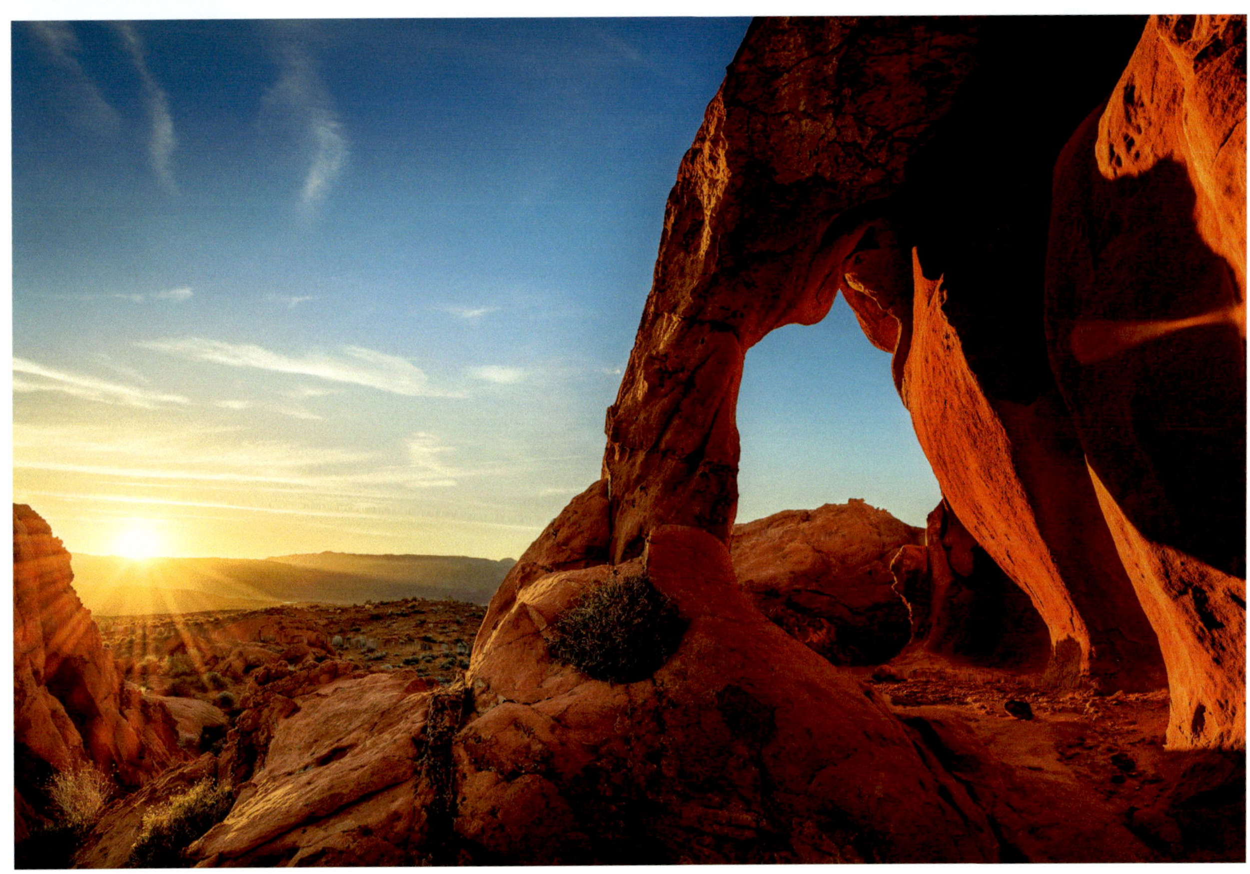

Photograph by Rochester Institute of Technology photography alumnus Kevin Young

Color management is a term that strikes fear and anxiety in photographers' hearts and minds. Like taking vitamins or getting a flu shot, many of us understand its importance but don't look forward to the follow through. Color management's reputation is one involving frustration and complexity: extra equipment, extra time, extra settings and configurations to keep straight. The good news is that excellent color management systems are increasingly accessible and streamlined for photographers that don't want to grow old attempting to understand a properly executed, color-managed workflow. A color-managed workflow is dictated by your specific needs in the context of a gallery exhibition, print publication or soft-copy client delivery and only requires a degree of diligence and attention to detail once established. This chapter is an overview of the concepts and components to make sense of the concepts, terminology and software settings used for maintaining accurate, predictable and desired color in photographic reproduction. By the end of this chapter, the instances of being surprised or frustrated by your photographic output should dramatically decrease.

Why Color Management Matters

The previous chapter laid out the many aspects of the human visual system that result in color vision. We've looked at ways of making color (mixing additive and subtractive primaries), metamerism and the CIE chromaticity diagram all in the service of creating a robust vocabulary and framework for working with color. Color management takes these concepts and provides a scaffolding to bolster our ability to retain and reproduce accurate, consistent color in our image-making endeavors. Now we need to establish new ideas like calibration, characterization, ICC profiles and rendering intents to take advantage of that scaffolding.

The cold, hard reality is this: we don't have true color matching from input (capture) to output (print or display).[1] The technologies used are varied and often cutting-edge, yet our tools lack the ability to reproduce every naturally occurring (or synthetically concocted) color and tone. Defining the boundaries and limitations of our materials and mitigating their shortcomings is the best available strategy. Sometimes this means altering image data to fit the constraints while other times it means accepting that one output is never visually equivalent to another. Color management is named appropriately; we don't yet have magical, infinite, perfectly true-to-life color solutions. Color management helps ensure predictable color reproduction.

Even the wealthiest photographer with unlimited ink cartridge funds appreciates minimizing wasted time. Printing and reprinting with incremental changes each time until an optimal print is made is an option, but it's time-consuming and wholly avoidable. Time is perhaps a more critical restraint than materials or monetary resources for highly scheduled productions like newspapers, magazines and online journalistic institutions: a client or publisher requires that a file be ready the first time, not after eight or nine iterations.

Who Governs Color Management?

Before going further, it helps to understand the origin of color management and who governs its standards. The International Color Consortium (ICC) is the governing body in the field of color management. Founded in 1993, the group oversees the field of color management and maintains the ICC profile specification (which we'll dive into later in this chapter). The ICC's mission is to "promote the use and the adoption of open, vendor-neutral, cross-platform color management systems".[2]

The five founding members of the ICC were Adobe Systems Incorporated, Agfa-Gevaert N.V., Apple Computer, Inc., Eastman Kodak Company and Microsoft Corporation. There are approximately 40 members today across the photography and printing industries. There are also 16 honorary members including Rochester Institute of Technology, home to the Munsell Color Science Laboratory.[3] These industry giants realized the need for all devices and software created by different companies to communicate with each other. To accomplish this, they developed the framework for a color management system that uses ICC profiles developed to a standard format. The current version of the standard is Specification ICC.1:2010-12 and can be found at www.color.org. Without this cross-company collaboration, color management could easily devolve into manufacturer-specific walled-gardens of workflow solutions and limited compatibility.

Reviewing Color Data Concepts

Let's take a quick look back at color concepts relevant to color management. Most tools used to examine the contents of a color profile use a chromaticity diagram to display a color gamut like the one in Figure 14-1. A color gamut describes all of the colors formed by mixing different amounts of the output primaries (typically RGB or

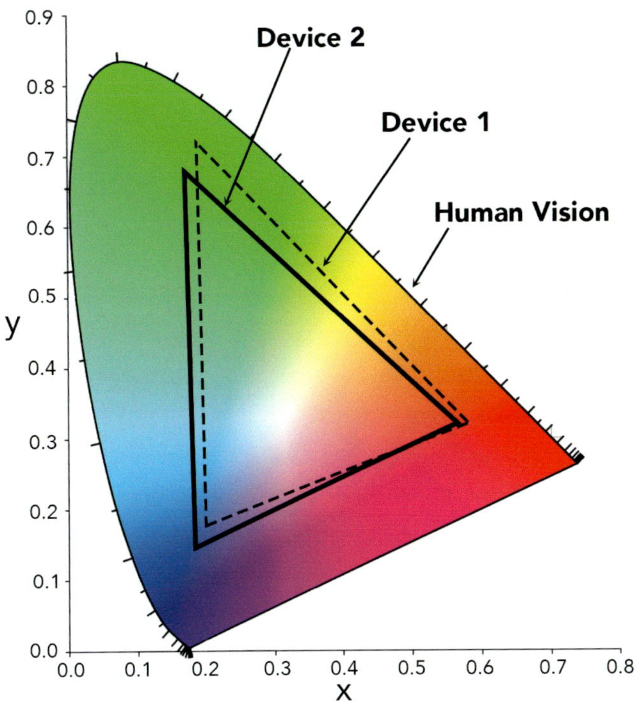

Figure 14-1 The CIE chromaticity diagram.

CMYK) and it's used to define the color reproduction capabilities of a device. In 1931, the CIE defined the CIEXYZ color space. Working with tristimulus values is difficult because they are not easily visualized. Most of us find it difficult if not impossible to identify a color represented by X, Y and Z tristimulus values.

Realizing this, the CIE also defined a method to transform tristimulus values into chromaticity coordinates. These values are *xyY*. The Y is a luminance value and is not plotted. The chromaticity coordinates *x* and *y* are calculated according to Equations 14.1 and 14.2 and can be plotted on a chromaticity diagram.

$$x = \frac{X}{X+Y+Z} \quad \text{(Eq. 14.1)}$$

$$y = \frac{Y}{X+Y+Z} \quad \text{(Eq. 14.2)}$$

These chromaticity coordinates allow for plotting any color on a chromaticity diagram independent of luminance. The chromaticity diagram is used in color management to illustrate color gamuts and white points.

Human vision's color gamut is the largest gamut that we consider. Unfortunately, there is no device available that can reproduce every visible color. The chromaticity coordinates of the pure red, green and blue primaries of a device are calculated and plotted on a chromaticity diagram. A device gamut is the triangle formed by connecting these three points. Any color that falls in the interior of the triangle is reproducible. Any color outside the triangle cannot be reproduced and is referred to as an *out-of-gamut color*. If a system, such as a printer, uses more primaries beyond cyan, magenta and yellow inks, the color gamut may be differently shaped.

Mismatched gamuts is one of the problems addressed by a color management workflow. For example, when the color gamut of the monitor is larger than the color gamut of the printer, how are the out-of-gamut colors going to print? This is handled using rendering intents, a set of behaviors or instructions that dictate the reproduction strategy.

Color Space Types

Chapter 13 introduced the CIELAB color space as a solution to modelling and describing color. CIELAB is a *device-independent* color space encompassing all of human vision. It does not describe the color reproduction capabilities of any one output device. In color management, there are two device-independent color spaces that use numeric values to model human vision: CIEXYZ and CIELAB. CIELAB is valuable as a universal translator sitting between the input media or device and the output device.

A *device-dependent* color space is based on the characteristics of the inks, in the case of a printer, or the filters, in the case of a display with color-filtered pixels. Every device defines its own device-dependent color space. The color space of a monitor, for example, is defined by a finite set of RGB values used to control its output. The same RGB values displayed on two unique monitors may appear different and have different measured tristimulus values, making the RGB values device-dependent.

sRGB, Adobe RGB and ProPhoto RGB

There are three standard color spaces that photographers are likely to encounter when capturing images: sRGB, Adobe RGB and ProPhoto RGB. These color spaces describe predefined color gamuts and are plotted together on a chromaticity diagram in Figure 14-2. Adobe RGB and sRGB share the same red and blue primaries. They differ in the green primary with Adobe RGB exhibiting the larger gamut. The sRGB color space (the "s" is for "standard") is the appropriate choice if a photograph is viewed on a projector or monitor. Although sRGB is the smallest gamut of the three, you do not risk the colors being poorly reproduced by delivering images with colors and tones beyond what the viewer's display is capable of reproducing. The Adobe RGB space provides greater headroom for editing and includes ranges of colors than can be reproduced in print. Many cameras offer settings to capture in either the Adobe RGB or sRGB space. We suggest setting your camera capture to Adobe RGB as you can always map to a smaller gamut later on. ProPhoto RGB is by far the largest color space. There is no printer available today that can print a gamut this large, however, it offers the most amount of data headroom for post-processing adjustments.

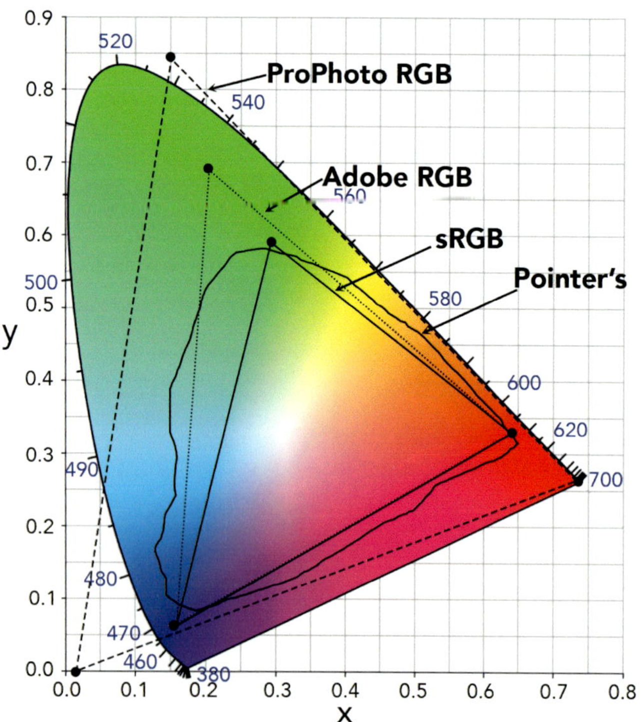

Figure 14-2 ProPhoto RGB, Adobe RGB and sRGB color spaces plotted on a chromaticity diagram. Pointer's Gamut is also plotted for reference.

Pointer's Gamut

Pointer's Gamut was developed by Michael R. Pointer in 1980 by measuring over 4,000 color samples.[4] The gamut represents all of the real surface colors visible to the human eye. These are colors reflected by the object's surface using subtractive color mixing. This color gamut is irregular in shape as shown in Figure 14-2 and is not defined with three primaries like all other color gamuts. It covers 47.9% of human vision.

Revisiting the ColorChecker

We introduced the X-Rite ColorChecker in Chapter 9 because its patches are valuable for color balancing and evaluating tone reproduction during post-processing edits. The ColorChecker target is also incredibly useful for color management and output reproduction assessment. The ColorChecker target patches are grouped into four sections: Memory Colors, Hard to Reproduce Colors, Gamut Colors and a Neutral Grayscale as shown in Figure 14-3.

Patches 1 through 4 represent dark skin, light skin, blue sky and foliage. These are colors that we all remember and are consequently critical when judging photo reproduction. Patches 5 through 11 are colors that film did not always adequately reproduce. Patch 5 represents a prized morning glory flower nicknamed "Heavenly Blue." The orange (patch 6), moderate red (patch 8) and orange-yellow (patch 11) represent oranges, grapefruits and lemons respectively. The third row of patches are the additive and subtractive primaries used to evaluate color gamuts. The last row are Munsell neutral patches that covered the dynamic range of film in the 1970s.

Each of these patches helps when assessing color and tone reproduction. The X-Rite ColorChecker is produced with published CIELAB values. The data can be evaluated against measured data from a reproduction to access

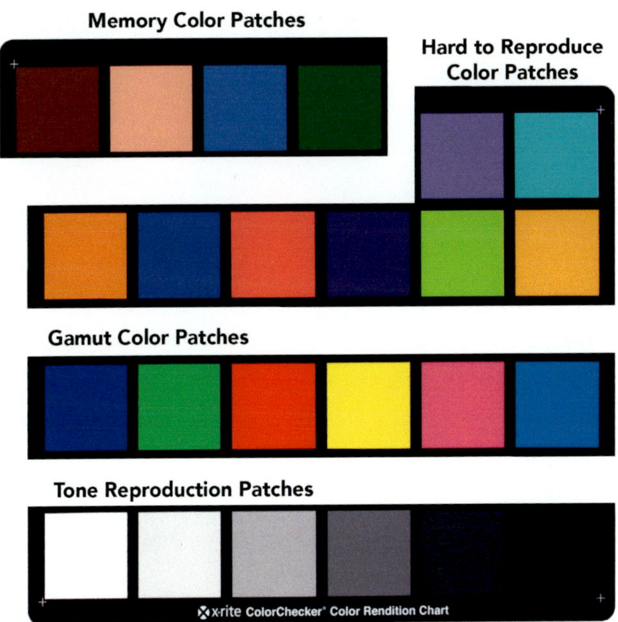

Figure 14-3 The X-Rite ColorChecker Color Rendition Chart.

accuracy objectively. For example, the ΔE or color difference can be calculated for all 24 patches. This provides insight into how well our profile performed and can assist in identifying any present color cast. The gamut patches are used to create a basic gamut plot. The neutral patches are used to create a tone reproduction plot to determine if the print brightness levels are matched to the original. Finally, a subjective visual assessment is performed using all patches. We outline all of these practices later in this chapter.

Defining Characterization and Calibration

The terms characterization and calibration are often used interchangeably in color management. They do not mean the same thing. *Characterization* is the process of determining how a device performs. This includes its capabilities and its limitations. We can characterize the performance of a camera by testing it for a linear response, measuring its spectral response, measuring its signal-to-noise ratios and the range of illuminances it can record. Characterization, then, describes the behavior of the device. In the context of color management, characterizing is determining the color gamut that a printer can reproduce, a monitor can display or an imaging device can capture.

Calibration is a process of returning a device to a known standard or its proper and optimal operating state. If you have a weight scale that no longer reads zero pounds when there's nothing on it, the scale is adjustable back to zero as a form of calibration. Similarly, if a printer, monitor or scanner can be adjusted back to a known state, it can be calibrated.

All the parts of a digital system—the camera, monitor, scanner, printer and any hardware used in the color management process—are describable in mathematical terms that a computer understands. This allows us to characterize all of these devices. The term used for this characterization is a *color profile*. When a device's characteristics change or drift, a new standard for calibration in the form of a color profile may be necessary. The need to recharacterize a device usually becomes apparent when the device can no longer be calibrated, often indicating that its performance characteristics have changed.

Characterization builds a profile of a device. A specific ICC profile identifies how a device reproduces color. It is only valid if the device exhibits consistent behavior. If something changes with the device between profile creation and producing the output product, the profile becomes invalid. A device that doesn't produce predictable results from one use to the next is a poor choice for a color-managed workflow; if it can't be trusted to do the same job over and over, it's nearly impossible to anticipate and accommodate its output capabilities. As long as a device can be calibrated back to the operating condition in which it was characterized, there is no need to create a new profile.

Color Management Systems

A *color management system*, or CMS, is software that controls the accurate reproduction and appearance of colors across different devices. The CMS's main responsibilities are twofold: to assign RGB or CMYK values to a specific color and to control the appearance of that color as it goes from one device to another so that it appears the same.

There are three components in a color management system: the *color management module* or *color matching model* (CMM), the *profile connection space* and the *color profiles*. The CMM is the overarching software that takes an input or source profile into the profile connection space and creates the output or destination profile. There are often several CMMs to choose from, however, the Adobe Color Engine (ACE) performs well and is often the default CMM.

The *profile connection space* (PCS) is a perceptually based, device-independent color space. The PCS uses either the CIELAB or CIEXYZ color space to function as the universal translator between devices. Other than appreciating that the PCS is where the color control magic happens, we never have to work directly with this part of the CMS.

Color profiles describe a device's behavior, be it a camera, printer, scanner or display device. These are real, physical devices. A profile can also be virtual, for example the sRGB or Adobe RGB spaces. The profile tells us the range of colors that a device can capture, display or print. All profiles conform to ICC specifications which ensures functionality with any encountered CMS.

An image's journey through the CMS is diagrammed in Figure 14-4. An input device passes its *source profile* into the CMM. The CMM converts this profile into the PCS. The PCS maps the input device to the output device through a *destination profile*. For example, an image is displayed on a monitor with its own source profile. The intent is to print this image. The CMM maps the monitor source profile to the destination printer profile that defines the output device such that the printer receives and understands the image data.

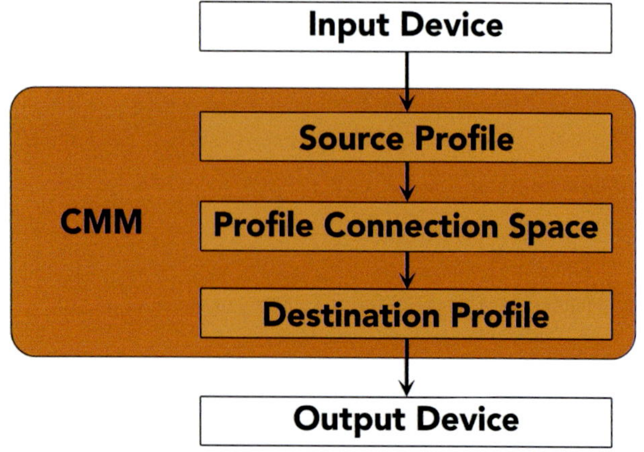

Figure 14-4 The color management module workflow that takes input image data and translates it to an output device.

The ICC Profile

The International Color Consortium released the first specification document in 1994. The consortium established the eponymous *ICC profile*: a cross-platform, vendor-neutral file format used to describe the color rendering behavior of a device.[5] ICC profiles are used in color management systems to formalize the translations and capabilities of our displays and printers.

An ICC profile allows an input image to be displayed or printed with consistent color reproduction. The profile defines the relationship between a color space, such as the RGB primaries of a monitor, to the corresponding values in a color space like CIELAB. Profiles can be device-dependent or device-independent. A device-dependent profile depends on the profiled equipment. A device-independent profile is one where the color designation is absolute in that it defines one color no matter where it is applied. The CIELAB and CIEXYZ color spaces are used to produce device-independent profiles.

We categorize profiles into three classes: input, display and output. Each plays a unique role in color management. Input profiles describe image-creation devices like scanners and cameras. These are one-way profiles; you cannot output image data to a scanner or camera. A one-way profile only maps the RGB pixel values of the device to its corresponding CIELAB values used in the PCS. Input profiles tell us how these image-creation devices record color (or "see" color, if you prefer to think of it that way).

Display profiles describe monitors and transmissive display devices. These are two-way profiles, as a display can act as both an input device and an output device. When editing an image viewed on your computer display, it's effectively an input device; it's contributing to the formation or interpretation of the image data. When displaying an image as a means of photographic output, the display acts as the output medium or device. A two-way profile must communicate data to the PCS and understand data coming from the PCS.

Finally, output profiles describe printers and printing press technologies. These are one-way profiles because they are used to move image data from the PCS to the output device. The output information is in a form that the output device requires. For printers, that form is typically CMYK.

Canned Profiles

Cameras and printers come with *generic* or *canned profiles* provided by the manufacturer (you may need to navigate their websites to download them). These profiles approximate the performance of the device, however, they are created by averaging the performance of a sample set of devices from the production line. A canned profile characterizes your make and model printer in a generic way, not your printer in particular.

In many cases, a generic profile works well in supporting a color-managed workflow. It's certainly better than not having any profile at all to guide your color output. A generic profile offers a sense of the output device's limitations. However, there are times when a unique, custom profile is necessary. For example, Epson creates its canned printer profiles using Epson inks. The canned profile may not produce satisfactory results if we switch to inks made by another manufacturer. It's also possible that your specific Epson printer is an operational outlier compared to the larger production line of that model and its performance differs from that of the canned profile.

The iccMAX Profile

The *iccMAX* profile was first introduced in 2017. The current version is ICC.2:2018 (iccMAX). The ICC created iccMAX to support a more flexible and extensible system than the current profile system provides to meet the evolving needs of the industry. The ICC approved a private tag in V5 profiles that accommodate the ability to embed an iccMAX profile, making them backward compatible with current software.

The additional functionality that iccMAX offers include:

- the ability to use actual illuminant and observer data
- incorporating a new gamut boundary description
- measurement data using the CxF format (Color Exchange format)[6]
- a new encoding of named color to support tints
- a Material Connection Space (MCS) to support identification and visualization of material amounts in addition to color
- support for bidirectional reflectance distribution functions (BRDF).

Although most of these go beyond the realm of photography, the ability to incorporate actual illuminant data may prove useful to account for the lighting used for viewing and displaying photographic work.

CMYK Profiles

Output to print media requires, more often than not, that your image data be translated into a language of cyan, magenta, yellow and black (CMYK): the subtractive primaries. A *CMYK profile* that matches the destination printing condition is required when sending images to a commercial offset printer. There are unique CMYK profiles for North America, Europe and Japan as each country uses different printing standards.

Printing in North America offers three options for CMYK profiles. Sheet-fed lithographic printing uses the *General Requirements for Applications in Commercial Offset Lithography* (GRACoL) setup for printing on coated paper. The Coated GRACoL 2006 profile is used for Grade 1 paper. When using web offset production presses, the *Specifications for Web Offset Publications*, or SWOP, setup is used for printing on lightweight papers. There are two options: Web Coated SWOP 2006 for Grade 3 and Web Coated SWOP 2006 Grade 5.

Most printers in Europe and the UK use the ISO 12647/2-2004 standard developed by FOGRA, a German printing research organization. They developed the FOGRA39 dataset which consists of two CMYK profiles: ISO coated v2 (ECI) for sheet-fed offset on coated papers and

ISO coated v2 300% (ECI) for web offset printing on whiter web offset papers.

Converting or Assigning Profiles

There are two options for using profiles with image files: converting an image to a profile color space or assigning the profile and embedding it in the file's metadata. Throughout this book, we've stressed the importance of maintaining original image data and editing images in a non-destructive manner. Profiles can be handled in the same way. When we convert an image to an output profile, the actual RGB pixel values are permanently altered. It bakes the changes into the pixel data and it cannot be undone. This method is the best option when you are delivering an image to a client or printer service to ensure that the image appears the way you intended.

The alternative is to assign a profile and embed it in the metadata. Assigning a profile to an image file is non-destructive and offers a translation guide to tell the image display software what the RGB values mean. The software applies the profile and adjusts the pixel values for display or for printing, however the original pixel values are left unaltered. This allows for needed flexibility. For example, perhaps you need to make a print for a gallery show that is 40x60 inches and also make 4x6 prints for giving out during the show. The two print types are likely printed on different printers and paper combinations. Assigning a profile at the time of printing allows you to use the same file for both sizes. Some web browsers read and correctly use embedded profiles but it's not a universal behavior of web browsers across desktop and mobile software today.

Creating Profiles with Color Measurement Tools

We introduced some measurement tools used to quantify light in Chapter 1. Here, we're interested in measuring color and density in our output media. Colorimeters measure emitted, reflected or transmitted light through a set of (approximately seven) color filters. They are primarily used for taking color readings off of computer displays.

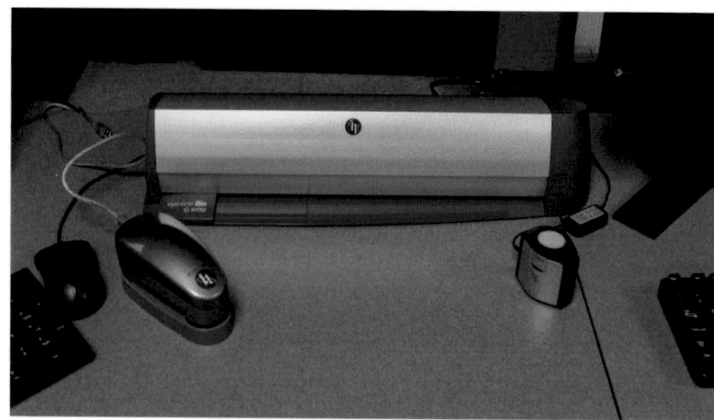

Figure 14-5 Spectrophotometers and colorimeters are used for measuring output color on displays and print.

Spectrophotometers measure color across a large set (>30) of discrete wavelengths and provide additional information from which colorimeter data can be calculated along with density measurements. A spectrophotometer can gather the same information as a colorimeter but not the other way around. Of course, the more capable device is more expensive. If basic display measurements are all that is needed, a cheaper colorimeter will suffice. Figure 14-5 shows examples of both types of color measurement devices.

Input Profiles for Cameras or Scanners

Building a camera profile is useful primarily for studio product photographers. An input profile helps characterize the camera's color reproduction under a highly specific and rigid set of conditions; if those conditions change, the profile is invalid. If you use the same two strobes and the same lens to shoot different products against the same white seamless day in and day out, then creating an input profile for your setup makes sense. Otherwise, the moment you change your lights or lens, your profile describes a situation different from the one you're photographing. X-Rite's i1Profiler software can be used for building input profiles although there are many options, both commercial and open source.

We photograph or scan a calibrated target like the Image Target 8 (or IT8 for short) shown in Figure 14-6 to create an input profile. The IT8 target is a ubiquitous name for calibration targets just as Kleenex refers to any brand

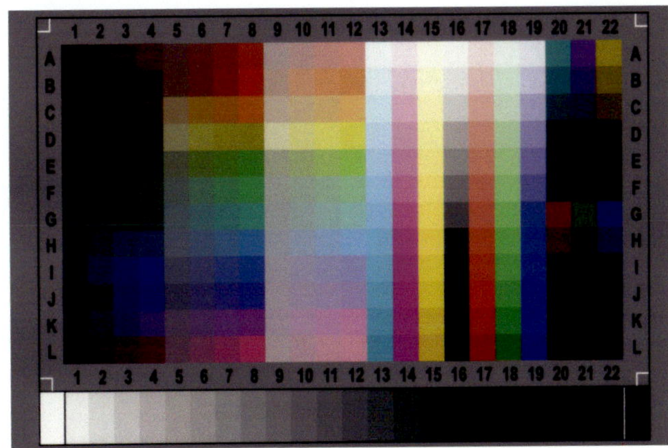

Figure 14-6 An IT8 target used for creating input profiles.

of tissue. The IT8 is the reference color set supplied by the manufacturer. Each color sample is accompanied by measured CIELAB and CIEXYZ values. Profiling software takes the input RGB values from the camera or scanner and maps them to the target's known values to create the profile. The generated profile is specific to the camera or scanner used.

A scanner profile, or any input profile, is not used to make the images look good. It does not correct color casts, improper exposure or poor contrast. Rather, the input profile allows software to display the input image file on your monitor in a way that matches the original.

Display Device Profiles

We promised at the start of this chapter that proper color management is increasingly user-friendly for photographers. Profiling a display requires a colorimeter or spectrophotometer to measure it. Unlike the calibrated target used for a camera or printer, the software sends color patches directly to the display that's measured by the colorimeter or spectrophotometer in turn. The profiling software requires the user to set certain parameters such as device type, gamma and white point. The brightness value is also adjusted. The profiling software then runs through neutral, red, green and blue color patches

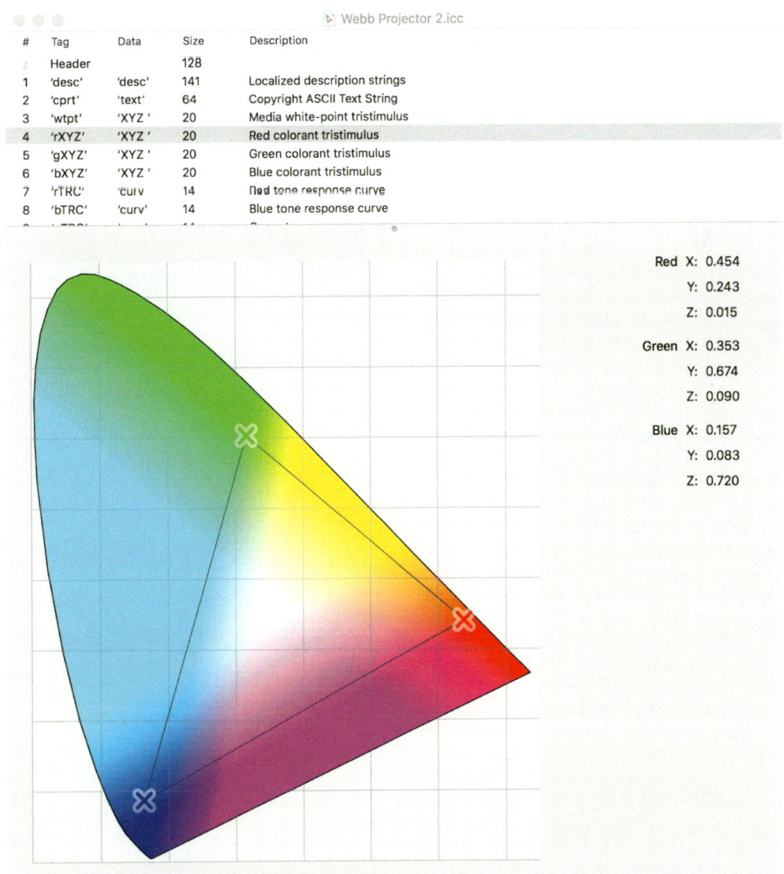

Figure 14-7 A display color gamut as measured by profiling software and stored in an ICC profile file.

that vary in brightness from 0 to the maximum digital count of the display. The CIEXYZ values are measured and CIELAB values calculated. The profile is created such that the PCS understands what color every RGB pixel combination represents. The operator is prompted to name the resulting ICC profile at the end of the process. We suggest including the monitor name, luminance value and calendar date for easy identification. Figure 14-7 illustrates the measured color gamut of the projector in the auditorium we use to lecture on photography topics. We're able to view the measured gamut in the operating system's profiler viewer utility.

Display characteristics change or drift as they age and require profiling on a regular basis. Most profiling software includes a 30-day reminder to make a new profile. The profile is also affected by the brightness and contrast settings on the display. These settings are typically controlled through software for built-in displays like the ones found on laptops and as hardware controls for external monitors. Once a profile is created, these controls cannot be changed or the profile becomes invalid. This detail is notable because we often like to vary our laptop screen brightness to conserve energy or boost visibility in brightly lit environments. This action invalidates the profile, meaning that we have to change this habit or avoid color-management-critical image editing work on our laptop computers.

Printer Profiles

Printers often come with a canned profile and paper manufacturers create profiles for their papers. Most times they work well. When they do not, or if the profile you need is not available, you may need to create a custom printer profile. Starting the process of profiling a printer begins with confirming that the printer is properly working. A printer with clogged or dirty nozzles causes banding in the print. Printing software utilities can run test prints to exercise the nozzles and confirm they are operating as expected. Printing profile software steps through the process of printing a test print needed to create a profile. This may include turning off color management, selecting the printer, the output media and the print quality.

There are often multiple test targets to select from. The adage "go big or go home" applies here. Selecting the largest test target with the most color patches results in a robust printer profile. A print should dry for 24 hours to ensure that there is no further shift in the color of the inks. Once dry, we measure the printed patches with a spectrophotometer or colorimeter and feed the values to the profiling software. The resulting ICC profile is specific to the paper and printer with which it was created and should be named accordingly for easy identification.

Gamut Handling and the Profile Connection Space

As introduced earlier, the profile connection space or PCS is the place where the input and output profiles are bridged using a universal color space. A device profile defines the relationship between a device and the PCS. For example, a camera profile defines the relationship between the RGB digital counts from the camera to the PCS; a printer profile defines the relationship between the PCS and the CMYK values required by the printer.

The ICC based the PCS on the ISO 13655 standard Graphic technology – Spectral measurement and colorimetric computations for graphic arts images. The PCS uses the 1931 CIE standard observer, D50 illuminant and either 0°/45° or 45°/0° color measurement geometries. It also requires a black backing behind prints when making reflectance measurements. The ISO 3664 standard is used to properly view prints created with ICC profiles. The viewing setup requires the D50 illumination at 500 lux on a 20% reflecting background.

Addressing the difference between input gamut and output gamut, especially when the output gamut is smaller, is the responsibility of rendering intent decisions discussed in the next section. First, though, we need clear strategies for handling out-of-gamut color information. One available strategy is *gamut clipping*. Every out-of-gamut color is mapped to the closest color that is in-gamut when using this strategy. Several different input colors may be mapped to the same output color. This can cause a loss of tonal variation in highly color-saturated areas.

The second strategy is *gamut compression*. The larger input gamut is compressed to fit inside of the smaller output gamut. Since this impacts all of the image's colors, including those which would have otherwise natively fit in the available gamut, some colors that were perfectly reproduced prior to the compression are changed or shifted after compression. Gamut compression can also lead to loss of some tonal variation in highly saturated areas.

Rendering Intents

Using output profiles and an optimal strategy for handling out-of-gamut information for that output involves the use of *rendering intents*. These are the specific rules that dictate what the color management module does with, say, the vibrant shades of green in a rainforest scene that your printer cannot faithfully reproduce. Without an exact, reproducible match for those colors, we turn to rendering intents for a treatment that yields a good looking print with vibrant greens—even if they are adjusted to a slightly different shade. The ICC specifies four rendering intents: perceptual, saturation, ICC-absolute colorimetric and media-relative colorimetric. Figure 14-8 illustrates these available approaches with two example color samples measured from an image. Consider how the out-of-gamut and in-gamut samples are treated by each approach as we describe them in greater detail.

The *perceptual rendering intent* employs a gamut compression strategy that works to maintain visual detail and luminance over hue and saturation. We've mentioned many times that our vision is more sensitive to luminance than it is to color, a characteristic that's exploited at many stages of image-making. In color management, we consider the perceptual rendering intent to be one of the most useful strategies because it plays to our visual system sensitivities. The perceptual rendering intent shifts in-gamut data to ensure that all out-of-gamut data is shown. This shift is a compromise to maintain the overall relationship of all the colors in the image. It may mean that in-gamut colors are desaturated.

The *saturation rendering intent* employs a gamut clipping strategy, preserving saturation over luminance. It's primarily used for graphics such as company logos or illustrations. The rationale here is that it's preferred to maximize saturated colors to grab attention and that graphical elements are not necessarily based on real-world color from which to compare. The saturation rendering intent moves out-of-gamut colors to the edge of the destination color gamut and may move in-gamut color out to the edge as well. This rendering intent is not concerned with the accuracy of color reproduction.

There are two colorimetric rendering intents: ICC-absolute colorimetric and media-relative colorimetric. Both rendering intents attempt to leave original colors unaltered when possible. The difference between them is how the color white is treated.

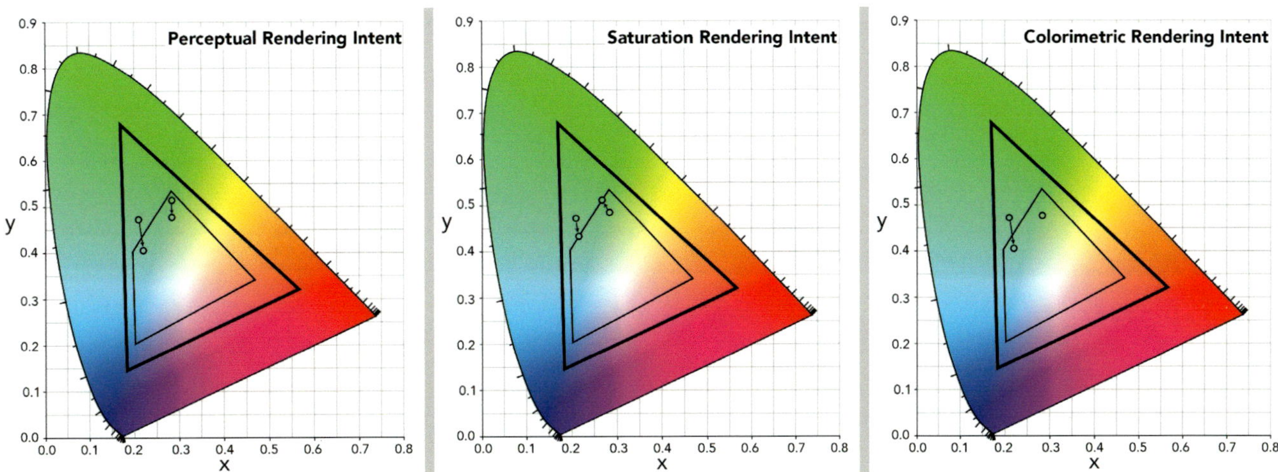

Figure 14-8 Example treatments for sampled image areas using different rendering intents.

The *ICC-absolute colorimetric rendering intent* recognizes that white in the image is a function of the substrate's white appearance. In other words, white is never pure and instead it takes on the base color of the paper on which the image is printed. For example, an image printed in a magazine must be proofed for reproduction on the magazine paper. We normally consider print output using photo-quality printers and white paper substrates. Magazines, though, tend to use cheaper paper with a darker, sometimes off-white white point. The absolute rendering intent maps the white in the image to the white of the print material. The remaining colors are left unaltered when possible and adjust those that require it.

The last rendering intent is *media-relative colorimetric*. In this rendering intent, the white in the image or source is mapped to the brightest white possible in the destination color gamut. This approach is referred to as *white point compensation*. All of the other colors in the image file are shifted accordingly. The result may be slightly brighter or darker than the original. Out-of-gamut colors are set to their nearest, in-gamut likeness. This intent often works well with photographic content.

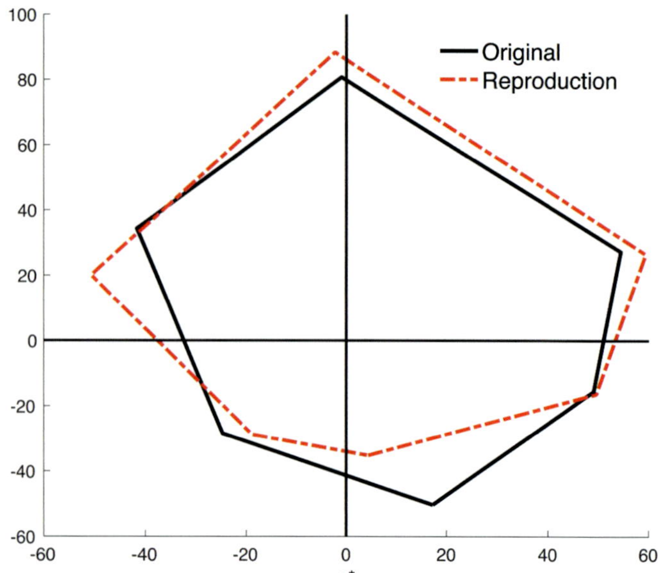

Figure 14-9 Example of a gamut comparison between an original and a reproduction. The reproduction is less capable of rendering some colors in the magenta region which may or may not be relevant to our photographic content.

Evaluating Color Reproduction

At the end of the day, there are two ways to evaluate the color reproduction of your photographs. The first is a simple visual inspection: does the output medium show the content as you intended it to look? The only tools required here are your artistic vision, your eyes and your subjective opinion. If objective color reproduction is deemed valuable or necessary, a quantitative approach is required.

Measuring and Comparing Color

There are several established methods for examining color differences. An overall color difference can be examined. The first step might be comparing the color gamut differences between the source and the reproduction. If a noticeable difference is identified, further analysis can determine if a sampled color's saturation changed using a chroma ratio. The hue of the original and the reproduction can also be calculated and compared. A tone reproduction curve can be generated to determine if the brightness is faithfully reproduced.

We quickly evaluate the relative color gamuts of an original versus its reproduction using a two-dimensional color gamut plot like the one shown in Figure 14-9. This plot uses the a* and b* values of the gamut colors (red, green, blue, cyan, magenta and yellow). Gamuts are defined as three-dimensional spaces, however, this simplified representation provides insight into areas where the color may be inaccurate.

The most common metric used to evaluate the accuracy of a color match is *Delta E* (or ΔE). Delta E is a measure of the difference between two samples. Refer back to Chapter 11, *Calculating Color Difference*, for a review of this metric. There are two ΔE options: ΔE_{ab} and ΔE_{00}. ΔE_{ab} is easily calculated by hand or with spreadsheet software. However, the CIE recommends a ΔE_{00} (Delta E 2000) calculation which is much more computationally rigorous and places heavier weight on luminance over chroma and hue values. Either metric provides valuable feedback on the accuracy of color reproduction.

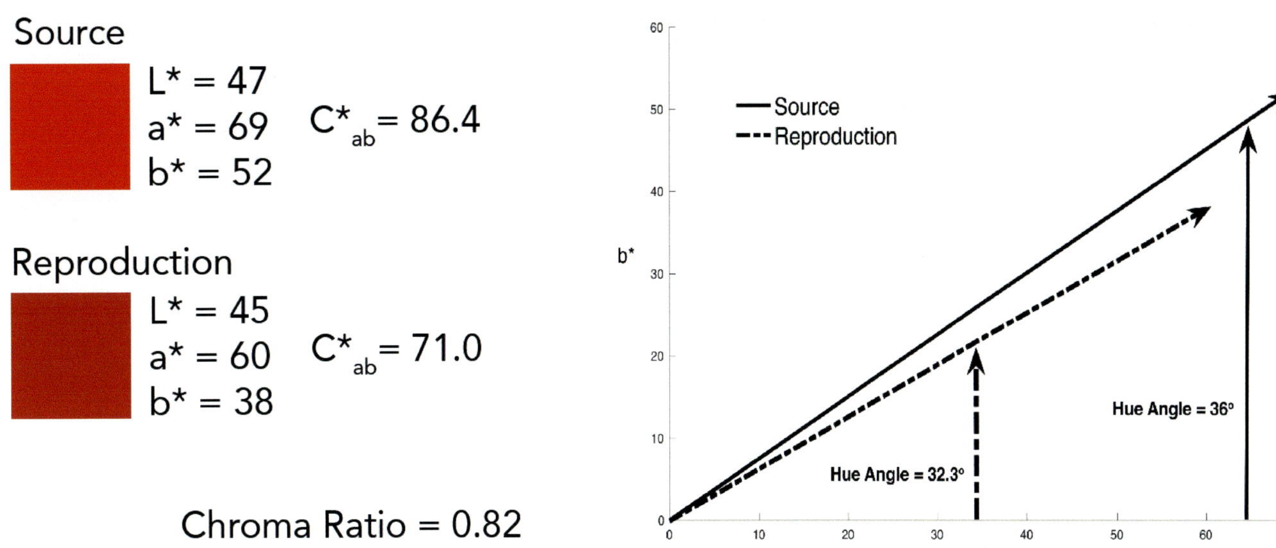

Figure 14-10 Calculating chroma and chroma ratio for a sampled color and its reproduction. We can conclude that the reproduction is less chromatic or saturated than the source.

Chroma (C^*) is a measure of the degree of saturation (see Figure 14-10). A *chroma ratio* provides insight into a saturation change in the reproduction. The formulas for calculating chroma and chroma ratio are provided in Equations 14.3 and 14.4. A chroma ratio equal to 1 indicates a perfect match between the reproduction and the original. A value greater than 1 indicates that the reproduction is more chromatic than the original and a value less than 1 indicates that the reproduction is less chromatic. Figure 14-10 shows these calculations applied to a sample color patch and its print reproduction. While a slight visual difference is apparent between the two red samples, calculating chroma and chroma ratio put objective numbers to support that observation.

$$c^*_{ab} = \sqrt{a^{*2} + b^{*2}} \quad \text{(Eq. 14.3)}$$

$$Chroma\ Ratio = \frac{c^*_{ab}\ Reproduction}{c^*_{ab}\ Original} \quad \text{(Eq. 14.4)}$$

Recall that a color sample representation in CIELAB consists of three elements: L* represents the brightness of the color while a* and b* describe the color information. A *hue angle* (h_{ab}) calculation identifies the sample's color or hue. Determining if there is a shift in hue means calculating and comparing the hue angles for the original and reproduction (see Equation 14.5). The change in hue angle is indicated in Figure 14-10.

$$h_{ab} = tan^{-1}\left(\frac{b^*}{a^*}\right) \quad \text{(Eq. 14.5)}$$

A *tone reproduction plot* is made using neutral patches included in a test print. L* values provide luminance or brightness information, therefore a plot of the original neutral patch L* values compared to the reproduction provides an easily interpreted visual to evaluate. The plot shown in Figure 14-11 (overleaf) shows that the original is lighter than the reproduction, signaling a change to the overall brightness in our reproduction that we can consider when making final image adjustments for the desired print.

Color Correction

Color corrections are made when we believe that our workflow is properly color managed and predictable. When all components produce a predictable output and

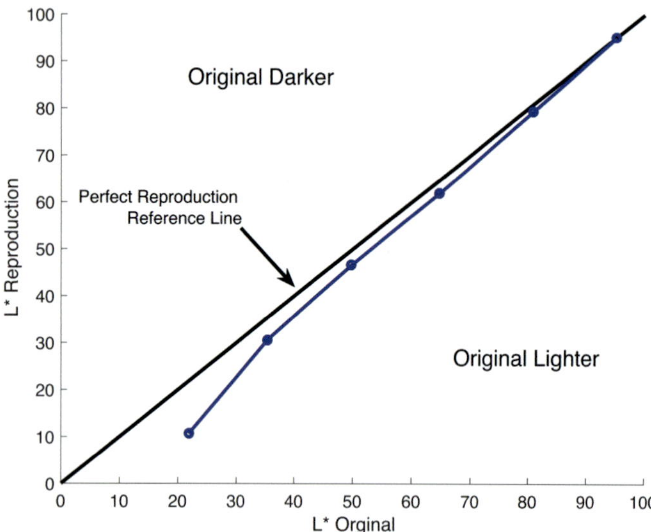

Figure 14-11 A tone reproduction plot. The reference line makes it easy to observe if the measured patches from the reproduction are lighter or darker than the original.

the result is still, say, too yellow, that's the time to go back and introduce more blue to the file. If the system is not properly color managed, for example, color corrections applied to your image can have an unforeseen outcome on your print. Color correction techniques are covered in Chapter 9.

Establishing an Appropriate Workspace Setup

Control and consistency are key when optimizing a workspace for a color-managed workflow. The ISO 3664 standard specifies standards for viewing color-managed images, some of which we can affordably implement while others we cannot.

Photography students tend to edit images wherever they can find a wall outlet to power their laptops. We do not suggest that anyone should do this with any expectations for accurate color reproduction in an editing workflow. The optimal workspace environment starts with a windowless room with neutral walls (ideally a midtone gray). The room lighting should be D50 according to the ISO standard. However, D50 illuminants are not found at your local hardware store. The alternative is a daylight balanced light with a brightness output between 30 and 65 lux. Figure 14-12 shows a great workspace environment for color-critical photo editing and output.

Lux levels are not described on light bulb packaging. Instead, they tend to advertise light output in lumens. For a 10x10' room, 30–65 lux is between approximately 278 and 603 lumens. As a point of comparison: a dinner candle gives off approximately 12 lumens and a single 60-watt soft white incandescent light bulb produces approximately 840 lumens. Choosing a desktop editing station environment that lacks windows ensures that the room illumination stays constant and is not subject to mixed source illumination. While we encourage photographers to get some sunshine, we want to avoid late-night editing sessions getting revised the following day due to ambient light changes from nearby windows. As a final detail, care must be taken to avoid direct reflections or glare due to lights positioned at complementary angles relative to those used when viewing the display.

The display used for image editing should be set to an output luminance between 80 and 120 cd/m^2. This is set by the software used to create the display profile and should not be modified between profiling sessions. Running through the profiling process for the first time, photographers are often surprised at how dim the room lighting and their screens appear when set to the appropriate light levels. Minutes later, their vision adapts to the lower light levels and the confusion and concern fades.

Finally, the software interface and the computer desktop background should be set to a neutral midtone gray to avoid simultaneous contrast effects. Image editing software

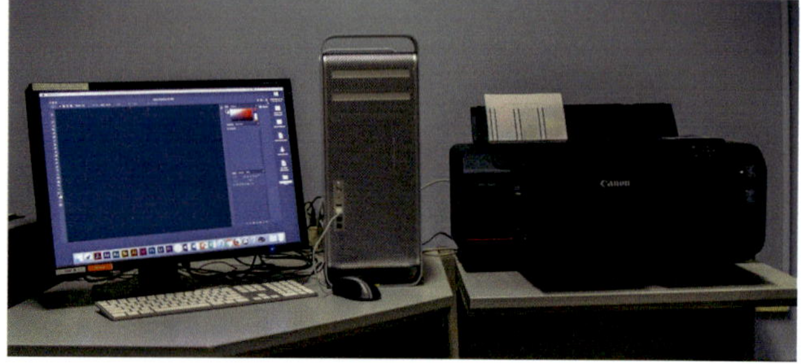

Figure 14-12 An example workspace ideal for editing and print or display output.

user interface settings often allow for alternating between different neutral tones (white, black and shades of gray in between).

Soft Proofing with Profiles

Proofing is the practice of testing or evaluating how the final product is going to look upon final output. When performing this on the computer display, it's considered *soft proofing*. Making a physical print on a substrate is *hard proofing*. Both are valuable exercises and are worth using hand in hand when considering photographic output adjustments as you work toward the best possible reproduction. Soft proofing minimizes printing costs when preparing media for physical media output and saves valuable time when prepping for display output as well.

Soft proofing offers an expectation of your image's appearance with a specified output, including print, even though it's conducted exclusively with a computer display. A major limitation to soft proofing is the difference between the additive, emissive color mixing of the monitor compared to the subtractive, reflective color mixing of the physical substrate and colorants. Even set to a low brightness, a display is brighter with a higher white point than any photo paper. To compensate, we must use the display output profile plus the print output profile to approximate an accurate appearance.

A Soft Proofing Workflow

Once the creative edits are finalized, we work to prepare the image for reproduction. The steps in a soft proofing workflow vary depending on the software used, though the ingredients are always the same: a properly characterized and profiled monitor, an environment optimized for image editing and an ICC profile for the printer/paper combination (or alternate display) intended for output.

Adobe Photoshop and Adobe Photoshop Lightroom both offer soft proofing tools. By using destination profiles for output devices or color spaces, we can see a simulated, visual approximation of how a photograph will render upon output. This allows for making adjustments in anticipation of the destination color space before committing to a conversion in the CMM. We don't ever want to convert to a profile until all image editing is complete, so soft proofing is a preemptive step toward getting a desirable output result.

We open our image file in Adobe Photoshop Lightroom, for example, and switch to its soft proofing mode through the Develop module. This introduces new settings shown for identifying the destination profile (from the ICC profiles available on your computer) and the preferred rendering intent strategy. In this case, the editing software offers the option to create a derivative version or copy of the image from which to make edits specific to your intended output. This is helpful when considering work that may see multiple avenues of reproduction; multiple copies can be kept separate with custom adjustments made to each as necessary for optimized output.

The software can indicate if there are any areas containing out-of-gamut colors, visualized with a colored pixel overlay toggled through the histogram panel and shown in Figure 14-13 (overleaf). There are many editing actions that can help correct this gamut issue. One option is to globally desaturate all colors. This is likely the least desirable approach, as it's guaranteed to negatively impact color reproduction relative to the original. We might instead desaturate or shift the hues of out-of-gamut colors selectively using the targeted adjustment tool or similar eyedropper style controls. Adobe Photoshop Lightroom offers a panel for adjusting hue, saturation and lightness: a combination of these three characteristics results in some of the photograph's pixels to be outside of the destination profile's color gamut. Working with one or a combination of all three can reign in the problematic pixels. Once the out-of-gamut warnings are minimized, we can assume that there won't be any surprising delta between the source and destination renderings of our image. Indeed, with a thoughtfully selected rendering intent and minor tweaks to hue, saturation or lightness, we can often create a prepared file that yields excellent output results with minimal visual changes or differences.

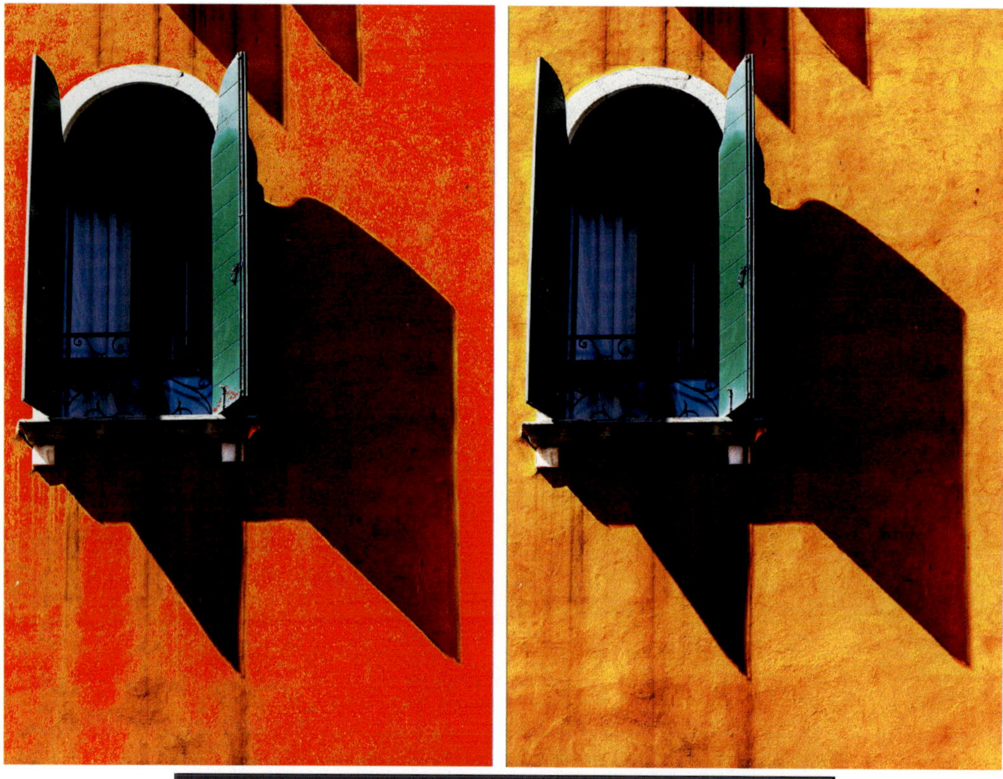

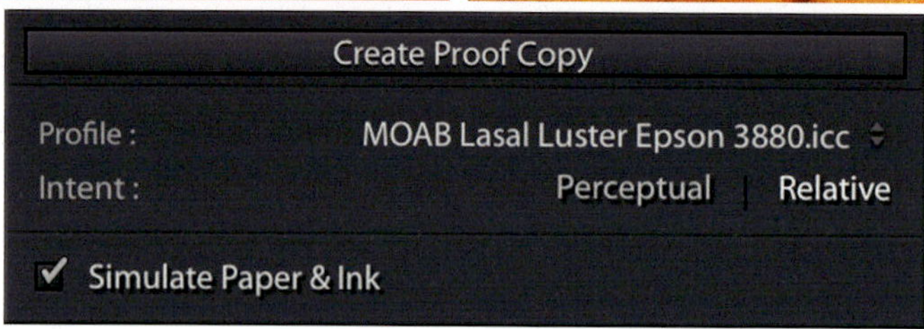

Figure 14-13 Simulating a reproduction using an Epson printer and luster photo paper profile. The out-of-gamut warning colors pixels that cannot be directly reproduced using the destination profile (left). After some edits to saturation and hue, the out-of-gamut pixels are minimized (right).

Notes

1 Murphy, Chris. "Top ten color management pros." *Color Remedies: Library*, Nov. 2001, colorremedies.com/library.html.

2 "International Color Consortium," color.org/.

3 "Program of color science." *Reasons Students Plagiarize or Cheat | Academic Integrity | RIT*, www.rit.edu/science/pocs/.

4 Pointer, M.R. "The Gamut of real surface colours." *Color Research & Application*, vol. 5, no. 3, 1980, pp. 145–155., doi:10.1002/col.5080050308.

5 The latest specification as of this publication is Specification ICC.1:2010.

6 "CxF – Color Exchange Format." *X-Rite*, www.xrite.com/page/cxf-color-exchange-format.

15 Display Technology

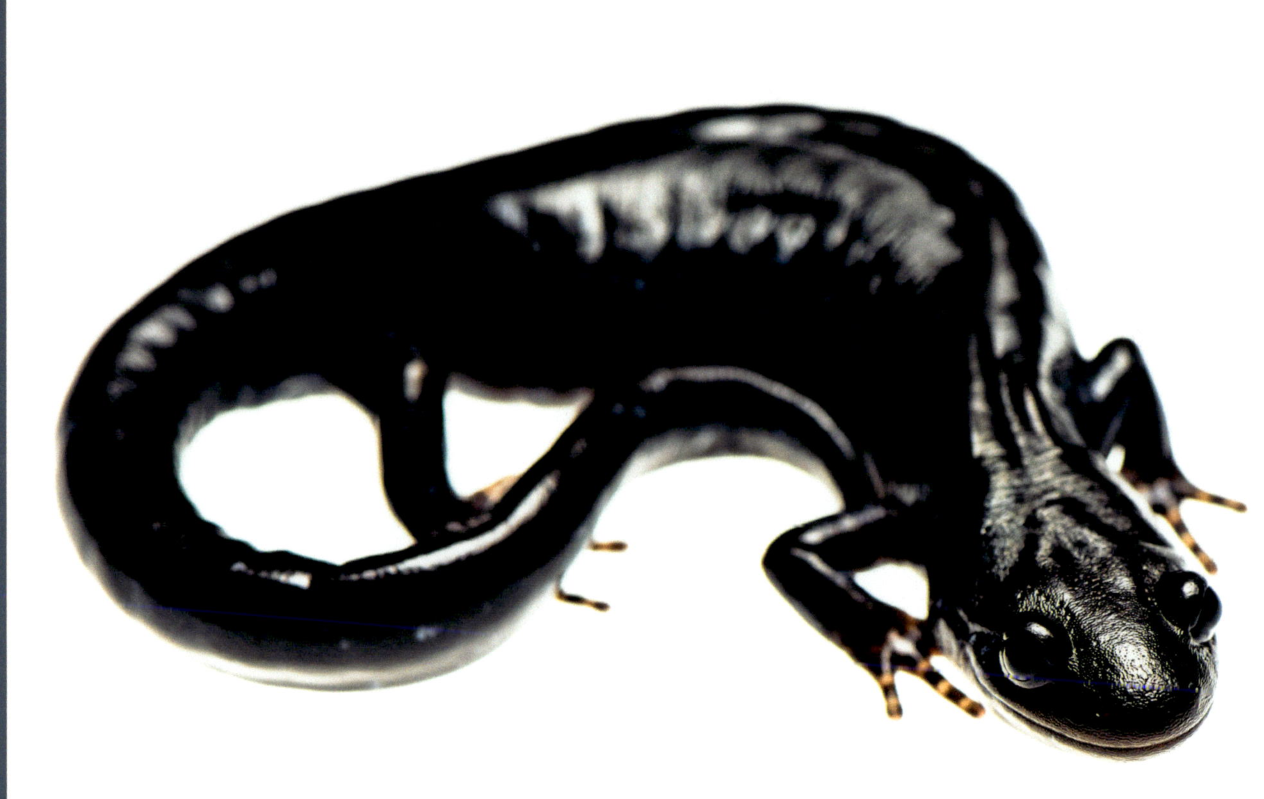

Photograph by Rochester Institute of Technology photography alumnae Jenée Langlois

Displays are incredibly important to photographers. We take for granted the number and variety of displays we encounter in day-to-day life, from watching television to using our phones and desktop computers. Photography and video content are experienced on all of these yet the most critical display is the one we use for reviewing and editing our work. A good display for a photographic workflow takes into consideration the specific display technology, resolution, dynamic range and color gamut to best serve our images. It must also be coupled with proper calibration and color management. Understanding displays requires a familiarity with the underlying technologies, industry standards, principles of color mixing and a sprinkling of color measurement. Here, we review the technologies and characteristics of displays as they relate to photographic reproduction. At the end of the chapter, we look at emerging trends and how mobile phone display capabilities have grown in recent years.

A cheap display can undermine a whole host of expensive equipment before and after its place in the processing pipeline. We consider computer hardware upgrades every few years and yet the desktop monitor's lifespan is often longer. Additionally, photographers rely on quality displays beyond their desktop computer setup. The camera preview screen, electronic viewfinders, laptops, tablets and television sets all play a role in a photographic workflow and output. Tethered capture and remote viewing are common methods of reviewing images during and after shooting sessions, either due to inconvenient camera positions, having a viewing audience or to preview captured frames with instant post-processing adjustments. These secondary or tertiary viewing displays may not be as keenly calibrated or optimized and yet as visual media practitioners we lean on them heavily for feedback. Their use means that one photographer may encounter or take advantage of a variety of display types, configurations and capabilities in their endeavors.

Relevant Display Technologies for Photographers

Let's go in chronological order of mass adoption as primary display technologies: cathode ray tube, liquid crystal display, organic light-emitting diode and quantum dot. All displays require an input signal sent from a computer's graphics processing unit (GPU) that is first held in a *frame buffer* in random access memory (RAM). The frame data is sent to the display which houses its own signal interpretation hardware to translate and command its display elements to drive brightness and color.

Cathode Ray Tube

The *cathode ray tube* (CRT) display uses an evacuated glass tube with a phosphorescent screen and an electron gun. Light is emitted when the electron gun fires electrons (the cathode ray) at the screen and excites its phosphors. The electron beam is modulated to display images or graphics and scans from the top of the screen to the bottom in rapid sequences, one line at a time. Recall from Chapter 1 that phosphorescence is a type of light energy emission that persists even after excitation. Using materials that have long afterglow emission times can cause image ghosting; CRT displays with phosphor emission times below 5–10 ms are desired for motion media.[1]

CRT technology started as a monochromatic method of rendering images and evolved to use three electron guns and three phosphor-coated color screens (red, green and blue emitting) to create color images in the mid-1950s. A thin metal grid called a *shadow mask* is sandwiched between the screen and electron gun to help create precise excitation elements for resolving image points.

The cathode ray tube was a ubiquitous display technology used for televisions, computer monitors and a variety of other uses. The technology offers very good viewing angles and fast response times. The CRT's peak brightness is 100 cd/m^2. The Rec.709 specification for color, discussed later in this chapter, is based on the display capabilities of CRT technology. CRTs are increasingly rare for personal or professional use, though some are found in specialized industries such as military, medicine and industrial engineering (such as oscilloscopes). Their large size and high power consumption are notable downsides compared to newer options.

Liquid Crystal Display

The CRT's popularity was eclipsed by *liquid crystal display* (LCD) technology that offers better picture quality in a smaller form factor. An LCD consists of an array of sub-pixels positioned in front of a light source. A layer of molecules aligned between two transparent electrodes and two polarizing filters comprise the display screen. The polarizing filters are aligned perpendicular to each other, blocking all light from passing through. The electrodes apply an electrical field to the liquid crystals which align to control the amount of light passing through the system like small, light-blocking shutters. This sandwiched layering of components is shown in Figure 15-1. A color filter layer sits atop the liquid crystal elements such that individual sub-pixels are filtered to be red, green or blue as seen under the microscope in Figure 15-2. This filtering strategy takes advantage of partitive mixing to appear as a

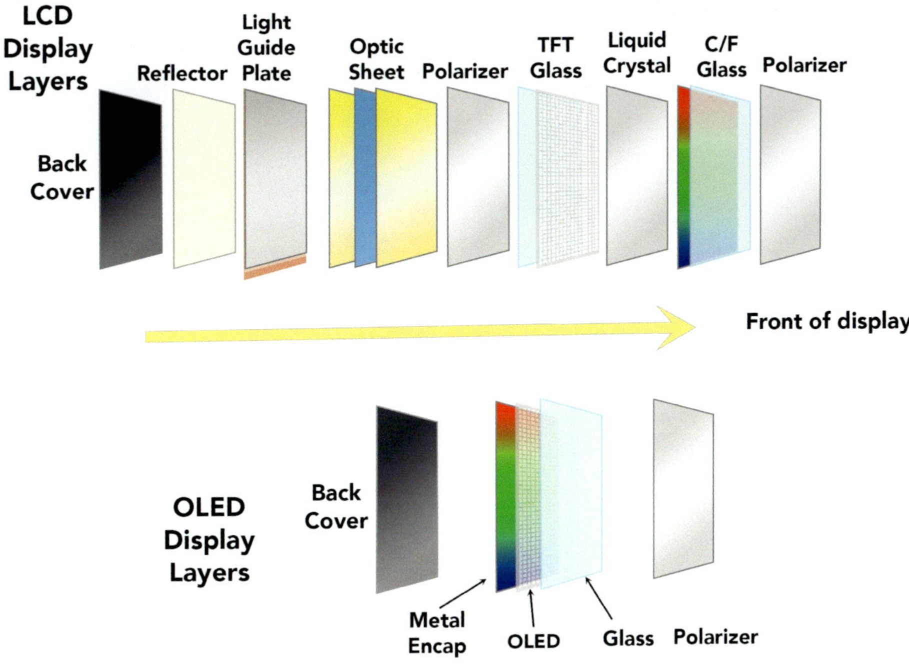

Figure 15-1 The fundamental layers of an LCD (top) and an OLED display (bottom). Illustration adapted from LG.com

wide variety of colors (including white) when viewed at a standard working distance as the pixels vary the amount of light transmitted.

Importantly, LCDs do not produce their own light. A few applications of LCD displays work just fine without light emission of any kind. The readout of a basic calculator, for example, instead relies on reflected light from the environment. Most applications, though, whether it's a microwave oven timer or a living room television, require backlighting to create an emissive light display. The backlight of a display used for photographic content provides even, bright white illumination that is diffused, polarized, filtered and transmitted through the layers stacked on top of it. Early LCD monitors used a *cold cathode fluorescent lamp* (CCFL) as a backlight source. Though cheap, CCFL is heavy and uses more power than newer *light-emitting diode* (LED) backlighting solutions. LED backlights are most commonly comprised of blue LEDs coated with yellow phosphors to produce a neutral, white light. These are power efficient but don't offer the full spectral distribution range that RGB LED backlights can; a limited spectral emission

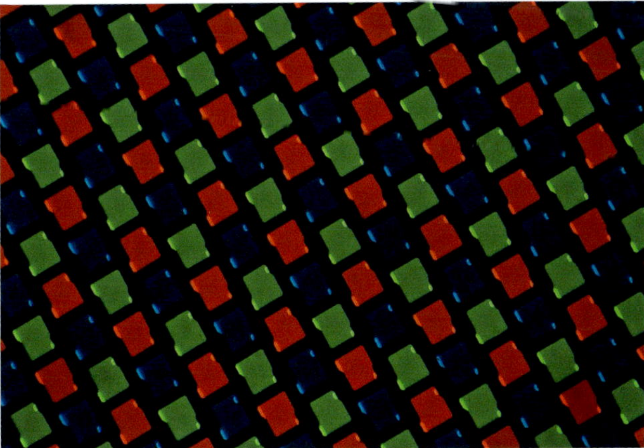

Figure 15-2 The surface of an LCD screen of a portable music player photographed through a reflected light microscope. Photograph by Rochester Institute of Technology photography alumnus Griffin Kettler

Figure 15-3 An LCD monitor displaying a pure black image and viewed in a dark room reveals backlight non-uniformity and an elevated black point.

range means poorer color reproduction. The use of LED backlights spawned confusing marketing terminology where displays are sometimes branded as "LED displays" even though the driving technology is LCD. Simpler LED backlights use arrays of lights along the outside borders of the active display area that get diffused with light-guiding sheets. This can lead to backlighting non-uniformity that becomes most apparent when displaying dark, uniform tones on screen (like the end credits to a film). An example of this backlight non-uniformity is seen in Figure 15-3 where an entirely black image is displayed in a dark room. More complex LED backlight solutions use a full array of controllable diodes behind the LCD.

A traditional backlight is only capable of *global dimming*. LED backlight panels with segmented, local zones whose luminance are independently controlled improve the dynamic range of LCDs. This feature is called *localized dimming*. The more finely divided (and thus more numerous) the zones, the greater the potential improvement over global dimming. The ability to drive backlight intensity in specific parts of the frame means that a landscape shot with a bright sky and dark foreground can be backlit separately to great effect. Figure 15-4 illustrates this concept using a simple grid array representing backlight luminances. In reality, the localized backlight zone boundaries are slightly blurred or softened by a layer of diffusion before the liquid crystal layer.

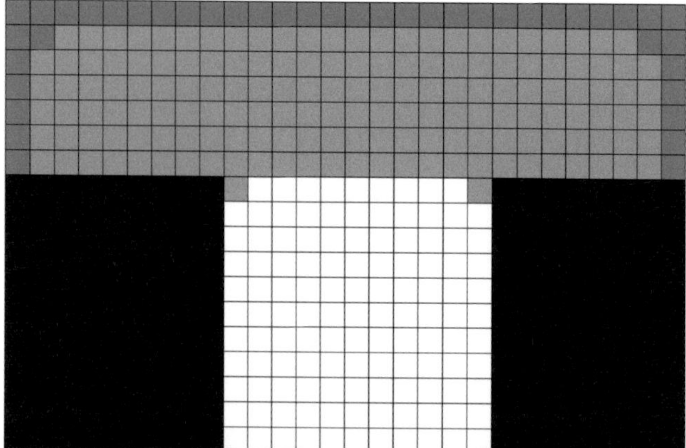

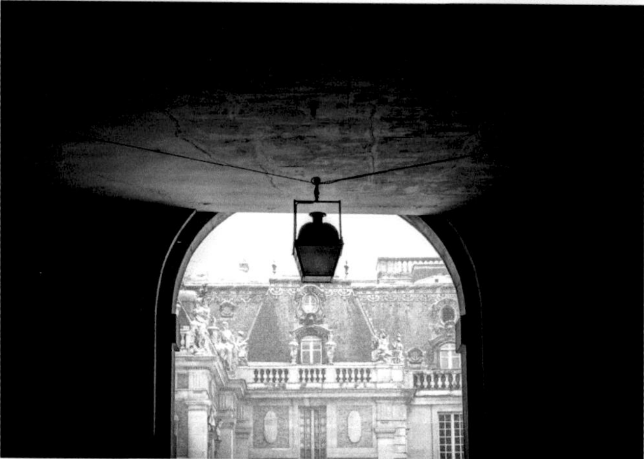

Figure 15-4 An illustration of an LED backlight panel with independently controlled zones. The brightness pattern acts like a low-resolution luminance interpretation of the on-screen content to enhance dynamic range.

LCD screens additionally employ different hardware designs for handling the liquid crystals: *in-plane switching* (IPS), *twisted nematic* (TN) and *vertical alignment* (VA). Although IPS is the most expensive to manufacture, it offers the best color reproduction and viewing angles among the three. IPS technology's recent evolutions include *Super IPS* (S-IPS), *Advanced Super IPS* (AS-IPS) and *IPS Pro*. IPS technology allows each pixel to display a value between 0 and 255 which results in a better color rendition over the TN and VA alternatives. LCDs with IPS are often not as bright, however, and the liquid crystals cannot change state as quickly as in an LCD with TN. Viewing angle is a critical characteristic when considering the increasing frequency of viewing displayed content on portable devices and those in our work or social environments; displays viewed head-on from a desktop or living room couch are far from their only use case.

High-quality LCD panels are made by manufactures including Eizo, BenQ, LG, Samsung and NEC. Professional photographers relying on an editing workstation for a color managed workflow must consider the appropriate display hardware offering. Some monitors, specifically marketed to photo and video editors, feature integrated, self-calibrating hardware and software.

Organic Light-Emitting Diode

Organic light-emitting diode (OLED) displays offer additional improvements over traditional LCD technology. The emissive electroluminescent layer in an OLED is made of a solid-state semiconductor film of organic compounds. The layer is typically a polymer substance that allows the organic compound to be deposited in rows and columns on a flat carrier that become individually addressable. The compound, a fluorescent or phosphorescent material, emits varying amounts of light when current from a cathode is applied. OLED displays do not require a backlight (the pixels are self-emitting) and they use less energy than an LCD display.[2] The organic compound layer is covered by a single polarizer and is typically sandwiched between a transparent cathode and an anode layer. Figure 15-1 shows the relatively fewer components present in an OLED panel design relative to LCD.

A consequence of OLED's self-emitting pixels is truly deep, dark black tones. Displaying black is accomplished by not sending any electric current through the organic material and thus the only brightness at that location comes from reflected light off of the screen surface. LCD cannot accomplish this because the backlight panel stays on to illuminate other pixels and the cross polarization is not 100% effective at blocking light.

OLED panels started showing up in camera hardware for the back-of-camera preview screens. They are increasingly found on smartphones and televisions. The lack of a backlight layer means that the panels can be thinner than their LCD counterparts. OLED technology can also be mounted on flexible substrates (like plastic) to produce curved or semi-bendable form factors. They can be manufactured without any backing at all to produce translucent displays (of questionable utility aside from the major science fiction wow-factor). The manufacturing process can additionally integrate a touch-sensing layer that makes a separately manufactured and assembled layer of touch screen technology unnecessary. LG Electronics, Inc. and Samsung Electronics Co., Ltd are the primary manufacturers of OLED panels today.

OLED technology's manufacturing complexity kept prices high and yields low until recent years. This fact also explains why they proliferated quickly for small panel applications like phones before becoming viable options for television panels. However, larger panels are becoming increasingly price-competitive with LCD options. OLEDs can be susceptible to image burn-in and early iterations saw short lifespans for the blue-emitting phosphorescent material.[3,4] Many mobile devices incorporate software solutions that keep any single pixel from displaying the exact same thing for too long in an effort to avoid burn-in degradation.

Quantum Dot

LCDs are one of the most commonly encountered display technologies today. Without technological advances, they may be feature-eclipsed by OLED. However, *quantum dot* (QD) technology is keeping LCDs in the running as contenders arise. Quantum dots are semiconductor nanoparticles that emit different colors when excited by incident blue light. The color emitted is dictated by the size of the crystals which range from 2–6 nm in diameter. The smaller the dots, the shorter the emitted wavelength of visible light: the largest dots emit red, the smallest, blue within narrow bands. The blue backlight itself is often used as the third primary alongside red and green emitting dots. Building a display using a variety of quantum dot sizes means that exciting all of them with blue backlight can produce any desired color. The nanoparticles absorb and reemit light energy with a high degree of quantum efficiency (nearing 100%). Green QDs fade or fail to emit earlier than red ones, meaning that a full color display may see a shortened lifespan, not unlike early OLED displays with fading blue emission.[5]

Quantum dot technology produces highly saturated colors which allows QD displays to render wide color gamuts (potentially wider, even, than OLED). The lack of filters means that they are more efficient in their use of the backlight to create an image. The primary method of creating quantum dots involves the use of cadmium, a potentially toxic metal. The undesirable risk of its use in consumer electronics spurred the development of cadmium-free quantum dot technologies. These variants exhibit reduced quantum efficiency and lessened color gamuts.[6]

QD technology is additionally being leveraged for lighting solutions with high Color Rendering Index (CRI) characteristics. Instead of driving a full color display, quantum dots' light emission can make for spectrum-tunable, flat-panel light fixtures.

Display Connection Standards

External monitors for desktop computing use High-Definition Multimedia Interface (HDMI), Digital Visual Interface (DVI) or DisplayPort connection protocols. Specialized products might offer some functionality via USB, WiFi or Bluetooth, though these are not common for continuous video display due to bandwidth and power limitations. HDMI and DisplayPort come in different flavors with newer versions offering higher throughput, power and daisy-chaining.

Display Resolution

The *display resolution* describes how many pixels comprise the screen in width and height. The more pixels in an array, the more information can be displayed. Similar to image sensors, displays have one set, native resolution when they're manufactured. Options to change resolution in operating system settings are actually just modifying the scale of rendered graphics and user interfaces. Describing display resolution as a function of area uses the measurement of *pixels per inch* (ppi).

The higher the *pixel density*, or number of pixels per given area, the more likely it is that your eyes cannot see the separate, discrete pixel boundaries at a normal working distance. Recall that pixels are a useful building block for images yet LCD displays are comprised of red, green and blue sub-pixels; pixel density considers a group of RGB sub-pixels as a single pixel. The standard pixel density used to be 72 ppi. This was generally the case for desktop displays for a number of years. Today, most desktop and laptop displays are 100+ ppi in pixel density. Smaller screens like those found on the smartphones and the backs of cameras often offer even higher pixel densities of 200–300 ppi or more. A combination of function and the realities of manufacturing challenges, small screens pack high spatial resolution into small spaces and hold up to close viewing distances. While a desktop monitor is likely to be viewed at a single distance, a phone or tablet invites variable viewing distances and needs to look good across all of them. High pixel density displays are also critical for wearable or head mounted display applications with very short viewing distances.

The higher the resolution, the more information can be shown at a time. Using a display that's lower resolution than the content, such as editing 4K video on a sub-4K monitor, makes it mathematically impossible to view the content pixels 1:1 on screen while showing the entire content frame. Photographers have long since understood that they have more pixels than they're viewing when zoomed out to fit images to the screen.

Aspect Ratio and Screen Size

We listed the standard resolutions and aspect ratios for video formats in Chapter 6. Displays vary greatly in aspect ratio depending on their application, though we generally see a trend toward wider formats in mobile and desktop applications. The closer a display aspect ratio comes to a film and video standard like 16:9, the more of the screen is active during playback of such content. Desktop displays in particular are used for much more than watching movies, however: extra screen real estate in vertical or horizontal dimensions can be valuable for additional user interface elements, panels or side-by-side application windows. It's also common for professionals to arrange multiple monitors side by side (supported in any modern operating system). This is an effective way to display an image as

Table 15-1 Common desktop display resolutions and aspect ratios.

Pixel Resolution (Width x Height)	Aspect Ratio	Category
1024x768	4:3	Full screen
1600x1200	4:3	Full screen
1920x1080	16:9	Widescreen
2560x1440	16:9	Widescreen
3840x2160	16:9	Widescreen
5120x2880	16:9	Widescreen
2560x1080	21:9	Ultra Widescreen
3440x1440	21:9	Ultra Widescreen
3840x1080	32:9	Ultra Widescreen

large as one display allows while relegating software windows and controls to another display.

CRTs were, by and large, 4:3 in aspect ratio. This is considered *full screen*. A 16:9 aspect ratio, perhaps the most common today with LCDs, is called *widescreen*. Displays featuring even wider dimensions are categorized as *ultra widescreen* and feature aspect ratios such as 18:9 or 21:9. Table 15-1 lists common screen resolutions and their aspect ratios.

Large displays are often described as a measurement of their diagonal dimension, from one top corner to the opposing bottom corner. Aspect ratio and pixel density are worth considering in the context of a display's diagonal dimension since size only tells part of the story. Larger displays do not necessarily come with increased pixel densities. A smartphone and living room television can feature similar display resolutions despite being dramatically different physical dimensions. The diagonal dimension is measured on the active display area (not including the bezel). The thinner a bezel, however, the more seamless the appearance becomes when placing multiple panels next to each other. Typical desktop display sizes include 24, 27, 32 and 34 inch diagonals. Televisions used as large review monitors in studios or editing suites can be 32, 43, 55, 65 and 75 inches in size (as well as sizes in between).

Refresh Rates and Response Time

A display's *refresh rate* defines the number of times per second that the display refreshes or draws successive images. Refresh rate is a measure of frequency in hertz (Hz). Motion in video is shown as differences between frames, therefore the refresh rate impacts the perception of smooth motion. The terms refresh rate and frame rate are sometimes confused: refresh rate is a characteristic of the monitor whereas frame rate is defined by the amount of information being sent to the monitor.

We perceive a slideshow-like display of sequential frames when displayed at frequencies less than 10 Hz. Starting at about 10 Hz, we begin to perceptually integrate the frames. A refresh rate of 24 Hz is the motion picture standard originally established in the 1920s. A common refresh rate for computer monitors, tablets and other mobile device screens is 60 Hz. Increasing things up to 90 Hz becomes important for fast motion with minimal flicker, a necessary behavior for head mounted displays (more on this later). Refresh rates of 120 Hz are offered on higher-end gaming monitors. Some televisions tout high refresh rates but don't necessarily have the temporally sampled content to match. Perceiving the apparent refresh rate of still frames results in *flicker*. It is more easily noticed in bright light and dim light environments and in one's peripheral vision. It becomes less noticeable with fatigue. Flicker is a function of the display's refresh behavior, not the capture method or frame rate.

High refresh rates are beneficial when rendering graphics, graphic user interfaces and video game content because graphics processing units are able to generate content at high rates. Televisions that attempt to reduce motion blur with artificial frame interpolation to achieve a 120 Hz signal can look unnatural or what many describe as the "soap opera effect." It is common for televisions to default to such artificial motion smoothing despite its unpleasant appearance for the sake of motion smoothing. High refresh rates mean more content per second. Especially at high resolutions (4K and above), high refresh rates demand considerable bandwidth. Such bandwidth is only supported on the latest connection protocols of HDMI and DisplayPort.

The most accurate term to describe the fastest refresh speed of LCD and OLED displays is *pixel response time*. Response times are the duration (in fractions of seconds) that it takes addressable display pixels to switch from one value to another. LCD technology offers pixel response times between 1–5 milliseconds on average, limited by how quickly the liquid crystal can change orientation and therefore light transmission. OLED can potentially refresh ten times as fast (0.01 ms). LCD and OLED displays use a *sample-and-hold* behavior that shows one image or video frame until the next is available. The display is continuously backlit for the first frame, the next frame when refreshed and any time in between. This contributes to a perception of motion blur or *ghosting* when viewing motion media or when playing real-time rendered video games. Minimizing this time in between can help, but other strategies are used to help further such as *black frame insertion*. A black, blank frame is displayed between two content frames at high refresh rates in an effort to lessen the appearance of ghost-like images with fast-moving content. Another approach is to rapidly strobe the backlight on and off. This can be done albeit with reduced luminance output relative to a display's non-strobing mode.[7] Dominant in the realm of gaming, such technologies are not as critical for normal photo and video editing or viewing. Additionally, they may introduce color shifts which is undesirable for color-critical work.

Display Dynamic Range, Brightness and Bit Depth

We introduced the measurement of luminance in terms of *candelas per unit area* in Chapter 1. It is increasingly common in the context of display brightness to use the term *nit* to describe this same measurement. One nit is equal to one candela per square meter. Nits are convenient (and less of a mouthful when discussing out loud) because displays are two-dimensional areas from which light is emitted. As discussed in Chapter 1, light measurement gets more complicated when dealing with bulbs that emit in all directions. This chapter uses *nits* and *cd/m²* interchangeably as they refer to the same light measurement. You may encounter both when shopping for, calibrating and evaluating professional displays.

The full range of scene brightnesses faces multiple stages of technological bottlenecks before a recording of that scene is viewed on a display. A high dynamic range (HDR) scene exposure necessitates a camera sensor capable of operating across a potentially huge spread of luminances. Sensors continue to improve, yet the next bottleneck shows up in how the recorded data is stored. Image file formats have maximum bit depths that define the number of discrete tones they can represent. Finally, the output display produces a limited range of luminances. Until recently, computer monitors and televisions supported *standard dynamic range* (retroactively referred to as *SDR-capable*). Due to display technology and standard definitions for broadcast television content, this limited the upper end of brightnesses to 100 cd/m².[8] OLED and QD technologies are pushing that upper brightness capability to 1,000 cd/m² and beyond. A benefit to such a bright luminance display is its increased visibility in brightly lit environments such as outdoors or in a living room with many windows. You do not want to edit photos in a dimly lit studio with the display shining at the full 1,000 cd/m², however.

Additionally, their ability to render darker black tones relative to older displays means that the total range of displayable brightnesses is significantly expanded. Marketing-speak sometimes describes this characteristic of a television as the *contrast ratio*. It's based on the *lowest possible display luminance* (L_{min}) and the *maximum possible display luminance* (L_{max}). The greater the ratio between these values, the wider the scope between bright and dark. LCDs, for example, tout contrast ratios of 1,000:1. Of course, taking advantage of such a capability means having high dynamic range source content to output. High dynamic range photo content has been achievable for a number of years while video recording in HDR is a more recent development.

HDR display standard adoption is in a state of flux as of this writing. The primary contenders are *Dolby Vision* (a proprietary solution requiring licensing), *HDR10* (an open source solution) and *Hybrid Log Gamma* (royalty free, co-developed by the British Broadcasting Corporation and the Japan Broadcasting Corporation). Dolby Vision supports up to 10,000 nits even though no available display is capable of reproducing that brightness and requires a specific hardware decoder in the display. HDR10, created by the Consumer Technology Association, supports up to 1,000 nits and can be decoded in display software. HDR10 was adopted by Netflix, LG, Samsung, Sony and Vizio, to name a few major players.[9] Many television manufacturers offer compatibility with both, at least until one becomes the dominant choice for mastering, distribution and broadcast.

It's important to separate maximum brightness or contrast ratios from bit depth. A display can show an extremely bright white and an inky black but its bit depth capabilities define how smooth the gradation is between these two extremes. Low bit depth translates to posterization, high bit depth means natural tone transitions and a wider range of displayable colors. Displays are 8-, 10- or 12-bit with developing technologies promising 14-bits and higher.

One of the challenges is deciding on a transfer function to convert the digital signal to optical energy given the variety of brightness capabilities of different display technologies. At the same time, some amount of backwards-compatibility with SDR displays is required at least for broadcast television.

The UHD Alliance is an organization of over 40 film and television studios, leading consumer manufacturers, content distributors and technology companies. The organization is working to establish "performance requirements for resolution, high dynamic range, color and other video and audio attributes with an eye toward giving consumers the best possible UHD with HDR experience."[10]

Display Color Gamut

Recall that the gamut defines the range of addressable colors; the color gamut of a display defines the colors it can accurately create and show from input media. There are several additional named color gamuts when discussing displays as shown in Figure 15-5.

The *NTSC* color gamut is perhaps the grandad of color gamuts, introduced in 1953 by the Federal Communications Commission. Developed by its namesake, the National Television Standards Committee, this is the standard color gamut for analog broadcast television. The NTSC is a wide gamut very similar to Adobe RGB, though they differ slightly in their red and blue primaries.

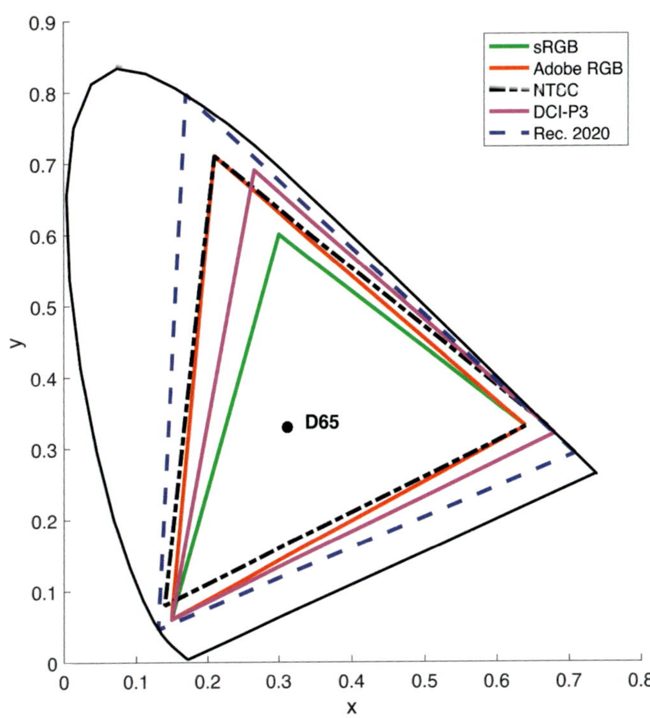

Figure 15-5 Comparison of the coverage of common color gamut standards.

Recommendation 709, also known as *Rec. 709*, was introduced in 1990 to provide a standard for HDTV.[11] Many use the terms sRGB and Rec. 709 interchangeably as they share the same RGB primaries and white point. Each uses a different gamma, however: 2.2 for sRGB and typically 2.4 for Rec. 709 (though the standard does not define it). Rec. 709 functions as the broadcast standard for SD and HD content and is used in the majority of broadcast content today.

DCI-P3 was developed for digital cinema projection in 2007 by the Digital Cinema Initiative and published by the Society of Motion Picture and Television Engineers.[12] The DCI-P3 gamut shares the same blue primary as sRGB and Adobe RGB. The red primary extends to the spectrum locus using a monochromatic light emission at 615 nm. DCI-P3 covers 45.5% of the chromaticity diagram (representing all of human vision), completely encompasses the sRGB color space and covers 90.1% of NTSC and 93.6% of Adobe RGB color spaces.

Rec. 2020 (ITU-R Recommendation BT.2020) was published in 2012 by the International Telecommunication Union (ITU).[13] It defines ultra-high-definition television (UHD TV) with wider dynamic range and *wide color gamut* (WCG). The standard defines expansions in color gamut, frame rates, bit depth (10 or 12), resolution, luma-chroma color representations and subsampling relative to previous broadcast standards. Rec. 2020 covers 75.8% of human vision, 52.1% of Adobe RGB and 99.9% of Pointer's gamut. We mentioned WCG in Chapter 6 when considering trends in motion video; film and television content is increasingly captured with extended color gamuts, mastered and streamed to viewers that are able to experience the difference on newer displays. This expansion of data throughput and output can require additional connection bandwidth in the form of network speeds and/or display interface connections and cables.

A display's ability to reproduce a range of colors or a percentage of a defined color space is directly related to the color primaries of its sub-pixel elements. The higher the saturation, color purity and range of luminances, the larger the pool of possible colors that the display can reproduce when needed. It's always a balancing act as highly saturated filters absorb more light and cause reduced brightness output while less saturated filters yield a smaller

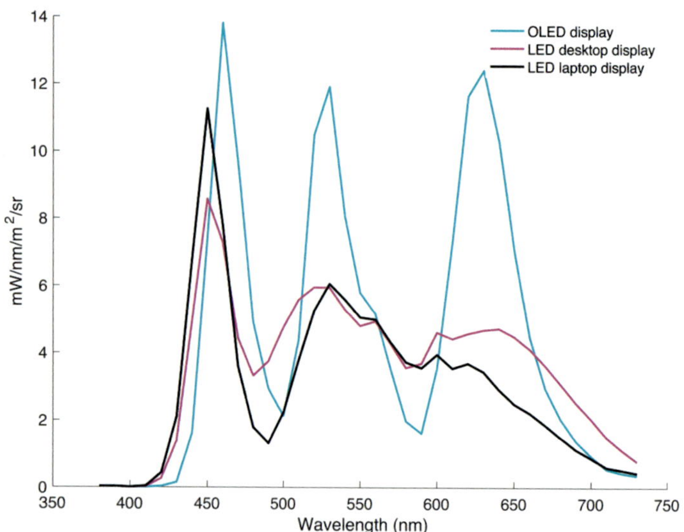

Figure 15-6 Measured spectral power distributions for the red, green and blue emissions of LCD and OLED displays.

color gamut. Figure 15-6 shows measured spectral power distributions for the additive primaries, red, green and blue, for three common displays. The measurements show that the OLED display emits narrow band wavelengths at each primary hue; the LED desktop and laptop measurements show that a shared display type may still show performance differences.

Defining the Display Viewing Conditions

Chapter 14 covered soft proofing and how to best manage a workspace environment for an optimal color management workflow and how to calibrate a display. Here, we address the physical size of a monitor in that space. Selecting the proper size display for the environment can be a topic of debate in many homes, particularly when it comes to a home theater or living room setup. Personal opinions aside, there are some objective guidelines that can settle the debate.

Viewing Angle

We first consider *viewing angle*, a characteristic defining the range at which the display can be viewed off-axis while retaining color and tone fidelity. A limited viewing angle means that colors and brightness may shift when viewing the display at any position other than head-on. Off-axis viewing can reveal a much dimmer and color-inaccurate view of displayed content. This is an important characteristic for displays in environments where viewer position is either varied or uncontrolled, such as movie theaters or in open spaces. It is less critical for the photographer sitting at a desk, well-centered and aligned with the monitor.

Viewing angle is dependent on the type of display panel technology. Twisted nematic panels exhibit the most restricted view angle. Vertical alignment display panels are considered to have moderate to good view angles. In-plane switching panels exhibit the best performance with many manufactures claiming a 178° view angle in both the vertical and horizontal directions.[14] It can also be a function of display shape: for a brief time, curved OLED panels were pushed by manufacturers for televisions and computer monitors. The former failed to catch on, perhaps because making a display that curves inwards on either side makes for a worse experience when sitting anywhere other than the center of the couch. Curved panels offer marginally improved utility on a desktop, on the other hand, as the curved sides provide a more consistent viewing distance in a user's periphery.

Viewing Distance

Viewing distance is also worth evaluating and is ideally consistent across sessions for both desktop workstations and home theater setups. There are many different methods for calculating *optimal viewing distance*, the distance where individual pixels cannot be seen and resolve to form a clear image. This distance depends on the pixel pitch and pixel density. *Pixel pitch* is the distance from the center of a pixel to the center of the next closest pixel. *Pixel density* defines how many pixels there are in a given area (an inch, for example) as illustrated in Figure 15-7. A smaller pixel pitch and a higher pixel density results in a shorter viewing distance just as a larger pixel pitch and low pixel density results in a larger viewing distance.

The simplest method is provided by display manufacturers in Equation 15.1. This method is put forth by Christie

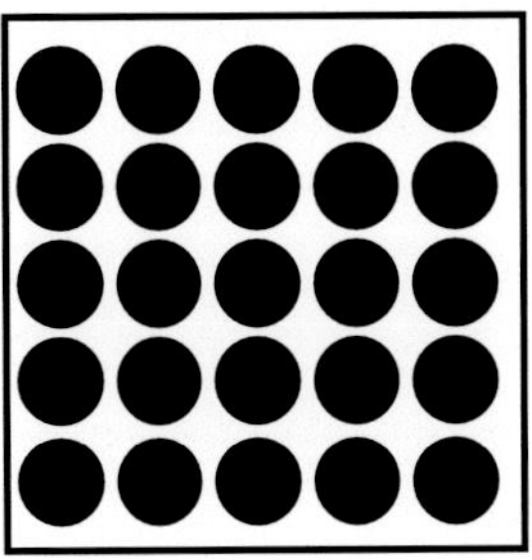

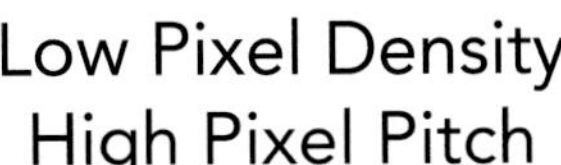

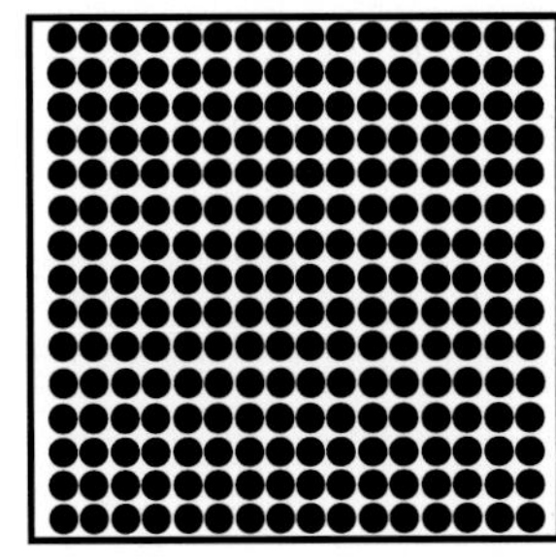

Figure 15-7 Keeping space between pixels minimal, larger pixels have low pixel density and high pixel pitch (left) while smaller pixels have a higher pixel density and lower pixel pitch (right).

Digital Systems and only requires the pixel pitch of the display.[15] Depending on the manufacturer, the pixel pitch is multiplied by a constant of 8, 10 or 15. This equation does not take into account human vision and is an estimation of distance.

$$\textit{Optimal viewing distance (in feet)} = \textit{Pixel pitch} \times 8 \quad \text{(Eq. 15.1)}$$

Optimal viewing distance depends on human vision which can resolve detail that is approximately 1 arc minute or 0.01670°. When determining optimal viewing distance, the pixel pitch must fit within this angle in the field of view. Individual pixels are visible if the pixel pitch exceeds 1 arc minute as illustrated in Figure 15-8 (overleaf).

Equation 15.2 is used to determine the proper viewing distance for a display with a known pixel pitch or to determine the required pixel pitch for a predetermined viewing distance. The goal is the same in either case: to have the proper combination of pixel pitch and viewing distance that results in good image quality.

$$\textit{Pixel pitch} = \textit{Viewing distance} \times \tan\left(\frac{\textit{1 arc minutes}}{\textit{60 arc minutes per degree}}\right) \quad \text{(Eq. 15.2)}$$

Viewing angle, viewing distance and environmental lighting all play a role in selecting and optimizing the performance and utility of your workspace displays. Many photographers have a desktop environment where

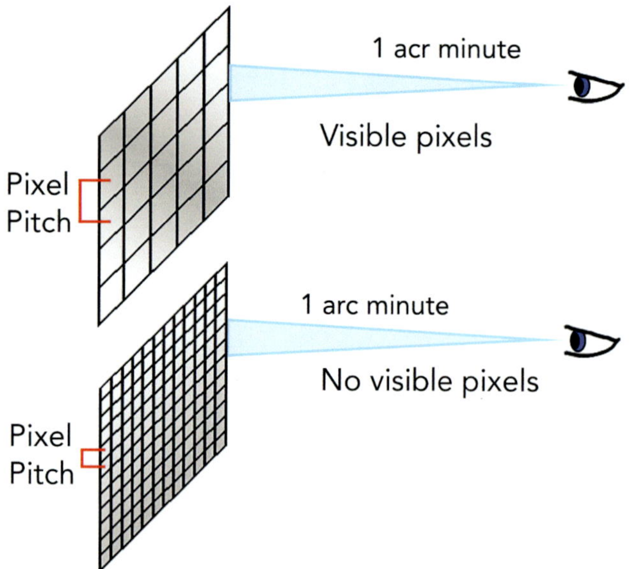

Figure 15-8 Individual pixels are not visible if the pixel pitch forms an angle with the eye of less than 1 arc second. Illustration adapted from Extron.com

they perform all of their image reviewing and editing. This allows for the selection of a display that best fits the environment, both in size, technology and capabilities. Laptops lack static or predictable viewing environments in exchange for portability—a tradeoff we're happy to accept for on-location shoots and when keeping up with the workload during travel.

Calibration and Configuration for Color Management

Display profile creation is inherently tied to color management and best practices for a photographic workflow. Calibration involves measuring and adjusting the display of brightness and color information from digital media files. Thankfully, the process of calibrating and characterizing our workstation monitors is aided by easy-to-follow software steps (assuming the measurement hardware is on-hand). Desktop operating systems support setting the custom ICC profiles created by this exercise as the default for your computer and monitor combination. The hardest part is often the discipline in revisiting the topic on a regular basis to counteract any drift or aging in the display hardware's performance.

More recently, color management software is integrated into mobile operating systems and display profiling solutions exist where they previously did not. This may seem excessive for the average user of a phone or tablet, but having color-critical settings and calibration is valuable when using these convenient displays for remote tethering or previewing of captured content.

The process of profiling a display involves some additional choices or options in addition to the measurement of color patches. Let's breakdown these other settings that impact the behavior and appearance of displayed content.

Recommended Settings and Conditions

Creating an accurate display profile requires a proper working environment. The recommended brightness setting for a color managed, photographic workflow is a luminance no higher than 120 cd/m^2.[16] This may look dim when working by the window at your favorite coffee shop or if you frequently keep your phone and laptop screens at maximum brightness. However, 120 cd/m^2 appears perfectly bright in a properly lit editing environment with neutral surrounding tones, no windows in your line of sight and the help of a *monitor hood* to further block stray light. Monitor hoods are purchasable accessories or can be constructed with foam board and flocking material to shield the monitor's top and side edges. Additionally, any objects in the room, including the table that the display is sitting on, should be neutral in color. Non-neutral colored objects may reflect a color cast onto the screen altering its appearance.

Display Profile Characteristics

Creating a display profile is driven by software. There are a few options to set prior to the calibration process. A common starting point is setting the white and black luminance levels of the monitor. This dictates the dynamic range available. This can be done prior to the calibration process or as the first step in the profiling software's step-by-step workflow. The contrast setting may also need adjustment before calibration. This is evaluated by determining if there is a difference between a white and slightly non-white when displayed by the monitor. The software determines if an adjustment is needed. Some display manufacturers do not provide the ability to adjust the contrast setting.

White point selection for a display profile sets the color temperature or the appearance of white. Most monitors range between 5000K and 6500K. The graphics industry traditionally uses 5000K while video and web publishing industries use 6500K. A white point of 5000K appears too warm for photographic applications while 6500K is too blue. Neither of these is ideal or recommended for photographic editing and display. A white point of 5500K is a good compromise between these two industry standards and should be selected if the native white point is unknown. Selecting the monitor's native white point provides the best dynamic range possible.

Additionally, the desired gamma or *tone response curve* (TRC) must be selected. This defines the behavior of the display between white (the brightest luminance) and black. In other words, gamma controls display contrast. A value of 2.2 is used for photography, video and web. A gamma of 1.8 is traditionally used by the graphic design industry.

The last step of creating a display profile is measuring a series of color patches. The profile created from these measurements defines the relationship between the RGB digital counts driving the monitor and the CIEXYZ or CIELAB values measured. The more patches measured, the more robust the profile created. Some high-end monitors designed for color critical work offer built-in color measurement hardware that moves a probe into position over the display and runs automatically at scheduled intervals. Such products may additionally use special lookup tables (LUTs) internally, stored in dedicated memory, to further control and optimize the translation from the computer's signal to displayable pixel values.

Emerging Display Trends and Applications

If you've ever purchased a television and then enviously eyed the Black Friday sales the following year, you're already familiar with the pace of consumer display technology development. Of course, most year-to-year changes or offerings are marketing gimmicks or largely incremental upgrades. Still, display capabilities, form factors and applications never stop evolving. Manufacturers are always looking to improve performance with regard to resolution, frame rate, dynamic range and color gamut. Here are a few additional categories to watch.

Night Modes and Reduced Blue Light Exposure

It didn't take long before we all became accustomed—possibly addicted—to staring at our smartphone screens and tablets late at night before bed. Scientists and restless Twitter users alike started wondering if exposure to bright computer screens late into the night influences sleep quality for the worse. Indeed, studies show that "watching a display at night can not only make it harder to fall asleep (up to 1.5 hours longer) but then the quality of sleep during the night is also reduced."[17] Furthermore, exposure to blue light (460–490 nm) in particular seems to disrupt the body's circadian rhythm by suppressing the production of melanin. Thus began the influx of mobile operating system software Band-Aids: adjusting the color profile to skew very warm during late night hours is thought to at least somewhat mitigate the problem. This is commonly done by limiting the use of the blue diodes in the display. While this works for comfort and possibly sleep quality, it is not ideal from a color management standpoint. We expect to be staring at displays long into the night for those endless photo editing sessions; future displays may include designs that minimize emission at the blue end of the spectrum for our health and well-being.

Electronic Viewfinders

One of the key features of the SLR design is its optical viewfinder. Putting an eye up to the viewfinder reveals a projected image of the scene as it gets recorded on the sensor at the time of exposure. Electronic viewfinders (EVFs) display a live video feed of the image along with information overlays like exposure settings, focus points and more. The display is quite small, as it resides inside the camera body and is only viewable when positioning an eye up to the viewfinder window. These small screens must have high pixel densities to deliver an experience worth abandoning that of our visual system viewing an optical image of the scene directly. Found in smaller camera form factors, EVFs are a solution to the fact that the newer, non-SLR camera designs lack the functional design of the pentaprism viewfinder. The pentaprism design allows for the photographer to see exactly what the sensor sees—critical for composing and framing. EVFs are an alternative that get back to this what-you-see-is-what-you-get visual feedback when shooting.

Head Mounted Displays

Computers continue to shrink, their ubiquity and integration into our personal and work lives means that wearable solutions are the next frontier. *Virtual reality* (VR) uses *head mounted displays* (HMDs) that completely envelop the user's vision. *Augmented reality* (AR) is similar but requires the integration of the real world by introducing see-through displays. Both VR and AR demand considerable and sometimes yet unseen display solutions.

It's too early to say if head mounted displays used for virtual reality and augmented reality experiences will have a major role in the photographic medium. The display hardware is considerable in its boundary-pushing refresh rates, resolutions and user-input tracking. The modern consumer HMD for virtual reality experiences came to life thanks to driven-down manufacturing costs of small display panels for smartphones, meaning that continued investment and adoption of such systems may lead to other unforeseen benefits to visual media. Display pixel densities are still below the threshold for appearing seamless at the very close viewing distances required of head mounted hardware, though this is quickly changing.

Many of us can detect a light source flickering below 60 Hz. This is especially true with our peripheral vision. The context of head mounted displays for virtual reality raises the minimum bar higher because flickering quickly leads to user motion sickness. Common HMDs today have refresh rates of at least 90 Hz to avoid this uncomfortable experience.

Proof of Concept: Documenting the Growth in Mobile Device Display Capabilities

We can use our color management tools to look at display gamut capabilities in a simple way that quickly reveals useful information. We've run an exercise in our classes for a number of years now that asks students to measure primary color patches (R, G, B) on their smartphone screens using photometers. We began this experiment as phone screens were getting bigger, more colorful and higher in resolution in the early 2010s. This logically coincided with a surge in visual media on mobile platforms and apps, even though the idea of mass media consumption on these devices just a few years earlier seemed far-fetched. As soon as phone screens were considered good enough to view and share photographs and motion media, their popularity exploded (as did the hunger for greater data bandwidth).

As photographers and avid media consumers, we hope that our smartphone screens are capable of representing photographic content accurately and completely. It's only in the last few years that mobile operating systems have incorporated mature color management software to ensure quality color reproduction. Much of this color management and interpretation of any available, embedded profiles is inaccessible to us as smartphone users. Still, we can get a general sense of their display capabilities with a simple set of measurements to find their color gamut.

First, we measure the tristimulus values for the additive primary colors: red, green and blue. We prepared a series of image files made in Adobe Photoshop where each consists

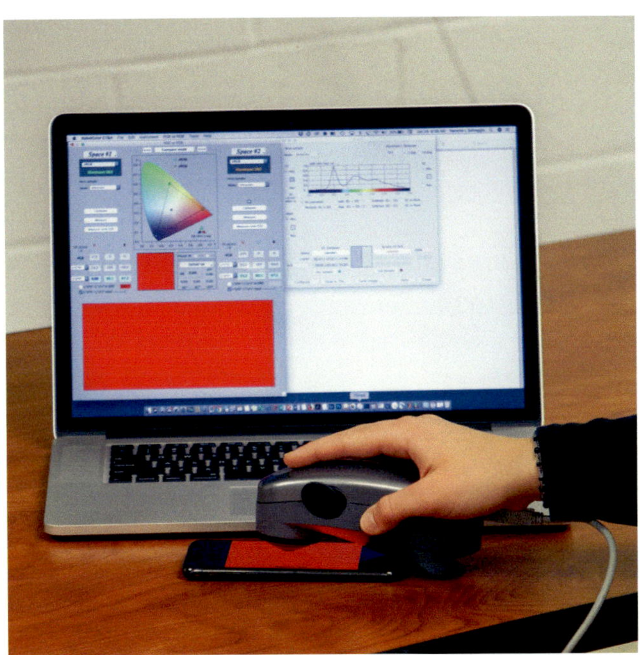

Figure 15-9 Measuring a smartphone display using prepared color patch images and a photometer.

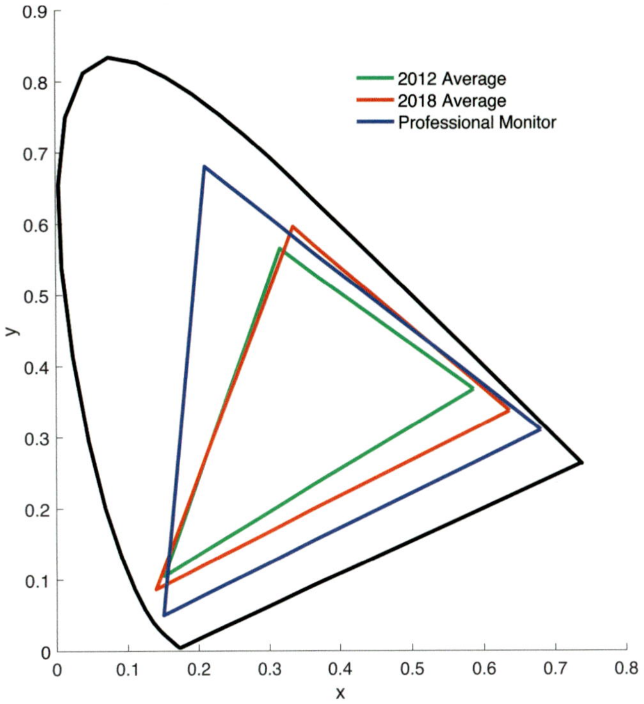

Figure 15-10 A chromaticity diagram showing the gamuts of our measured displays: a high-end desktop monitor, the average gamut for phones in 2012 and again in 2018.

of a single color. These colors are the purest red, green and blue (respective color channel value: 255). We loaded these image files onto our devices and, one by one, measured them displayed full screen at 100% brightness with a photometer as shown in Figure 15-9. The photometer outputs tristimulus values for each patch. With XYZ values in-hand, we calculate chromaticity coordinates (*x* and *y*) and plotted them on a chromaticity diagram.

Table 15-2 lists XYZ values averaged from the ones measured by our students in 2012 and 2018. It also shows measured data from a professional desktop display (an LCD). We think it's interesting to have a point of reference, even if we don't expect our phones to keep up with the capabilities of professional, dedicated display hardware.

Figure 15-10 shows aggregate results from running this exercise over a number of years. We took student-collected data—hundreds of measured phone screens across a variety of models and operating systems—and plotted the average tristimulus values for the 2012 and 2018 school years. While this does not represent every available device from those years, the data is notably varied in models and screen types.

Table 15-2 Measured tristimulus values and calculated chromaticity values for the average mobile phone in 2018 and a professional desktop LCD.

	Color Patch	X	Y	Z	x	y
Mobile Phone (2018)	Red	41.2	21.3	1.99	0.64	0.33
	Green	33.3	60.1	9.85	0.32	0.58
	Blue	15.4	7.38	77.5	0.15	0.07
24" Professional Grade LCD Monitor	Red	56.39	25.64	0.93	0.68	0.31
	Green	21.03	68.08	10.32	0.21	0.68
	Blue	17.36	5.69	92.79	0.15	0.05

This idea can be further extended by measuring a series of grayscale patches ramping from black to white to gather data on contrast, maximum luminance and white points. We additionally measure a pure white patch to investigate color casts and the behaviors of "night modes" or "true color" color temperature adjustment software frequently found on mobile operating systems today.

Questions to consider from this exercise and our collected data:

- What do you think is the primary contributing factor to the increase in color gamut capabilities on mobile screens?
- Have the increasing capabilities of small displays led to their increased use for visual media viewing?
- Do you think that the average consumer notices the difference or improvements over the last few years?
- Do you believe that portable device displays are headed toward professional-grade color reproduction and other higher-end display characteristics? Are there characteristics beyond color gamut described in this chapter that are important for these displays?

Notes

1 Allen, Elizabeth and Sophie Triantaphillidou. *The Manual of Photography*. Elsevier/Focal Press, 2017, p. 292.

2 Young, Ross, et al. "White paper release: QLEDs – Quantum dot technology and the future of TVs." *Display Supply Chain Consultants*, Nov. 15, 2017, www.displaysupplychain.com/white-paper-release.html, p. 4.

3 Young, Ross, et al. "White paper release: QLEDs – Quantum dot technology and the future of TVs." *Display Supply Chain Consultants*, Nov. 15, 2017, www.displaysupplychain.com/white-paper-release.html, p. 6.

4 Chinnock, Chris. "Insight media releases technical white paper on quantum dot technology." *Insight Media Releases Technical White Paper on Quantum Dot Technology*, Nov. 14, 2016, www.insightmedia.info/insight-media-releases-technical-white-paper-on-quantum-dot-technology/.

5 Young, Ross, et al. "White paper release: QLEDs – Quantum dot technology and the future of TVs." *Display Supply Chain Consultants*, Nov. 15, 2017, www.displaysupplychain.com/white-paper-release.html. p. 7.

6 Chinnock, Chris. "Quantum dots will power display products to the next level." *Insight Media Releases Technical White Paper on Quantum Dot Technology*, Nov. 2016, www.insightmedia.info/insight-media-releases-technical-white-paper-on-quantum-dot-technology/., p. 18

7 Baker, Simon. "Response time measurement." *TFT Central Monitor Panel Part Database*, Jan. 2013, www.tftcentral.co.uk/articles/response_time.htm.

8 Nilsson, Mike. "Ultra high definition video formats and standardization " *Slidelegend.com*, BT Media and Broadcast Research Paper, Apr. 2010, slidelegend.com/ultra-high-definition-video-formats-and-standardisation-bt-media-_59bf6bef1723dd5242bdfbc0.html.

9 Brennesholtz, Matthew. "HDR10 vs Dolby Vision." *DisplayDaily*, Aug. 10, 2016, displaydaily.com/article/display-daily/hdr10-vs-dolby-vision.

10 "Members." *UHD Alliance*, alliance.experienceuhd.com/members.

11 *BT.709: Parameter Values for the HDTV Standards for Production and International Programme Exchange.* International Telecommunications Union, June 2006, www.itu.int/rec/R-REC-BT.709/en.

12 The Society of Motion Picture and Television Engineers (2010), SMPTE-EG-0432-1:2010 Digital Source Processing – Color Processing for D-Cinema.

13 *BT.2020: Parameter Values for Ultra-High Definition Television Systems for Production and International Programme Exchange.* International Telecommunications Union, Oct. 14, 2015, www.itu.int/rec/R-REC-BT.2020-2-201510-I/en.

14 Jackson, Harry. "Viewing angle defined and explained." *Monitors for Photo Editing, Helps You Choose the Best Monitor for Photo Editing and Photography*, Feb. 11, 2018, www.monitorsforphotoediting.com/monitor-viewing-angle-defined-explained/.

15 "LED displays." *Christie – Digital Projection and Integrated Visual Display Solutions*, www.christiedigital.com/en-us/digital-signage/visual-display-technology/resources/LED-displays.

16 Ashe, Tom. *Color Management & Quality Output: Mastering Color from Camera to Display to Print.* Focal Press, 2014.

17 Soneira, Raymond M. "Watching displays at night." *DisplayMate LCD Advantages and Disadvantages*, www.displaymate.com/Displays_At_Night_1.htm.

16 Printing and Physical Media

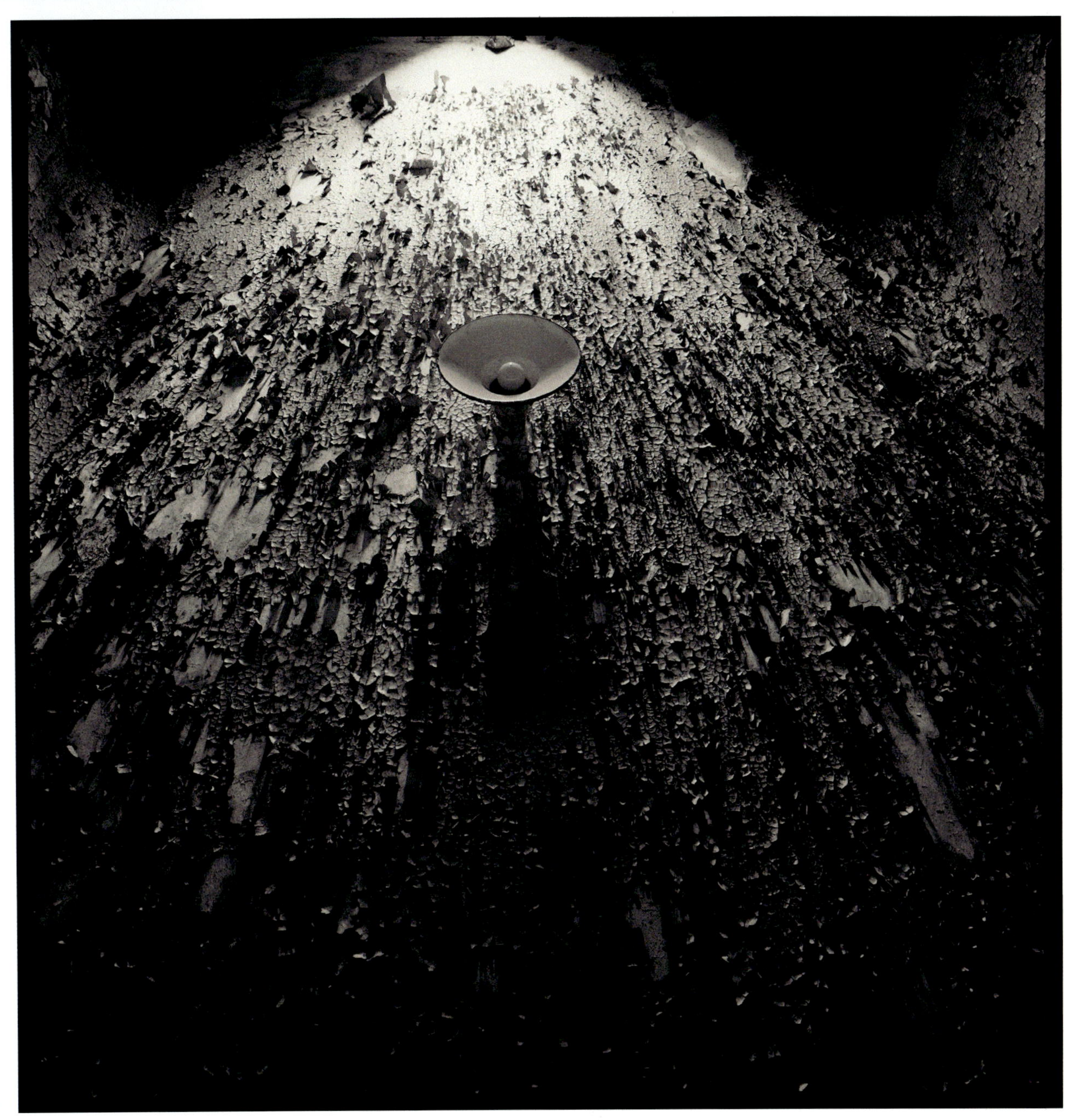

Photograph by Eric Kunsman

This chapter was written in collaboration with Eric Kunsman, Lecturer at Rochester Institute of Technology and owner of Booksmart Studio, Inc. in Rochester, New York.

—

Printing technology is expanding rapidly to meet the demands of the average consumer, the professional photographer and everyone in between. Photographic prints, once created solely with light-sensitive materials, now employ various forms of ink or toner and sophisticated printer hardware. High-quality printing is now easily achieved in a home studio or office. The print media industry is constantly improving printing technologies, whether they are printer manufacturers, ink and toner developers, paper companies or print finishing companies. The push for "larger is better" has never been as true in the output field as it's been since the beginning of the twenty-first century.

This chapter aims to inform photographers about available printing media and technologies and to provide insight into their best strengths and applications. We review the fundamentals of what it means to output images to print media, the printer hardware, the papers and other substrates used and a variety of other factors to consider. Printing to physical media represents a key balance of vision, craft and technical precision; it's how a great deal of photography is discovered and experienced even in our increasingly digital world.

The Fundamentals of Printing

Printing for photographic output is a subtractive color mixing process that lays down color material onto a receiving substrate. A *substrate* is any surface onto which an ink or dye can be printed. The fidelity of the printed reproduction of an image file is dictated by its detail, color, tonality and sharpness, among other criteria.

A camera captures an image with a set resolution defined by the size and density of the photosites across the area of a digital sensor. The native sensor resolution dictates the maximum available pixel dimensions of our captured image file. Often, photographers only care about the number of megapixels (a measure of pixels dimensions, width multiplied by height). From pixel dimensions we determine print size when choosing how many *pixels per inch* (ppi) to send to the printer for a given print size. There is great debate between photographers as to the proper pixels per inch needed to print. Today, Epson printers render upwards of 360 ppi and Canon 300 ppi of spatial resolution on a high-end glossy substrate. Print resolution is a logical place to start an overview of printing fundamentals.

Pixels Per Inch and Dots Per Inch

Pixels per inch is a measure of the resolution of a display, scanner or image sensor; it's a count of how many pixels exist in a square inch of space. This is different from *pixel density* which is a function of the number of pixels in height and width that are then rendered using dots of inks when printing. We must decide on the printed spatial resolution to use with a 3,600x4,800-pixel image file, for example. If we send the file to the printer at 300 ppi, we divide the pixel resolution by 300 to determine the print dimensions in inches as calculated in Equation 16.1.

$$\frac{3600\ \text{pixels}}{300\ \text{pixels per inch}}\ by\ \frac{3800\ \text{pixels}}{300\ \text{pixels per inch}} = 12 \times 18\ \text{inch print} \qquad \text{(Eq. 16.1)}$$

This calculation indicates the print dimensions possible with the native pixel resolution, though we always have the option of interpolating and upscaling the image data. Print size relative to viewing distance is discussed later in this chapter.

The number of ink dots that physically fit in an inch on the substrate is measured as *dots per inch* (dpi). This is a logical way to talk about print resolution in terms of the physical printing mechanics. As a printer does not print pixels, dots per inch is an appropriate term to describe printing behavior. The greater the dots per inch metric, the more dots of ink a printer lays down in a square inch area of the receiving substrate. Dots per inch does not tell us anything about pixel resolution.

Continuous Tone and Halftone Printing

Printing dots is accomplished in one of two ways: *continuous tone* or *halftone*. Continuous tone digital printers produce output similar to the analog color photographic process by writing individual image dots directly to paper or film. The dots vary in density and the dyes used are transparent. This allows for placing one color directly on top of the previous color. A printer using the three subtractive primary colors of cyan, magenta and yellow is theoretically capable of reproducing more than 16.7 million colors. The color gamut of the dyes used determines the actual number of reproducible colors. Photosensitive light written and thermal transfer printing technologies are continuous tone options available today outside of the traditional darkroom print. The use of a light source writing the image to a photosensitive material aids in the creation of continuous tone.

Halftone printing uses opaque dots that do not vary in density. Halftone dots can't be placed on top of one another without obscuring the previous dots. These dots are printed in patterns that blend to the eye and are perceived as various colors when viewed from a distance. The process of printing these small dot patterns is called *halftone screening*. Halftone screening does not allow for continuous tone density because the ink dots are overlapping, sized differently or spaced differently to create the illusion of continuous tone. The finer the dot (or dot size) and the higher the frequency (the dots per inch), the more the image appears as continuous tone to the viewer. The space between the dots of ink reveals the underlying substrate is a part of the process whereby our visual system creates the illusion of continuous tone.

Halftone printing uses *amplitude modulation* (AM) or *frequency modulation* (FM) screening methods. A loupe or magnifying glass is necessary to distinguish between the two. The AM screening method was first used for early offset lithography; the image was exposed through screens onto film with a grid-like pattern and a uniform spacing between differently sized dots. This grid-like pattern is called *lines per inch* (lpi) as this trait determines the space between dots and their size. The higher the lines per inch, the finer the dot size. The physical dot size is determined by the exposure of that dot. A film, also called a *screen*, is

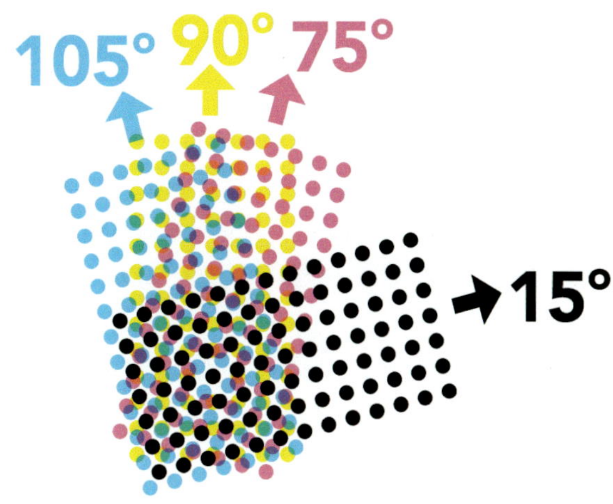

Figure 16-1 An example orientation for halftone screen ink dot patterns.[1]

created for each color used. These screens break the image up into a series of dots of varying frequencies and sizes corresponding to the amount of that particular color in the image. The resulting films are used to expose printing plates. Each color uses its own angle to prevent the dots from perfectly overlapping. Figure 16-1 illustrates one possible combination of halftone ink dot orientations. The angles are adjustable depending on the lines per inch to avoid introducing printing artifacts like moiré patterns.

The AM screening method is used today for traditional *offset lithography* and by the HP Indigo printing press. Offset lithography does not print directly onto the substrate or paper. Instead, a *printing plate* is created for each color which initially receives the ink. The ink is then transferred onto the *printing blanket*, typically made of rubber, which then comes in contact with the substrate to transfer the ink. The contact between the printing blanket and the substrate is facilitated by an *impression cylinder* that creates contact pressure between them. The printer must transfer all of the toner from the blanket to the substrate and therefore employs the AM halftone method. The HP Indigo supports on-the-fly changes to screening resolution and the angles of each color during a print job.

FM screening is also known as *stochastic screening*. The method came about when computers were first used to create the films that then made the printing plates for offset lithography. FM screening uses a random dot

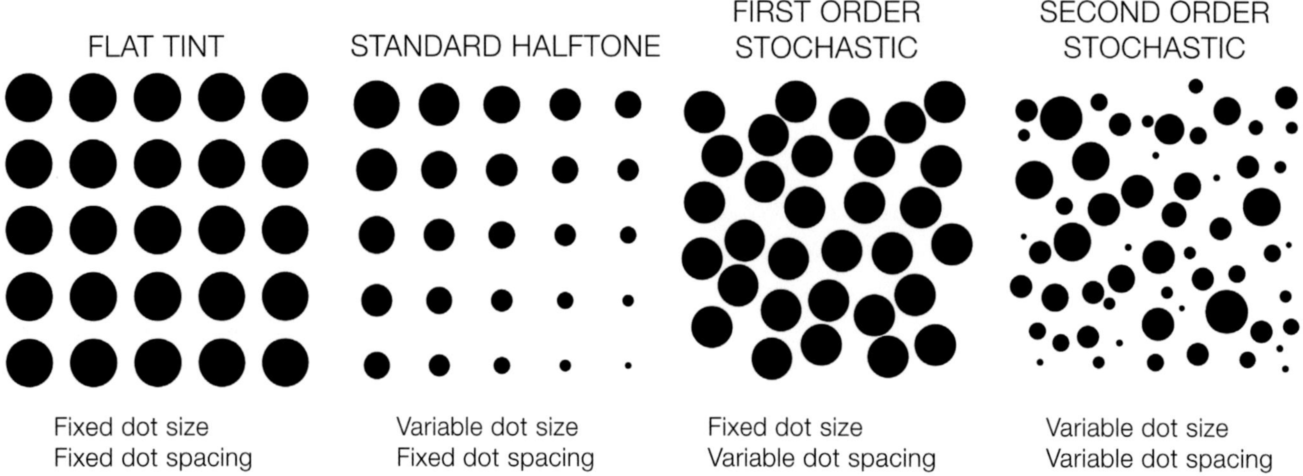

Figure 16-2 Amplitude modulation screening patterns compared to frequency modulation screening patterns. Illustration courtesy of Tom Ashe

pattern to create a frequency modulation that provides an improved, continuous tone appearance when compared to AM screening patterns. Inkjet printers and dry toner electrophotographic printers (described later in this chapter) use a newer method of FM screening that leverages dithering to further improve the continuous tone appearance.

Dithering is a technique of printing a series of tiny dots to create the illusion of a color that can't be directly produced by the printer. Altering the dither pattern changes the color appearance thanks to partitive mixing. Dithering, combined with stochastic screening, creates a random dot pattern and spacing with variable dot sizes. Figure 16-2 illustrates the traditional halftone AM screening, traditional FM stochastic screening and the newer dithering and stochastic method.

Manufacturers are constantly working on dot size and halftone methods to create the most continuous tone image possible with each new generation of inkjet printers. This requires developing ink formulations that allow for smaller printer nozzles and incorporating the capabilities into their screening and printing software solutions.

For many years, almost all technologies using ink or toner introduced additional colors like orange, light magenta and light cyan to improve color gamut and tonality. This practice became less common over the last decade, however, as the quality and gamut capabilities of the traditional subtractive primary colorants improved.

Printer Technologies

There are numerous printing technologies used in the diverse world of printing applications. This chapter concentrates on inkjet printing used for professional photographic output but we'll also describe light-sensitive printing, electrophotographic and thermal transfer printing technologies.

Inkjet Printing

Inkjet printing uses a *printhead* that deposits small amounts of colorant onto a receiving substrate. The mechanics of inkjet printing allow for a wide range of print sizes: since the printhead is mounted and travels along a linear rail, the maximum print width is extended by making the rail longer. Conversely, inkjet printers can be sized to sit on a desktop and output smaller prints. The former approach is considered *wide format inkjet*, the latter, *desktop inkjet*. Wide format inkjet printers are categorized by their ability to output print sizes 24 inches wide or larger. Inkjet printing is a rapidly evolving technology because of the enormous amount of development dollars spent on it. It's also one of the few affordable technologies for the home user.

There are two inkjet printhead technologies to consider and both use *drop-on-demand* (DOD) mechanisms to deposit ink in a controlled manner. The first printhead technology is the *thermal* or *bubble jet* system found in printers made by companies including Canon and Hewlett-Packard (HP). Each ink cartridge in a desktop inkjet printer contains a series of tiny nozzles and an electrical connection to the printer. The ink is routed into individual chambers, each with a tiny resistive heating element. Applying a pulsed current to the heating element heats the ink until it vaporizes, causing a bubble to form. The expanding bubble forces the ink through the small opening in the chamber and sprays it toward the paper as illustrated in Figure 16-3. The vacuum created in the chamber draws more ink into the nozzle to repeat the process. This process allows for depositing variable droplet sizes onto the substrate.

Thermal printheads use self-detection mechanisms to monitor for clogged nozzles, a commonly encountered

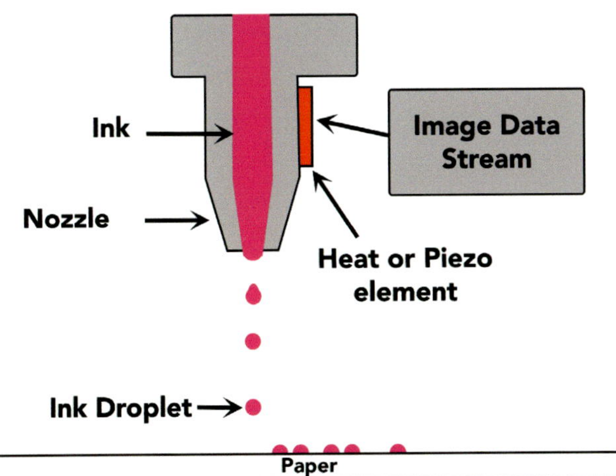

Figure 16-3 Drop-on-demand inkjet printheads use a heating element to create a bubble of ink or a piezo element pushes a drop of ink onto the paper when requested by the image data stream. Not illustrated is the printhead's ability to vary ink droplet size.

operating challenge with inkjet printers. The printhead switches to one of its many extra nozzles if a clogged nozzle is detected. Despite these extra nozzles, thermal printheads eventually run out of unclogged ones and must be replaced by the user; these printheads are a consumable printer component. Canon and HP home desktop printer printheads are built into the ink cartridges which drives the cost of replacement cartridges higher. The printhead hardware is replaced when the ink cartridges are replaced even though it may have useful operating life left. Professional-grade printers employ different printhead design approaches. Canon uses either a single or double printhead for up to 12 colors; HP models use one printhead for every two colors.

Instead of using a heating element to force ink out of the nozzle, *piezoelectric inkjet* printers use a small piezoelectric crystal that expands and changes shape when a current is applied. This change forces ink out of the nozzle chamber while also refilling the chamber for the next firing of the nozzle. The piezoelectric jet is like a small electromechanical pump that precisely delivers a small amount of ink. Since the shape of the piezoelectric element changes based on the amount of charge applied, the size of the ink dot is variable. This technology is used by many printer manufacturers in their desktop, wide format and high-speed inkjet printers. The difference between manufacturers' offerings is the number of nozzles per inch for various ink types and viscosities. Epson printers traditionally use 360 nozzles per inch that force ink droplets out of the chamber at a size of 3.5 picoliters (the physical size of a picoliter is approximately 20 microns).

Current piezoelectric technology is capable of resolutions up to 2880 dpi. The printer spatial resolution can produce upwards of 360 ppi accurately rendered with dots of ink as compared to the 300 ppi possible using thermal printhead technologies. The print quality between piezoelectric and thermal printheads is indistinguishable to the human eye without the use of a magnifying loupe.

Continuous-flow inkjet printers pump a continuous stream of electrically charged ink droplets (64,000–165,000 per second) at the paper as illustrated in Figure 16-4 (overleaf). A magnetic field controls ink placement on the page; unused ink is directed to a recovery reservoir.

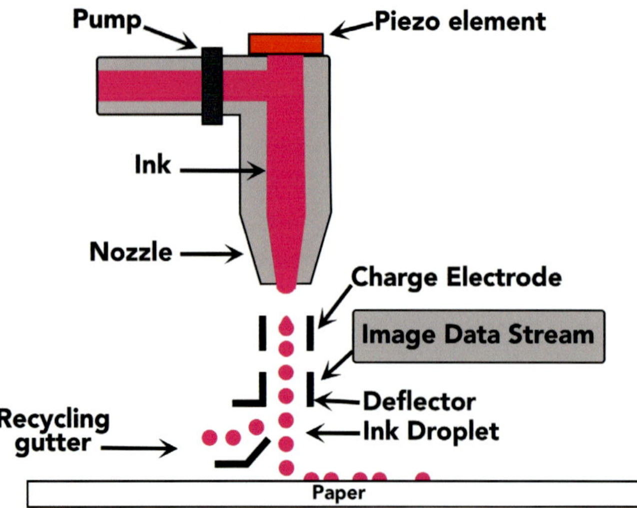

Figure 16-4 A continuous-flow inkjet printhead pumps a stream of ink droplets that get redirected by a magnetic field to get deposited on the substrate or recycled.

Continuous-flow inkjet printers are available for several distinct applications. The high-speed, low-resolution variety is used to print product identification (labels), personalized direct mail and magazines. High-resolution, low-speed printers like the Iris series by Scitex were used for proofing and fine art printing for many years. Iris printers produced multiple spots per dot and achieved effective resolutions of up to 1,800 dpi. In part because of the great number of paper surfaces on which it printed (especially heavier weight, fine art watercolor papers), the Iris is the printing technology that facilitated the acceptance of fine art reproduction by museums and collectors. Continuous-flow technology is also employed by some high-speed inkjet printers to help deliver faster output speeds.

Photosensitive Light Writing Printing

One of the more cost-effective continuous tone printing methods available today is *photosensitive light writing printing*. An RGB laser or set of light-emitting diodes (LEDs) exposes an image onto light-sensitive material. The light-sensitive material is then processed using RA-4 development chemistry just like a traditional darkroom print. This process produces prints on chromogenic papers as well as silver gelatin papers for black and white reproduction.

The Durst Lambda printer is one popular laser imaging photosensitive digital printer on the market. Using a series of laser diodes to write an image onto photographic paper, the Lambda printer handles rolls of paper up to 50 inches wide, exposing the paper as it moves past the lasers. The paper materials are sensitized depending on the light source used. The resulting *chromogenic print*, otherwise known as a *digital c-print*, uses color coupler dyes (cyan, magenta and yellow) in an emulsion layer with light-sensitive silver halide crystals. Digital chromogenic prints are made on traditional paper substrates or translucent materials.

Light-sensitive silver halide crystals are suspended in a gelatin emulsion which is then coated onto a *carrier substrate* (the supporting material). A chemical layer of barium sulfate also known as *Baryta* is applied to the carrier substrate to create a surface on which the light-sensitive layer sits. This is different from inkjet papers that use a microporous coating atop the Baryta layer. Once the image is exposed, the paper is developed with a chemical process that transforms the exposed areas into silver metal. The unexposed silver halide is removed. Fiber-based prints are considered much more archival than their resin-coated counterparts but they require an extensive washing stage to remove residual chemistry. These prints are as archival as traditional darkroom prints, around 25 years, and offer better scratch resistance than inkjet prints thanks to the emulsion layer.

Printer hardware like Kodak's Pegasus LED Printer print directly onto special digital photographic paper using a small array of LEDs. The paper is fed into a drum where a vacuum pump pulls the paper tight against the inside of the drum. The Pegasus handles roll sizes up to 20 inches wide and the drum accommodates a 33-inch long piece of paper, allowing for a maximum 33x20 inch print size. LVT is another company manufacturing printers that use LEDs to expose photographic film and paper. Instead of the paper being drawn by a vacuum to the inside of a drum, LVT's printers wrap the paper around the outside of a drum.

LED printers expose the image onto the paper using a small array of four red, four green and four blue LEDs mounted at the end of a counterbalanced arm. The output of the red, green and blue diodes is combined with an optical lens assembly to create a single, focused spot. The arm spins on a spiral track at approximately 1,350 revolutions per minute (RPM) and the LED assembly is positioned just above the paper's surface. The image is written as the arm travels down the length of the drum on the spiral track. Once the image is written and the paper exposed, it's advanced into an attached processor for development. It exits from the machine fully dried in about 6 minutes.

Electrophotographic Printing with Dry Toners

There are two main types of *electrophotographic printing* technologies today: those that use *dry toner* and those that use *liquid toner*. Dry toner technology is used by a variety of manufacturers with each having slight differences in their mechanics. With either toner type, electrophotographic technologies allow for *print on demand* (POD) workflows because each time an impression or image is written with a new charge to the imaging drum.

Dry toner technology was initially developed for photocopiers but found its way into desktop printers in 1985 with the introduction of the laser printer. A laser, directed via a spinning mirror, alters the magnetic charge on a rotary drum. Toner particles are attracted to these areas of the drum. Toner particles are transferred to the paper as the drum rotates into contact with it. The paper is then transported through a pair of heated rollers which fuse the toner particles to the paper. The color process version adds cyan, magenta and yellow toners and requires exposing the electrostatic drum once for each color.

Dry toner machines use FM screening just like inkjet printers. Initial dry toner technology was limited to CMYK toners; some printers now offer silver, gold, green, orange and white toners that expand color gamuts. Manufacturers are also working on toner development to increase the color gamut of dry toner printers.

Prints made with fused toner are relatively inexpensive per sheet compared to other technologies discussed in this chapter. Dry toner electrophotographic machines are migrating from older laser and mirror technologies to LEDs to write to the imaging drum. Newer printers also use belts instead of rotary drums to pass the substrate between the imaging roller and a charge corotron (a component that regulates voltage).

Electrophotographic Printing with Liquid Toners

The only liquid toner printing press available at the time of writing is the HP Indigo digital press. HP Indigos are used in commercial production for print applications such as marketing collateral (brochures, business cards, posters), direct mail, labels, folding cartons, flexible packaging, books, manuals and specialty applications. The Indigo's ability to print without films and printing plates enables personalized short runs with variable data by changing text, images and jobs without having to stop the press. Photographers enjoy the HP Indigo press when printing photography books because of their ability to mimic a traditional offset lithography press and to leave the substrate characteristics intact.

Each press consists of up to seven color stations which use cyan, magenta, yellow, black and a variety of *spot color* inks. Spot colors are either premixed inks or specific pure colors that may be difficult to create by mixing the available CMYK inks. Presses may also use special inks such as white, UV red, security colors and transparent (for a *spot varnish*). The ability to use spot colors is common with non-digital offset lithography presses and is one of the features that distinguishes the HP Indigo digital press.

The Indigo's electrophotographic liquid toner technology is based on HP's ElectroInk which uses charged pigment particles suspended in imaging oil that's attracted or repelled by means of a voltage differential. The liquid toner solution starts out as a mixture of 80% imaging oil and 20% toner along with the proper amount of imaging agent to make sure that its conductivity is at the proper level. The ink particles are small to ensure that the printed image does not mask the underlying surface texture of the paper (as is possible with some toner-based processes). Additionally, the press creates a thin, smooth plastic layer on the substrate surface to accept the ink. The physical ink particles make up a halftone pattern and larger dots that mimic conventional offset lithography. The physical ink particles are smaller than dry toner because they are suspended in imaging oil and cannot become airborne.

The process begins with electrostatic charging of the electrophotographic *photo imaging plate* (PIP) mounted on the imaging cylinder. The initial charge is completed by

Scorotrons at 5,000–5,800 volts. The initial charge is negative and floats on top of the PIP and a thin layer of imaging oil. The PIP is light-sensitive and the charge is controlled by an auto-bias. The PIP is exposed by a scanned array of lasers shooting through the negative charge. These lasers are controlled by the raster image processor which converts instructions from a digital file into on/off instructions for the lasers (described in more detail later in this chapter). The positively charged, exposed image area attracts the ink. Inking of the PIP occurs via the highly charged *binary ink developer* (BID) roller.

Printing begins when the mechanical roller pushes ink through the BID while applying a negative charge to the ink. A squeegee removes the imaging oil and applies a negative charge to it, forcing the imaging oil away and the toner particle toward the *developer roller*. The developer roller creates the positive charge for the toner particles as the imaging oil is removed. At this point, the ink solution percentages are reversed to 80% toner and 20% imaging oil. The BID moves closer so that the toner can jump to the PIP's image areas.

Next, the PIP transfers the inked image to the blanket on the blanket cylinder which is heated and helps to create a thin layer of plastic. The heated inked image is transferred to the substrate held by an impression cylinder. The impression cylinder must have the right amount of contact to properly transfer the image. Most HP Indigo presses transfer each color one at a time using this process. However, roll-to-roll and other presses allow for printing using a process called *one-shot*. One-shot collects all of the colors onto the blanket and only requires one round of contact with the substrate. This allows for perfect registration and the ability to work with substrate rolls. If duplexing is required, the substrate waits in the *perfecting unit* while a second sheet is started. Once the second sheet's first side is printed, it releases the first sheet to print the second side.

The technical process described earlier gets the toner onto the substrate. There are many consumables on these presses and many controls not discussed here that ultimately determine print quality. The electrophotographic liquid toner press requires a trained technician to maintain it—unlike most dry toner machines.

Thermal Dye-Diffusion Printing

Sony and Kodak both introduced printers in the mid-1980s that produced a continuous tone image from a video source using a *thermal dye-diffusion* process (also called *thermal transfer*). The thermal dye-diffusion process uses a two-part medium. The first part is a clear mylar film called a *donor ribbon* onto which consecutive transparent cyan, magenta, yellow and optimizer dye patches are coated. The second part is a paper-based material called the *receiver*. The donor material resides on a motor-driven spool. A thermal printhead containing thousands of individually controllable resistive elements heats the dyes on the donor material which causes the dye to transfer from the donor to the receiver (see Figure 16-5). The amount of transferred dye is controlled by varying the amount of current (and thus heat) sent to each of the resistive elements on the printhead. The process prints one color at a time and the paper is rewound back to precisely the same starting point so that the next color is placed in registration.

The dyes in a thermal dye-diffusion printing process are transparent and their printed densities are variable by up to 255 different levels for each color. The color dots are placed on top of one another, combining to create any of the 16.7 million theoretically possible colors in a 24-bit image. Figure 16-6 shows the resulting image viewed under magnification. The image is somewhat blurred due to the nature of the solid-to-gas-to-solid events of dye-diffusion.

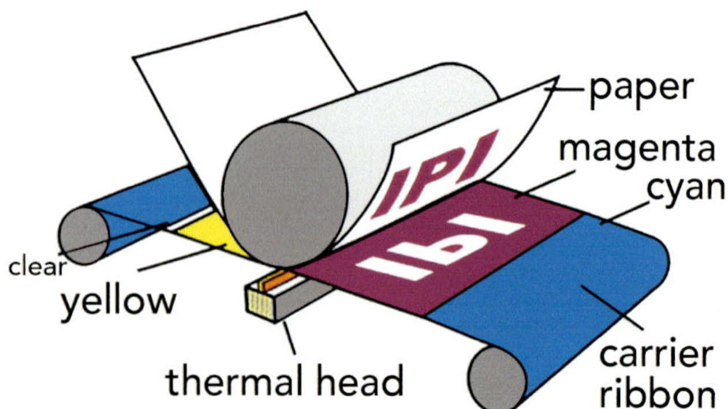

Figure 16-5 The donor ribbon transfers dye to the receiver paper when heated. Illustration courtesy of the Image Permanence Institute

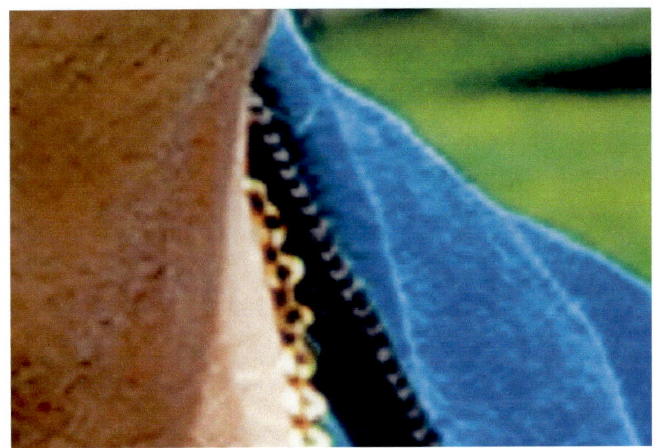

Figure 16-6 A magnified look at a thermal dye-diffusion printed image. Photograph courtesy of the Image Permanence Institute

Dye Sublimation Printing

Dye sublimation printing, also called *dye diffusion*, is a process that first prints onto transfer paper with unique dye sublimation inks. Using a heat press, typically around 400ºF, the transfer paper is placed on top of the receiver substrate. Heat and applied pressure cause the dyes to sublimate into the substrate fibers. This yields an image with vibrant color and good durability. The heated printing process turns solid ink into a gas, avoiding a liquid stage.

In traditional dye sublimation printing, the fabrics needed to be white or light in color and made of 100% polyester or a 50% polyester, 50% cotton mix. Today, microfiber and nylon are potential options as well. The process can also be used on ceramic, wood, glass and metal as long as they have a special polymer coating to accept the ink in its gas stage. Transfer papers and ink formulations now exist for popular elastic fabric materials and for all kinds of fabrics including natural fiber fabric like cotton, silk, linen and wool.

Ink Technology

Colorants, inks and pigments are three commonly used terms when explaining ink technologies and materials. It's important to clarify the distinctions between them. A *colorant* is any substance used to add color. Inks, dye and pigments are all types of colorants. Photographic printing technology takes advantage of this variety of colorants depending on the application and intended appearance.

When discussing photographic printers, a *dye-based ink* is a water-based or aqueous solution into which a dye, the colorant, is dissolved. The dye attaches to the water carrier and stays suspended in the solution. This is similar to adding sugar into a cup of coffee: it cannot be removed or separated once dissolved. Different dye colorants create a variety of ink colors. Dye-based inks are absorbed into a paper substrate while the water evaporates, leaving the colorant behind. Dye-based inks offer great vibrancy in color but are prone to damage from exposure to ultraviolet (UV) radiation.

A *pigment* is a compound of many molecules clumped together and forms a finely ground powder colorant. Pigment particles are often many times larger than dye particles. A *pigment-based ink* is comprised of a pigment suspended in water in the context of photographic printing. The pigment settles out from the water given enough time. When printed, pigment often sits on top of the paper and bonds to the surface in a thin film. Pigments are not as severely affected by UV exposure relative to dye and do not easily smear. They tend to be more expensive than dye-based inks.

Aqueous Inkjet Inks

Aqueous inkjet printers are the most widely used inkjet technology and are commonly found in homes and photography studios. They are affordable entry-level options but the substrates and inks used are the most expensive of all inkjet printing technologies. Aqueous inkjet inks use a water-based carrier for the colorant. Special coatings on the paper are used to accept the colorant while allowing the water to evaporate. These coatings drive up the cost. Both dyes and pigments are used as colorants in aqueous inkjet inks with most printer manufacturers moving to pigment-based inks. Canon, Epson and HP are constantly introducing new inkjet printers to the aqueous inkjet market. Often times, new versions or generations see upgrades in the ink technology used in an effort to improve printer color gamut capabilities. Inkjet inks are not 100% opaque, allowing for the blending of colors and densities by overlaying inks.

Dye-based inks offer a larger color gamut than pigment-based inks but tend to fade at a faster rate. Pigment-based inks are more stable as they have larger insoluble organic particles, however, this makes them more prone to scratches and scuffs. They also require a microporous coating rather than a swellable polymer. Therefore, pigment-based inks are never truly encapsulated within the inkjet receptive coating. Both dye-based and pigment-based aqueous inks offer a wider color gamut when compared to other available inks thanks to the introduction of colorants such as green, orange, red or blue into the printers.

Solvent Inks

Solvent inks are the backbone of the digital inkjet printing industry for outdoor signage applications. Solvent inks use an oil-based solution to hold the pigment and resin. Solvent inks are used to print on different uncoated banners, papers, flexible vinyl substrates, vehicle wraps and adhesive decals. This technology is fade-resistant, waterproof and abrasion-resistant: all important qualities for outdoor usage. Unlike many aqueous inks, prints made using solvent-based inks are generally waterproof and UV-resistant without special over-coatings. Solvent inks emit volatile organic compounds and ventilation is required when working with them. The substrate used when printing with solvent inks is often heated immediately before and after the printheads apply ink; the high print speed of many solvent printers demands special drying equipment.

Solvent inks are offered in the standard cyan, magenta, yellow and black. Additional colors such as orange, green, violet, light cyan, light magenta, light black, white and even silver or metallic are also available options.

Solvent inks are subdivided into two categories: *hard solvent ink* offers the greatest durability without specialized over-coatings but requires special ventilation of the printing area to avoid exposure to hazardous fumes. *Mild* or *eco-solvent* inks are intended for use in enclosed spaces without special ventilation. They are sometimes called *low-solvent* or *light-solvent* inks. Outgassing continues for up to 24 hours on both solvent and eco-solvent inks, so there is a waiting period before beginning any finishing processes, particularly lamination.

The popularity of eco-solvent inks grew in the last decade as their color quality and durability increased while their cost concurrently decreased. Eco-solvent inks contain solvents and binders made from renewable crops like corn. However, the liquid solution in eco-solvent ink comes from ether extracts taken from refined mineral oil, so it's inaccurate to think that this is an entirely ecologically friendly alternative. Printers using eco-solvent inks use heat to evaporate the solution. Eco-solvent ink is usable on many uncoated substrates but takes longer to dry than solvent ink. Prints made with eco-solvent ink last for approximately two to three years before beginning to fade.

Ultraviolet Curable Inks

Ultraviolet curing is a photochemical process that uses a high-intensity ultraviolet energy source to instantly cure or dry inks. Liquid monomers and oligomers are mixed with a small percentage of *photoinitiators* and exposed to UV energy. The ink instantly hardens to become solid polymers in just a few seconds of exposure. This process is widely used in the silkscreen industry. In fact, UV cure inkjet printing is now the fastest growth area in both usage and technological advancements since 2015.[2] The inks and light sources are constantly improving in performance.

UV curable inks do not evaporate but rather set as a result of the chemical reaction. No material is evaporated or removed, therefore 100% of the delivered ink volume is used to produce the printed dot. The curing reaction happens very quickly, leading to instant drying that results in a completely cured print in seconds. This allows for immediate print quality inspection. The fast chemical reaction prevents ink from penetrating the substrate, allowing for highly controlled dot placement.

UV curable inks were created as an alternative to solvent-based products for the signage industry. They contain no solvent or water, meaning that there is no loss of ink thickness or substrate shrinkage and substrate edges do not curl. UV curable ink manufacturers are constantly working to improve on flexibility, durability, color gamut, reducing surface texture and printability.

UV cure printers are expensive compared to aqueous and solvent printers and the cured ink's thicker viscosity leaves a slight relief on the print surface. The viscous inks are more susceptible to cracking if applied to a flexible substrate relative to solvent inks, though the new formulations to address this issue are being actively developed. There are two main classifications of inks used in this process: *free radical* and *cationic*; there are likely to be more alternatives in the coming years.

The free radical UV curable ink is sensitive to oxygen, so the curing process must be quick. This often means using a greater intensity UV source and more photoinitiators in the ink that allow for oxygen quenching. The increased intensity causes more heat on the substrate and some substrates are not built to accept that heat. Adding more photoinitiators to the ink adds to the cost and produces more of an odor.

Cationic inks are not sensitive to oxygen, require less UV energy to initiate the curing process and are fully cured after exposure. These inks are also known to provide improved flexibility, adhesion, hardness, chemical resistance and opacity with a higher gloss and less of an odor than free radical inks. However, cationic inks are known to cure slower than free radical inks and may require pre-heating of the substrate to accept the ink. The ink formulations are often more expensive and are sensitive to moisture along with acids and bases.

Latex Inks

One of the latest developments in inkjet technology are aqueous *latex inks* that use latex as the pigment carrier solution. These inks offer an alternative to solvents and UV curable inks in the signage market. The goal is to replace solvents and reactive ingredients with less hazardous materials and water. This technology offers comparable durability to solvent inks on numerous substrates, including uncoated vinyl. The use of water-based formulations in latex inks allows for a more environmentally friendly finished print that requires no ventilation. This is good for items used indoors such as printed wallpaper or signage and items are durable for indoor or outdoor usage.

Latex inks require heaters in the printers as the substrate becomes receptive to the ink through a pre-heating step. A post-heating step allows the ink to properly dry. A substrate that exhibits rapid expansion or contraction due to heat is problematic when using latex inks. At the same time, these machines have higher electricity demands compared to other inkjet technologies because of the need for the heating elements.

HP was the first printer company to introduce latex printing technology and only within the past few years have competitors started to offer their own versions. Ricoh and Mimaki introduced a machine that requires a lower amount of heat; Mimaki's latest machine states that it only needs 60°C while the HP printers need around 120°C.

Dye Sublimation Inks

There are various types of ink chemistry used for the dye sublimation process when printing on textiles. Using the proper combination of inks with the transferred fabric type is important. Cotton, rayon, linen and silk must undergo a pretreatment prior to printing and often use reactive dyes in their manufacturing. Acid and reactive dyes are essentially steamed to fix the dyes to the fabric and must be washed afterwards to remove any extra or non-fixed ink remaining on the fabric. Dye sublimation manufacturers offer a variety of fluorescent colors to help with matching of a specific brand color, as well as expanding the overall color gamut of their machines.

Printing Substrates

Each printing technology presents unique requirements for preparing the substrate surface to accepting the colorant. Inkjet substrate coatings, for example, help the dye or pigment colorant to penetrate the surface without penetrating too far thus preventing proper drying. Choosing the proper paper for your work is overwhelming as there are many choices available for photographic output. Here, we explore the primary physical media substrate types to consider before diving into specific characteristics in the next section.

Note that the term *photo paper* previously referred exclusively to light-sensitive substrates used to print in the darkroom. Today, the term includes these options but also extends to papers used with ink-based digital printing processes. *Fine Art photo papers* used in inkjet printing are specially coated to receive dye-based or pigment-based inks and can be made of cotton, alpha cellulose, bamboo, sugar cane, silk, rice and many other materials.

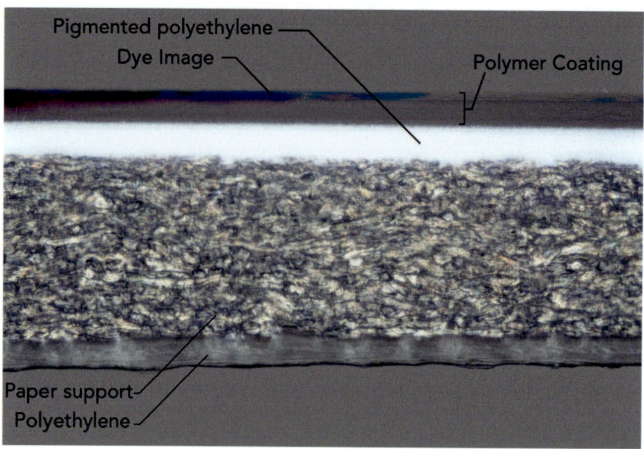

Figure 16-7 A 200x magnified cross section of RC swellable polymer coated paper. Photograph courtesy of www.graphicsatlas.org

Aqueous Inkjet Substrates

There are two main coating types for aqueous inkjet printing: *swellable polymer* used for dye-based inks and *porous inkjet* used for dye or pigment-based inks. The subcategories of porous substrates compatible with pigment-based inks are *microporous* and *nanoporous*. *Macroporous* is compatible with dye-based inks.

A swellable inkjet coated paper absorbs dye-based ink as it is sprayed onto the paper. This results in the paper swelling around the ink. Swellable paper requires time to dry and smears if handled while wet (though some instant-drying papers exist). Swellable papers offer high gloss surfaces and are resistant to scratching and fading once dry. Swellable papers cannot be used with pigment-based inks as the pigment is not absorbed into the paper and can rub off; the process of swelling and encapsulating works because of how thin dye colorant is compared to pigment.

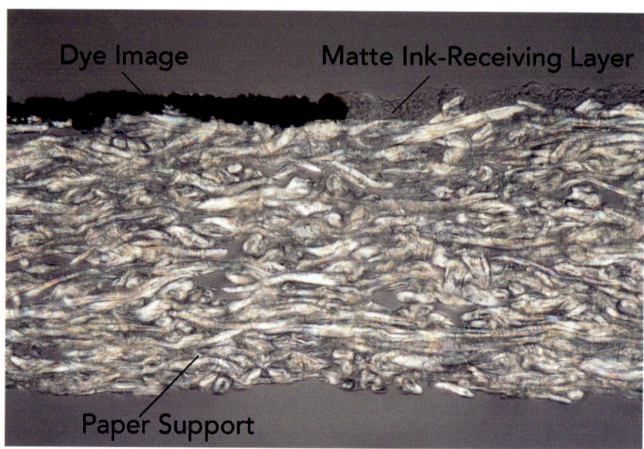

Figure 16-8 A 200x magnified cross section of uncoated paper printed with dye ink. Photograph courtesy of www.graphicsatlas.org

Both swellable and porous paper types may embed *resin-coated* (RC) layers. The top RC layer sits directly under the swellable or porous coating to prevent moisture from absorbing into the paper base (moisture causes the paper to curl). The second RC layer is applied to the back of the paper for the same reason. This layer is clear.

Figure 16-7 shows how the printed dye sits in a swellable polymer coating and does not absorb lower into the paper support. Attempting to print with pigment ink results in the colorant sitting on top of the coating that will not dry. Figure 16-8 shows the result of printing onto an uncoated paper—the dye ink sits on the top surface on the substrate without completely absorbing into the paper support.

Microporous coatings are commonly used for pigment-based inks. The ink is absorbed into the coating layer and remains there once dry. Figure 16-9 shows pigment ink printed onto the coating; it does not absorb past it to the polyethylene or paper support base layers below. Microporous coatings are often employed with RC glossy and luster papers. You can often identify them by the backing polyethylene coating because it feels like plastic.

Figure 16-10 shows a matte surface paper where the microporous coating sits directly on top of the paper

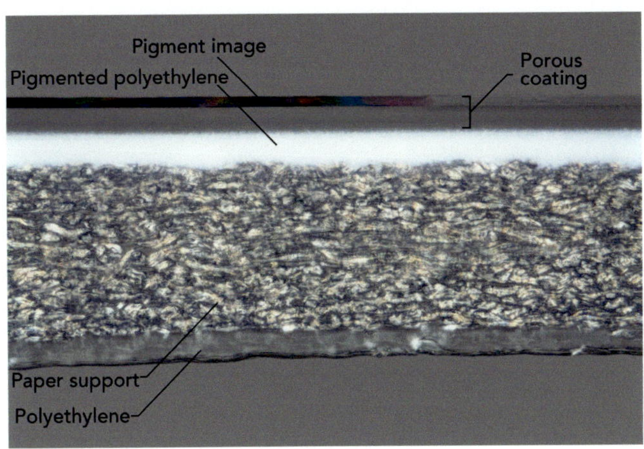

Figure 16-9 A 200x magnified cross section of RC microporous coated paper. Photograph courtesy of www.graphicsatlas.org

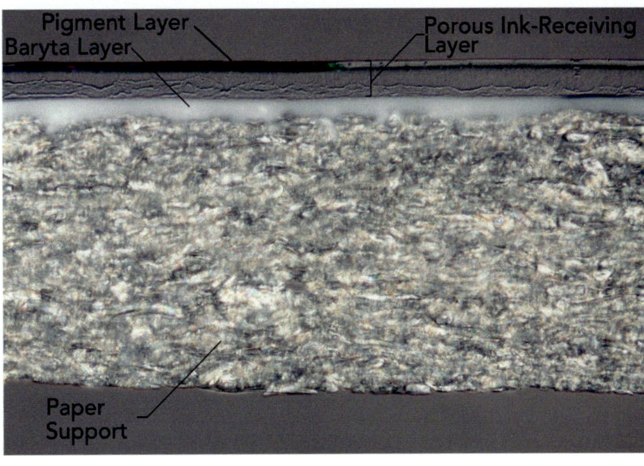

Figure 16-11 A 200x magnified cross section of a Baryta microporous coated paper. Photograph courtesy of www.graphicsatlas.org

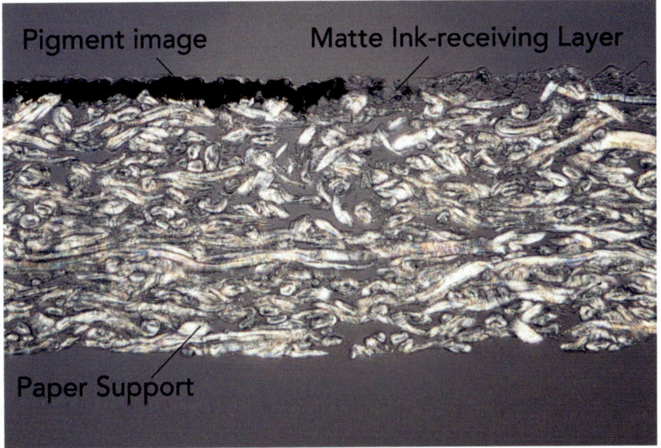

Figure 16-10 A 200x magnified cross section of matte microporous coated paper. Photograph courtesy of www.graphicsatlas.org

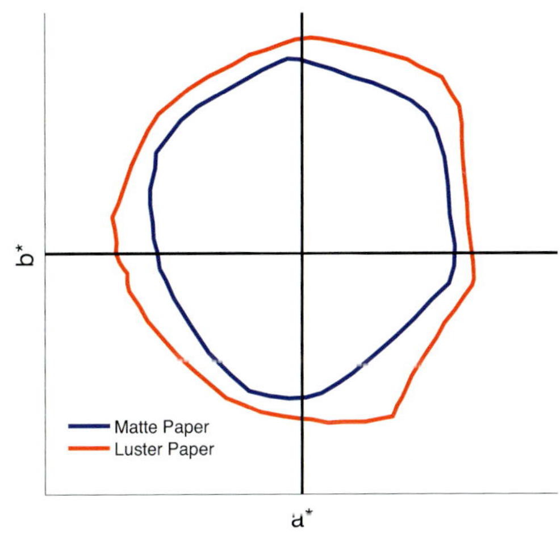

Figure 16-12 A comparison of measured color gamuts between luster and matte photo papers using an Epson 9900.

support. The pigment ink absorbs into the microporous coating and possibly some of the paper support depending on the coating quality. Higher-end papers allow for the pigment ink to absorb to the bottom of the microporous coating and for the top to harden allowing for a more scuff-resistant print.

Figure 16-11 shows a substrate with a special chemical coating typically comprised of barium sulfate (*Baryta*) under the porous ink-receiving layer. Such substrates are commonly used by photographers because they yield an image that renders similarly to a photographic process without using darkroom chemistry. Figure 16-12 highlights the noticeable difference in color gamut when ink is absorbed into the coating compared to when it sits in the microporous coating.

Chromogenic Substrates

Chromogenic substrates are light-sensitive papers that require a photochemical development process to create a final image. Chromogenic paper consists of a gelatin emulsion layer containing color dyes coated onto a cellulose acetate support seen in Figure 16-13 (overleaf). Exposing the emulsion to light using lasers or LEDs activates the dye

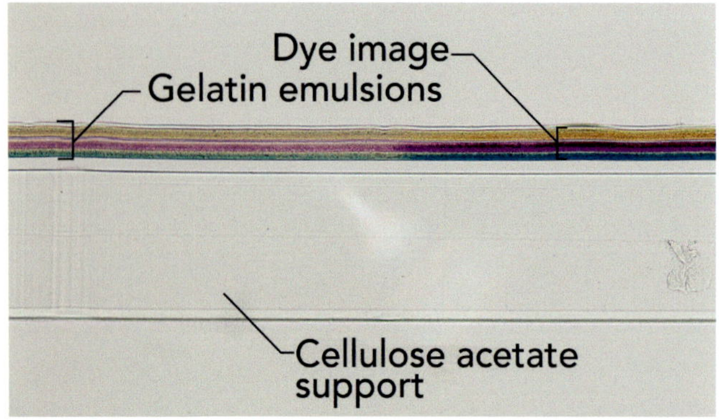

Figure 16-13 A 200x magnified cross section of chromogenic paper. Photograph courtesy of www.graphicsatlas.org

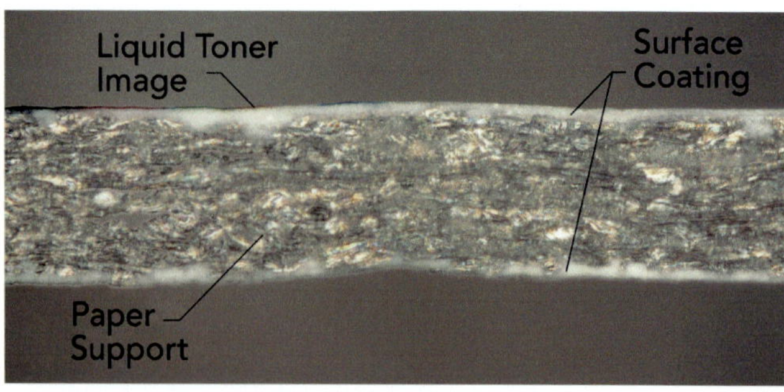

Figure 16-14 A 200x magnified cross section of a matte paper treated for liquid toner. Photograph by www.graphicsatlas.org

layer. The paper is then developed using the RA-4 process to create the print. Chromogenic papers used for digital image printing have a different chemical makeup compared to those used in a traditional darkroom context.

Liquid Toner Substrates

A special treatment is required for substrates used with liquid toner unless *super calendering* (rolling and compressing the surface) of the substrate allows for the toner/plastic layer to transfer from the blanket to the substrate. The treatment also allows the toner to adhere to the substrate to create a scratch resistance surface.

Substrates for the HP Indigo press, which use liquid toners, are subject to a certification process specified by HP. The Printing Applications Lab at Rochester Institute of Technology is responsible for this certification process.[3] Certified substrates are treated to allow the thin plastic film to adhere to it. Therefore, the qualifications for the certification are: *runablity* (does it feed through the press), *blanket wear* (does the substrate destroy the blanket), *adhesion* (does the toner adhere to the substrate and how well at different time intervals). Figure 16-14 shows that both sides of the substrate are treated. The surface treatment that accepts liquid toner is not the same as surface coatings needed for aqueous inkjets.

Dry Toner Substrates

Dry toner substrates are the easiest to find and can be purchased in any office supply store by the ream for just a few dollars. The paper does not require any special coatings or treatment as the dry toner printing process fuses the toner to the paper as seen in Figure 16-15. This fusing makes the final print more scratch-resistant compared to liquid toner prints. The substrates used are often standard color copier paper but higher-end options exist; pearlized paper, Kraft paper, transparency, vellums and Fine Art papers are available for dry toner printing.

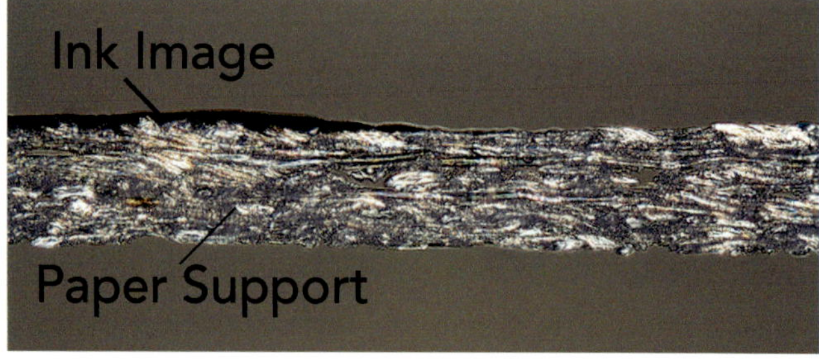

Figure 16-15 A 200x magnified cross section of a matte paper with a fused image from dry toner. Photograph by www.graphicsatlas.org

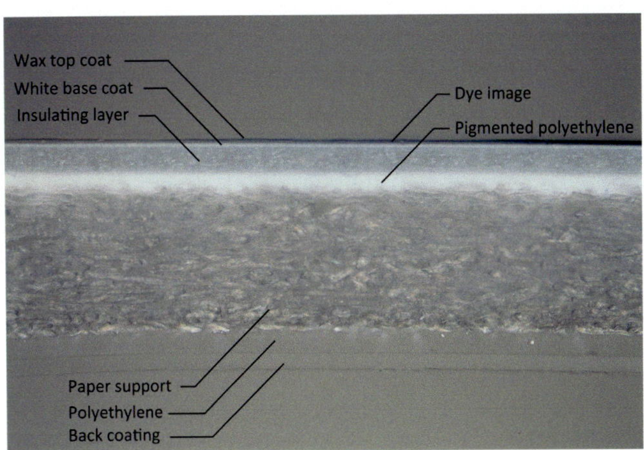

Figure 16-16 A 200x magnified cross section of dye sublimation paper. Photograph by www.graphicsatlas.org

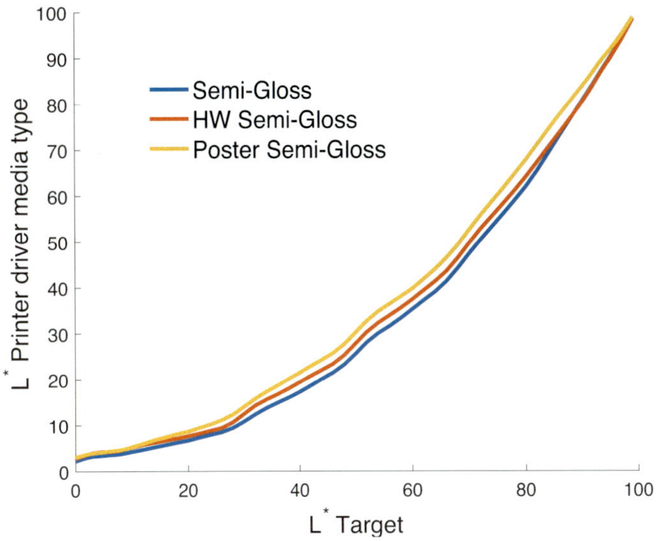

Figure 16-17 The measured and plotted data from a tone reproduction scale printed with different printer driver setting media types.

Dye Sublimation Substrates

Dye sublimation substrates are coated to allow for the encapsulation of the dye when it's in its sublimation state. Figure 16-16 shows the dye image sitting on top of the substrate surface—dye doesn't get absorbed into the paper support. Both sides of the paper have a polyethylene layer. The back of the paper features a back coating while the front features an insulating layer below the top coatings. The insulating layer is critical during the printing process when heat is applied for each dot of transferred dye. The amount of heat determines how much dye is transferred.

Photo Paper Characteristics

We consider a variety of paper characteristics beyond the basic swellable and porous categories. Importantly, paper types dictate how much ink is appropriate to lay down (controlled by printer ink settings). In Figure 16-17, the same tonal reproduction scale is printed with different media types chosen from the printer driver software and the resulting L* values are measured. The difference in media type additionally impacts color gamut. Some media type settings offer subtle differences and making small tweaks to the available ink controls may be necessary if over- or under-inking is observed.

Other key substrate characteristics include paper weight, thickness, surface sheen, texture and base tint or white point. Manufacturers often offer samples to examine and assist in selecting a photographic paper and we recommend seeking out these paper sample books when planning photographic output.

Paper Weight and Thickness

Paper stock is characterized by the base substrate thickness in accordance with ISO 18055-1:2004 Photography and Imaging – Inkjet Media: Classification, Nomenclature and Dimensions – Part 1: Photo-Grade Media (Paper and Film). One way to measure thickness is using the *mil*, a unit of length where 1 mil is equal to one-thousandth of an inch (0.001 inch). A photo paper may be approximately 10 mil thick, for example, while a U.S. dollar bill is 4.3 mil.[4] Paper weights are described by basis weight in *grams per square meter* (g/m^2). Paper used for documents and text is typically around 80 g/m^2; photo papers range in weight from 190 to 270 g/m^2.

Table 16-1 Surface sheen categories and their appearance.

	Category	Appearance
Coated Papers	Gloss	High sheen surface
	Satin	Less shiny than gloss
	Matte	Flat, little sheen
Uncoated Papers	Smooth/Woven	Very smooth surface
	Laid	Textured lines
	Linen	Fine lines

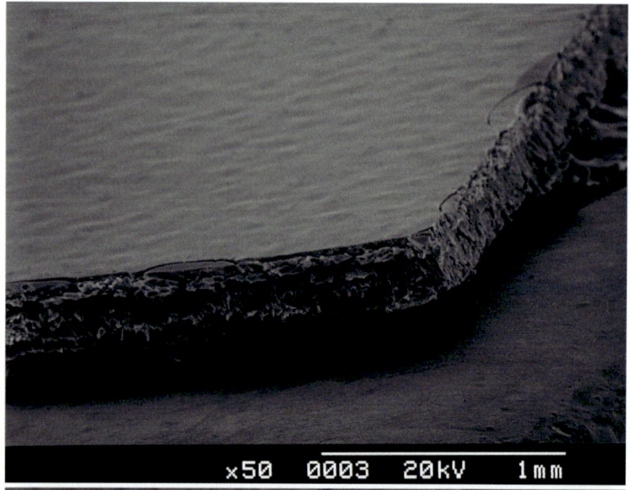

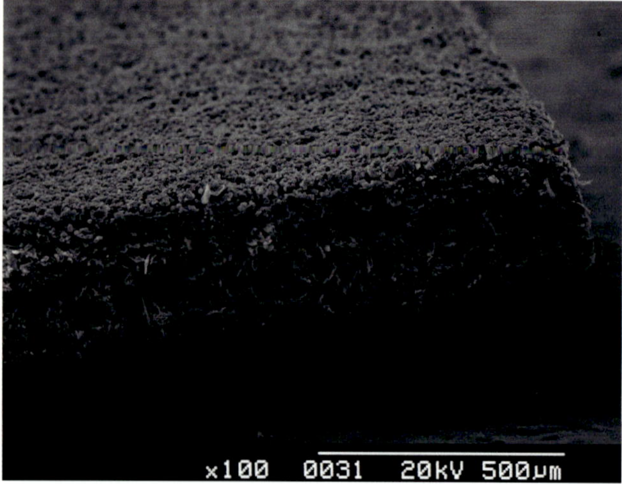

Figure 16-18 Highly magnified scanning electron microscope images of photo paper substrates: a semi-gloss (top) and a matte (bottom). Photographs by Rochester Institute of Technology photography alumnae Lia DiRico

Surface Sheen

A substrate's ability to reflect light defines its *surface sheen*. The categories of sheen are specific to traditional printing processes for coated or uncoated printing papers. Coated papers are categorized as *gloss*, *satin* or *matte*. Uncoated papers exhibit surface sheen categories of *smooth* or *woven*, *laid* and *linen*. Table 16-1 identifies the main categories of surface sheens and their appearances. Inkjet substrates borrow the gloss, satin and matte descriptors despite differences in material composition. Figure 16-18 shows two photo papers photographed using a high magnification scanning electron microscope to reveal their topographic differences.

Surface Texture

Texture is the feel of the paper surface. Some photo papers have the look and feel of traditional light-sensitive photo paper where others offer an appearance of a paint canvas or watercolor paper. While many photographic prints are not intended to be handled by viewers, texture is often visually inferred based on the play of light and shadows across the paper surface. On the other hand, texture and paper weight are key elements of the photo book experience as the reader holds and turns the pages.

Brightness and Optical Brightening Agents

Paper is not inherently white and its color varies depending on the region of the world from which its raw materials are purchased. To produce a paper with a pure white, papers are often tinted with chemicals like titanium dioxide. Papers may also be dyed to create a warmer paper base like an off-white or cream color.

It's common to incorporate some amount of *optical brightening agents* (OBAs) in paper surfaces with the goal of intensifying the paper's apparent brightness. These colorless chemical compounds are similar to laundry detergent brighteners that promise to keep white fabrics looking new. The effect is produced by using a dye or chemical substance that fluoresces upon exposure to ultraviolet energy (present to some extent in most light sources). That is, the chemical component absorbs incident

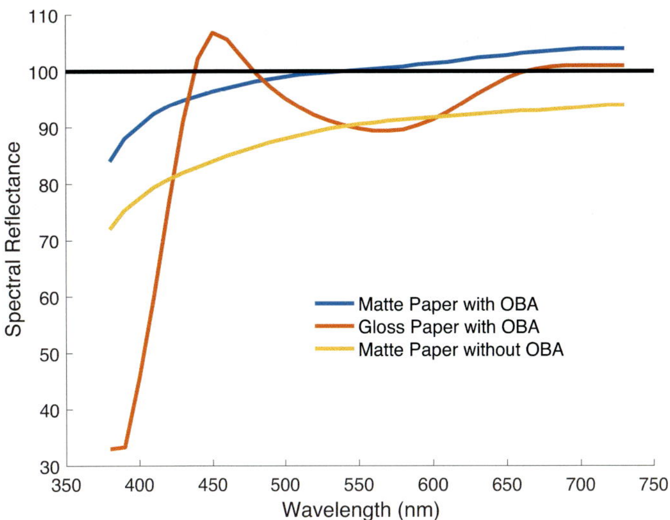

Figure 16-19 Measuring the spectral reflectance of different photo papers reveals the impact of OBAs. A 100% reflectance line is included for reference.

UV energy and re-emits it as visible light energy, primarily in the blue range. This causes the spectral reflectance of papers with OBAs to exceed 100% as measured in Figure 16-19. The presence of brightening agents results in paper looking brighter than materials nearby in its environment. OBAs are not archival and fluoresce less over time due to airborne pollutants or simply exposure to oxygen or light. The lessening chemical reaction reveals the natural, likely yellowish substrate base color.[5] On the other hand, framing a print behind archival, UV-blocking glass prevents the fluorescence reaction altogether and negates the utility of any present OBAs.

Mineral Whiteners

Paper companies alternatively or additionally use chemical additives such as calcium carbonate to maintain consistency in substrate whiteness. This degree of substrate color control prevents the need to create a new ICC profile for each batch of paper. These *mineral whiteners* are more stable than the optical brightening agents described earlier and do not necessarily modify the spectral reflectance of the substrate. The Canson® Infinity line of archival photo papers uses mineral whiteners and is OBA-free. Mineral whiteners create a dust when the paper is cut that may cause production issues in large-scale printing operations and their presence dulls paper cutting blades faster.

Paper White Point

The color of a paper's base tint is called the *paper white* or *paper white point*. The paper white point is identified in a paper's ICC profile. ICC profiles and the color management module software use its color characteristics to correctly render the white point in an image and to adjust all colors accordingly for the most accurate reproduction when soft proofing and printing. The paper white point is typically provided using CIELAB values. Newspaper is a notable example of a paper substrate with a paper white that is far from bright or pure white.

Understanding Printer Settings

Navigating software options presented to the user moments before sending a file to print is daunting even with a solid understanding of the materials and technologies covered thus far. Here, we describe some of the major options available when configuring the software to output to your paper of choice. These include selecting between photo or matte black inks, printhead height, bit depth, manufacturer-specific options like Super MicroWeave, high-speed printing, output resolution and proprietary printer drivers.

Photo Black and Matte Black Inks

The popular photo printer manufacturers, Epson, HP and Canon, use two distinct blacks in their printers: *Photo Black* (PK) and *Matte Black* (MK). The difference lies in the type of paper each of the inks is formulated to work with. Photo Black (or non-absorbent black) is meant for papers where the ink sits on top of the microporous coating and doesn't penetrate into the paper fiber. Resin-coated and Baryta-type papers should receive Photo Black ink. Matte Black (or absorbent black) is formulated for papers in which the ink sits within the microporous coating. It's also intended to

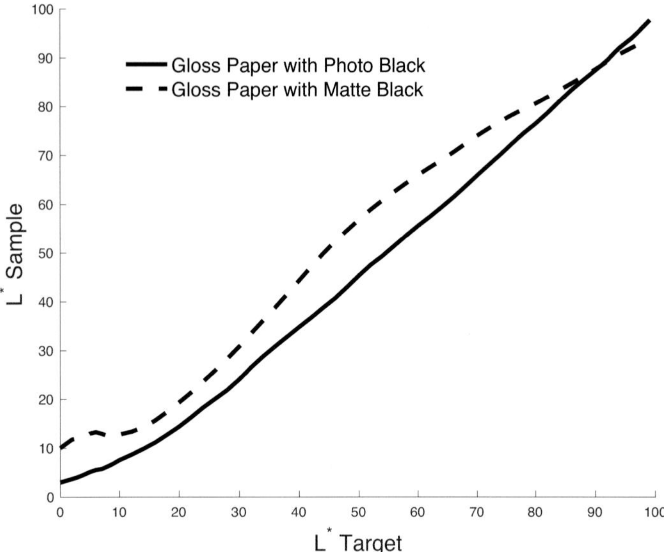

Figure 16-20 A comparison of tone reproduction when printing on Hahnemühle Photo Rag Baryta using MK and PK inks.

get somewhat absorbed into the paper fibers. Matte Black should be used with cotton and matte papers.

Each of the ink formulations provides the maximum black when used on the correct paper and helps to avoid printing defects like bronzing. Accidentally printing with Matte Black on a paper that is non-absorbent means that the black ink rubs off with the slide of a finger across its surface. Figure 16-20 demonstrates how using PK ink on a matte paper drastically changes the black density and therefore the overall tonal reproduction. Many paper profiles pick the proper ink automatically to avoid accidental use of the incorrect black.

Printhead Height

The printhead height setting controls the height of the printhead in relation to the substrate. This can be important to adjust depending on the thickness of the paper and environmental conditions. The thicker the substrate, the higher the printhead height must be set. Changing the printhead height also helps prevent *head strikes* where the printhead comes in contact with the substrate and creates ink buildup on the edges of the paper or scratched lines in the print area. Head strikes are also introduced by high humidity in which the edges of the substrate curl, emphasizing the importance of controlling the temperature and humidity in a printing environment. Head strikes indicate a need to adjust the printhead height setting to prevent damage to the printheads and the substrate. If the printhead it too far away, on the other hand, the inkjet spray exhibits *over-misting* which results in a much softer printed edge.

Printing Bit Depth

Bit depth settings control how much tonal data is sent to the printer. The printer uses the image data to create the maximum tonal range for the selected substrate. Current printers are really only capable of printing upwards of 12-bits worth of image data when working on a luster or glossy photo paper.

Super MicroWeave and Finest Detail

The *Super MicroWeave* and *Finest Detail* settings offered by Epson printers dictate how the dots of inks are laid down on the substrate using screening and variable dot size controls. The effect is more easily observed on a luster or glossy paper surface than on a matte surface. Figure 16-21 shows the Finest Detail setting turned on and off when printing with Super MicroWeave enabled, highlighting the difference in how the ink dots are laid down.

High-Speed Printing

The high-speed printing option dictates whether the printer uses unidirectional or bidirectional printing. Think about eating corn on the cob: do you eat it in both directions or in one direction and return back to the other side to start again like a typewriter? The two approaches demonstrate unidirectional and bidirectional action. The latter method gets more accomplished with a similar range of movement as the former. Bidirectional printing translates to high-speed printing because the printhead lays down ink in both directions as it moves back and forth over the paper. Some photographers swear that bidirectional printing creates image softness if the head is not laying the ink down in the proper spot on the return passage of the printhead. That is a possibility, however, a software utility

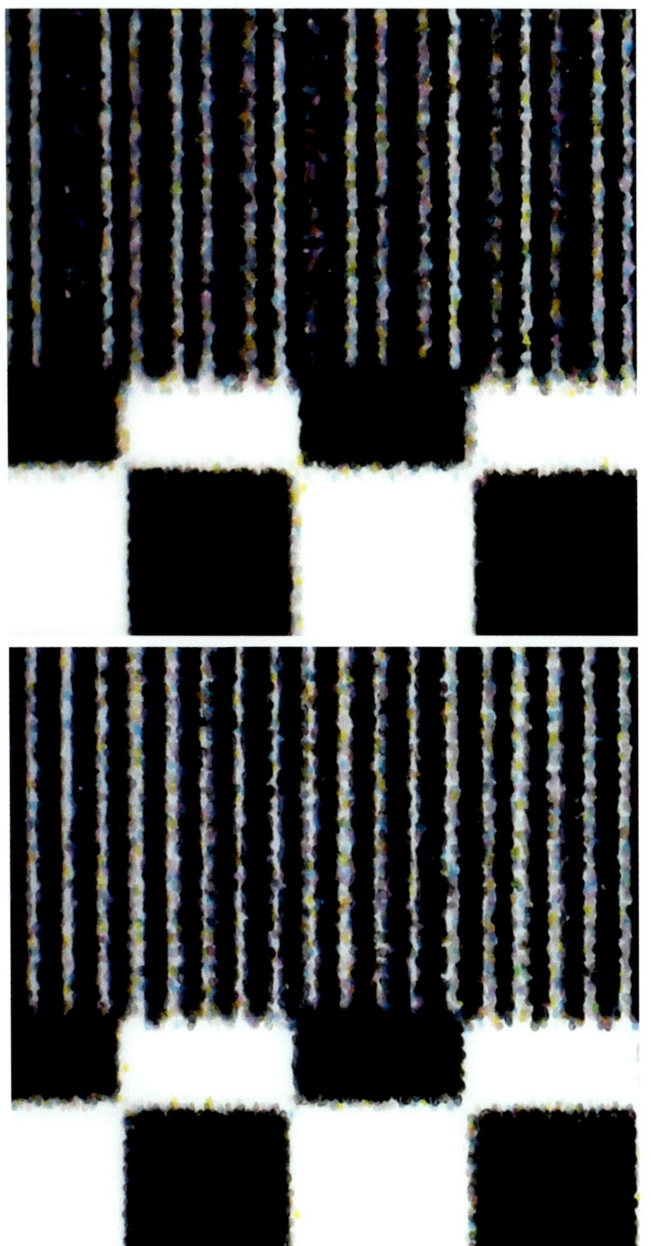

Figure 16-21 High magnification views of prints made with an Epson 4880 at 1440 dpi and using Super MicroWeave on Ilford Gold Fiber Silk. The test target is printed fine detail turned off (top) and with fine detail turned on (bottom). Photographs by Eric Kunsman

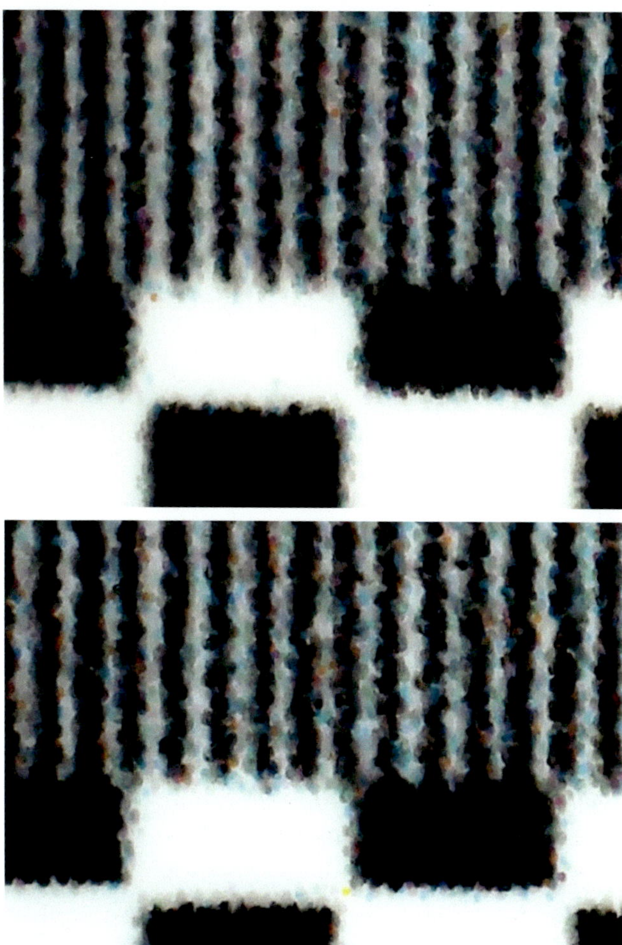

Figure 16-22 High magnification views of prints made at 1440 dpi (top) and at 2880 dpi (bottom) on Epson Premium Luster photo paper. Photographs by Eric Kunsman

exists to ensure proper alignment. Running a printhead alignment when set up for bidirectional printing negates this potential print quality problem. High-speed printing can reduce total print time (which is considerable for large print sizes).

Output Resolution

The most common output resolutions for photographic purposes are 1440 or 2880 dpi. Printing at higher output resolutions slows the print speed down. The print resolutions offered by an example Epson printer are 360, 720, 1440 and 2880 dpi. For viewing distances greater than 10–15 feet, print output resolutions as low as 360 or 720 dpi yield acceptable quality.

Some believe that photographers must use 2880 dpi for the finest prints. In the end, think about the substrate and how well it holds the dot definition. There is little to no difference in detail between 1440 and 2880 dpi when working with matte fine art papers, for example. Working with a luster RC paper, on the other hand, and you may distinguish the difference. Figure 16-22 shows the difference in print resolution settings on a Luster RC paper under magnification. Most users only see a difference under a loupe or magnification and therefore use the 1440 dpi resolution setting most of the time. Photographers should test the available settings using their selected substrate and printer combinations to establish a preferred resolution.

Printer Drivers

Canon, Epson and HP provide *printer drivers* to best configure the printer hardware for optimal print media output. These are custom software commands that interface with the printer hardware. It's worth the time to test and compare the different controls offered by the printer driver to understand how they alter the image quality on a given substrate. For instance, choosing your substrate type effectively sets an ink limitation and ink conversion table specific to that paper control. Therefore, when building a color managed workflow, make sure that you use the same paper controls that were used to build the ICC profile at the start. If you use generic paper profiles downloaded from the paper manufacturer's website, use the settings they used to create that profile to maximize the profile's potential. Ultimately, the printer driver is a black box with predefined controls that we try to adjust for a specific substrate. Once you determine the options that you feel create the best image, stick with them.

Print Size and Viewing Distance

Always consider viewing distance when talking about a print's pixels per inch and dots per inch characteristics. At what distance do you expect viewers to experience the print? The answer varies wildly depending on the venue, presentation and photographic subject matter. There's always an individual at an exhibition that looks at a 24x36 inch print from half an inch away, judging the characteristics of the print. Prints on display should be viewed and considered as a function of showing the image, not as an exercise in print characteristics.

The traditional calculation for viewing distance multiplies the diagonal of the print by 1.5. For example, a 17x22 inch print with a diagonal of 28 inches equates to a viewing distance of 42 inches. This is a general rule of thumb as many factors impact viewing distance including paper type (texture and gloss level), print resolution and a photograph's contrast or dynamic range. The higher the pixels per inch and dots per inch, the closer one can view the image and discern detail.

In the early 2000s, Nikon introduced a point-and-shoot digital camera called the Nikon 950. They printed a photograph taken with the camera onto a large billboard on the side of a building several stories tall about two blocks from the Photo Plus Expo in New York City. People walking out of the trade show buzzed about buying that camera because it created photographs capable of being printed so large. They failed to consider the substantial viewing distance as a primary contributor in making the image look so good at that size.

We use this anecdote to consider another factor related to viewing distance: the pixels per inch required for the viewing distance as a function of the human visual system's resolving power. Equation 16.2 is used for a high contrast print with optimal lighting conditions.

$$\text{Pixels Per Inch} = \frac{1}{\frac{(\text{Distance} \times 0.00029)}{2}} \qquad \text{(Eq. 16.2)}$$

Alternatively, Equation 16.3 rewrites this equation to solve for distance:

$$\text{Distance} = \frac{2}{\text{Pixels per Inch} \times 0.00029} \qquad \text{(Eq. 16.3)}$$

These equations are based off of studies conducted by Ed Grainger in the 1970s regarding the human bandpass characteristic whereby we see certain spatial frequencies better than others for subjective print sharpness. Table 16-2 provides guidelines for a range of viewing distances based on Equation 16.3.

Table 16-2 Viewing distance guidelines based on pixel resolution.

Viewing Distance (inches)	Resolution (pixels per inch)
6	1,145
12	573
18	382
36	191
48	143
60	115
96	72
120	57

Raster Image Processing

Raster image processing transforms the image data into a language that the printer speaks, compatible with its method of printing (ink drops, laser, etc.). The *raster image processor* (RIP), a software solution, takes the image file and translates it to the various controls offered by the printing hardware: resolution, ink colors, screening pattern and color profiles are all factored into the preparation. RIP functionality comes in the form of printer firmware or desktop software. The act of "RIPing" means passing the image file through this layer of interpretation as it heads to the printer hardware.

A printer driver provides a starting point with controls predetermined by the manufacturer. A RIP, depending on the level of control desired, may offer finer tuning and a greater level of low-level settings to maximize your substrate and printer combinations' output quality. Photographers opt to work with a RIP when the manufacturer's printer driver doesn't offer the control they need or when working in a lab environment where queue management and auto-layout to maximize print area are used.

RIPs can be organized into three tiers with each level adding additional controls and capabilities. A basic RIP provides minimal control of ink amounts and drop layout. Mid-level RIPs provide custom ICC profile creation tools and the ability to linearize the printer. Mid-level RIPs provide the ability to set ink limitations, and create custom ICC profiles. High-end RIPs additionally offer control of each ink channel along with ink drop size, dot structure and screening patterns. Higher tiers of RIP software typically correspond with higher price tags.

Hard Proofing

We've talked a lot about creating output profiles and this is the stage where they get to flex their color-managed muscles. An image must be interpreted by the output profile before sending the information to the printer. This profile, remember, is a characterization of the specific printer and paper combination you're using to print the image. Sometimes this step of converting the photo to the output profile is not obvious: Adobe Photoshop waits until you're at the "Print" screen to ask about the output profile to apply, for example.

A *hard proof*, also called a *proof print* or *match print*, is a printed simulation of your final intended output in order to review image processing, print settings and any other relevant details. A hard proof ensures that the final product is the highest quality physical media output of your photographic work. Soft proofing always faces an uphill battle by virtue of relying on additive color mixing (via display) when the final output uses subtractive color mixing (via colorants and substrates). Options to simulate paper color or paper texture are inherently less accurate than making actual print. Soft proofing is a valuable precursor to making a test print (or two, or ten) while keeping an eye on the prize: optimal color and tone reproduction of your images. As each photograph is unique and circumstances regarding print size, file size and tone reproduction are variable, hard proofing is a critical part of the output process to get everything optimized.

Hard proofs are different for commercial use and fine art use. A commercial hard proof is often made using inkjet printers with an aqueous inkjet paper that emulates the intended output substrate for traditional printing processes. A hard proof is not created on a printing press due to the make-ready process of RIPing the job; creating printing plates and mounting the plates on the press is prohibitively expensive. If the final output is on a digital press, hard proofs are often made using the same printer hardware and with the substrate used in production. These are used as *contract proofs* which act as an agreement between the printing house and the client regarding how the production should ultimately look.

In a fine art print studio, the printer and substrate combination are used to hard proof and all final adjustments are judged on the exact substrate. This is critical for artists and photographers that work with open editions because the print studio makes copies as demand for the print arises. The fine art hard proof is used to ensure that the edition always matches from start to finish; printing technology may change if the edition is open for a long period of time and this practice facilitates consistency.

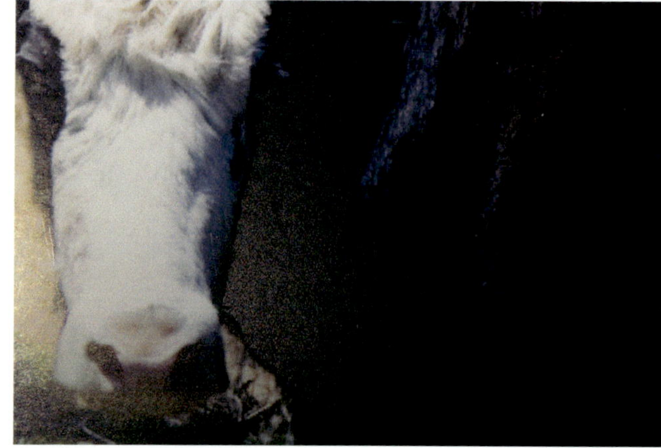

Figure 16-24 A visible gloss differential. Photograph courtesy of the Image Permanence Institute

Printing Issues

There are three common issues that occur in physical media output: abrasion, bronzing and gloss differential. Let's step through each one.

Bronzing describes when the ink appears bronze in color when viewed at an angle. Figure 16-23 shows bronzing due to printing with a matte black ink on a glossy photo paper. Bronzing occurs when certain light wavelengths are trapped under the ink that sits on the microporous coating and reflect at a different angle. This creates more of a metallic look relative to the ink sitting on the substrate surface. Additionally, some printer companies are formulating their new inks to sit on the paper surface which can also inadvertently introduce the characteristic.

Figure 16-25 Minor abrasion on a print surface. Photograph courtesy of the Image Permanence Institute

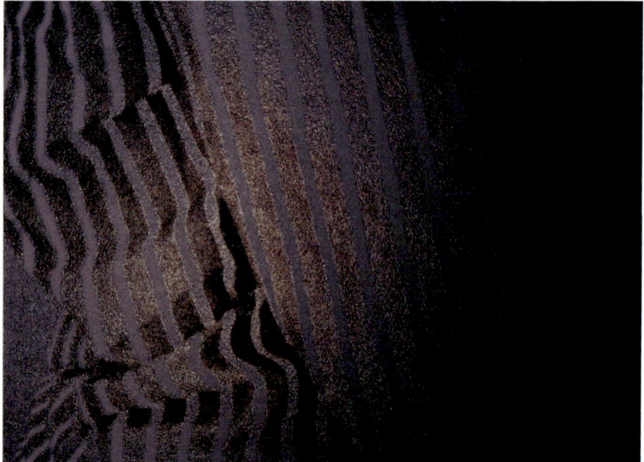

Figure 16-23 An example of bronzing introduced by printing with a matte black ink on a glossy photo paper. Image courtesy of the Image Permanence Institute

Gloss differential is an unwanted appearance that occurs when the printed ink changes the gloss level of the paper surface. It's a consequence of the pigment's gloss level differing from that of the substrate. If the pigment sits on

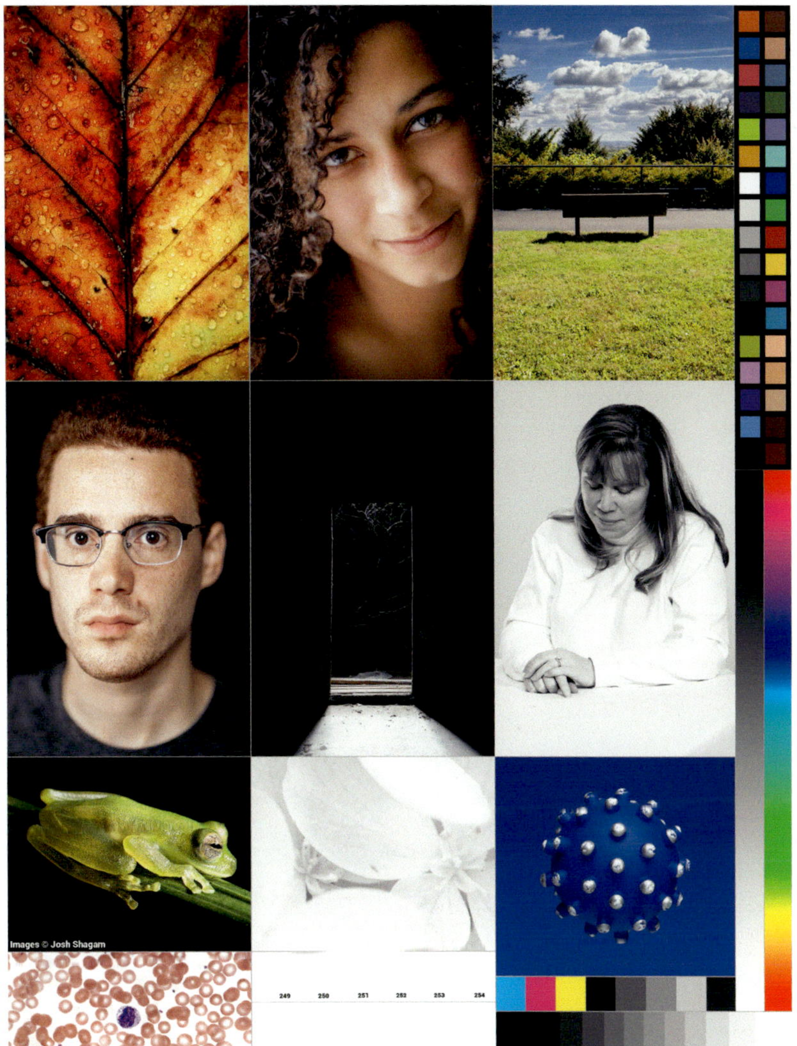

Figure 16-26 An example test print created based on the recommendations found in the textbook *Color Management & Quality Output*.[6]

top of the microporous coating, the different gloss levels are visible as unequal reflectivity as seen in Figure 16-24. Printer companies combat this problem by applying a clear coat ink (called a *gloss optimizer* or *chrome enhancer*) after all of the color inks are applied. The gloss optimizer creates a uniform surface off of which light reflects.

Abrasion occurs when ink sits on top of the microporous coating or even within the coating. The surface is damaged by physical contact and the colorant is scratched or completely removed. Figure 16-25 shows an example of minor abrasion to the surface of a printed image. Abrasion comes from head strikes or a lack of careful handling and storage of the final print.

Evaluating Paper and Print Quality

One question that we frequently hear from photography students is: what's the best paper for printing? There is no simple or easy answer as there are many factors to consider including personal preference and artistic intent. A classic paper study helps answer the question on a technical, physical media level, which offers an insightful starting point. We first run a customized test print like the one shown in Figure 16-26 for every paper and printer combination we use or intend to evaluate for use in our practice.

The test print provides us with everything necessary to objectively and subjectively evaluate image quality as

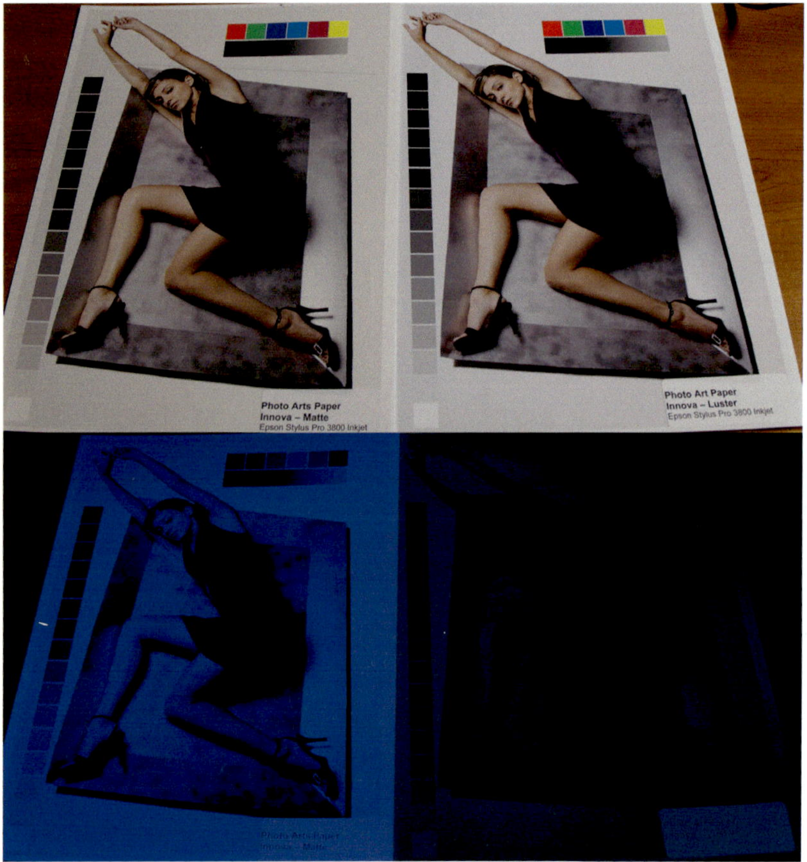

Figure 16-27 The presence of OBAs is easily detected using a standard UV blacklight. The photo paper on the left fluoresces while the one on the right does not.

a function of paper characteristics. It includes high key and low key images, skin tones, black and white images, challenging saturated colors and memory colors like blue sky and green grass. The test print layout also includes ColorChecker patches, grayscale and a full color gradients. We suggest building a test print document in Adobe Photoshop and replacing or revising elements as your printing skills and needs evolve.

Testing for OBAs

We test for the presence of optical brightener agents by placing the paper under a UV light source. A paper with chemical brighteners fluoresces or glows brightly under a UV source such as a blacklight. We find that manufacturers' claims here are not always reliable. Printing with papers containing OBAs is not necessarily problematic but it is a helpful to know if long-term durability and print quality are priorities and if the product description is unclear on their use. Figure 16-27 shows our low-tech test for identifying photo papers with OBAs.

Measuring Color Gamut and White Point

Next, we measure CIELAB values for the red, green, blue, cyan, magenta and yellow patches using a spectrophotometer to create a gamut plot. The measured CIELAB values for a white patch indicate the white point or neutrality of the paper or it identifies a notable base tint. A perfect white in CIELAB space is indicated by a* and b* values of 0. Knowing the paper's white point assists in determining if a print on the same photo paper will be neutrally color balanced.

Measuring Black Point Density and Gloss

Following gamut plots and white point measurements, we use a densitometer and the grayscale patches on our test print to determine the black point density and to evaluate the dynamic range of the paper and printer combination. The black point density is largely driven by the paper surface. A glossy paper yields a darker black than a matte paper due to the first surface reflections of the substrate. Prints are typically viewed on the perpendicular with lighting off-axis. Most of the incident light that strikes a high gloss paper with a smooth top surface bounces off at the same angle as it approaches with very little light reflecting to the viewer's eyes (see Figure 16-28). This results in a deeper, darker black and a higher dynamic range because areas of high ink or pigment density appear dark to the viewer. A textured paper surface like the kind found on a matte paper causes the incident light to reflect back at many different angles. Some of that light reaches the viewer's eyes as flare and some of it scatters, resulting in a perceived low black point.

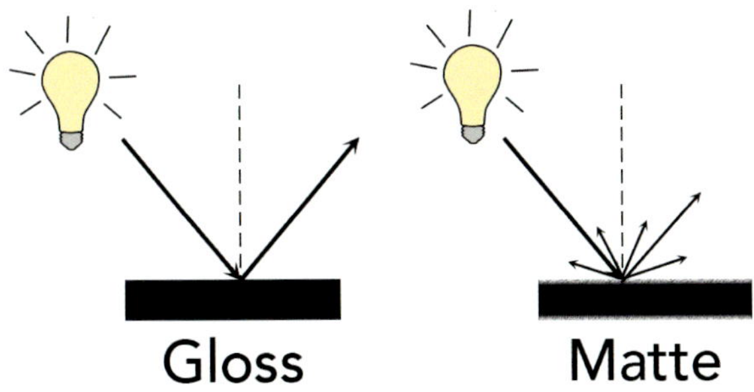

Figure 16-28 The interaction of incident light on paper surfaces changes the perceived density.

Photo paper manufacturers typically label their papers as gloss, luster (or satin) and matte. The definitions of these categories are not dictated by the ISO and are at the discretion of the manufacturer, so going purely off of marketing terms could mean that one photographer's satin is

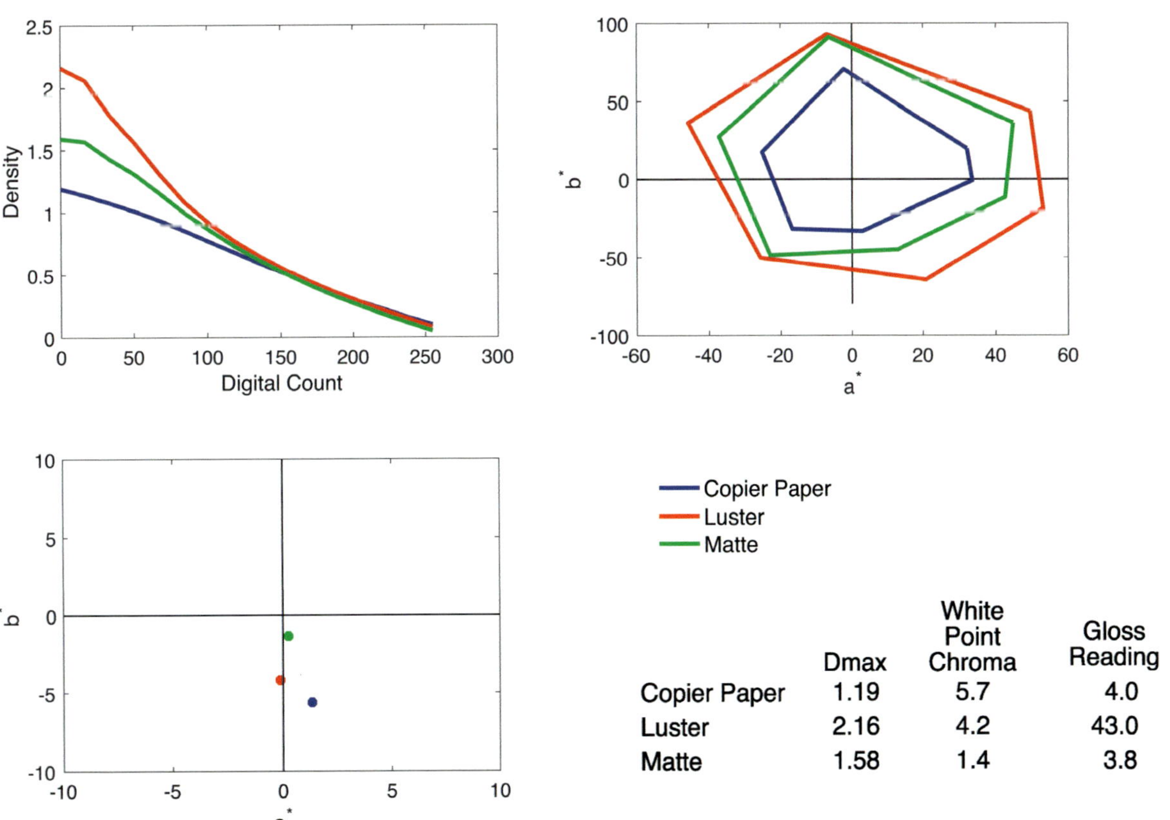

	Dmax	White Point Chroma	Gloss Reading
Copier Paper	1.19	5.7	4.0
Luster	2.16	4.2	43.0
Matte	1.58	1.4	3.8

Figure 16-29 A compilation of print quality measurements designed to reveal key characteristics of our substrates using the same inkjet printer. Clockwise from top left is a tone reproduction plot, a gamut plot, a table listing D_{max}, white point chroma and gloss readings and a paper white point plot.

another's glossy. In light of this, the Technical Association of Pulp and Paper Industry's T-480 offers a published standard for measuring gloss for papers, both coated and uncoated.[7] A *gloss meter* is used to classify a paper surface according to its reflectance at specific angles. It measures the specular reflections on a surface at a range of angles and reports its measurements in *gloss units* (GU).

The gloss meter offers us the chance to create a uniform gloss name categorization across our most-used papers. It takes measurements at 20°, 60° and 85° and returns gloss unit values ranging from 0–100. Semi-gloss surfaces are measured at 60° and should fall between 10–70 GU. Matte surfaces measuring below 10 GU at 60° should be measured at 85°; highly reflective surfaces with measured values exceeding 70 GU at 60° should be measured at 20°.

Figure 16-29 shows the compiled results from conducting some of the tests and measurements described here on copier paper, a luster photo paper and a matte photo paper. It borrows concepts and practices described in Chapter 13 and Chapter 14, using CIELAB measurements and chroma calculations. From this data we begin to draw conclusions and form an understanding of the photo papers we regularly work with: their potential tonal range, white point neutrality, color gamut and gloss characteristics. While we wouldn't recommend seeking to create high-quality photographic reproduction on cheap copier paper, we included it in our investigation as a point of reference—it emphasizes the power of the substrate in addition to the capabilities of the printer.

Critically Evaluating Color and Contrast

Additional characteristics such as contrast, color casts and accurate color reproduction are important to evaluate with the test print. In an image with skin tones, getting the proper color balance is key. Look for artifacts like posterization or banding in smooth tones and gradual tone or color transitions. Keep a critical eye on how dark and how bright the high and low key details render; maintaining image pixel information in these extremes is not equivalent depending on the paper type, color management decisions or editing decisions made prior to printing. A professional workflow involving hard proofing means making derivative image files that tweak and revise edits when the test prints are subpar. If you've followed the text thus far, you likely have an appreciation for holding onto detail and image information from the beginning of the image-making process—don't leave anything on the table at this last output stage.

Simultaneous contrast, defined in Chapter 13, is important to keep in mind when hard proofing and when considering display environments for your work. The background or surrounding area in front of which a print is viewed changes the perception of that print. The phenomenon can change your perception of both color (hue and saturation) and lightness/density.

The best option when doing critical print evaluation is to use a designated light booth (sometimes called a *viewing station*) with neutral surround and controlled illumination. These offer the best chance to evaluate the print without outside factors introducing bias or misleading representations. A calibrated viewing station is shown in Figure 16-30. The best practice is to evaluate prints under the illumination type that will be used to illuminate them when viewed by others. As a consequence, viewing stations are equipped with multiple standardized illuminants like D65. Newer models include UV sources for detecting the presence and effect of OBAs.

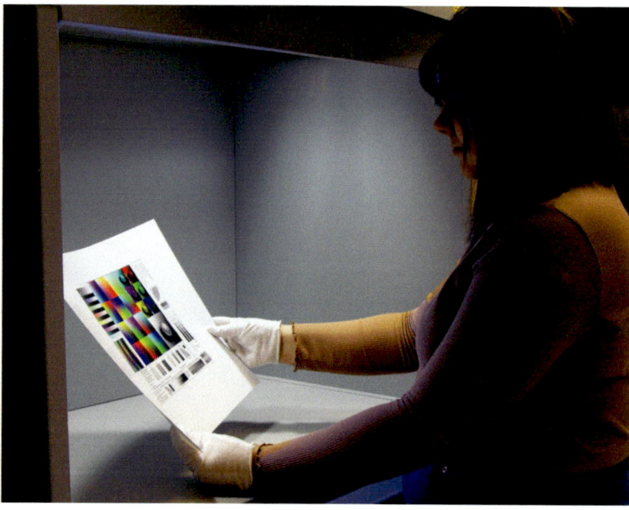

Figure 16-30 Evaluating a test print using a calibrated viewing station. Some viewing stations include multiple light sources including UV.

Finally, there is more to print quality than just objective measurements. There are many subjective qualities that make a great print. We have touched on many of them throughout this text. The dynamic range of a paper may be considerable, for example, yet a poor print or poorly edited file can render everything too dark or muddy and low contrast. Texture is another area that must be seen and experienced to appreciate if it enhances or distracts from the printed content.

Our favorite resource that goes into more detail with excellent exercises and examples is *Color Management & Quality Output: Working with Color from Camera to Display to Print* by Tom Ashe, published by Focal Press in 2014.

Notes

1 "Real world print production." *Real World Print Production*, by Claudia McCue, Peachpit Press, 2009, p. 31.

2 "Global UV cured printing inks market (2018–2023): The market is expected to grow at a CAGR of over 10% – ResearchAndMarkets.com." *Business Wire*, Sept. 7, 2018, www.businesswire.com/news/home/20180907005221/en/Global-UV-Cured-Printing-Inks-Market-2018-2023.

3 "Printing applications laboratory.", www.rit.edu/gis/printlab/.

4 "United States one-dollar bill." *Wikipedia*, Wikimedia Foundation, Feb. 13, 2019, en.wikipedia.org/wiki/United_States_one-dollar_bill.

5 Work, Roy. "To brighten or not to brighten." *LexJet Blog*, July 2000, https://blog.lexjet.com/wp-content/uploads/2009/10/sbjuly43-45.pdf.

6 Ashe, Tom. *Color Management & Quality Output: Working with Color from Camera to Display to Print*. Focal Press, 2014, p. 51.

7 "Specular gloss of paper and paperboard at 75 degrees, test method TAPPI/ANSI T 480 Om-15." *Thickness (Caliper of Paper, Paperboard, and Combined Board, Test Method TAPPI/ANSI T 411 Om-15*, imisrise.tappi.org/TAPPI/Products/01/T/0104T480.aspx.

Index

Q

R

S

T

U